TRUTH COMMISSIONS AND
PROCEDURAL FAIRNESS

This is the first law book devoted entirely to the subject of truth commissions. The book sets forth standards of procedural fairness aimed at protecting the rights and interests of those who come into contact with truth commissions – primarily victims and their families, witnesses, and perpetrators. The aim of the book is to provide recommended criteria of procedural fairness for five possible components of a truth commission's mandate: the taking of statements, the use of subpoenas, the exercise of powers of search and seizure, the holding of victim-centered public hearings, and the publication of findings of individual responsibility in a final report (sometimes called the issue of "naming names"). The book draws on the experience of past and present truth commissions, analogous national and multilateral investigative bodies, and international and comparative standards of procedural fairness.

Mark Freeman is an international lawyer, author, and lecturer specializing in human rights and transitional justice. He is co-author of the first comprehensive Canadian textbook on international human rights law, as well as a companion volume of texts, cases, and materials. He has conducted missions to more than a dozen countries to provide advice and training on the establishment and operation of truth commissions and other transitional justice mechanisms. He currently heads the Brussels office of the International Center for Transitional Justice.

TRUTH COMMISSIONS and PROCEDURAL FAIRNESS

Mark Freeman

CAMBRIDGE
UNIVERSITY PRESS

CAMBRIDGE UNIVERSITY PRESS
Cambridge, New York, Melbourne, Madrid, Cape Town, Singapore, São Paulo

Cambridge University Press
32 Avenue of the Americas, New York, NY 10013-2473, USA

www.cambridge.org
Information on this title: www.cambridge.org/9780521850674

First published 2006

Printed in the United States of America

A catalog record for this publication is available from the British Library.

Library of Congress Cataloging in Publication Data
Freeman, Mark, 1968–
Truth commissions and procedural fairness / Mark Freeman. – 1st ed.
   p. cm.
Includes index.
ISBN 0-521-85067-3 (hardback : alk. paper)
1. Truth commissions. I. Title.
JC580.F74 2006
323.4′9 – dc22   2005028817

ISBN-13 978-0-521-85067-4 hardback
ISBN-10 0-521-85067-3 hardback

ISBN-13 978-0-521-61564-8 paperback
ISBN-10 0-521-61564-X paperback

... for truth is truth
to the end of reckoning.

– WILLIAM SHAKESPEARE,
MEASURE FOR MEASURE

Contents

Foreword	*page* xi
Preface	xiii
Acknowledgments	xix
Abbreviations	xxi

PART I

1 Truth Commissions   3
Introduction   3
Section 1: Overview of Transitional Justice   4
Section 2: Overview of Truth Commissions   11
Section 3: Distinguishing Truth Commissions from Other
    Human Rights Investigations   40
Section 4: Distinguishing Truth Commissions from Courts   69
Conclusions   87

2 Procedural Fairness   88
Introduction   88
Section 1: Relevant International Standards   89
Section 2: Selected Domestic Models of Fairness   108
Section 3: Toward a Conception of Procedural Fairness
    for Truth Commissions   131
Conclusions   154

PART II

3   Statement Taking   159
   Introduction   159
   Section 1: Publicity and Outreach   162
   Section 2: Accessibility   168
   Section 3: Information on Possible Consequences
       of Giving a Statement   171
   Section 4: Procedures for Taking and Recording Statements   175
   Section 5: Receipt and Preservation of Confidential and
       Anonymous Statements   181
   Section 6: Support and Referrals   186

4   Subpoena Power   188
   Introduction   188
   Section 1: Procedure for Issuing and Serving Subpoenas   191
   Section 2: Subpoena Content and Scope   193
   Section 3: Enforcement Powers   197
   Section 4: Recipient Rights   202

5   Search and Seizure Power   205
   Introduction   205
   Section 1: Procedure for Issuing Warrants   208
   Section 2: Scope of a Warrant   212
   Section 3: Procedure for Executing Warrants   215
   Section 4: Rights of the Subject of the Search   219

6   Public Hearings   222
   Introduction   222
   Section 1: Selection and Preparation of Those Who Will Appear   226
   Section 2: Notification to Implicated Persons: Timing,
       Method, and Content   230
   Section 3: Nature and Scope of the Right of Reply   235
   Section 4: Oaths and Affirmations   240
   Section 5: Right to Legal Representation   242
   Section 6: Admissible Evidence   245
   Section 7: Privileges Based on Contexts and Relationships
       of Confidentiality   248
   Section 8: Use Immunity and the Privilege against
       Self-Incrimination   251
   Section 9: Protective Measures   258
   Section 10: Victim Emotional and Psychological Support   265

7 Publication of Findings of Individual Responsibility   268
   Introduction   268
   Section 1: Types of Evidence   276
   Section 2: Standard of Proof   280
   Section 3: Notification of Intent to Name: Timing,
      Method, and Content   284
   Section 4: Nature and Scope of the Right of Reply   288
   Section 5: Investigation of Replies   290
   Section 6: Mode of Naming in a Final Report   291
   Section 7: Judicial Review   298

Summary of Recommendations   301
   Statement Taking   301
   Subpoena Power   304
   Search and Seizure Power   306
   Public Hearings   308
   Publication of Findings of Individual Responsibility   313

Appendix 1: Table of Truth Commissions   317

Appendix 2: Primary Materials on Truth Commissions   327
   The Truth and Reconciliation Commission Act 2000
      (Sierra Leone)   327
   From Madness to Hope: The 12-Year War in El Salvador –
      Report of the Commission on the Truth for El
      Salvador (1993) [Excerpts]   339

Appendix 3: Primary Materials on Other Commissions of Inquiry   353
   UK Inquiries Act (2005) [Excerpts]   353
   Report of the International Commission of Inquiry on
      Darfur to the United Nations Secretary-General
      (2003) [Excerpts]   376

Index   393

Foreword

Transitional justice has become a feature of the past three decades. It is a consequence of the significant number of nations that have struggled to make the transition from war to peace or from oppression and discrimination to forms of democratic government. The challenge facing such societies is the manner in which they should treat past serious human rights violations. The perpetrators seek blanket amnesties and the victims seek prosecution of the former leaders.

It is tempting in that context to forget the past in favor of building a new and better future. It is the line of least resistance. It is also a recipe for future disaster. Where past human rights violations are ignored and the victims forgotten, there is a cancer in such a society that remains dormant and available for use or abuse by some or other future despotic, nationalistic leader. Examples are there for the choosing the Balkans, Rwanda, the Middle East.

More enlightened leaders have sought a third way between national amnesia and criminal prosecutions – the establishment of a truth commission. In Chapter 1 of this work there is an excellent and concise history of truth commissions and an explanation of their relationship to courts and other forms of official and nonofficial truth-seeking mechanisms.

One of the challenges facing a truth commission is the fairness of its proceedings. It is all too easy to allow it to be used as a political platform to castigate the former regime. It is a complex and sensitive process to assure victims they will receive protection and respect for their dignity when they testify. It is no exaggeration to state that the success or failure of a truth commission will crucially depend upon the fairness of its proceedings.

This study could not be timelier. It would have been a great resource for the leaders of earlier truth commissions as they went about their work. I have no doubt that it will be regarded in that way by those still to come.

This book, however, has a wider relevance. It contains a thorough overview of the international law of procedural fairness that applies not only to truth commissions but also to other forms of nonjudicial inquiry. It has become evident that many international organizations fail to observe procedural fairness – whether committees of the United Nations that make decisions affecting the lives of many thousands of persons or committees of investigation set up by other international or regional organizations. There are many domestic committees of investigation that also fail to observe rules of fairness. I have in mind investigations set up by national legislatures and especially in the United States where congressional committees conduct scores of investigations annually. This book should be made compulsory reading for those who conduct such investigations and the members of their staff.

The author does not pontificate, yet makes no concessions on matters of principle. He is well aware of and takes into account the practical and pragmatic problems faced by truth commissions. I have in mind questions such as the appropriate burden of proof, the admissibility of evidence, and notice to those who might be adversely affected by evidence or the findings. There are a host of other practical issues that are treated with thoroughness and thoughtfulness.

I recommend this book to anyone who has an interest in transitional justice and, in particular, truth commissions. I also believe *Truth Commissions and Procedural Fairness* will be a useful and insightful work for lawyers, legislators, and members of the public who have an interest in the fairness of institutions that continue to multiply and affect the daily lives of millions of people around the world.

Richard J. Goldstone

Preface

Since the Nuremburg trials and even more so since the end of the Cold War, formal mechanisms to address human rights abuses have increased dramatically, both in number and variety. Today there are, for example, a permanent International Criminal Court, two *ad hoc* international criminal tribunals (the International Criminal Tribunals for the former Yugoslavia and for Rwanda), and several mixed national-international criminal tribunals. There are three regional human rights courts: the European and Inter-American Courts of Human Rights, and the African Court on Human and Peoples' Rights. There is also a multitude of quasi-judicial and nonjudicial human rights mechanisms, including seven UN treaty bodies and two regional human rights commissions.

Most contemporary mechanisms for the vindication of human rights follow well-established rules of procedure. International criminal tribunals, for example, abide by internationally recognized standards of a "fair trial." Regional human rights courts and commissions have followed essentially the same rules of procedure for, in some cases, more than three decades. Yet there are a number of human rights mechanisms for which rules of procedure remain *ad hoc* and vague. This book constitutes a systematic attempt at outlining fair procedures for one such mechanism: the truth commission.

A truth commission is an *ad hoc*, autonomous, and victim-centered commission of inquiry set up in and authorized by a state for the primary purposes of (1) investigating and reporting on the principal causes and consequences of broad and relatively recent patterns of severe violence or repression that occurred in the state during determinate periods of abusive rule or conflict, and (2) making recommendations for their redress and future prevention.

Particularly since the Truth and Reconciliation Commission in South Africa, the subject of truth commissions has attracted worldwide interest. Today it is widely believed that truth commissions can contribute not only to the clarification of contested historical events but also to criminal justice efforts, victim reparation, reform of dysfunctional public institutions, and national reconciliation. Remarkably, several truth commissions have done so. If it were otherwise, their general popularity among human rights activists would be difficult to explain. Yet truth commissions are only one tool among many available to help a society confront its past. Truth commissions, in fact, are part of the broader field of transitional justice, which focuses on the complex question of how states come to grips with a legacy of mass abuse.

Observers and sponsors of truth commissions have rarely taken a hard look at issues of procedural fairness for truth commissions. There are some exceptions. Priscilla Hayner, the leading authority on truth commissions, has examined fairness issues that arise for commissions that publish findings of individual responsibility in their final reports. The South African Truth and Reconciliation Commission's terms of reference were the result of extensive parliamentary and public debate on issues of fairness, and local courts rendered important judgments on questions of fair procedure that arose in the commission's course of operation. There have also been sporadic attempts at the UN Commission on Human Rights to codify a limited number of relevant procedural standards. But overall, there remains no sustained account of procedural fairness for truth commissions.

This book recognizes the fact that no two truth commissions – nor, for that matter, two political contexts – are identical. Some truth commissions are established by the executive branch of government, others by the legislature; some truth commissions run for less than a year, others for several years; some comprise three commissioners, others more than twenty; some hold public hearings, others only operate in private; some "name names," others do not; some have subpoena and search and seizure powers, others lack them; some operate in contexts marked by serious and ongoing security threats, others operate in more settled environments. The world of truth commissions is, in short, marked by diversity. Yet the fact is that the similarities between truth commissions are far greater than the differences. As this book demonstrates, truth commissions resemble nothing so much as each other. For this reason, and despite the apparent diversity of models, it is possible to develop a set of guiding principles on procedural fairness for truth commissions.

My interest in developing fairness standards for truth commissions was borne of an appreciation for international fair trial standards, and a recognition that the world of trials was at least as diverse as the world of truth commissions.

There are criminal trials and civil trials; group trials and individual trials; full-length trials and summary trials; trials in common law jurisdictions and trials in civil law jurisdictions; trials in person and trials *in absentia*; trials by specialized tribunals and trials by ordinary tribunals; trials in public and trials *in camera*; trials by judge and trials by jury; and so forth. None of this diversity has led any serious scholar to suggest the futility or irrelevance of having international fair trial standards. The same goes for truth commissions. Those who create or run truth commissions require guidelines on fairness no less than those engaged in trial proceedings.

This book does not cover all aspects of a truth commission's mandate or operation. Instead, it offers recommended criteria of procedural fairness for five possible components of its work that bear directly on issues of procedural fairness: the taking of statements, the use of subpoena powers, the use of powers of search and seizure, the holding of public hearings, and the publication of findings of individual responsibility in a final report. In examining these functions, the book explores the notion of procedural fairness for persons who might be adversely impacted by them, but it gives equal attention to the procedural fairness interests of witnesses and of victims and their next-of-kin.

Certain of these five components arise more frequently than others. For example, every truth commission conducts some form of statement taking, but not all have wielded subpoena or search and seizure powers; some commissions have the power to make findings of individual responsibility, others do not; some hold public hearings, others do not. At the same time, it is rare for truth commission sponsors to bypass consideration of any of the five attributes. Moreover, truth commission mandates increasingly encompass most, and in some cases all, of these attributes, thus increasing the need for attention to issues of procedural fairness. Admittedly, the quality of the justice system in most transitional contexts tends to be low, making resort to the courts on procedural fairness violations unlikely when the commission is still in operation. But this is beside the point. Truth commissions, no less than courts, should apply high standards of procedural fairness for their own sake. No one would suggest that fair trial standards are irrelevant because they are difficult to discharge. The same logic should apply to truth commissions.

Some readers may note this book's omission of more controversial and atypical aspects of some recent truth commission mandates. For example, there is no in-depth analysis of the truth-for-amnesty procedure used by the South African Truth and Reconciliation Commission. Nor does the book examine the Timor-Leste Commission on Reception, Truth, and Reconciliation's power to formalize contracts of community service for perpetrators. Nor, finally, does it cover the compensation-granting power wielded by the Moroccan Commission on Fairness and Reconciliation. The primary reason for not examining these unique attributes here is their adjudicative character (*i.e.*, the fact that they involve the settling of legal rights). The focus of this book is limited to the nonadjudicative aspects of truth commission work.

In light of the wide range of possible truth commission objectives, attributes, and budgets, and given the importance of local participation in any commission's conception, this book does not provide a blueprint for the design of an "ideal" truth commission. Rather, it aims to provide a practical reference tool for local sponsors, advocates, and members of truth commissions, as well as for international human rights scholars and practitioners. Some of the material in the book will be of most use at the "design stage" (*i.e.*, for sponsors and advocates of a truth commission prior to its establishment). Some will be of most use at the "implementation stage" (*i.e.*, for appointed commissioners and staff and for a commission's many external stakeholders). And some of it will be most relevant to the "postcommission" stage (*i.e.*, for governments and others dealing with implementation of the final report and any attendant legal challenges). All of it, however, will be relevant to persons who accept the importance of procedural fairness and who wish to depoliticize what is an inherently controversial public exercise.

A very diverse, if nonexhaustive, range of relevant mechanisms and sources was consulted in the research for this book. Particular attention was paid to the experiences of (1) past truth commissions; (2) analogous domestic, multilateral, and nongovernmental human rights investigations; and (3) relevant international human rights and criminal law standards. An effort was also made to consult legal sources from different legal traditions. Admittedly, however, the book has a common law bias corresponding to the legal education of its author. I hope that bias is overcome in part by the selection of sources: the truth commissions and the analogous bodies examined in the book operate in civil and common law countries alike, and the referenced international standards represent the closest approximation to "universal" standards.

One final remark by way of introduction. While its immediate topic is truth commissions, much of the book is also directly relevant to human rights investigations by analogous bodies such as nongovernmental organizations, Commonwealth commissions of inquiry, national human rights commissions, coroners, international commissions of inquiry, vetting bodies, and compensation commissions – many of which operate according to *ad hoc*, and not especially victim-sensitive, standards of procedural fairness. My discovery in writing this book was that truth commissions have as much to teach as to learn in relation to these and other investigative bodies.

The book comprises two principal parts. Part I provides an overview of the book's two main themes: truth commissions and procedural fairness. Part II examines the five previously noted possible components of a truth commission mandate. Each chapter in Part II consists of a detailed analysis of specific issues, followed by concrete recommendations. Although consistent themes emerge throughout Part II, the chapters and sections are intentionally self-contained and can, for the most part, be read independently of one another. At the end of the book are three appendices. Appendix 1 is a table of past and present truth commissions and their key attributes. Appendix 2 consists of a small selection of primary materials on truth commissions. Appendix 3 contains a sampling of primary materials on analogous commissions of inquiry.

This work is current as of 1 January 2006 except where otherwise noted.

Acknowledgments

As with any book, this one benefited immensely from the contributions of many individuals.

I am compelled to start with a special tribute to Patricia E. Ronan, as well as to Cynthia M. Reed. Both made major contributions to the preparation of initial versions of Part II of this book. I am indebted to both of them, and I hope they will find the final results worthy.

Heartfelt thanks are also owed to Orla Bannan and Jedediah Purdy, as well as to Mike Halberstam, Paul Lall, Renate Lunn, Stuart Naifeh, and Sandra Sheldon. Early in the process, they too made noteworthy contributions to selected chapters in Part II of the book.

Along the way, many other friends and colleagues have provided invaluable assistance or advice. I am deeply grateful to all of them. These include Patrick Burgess, Irina Ceric, Gibran van Ert, Kirsten Fisher, Jordan Glick, Eduardo González, Pablo de Greiff, Daina Groskaufmanis, Priscilla B. Hayner, Oscar Bañez Herráez, Luc Huyse, Diana Juricevic, Hugo Leal-Neri, Renu Mandhane, Andrew Matheson, Anita McBride, Tamara Morgenthau, Michael Nesbitt, Joanna R. Quinn, Ronald C. Slye, Henry F. Smith, Emilie Taman, Darren Thorne, Paul van Zyl, and Marieke Wierda. Others who have kindly assisted include Yousuf Aftab, Claire Freeman, Alejandro Garro, Ena Paul, and Andrew Pinto.

I would additionally like to acknowledge the International Center for Transitional Justice for the initial encouragement and support that helped get this research underway. I am also indebted to Paul, Weiss, Rifkind, Wharton & Garrison LLP for its valuable *pro bono* support.

John Berger at Cambridge University Press has been a fervent supporter of this work from the moment it arrived on his desk. My gratitude to him, and to my editors Susan Greenberg and Holly Johnson, is immense.

Last, but certainly not least, I would like to thank my wife, Annamie Paul. Without her, this moment would never have arrived. The book is lovingly dedicated to her, and to our two children, Malachai and Jonas.

Abbreviations

ACHR	American Convention on Human Rights 1969
AfrCHPR	African Charter on Human and Peoples' Rights 1981
AJIL	*American Journal of International Law*
AmDR	American Declaration on the Rights and Duties of Man 1948
CAT	Convention Against Torture and Other Cruel, Inhuman or Degrading Treatment or Punishment 1984
CEDAW	Convention on the Elimination of All Forms of Discrimination Against Women 1979
CERD	International Convention on the Elimination of All Forms of Racial Discrimination 1966
Charter	See "Mandate"
Commonwealth commission of inquiry	A commission of inquiry established in an English or Commonwealth jurisdiction pursuant to a statute generally entitled *Commissions of Inquiry Act* or *Tribunals of Inquiry Act*
CRC	Convention on the Rights of the Child 1989
ECHR	European Convention for the Protection of Human Rights and Fundamental Freedoms 1950
ECOSOC	UN Economic and Social Council

ETS	European Treaty Series
EU Charter of Rights	Part II (Charter of Fundamental Rights of the Union) of the draft Treaty establishing a Constitution for Europe 2004
EurSC	European Social Charter 1996
GA res.	UN General Assembly resolution
ICC	International Criminal Court
ICCPR	International Covenant on Civil and Political Rights 1966
ICESCR	International Covenant on Economic, Social and Cultural Rights 1966
ICJ Rep	International Court of Justice Law Reports
ICTR	International Criminal Tribunal for Rwanda
ICTY	International Criminal Tribunal for the former Yugoslavia
ILM	International Legal Materials
ILO	International Labour Organization
Mandate	The legal instrument(s) by which a truth commission is established and in which can be found its objectives, functions, and powers
Mutatis mutandis	"Making the necessary alterations"
NGO	Nongovernmental organization
OAS	Organization of American States
OAS TS	OAS Treaty Series
Rome Statute	Rome Statute of the International Criminal Court 1998
SC res.	UN Security Council resolution
Terms of reference	See "Mandate"
TRC	Truth and Reconciliation Commission
UDHR	Universal Declaration of Human Rights 1948
UN Charter	Charter of the United Nations 1945
UNTS	United Nations Treaty Series

PART I

1

Truth Commissions

INTRODUCTION

It is common today for countries emerging from periods of conflict or repression to consider the possibility of establishing a truth commission. In such contexts the near impossibility of mounting prosecutions on a large scale makes consideration of such commissions almost inevitable. It is for this and other reasons that truth commissions form an integral part of the broader topic of transitional justice, which is the focus of the first part of this chapter.

Despite the apparent popularity of truth commissions, their nature often remains obscure to lawmakers and laypersons alike. There is, for example, a continuing tendency to assume that all truth commissions look and function like the South African Truth and Reconciliation Commission. The second part of this chapter will address such fallacies, provide a definition of truth commissions, and canvass the actual diversity of truth commission models.

Since truth commissions are but one form of human rights investigation, and not always the most appropriate one, it is important to understand what distinguishes them from other forms of national and international human rights investigation. To that end, the third part of this chapter will posit a taxonomy of human rights investigation and attempt to situate truth commissions within it.

The chapter will conclude by distinguishing truth commissions from courts. Truth commissions, at times seen as substitutes for criminal justice, naturally elicit controversy. This book challenges the notion of truth commissions as surrogates for criminal justice, and also seeks to explain the distinct, yet complementary, roles that truth commissions and courts can play in achieving the broader objectives of transitional justice.

SECTION 1: OVERVIEW OF TRANSITIONAL JUSTICE

It would be injudicious to examine the subject of truth commissions in isolation from the broader subject of transitional justice. Indeed, one of their characteristics is that truth commissions are usually established during periods of political or postconflict transition. This fact is best explained by an analysis of the justice-related challenges that attend such transitions.

The term "transitional justice" is of recent origin. In the past two decades, a veritable cottage industry of literature has developed on the subject.[1] In general, transitional justice concerns how states in transition from war to peace or from authoritarian rule to democracy address their particular legacies of mass abuse.[2] Like the broader topic of human rights, of which it forms part, transitional justice is a multidisciplinary field of study and practice that encompasses aspects of law, policy, ethics, and social science.

The field of transitional justice arose as a result of many global developments, including the events and aftermath of the Second World War – which saw major war crimes trials, massive reparation programs, and widespread purges – as well as transitions out of war in places ranging from El Salvador to the former Yugoslavia to Sierra Leone. The development of transitional justice was also prompted by transitions (or returns) to democracy in Southern Europe

---

1   *See, e.g.*, Aspen Institute, *State Crimes. Punishment or Pardon: Papers and Reports of the Conference, November 4–6, 1988, Wye Centre, Maryland* (Queenstown, MD: Aspen Institute, 1989); B. Ackerman, *The Future of Liberal Revolution* (New Haven: Yale University Press, 1992); N. Kritz, ed., *Transitional Justice: How Emerging Democracies Reckon with Former Regimes*, 3 vols. (Washington, DC: US Institute for Peace Press, 1995); N. Roht-Arriaza, ed., *Impunity and Human Rights in International Law and Practice* (New York: Oxford University Press, 1995); A. McAdams, ed., *Transitional Justice and the Rule of Law in New Democracies* (Notre Dame, IN: University of Notre Dame Press, 1997); R. Rotberg and D. Thompson, eds., *Truth v. Justice* (Princeton, NJ: Princeton University Press, 2000); R. Teitel, *Transitional Justice* (New York: Oxford University Press, 2002); A. Henkin, ed., *The Legacy of Abuse* (New York: Aspen Institute and NYU School of Law, 2002); M. C. Bassiouni, ed., *Post-Conflict Justice* (Ardsley, NY: Transnational, 2002); R. Mani, *Beyond Retribution: Seeking Justice in the Shadows of War* (Malden, MA: Polity, 2002); J. Elster, *Closing the Books: Transitional Justice in Historical Perspective* (Cambridge: Cambridge University Press, 2004).

2   These are the standard categories of transition. In fact, there are many other "transitional" contexts that do not fit neatly into either category, but to which the methodology of transitional justice applies. These include, for example, more subtle transitions from a democracy in which human rights are weakly observed to one in which they are more effectively observed.

in the 1970s, Latin America in the 1980s, and Africa, Asia, and Central and Eastern Europe in the 1990s and beyond.[3]

On one level, there is little that unites any single transitional context to another; the differences are greater than the similarities. Sometimes the transition is quick and relatively unconstrained (*e.g.,* Greece's return to democratic rule in the 1970s), other times it is slower and more constrained (*e.g.,* the return to democratic rule in Chile in the 1990s). Sometimes the United Nations is deeply involved (*e.g.,* in negotiating the end of civil war in Guatemala), other times not (*e.g.,* the return to multiparty democracy in Ghana in the 1990s). Sometimes the transition is catalyzed by foreign intervention (*e.g.,* Afghanistan), other times by internal armed rebellion (*e.g.,* South Africa), by scandal (*e.g.,* Peru), or by general elections (*e.g.,* Serbia and Montenegro). Sometimes the scale of violations is massive (*e.g.,* Cambodia), other times less so (*e.g.,* Panama). In some instances, the worst violations occurred long before the transition (*e.g.,* Spain); in other cases, they have continued right up until the moment of transition (*e.g.,* Timor-Leste). Sometimes state actors have committed the bulk of violations (*e.g.,* El Salvador); other times it has been nonstate actors (*e.g.,* Sierra Leone); and at times responsibility has also been shared more or less equally by state and nonstate actors (*e.g.,* Mozambique).

Despite these and other differences, there is one feature that unites all these contexts: the legacy of widespread violence and repression. It is this feature that led to the development of the field of transitional justice. In many of these countries the ordinary tools of justice – primarily, the courts – were simply not up to the task of meting out a form of justice commensurate with the scale of violations committed. The contexts demanded other tools, other responses, other mechanisms.

Truth commissions constitute one such response or mechanism. Transitional justice is not, however, synonomous with truth commissions; truth commissions are but one component of the field of transitional justice.

In theory and in practice, transitional justice focuses on four main mechanisms:

1. *Trials* – whether civil or criminal, national or international, domestic or foreign
2. *Fact-finding bodies* – whether truth commissions or other similar national or international investigative bodies

---

3   *See, e.g.,* G. O'Donnell and P. Schmitter, eds., *Transitions from Authoritarian Rule: Tentative Conclusions about Uncertain Democracies* (Baltimore: Johns Hopkins University Press, 1986); S. P. Huntington, *The Third Wave: Democratization in the Late Twentieth Century* (Norman: University of Oklahoma Press, 1991); J. Linz and A. Stepan, *Problems of Democratic Transition and Consolidation* (Baltimore: Johns Hopkins University Press, 1996).

3. *Reparations* – whether compensatory, symbolic, restitutionary, or rehabilitative in nature
4. *Justice reforms* – including legal and constitutional reforms, and the
   removal of abusers from public positions through vetting or lustration
   procedures

Transitional justice also intersects with other subjects such as amnesty, reconciliation, and the preservation of memory, as well as democratization and
peacebuilding.[4]

The four main mechanisms of transitional justice closely correspond to state
obligations under international human rights law. Trials are a means by which
states implement their obligation to investigate and punish perpetrators of
serious human rights violations. Fact-finding bodies such as truth commissions
are a means by which states implement their obligation to investigate and
identify perpetrators of serious human rights violations and their victims.
Reparations are a means by which states implement their obligation to provide
restitution and compensation for serious human rights violations. And justice
reforms are a means by which states implement their obligation to take effective
measures to prevent future serious human rights violations.

Each of these obligations corresponds, in turn, to an individual right. The
obligation to investigate, prosecute, and punish serious human rights violations
corresponds to the right to justice (or the right to an effective remedy); the
obligation to investigate and identify victims and perpetrators of serious human
rights violations corresponds to the right to truth (or the right to know);
the obligation to provide restitution and compensation for serious human
rights violations corresponds to the right to reparation; and the obligation to
prevent serious human rights violations corresponds to the right to guarantees
of nonrepetition.[5]

The right to truth, which is of primary interest in this book, has been
interpreted very broadly, if erratically, by domestic and regional courts and
multilateral human rights supervisory organs. The right – affirmed in 2005 in

---

4   For example, the themes and mechanisms of transitional justice form part of the man-
    date of the proposed UN Peacebuilding Commission. *See* World Summit Outcome: Final
    Document, GA res. 60/1 (2005), paras. 97 and 98.
5   For a review of most of these obligations and their corresponding rights, *see* L. Joinet,
    "Set of Principles for the Protection and Promotion of Human Rights Through Action
    to Combat Impunity," UN doc. E/CN.4/Sub.2/1997/20/Rev. 1 (1997) [Joinet Principles],
    which was updated in 2005 by UN expert D. Orentlicher, "Updated Set of Principles for
    the Protection and Promotion of Human Rights Through Action to Combat Impunity,"
    UN doc. E/CN.4/2005/102/Add.1; and "Basic Principles and Guidelines on the Right to
    a Remedy and Reparation for Victims of Violations of International Human Rights and
    Humanitarian Law," annexed to GA res. A/C.3/60/L.24 [Bassiouni Principles].

an unprecedented resolution of the UN Commission on Human Rights[6] and in the draft International Convention for the Protection of All Persons from Enforced Disappearance[7] – has been found to encompass an individual's right to have serious human rights violations effectively investigated by the state,[8] to be informed of the fate of missing or forcibly disappeared relatives,[9] to be kept informed of the state of official investigations into disappearances and other serious violations,[10] to be provided with the "mortal remains" of loved ones once they have been located,[11] and to know the identity of those responsible for the violations.[12] It has also been found to include a societal right to know

6   Resolution 2005/66, "Right to the Truth." The resolution was adopted without a vote. The resolution calls upon the Office of the UN High Commissioner for Human Rights "to prepare a study on the right to the truth, including information on the basis, scope and content of the right under international law, as well as best practices and recommendations for effective implementation of this right . . ."

7   UN doc. E/CN.4/2005/WG.22/WP.1/REV.4 (23 September 2005), article 24(2): "Each victim has the right to know the truth regarding the circumstances of the enforced disappearance, the progress and results of the investigation and the fate of the disappeared person. Each State Party shall take appropriate steps in this regard." In addition, the preamble affirms "the right to know the truth about circumstances of an enforced disappearance and the fate of the disappeared person, and the respect of the right to freedom to seek, receive and impart information to this end."

8   See, e.g., McCann and others v. United Kingdom, 18984/91 [1995] European Court of Human Rights (27 September 1995), at para. 161; Laureano v. Peru, UN Human Rights Committee, UN doc. CCPR/C/56/D/540/1993 (1996), at para. 8.3; Rodriguez v. Uruguay, UN Human Rights Committee, UN doc. CCPR/C/51/D/322/1988 (1994), at para. 12.3.

9   See, e.g., Quinteros Almeida v. Uruguay, UN Human Rights Committee, Communication no. 107/1981 (2003); Bámaca Velásquez v. Guatemala, Inter-American Court of Human Rights, vol. 70, Series C, paras. 159–66 (25 November 2000); the Srebrenica cases, Human Rights Chamber (BiH), Cases Nos. CH/01/8365 et al., Decision on Admissibility and Merits (7 March 2003), at paras. 191 and 220 (4). Article 3 of the Inter-American Convention on Forced Disappearance of Persons 1994, (1994) 33 ILM 1429, provides that the offense of forced disappearance "shall be deemed continuous or permanent as long as the fate or whereabouts of the victim has not been determined." Article 32 of Protocol Additional to the Geneva Conventions of 12 August 1949, and relating to the Protection of Victims of International Armed Conflicts (Protocol I) 1977, 1125 UNTS 3, provides for "the right of families to know the fate of their relatives." See also art. 33, which requires parties to international conflicts to search for missing persons. See also Principle 16(1) of the Guiding Principles on Internal Displacement, UN doc. E/CN.4/1998/53/Add.2.

10 See, e.g., the Del Caracazo case, Inter-American Court of Human Rights, vol. 95, Series C (Reparations) (2002), at para. 118; Kurt v. Turkey, 24276/94 [1998] European Court of Human Rights 44 (25 May 1998), at para. 140.

11 See, e.g., Bámaca Velásquez case, Inter-American Court of Human Rights, vol. 91, Series C (Reparations), para. 79 (22 February 2002). See also Law on Missing Persons, Bosnia and Herzegovina, Official Gazette 50/04, art. 3.

12 See, e.g., Ellacuría and others v. El Salvador, Inter-American Commission of Human Rights, Case 10.488, OEA/ser.L/V/II.106 (1999), at para. 221.

the full truth concerning serious violations, both for its own sake and to avoid the future recurrence of such violations.[13] Violations of the right to know have been deemed, among other things, violations of the prohibition on torture,[14] the right to respect for private and family life,[15] the right to life,[16] the right to an effective remedy,[17] and the right to reparation.[18] Like most human rights, however, the right to truth is probably not absolute. It may be subject to limitations in the broader public interest.[19]

The Inter-American Court of Human Rights articulated the first truly comprehensive statement of a state's human rights obligations in the landmark case of *Velásquez Rodríguez v. Honduras*.[20] The case dealt with a Honduran student who was apparently detained without warrant, tortured by police, and ultimately forcibly disappeared. In a unanimous judgment, the court found Honduras in violation of several articles of the American Convention on Human Rights 1969 (ACHR),[21] and directed it to pay fair compensation to Velásquez's next-of-kin.

The Court grounded its judgment in an analysis of ACHR article 1(1), by which states parties to the convention "undertake to respect the [ACHR's]

---

13   *See, e.g., Ellacuría,* above note 12, at paras. 223 and 226; *Romero v. El Salvador,* Inter-American Court of Human Rights, Case 11.481, OEA/ser.L/V/II.106 (2000), at para. 144 ("The right to the truth is a collective right that enables society to have access to information essential to the development of democracies."); the *Srebrenica* cases nos. CH/01/8365 *et al.,* above note 9, para. 212. The societal right to truth is also linked to the right of access to information. *See* T. M. Antkowiak, "Truth as Right and Remedy in International Human Rights Experience" (2002) 23 *Mich. J. Int'l. L.* 977, at 994. *See also* Orentlicher, "Updated Set of Principles," above note 5, Principles 2 ("The Inalienable Right to the Truth") and 3 ("The Duty to Preserve Memory").

14   *See, e.g., Cyprus v. Turkey,* 25781/94 [2001] European Court of Human Rights 327 (10 May 2001), at paras. 157–8; the *Srebrenica* cases, above note 9, at paras. 191 and 220 (4).

15   *See, e.g., Srebrenica* cases, above note 9, at paras. 181 and 220 (3). *See also* UN docs. E/CN.4/1435 and E/CN.4/1983/14, para. 134.

16   *See, e.g., Cyprus v. Turkey,* above note 14, at para. 136.

17   *See, e.g., Parada Cea et al. v. El Salvador* (case 10.480), Inter-American Commission on Human Rights, report no. 1/99, at para. 152; *Aksoy v. Turkey,* 26 European Court of Human Rights 2260 (1996), at 2287; and *Mentes et al. v. Turkey,* 59 European Court of Human Rights 2689 (1997), at 2716. *See also* the African Commission on Human and Peoples' Rights, Principles and Guidelines on the Right to a Fair Trial and Legal Assistance in Africa, DOC/OS (XXX) 247, Principle C.

18   *See, e.g., Monsignor Oscar Arnulfo Romero y Galdámez v. El Salvador* (case 11.481), Inter-American Commission on Human Rights, report no. 37/00, paras. 147–8; *Myrna Mack Chang* case, Inter-American Court of Human Rights, vol. 101, Series C, paras. 274–5 (23 November 2003).

19   On such limitations generally, *see* M. Freeman and G. van Ert, *International Human Rights Law* (Toronto: Irwin Law, 2004), at 33–5. The right to truth could also conflict with other human rights, including privacy and reputation rights. *See* Chapter 2, Section 1.

20   (1988) I/A Court HR Series C no. 4 [*Velásquez Rodríguez*].

21   OAS TS no. 36.

rights and freedoms" and "ensure to all persons subject to their jurisdiction the free and full exercise of those rights and freedoms" without discrimination. Its most important holding for present purposes was the following:

> The state has a legal duty to take reasonable steps to prevent human rights violations and to use the means at its disposal to carry out a serious investigation of violations committed within its jurisdiction, to identify those responsible, to impose the appropriate punishment and to ensure the victim adequate compensation.

The essence of *Velásquez Rodríguez*, implicit in the main UN and regional human rights treaties, has been affirmed, *inter alia*, in the Joinet Principles[22] and the Bassiouni Principles.[23] Though nonbinding, these Principles probably constitute the most comprehensive and widely accepted description of a state's human rights obligations and an individual's human rights.[24]

The field of transitional justice is conceptually wedded to the broad approach to human rights articulated in *Velásquez Rodríguez* and affirmed in the Joinet and Bassiouni Principles. Transitional justice, in other words, includes – but extends well beyond – the realm of criminal justice. This is unsurprising, because in nearly all transitional contexts there is a virtual guarantee of "incomplete justice." There are many reasons for this. In transitional contexts there are often thousands of victims, as well as hundreds if not thousands of perpetrators. The abusive forces of the past often continue to wield some measure of political authority and military or police power. The administration of justice – from police to prosecutors to judges – is typically weak and frequently plagued by corruption. Transitional contexts are usually marked by widespread unemployment and scarce public resources too, making it difficult to meet or justify the costs associated with a program of retroactive justice.

22 *See* note 5 above. The Joinet Principles specify four rights: the "right to know," the "right to justice," the "right to reparations," and the right to "guarantees of non-recurrence" of violations.

23 *See* note 5 above. Principle 3 of the Bassiouni Principles provides: "The obligation to respect, ensure respect for and implement international human rights law and international humanitarian law as provided for under the respective bodies of law, includes, *inter alia*, the duty to: (a) Take appropriate legislative and administrative and other appropriate measures to prevent violations; (b) Investigate violations effectively, promptly, thoroughly and impartially and, where appropriate, take action against those allegedly responsible in accordance with domestic and international law; (c) Provide those who claim to be victims of a human rights or humanitarian law violation with equal and effective access to justice, as described below, irrespective of who may ultimately be the bearer of responsibility for the violation; and (d) Provide effective remedies to victims, including reparation . . ."

24 *See* D. Orentlicher, "Promotion and Protection of Human Rights: Impunity," UN doc. E/CN.4/2004/88 (2004), at "Summary."

Rising criminality is also a common feature of countries in transition, placing governments in the invidious position of having to confront massive numbers of past as well as present crimes. Key documents are often destroyed and crime scenes altered to conceal evidence. Witnesses may still fear the potential repercussions of testifying, even in the absence of persistent intimidation, and judges and prosecutors may face death threats. There are often legal obstacles to achieving justice as well, whether in the form of amnesty laws, lapsed prescription periods for prosecuting certain crimes, or lacunae in the reception of international norms into domestic law.

In the face of these myriad challenges, it is little wonder that societies in transition are breeding grounds for new models and broader conceptions of justice. At the same time, criminal justice retains an appropriately unique place in the range of responses to mass atrocity. In the last fifteen years alone, the world has witnessed the establishment of *ad hoc* international criminal tribunals for the former Yugoslavia and Rwanda, a permanent international criminal court in The Hague, and hybrid criminal tribunals in Kosovo, Sierra Leone, Timor-Leste, Bosnia-Herzegovina, and Cambodia. Alongside these developments, domestic prosecutors and judges have become increasingly important actors in the transitional justice arena in relation to international crimes committed both within and outside national borders.[25] In short, the importance of criminal trials remains unrivaled. No other mechanism is perceived to have a greater impact on specific and general deterrence, public confidence in the state's ability and willingness to enforce the law, and a victim's sense of justice.

Yet if criminal trials were alone sufficient, the field of transitional justice would never have emerged. The fact is that other responses, beyond criminal justice, are required. Justice systems simply are not designed to remedy violations committed on the massive scale typical of transitional contexts. Rather, justice systems are designed to handle crime as an exceptional occurrence.[26] The relatively slow pace, minimal victim participation, and weak rehabilitative or reconciliatory capacity that tend to be endemic to criminal prosecutions also limit the depth and reach of their impact, no matter the context. Accordingly, the recourse of transitional governments to complementary nonjudicial mechanisms such as truth commissions is natural.

---

25 *See* Section 4 below.
26 M. Freeman and P. van Zyl, "Conference Report," in Henkin, *The Legacy of Abuse*, at 5. *See also* A. Boraine, *A Country Unmasked* (Oxford: Oxford University Press, 2000), at 434: "In trying to come to terms with genocide, crimes against humanity, and other massive atrocities, not only does our moral discourse appear to reach its limit, but ordinary measures that usually apply in the field of criminal justice become inadequate. Abnormal atrocities demand abnormal measures."

SECTION 2: OVERVIEW OF TRUTH COMMISSIONS

Despite its Orwellian name, the truth commission has become a preferred fixture of international law and politics alongside international and hybrid criminal tribunals. Particularly since the advent of South Africa's Truth and Reconciliation Commission (TRC) in the 1990s, it is difficult to conjure an example of a political or postconflict transition in which the idea of establishing a truth commission has been overlooked.[27] For the most part this is a good thing. The majority of truth commissions have done important work in their respective contexts. They have often rebutted the misrepresentations of the old order through investigation, public hearings, and detailed reports. Some have spurred significant national debates and helped push governments to take corrective and preventive actions in the areas of justice, reparation, and institutional reform. Many truth commissions have also contributed to a sense of "historical justice" on the part of victims and society when criminal justice was not a viable option.[28]

At the same time, some people's expectations of what a truth commission can achieve exceed the bounds of reason. There is often a sense that truth commissions can do magic: heal nations, reconcile victims and torturers, ensure the rule of law, and establish a culture of human rights.[29] It is also often imagined that truth commissions can help "refound" a broken polity,[30] or construct a kind of psychological bridge between a country's past and its future, without which the future remains volatile.[31] With expectations so high, it is little

---

27 This is not to suggest that truth commissions command universal appeal. Countries in the former Eastern Bloc of communist states did not (with the exception of Germany) establish truth commissions. This is often explained by factors such as the public distrust of official "truths" (after years under Soviet rule) and the fact that responsibility and victimization were spread across almost the entire population. *See, e.g.*, H. Steiner, ed., *Truth Commissions: A Comparative Assessment* (Cambridge, MA: Harvard Law School Human Rights Program, 1997), at 39–41. Also, "In cases where a clear victor emerges, no truth commission is established. The winners simply prosecute the losers. Truth commissions have been established in situations where there is no clear victor" (Jose Zalaquett, cited in *ibid.*, at 70).

28 *See* Teitel, *Transitional Justice*, at 81–92. Teitel distinguishes between criminal justice, historical justice, reparatory justice, administrative justice, and constitutional justice. Historical justice, in brief, refers to a perception on the part of victims and society that the worst crimes of the past have been adequately identified and acknowledged.

29 Such outcomes tend to be presumed, rather than tested in a serious manner. For a proposed research agenda to test some of the claimed benefits of truth telling, *see* P. de Greiff, "Truth-Telling and the Rule of Law," in T. A. Borer, ed., *Telling the Truths: Truth Telling and Peacebuilding in Post-Conflict Societies* (Notre Dame, IN: University of Notre Dame Press, 2005).

30 Jose Zalaquett, cited in Steiner, *Truth Commissions*, above note 27, at 30.

31 *See, e.g.*, the preamble to the *Promotion of National Unity and Reconciliation Act*, 1995 (South Africa), which created the South African TRC. It declares in part: "Since the Constitution of

wonder that a sense of disappointment sometimes emerges in the aftermath of a truth commission process, when the public inevitably confronts the fact that becoming a "normal" or "reconciled" society will take more than a few years.[32]

A proper understanding of the limitations of truth commissions can help curb such expectations. With this in mind, the next section of the chapter offers a comprehensive definition of the subject. This is followed by a brief historical survey of the origins and contemporary forms of the truth commission, and then by a discussion of challenges and limitations that can be reasonably expected.

Definition

The standard definition of truth commissions is provided by Priscilla Hayner, the leading authority on the subject. In *Unspeakable Truths*,[33] Hayner defines truth commissions as bodies that share the following characteristics: (1) they examine only past events;[34] (2) they investigate patterns of abuse committed

---

the Republic of South Africa, 1993 (Act No. 200 of 1993) provides an historic bridge between the past of a deeply divided society characterized by strife, conflict, untold suffering and injustice, and a future founded on the recognition of human rights, democracy and peaceful co-existence for all South Africans, irrespective of colour, race, class, belief or sex . . . And since it is deemed necessary to establish the truth in relation to past events as well as the motives for and circumstances in which gross violations of human rights have occurred, and to make the findings known in order to prevent a repetition of such acts in future . . ."

32   This is one reason to be skeptical of the prevalent use of the term "reconciliation" in a truth commission's title. Few truth commissions actually focus in any depth on reconciliation activities (the commission in Timor-Leste being at least one prominent exception). Instead, truth commissions, as much by necessity as by choice, tend to focus and deliver primarily on the "truth" part of their mandate.

33   P. Hayner, *Unspeakable Truths: Facing the Challenge of Truth Commissions*, 2d ed. (New York: Routledge, 2002), at 14.

34   In an earlier article, Hayner listed the Philippine Presidential Committee on Human Rights as a truth commission despite the fact that it was mandated to investigate not only past abuses but also, for an indeterminate period, future abuses. *See* P. Hayner, "Fifteen Truth Commissions – 1974 to 1994: A Comparative Study" (1994) 16 *Human Rights Quarterly* 597, at 620. In Hayner, *Unspeakable Truths*, above note 33, the Committee is not included as a truth commission, but for a different reason. "[The] Committee was not expected to produce an overall report nor to document the pattern of past abuses, but rather focused its work on responding to individual cases . . ." *Ibid.*, at 270. Query how best to categorize the current TRC in the Democratic Republic of Congo (DRC). Established in 2004, the commission is authorized to investigate violations committed between 1960 and 2006, when the country's formal political transition is scheduled to conclude. Applying Hayner's definition, the TRC in the DRC would not be characterized as a truth commission.

over a period of time, as opposed to a particular event;[35] (3) they are temporary bodies that finish their work with the submission of a report containing conclusions and recommendations; and (4) they are "officially sanctioned, authorized, or empowered by the state (and sometimes also by the armed opposition, as in a peace accord)."[36] Hayner identifies three more common elements of the truth commissions examined in her book: (1) they focus on recent events, (2) they investigate politically intentioned or targeted violations, and (3) they operate in contexts marked by widespread violations.[37] Finally, she notes that truth commissions are usually established at, and serve as a central component of, a period of political or postconflict transition.[38]

---

35 As explained in Section 3 below, most event-specific inquiries cover surrounding circum-stances or events, but that does not make them inquiries into abuses "committed over a period of time" in the manner typical of truth commissions. This author, therefore, ques-tions Hayner's description of the 1995 international commission of inquiry "to establish the facts relating to the assassination of the President of Burundi on 21 October 1993 [and] the massacres and other related serious acts of violence which followed" as an exam-ple of a truth commission. It should be considered more akin to the investigation of a single event rather than "patterns of abuses committed over a period of time." This dis-tinction is discussed in more depth later in this chapter. On the Burundi inquiry, *see* Hayner, *Unspeakable Truths*, above note 33, at 67–8. The inquiry's full report is avail-able at http://www.usip.org/library/tc/doc/reports/burundi_coi/burundi_coi1996toc.html. That inquiry was preceded by two other UN inquiries on the same subject. *See* UN docs. S/1995/157(1995) and S/1995/631(1995).

36 *See also* Hayner, "Fifteen Truth Commissions," above note 34, at 604: ". . . a truth commission is always vested with some sort of authority, by way of its sponsor, that allows it greater access to information, greater security or protection to dig into sensitive issues, and a greater impact with its report." It is this official character of a truth commission – combined with the fact that the general array of past violations is already thought to be known – that has led many observers to assert that a truth commission is as much about *acknowledging* the truth as about finding it. *See, e.g., ibid.,* at 607; Hayner, *Unspeakable Truths,* above note 33, at 25 ("In some countries, rights activists insist that a truth commission does not find new truth so much as lift the veil of denial about widely known but unspoken truths.")

37 Hayner, *Unspeakable Truths,* above note 33, at 17. It is not clear why Hayner lists these elements outside of her definition.

38 *Ibid.* This is logical, since tyrants generally prefer not to expose their human rights records to independent scrutiny while in power. As for wartime contexts, "The utility of a truth commission in a context where an intense armed conflict is ongoing is . . . dubious because it would be virtually impossible to achieve the appearance of neutrality, or to ensure victim and witness participation and security. In addition, geographical access and access to key information is likely to be severely limited in such a context." M. Freeman and P. Hayner, "Truth-Telling," in *Reconciliation After Violent Conflict: A Handbook* (Stockholm: Institute for Democracy and Electoral Assistance, 2003), at 127.

Hayner's definition provides a useful starting point. However, it omits other essential truth commission attributes. These attributes derive from past and present truth commission experiences. When they are incorporated into the definition, a more precise understanding of the truth commission phenomenon emerges.[39]

A first element omitted from Hayner's definition is the fact that truth commissions are *commissions of inquiry* whose primary function is investigation.[40] As such, truth commissions are easily distinguishable from courts and administrative tribunals, whose primary function is adjudication. Truth commissions, by definition, are never equivalent to courts or tribunals.[41]

A second omitted element from Hayner's definition is the fact that truth commissions *focus on severe acts of violence or repression.* Such acts may take many forms, ranging from arbitrary detention to torture to enforced disappearance to summary execution. Depending on the context, such acts may constitute violations of international or domestic human rights, humanitarian, or criminal law.[42] Truth commissions invariably, and appropriately, focus primarily on direct acts of physical violence.[43] However, some have examined other forms of repression too, including expropriation of property without

---

39   Some of the attributes described below are implied in Hayner's analysis, but they are not made explicit in her definition.

40   The one prominent exception is the TRC in the DRC which, since its establishment, has focused primarily on reconciliation and mediation activities rather than on investigation. With some reluctance, however, it is treated as a truth commission in this book; for even if it chooses to limit its investigative work, its mandate makes plain that it was intended to function as a commission of inquiry. Just as importantly, it has been consistently characterized as a truth commission – simply a bad example of one.

41   *See* Section 4 below. The abandoned mandate of a truth commission in Burundi envisaged the conversion of the commission from an investigative body into the equivalent of a court for purposes of assessing damages payable to the identified victim of a presumed perpetrator. In this respect, it resided somewhere between a court and a truth commission, without necessarily being one or the other. *See Law no. 1/018 (2004) Concerning the Mission, Composition, Organization and Functioning of the National Truth and Reconciliation Commission* (Burundi), chapter V.

42   On the distinctions between international human rights, humanitarian, and criminal law, *see* Freeman and van Ert, *International Human Rights Law*, above note 19, c. 7.

43   *See, e.g.,* Orentlicher, "Updated Set of Principles," above note 5, Principle 8(d): "Commissions of inquiry may have jurisdiction to consider all forms of violations of human rights and humanitarian law. Their investigations should focus as a matter of priority on violations constituting serious crimes under international law, including in particular violations of the fundamental rights of women and of other vulnerable groups." For a contrary view about the appropriateness of focusing on violations of bodily integrity, *see, e.g.,* M. Mamdani, *Citizen and Subject* (Princeton, NJ: Princeton University Press, 1996).

compensation,[44] unjust dismissal and government harassment,[45] and forced displacement.[46]

A related omission from Hayner's definition concerns the contexts in which such acts of violence or repression occur. Truth commissions focus primarily on acts that occurred *during recent periods of abusive rule or armed conflict*. In most instances, those periods have drawn to a close. However, that is not always the case.[47] Nor is it always the case that a truth commission mandate covers all of the "dark" periods in a country's relatively recent past. For example, Haiti's truth commission covered only three years out of many decades of repressive rule. However, the prototypical truth commission examines all of the key periods of recent conflict or repression, precisely at a moment of transition toward ostensibly better times.

A further omitted element of Hayner's definition is the fact that truth commissions are concerned not only with sorting out the facts of individual cases but also with providing an account of the *broad causes and consequences* of the violations that occurred. Inquiries that do not seek to provide an overarching narrative of the historical periods under consideration are not truth commissions.

Another element of a complete definition of truth commissions is the fact that they focus on *violations committed in the sponsoring state*. This focus applies

---

44 *See, e.g.*, art. 4(a) of the mandate of the *National Reconciliation Commission Act*, 2002, Act 611 (Ghana), which provides that the commission shall "investigate violations and abuses of human rights relating to killings, abductions, disappearances, detentions, torture, ill-treatment and *seizure of properties suffered by any person* within the specified periods" (emphasis added). *See also* the *Report of the Task Force on the Establishment of a Truth, Justice and Reconciliation Commission*, Republic of Kenya (2003), Recommendation 13: "That the TJRC have the power to investigate human rights violations and violations of economic, social and cultural rights." *See also* Recommendation 18: "That the TJRC be empowered to negotiated with perpetrators of economic crimes for the return of stolen property and funds in exchange for recommendations of limited amnesty and immunity."

45 *See, e.g.*, Hayner's discussion of Germany's truth commission. *Unspeakable Truths*, above note 33, at 61–2. *See also* Nigeria: *Judicial Commission of Inquiry for the Investigation of Human Rights Violations, Final Report* (2002), Synoptic Overview, ch. 2, at 58, where the commission notes that it received and investigated "over 600 memoranda from civil servants alleging that the federal government and state governments had violated their right to work."

46 In Sierra Leone, the TRC documented not only forced displacement (which accounted for almost 20% of the violations reported to the commission), but also destruction of property and looting of goods. *Sierra Leone Truth and Reconciliation Commission Final Report* (2004), vol. 2, ch. 2, paras. 86–7.

47 For example, the TRC in the DRC is operating despite the fact that armed conflict continues in parts of the country.

irrespective of whether the violations are predominantly committed by the state (*e.g.*, Chad), by nonstate actors (*e.g.*, Peru), or by a former occupying power (*e.g.*, Timor-Leste).[48] A commission of inquiry established in state X to focus primarily or exclusively on violations committed in state Y is not a truth commission. A truth commission has an inherent self-assessment or self-investigation character; it involves a state or society trying to repair or regenerate itself in some way.[49]

A related defining element of truth commissions concerns their place of operation. Truth commissions are not only authorized or empowered *by* states, they are also set up *in* them. Indeed, it would be a mischaracterization to describe an inquiry as a truth commission if its office and staff were predominantly or exclusively located outside the sponsoring state.[50] Admittedly, truth commissions may conduct part of their operations extraterritorially, whether by choice[51] or by necessity.[52] But a fundamental element of a truth commission is its domestic, or "on-site," character.

---

48 Many truth commissions have also examined the responsibility of foreign states. For example, the Guatemalan truth commission revealed US involvement in the violations being investigated, while the TRC in Sierra Leone made critical findings of governments in Liberia, Libya, and the UK, as well as of the United Nations. *Sierra Leone Truth and Reconciliation Commission Final Report* (2004), vol. 2, ch. 2, paras. 364–72.

49 This may involve examining violations committed by the sponsoring state in neighboring jurisdictions too. For example, the South African TRC investigated atrocities in Mozambique and Namibia that were committed by the prior apartheid governments, and the Chilean TRC examined violations committed throughout the Southern Cone by the prior military government. *See* R. Mattarollo, "Truth Commissions," in Bassiouni, *Post-Conflict Justice*, above note 1, at 297–8.

50 Admittedly, a future truth commission could be established by more than one state (*e.g.*, a regional truth commission for the states comprising the former Yugoslavia). Provided that the commission's offices and staff members were predominantly or exclusively located in the participating states (as opposed to in third states), it would be consistent with this book's truth commission definition. Such is the case for the Commission on Truth and Friendship between Timor-Leste and Indonesia. The commission consists of ten members, five from each sponsoring state, operating within the two sponsoring states. (Note, however, that the Commission on Truth and Friendship is an event-specific inquiry, not a truth commission. Article 12 of its mandate sets its primary objective as the establishment of "the conclusive truth in regard to the events prior to and immediately after the popular consultation in 1999." The mandate is available online at http://www.etan.org/et2005/march/06/10tor.htm.)

51 For example, the truth commissions of Argentina, Chile, Guatemala, and Morocco authorized statement taking by embassies or foreign organizations. Such an approach enables members of a large diaspora of nationals (including refugees) to participate in the truth commission's work.

52 El Salvador's truth commission, faced with serious security concerns, had to physically move its operations out of the country partway through its work. This of course does not alter fact that the commission was set up to operate *in* El Salvador.

A further element that should be added to Hayner's definition is the fact that truth commissions are *victim-centered* bodies.[53] Being victim-centered means that most of a truth commission's time and attention is focused on victims – their experiences, their views, their needs, and their preferences.[54] It does not mean that a truth commission is always self-consciously victim-centered (because some are not), nor does it mean that a truth commission is concerned only with victims (because they are not).[55] It simply means that victims, as opposed to witnesses and perpetrators, constitute the primary focus of a commission's work.

Another defining characteristic of a truth commission concerns its *relative independence from the state*. Where state crime is involved, whether in the context of repressive rule or armed conflict, turning to the ordinary or standing investigative organs of the state (*e.g.*, police, gendarmes, Department of Justice) can undermine the appearance or reality of an independent investigation. It can create a "cloud of suspicion" around the investigation. In authorizing the establishment of a truth commission – by definition an *ad hoc* body – the sponsor seeks to create the appearance of a semi-independent or arm's length investigation.[56] While some may query how a truth commission created or authorized by the state can be independent of it, such logic is flawed. For example, the fact that a judge is appointed by the state to serve on a court is hardly an indication of an absence of judicial independence. In assessing the degree of independence of any public body, a multitude of other factors needs to be taken into account, including its composition and the degree of its financial, legal, and operational autonomy.[57]

---

53 Relatives of the direct victim may also themselves be defined as victims, especially in cases of death or forced disappearance. *See, e.g.*, Principle 8 of the Bassiouni Principles, above note 5.

54 This may be by choice (*i.e.*, a commission may prefer to focus on victims), necessity (*i.e.*, a commission may focus on victims because independent witnesses and perpetrators generally shun it), or a combination of both.

55 For example, the truth commissions in South Africa and Timor-Leste focused significant attention on alleged perpetrators – the former through its amnesty procedure, the latter through its community reconciliation panels. Yet each commission consistently described itself as a victim-centered body.

56 *See, e.g., A Hard Journey to Justice: First Term Report by the Presidential Truth Commission on Suspicious Deaths of the Republic of Korea* (2004), at 60: "The main body conducting the fact-finding investigation had to be independent of the government authorities, which were themselves related to the suspicious deaths. In this respect, the public prosecutor's reinvestigation was not recommended . . . It was not a good idea, therefore, to form a special committee or team within the National Assembly or the National Human Rights Commission of Korea. It was agreed eventually that a new and independent special commission should conduct the inquiry."

57 *See* Chapter 2, Section 3.

A final point concerns the reconsideration of an element included in, as opposed to omitted from, Hayner's definition. As previously noted, Hayner defines truth commissions as bodies "officially sanctioned, authorized, or empowered by the state (*and sometimes also* by the armed opposition, as in a peace accord)."[58] On the face of it, this seems a sound criterion. For instance, the armed opposition in each of El Salvador, Guatemala, Sierra Leone, Burundi, the Democratic Republic of Congo (DRC), and Liberia agreed to the establishment of a truth commission as part of a comprehensive peace accord. Yet Hayner treats two commissions of inquiry created by the African National Congress (while still a liberation army) as truth commissions, despite the fact that no state, least of all South Africa, sanctioned, authorized, or empowered them.[59] The only way to classify these inquiries as truth commissions while remaining true to her definition is to treat the words "and sometimes also" to mean "and/or," so that a truth commission can be a body set up by the state *or* by the armed opposition (as opposed to a body set up by the state alone, or by the state *and* the armed opposition acting jointly as in a peace accord). This does not make sense. The ANC inquiries are nonstate inquiries – period. Their nonstate character sets them apart from all other truth commissions Hayner describes in her book, and their inclusion serves to confuse an otherwise cogent, if incomplete, definition.[60]

Based on the preceding considerations, this book defines a truth commission as follows:

A truth commission is an *ad hoc*, autonomous, and victim-centered commission of inquiry set up in and authorized by a state for the primary purposes of (1) investigating and reporting on the principal causes and consequences of broad and relatively recent patterns of severe violence or repression that occurred in the state during determinate periods of abusive rule or conflict, and (2) making recommendations for their redress and future prevention.[61]

---

58   Emphasis added by author.
59   See Hayner, *Unspeakable Truths*, above note 33, at 60–4. In an earlier article, Hayner characterized another purely nongovernmental investigation in Rwanda as a truth commission. *See* Hayner, "Fifteen Truth Commissions," above note 34, at 629–32. She does not, however, list it as a truth commission in *Unspeakable Truths*, because "this commission was ultimately a nongovernmental effort . . ." (271).
60   This aspect of Hayner's definition may account for why some continue to refer to other nonstate investigations that mimic truth commissions (*e.g.*, the one which produced Brazil's *Nunca Mais* report) as truth commissions. *See, e.g.*, M. Minow, *Breaking the Cycles of Hatred: Memory, Law, and Repair* (Princeton, NJ: Princeton University Press, 2002), at 24.
61   Compare this to the similar, and relatively complete, definition of truth commission found in the Report of the UN Secretary-General, "The Rule of Law and Transitional Justice in Conflict and Post-Conflict Societies," UN doc. S/2004/616 (2004): "Truth commissions are

Like any definition, this one purports to be authoritative. It is not, however, meant to serve as the last word on the subject. The phenomenon of truth commissions is ever changing, and minor refinements may be necessary in the future. The essence of the definition should, however, hold.

Some additional qualifications are in order. First, the definition is not normative in character. It is not a description of what truth commissions *should* be. It is descriptive only. Its singular aim is to improve – to help make more precise – our collective understanding of the truth commission phenomenon.

Second, the definition used here is not meant to convey any kind of superior status for truth commissions. Thus, to characterize a human rights inquiry as something other than a truth commission – as this book frequently does – is not to denigrate the inquiry's moral, social, or political value. It is simply a matter of definitional clarity. An unbiased investigation by the police, a national human rights commission, or an NGO is better than a biased investigation by a truth commission. Truth commissions, in other words, do not automatically or necessarily sit atop a normative hierarchy of investigation. In fact, a human rights inquiry that corrresponds to the truth commission definition may not even be a creditable body at all. For example, a commission that meets the technical definition may, nevertheless, fail due to insufficient staff or material resources. Alternatively, a commission may conduct its operations in a discriminatory, nontransparent, or half-hearted fashion. In other cases, the commission may be nothing more than a public relations exercise aimed to appease an international community that has become increasingly demanding in the areas of truth and justice.[62]

A final qualification concerns the application of the truth commission definition in "borderline" cases. Specifically, it is important to consider how to classify a body that could be said to meet the definition of a truth commission when there is broad domestic and international consensus that it is *not* a truth commission. A few examples can help illustrate the point.

In Algeria in September 2003, an *ad hoc* committee presided over by the head of the national human rights commission was established to assist families of the missing and disappeared. The committee's role was to verify cases of missing persons and recommend compensation for families of the missing in

---

official, temporary, non-judicial fact-finding bodies that investigate a pattern of abuses of human rights or humanitarian law committed over a number of years." A very similar definition is found in Orentlicher, "Updated Set of Principles," above note 5, at 6.

62 A case in point is the unconvincing Truth and Reconciliation Commission established in 2001 in the Federal Republic of Yugoslavia (FRY), now Serbia and Montenegro. Although the commission was ultimately discredited, the initiative (and the title) helped buy time for a government in need of continuing aid dollars. *See* M. Freeman, *Serbia and Montenegro: Selected Developments in Transitional Justice* (International Center for Transitional Justice, 2004), at 7–9.

confirmed cases.[63] Although the Algerian government periodically described the committee as a truth commission, and although the mandate of the committee largely conformed to that of a truth commission, it was not broadly viewed as such, either domestically or internationally.[64]

Consider a slightly different example. A recent National Commission on Political Imprisonment and Torture in Chile investigated the systematic use of torture during the period of military rule in the country.[65] It investigated cases that Chile's previous TRC was precluded from documenting in its final report, namely, the cases of torture survivors.[66] Without reviewing all of its attributes, suffice it to say that the Torture Commission appears to conform to this book's definition of a truth commission. It seems, however, that it was broadly viewed as something different from a truth commission.[67] It was viewed more as an auxiliary investigation to the country's earlier TRC. The Torture Commission's job was to finish an investigation that was started, but left incomplete, by the TRC (on account of its limited mandate). Here again the question arises as to whether it makes sense to classify the body as a truth commission.

Lastly, consider a reverse scenario, namely, where a body that some might have previously considered to be a truth commission is "displaced" by a body that most, if not all, persons view as a truth commission. For example, Hayner

---

63   The committee's mandate is annexed to Human Rights Watch, *Truth and Justice on Hold: The New State Commission on Disappearances* (9 December 2003).

64   In practice, the committee operated merely as an "interface" between the state and families of the missing rather than as an investigator. *See* Fédération Internationale des Ligues des Droits de l'Homme, *Rapport: Les commissions de vérité et de réconciliation: L'expérience marocaine* (July 2004), at 53; International Center for Transitional Justice, *Annual Report* (2003/4), http://www.ictj.org, at 33. A similar borderline case comes from Lebanon. In January 2001, a committee was established to investigate submissions from families of disappeared persons who had reason to believe their loved ones remained alive. The committee was chaired by the minister of the interior and included among its members the public prosecutor, representatives of security services, and some lawyers appointed by the Beirut and Tripoli law societies. Its work ended in June 2002, but as of this writing it has not issued a report on the issues within its remit. *See* Fédération Internationale des Ligues des Droits de l'Homme, *Rapport*, at 52.

65   The commission, headed by Monsignor Valech, delivered its final report to President Ricardo Lagos in late 2004. Shortly thereafter, Chile's Congress voted to grant reparations to more than 28,000 people identified in the report as torture survivors. The reparations law also includes a controversial clause that keeps evidence gathered for the report secret for fifty years. "Transitional Justice in the News" (http://www.ictj.org), 15 November 2004 and 13 January 2005.

66   The TRC's mandate was limited to " . . . disappearance after arrest, execution, and torture leading to death committed by government agents or people in their service, as well as kidnappings and attempts on the life of persons carried out by private citizens for political reasons . . .": art. 9. The TRC did, however, interview survivors of torture.

67   In the extensive news coverage of the Torture Commission in Chile, this author could not find any sources that referred to the Torture Commission as a truth commission.

characterizes a 1985 parliamentary commission in Uruguay as a truth commission.[68] To the extent that the commission was ever broadly perceived as a
truth commission (the evidence of which is slight),[69] that perception appears
to have altered. A "Peace Commission" established in 2000 in Uruguay is, today,
broadly viewed as Uruguay's only "real" truth commission.[70] The same type of
displacement or reversal appears to have occurred in Uganda. Hayner describes
President Idi Amin's 1974 "Commission of Inquiry into the Disappearance of
People in Uganda since 25th January, 1971" as a truth commission.[71] Yet within
and outside of Uganda, it is rarely (and only awkwardly) so classified. Instead,
Uganda's 1986 Commission of Inquiry into Violations of Human Rights is
broadly viewed as the country's only truth commission.[72]

There is, admittedly, more than one possible conclusion that can be drawn
from the preceding cases. For example, one could view the Chilean Torture
Commission as a continuation of Chile's TRC or, alternatively, as a second
national truth commission. One could make the same arguments for the
Uruguayan and Ugandan examples. Although those are not conclusions drawn
by this author, reasonable people can disagree on the matter. After all, classification of political phenomena is an inherently contested endeavor.

What should be clear, however, is the importance of going beyond technical definition. In seeking to assess whether a body is a truth commission, both
objective *and* subjective criteria should be evaluated. The ultimate classification
should, in other words, be internally coherent (*i.e.*, the body in question should
reasonably conform with the technical definition of a truth commission) and
externally coherent (*i.e.*, the classification of the body as a truth commission
should reasonably correspond to a broad domestic and international consensus
about that classification). Consequently, the determination of whether a particular body is a truth commission should proceed as follows. First, one should
assess whether the body in question conforms with the technical definition. If
it does not, then it cannot be properly characterized as a truth commission,
whatever its other virtues. If it *does* correspond to the technical definition, one
should gauge – as best as possible – whether there is also broad domestic and

---

68   Hayner, *Unspeakable Truths*, above note 33, at 54.
69   Hayner acknowledges in her book that the commission was perceived as "a political exercise."
      Ibid.
70   For background on the Peace Commission, *see* "Transitional Justice in the News"
      (http://www.ictj.org), 30 April 2003.
71   Hayner, *Unspeakable Truths*, above note 33, at 51–2.
72   In fact, a commissioner on the 1986 commission apparently wrote that his was the "second"
      truth commission after Argentina. Hayner, *Unspeakable Truths*, above note 33, at 276. A
      similar displacement can also be expected to occur in Zimbabwe. In that country, there
      was a limited commission of inquiry that Hayner describes as a truth commission. *Ibid.*, at
      55. Yet it has never been broadly viewed as a truth commission and is not listed as such in
      Appendix 1 to this book.

international consensus that it is a truth commission.[73] If such consensus is evident, then it is a truth commission. If such consensus is not evident, then, on this account, its proper classification would be open to question.

History

The history of truth commissions is still being written. New commissions, arising in ever more diverse contexts and with increasingly unique mandates and structures, continue to be created. A complete list of truth commissions, together with information about some of their key attributes, is included in Appendix 1.

In explaining the origins of truth commissions, one is again compelled to begin with Hayner's work. Starting with a case study of the 1974 commission of inquiry established by former Ugandan president Idi Amin, her work offers extensive analysis of it and various cases that followed. Hayner does not, however, address the significant influence of, or similarities between, Commonwealth commissions of inquiry and truth commissions. She also does not trace the important connection between the Commonwealth model and the design and subsequent global influence of the South African TRC.

Commonwealth commissions of inquiry (also sometimes called "tribunals" of inquiry) originated, as one might expect, in the United Kingdom.[74] Commonwealth commissions of inquiry are set up by governments as an exceptional recourse in response to particularly urgent public controversies or concerns. They are usually established by order in council under powers provided by statutes[75] or constitutions.[76]

---

73   In making that assessment, however, it may be important to distinguish two types of perception: (1) the perception that an investigation is not a truth commission, despite its apparent correspondence to the technical definition; and (2) the perception that it is a truth commission, but just a flawed version of one. We have already discussed the former case. As for the latter, the issue is straightforward: it is a truth commission. Here there is both internal and external coherence. The only disputes are normative (*i.e.*, they concern only the perceived vices and virtues of the particular truth commission); they are not definitional.

74   *Report of the Royal Commission on Tribunals of Inquiry*, 1966 (Cmnd 3121 London). Before the promulgation of commission of inquiry legislation in the UK, most investigations of public mischief were conducted through Select Committees of Parliament. The *Tribunal of Inquiry (Evidence) Act* 1921 (UK) – recently repealed by the *Inquiries Act*, 2005 (UK) – was passed with the aim of removing the political or partisan elements of public inquiries on controversial events and issues. L. Blom-Cooper, "Public Inquiries" (1993) 46 *Current Legal Problems* 204, at 206. Excerpts of the *Inquiries Act*, 2005 (UK) are included in Appendix 3 to this book.

75   *See, e.g.*, the Ontario *Public Inquiries Act*, RSO 1990, as amended. This is a prototypical commission of inquiry statute. As such, frequent reference is made to it in subsequent chapters of the book.

76   *See, e.g.*, Constitution of Ghana, arts. 278–83.

Commonwealth commissions of inquiry greatly resemble the modern truth commission. They are typically vested with subpoena powers, the authority to conduct public and *in camera* hearings, and the discretion to determine responsibility and make recommendations in a final report.[77] Since the advent of such commissions, Commonwealth member states have established scores of them in response to proven or alleged human rights abuses.[78] Some of these – commissions of inquiry in Uganda (1974 and 1986),[79] Zimbabwe (1984),[80] Nepal (1990),[81] Sri Lanka (1994),[82] and Nigeria (1999)[83] – Hayner has characterized as truth commissions. But in their particular contexts, they resembled something older and more familiar: standard commissions of inquiry into public controversies.

In other Commonwealth countries – for example, South Africa and Sierra Leone – truth commissions were established under fresh legislation rather than under extant commissions of inquiry statutes.[84] Yet the influence of the Commonwealth commission of inquiry tradition in these places is apparent. In

---

77 They may also occasionally wield powers of search and seizure. *See generally* Chapters 4 to 7.

78 For example, in Canada alone, over the last two decades there have been scores of federal and provincial inquiries into, *inter alia*, wrongful conviction (*e.g.*, Donald Marshall Jr. inquiry, Thomas Sophonow inquiry, Guy Paul-Morin inquiry), prison disturbances (*e.g.*, the Kingston Prison for Women), torture (*e.g.*, the deportation and extraterritorial torture of Maher Arar), and murder (*e.g.*, the torture and killing of a local teenager by Canadian peacekeeping forces in Somalia, the killing of aboriginal protester Dudley George by police in Ontario). Human rights have also been the subject of commissions of broader scope in Canada, including the Commission of Inquiry on War Criminals in the 1980s and the Royal Commission on Aboriginal Peoples in the 1990s. In Ontario alone, one of the ten Canadian provinces, more than two hundred commissions of inquiry have been established since 1867. R. Centa and P. Macklem, "Securing Accountability Through Commissions of Inquiry: A Role for the Law Commission of Canada," in A. Manson and D. Mullan, eds., *Commissions of Inquiry: Praise or Reappraise?* (Toronto: Irwin Law, 2003), at 80.

79 *See generally* Hayner, *Unspeakable Truths*, above note 33, at 50–1; J. R. Quinn, "The Politics of Acknowledgement: Truth Commissions in Uganda and Haiti," Ph.D. diss., McMaster University, 2003, at 120–1 (copy on file with the author).

80 *See* Hayner, *Unspeakable Truths*, above note 33, at 55; R. Carver, "Zimbabwe: Drawing a Line Through the Past," in Roht-Arriaza, *Impunity and Human Rights in International Law and Practice*, above note 1, at 258, 260–1.

81 *See* Hayner, *Unspeakable Truths*, above note 33, at 57. Nepal is not a Commonwealth member state, but it has a similar commission of inquiry tradition due to the special historical influence of the British.

82 *See ibid.*, at 64–6.

83 *See ibid.*, at 69–70, 265–66.

84 Ghana is a more complicated case. Ghana's truth commission is called the National Reconciliation Commission, and it was established pursuant to the *National Reconciliation Commission Act*, 2002, Act 611 (Ghana). The Act had to conform to the commission of inquiry provisions of Ghana's Constitution (arts. 278–83).

each instance, the drafting of the truth commission legislation was influenced by commission of inquiry legislation.[85] At the same time, their long experiences with commissions of inquiry also made the countries cognizant of the commissions' habitual limitations (*e.g.*, overly adversarial proceedings, excessive costs and delays, final reports that are largely disregarded). For this and other reasons, it made sense to create fresh legislation that could borrow the helpful parts of Commonwealth commissions of inquiry statutes (*e.g.*, summons or subpoena powers, public hearing provisions, confidentiality obligations, general provisions about their operation) and leave behind the rest. The use of fresh legislation also permitted the introduction of new elements drawn from past truth commission experiences in other countries (*e.g.*, broad consultation requirements in the selection of commissioners, victim support and protection mechanisms, governmental obligations related to the commission's final report).

There is still more to the story. If one examines the truth commissions before South Africa's (at least those labeled as such by Hayner), the only ones that held public hearings as part of their work were, with the exception of Germany, Commonwealth states.[86] All those that did not hold public hearings – namely, the commissions in Argentina, Bolivia, Uruguay, El Salvador, Chile, Chad, and Haiti – were non-Commonwealth states. Everything then changed with South Africa's TRC, the first truth commission with a truly international, as opposed to local or regional, impact.[87] After the TRC, the idea of a truth commission holding public hearings – especially victim-centered hearings – became the norm. This was true not only in Commonwealth states like Ghana and Sierra Leone (where public hearings would be expected irrespective of the subject of inquiry) but also in non-Commonwealth states lacking the same tradition of commissions of inquiry (*e.g.*, Peru, Timor-Leste, Morocco, and Paraguay).[88] The only exceptions are Ecuador and Panama, where truth commissions were

---

85   A facial comparison of the *Commissions Act*, Act no. 8 of 1947 (South Africa) and the *Promotion of National Unity and Reconciliation Act*, 1995 (South Africa) can leave no other impression.

86   The others were the truth commissions of Uganda and Sri Lanka.

87   El Salvador's truth commission also generated widespread attention in its day but still nothing on the order of the South African TRC. *See* Hayner, "Fifteen Truth Commissions," above note 34, at 598.

88   It is important to also acknowledge here the special influence of NGOs such as the International Center for Transitional Justice, which provides comprehensive assistance in setting up and running effective truth commissions. The Center, along with other experts, offers information and guidance on the pros and cons of public hearings, based on lessons learned from the South African TRC and also from other commissions that have held public hearings. Thus, there is admittedly more at work here than the singular influence of the South African TRC.

created with reference only to prior Latin American experiences, none of which involved public hearings.[89] This gives an indication of the influence of South Africa's TRC, which not only brought the power of public hearings to global attention but also demonstrated that a commission could be victim-centered and public at the same time.[90] What the preceding discussion also reveals is the influence of the Commonwealth commission of inquiry model on the modern truth commission. In the absence of the Commonwealth model, it is far from clear that truth commissions would be holding public hearings – a feature of contemporary practice whose absence would render the modern truth commission not only unrecognizable but also, for many, less attractive. For this and other reasons, special attention is devoted to the Commonwealth model in later chapters of this book.[91]

Comparative mandates and models

Since the 1980s, over two dozen truth commissions have been formed, a majority of them in Latin America and sub-Saharan Africa. In the past five years, an average of nearly three truth commissions has been established each year. Many of these commissions have benefited from substantial resources and, since the advent of South Africa's TRC, increasingly robust mandates. At the time of writing there are truth commissions in operation in Paraguay, the DRC, and Liberia. There are also expected truth commissions in Indonesia and Fiji.[92]

Most experts agree that truth commissions first commanded attention with the experience of the National Commission on the Disappearance of Persons in Argentina in the early 1980s.[93] That commission inspired several subsequent

89 Guatemala is another exception to the public hearing trend. It too began work after the South African TRC. But its mandate was established in 1994, one year before that of South Africa.

90 South Africa also set an important precedent by the broad public debate that accompanied both the drafting of the truth commission's terms of reference and the appointment of its commissioners. Freeman and Hayner, "Truth-Telling," at 129–30. Writing just prior to the establishment of the South African TRC, Hayner noted: "To date, in fact, no truth commission has been founded through a process of public debate on terms." See "Fifteen Truth Commissions," above note 34, at 639.

91 This does not, however, diminish the importance and influence of the early Latin American truth commission experiences in Argentina, Chile, and El Salvador, from which the South African TRC and subsequent commissions drew – and continue to draw – important lessons.

92 The prospect of a truth commission has been actively, if inconclusively, debated in several other places too, including Algeria, Bahrain, Bosnia and Herzegovina, Burundi, Canada, Honduras, Iraq, Mexico, Namibia, Northern Ireland, and Spain.

93 See Hayner, Unspeakable Truths, above note 33, at 33–4. See more generally Nunca Más: The Report of the Argentine National Commission on the Disappeared, trans. E. Canetti (New York: Farrar Straus Giroux, 1986).

commissions, including ones in El Salvador and Chile. Its influence was, however, mostly limited to Latin America. As just noted, it was only with the experience of the South African TRC in the mid-1990s that truth commissions, for the first time, attained worldwide prominence. Though its work concluded several years ago, and though it remains the only commission to have used a truth-for-amnesty procedure,[94] to this day the South African TRC remains the most well-known truth commission. In a sense, one can divide the history of truth commissions into two periods: before South Africa, and after. Before South Africa, truth commissions did not conduct victim-centered public hearings; after South Africa, truth commissions have almost always conducted such hearings.[95] This highlights perhaps the clearest demarcation of competing truth commission models: there are those that conduct public hearings (the contemporary model), and those that do not (the early model). As explained in more detail in chapter 6, whether or not a commission conducts public hearings – especially victim-centered hearings – has an unparalleled impact on the level of public awareness and engagement in a truth commission process.

In the sections that follow, the main features of truth commission practice are briefly reviewed. The sections examine who establishes truth commissions, who appoints commissioners and staff, who provides financing, how long truth commissions operate, what span of history they examine, what violations they

94   The TRC – or more specifically, its Amnesty Committee – had the power to grant amnesty to persons who confessed to their involvement in politically motivated past crimes. For particularly serious crimes, the applicant was required to appear in a public hearing to answer questions from the TRC, from victims and families, and from their legal counsel. Applicants did not need to express remorse as a condition of obtaining amnesty. Freeman and Hayner, "Truth-Telling," at 141. No subsequent truth commission has adopted the truth-for-amnesty formula, although as of this writing, Fiji is considering doing so. *See also* article 8(g) of *Law 04/018 (2004) Concerning the Organization, Powers and Functions of the Truth and Reconciliation Commission* (DRC), which empowers the TRC to "propose to the competent authority to accept or refuse any individual or collective amnesty application for acts of war, political crimes, or crimes of opinion." Translated from the original French, in F. Borello, *A First Few Steps: The Long Road to a Just Peace in the DRC* (International Center for Transitional Justice, 2004), at 43. The DRC amnesty power differs from the South African model in two key respects: first, it is a power to propose, not to grant, amnesty; second, amnesty is available for a different and less serious set of crimes. *See also An Act to Establish the Truth and Reconciliation Commission of Liberia* (2005), s. 26(g); and *Terms of Reference for the Truth and Reconciliation Commission* (Grenada), s. 3(d). A recent Indonesian law to establish a TRC also creates a power to recommend, but not to grant, amnesty.

95   To be sure, the South African experience does not dominate local debates and approaches regarding the design and operation of a truth commission or its public hearings. Rather, it tends to provide a starting point. More typically, the design and operation of a new truth commission is shaped by the study of many other truth commission experiences. Lessons learned from all of these experiences are then weighed in light of local preferences and constraints.

investigate, what objectives they pursue, what legal attributes they possess, and what activities they mainly pursue.

Who establishes truth commission mandates?

As noted earlier in the chapter, the state in which a truth commission operates plays a formal legislative or sponsoring role in the establishment of its mandate. Truth commission mandates (also called charters, or terms of reference) are most commonly established at the domestic level, whether by the executive branch of government (*e.g.*, Chile), the legislative branch (*e.g.*, South Africa), or even by a monarch (*e.g.*, Morocco).[96] Sometimes the truth commission mandate also reflects hybrid authority, as when a president sets out the commission's mandate by order in council under powers provided by parliamentary statute (*e.g.*, Nigeria), or when the legislative and executive branches jointly endorse a truth commission (*e.g.*, the DRC).[97] All or part of a commission's mandate may also be set out in a peace agreement without further domestic legislative implementation (*e.g.*, El Salvador) or, alternatively, in a law that codifies and expands the relevant terms of a peace agreement (*e.g.*, Sierra Leone).[98]

None of these means of establishing a truth commission is inherently preferable to the others. In one context the executive branch may be seen as more credible than the legislative branch; in other cases, the reverse may be true. In some contexts the need to implement in law the relevant terms of a peace accord could be essential; in other cases, this may not be so. Also, in some cases

96 The ultimate law (*dahir*) governing the truth commission in Morocco was issued by the king, but its content was formulated by the members of the commission, who had been appointed to their posts a few months prior.

97 In arguably the broadest expression of domestic legal and political support for a truth commission, Timor-Leste's mandate was established by a UN interim authority, pursuant to a recommendation of the pre-government body called the National Council. Subsequently it was written into the country's Constitution. What is more, "The Government, Parliament, Political parties, key political figures, civil society and the Church also gave (the Commission) excellent cooperation at all times, both morally and practically. Such was the cooperation given to the Commission that at no point did (the Commission) have to consider activating its inquiry related search and seizure powers." Text of address by Aniceto Guterres Lopes, chair of Timor-Leste's truth commission, upon the presentation of the commission's final report to the president of the Republic (31 October 2005).

98 In a particularly bizarre formulation, section 2.3 of the "Memorandum of Understanding between the Government of the Republic of Indonesia and the Free Aceh Movement," dated 15 August 2005, calls upon the future Indonesian Commission of Truth and Reconciliation to establish a commission for Aceh "with the task of formulating and determining reconciliation measures." The Aceh commission, if it is ever established, would presumably operate as a committee of its Indonesian sponsor. Its only assigned task – "formulating and determining reconciliation measures" – leaves in doubt whether it would be an investigative body, and thus whether it could properly be characterized as a truth commission.

the most respected public authority may be the most difficult to engage for the purpose of establishing a truth commission mandate; thus, for example, the executive branch may need to establish a truth commission mandate because of deep divisions within parliament. Under the constitutions of most states, however, only the legislative branch holds the power to imbue a commission with investigative powers such as the power to compel testimony or to search premises and seize evidence. At the same time, putting a bill through a multiparty legislative process will tend to take more time at a moment when prompt action may be required. It may also jeopardize important elements of the mandate in the process of multipartisan negotiation.[99]

Whatever the case, the authority that establishes the mandate has a direct impact on a truth commission's perceived legitimacy. This is unavoidable; truth commissions are highly politicized ventures. What is essential is for the sponsoring authority to enjoy the minimal credibility necessary to avoid a "stillborn" commission.[100]

Who appoints commissioners and staff?

The state in which a truth commission operates will usually, but not always, play a formal role in the appointment of commissioners. Commissioners may be appointed by the executive branch acting alone (*e.g.*, Panama), by the executive branch acting jointly with the legislative branch (*e.g.*, South Africa), by the legislative branch acting alone (*e.g.*, Germany), or by the monarchy (*e.g.*, Morocco). Commissioners may also be appointed by, or in coordination with, international authorities such as the United Nations (*e.g.*, El Salvador), or by a mix of international and national authorities (*e.g.*, Sierra Leone). Sometimes commissioner selection is preceded by a formal and independent nomination and selection process (*e.g.*, Timor-Leste); other times this is not the case.

---

99 For an appreciation of the pros and cons of each approach, *see, e.g.,* the *Report of the Task Force on the Establishment of a Truth, Justice and Reconciliation Commission,* Republic of Kenya (2003), at 27: "Many Kenyans felt that the truth commission ought to be established through an Act of parliament. They felt that legislating a truth commission would give it adequate powers and insulate it from the whims of the executive, a fate that has all too often met past presidential commissions under KANU governments. But they also wanted a truth commission established immediately. The Task Force then had to reconcile these two positions. The Task Force rejected the legislative route because it is of the view that the Kenyan parliament has too many competing, vested, and self-protective interests that would delay, scuttle, or give the country a truth commission that would be devoid of any meaningful powers."

100 Such credibility was absent in the case of the Truth and Reconciliation Commission established in 2001 by former Federal Republic of Yugoslavia President Kostunica. The commission was quietly dissolved in 2003. *See* Freeman, *Serbia and Montenegro,* above note 62, at 7–9.

Sometimes the commissioners are selected in accordance with explicit criteria and procedures set out in a truth commission's mandate (*e.g.*, Ghana); other times no such criteria or procedures exist (*e.g.*, Nigeria). In yet other cases, commissioners are selected even before the mandate itself has been created (*e.g.*, the DRC).[101] The key lesson from past experiences is that a commission will tend to enjoy greater public and international support where its members are selected through a broad process of consultation aimed at ensuring a fair balance in the representation of political constituencies, ethnic or religious groups, and gender.[102] A meritorious appointment process can also enhance the ability of future triers of fact to rely on the commission's findings.[103]

The ultimate composition of a commission can vary greatly. There may be more than a dozen commissioners (*e.g.*, Germany), or only a few (*e.g.*, Guatemala). The commissioners may all be nationals (*e.g.*, Uganda), all foreigners (*e.g.*, El Salvador), or a mix of the two (*e.g.*, Sierra Leone). There may be a reasonable balance of male and female commissioners (*e.g.*, South Africa, where seven of the seventeen commissioners were female), or not (*e.g.*, Morocco, where only one of the seventeen commissioners was female). Commissioners may come from a wide cross-section of religious, racial, cultural and socio-economic communities (*e.g.*, South Africa), or a narrow one (*e.g.*, the former Federal Republic of Yugoslavia, where all of the original commissioners were Serbs). Commissioners tend to come from a wide range of educational and professional backgrounds, including law, academia, human rights, psychology,

---

101 This practice is highly exceptional. It can also have a negative effect on a commission's credibility. *See, e.g.*, Borello, *A First Few Steps*, above note 94, at 41–2.

102 Freeman and Hayner, "Truth-Telling," above note 38, at 129. *See also* Orentlicher, "Updated Set of Principles," above note 5, Principle 6: "To the greatest extent possible, decisions to establish a truth commission, define its terms of reference and determine its composition should be based upon broad public consultations in which the views of victims and survivors especially are sought. Special efforts should be made to ensure that men and women participate in these deliberations on a basis of equality." *See also* Principle 7(c): "In determining membership, concerted efforts should be made to ensure adequate representation of women as well as of other appropriate groups whose members have been especially vulnerable to human rights violations." The law establishing Liberia's truth commission implemented this principle directly: "The TRC shall comprise nine (9) commissioners, with not less than four (4) women making up its entire composition." *An Act to Establish the Truth and Reconciliation Commission of Liberia* (2005), s. 7.

103 *See, e.g.*, the findings of the Inter-American Commission on Human Rights in *Ellacuría* above note 12, at para. 78: "Given the rigorous methodology used by the (Salvadoran) Truth Commission and the guarantee of its impartiality and good faith resulting from the manner in which its members were appointed (and in which the State itself participated), the (Commission) considers that its investigation into this case is credible and as such must be taken into account, together with the alleged facts and other evidence submitted. Moreover, it should be noted that the State has not presented any allegations or evidence that would cast doubt on the conclusions of the Truth Commission, which the State itself created."

and medicine.[104] Commissioners may also, sometimes, receive assistance from the United Nations[105] or from special advisers.[106]

The final makeup of a truth commission will, of course, profoundly affect the appearance and reality of its independence,[107] but so too will the person who serves as the commission's chair or president. In addition to setting the commission's overall direction and priorities, the chair often becomes the public face of the commission.[108] Indeed, his or her name frequently constitutes the central element of the commission's unofficial title (*e.g.*, in Chile, the "Rettig Commission" rather than the National Truth and Reconciliation Commission).[109] The best practice, in any case, is to select a respected leader who can work alongside a diverse mix of persons of similarly high moral probity and public or professional stature. To date, no truth commission has had a female chair or president.

Besides commissioners, truth commissions employ staff. Commissioners generally hire the staff. A commission with inadequate funding may, however, be unable to hire staff; it may need to rely on seconded bureaucrats who are

104 Although commissioners tend to be well educated, it is not always so. For example, the original, and ultimately abandoned, slate of commissioners for Liberia's truth commission included illiterate persons.

105 For example, the members of the Sierra Leonean TRC received assistance from the Office of the High Commissioner for Human Rights. Even before the work of the commission had started, the Office had funded not only public education and sensitization campaigns about the TRC but also a preliminary investigation to obtain initial evidence on certain key events. The Office was also directly involved in the selection of the TRC's commissioners. *See generally Sierra Leone Truth and Reconciliation Commission Final Report* (2004), vol. 1, ch. 2.

106 For example, a small Advisory Council of well-known national and international figures assisted Timor-Leste's truth commission. Similarly, the mandate of Liberia's truth commission requires the establishment of an "International Advisory Committee." *An Act to Establish the Truth and Reconciliation Commission of Liberia* (2005), s. 10.

107 *See* Chapter 2, Section 3.

108 For this reason, his or her perceived independence and impartiality is especially important. In Sierra Leone, for example, this became an issue, notwithstanding a broadly consultative process of commissioner selection. "[A]lthough the government has not been particularly supportive of the TRC, there were strong concerns among both Sierra Leoneans and international experts that the TRC's national commissioners were too close to the ruling Sierra Leone Peoples' Party (SLPP) government. The TRC Chairman, for example, supported Sierra Leone's President Kabbah when he refused to apologize for the war on behalf of the state, and on another occasion the Chairman thanked the pro-government militia, the Civil Defence Forces (CDF), for having 'defended the country.'" R. Shaw, "Rethinking Truth and Reconciliation Commissions: Lessons from Sierra Leone" (United States Institute for Peace, February 2005), at 5–6.

109 In Latin America, truth commissions have tended to be chaired by intellectuals; in Commonwealth countries, by judges; and in various jurisdictions since the South African TRC, by religious clerics. Yet there is no hard-and-fast rule. In Morocco, for example, the president of the truth commission was a former political prisoner and torture survivor.

selected and deployed there in coordination with the government. The process of selecting staff can also have an impact on the perceived legitimacy of the commission, albeit not nearly as much as the selection of commissioners, who wield the key decision-making powers and serve as the commission's public face.

A truth commission's staff may comprise nationals, foreigners, or a mix, and it may or may not be balanced in terms of gender, demographic, educational, or professional background.[110] Staff usually far outnumbers commissioners, and increasingly staff can reach into the hundreds at the peak of a commission's operation.[111] Beyond the paid staff members of the commission, there may also be consultants, interns, and volunteers who play important roles at different stages of its life.

Who finances truth commissions?

In the past, truth commissions often operated on relatively small budgets. But as the size and complexity of truth commissions have increased, so too has the need for larger budgets. Today's typical truth commission budget tends to be in the range of US$5 million to $10 million.[112] Virtually every truth commission has lamented the insufficiency of funds to carry out its mandate.

The source of a commission's funding varies widely. Some truth commissions have been financed purely by the national government (*e.g.*, Argentina), others purely by international authorities (*e.g.*, El Salvador), others by a mix of national and foreign governments (*e.g.*, Peru), and some by private foreign donors (*e.g.*, Nigeria).[113]

---

110 Section 34 of *An Act to Establish the Truth and Reconciliation Commission of Liberia* (2005) uniquely provides: " . . . the TRC shall ensure and accord due consideration and preference to the appointment of a competent woman as Executive Secretary . . ."

111 At its peak, the Peruvian truth commission had around 500 staff persons. International Center for Transitional Justice, *Annual Report* (2003/4), http://www.ictj.org.

112 Freeman and Hayner, "Truth-Telling," above note 38, at 132. As of this writing, Canada stands to launch a "Truth and Reconciliation process" to deal with the legacy of so-called Indian Residential Schools (IRS), wherein tens of thousands of aboriginal children once suffered systemic physical and sexual abuse and violations of cultural and other rights. An "Agreement in Principle" between the government, churches, aboriginal groups, and their counsel proposes CDN $60 million for a truth and reconciliation process to deal with the legacy of IRS abuse. It also proposes nearly CDN $2 billion in reparation payments for victims and survivors. *See generally* the website of the Federal Representative on the IRS issue: http://www.iacobucci.gc.ca.

113 The Ford Foundation and the Open Society Institute, for example, have made direct contributions to truth commissions as well as to local NGOs working alongside them. "Truth Commissions and NGOs: The Essential Relationship" (International Center for Transitional Justice, April 2004, available at http://www.ictj.org), at 26.

How long do truth commissions operate?

Truth commissions are temporary bodies, but some are more temporary than others. Truth commissions that do not conduct public hearings tend to have mandates lasting one year or less. By contrast, truth commissions that hold public hearings – whether of the lawyer-dominated Commonwealth commission of inquiry variety, or the more contemporary victim-centered variety – require much more time to operate, usually in the range of two years. Many mandates envisage an additional preparatory phase of a few months.[114] Often commissions also have the discretion to extend their operations by as many as six months. Some commissions, such as those in Uganda, South Africa, and Timor-Leste, have operated for several years.[115]

What span of history do truth commissions examine?

As already explained, all truth commissions focus on the main periods of state repression or armed conflict in a country's relatively recent past. An inquiry that examines only events that took place more than a generation ago is better characterized as a historical (or sociohistorical) commission of inquiry.[116] At the same time, it would be misleading to suggest that truth commissions examine only events of very recent occurrence. Most truth commissions examine a mix of recent and historical violations, in some cases events stretching back as many as four decades. For example, Morocco's truth commission examined violations committed from 1956 to 1999, the South African TRC examined violations from 1960 to 1994, Guatemala's truth commission examined violations from 1962 to 1996, and Germany's truth commission examined violations from 1949 to 1989. In the best instances, the particular span of time corresponds to

---

114 Common activities during this phase include "development of a staffing plan and hiring of staff; drafting internal regulations and policies; adoption of a work plan; design and installation of an effective database for the storage, organization and retrieval of records and data; preliminary background research; collection of existing documentation from national and international non-governmental organizations (NGOs), the UN, foreign governments and other sources; design of a public education campaign; and fund-raising and budget preparation." Freeman and Hayner, "Truth-Telling," above note 38, at 132–3.

115 The Ugandan commission operated for the longest period of any commission. It lasted more than eight years, albeit with intervening stoppages due to lack of resources. As one might expect, by the time the commission reported, it had long since lost the public's interest. "When the Report was finally produced . . . it was without significant fanfare – people had already largely forgotten about the struggling Commission." J. R. Quinn, "Constraints: The Un-Doing of the Ugandan Truth Commission" (2004) 26 *Human Rights Quarterly* 401, at 416.

116 *See* Section 3 below.

periods in a country's modern history when the worst or greatest number of violations occurred.[117]

What types of violations do truth commissions examine?

We have already observed that truth commissions mainly focus on acts of extreme physical violence or repression, and that they may also examine other types of violations, including property crimes.[118] The most commonly investigated crime by a truth commission is that of enforced disappearance.[119] This flows logically from the nature of the crime itself: the person's fate remains unknown, thus necessitating inquiry. Beyond the crime of enforced disappearance, truth commissions tend to focus on gross violations committed on a systematic scale. Most often these are cases of torture, rape, prolonged arbitrary detention, and various forms of killing, such as summary executions and large-scale massacres, whether committed in the context of state repression or of civil war.[120]

In cases of civil war or low-level conflict, truth commission mandates (appropriately) require the investigation of violations committed by all sides. In contexts in which there has been no armed conflict, but only state repression, truth commission mandates are naturally limited to state actions.

What are a truth commission's primary objectives?

As with any human rights inquiry, there are many possible objectives a truth commission may pursue. Two invariable and interrelated objectives are the investigation or clarification of serious past violations, and the prevention of similar violations in the future. Beyond that, a truth commission may be established to help achieve a variety of other objectives. These can include national reconciliation (*e.g.,* Chile), reconciliation between victims and perpetrators (*e.g.,* Timor-Leste), criminal justice (*e.g.,* Argentina), the dignifying of victims (*e.g.,* Peru), and the consolidation of peace and democracy (*e.g.,* DRC). A commission's objectives serve to guide its work; they also constitute the benchmark that will be used to measure its achievements.

Given its brief period of operation and its inability to enforce the recommendations it makes, a truth commission's attainment of any of these objectives

---

117 Freeman and Hayner, "Truth-Telling," above note 38, at 131.
118 On the risks involved in having a truth commission focus on economic crimes, *see* P. Hayner and L. Bosire, "Should Truth Commissions Address Economic Crimes? Considering the Case of Kenya," 26 March 2003, available at http://www.tikenya.org.
119 *See* Appendix 1, which illustrates that several of the earlier truth commissions were focused primarily or exclusively on the crime of enforced disappearance.
120 *See* Hayner, *Unspeakable Truths,* above note 33, at 316–19.

is less than assured. For example, only some, not all, violations will usually be discovered.[121] Moreover, national reconciliation, an inherently long-term process, may not emerge as a natural consequence of historical clarification.[122] But if a truth commission's varied objectives are unattainable strictly by dint of its own efforts, they are nevertheless important in setting the tone and context for the commission's work.

As later chapters reveal, the objectives of a truth commission – whether predominantly retributive or restorative – may also have important implications in the area of procedural fairness.

What legal attributes do truth commissions possess?

The early truth commissions of Latin America possessed few investigative powers. By contrast, truth commissions in Commonwealth countries, both before and particularly after the TRC experience in South Africa, have wielded a range of important investigative powers including summons or subpoena powers (with concomitant penalties for noncooperation), search and seizure powers, and even witness protection powers. Some of these powers are becoming standard for truth commissions in non-Commonwealth countries as well (*e.g.*, Timor-Leste, the DRC).[123] The other significant legal attributes a truth commission may possess are the ability to conduct public hearings and the ability to determine individual responsibility for human rights violations. Those subjects, and their implications for procedural fairness, are examined in detail in Chapters 6 and 7, respectively.

If a truth commission's work has historically been focused on research and investigation, and if its powers have mostly been linked to truth-seeking activities, that situation is beginning to change. In recent years there have been truth commissions wielding "adjudicative" powers (*i.e.*, the power to settle legal rights). These include the power to grant amnesty to perpetrators of gross human rights violations (*i.e.*, South Africa), the power to formalize contracts of community service and reparation between eligible perpetrators and specific beneficiary communities (*i.e.*, Timor-Leste),[124] and the power to grant financial

---

121 Even relatively well-resourced truth commissions, such as those of Guatemala and Peru, documented only a percentage of the total estimated number of serious violations of human rights or humanitarian law.

122 The belief that truth will lead to reconciliation or is a precondition to its attainment is rarely realized in reality. *See, e.g.*, Freeman and Hayner, "Truth-Telling," above note 38, at 122–3. Nevertheless, most contemporary truth commissions are expected to at least help advance the cause of national reconciliation.

123 *See* Chapters 4 and 5.

124 Note also that article 41 of the law establishing the TRC in the DRC stipulates that anytime a victim and perpetrator agree on a reparation arrangement "under the aegis of the TRC," it will have the value of a binding contract. *See* Borello, *A First Few Steps*, above note 94, at 44–5.

compensation to victims (*i.e.*, Morocco).[125] While such added powers can deepen and broaden the impact that a truth commission can have on victims, perpetrators, and society at large, they can also complicate its work by distracting from what is often viewed as a truth commission's central task: clarification about the main causes and effects of past periods of mass abuse or conflict.[126] The aforementioned adjudicative powers are not examined in this book. As explained in the Preface, the focus of this work is limited to the nonadjudicative aspects of truth commission procedures. In the case of South Africa, its amnesty-granting power depended for its success on the credible threat of prosecution. That threat will rarely be present in a transitional environment.[127] Moreover, the amnesty dimension of the South African TRC process has already been the subject of extensive commentary.[128] The Timor-Leste "community reconciliation agreement" model, however compelling, is also unlikely to be replicated in the same form in other contexts because it was designed to address a unique set of historical and cultural circumstances.[129] The Moroccan model may also turn out to be an isolated example, for it

125 The draft mandate of a planned truth commission in Fiji also contemplates imbuing the body with a direct compensation-granting power.

126 As Hayner writes, "The central aim of a truth commission is not therapy. It is, instead, to gather as much detailed information from the greatest number of victims as possible to allow an accurate analysis of abuses over a period of time." *Unspeakable Truths*, at 139.

127 Note, however, that in some circumstances it is the absence, rather than the presence, of a threat of prosecution that might entice perpetrators to give statements or testify at a public hearing. This was to some extent the case in Sierra Leone, where perpetrator participation with the TRC increased as the likelihood of prosecution or of information sharing with the parallel Special Court decreased. P. Hayner, International Center for Transitional Justice, *The Sierra Leone Truth and Reconciliation Commission: Reviewing the First Year* (January 2004), at 4. *See also* W. A. Schabas, "A Synergistic Relationship: The Sierra Leone Truth and Reconciliation Commission and the Special Court for Sierra Leone," in W. A. Schabas and S. Darcy, eds., *Truth Commissions and Courts: The Tension between Criminal Justice and Truth* (Dordrecht: Kluwer, 2004), at 30, 41, 42.

128 *See, e.g.*, R. A. Wilson, *The Politics of Truth and Reconciliation in South Africa: Legitimizing the Post-Apartheid State* (Cambridge: Cambridge University Press, 2001); R. Slye, "Amnesty and Justice," in C. Villa-Vicencio and W. Verwoerd, eds., *Looking Back, Reaching Forward: Reflections on the Truth and Reconciliation Commission of South Africa* (Cape Town: University of Cape Town Press, 2000); Boraine, *A Country Unmasked*, above note 26, c. 8.

129 These circumstances include the fact that the vast majority of perpetrators reside in another state (*i.e.*, Indonesia), that the process is integrated with a traditional indigenous model of local conflict resolution, and that a large number of the lower-level perpetrators were nationals who were prepared to return home, confess their crimes, and enter contracts of community service. The absence of all these factors should not, however, discourage the study and transfer of the principles and objectives that underlie the Timorese model. In particular, the commission's multilayered emphasis on community participation, perpetrator reintegration, truth telling, and the integration of local customs and spiritual values merits serious study by any society in the process of democratic or postconflict transition.

followed, rather than preceded, a state compensation body, whose inadequacies it was intended to redress.[130]

What are a truth commission's main activities?

As just noted, truth seeking and truth telling remain the core functions of all truth commissions, even of those with additional functions and powers such as those of South Africa, Timor-Leste, and Morocco. It is important to understand, however, what truth seeking and truth telling entail in practical terms.

A truth commission, whether or not it holds public hearings, will invariably expend enormous time and resources on statement taking from victims and their family members, witnesses, and, where possible, perpetrators. Many truth commissions also conduct varying degrees of public outreach, academic-style research, police-like investigation, data processing, quantitative analysis, and selected exhumations. The provision of psychological and medical support, the organization of public hearings, and the writing of the final report are other common activities of truth commissions. All of these functions are discussed in more detail in Part II of the book.[131]

Some commissions have undertaken other, more unique, projects. For example, in Sierra Leone, the truth commission created the "National Vision for Sierra Leone" project, which invited the public to submit written and artistic expressions of their vision of the country's future.[132] Peru's truth commission organized a major photography exhibition, "To Be Remembered," documenting the violence of the period under investigation.[133] Many truth commissions also organize public debates on key subjects.[134] The truth commission in

---

130 M. Freeman and V. Opgenhaffen, *Transitional Justice in Morocco: A Progress Report*, International Center for Transitional Justice (November 2005), at 10–14.

131 *See also* Hayner, *Unspeakable Truths*, above note 33; Freeman and Hayner, "Truth-Telling," above note 38.

132 The commission also made use of local traditional leaders. A number of reconciliation ceremonies were held in which victims and perpetrators would meet, and in which perpetrators who confessed their crimes would sometimes be ritually purged through cleansing ceremonies before being readmitted into the community. International Center for Transitional Justice, *The Sierra Leone Truth and Reconciliation Commission*, above note 127, at 5. The commission also collaborated with the nongovernmental organization WITNESS to produce a one-hour video version of the final report entitled "Witness to Truth." It also worked with UNICEF to establish a children's version of the final report. *See* http:// http://www.unicef.org/voy/media/TRCCF9SeptFINAL.pdf.

133 More than 18,000 people visited the exhibition during its eighty days on display. *See* "Truth Commissions and NGOs," above note 113, at 34. The truth commission in Timor-Leste also held a photo exhibition in connection with its public hearing on internal political conflict.

134 For example, the truth commission in Morocco organized public debates on subjects such as prison literature, state violence, the meaning of truth, and political trials. *See* http://www.ier.ma. The commission also organized the staging of a play in conjunction with one of the public debates.

Timor-Leste, perhaps the most broad-ranging commission since South Africa, undertook a wide range of specialized activities. It ran a program called "community profiles" in which it arranged for victim communities to sit together and construct, in a participatory way, a history of the conflict as it affected particular villages. It also organized several "healing workshops" in which the worst-affected victims from local villages came to the capital in Dili to take part in multiday sessions that combined interactive discussions, group counseling, singing, and painting.[135]

Perceived advantages and disadvantages of truth commissions

A truth commission is a high-risk endeavor. For some governments and societies, it is a risk best avoided. For others, however, the potential gains are seen to outweigh any palpable risks. In this section, there is an analysis of the main potential benefits, as well as of the perceived risks, of truth commissions. The analysis covers the perspectives of both government and civil society.

Truth commissions are inherently political enterprises, and they may be created with diverse motives. For example, a government may establish a commission as a means to effectively "outsource" the responsibility of historical justice to a third party. Once the commission is set up, a government gains "breathing space"; it can answer difficult questions by saying that the matter is before the commission. In addition, any investigative or reporting failures become attributable to the commission rather than the government. A government may also establish a truth commission on the presumption that the commission will be less threatening than trials and less expensive than compensation, and not because it believes that either victims or society has a right to know the truth. Similarly, a cynical government may hope that a truth commission will help exhaust public interest in greater measures of political and legal accountability.

A government may also choose to create a truth commission in order to control both the investigators and the scope of the investigation by, for example, focusing the mandate on periods and events embarrassing to political enemies rather than to itself, or appointing persons "anxious enough about their next piece of government patronage to go lightly on their criticism."[136] Successor governments may alternatively establish truth commissions simply as a way to "show their democratic *bona fides* and curry favour with the international community."[137] A truth commission may also be established in the hope that

---

135 *See* CAVR Update, June–July 2003 (http://www.easttimor-reconciliation.org). The commission also held a healing workshop exclusively for women. *See* CAVR Update, December 2003–January 2004.

136 B. Schwartz, "Public Inquiries," in Manson and Mullan, *Commissions of Inquiry*, above note 78, at 448.

137 J. Tepperman, "Truth and Consequences" (March/April 2002) *Foreign Affairs* 128, at 128.

it will perform the same entertaining and distracting function as bread and circuses did in ancient Rome.

Of course, governments do not establish truth commissions only to score political points, save face, or distract the public. A government may institute a truth commission on the basis of more noble motives. A government may believe that a truth commission is an effective mechanism for preventing the recurrence of repression or armed conflict, restoring public confidence in the state, or fostering national reconciliation and social solidarity with victims. Alternatively, it may believe that a truth commission will produce the evidentiary record and public support needed for criminal justice, reparation, and institutional reform efforts to follow. A government may also believe that truth commissions represent the next best approximation of criminal justice in a context where an entrenched amnesty law ousts the jurisdiction of courts to try past human rights crimes. A government may alternatively be attracted to the flexibility of the truth commission model, whose form it can freely tailor to the legal, political, historical, and sociocultural nuances of the particular context.

Whether the motives of a government are cynical or laudable, in practice a truth commission – like any semi-independent investigation – may end up surprising its sponsors. It may pursue its own agenda, call public attention to the state's past human rights record, and make unexpected findings. A truth commission established to relieve public pressure on the government may end up increasing pressure on it, for example, through embarrassing public hearings. A commission created with a narrow mandate, or with limited operational and financial independence, could end up taking a broad interpretation of its mandate and securing external sources of funding to enable it to carry out its own vision of the mission. A commission put in place to bring closure with the past could end up reopening it, whether in the short term or, as is often the case, over the long term.

Alternatively, a truth commission set up to facilitate and inspire subsequent justice and reparation measures could have the contrary effect of producing "compassion fatigue" and a concomitant public preference to focus on the future and put the past to rest. The commissioners appointed to carry out the mandate could also turn out to be incompetent or biased, which could generate public distrust and allegations of a "witch hunt." And rather than providing a sense of historical justice, a truth commission could finish by disappointing victims and the general public.[138] Alternatively, a truth commission premised

---

138 This is true even for some of the more objectively successful truth commissions, such as that of Peru. *See, e.g.,* T. Bridges, "Critics: Truth Commission Wheels of Justice Are Slow," *Miami Herald,* 9 October 2004, describing various public disappointments that followed the completion of the Peruvian TRC's work in 2003. The disappointment is all the more surprising in the case of Peru because the contribution of its TRC exceeds that of many

on the importance of knowing the truth could conflict with local healing and reconciliation practices that emphasize "social forgetting" as a means to ensure social peace.[139] And in a worst-case scenario, a truth commission's impact could be eclipsed by the subsequent passage of a broad amnesty law.[140]

In this author's view, truth commissions should generally focus on the objective of providing a measure of impartial, historical clarification to countervail false or revisionist accounts of the past.[141] This is, arguably, what truth commissions do best. Indeed, if a commission fails in the mission of historical clarification, it is almost sure to have failed in parallel or subsidiary missions such as to bolster accountability, reform, or reconciliation.

Yet the reality is that every truth commission will fall short even in the realm of historical clarification. This is partly due to factors endemic to the investigation of any crime, such as insufficient perpetrator cooperation, imperfect victim and witness memories, and missing documentary and physical

---

other places. For example, criminal prosecutions have progressed in several cases; there is public access to the TRC's archives; exhumations of massacre sites continue; the president has issued a formal apology on behalf of the state; a national Day of Reconciliation has been established; and a victim reparation law has been passed.

139   In a critique of the assumptions underlying the need for a truth commission in Sierra Leone, one commentator queries, "Do local techniques of post-conflict healing, reconciliation, and reintegration resolve the need for justice and accountability? Here, I would argue, a distinction should be drawn between the need to make states and leaders accountable for mass violence on the one hand, and the treatment of rank-and-file perpetrators on the other. If most survivors of the violence want some form of retributive justice against the latter, then a truth commission or TRC is unlikely to be an adequate response. But in Sierra Leone, as in Mozambique, most survivors wanted reintegration and peace. Here, a truth commission – especially one with public hearings – was popularly felt to be a destructive process." Shaw, "Rethinking Truth and Reconciliation Commissions," above note 108, at 11.

140   Five days after the publication of the final report of El Salvador's truth commission, the legislature promulgated a "broad, absolute, unconditional amnesty in favor of all persons who participated in any way in the commission of political crimes, related common crimes and other common crimes committed by groups of no less than 20 persons." *Ley de Amnistía General para la Consolidación de la Paz*, Legislative Decree no. 486 (1993), article 1.

141   For example, "The testimony of victims in South Africa has made it impossible to deny that torture was officially sanctioned and that it happened in a widespread and systematic fashion. The commissions in Chile and Argentina rebutted the myth that opponents of the military regimes fled these countries or went into hiding. These commissions conclusively established that opponents were 'disappeared' and killed by members of the security forces as part of an official policy." P. van Zyl, "Transitional Justice: Conflict Closure and Building a Sustainable Peace," in (2003)a *Dispute Resolution Magazine*, 6, at 7. *See also Sierra Leone Truth and Reconciliation Commission Final Report* (2004), vol. 1, ch. 1, para. 26: "While it may be illusory to think that bodies like truth commissions can establish a complete historical record, they can nevertheless discredit and debunk certain lies about conflicts. If they can accomplish only this, their work may contribute validly to the rebuilding of a stable social environment on the ruins of conflict and war."

evidence. Other more institutional factors may also preclude the achievement of full historical clarification. First, as already noted, most mandates limit a truth commission's duration to an average of around two years. However, the scope of the commission's investigation may be quite vast – spanning several decades and involving thousands of incidents and individuals. As a result, it is virtually impossible to ensure that all sources of information – all locations, victims, witnesses, and perpetrators – are sought out and surveyed. Moreover, in most cases only a small fraction of the total number of cases identified by a commission can be investigated in any depth. A second major institutional limitation is in the area of resources. The process of investigating, coding, analyzing, and corroborating information can be costly, generally involving the enlistment of a large staff of statement takers, lawyers, investigators, researchers, analysts, and technical and support staff. As explained in more detail in Chapter 2, Section 3, these and other constraints not only limit the amount of truth a commission can deliver; they also limit the scope of procedural fairness a truth commission can ensure.

Despite the foregoing, in the hearts and minds of most human rights advocates, the perceived advantages of truth commissions appear to outweigh any potential disadvantages or limitations. Through their hard-fought contributions to truth, justice, reparation, reform, and reconciliation, truth commissions have earned a justifiably privileged place in the arsenal of responses to mass atrocity.

SECTION 3: DISTINGUISHING TRUTH COMMISSIONS FROM OTHER HUMAN RIGHTS INVESTIGATIONS

Earlier in this chapter, a definition of a truth commission was provided, which highlighted its core attributes. However, to have a clear understanding of what a truth commission is, it may also help to understand what it is not. In this section, an attempt is made to distinguish truth commissions from other human rights investigations. The term "human rights investigation" is used here to signify any body that investigates human rights and related violations as part of its work, irrespective of whether investigation is a primary or subsidiary component of the overall mission. The aim is to develop a coherent, if nonexhaustive, taxonomy of human rights investigation in order to situate truth commissions within a broader context.[142] The taxonomy should also assist the reader when,

---

142 National and international judges and prosecutors are not included in the taxonomy, although many of them conduct human rights investigations in this book's sense of the term. *See* Section 4 below. Other bodies that sometimes conduct human rights–related investigations (and that are not discussed here) include amnesty commissions (*e.g.*, in Brazil) and

in later chapters, a comparison is made between the procedural fairness standards and practices of various human rights investigations and those of truth commissions.

Another reason for examining other human rights investigations is that a truth commission is only one of many possible mechanisms available to satisfy, or contribute to, the vindication of the individual and societal "right to truth." Sometimes a truth commission will be the ideal vehicle to vindicate the right, other times not. Whatever the case, there is no denying that other human rights investigations – whether *ad hoc* or standing, governmental or nongovernmental, domestic or multilateral – are important in their own right. Truth commissions were not the first, nor are they necessarily the most important, kind of human rights investigation.

This book divides the universe of human rights investigations into the following categories:

1. Nongovernmental human rights investigations
2. National human rights commissions, ombudsman offices, and hybrid variations
3. Standing and *ad hoc* multilateral human rights monitors
4. *Ad hoc* national human rights–related commissions of inquiry
5. Coroners and medical examiners
6. *Ad hoc* multilateral human rights–related commissions of inquiry
7. Standing and *ad hoc* multilateral and national human rights compensation and reparation bodies
8. Standing and *ad hoc* multilateral and national human rights vetting and lustration bodies
9. Standing and *ad hoc* multilateral human rights complaint procedures
10. State reports on the human rights practices of foreign states
11. Standing national human rights–related administrative tribunals

Truth commissions tend to fit into the category of *ad hoc* national human rights–related commissions of inquiry. For that reason, later chapters pay especially close attention to the procedural fairness standards and practices of bodies falling within that category.

Sometimes truth commissions are preceded by, and benefit from, the prior work of these other human rights investigations. Other times it is truth commissions that come first. And in many instances, multiple human rights

---

disarmament, demobilization, and reintegration commissions (*e.g.,* the Colombian National Commission of Reparation and Reconciliation established under the 2005 Justice and Peace Law: Law no. 275). The latter has responsibilities in the areas of victim participation, truth telling, victim reparation, and reintegration of ex-combatants.

investigations are taking place simultaneously – and sometimes even collaboratively.[143] Whatever the case, truth commissions are not alone; they are one among many possible tools to advance the cause of truth.

Nongovernmental human rights investigations

In contexts where official truth seeking is not possible, human rights investigations by nongovernmental actors can be particularly important. They may provide the only dependable record of past violations.

However, nongovernmental bodies, no matter how much they seek to emulate truth commissions, are not and cannot become truth commissions. They are not "official" bodies like truth commissions. In addition, they lack other important (though not invariable) characteristics of truth commissions, such as privileged access to government and court files, the possession of quasi-judicial investigative powers, legal immunity for good faith acts or omissions, the authority to guarantee confidentiality, and the promise of some form of government reply to their final report.[144] In other respects, however, nongovernmental human rights investigations can resemble truth commissions. They might, for example, conduct public hearings, "name names" in a final report, or catalyze important reforms.[145] They might even call themselves truth commissions.[146]

---

143 For example, in 1993 in El Salvador, a so-called Joint Working Group investigated and reported on the actions of politically motivated illegal armed groups. The Group – which comprised the human rights ombudsman, two independent government representatives, and the director of the Human Rights Division of the UN's Mission (ONUSAL) – was established in El Salvador in 1993 following the murder of two rebel (FMLN) leaders. M. Popkin, "El Salvador: A Negotiated End to Impunity," in Roht-Arriaza, *Impunity and Human Rights in International Law and Practice*, above note 1, at 215.

144 Nongovernmental bodies may also lack equivalent access to national media and state resources. *See* L. Bickford, "Unofficial Truth Projects" (unpublished paper on file with the author).

145 For example, the Archdiocese of São Paolo's *Nunca Mais* report on torture in Brazil created sufficient public revulsion about torture to compel the country's president to sign the Convention Against Torture and Other Cruel, Inhuman or Degrading Treatment or Punishment 1984. L. Weschler, *A Miracle, A Universe: Settling Accounts with Torturers*, 2d ed. (Chicago: University of Chicago Press, 1998), at 75. The same report also named individuals presumed responsible for torture.

146 For example, in 2004, a group of civic leaders from Greensboro, North Carolina created the Greensboro Truth and Reconciliation Commission. The commission is investigating a single event: the 1979 shooting deaths of five protestors and the wounding of several others by the Ku Klux Klan and the American Nazi Party. Although headed by a local district court judge, the commission is in every sense nongovernmental. The International Center for Transitional Justice website describes the commission as an "attempt to apply the methodologies of other countries' truth commissions to deal with past human rights

The universe of nongovernmental bodies that conduct human rights investigations is vast. The prototypical example is the human rights nongovernmental organization (NGO).[147] Although NGO activities and mandates run the gamut, a majority of domestic and international NGOs focus on the investigation, documentation, and publication of human rights abuses. At the domestic level, there are simply too many NGOs to name. At the international level, Amnesty International[148] and Human Rights Watch[149] are paradigmatic examples. One of their main objectives is to produce accurate and authoritative reports that will both shame governments and push the domestic and international public to demand justice. In their investigative work they often rely on, and work closely with, domestic NGO partners.

NGOs also approach investigation and reporting in other ways. In Uruguay, for example, an NGO sought to emulate Argentina's truth commission. It employed a similar investigative methodology and even adopted the same title for its final report: *Nunca Más*, meaning "Never Again."[150] In Morocco, local NGOs organized truth caravans (*caravanes de vérité*) to former detention centers where they conducted and recorded testimonial sessions akin to truth commission public hearings.[151] Some NGOs conduct highly specialized investigations, such as the National Security Archive, a United States–based NGO with expertise in the declassification of US government documents that often assists other NGOs and truth commissions.[152] Other NGOs function primarily as documentation centers, with the primary goal of gathering and preserving documents in order to safeguard the collective memory of a prior period of

---

violations in the United States." *See* http://www.ictj.org/americas/us.asp. Needless to say, the mere fact that an investigative body uses the same methods as a truth commission does not make it one, just as an unofficial public tribunal that uses the same methods as a criminal tribunal does not make it a criminal tribunal. *See* the discussion of the Women's International War Crimes Tribunal below.

147 *See generally* W. Korey, *NGOs and the Universal Declaration of Human Rights* (London: St. Martin's Press, 1998); M. F. Keck and K. Sikkink, *Activists Beyond Borders: Advocacy Networks in International Politics* (Ithaca, NY: Cornell University Press, 1998).

148 *See* http://www.amnesty.org.

149 *See* http://www.hrw.org.

150 *Recall* also the unofficial Brazilian report, discussed above in note 145, which used the same title: *Nunca Mais*. "Though Brazil and Uruguay's truth-tellings were unofficial, they emulate official accounts on the continent, such as Argentina's, conveying how even private reporting will be perceived as social truth so long as it follows the authoritative transitional form. Both the Brazil and Uruguay reports appropriate the features of the official governmental report . . . [B]oth reports expressly follow Argentina's first such report: in title, organization, scope of mandate to investigate what happened during prior rule, and sources of evidence, deriving from official governmental sources." Teitel, *Transitional Justice*, at 80.

151 Freeman and Opgenhaffen, *Transitional Justice in Morocco*, above note 130, at 12.

152 *See* http://www2.gwu.edu/~nsarchiv/.

terror or war.[153] The International Committee of the Red Cross (ICRC), an NGO with a *sui generis* international legal status and role, is another important example. It conducts confidential inspections of prisons and reports its findings in private to the concerned state. It publishes the findings only if the state attempts to mislead the public.[154]

Faith-based institutions, especially in Latin America, have occasionally carried out important human rights investigations too.[155] For example, the human rights office of the archbishop of Santiago, Chile, tracked disappearances that occurred under military rule and eventually passed its files to the country's TRC.[156] A larger-scale, faith-based undertaking was the Recovery of Historical Memory Project (REMHI, by its Spanish acronym), a project of the Human Rights Office of the Archbishop of Guatemala. REMHI was supported by dozens of churches and NGOs from around the world. Hundreds of trained statement takers, mostly indigenous, collected some sixty-five hundred testimonies, and overall the project documented fifty-five thousand cases and recovered five hundred massacre sites.[157] Taking its cue from prior regional experiences, the project concluded with a massive final report entitled *Guatemala: Nunca Más*, upon which Guatemala's truth commission placed significant reliance.[158]

Various other nongovernmental actors conduct human rights investigations too. Private lawyers and legal associations sometimes do so.[159] Organizations of forensic anthropologists, such as the Argentine Forensic Anthropology Team, combine physical anthropology, forensic archaeology, and forensic pathology in the investigation of massacres and other serious human rights

---

153 *See* Bickford, "Unofficial Truth Projects," where the author discusses various examples of such centers, including the Documentation Center of Cambodia and the Iraq Memory Foundation.

154 *See* http://www.icrc.org/.

155 Some of these are also NGOs. Being faith-based does not mean not being an NGO (*e.g.*, the Human Rights Office of the Archbishop of Guatemala, mentioned below).

156 Hayner, *Unspeakable Truths*, above note 33, at 237.

157 Mani, *Beyond Retribution*, above note 1, at 116.

158 A summary of the full report is available on the website of the Human Rights Office of the Archbishop of Guatemala at http://www.odhag.org.gt/. The project's leader, Bishop Gerardi, was assassinated two days after the release of the final report. *Ibid.*, at 117. Nevertheless, members of the REMHI project continued to carry out various activities including workshops and skits, distribution of pamphlets and posters, and the provision of legal and mental health assistance to victims. *See* M. Ballengee, "The Critical Role of Non-Governmental Organizations in Transitional Justice: A Case Study of Guatemala" (2000) 4 *UCLA J. Int'l L. & Foreign Aff.* 477.

159 For example, the International Bar Association – which comprises 16,000 individual lawyers and over 190 bar associations and law societies worldwide – conducts fact-finding missions through its Human Rights Institute. *See* http://www.ibanet.org.

violations around the world.[160] The investigative work of print, radio, and television journalists sometimes reveals significant human rights abuses too.[161] Many documentary filmmakers also make important contributions to truth telling.[162] So too do universities, which may have human rights centers and law clinics that undertake investigations.[163] Even private banks have established human rights–related inquiries.[164] The African National Congress, when it was still a national liberation movement, organized two commissions of inquiry into abuses attributed to its own forces.[165] Individual historians, too, have sometimes conducted important human rights investigations.[166]

160 The work typically comprises three distinct phases: a preliminary investigation, an archaeological examination, and lab work. *See generally* the website of the Argentine group: http://www.eaaf.org/. *See also* J. R. Quinn and M. Freeman, "Lessons Learned: Practical Lessons Gleaned from Inside the Truth Commissions of Guatemala and South Africa" (2003) 25 *Human Rights Quarterly* 1117, at 1139–40.

161 In the United States, for example, television programs like *60 Minutes* (which is highly regarded for its weekly investigative reports on the day's major public controversies), radio journalists like Robert Parry (who is credited with breaking the story of the Iran-Contra affair), and print journalists like Seymour Hersh (who famously exposed the 1968 My Lai massacre and its cover-up during the US-Vietnam war) are prime examples of investigative journalists. *See also* P. Rodríguez, "Un libro que fue clave para el arresto de Pinochet: Los zarpazos de una periodista" (http://www.pagina12.com.ar/2000/00-12/00-12-04/pag21.htm), which describes the work of the award-winning investigative Chilean journalist Patricia Verdugo, whose book *Los Zarpazos del Puma* was critical to the indictment of General Pinochet in Chile.

162 For example, Barbara Trent's film "The Panama Deception" investigated the claims of the US government concerning civilian casualties during the US invasion of Panama in 1989. The international NGO, Human Rights Watch, organizes an annual human rights film festival in which many important human rights–related documentaries are publicly screened. There have also been documentaries about truth commissions including, for example, Bill Moyers' "Facing the Truth" about the South African TRC process.

163 For example, Northwestern University law school's Center for International Human Rights convened an unofficial Tribunal of Opinion to investigate and "judge" a massacre that took place in Santo Domingo, Colombia, in 1998. *See* http://www.law.northwestern.edu/depts/clinic/ihr/.

164 For example, Deutsche Bank AG, Frankfurt am Main, created a historical commission to investigate the bank's gold transactions during the Second World War to determine, *inter alia*, whether it received (and failed to return) gold stolen from Holocaust victims and survivors. *See generally* J. Steinberg, "Reflections on Intergenerational Justice," in Henkin, *The Legacy of Abuse*, above note 1. Some private banks also have established ombudsman offices to investigate customer complaints that may involve human rights issues such as discrimination in the provision of services.

165 Hayner, *Unspeakable Truths*, above note 33, at 60–64.

166 For example, the book *Neighbors* (Princeton, NJ: Princeton University Press, 2001) by the historian Jan Tomasz Gross, had a profound impact on Polish awareness about their role in the Holocaust. The book documents how a 1941 massacre of Jews in a small Polish town called Jedwabne was voluntarily committed by the Poles of that town, and not by its German

There are also unique instances of nongovernmental collaboration in the area of human rights investigation, such as the Women's International War Crimes Tribunal, a mock court established by NGOs from eight countries to "judge" Japan's use of sex slaves during the Second World War.[167] A slightly different example is the Independent International Commission on Kosovo, a commission arranged by the Swedish government but operated entirely by nonstate actors working in their personal capacity.[168] The commission examined war crimes and other aspects of the 1999 conflict in Kosovo.[169]

National human rights commissions, ombudsman offices, and hybrid variations

In many states today, there exists a wide array of national (and subnational) institutions that promote and monitor domestic human rights conditions. These bodies are generally described as "national human rights institutions." There are three such institutions considered in this section: national human rights commissions, ombudsman offices, and hybrid offices.[170] These bodies have divergent mandates, but virtually all hold the authority to receive and investigate human rights–related complaints from citizens and residents of the state in which they operate. As will be demonstrated, in some contexts these bodies have played important roles akin and complementary to truth commissions.

National human rights commissions, omnudsman offices, and hybrid offices differ from truth commissions in a number of important ways. First

---

occupiers. According to a Polish journalist who covered the story extensively in the largest national newspaper, "Before *Neighbors*, the idea that Poles had killed Jews during the war was unthinkable . . . At first the allegations provoked great anger and fear. But over time those feelings passed, and many Poles began to realize that Gross' book was true." Cited in A. Barnett, "Recovered Memory," *Princeton Alumni Weekly* (14 September 2005), at 34–5.

167 The tribunal held hearings in Tokyo (2000) and The Hague (2001). Victims testified about Japan's Second World War use of an estimated 200,000 Korean and Chinese women as sexual slaves in Japanese military brothels. *See* "Japan Found 'Guilty' of Sex Slave Crimes," *BBC News World Edition* (http://news.bbc.co.uk), 4 December 2001. In a similar vein, the well-known Permanent Peoples' Tribunal has held more than thirty unofficial trials on human rights violations committed in different countries around the world. *See* http://www.grisnet.it/filb/sentenze_eng.html.

168 The Swedish government appointed the chairman (Richard Goldstone) and co-chairman (Carl Tham). The appointment of the other eleven members was made through invitations from the chairman and co-chairman.

169 *See* Independent International Commission on Kosovo, *The Kosovo Report: Conflict, International Response, Lessons Learned* (New York: Oxford University Press, 2000). The commission's work was based entirely on documents available in the public domain.

170 *See generally* L. Reif, "Building Democratic Institutions: The Role of National Human Rights Institutions in Good Governance and Human Rights Protection" (2000) 13 *Harv. Hum. Rts. J.* 1.

they are permanent or freestanding bodies. Thus, their staff is already in place and their duration of operation is not limited in time as a truth commission's is. As permanent bodies, they are generally authorized to examine ongoing human rights violations, whereas a truth commission is focused on past violations. And while human rights commissions, ombudsman offices, and hybrid offices may be victim-centered in their activities, it is not a defining characteristic.

Human rights commissions are perhaps the most familiar of the three institutions. Many such commissions conform to the international "Paris Principles" standards on the status and functioning of national institutions for the promotion and protection of human rights.[171] In contrast to the broader concerns of ombudsman offices, the subject of human rights constitutes the explicit focus of national human rights commissions, as their name implies. Such commissions exist in dozens of countries today – from Canada to Morocco to the Philippines – and may go under a variety of names.[172] Commission mandates typically encompass, among other things, public education about human rights and the investigation of human rights complaints. In some cases, these may cover both the private and the public sector, but not necessarily in respect of all types of human rights.[173] National human rights commissions usually lack quasi-judicial decision-making powers; instead, their power tends to be limited to nonlitigious dispute resolution methods such as mediation and conciliation. In some cases they may also have the power to refer matters to binding forms of settlement such as human rights tribunals and courts.[174]

A number of states have established ombudsman offices in addition to, or instead of, national human rights commissions. The ombudsman idea, which originated in Sweden, today connotes national institutions that monitor public

---

171 "Paris Principles" is the term used to refer to GA res. 134, UN GAOR, 48th Sess., 85th mtg., UN doc. A/RES/48/134 (1993). The resolution sets out guiding principles concerning, for example, the competence, responsibilities, independence, and methods of operation of a national human rights institution.

172 For a full listing of such commissions, including their weblinks, see http://www. law.ualberta.ca/centres/ioi/eng/resources.html. Note that the Commission on Human Rights in the Philippines grew out of a truth commission–like body called the Presidential Committee on Human Rights, which functioned as a freestanding investigative and advisory body for the president. See above note 34. Executive Order no. 163 (1987) abolished the committee and enabled the Human Rights Commission to take over its functions. On the work of the committee, see B. Aquino, "The Human Rights Debacle in the Philippines," in Roht-Arriaza, *Impunity and Human Rights in International Law and Practice*, above note 1, at 232–3.

173 In Canada, for example, the mandates of some provincial human rights commissions are limited to the investigation of acts of discrimination, whether committed in the public or the private sector. See Freeman and van Ert, *International Human Rights Law*, above note 19, at 208–12.

174 Reif, "Building Democratic Institutions," above note 170, at 10–11.

administration. Ombudsman offices exist in over one hundred countries,[175] and may go by a variety of names.[176] An ombudsman office has the authority to conduct investigations of alleged abuse by public servants or by publicly regulated agencies. It typically does so in response to complaints, but it may also do so on its own initiative. Ombudsman offices also generally have the power to make corrective recommendations in their reports to the government or legislature. Like a human rights commission, however, an ombudsman office usually lacks the power to issue binding decisions. Since its mandate focuses on public administration, human rights issues unavoidably arise – including, for example, issues of discrimination or detention center abuse – but ombudsman offices do not have mandates that explicitly focus on human rights abuse.

In recent years, particularly in Latin America and Central and Eastern Europe, hybrid versions of the national human rights commission and the ombudsman have appeared. A leading commentator refers to these as "hybrid human rights ombudsmen."[177] As their name suggests, these bodies perform two primary roles: monitoring of public administration, and protection and promotion of human rights. They may, in addition, wield powers not generally possessed by the classic ombudsman or human rights commission, such as the power to contest legislation before constitutional courts, issue public censures for unconstitutional acts, and submit opinions on draft laws that deal with human rights. Examples of such hybrid bodies include the *Defensor del Pueblo* (Spain and many Latin American states including Colombia and Argentina), the *Procurador para la Defensa de los Derechos Humanos* (El Salvador, Guatemala), the Commissioner for Civil Rights Protection (Poland), the Human Rights Ombudsman (Slovenia), the Advocate of the People (Romania, Albania), and the Commission for Human Rights and Administrative Justice (Ghana).

Many human rights commissions, ombudsman offices, and hybrid offices have carried out work similar to truth commissions. A human rights ombudsman in Honduras conducted a full investigation of cases of enforced disappearance and produced a final report that included the names of those alleged to be responsible.[178] In Australia, a national human rights commission completed a major investigation and report on the state's practice of forcibly

---

175 For a full listing of ombudsman offices, including their websites, *see* http://www.law. ualberta.ca/centres/ioi/eng/resources.html.

176 The Parliamentary Commissioner for Administration (Sri Lanka), the Public Protector (South Africa), the *Protecteur du Citoyen* (Quebec, Canada), the *Volksanwaltschaft* (Austria), and the *Difensore Civico* (Italian regions and provinces) are all examples of ombudsman offices. Reif, "Building Democratic Institutions," at 9.

177 *See* Reif, "Building Democratic Institutions," above note 170, at 2.

178 N. Roht-Arriaza, "Overview," in Roht-Arriaza, *Impunity and Human Rights in International Law and Practice*, above note 1, at 154.

separating aboriginal children from their families between 1910 and 1970.[179] In Mexico, a national human rights commission investigated and published a three thousand–page report on acts of political violence committed by security forces during the country's "dirty war" of the 1970s and early 1980s.[180] In Peru, a far-reaching report by the *Defensoría del Pueblo* on enforced disappearances from 1980 to 1996 proved very useful to the work of the Peruvian TRC.[181] These are only a few examples of the useful contributions these bodies can make.

As a final note, it is important to acknowledge that human rights commissions, ombudsman offices, and hybrid offices exist alongside other similar, standing national institutions. Privacy commissions, correctional service investigators, police complaints commissions, and similar bodies also investigate human rights–related abuses in many countries. In some states, for example in many of those in the former Yugoslavia, there are standing commissions or institutes charged with investigating and documenting cases of persons who went missing during periods of armed conflict.[182] There are also *sui generis* bodies, such as the Polish Institute of National Remembrance. Established by the Polish parliament in 1998, its mission includes the investigation of serious human rights violations committed during and immediately after the Second World War.[183]

Standing and *ad hoc* multilateral human rights monitors

Complementing the work of domestic human rights bodies, there exists a wide variety of multilateral human rights monitors, some standing and others

---

179 Hayner, *Unspeakable Truths*, above note 33, at 17–18. The 1997 final report was entitled *Bringing Them Home*. The full report is available at http://www.hreoc.gov.au/bth/text%5Fversions/. It was the commission's conclusion that between 10 percent and one-third of aboriginal children were stolen from their homes during this time.

180 *Comisión Nacional de Derechos Humanos*, "Informe Especial Sobre las Quejas en Materia de Desapariciones Forzadas Ocurridas en la Década de los 70 y Principios de los 80." *See* http://www.cndh.org.mx/Principal/document/informe/infl.htm

181 Orentlicher, "Promotion and Protection of Human Rights: Impunity," above note 24, at para. 62.

182 *See generally A Report on Local, Regional and International Documentation of War Crimes and Human Rights Violations in the Former Yugoslavia* (International Center for Transitional Justice, 2002). *See also* the website of the International Commission on Missing Persons: http://www.ic-mp.org. The commission is an intergovernmental organization that addresses the issue of persons missing in the former Yugoslavia, primarily through the use of DNA technology. Other countries with standing commissions on missing persons like those of the former Yugoslavia include Brazil (the Commission on the Death and Disappearance of Political Prisoners) and Nepal (the Investigative Commission on Disappearances).

183 In 2002, the institute published a 1,500-page report in which it declared, to the apparent surprise of many, that at least thirty wartime massacres against Polish Jews had been perpetrated by locals rather than by Nazi occupiers. *See* "Poles Blamed for Wartime Massacres," *BBC News World Edition* (http://news.bbc.co.uk), 2 November 2002.

ad hoc. Some of these bodies focus on the full range of human rights (*e.g.,* the Inter-American Commission on Human Rights), while many others focus on specific categories of human rights (*e.g.,* the UN Committee Against Torture). Although multilateral bodies do not displace a state's international legal obligation to investigate and report on human rights violations, the work of these bodies can have a significant political and legal impact by helping to fill the so-called "impunity gap" in some states. Many of these human rights monitors also play important roles in the global promotion and mainstreaming of human rights.[184]

Multilateral human rights monitors are complementary to, but different from, truth commissions. Many of the most important ones are standing, rather than *ad hoc,* bodies. They tend to focus on past as well as on continuing violations. They generally lack quasi-judicial investigative powers, and operate mostly or entirely outside the state being investigated. Multilateral monitors investigate acts of severe violence or repression committed in contexts of authoritarian rule or armed conflict, but they might just as likely investigate violations committed in democratic states at peace. And while many monitors issue major reports on their investigations, these reports do not generally mark the body's demise; rather, they comprise an ongoing function, just as with NGOs, ombudsman offices, and national human rights commissions. In all of these respects, standing and *ad hoc* multilateral monitors differ from truth commissions.

In the UN system, there is a wide array of monitors that conduct some form of human rights investigation. The principal ones include the Office of the High Commissioner for Human Rights,[185] the various UN treaty bodies (in their capacity of reviewing state performance reports and investigating systematic violations),[186] the Commission on Human Rights (*e.g.,* through its "1503

---

184 *See generally* Freeman and van Ert, *International Human Rights Law,* above note 19, cc. 14–16.

185 *See ibid.,* at 408–10. The High Commissioner for Human Rights will sometimes dispatch *ad hoc* fact-finding missions in response to alleged atrocities (*e.g.,* Togo in 2005). *See* http://www.ohchr.org.

186 There are seven UN treaty bodies: the Human Rights Committee (which monitors compliance with the International Covenant on Civil and Political Rights 1966 and its optional protocol on the death penalty), the Committee on Economic, Social and Cultural Rights (which monitors compliance with the International Covenant on Economic, Social and Cultural Rights 1966), the Committee Against Torture (which monitors compliance with the Convention Against Torture and Other Cruel, Inhuman or Degrading Treatment or Punishment 1984 and its optional protocol), the Committee on the Elimination of Racial Discrimination (which monitors compliance with the International Convention on the Elimination of All Forms of Racial Discrimination 1966), the Committee on the Rights of the Child (which monitors compliance with the Convention on the Rights of the Child 1989 and its optional protocols), the Committee on the Elimination of Discrimination Against Women (which monitors compliance with the Convention on the Elimination of All Forms

procedure"),[187] working groups of the Commission on Human Rights (such as the Working Group on Enforced or Involuntary Disappearances),[188] independent monitors of the Commission on Human Rights or the Secretary-General (such as special representatives on particular countries and themes),[189] working groups of the Sub-Commission on the Promotion and Protection of Human Rights (such as the Working Group on Contemporary Forms of Slavery),[190] the Commission on the Status of Women,[191] and the Special Committee to Investigate Israeli Practices Affecting the Human Rights of the Palestinian People and Other Arabs of the Occupied Territories.[192] UN human rights field operations have also played important investigative roles in many states.[193]

Regional multilateral systems encompass a range of human rights monitors that conduct human rights investigations too. In the Inter-American human

---

of Discrimination Against Women 1979 and its optional protocol), and the Committee on the Protection of the Rights of All Migrant Workers and Members of Their Families (which monitors compliance with the International Convention on the Protection of the Rights of All Migrant Workers and Members of Their Families 1990). On their role in the review of state performance reports, *see* Freeman and van Ert, *International Human Rights Law*, above note 19, at 386–91; on their role in investigating systematic violations, *see ibid.*, at 391–3.

187 The procedure, which functions under the auspices of the UN Commission on Human Rights, deals with "consistent patterns of gross and reliably attested violations of human rights": ECOSOC res. 1503 (XLVIII) (1970) as amended by ECOSOC res. 2000/3 (2000). *See generally* Freeman and van Ert, *International Human Rights Law*, above note 19, at 404–5.

188 *See generally* Freeman and van Ert, *International Human Rights Law*, above note 19, at 405–7. *See, e.g.*, the 2005 report of the Working Group on Enforced or Involuntary Disappearances, at UN doc. E/CN.4/2005/65.

189 *See generally* Freeman and van Ert, *International Human Rights Law*, above note 19, at 405–7. There have been independent monitors on topics ranging from the independence of judges and lawyers, to violence against women, to internally displaced persons. There have been independent monitors on countries ranging from Iraq, to Haiti, to Somalia. Independent monitors conduct on-site investigations with the permission of the host state and then file reports on their findings to the Commission on Human Rights. In 2004, the UN Secretary-General also established the non-Commission-related office of the Special Adviser on the Prevention of Genocide.

190 *Ibid.*, at 403–4. *See, e.g.*, the 2005 report of the Working Group on Contemporary Forms of Slavery, UN doc. E/CN.4/Sub.2/RES/2004/19.

191 *See generally* Freeman and van Ert, *International Human Rights Law*, above note 19, at 407–8. *See, e.g.*, the commission's report on the "Situation of Women and Girls in Afghanistan," UN doc. E/CN.6/2004/L/1/REV.1 (2004).

192 The UN General Assembly established the committee under GA res. 2443 (XXIII) (1968). *See generally* http://www.unhchr.ch/html/menu2/7/a/moatsc.htm.

193 *See, e.g.*, I. Martin, "Closer to the Victim: United Nations Human Rights Field Operations," in Y. Danieli and others, eds., *The Universal Declaration of Human Rights: Fifty Years and Beyond* (Amityville, NY: Baywood Publishers, 1999), at chapter 8. In El Salvador, Haiti, Guatemala, and Sierra Leone, the UN's field missions (ONUSAL, MICIVIH, MINUGUA, and UNAMSIL, respectively) operated alongside truth commissions, albeit focusing mainly on ongoing, as opposed to past, violations. *See* Mattarollo, "Truth Commissions," in Bassiouni, *Post-Conflict Justice*, above note 1, at 296–7.

rights system, the principal such bodies are the Inter-American Commission on Human Rights (in its capacities of undertaking country studies and in-country investigations, and of reviewing state performance reports filed pursuant to the Additional Protocol to the American Convention on Human Rights in the Area of Economic, Social and Cultural Rights 1988)[194] and its special rapporteurs.[195] In the Council of Europe human rights system, the principal relevant bodies are the European Committee of Social Rights (in its capacity of reviewing state performance reports filed pursuant to the revised European Social Charter 1996),[196] the Commissioner for Human Rights,[197] the European Commission Against Racism and Intolerance,[198] the Committee of Experts Responsible for Supervising Adherence to the European Charter for Regional or Minority Languages 1992,[199] the Special Advisory Committee Concerning the Framework Convention for the Protection of National Minorities 1995,[200] and the European Committee for the Prevention of Torture and Inhuman or Degrading Treatment or Punishment.[201] In the Organization for Security and Cooperation in Europe's human rights system, the principal relevant bodies are the Human Dimension Mechanism,[202] the Office of the High Commissioner

---

194 *See generally* Freeman and van Ert, *International Human Rights Law,* above note 19, at 426–33.

195 There are currently two permanent special rapporteurs: the Rapporteurship on the Rights of Women, and the Special Rapporteur for Freedom of Expression. Both conduct in-country investigative missions and report their findings. *See ibid.,* at 433. There is also an *ad hoc* Special Rapporteurship on Migrant Workers and Their Families.

196 ETS no. 163. The Charter was preceded by the European Social Charter 1961 (ETS no. 35), the Additional Protocol to the Charter 1988 (ETS no. 128), the Protocol Amending the European Social Charter 1991 (ETS no. 142), and the Additional Protocol Providing for a System of Collective Complaints 1995 (ETS no. 158). On the work of the committee, *see* Freeman and van Ert, *International Human Rights Law,* above note 19, at 441–2; D. Harris, "Lessons from the Reporting System of the European Social Charter," in P. Alston and J. Crawford, eds., *The Future of UN Human Rights Treaty Monitoring* (Cambridge: Cambridge University Press, 2000).

197 *See* Freeman and van Ert, *International Human Rights Law,* above note 19, at 442–3. The commissioner's website is http://www.coe.int/T/E/Commissioner_H.R.

198 *See* Freeman and van Ert, *International Human Rights Law,* above note 19, at 443. The commission's website is http://www.coe.int/t/E/human_rights/ecri/.

199 ETS no. 148. On the work of the committee, *see* Freeman and van Ert, *International Human Rights Law,* above note 19, at 443–4.

200 ETS no. 157. On the work of the committee, *see* Freeman and van Ert, *International Human Rights Law,* above note 19, at 444.

201 *See* Freeman and van Ert, *International Human Rights Law,* above note 19, at 444. The committee's website is http://www.cpt.coe.int/en/default.htm.

202 *See* Freeman and van Ert, *International Human Rights Law,* above note 19, at 446. In certain circumstances, an independent investigator can be appointed to investigate alleged violations of human rights.

for National Minorities,[203] and the Representative on Freedom of the Media.[204] Finally, in the human rights system of the African Union (AU), the main relevant bodies are the African Commission on Human and Peoples' Rights (in its capacity of reviewing state performance reports and undertaking in-country investigative missions),[205] special rapporteurs of the commission,[206] and the African Committee of Experts on the Rights and Welfare of the Child (in its capacity of reviewing state performance reports).[207]

In addition to these bodies, there are multilateral monitors that conduct investigations in human rights–related fields such as international labor and refugee law. Examples of such monitors include: (1) International Labour Organization (ILO) bodies such as the Committee of Experts on the Application of Conventions and Recommendations,[208] and the Conference Committee on the Application of Conventions and Recommendations;[209] (2) North American bodies such as the Commission for Labor Cooperation;[210] and (3) refugee-related bodies such as the UN Office of the High Commissioner for Refugees.[211] The Commonwealth is another multilateral organization that monitors and periodically investigates serious human rights abuses.[212]

Ad hoc national human rights–related commissions of inquiry

A truth commission is one kind of *ad hoc* national human rights–related commission of inquiry. But there are at least four other major types of such inquiry: event-specific, thematic, sociohistorical, and institutional. The legal basis of any one of these may vary. The inquiry may take the form of a Commonwealth commission created by order in council under an extant commission of inquiry statute. It may take the form of a parliamentary inquiry or congressional committee of investigation, depending on the particular state's constitutional

203 *See ibid.*, at 446. The commissioner's website is http://www.osce.org/hcnm/.

204 *See* Freeman and van Ert, *International Human Rights Law*, above note 19, at 446. The representative's website is http://www.osce.org/fom/.

205 *See* Freeman and van Ert, *International Human Rights Law*, above note 19, at 448–52.

206 As of this writing, there are special rapporteurships on six issues: extrajudicial, arbitrary, and summary executions; prison conditions; the rights of women; freedom of expression; the situation of human rights defenders; and refugees, asylum seekers, and internally displaced persons. *See* http://www.achpr.org.

207 *See* Freeman and van Ert, *International Human Rights Law*, above note 19, at 452.

208 *See ibid.*, at 455.

209 *See ibid.*, at 455–6.

210 *See ibid.*, at 458. The commission was created pursuant to the North American Agreement on Labor Cooperation 1993.

211 *See ibid.*, at 460–2.

212 *See ibid.*, at 464–5. The Commonwealth has periodically investigated "serious and persistent violations" of human rights in selected member states. *See* http://www.thecommonwealth.org.

structure. It may also take the form of a presidential commission of inquiry or, in cases of suspected military abuse, a military inquiry.[213] The inquiry might also take the form of an internal departmental or multidepartmental inquiry set up on an *ad hoc* basis by one or more ministers.[214] Whatever the particulars, the common elements of such inquiries are their temporary character and their mandate to investigate and submit a report containing conclusions and recommendations. Other possible common elements may include, for example, the ability to hold public hearings or to publish findings of individual responsibility.

Event-specific inquiries

Unlike truth commissions, event-specific inquiries involve investigating and reporting on a particular event (*e.g.*, the police shooting of an unarmed civilian) or a short series of related events (*e.g.*, violent clashes over a period of months in a particular region), as opposed to a longer period of history or a broader range of events. Usually the event or events being probed are of recent occurrence, but they may also be historical events of singular notoriety (*e.g.*, the so-called November 17 Commission established in Czechoslovakia in the early 1990s to examine the 1989 "Velvet Revolution").[215]

Often a principal objective of event-specific inquiries is to determine whether there is any need for legal proceedings of a criminal, civil, or disciplinary nature; they may not, therefore, be as victim-centered as truth commissions. But like truth commissions, event-specific inquiries usually involve the examination of underlying causes, surrounding facts, and social consequences of the specific event or events. The investigation might thereby result in larger truths about past repression, in the same way a truth commission investigation might.

There are thousands of examples of event-specific human rights–related inquiries. In Commonwealth countries like Canada, for example, there are often several such inquiries operating in any given year.[216] One of the earliest known instances of event-specific, human rights–related inquiry was the popularly called Governor Eyre Inquiry concerning the suppression of the Morant Bay uprising in Jamaica in 1865.[217] More contemporary and pertinent instances

---

213 *See, e.g.*, K. J. Greenberg and J. L. Dratel, eds., *The Torture Papers* (New York: Cambridge University Press, 2005), which contains the reports of various military and other investigations of alleged US military abuse of Iraqi detainees in Iraq and elsewhere.

214 For example, Parts I and II of *Inquiries Act*, RS 1985, c. I–11 (Canada) explicitly contemplate such inquiries, as does the *Inquiries Act*, 2005 (UK). *See* Chapter 2, Section 2.

215 *See* Teitel, *Transitional Justice*, above note 1, at 94.

216 *See above* note 78.

217 "In 1866 early in January, a Royal Commission arrived from England to enquire into the origin and suppression of the rebellion. Governor Eyre was suspended, and the head of the Commission, Sir Henry Stokes, became temporary Governor. After thoroughly going into the matter, the Commission found that 'the disturbances had their immediate origin in a

from around the world include: the 1968 Peers Commission of Inquiry regarding the killing of Vietnamese civilians at My Lai;[218] the 1983 Kahan Commission of Inquiry in Israel regarding massacres of civilians at two Lebanese refugee camps;[219] the 1998 Bloody Sunday inquiry established by the UK government to investigate the 1972 killing of fourteen protesters in Northern Ireland;[220] the 2000 Nanavati Commission of Inquiry into anti-Sikh riots that occurred in 1984 in India and resulted in thousands of deaths;[221] the 2001 Sri Lankan presidential "Truth Commission on Ethnic Violence," which focused on the 1983 riots that sparked Sri Lanka's civil war;[222] and the 2003 Republika Srpska "Commission for Investigation of the Events in and around Srebrenica between the 10th and 19th of July, 1995."[223]

---

planned resistance to lawful authority; but that the punishments inflicted during Martial Law were excessive; that the punishment of death was unnecessarily frequent; that the floggings were reckless, and at Bath positively barbarous; and that the burning of 1,000 houses was wanton and cruel.' Eyre was then recalled and dismissed from the Imperial Service." Jamaica Royal Commission Report 1866, HMSO, 2 vols., London. *See also* A. Hochschild, *King Leopold's Ghost* (New York: Mariner Books, 1998), at 250–255, where the author describes a 1904 commission of inquiry on allegations of systemic and widespread abuse in the Belgian Congo.

218 In March 1968, during the Vietnam War, US troops reportedly massacred 400 to 500 Vietnamese peasants and Viet Cong guerrillas in the village of My Lai. General William R. Peers (and others) conducted an investigation into the massacre and the subsequent cover-up of information by several military officers. The investigation was completed in 1970 but remained confidential until 1974. *See Microfilm Guide to Vietnam War Research Collections: The Peers Inquiry of the Massacre at My Lai*, Microfilm DS 557.8 M9 P428 1996.

219 *Report of the Kahan Commission of Inquiry*, 1983 (Israel). The full report is available at http://www.jewishvirtuallibrary.org/jsource/History/kahan.html. *See* Chapter 7, note 27, for discussion of the commission's final report.

220 The inquiry was established in 1998 by UK prime minister Tony Blair under the *Tribunals of Inquiry (Evidence) Act*, 1921 (UK), as revised. Its purpose was to investigate the 1972 event known as "Bloody Sunday," when protesters were killed in Londonberry, Northern Ireland, apparently by the British army. *See* the inquiry's website at http://www.bloody-sunday-inquiry.org. A 1972 commission of inquiry into the same event was widely considered biased. *See* A. Hegarty, "Truth, Law and Official Denial: The Case of Bloody Sunday," in Schabas and Darcy, *Truth Commissions and Courts*, above note 127, 199 at 206–8, 212–14.

221 The commission was given a broader mandate than several previous inquiries appointed to investigate the anti-Sikh riots of 1984, which followed the assassination of former prime minister Indira Gandhi. The commission submitted its final report in 2005. *See* "Transitional Justice in the News" (http://www.ictj.org), 15 February 2005.

222 The truth commission moniker is an ill fit, not only because of the commission's subject matter (which required it to focus primarily on riots that occurred in July 1983), but also because the commission was established eighteen years after the event. Not surprisingly, victims and NGOs in Sri Lanka continue to call for a national truth commission that would cover the almost twenty years of civil war that followed the 1983 riots.

223 The commission was established by the Republika Srpska (BiH) National Assembly at its 25 December 2003 session, acting under pressure from the Office of the High Representative. Its final report led to unprecedented acknowledgments of responsibility by RS authorities.

Thematic commissions of inquiry

Thematic commissions of inquiry involve the examination of particular social policy issues that are mired in public controversy (*e.g.*, systemic discrimination against a particular racial, ethnic, or religious group). Like truth commissions, thematic inquiries examine policies and practices employed over a period of time. Unlike truth commissions, however, such inquiries tend to focus more on analysis of public policy than on victims or on individual fact-finding. Also, their work is not necessarily focused on the examination of violations committed during periods of abusive rule or armed conflict (unless the theme under review so corresponds).

There are scores of examples of such inquiries. Some relevant instances from around the world include the 1991 Royal Commission on Aboriginal Peoples in Canada,[224] the 1975 Commission of the Black Book of Fascism in Portugal,[225] and the 2001 government-appointed panel established in Turkey to examine questions of human rights and identity in the country.[226]

See generally M. Freeman, *Bosnia and Herzegovina: Selected Developments in Transitional Justice*, (International Center for Transitional Justice, 2004), at 8–10.

224 *See* Royal Commission on Aboriginal Peoples, *People to People, Nation to Nation: Highlights from the Report of the Royal Commission on Aboriginal Peoples* (Ottawa: The Commission, 1996). The commission held 178 days of public hearings in ninety-six communities across Canada. At several of its hearings, survivors of physical and sexual abuse at Canada's former Indian Residential Schools (IRS) courageously told of their experiences. As noted earlier, as of this writing Canada is considering a truth and reconciliation process as part of a comprehensive package to deal with the IRS legacy.

225 *See* A. C. Pinto, "Settling Accounts with the Past in a Troubled Transition to Democracy: The Portugese Case," in A. Brito and others, eds., *The Politics of Memory and Democratization* (Oxford: Oxford University Press, 2001), at 81. The commission comprised intellectuals and politicians of the republican and socialist left. It had access to the dictatorship's archives and ultimately published dozens of books about past repression in Portugal.

226 "The board's report, released this month, said things that were almost unsayable, triggering a sharp backlash. For example, the report implies that if the Lausanne treaty of 1923 – the basis of the Turkish state and its foreign relations – had been fully implemented, bloodshed between Turks and Kurds might have been avoided . . . It also says that articles which supposedly protect non-Muslim minorities have been read too narrowly: as well as covering Jews, Armenians and Greeks, these articles should have been applied, for example, to Syrian Orthodox Christians. More controversially still, it suggests replacing the term 'Turk' with a more inclusive word to cover all ethnicities and faiths, such as '*Turkiyeli*' – 'of Turkey'. It was more than some Turks could bear. Even as Ibrahim Kaboglu, the jurist who heads the board, was reading the report at a press conference, a fellow member snatched it and tore it into shreds. Both Mr Kaboglu and Baskin Oran, a political scientist who wrote the report, have been bombarded with threatening phone calls and mail . . . Prosecutors in Ankara are investigating claims that both academics may have committed treason. Ilker Basbug, a top general, has joined the fray, saying Turkey's unity should not be tampered with. The government, frightened by the reaction, has washed its hands of the report and denied

Sociohistorical commissions of inquiry

Sociohistorical commissions of inquiry involve the investigation of an important period in a country's history and, perhaps, its impact on a particular demographic group. Sociohistorical commissions of inquiry are distinguishable from truth commissions in that they are created a generation or more after the "immediate period" of political or postconflict transition, and hence they look back at a period that is, at the commission's moment of creation, more historical than contemporary in its character and in its implications for the government of the day.[227] Some pertinent examples from around the world include the 1982 US Commission on Wartime Relocation and Internment of Civilians,[228] the 1989 Czechoslovak Commission for the Investigation of the Events of 1967–70,[229] and the 1997 Commission of Inquiry into Nazi Activities in Argentina.[230] In 2005, there was also a call for a commission of inquiry in Spain to examine violations committed under former dictator General Francisco Franco between 1939 and 1975.[231]

Institutional commissions of inquiry

Unlike truth commissions, institutional commissions of inquiry are limited to investigating and reporting on events occurring within a particular institution. They do not, in other words, examine a broad range of abuses committed by multiple and possibly unrelated actors or institutions.

Institutional inquiries may be established by authorities external to the institution (*e.g.,* a president may establish an inquiry into racism within the

---

commissioning it": "Trouble over Turkish History," *The Economist*, 11 November 2004, at 56–7.

227 There will almost always be some political implications for a government that establishes a sociohistorical inquiry, but these will usually be less significant compared to the implications of inquiries into more recent periods of violence or repression.

228 The US Congress established the commission through H.R. 5499 (1982). The commission heard from hundreds of witnesses and conducted public hearings in several US cities. The commission recommended that the government apologize and provide reparations for surviving internees, which it eventually did. *See Personal Justice Denied: Report of the Commission on Wartime Relocation and Internment of Civilians* (Seattle: University of Washington Press, 1997). The original report was issued in 1983.

229 *See generally* Teitel, *Transitional Justice*, above note 1, at 94.

230 The commission's title in the original Spanish is *Comisión para el Esclarecimiento de las Actividades del Nazismo en la República Argentina* (CEANA). The commission tracked shipments of looted Nazi gold, determined how many war criminals arrived in Argentina, and found evidence of government complicity in assisting war criminals and Nazi collaborators to settle in Argentina in the immediate post–Second World War period. The commission's full report can be found at http://www.ceana.org.ar/.

231 The Spanish judge Baltasar Garzón launched the appeal for such a commission. *See* "Spain's Garzon Calls for 'Truth Commission' on Franco," Reuters (http://www.reuters.com), 27 February 2005.

national police force) or by superiors or persons in charge of the institution itself (*e.g.*, an army general may establish an inquiry into allegations of sexual harassment of female army recruits). There are countless such inquiries created in states around the world in any given year.

Coroners and medical examiners

In most common law jurisdictions, coroners and medical examiners conduct investigations and hold formal public inquests in cases of suspicious deaths. All coroner systems derive from the English system; they appear to have no functional equivalents in the civil law tradition.[232] Unlike truth commissions, the offices of coroners and medical examiners are permanent, not temporary, bodies. In addition, their focus is not on broad periods of history, but rather on isolated instances of death that do not always have a human rights dimension.[233] Like truth commissions, however, they are, above all, investigative bodies.

The investigative powers of coroners and medical examiners typically encompass the ability to enter places where bodies are located, disinter or exhume remains, inspect and extract information from records or writings relating to the deceased, and seize relevant artifacts.[234]

A coroner's inquest is a special hearing to determine the circumstances surrounding a particular death. Inquests may be conducted by a coroner or medical examiner "sitting alone." They may also be held with a jury, summoned in the same way as a criminal jury.[235] The jury hears evidence from witnesses and makes factual determinations.[236] The jury does not assign fault, but it may make recommendations to prevent similar deaths in the future. These recommendations are included in a nonbinding "verdict."[237] Often a coroner's inquest is mandatory when a person dies in prison or in police custody or

---

232 In civil law systems, death inquiries are typically conducted by police, magistrates, or prosecutors as a part of the routine investigation of crime. Unlike coroners' inquests, such investigations are conducted in private, although the conclusions may be made public. P. Matthews, *Jervis on Coroners*, 12th ed. (London: Sweet & Maxwell, 2002), at 11, 477, 486–9.

233 Freeman and van Ert, *International Human Rights Law*, above note 19, at 366–7: "Coroners and medical examiners do not investigate all deaths; only those that are unnatural, unexpected, unexplained, or warrant investigation for other reasons."

234 *Ibid.*, at 367.

235 Although originally every inquest was held with a jury, today most inquests are conducted without juries. Matthews, *Jervis on Coroners*, above note 232, at 218.

236 Similar proceedings take place in medical examiner jurisdictions, although they are often conducted by a judge sitting without a jury.

237 Matthews, *Jervis on Coroners*, above note 232, at 465–6. Evidence from coroner inquests is not admissible in a court of law. *Ibid.*, at 466.

dies violently or unnaturally. Otherwise it is established at the discretion of the investigating coroner.[238]

Ad hoc multilateral human rights–related commissions of inquiry

Human rights–related commissions of inquiry exist not only at the national level but also at the regional and international level. Multilateral commissions of inquiry resemble truth commissions less than do their national equivalents, but have in common with truth commissions the mandate to conduct investigations and report their findings and recommendations. Like truth commissions, but unlike other national commissions of inquiry, multilateral inquiries tend to focus on broad and recent patterns of abuse (although some focus only on specific events). Given their multilateral character, they typically operate outside of the concerned state, except when on a mission. Their investigative powers tend to be very weak,[239] and they do not conduct anything equivalent to truth commission or Commonwealth-type public hearings. At the same time, in the absence of effective national investigation – whether due to incapacity or unwillingness – multilateral inquiries can play a critical role in advancing truth and preserving evidence for later accountability efforts.

Multilateral human rights–related commissions of inquiry may take many forms. One of the earliest such commissions was the *ad hoc* Commission on the Responsibility of the Authors of the War and on Enforcement of Penalties, which was established after the First World War to examine wartime atrocities.[240] The United Nations, the most universal multilateral organization, has established many human rights–related commissions of inquiry through organs such as the Security Council, the Secretary-General, and the Commission on Human Rights. Since the end of the Cold War, there have been UN-sponsored commissions for the broad investigation of war crimes and similar atrocities committed, *inter alia*, in the former Yugoslavia (1992),[241] Rwanda

---

238 *Ibid.*, at 83 and 218.

239 *See, e.g., Report of the International Commission of Inquiry on Darfur to the United Nations Secretary-General* (2005), para. 6: "The Commission has not been endowed with the powers proper to a prosecutor (in particular, it may not subpoena witnesses, or order searches or seizures, nor may it request a judge to issue arrest warrants against suspects)." Excerpts of the final report appear in Appendix 3 to this book.

240 *See* Report Presented to the Preliminary Peace Conference, 29 March 1919, reprinted in (1920) 14 *AJIL* 95. The commission found evidence sufficient for prosecution of some 20,000 war criminals. M. C. Bassiouni, "The United Nations Commission of Experts on the Former Yugoslavia," in Bassiouni, *Post-Conflict Justice*, above note 1, at 433–6. The other major international war crimes commission of the first half of the last century was the so-called United Nations War Crimes Commission of 1943. *See ibid.*, at 436–8.

241 *See* Final Report of the United Nations Commission of Experts Established Pursuant to Security Council Resolution 780 (1992), 27 May 1994. The full report is available

(1994),[242] Burundi (1995),[243] East Timor (1999),[244] and Sudan (2004).[245] In contrast to truth commissions, which are focused on past events, these multilateral inquiries tend to investigate and document both past and ongoing violations, often in preparation for subsequent domestic or international prosecution.[246] The fact of ongoing conflict is a serious complicating factor for such commissions in their efforts to gather evidence.[247]

The UN and other multilateral organizations have created international commissions of inquiry to examine isolated past events too, including in Togo

---

at http://www.un.org/Docs/sc/missionreports/25700e.pdf. "The Commission worked for two years, during which it conducted thirty-five field investigations, established the most extensive database for gathering evidence and information about violations of international humanitarian law, identified over 800 places of detention, estimated 50,000 cases of torture and 200,000 deaths, estimated two million displaced persons as a result of ethnic cleansing that was documented in connection with some 2,000 towns and villages where the practices took place, and conducted the world's first and most extensive investigation into systematic rape": M. C. Bassiouni, "Appraising UN Justice-Related Fact-Finding Missions" (2001) 5 *Wash. U. J. L. & Pol'y* 35, at 46–7. The atrocities cited in the commission's report apparently bear strong resemblance to those documented by a similar inquiry established by the Carnegie Endowment for International Peace in 1913 to investigate the events of the First and Second Balkan Wars of 1912 and 1913. Bassiouni, "The United Nations Commission of Experts on the Former Yugoslavia," above note 240, at 438–9.

242 *See* UN Secretary-General, "Final Report of the Commission of Experts Established Pursuant to Security Council Resolution 935 (1994)," UN doc. S/1994/1405 (1994). The commission operated for three months and made only a one-week visit to Rwanda. It conducted virtually no fact-finding. The underlying purpose of the commission may have been to buy extra time for the Security Council to sort out the mandate of the planned International Criminal Tribunal for Rwanda. *See* Bassiouni, "Appraising UN Justice-Related Fact-Finding Missions," above note 241, at 42–5.

243 *See* above note 35.

244 *See* Report of the Commission on Human Rights on Its Fourth Special Session, UN doc. E/CN.4/1999/167/Add.1,E/1999/23/Add.1 (1999). The commission's full report is available at http://www.unhchr.ch. The commission was established by the UN Secretary-General at the recommendation of the Commission on Human Rights. The commission found that there had been "gross violations of human rights and breaches of humanitarian law" attributable to the Indonesian army and related militias. The commission worked for a total of seven weeks.

245 *See Report of the International Commission of Inquiry on Darfur to the United Nations Secretary-General* (2005). The commission's purpose was to investigate violations of human rights and humanitarian law, determine whether genocide occurred, and identify perpetrators.

246 M. C. Bassiouni, "Accountability for Violations of International Humanitarian Law and Other Serious Violations of Human Rights," in Bassiouni, *Post-Conflict Justice*, above note 1, at 31.

247 M. C. Bassiouni, "The Commission of Experts Established Pursuant to Security Council Resolution 780: Investigating Violations of International Humanitarian Law in the Former Yugoslavia" (1994) 5 *Crim. L. Forum* 279, at 300.

in 2000[248] and in the Ivory Coast in 2004.[249] Their closest functional equivalent would be a national event-specific inquiry.

The ILO Governing Body also periodically appoints *ad hoc* commissions of inquiry to examine the performance of member states accused of persistent and serious violations of fundamental ILO conventions.[250] International humanitarian law also includes a commission of inquiry mechanism. Article 90 of the Protocol Additional to the Geneva Conventions of 12 August 1949, and relating to the Protection of Victims of International Armed Conflicts (Protocol I) 1977,[251] establishes the International Humanitarian Fact-Finding Commission, a body whose members have been elected but which has yet to be called upon by parties to an international conflict.[252]

Multilateral human rights–related commissions of inquiry have also been established at the regional level. A prominent example is the investigation and report done by the International Panel of Eminent Personalities appointed by the Organization of African Unity (now the African Union) to investigate the 1994 genocide in Rwanda.[253] Another example is the Organization of

---

248 The UN and the Organization of African Unity (now the African Union) established a commission of inquiry tasked with "verifying the truth of allegations of hundreds of extra-judicial executions, which allegedly took place in Togo during 1998, made by Amnesty International's report published on 5 May 1999." In its 2001 final report, the commission confirmed the "existence of systematic violations of human rights in Togo during 1998." The Togolese government later established a national commission of inquiry to investigate the same events.

249 The commission was established by the UN Security Council in 2004 at the request of Ivory Coast President Laurent Gbagbo. It examined recent violations committed by both sides of the country's internal armed conflict. In a confidential annex to the report (which was later leaked to the press), there are the names of 95 individuals allegedly responsible for serious violations, including the president's wife. See "Ivory Coast First Lady Leads Death Squad, Report Alleges," *Washington Post*, http://www.washingtonpost.com, 29 January 2005.

250 The ILO commission of inquiry procedure usually involves hearings in Geneva as well as in-country investigation. The commission prepares a final report containing conclusions and recommendations, which it submits to the Governing Body. The government in question may accept the recommendations or file an appeal to the International Court of Justice, whose decision is final. See, e.g., the July 1998 Report of the "Commission of Inquiry Appointed under ILO Constitution Art. 26 to Examine the Observance by Myanmar of the Forced Labour Convention (no. 29) 1930." Available at http://www.ilo.org/public/english/standards/relm/gb/docs/gb273/myanmar.htm.

251 1125 UNTS 3, *entered into force* 7 December 1978.

252 Article 90(2)(a) of Protocol I provides: "The High Contracting Parties may at the time of signing, ratifying or acceding to the Protocol, or at any other subsequent time, declare that they recognize ipso facto and without special agreement, in relation to any other High Contracting Party accepting the same obligation, the competence of the [commission] to enquire into allegations by such other Party, as authorized by this Article." The commission's website is http://www.ihffc.org/.

253 A commission's final report, *Rwanda: The Preventable Genocide*, was published in 2000. Its executive summary is available at http://www.iss.org.za/AF/profiles/rwanda/IPEPRwanda.pdf.

American States (OAS) commission of inquiry into a massacre that took place on 17 December 2001 in Haiti.[254] In Europe, an example is the International Commission on Kidnapped and Other Missing Persons, which was established by the European Union (EU) in 2001 to investigate the fate of persons missing as a result of the brief armed conflict in 2001 in the Former Yugoslav Republic of Macedonia.[255]

Standing and *ad hoc* multilateral and national human rights compensation and reparation bodies

Victim reparation is an important tool of transitional justice and, as we have seen, encompasses compensation, rehabilitation, restitution, and various possible symbolic measures.[256]

Compensation is the dominant form that reparation takes in state practice. A number of states have established out-of-court programs to compensate victims of gross and systematic human rights violations. Compensation bodies may take the form of nonjudicial commissions or quasi-judicial tribunals. In either case, the investigation and corroboration of human rights violations will be an intrinsic function (though not always a primary one).[257] Unlike truth

---

254 The commission's final report (dated 1 July 2002) is available at http://www.oas.org/ OASpage/Haiti_situation/cpinf4702_02_eng.htm. The Inter-American Commission on Human Rights also announced in 2005 that it will reopen an inquiry into the 1981 massacre of hundreds of peasants in El Mozote, El Salvador. *See* I. Urbina, "OAS to Reopen Inquiry into Massacre in El Salvador in 1981," *New York Times*, 8 March 2005.

255 A Swedish ambassador chaired the commission. In its final report, the commission attributed its inability to determine the exact fate of any of the kidnapped or missing persons to lack of cooperation by local government officials. The information gathered by the commission was forwarded to the ICTY. A copy of the July 2002 final report is on file with the author.

256 *See* Section 1.

257 Consider the case of Argentina: "Requests for benefits were to be presented to the Office of Human Rights at the Ministry of the Interior. Petitioners had to declare under oath that they had been detained under the conditions established by the law somewhere between November 6, 1974, and December 10, 1983. Broad criteria of evidence were established, such that detention could be proven with habeas corpus petitions or the corresponding sentence, documents from [the truth commission's] files, from judicial and administrative files, and documents filed with the Inter-American Commission on Human Rights and the Inter-American Court of Human Rights. Documents found in national and international human rights organizations, journalistic materials, and bibliographic material were evaluated together with the other approved evidence. Grave injury could be proven with the clinical histories of the place of detention, a copy of the judicial sentence, or the medical or clinical history dated at the time of the detention by an official health institution. If necessary, it was possible to convene a medical panel, for which purposes the under secretary of human rights could enter into agreements with public hospitals. The partial or complete denial of

commissions, compensation bodies do not generally hold powers of subpoena or search and seizure, and they generally do not organize public hearings, prepare a final report on their investigations, or make findings of institutional responsibility.[258] Indeed, their primary function is to compensate individual victims, and not to conduct a broad national truth-telling process. But like truth commissions, compensation bodies primarily focus on victims, rather than perpetrators. The evidence gathered by such bodies can be shared with truth commissions (*e.g.*, Morocco).[259] More typically, however, the compensation commission or tribunal comes after the truth commission, and thus the sharing of information tends to be in the opposite direction (*i.e.*, truth commission files are forwarded to the subsequent compensation body, as occurred in Chile).

National-level *ad hoc* human rights compensation bodies have been established, *inter alia*, in Germany (for Holocaust survivors),[260] Chile (for familes of the disappeared and killed),[261] Argentina (for various victims of military repression),[262] Brazil (for families of the disappeared),[263] Malawi (for victims of the regime of President H. Kamuzu Banda),[264] and the United States and

---

any benefit under the law could be appealed to the National Administrative Appellate Chamber." P. de Greiff, "Reparations Efforts in International Perspective: What Compensation Contributes to the Achievement of Imperfect Justice," in C. Villa-Vicencio and E. Doxtader, eds., *To Repair the Irreparable* (Cape Town: New Africa Books, 2004).

258 Needless to say there are exceptions to this. For example, a Moroccan human rights compensation tribunal – the *Instance d'Arbitrage Indépendante* – prepared a final report on its work. But like other compensation tribunals, all of its proceedings were conducted in private.

259 The Moroccan compensation tribunal awarded nearly US$100 million to victims of arbitrary detention and to families of the forcibly disappeared in some 3,700 cases during its four years of operation (1999–2003). Freeman and Opgenhaffen, *Transitional Justice in Morocco*, above note 130, at 10, 11. Although the commission was not established as a court of appeal for the tribunal's decisions, it did reverse some of its findings in individual cases.

260 *See, e.g.*, R. Zweig, *German Reparations and the Jewish World: A History of the Claims Conference* (Boulder, CO: Westview Press, 1987); A. Baker, *Unfinished Business: Compensation and Restitution for Holocaust Survivors* (New York: American Jewish Committee, 1997); C. Pross, *Paying for the Past: The Struggle over Reparations for Surviving Victims of the Nazi Terror*, trans. B. Cooper (Baltimore: Johns Hopkins University Press, 1998).

261 *See generally* Hayner, *Unspeakable Truths*, above note 33, at 172–4. In 2005, in response to the Torture Commission discussed in Section 2, the Chilean parliament established a comprehensive (albeit less generous) reparation package for torture survivors who were ineligible under the program for families of the disappeared and killed.

262 *See ibid.*, at 174–8. *See also* M. J. Guembe, "Economic Reparations for Grave Human Rights Violations: The Argentine Experience," in P. de Greiff, ed. *The Handbook of Reparations* (Oxford: Oxford University Press, forthcoming 2006).

263 *See* I. Cano and P. Ferreira, "The Reparations Program in Brazil," in de Greiff, *Handbook of Reparations*, above note 262.

264 *See* D. Cammack, "Reparations in Malawi," in *ibid.*

Canada (for Americans and Canadians of Japanese ancestry who were sent to internment camps during the Second World War).[265] There are also, at the national level, instances of standing human rights–related compensation bodies such as criminal injury compensation boards.[266]

Examples of multilateral human rights–related compensation bodies include the *ad hoc* UN Compensation Commission[267] and the Iran–United States Claims Tribunal.[268]

Standing and *ad hoc* multilateral and national human rights vetting and lustration bodies

A vetting procedure is an important, if sometimes controversial, transitional justice mechanism. In its most familiar form, vetting is the practice of screening individuals responsible for serious misconduct from police and prison services and similar public institutions. The vetting process typically involves a comprehensive background check that relies on diverse sources of information and evidence to ensure, among other things, that the applicant has a record free of serious human rights violations. Persons being considered for hiring or firing, as the case may be, are made aware of the evidence against them and given an opportunity to refute it in writing or in person before any decision is made.[269] "Lustration," a term used primarily in Eastern and Central Europe, is somewhat different. It involves wide-scale dismissal and disqualification primarily on the basis of party affiliation, political opinion, or association with a former secret service, rather than on the basis of one's individual record. International and national authorities have often been critical of lustration programs for these and other reasons.[270]

265 *See* E. Yamamoto, "Report on Redress: The Japanese-American Internment," in *ibid.*, regarding the US program. *See* Freeman and van Ert, *International Human Rights Law*, above note 19, at 373–4 regarding the Canadian program.

266 For example, Denmark, the UK, and Canada have created such bodies. Their typical mandate is to provide out-of-court compensation to victims of private crime.

267 *See generally* D. Shelton, *Remedies in International Human Rights Law* (Oxford: Oxford University Press, 1999), at 337–45. *See also* H. van Houtte and others, "The United Nations Compensation Commission," in de Greiff, *Handbook of Reparations*, above note 262. The commission's website is http://www2.unog.ch/uncc/.

268 The tribunal's website is http://www.iusct.org/background-english.html.

269 *See* Report of the UN Secretary-General, "The Rule of Law and Transitional Justice," above note 61, at 17–18. *See also* M. Freeman, *Making Reconciliation Work: The Role of Parliaments*, published by the Inter-Parliamentary Union and the Institute for Democracy and Electoral Assistance (2005), http://www.idea.int, at 16.

270 *See generally* R. David, "Transitional Injustice? Criteria for Conformity of Lustration to the Right to Political Expression" (2004) 56 *Europe-Asia Studies* 789; C. Gonzalez-Enriquez,

The bodies that administer vetting and lustration procedures may take various forms. Vetting and lustration bodies generally have a nonjudicial character. They tend not to wield powers of subpoena or search and seizure, organize public hearings, prepare a final report on their investigations, or make findings of institutional responsibility in the way that truth commissions often do. But their key difference from truth commissions lies in the impact of their decisions on the individual: unlike truth commissions, vetting and lustration bodies can impose sanctions, ranging from job termination to bans on employment, that directly affect individual legal rights.[271]

Historical examples of vetting or lustration bodies include the post–Second World War "defascization" and "denazification" committees established in countries such as Italy[272] and Germany,[273] and the committees used to purge Nazi collaborators in countries such as Belgium and France.[274] Similar strategies were employed in the 1970s in Portugal and Greece during their transitions from military rule to democracy.[275] After the end of the Cold War, "decommunization" laws and "lustration" commissions came in vogue in

---

"De-communization and Political Justice in Central and Eastern Europe," in Brito and others, *The Politics of Memory and Democratization*, above note 225, at 218–47.

271 Lustration bodies have sometimes "named names" in public, much like truth commissions. Under Hungary's lustration law, for example, those deemed "collaborators" could be asked to resign from their posts within thirty days or risk having the evidence of their alleged collaboration publicized by the state media. *See generally* G. Halmai and K. L. Scheppele, "Living Well Is the Best Revenge: The Hungarian Approach to Judging the Past," in McAdams, *Transitional Justice and the Rule of Law in New Democracies*, above note 1, at 171–8.

272 *See, e.g.*, C. Nino, *Radical Evil on Trial* (New Haven, CT: Yale University Press, 1996), at 10–11.

273 Thirteen million Germans were obliged to complete screening forms to determine levels of culpability in terms of Nazi participation. In all, approximately 600,000 of them were subjected to a range of sanctions, including dismissals, demotions, reduction of incomes and pensions, confiscation of assets, obligatory payments to compensation funds, and various bans on public service employment. "Implementation of the Nazi War Crimes Disclosure Act: An Interim Report to Congress," October 1999, available at http://www.archives.gov.

274 In France, approximately 11,000 persons suspected of collaboration with the Vichy regime were subjected to some form of sanction for their wartime activities. Nearly 1,000 politicians, 6,000 teachers, and 500 diplomats were removed from their positions. Judges who enthusiastically implemented the policies of the Nazi occupying power were also purged from their positions. *See* Nino, *Radical Evil on Trial*, above note 272, at 11–13.

275 In Greece, following the demise of the military *junta* in the 1970s, the successor government purged over 100,000 individuals from military and government positions. Specifically, it dismissed, transferred, or disciplined all senior office holders under the *junta*, as well as most senior managers employed by the *junta* in public agencies and corporations. The government also retired or demoted selected senior military officials who had been part of the *junta*. *See* N. Alivizatos and P. Diamandouros, "Politics and the Judiciary in the Greek Transition to Democracy," in McAdams, *Transitional Justice and the Rule of Law in New Democracies*, above note 1, at 39–40.

countries ranging from the Czech Republic to Albania to Poland.[276] Controversy still surrounds these efforts for the reasons noted earlier. Nevertheless, new and equally problematic examples continue to arise.[277]

Somewhat less controversial have been the justice and security sector vetting procedures used in recent years in postconflict states, often under UN supervision. Prominent examples include those established in El Salvador[278] and Bosnia and Herzegovina,[279] and those underway in Afghanistan and Liberia.[280]

Standing and *ad hoc* multilateral human rights complaint procedures

There exists a wide variety of multilateral human rights complaints procedures that involve fact-finding. As noted earlier, most of them are operated by

276 *See, e.g.*, M. Ellis, "Purging the Past: The Current State of Lustration Laws in the Former Communist Bloc" (1996) 59 *Law & Contemp. Probs.* 181; R. Boed, "An Evaluation of the Legality and Efficacy of Lustration as a Tool of Transitional Justice" (1999) 37 *Colum. J. Transnat'l L.* 357.

277 See, *e.g.*, E. Stover and others, "Bremer's 'Gordian Knot': Transitional Justice and the US Occupation of Iraq" (2005) 27 *Human Rights Quarterly* 830, which criticizes the so-called "debaathification" process in Iraq.

278 An Ad Hoc Commission on the Purification of the Armed Forces was established as part of the 1991 peace accords. The commission, which comprised three Salvadoran nationals, recommended the forced retirement of over 100 senior military officers (including the minister of defense) based on their past involvement in human rights abuses. *See* Popkin, "El Salvador: A Negotiated End to Impunity?", above note 278, at 198; Mani, *Beyond Retribution*, above note 1, at 115.

279 In the aftermath of the Bosnian armed conflict (1992–5), two significant vetting programs were established: one targeted at police services, the other at judges and prosecutors. The vetting of police took place between 1999 and 2002 and involved the examination of approximately 24,000 individual officers. The UN Mission in Bosnia and Herzegovina (BiH) ran the program in cooperation with locals. The process involved three steps: completion of a mandatory registration form, prescreening for purposes of granting or denying provisional authorization to continue work, and decisions on final certification or decertification on the basis of criminal background checks and performance assessments. Concerning the vetting of judges and prosecutors, in 2002 three permanent High Judicial and Prosecutorial Councils were established to screen the appointments of approximately 1,000 judges and prosecutors. The councils, which comprised nationals and internationals, had jurisdiction to appoint, transfer, train, remove, and discipline judges and prosecutors. Persons seeking appointment or reappointment to judicial or prosecutorial posts submitted application forms involving detailed disclosures on matters such as their wartime activities. These files, along with information obtained from external sources, were reviewed by the councils prior to making decisions on appointments. The councils continue to operate as the standing appointment and discipline bodies for judges and prosecutors and are now operated exclusively by nationals of BiH. *See* Freeman, *Bosnia and Herzegovina*, above note 223, at 12–14.

280 *See* http://www.ictj.org.

standing bodies focused on a subset of the full panoply of human rights.[281] Unlike truth commissions, these are not victim-centered bodies, but rather neutral dispute resolution bodies. They do not investigate and report on broad patterns of abuse, but only on individual cases, none of which is necessarily connected to periods of abusive rule or armed conflict. The decisions of multilateral human rights complaint procedures are not legally binding, but they carry significant weight. Here the focus is on their role in examining petitions made by individuals and NGOs alleging human rights violations by a particular state.[282] The availability of the complaint procedures in any particular case is generally contingent on the participation by one's state of nationality in the relevant multilateral system (and ratification of any relevant treaty).

In the UN system, the principal complaints procedures are those of the seven treaty bodies previously discussed.[283] Upon receipt of admissible petitions, the state alleged to be in violation of its treaty obligations is given an opportunity to respond, before the treaty body issues its ultimate finding in the case. A non-treaty body, the Commission on Human Rights' Working Group on Arbitrary Detention, formulates "opinions" in individual cases too.[284] The UN Educational, Scientific and Cultural Organization (UNESCO) also operates a human rights complaint procedure, which deals with human rights violations in the realms of education, science, culture, or information.[285] In the ILO system, the principal relevant body is the Committee on Freedom of Association, which acts in conjunction with the Fact-Finding and Conciliation Commission on Freedom of Association to treat complaints about violations of the right to freedom of association.[286]

In the Inter-American system, the Inter-American Commission on Human Rights operates the key complaints procedures.[287] Victims of violations of the American Declaration on the Rights and Duties of Man 1948 (AmDR),[288] the American Convention on Human Rights 1969 (ACHR), or certain other Inter-American human rights treaties may file complaints with the commission.[289]

281 See "Standing and ad hoc multilateral human rights monitors" above.

282 There are also a variety of interstate complaints procedures. These are rarely used, and they are omitted from the present discussion.

283 On the bodies' individual and NGO petition procedures, see Freeman and van Ert, *International Human Rights Law*, above note 19, at 393–7.

284 *Ibid.*, at 406.

285 *Ibid*, at 422–3.

286 *Ibid.*, at 457.

287 The Inter-American Court of Human Rights is discussed in Section 4 below.

288 O.A.S. Res. XXX, adopted by the Ninth International Conference of American States (1948), *reprinted in* Basic Documents Pertaining to Human Rights in the Inter-American System, OEA/Ser.L.V/II.82 doc.6 rev.1 at 17 (1992).

289 *See generally* Freeman and van Ert, *International Human Rights Law*, above note 19, at 426–33.

In the Council of Europe's human rights system, the European Committee of Social Rights operates the principal complaints procedure.[290] In the AU human rights system, the principal relevant body is the African Commission on Human and Peoples' Rights.[291] The African Committee of Experts on the Rights and Welfare of the Child also operates an individual complaints procedure.[292]

State reports on the human rights practices of foreign states

Another important type of human rights investigation is that conducted by some government departments, particularly the US Department of State, which publishes annual "country reports" on the human rights practices of most states around the world. The reports are submitted pursuant to congressional requirements.[293] US embassies collect information throughout the year from a range of sources including government officials, public servants, journalists, human rights organizations, academics, and labor activists. They also rely on investigations conducted by US foreign service officers. The embassies' draft reports are analyzed, corroborated, and edited by the Department of State, which also examines reports provided by NGOs, foreign governments, multilateral organizations, and others.

State Department investigations differ from truth commission investigations in obvious ways. They are state-run investigations, not state-sponsored ones; they are perennial, not temporary, investigations; they do not focus on a wide expanse of time, but only on the prior year; they do not involve the use of any powers of investigation or public hearings; and they focus on foreign states only.[294] That said, the impact of these reports can be significant.

Few states follow the US State Department model. Instead, state reports on the human rights practices of foreign states tend to be more limited and *ad hoc*

---

290 *Ibid.*, at 441–2. The European Court of Human Rights is discussed in Section 4 below.

291 *Ibid.*, at 448–52. The African Court on Human and Peoples' Rights is discussed in Section 4 below.

292 *Ibid.*, at 452.

293 Specifically, they are submitted in compliance with sections 116(d) and 502B(b) of the Foreign Assistance Act of 1961, as amended, and section 504 of the Trade Act of 1974, as amended. The Secretary of State is required to transmit to the Speaker of the House of Representatives and the Senate Committee on Foreign Relations "a full and complete report regarding the status of internationally recognized human rights, within the meaning of subsection (A) in countries that receive assistance under this part, and (B) in all other foreign countries which are members of the United Nations and which are not otherwise the subject of a human rights report under this Act." The Department of State often includes reports on additional countries that do not fall into these categories.

294 There have, however, been some self-evaluative State Department human rights investigations established outside of the "country reports" process. An apposite example is the department's assessment of the implications of the El Salvador truth commission's final report on US foreign policy. *See* US Department of State, *Report of the Panel on El Salvador* (1993).

in character. For example, in the 1990s the governments of Austria, Germany, and Sweden employed teams of lawyers and police officers to investigate and report on allegations of war crimes in the former Yugoslavia.[295] Similarly, in 2005, the UK Parliament's International Development Committee investigated and reported on claims of genocide in the Darfur region of Sudan, finding the death toll to have been "grossly underestimated" by the United Nations.[296]

Standing national human rights–related administrative tribunals

Administrative tribunals are usually classified as quasi-judicial bodies. Regardless of their focus (whether discrimination, labor rights, refugee rights, housing rights, and so on), they are more analogous to courts than to truth commissions – and yet unlike both. Differences between truth commissions and administrative tribunals are discussed in Chapter 2. The point of their mention here is to underscore that, like the other bodies examined in this section, some administrative tribunals conduct forms of human rights investigation as well.

SECTION 4: DISTINGUISHING TRUTH COMMISSIONS FROM COURTS

After all that has been said about truth commissions, it is plain that truth commissions are not courts. Nevertheless, there are important similarities between them, as well as overlap in their respective missions. This section examines the main differences and similarities between the two, and explores to what degree they are, or can be, complementary.

Judicial forums

In the last fifteen years there has been a notable expansion in the variety and use of national and international courts to try human rights and related violations. Much of this expansion was spawned by the UN Security Council's unprecedented decision to establish the *ad hoc* International Criminal Tribunal for the former Yugoslavia (ICTY) in 1993.[297] This action presaged the subsequent creation – once again by the Security Council – of the *ad hoc* International Criminal Tribunal for Rwanda (ICTR).[298] These precedents, in turn, paved the way for the establishment of the permanent

---

295 *See* Bassiouni, "The United Nations Commission of Experts on the Former Yugoslavia," above note 240, at 450.

296 *See* "MPs Rap UN over Darfur Death Toll," *BBC News World Edition* (http://news.bbc.co.uk), 31 March 2005.

297 *See generally* Freeman and van Ert, *International Human Rights Law*, above note 19, at 468–74.

298 *See ibid.*, at 474–7.

International Criminal Court (ICC).[299] Lessons learned from the experiences of the two *ad hoc* international criminal tribunals, and their high cost to UN member states, resulted in turn in the creation of hybrid national-international criminal tribunals. Such tribunals have been established in Kosovo ("Regulation 64" panels),[300] Timor-Leste ("Serious Crime Panels"),[301] Sierra Leone (the "Special Court"),[302] Bosnia and Herzegovina ("War Crimes Chamber"),[303] and Cambodia ("Extraordinary Chambers").[304]

The spirit of international justice launched by the ICTY also coincided with a notable invigoration of national courts, in trying both domestic and extraterritorial human rights–related crimes. For example, in countries like Rwanda, thousands have been tried before domestic courts for genocide,[305] and now many thousands more are being tried by a village-level accountability mechanism called *gacaca*, which is partly based on a traditional Rwandan dispute resolution model.[306] Recently in many countries in Europe and Latin America (and elsewhere), domestic criminal courts have also entertained an unprecedented number of human rights–related actions on the basis of universal jurisdiction or similar jurisdictional principles.[307]

While criminal trials are the natural and appropriate response for dealing with perpetrators of gross violations of human rights, non-criminal proceedings can also be important. The International Court of Justice, a court that resolves disputes between states, has become increasingly engaged in human rights–related claims.[308] At the regional level, the Inter-American and European Courts of Human Rights have long played an effective role in redeeming human rights claims in their respective regions,[309] and it is envisaged that the

---

299 *See ibid.*, at 477–83.

300 *See ibid.*, at 484–5.

301 *See ibid.*, at 485–7.

302 *See ibid.*, at 487–8.

303 *See* Freeman, *Bosnia and Herzegovina*, above note 223, at 4–5. On the heels of a 2004 UN assessment mission, a hybrid tribunal – the "Special Chamber" – has been recommended for Burundi as well. *See* UN SC res. 1606 (2005).

304 *See* Freeman and van Ert, *International Human Rights Law*, above note 19, at 484.

305 *See* N. Kritz, "Where We Are and How We Got Here: An Overview of the Developments in the Search for Justice and Reconciliation," in Henkin, *The Legacy of Abuse*, above note 1, at 31.

306 *See* Freeman and van Ert, *International Human Rights Law*, above note 19, at 477. *See also* "Transitional Justice in the News" (http://www.ictj.org), 31 January 2005: "Rwanda's traditional Gacaca courts, set up to try crimes committed during the 1994 genocide, have begun systematic investigations nationwide. In the current investigative phase, communities hold public meetings where residents identify victims and suspects. In the trial phase, victims and suspects will face each other and talk before a panel of locally elected judges, who will issue verdicts."

307 *See* Freeman and van Ert, *International Human Rights Law*, above note 19, at 497–500.

308 *See ibid.*, at 417–19.

309 *See ibid.*, at 434–7 and 438–41, respectively.

emergent African Court on Human and Peoples' Rights may eventually do the same.[310] At the domestic level too, civil lawsuits are potentially important means for vindicating human rights claims. In at least one country – the United States – there is also the equivalent of universal jurisdiction in tort for certain human rights violations such as torture and enforced disappearance.[311]

There are still other forums that can perform functions similar to courts in the resolution of human rights–related claims. For example, a variety of formal proceedings are grouped under the heading of "alternative dispute resolution" (ADR). These include facilitated negotiation, conciliation, mediation, nonbinding arbitration, and binding arbitration.[312] There are also numerous *sui generis* proceedings described under the broad rubric of "restorative justice," including victim-offender mediation and sentencing circles.[313]

Some significant differences between courts and truth commissions

All courts differ from all truth commissions in a few fundamental ways. First, in a truth commission process there are no plaintiffs, no prosecution, no defense, and no trial. There is simply the investigation and reporting of facts.[314]

Second, a truth commission's findings produce very different consequences from those of a court. Courts have the authority to impose binding sanctions on individuals, often involving a loss of property or liberty. Truth commissions, by contrast, cannot impose civil or criminal penalties.[315] Even when a truth commission places someone's name on a list of abusers, the designation generally has no intrinsic legal effect. That is not to say that the social and political effect of a truth commission's findings may not be great; but that is a question of context, not law.

Another major difference between courts and truth commissions is that truth commissions have functions that are, by and large, alien to courts. A truth

---

310 *See ibid.*, at 447–8.

311 *See ibid.*, at 500–6.

312 *See generally* J. M. Nolan-Haley, *Alternative Dispute Resolution in a Nutshell*, 2d. ed. (St. Paul, MN: West Publishing Co., 2001). In some jurisdictions (*e.g.*, Canada), prior resort to ADR is often required as part of the pretrial process.

313 *See, e.g.*, B. Galaway and J. Hudson, eds., *Restorative Justice* (Monsey, NY: Criminal Justice Press, 1996).

314 A commission's public hearings may, nevertheless, take on the appearance of a trial. *See* Chapter 6.

315 The mandates of many truth commissions often explicitly state that they have no judicial authority. *See, e.g.*, Supreme Decree no. 0065-2001-PCM (Peru), as amended, art. 3: "[T]he Commission has no jurisdictional powers, therefore it does not substitute the functions of the Judicial Power and the Public Ministry" (Unofficial translation from Spanish by Lisa Magarrell.) *See also* Mexico Peace Agreements (1991), Provisions Creating the El Salvador Commission on Truth, S. 5: "The Commission shall not function in the manner of a judicial body." *See also* Presidential Executive Order Establishing the Truth and Justice Commission, 1995 (Haiti), art. 9.

commission may, for example, be expected to analyze the social causes of a conflict, contribute to national reconciliation, or dignify victims through victim-centered public hearings. While criminal courts might occasionally aspire to fulfill some of these functions, they are necessarily ancillary to a court's main purpose: to make determinations of the responsibility of the individual who is accused. A criminal court is required to answer one question: whether there is proof beyond a reasonable doubt (or equivalent evidentiary standard) that the accused committed the crimes of which he or she is charged.[316] This is true even for criminal trials involving "system crimes," such as crimes against humanity, which generally require proof of the commission of a proscribed act (*e.g.,* killing) and the existence of a broader context (*i.e.,* "committed as part of a widespread or systematic attack directed against any civilian population, with knowledge of the attack").[317] The individual, not the system, is actually on trial, even if the trial improves public understanding of the broader context in which the violation occurred.

The evidence upon which a truth commission rests its conclusions also tends to be qualitatively different from that used in courts. The attempt to heal a violence-ridden society, and to facilitate social consensus, involves concerns that are quite distinct from the localized, more insular, and more precedent-based reasoning of courts. A truth commission's heightened concern with victims' experiences contradicts the usual imperative of courts to neutrally probe and question the testimony of witnesses. In a victim-centered mode, the victim's storytelling itself may be deemed important – regardless of its precision or admissibility as evidence in court – and his or her testimony accorded a presumptive veracity.[318]

Some significant similarities between courts and truth commissions

The similarities between truth commissions and courts are often under-appreciated. Both bodies have the potential to contribute to the objectives

---

316 R. May and M. Wierda, *International Criminal Evidence* (Ardsley, NY: Transnational Publishers, 2003), at 14–15.

317 Rome Statute of the International Criminal Court 1998, 2187 UNTS 3, art. 7(2). *See also* Rome Statute art. 8(1), which provides that the proscribed acts (*e.g.,* torture) must have been committed "as part of a plan or policy or as part of a large-scale commission of such crimes" in order to constitute a war crime.

318 For example, at the South African TRC's victim hearings, commissioners rose in greeting as victims entered to testify, sometimes embracing them. Victims were "permitted to ramble, cry, and scream. Although commissioners did ask occasional clarifying questions, sometimes attempting to elicit names of perpetrators and corroborating witnesses, the witnesses were not subject to cross-examination." Sometimes traditional music was also played. T. G. Phelps, *Shattered Voices: Language, Violence, and the Work of Truth Commissions* (Philadelphia: University of Pennsylvania Press, 2004), at 109–10.

of truth, justice, reparation, reform, public debate, and the validation of victim experiences.[319]

Truth

Although it is frequently observed that truth commissions are powerful vehicles for broad truth telling, trials can perform a similar function. Sometimes one of a trial's main purposes is, indeed, to teach a country about its past and foster public introspection. The trials of the Nuremberg and Tokyo tribunals, though controversial from the standpoint of due process, are often characterized in this fashion.[320] So too are the trials of the former Nazi official Adolf Eichmann, who was tried in Israel in the 1960s,[321] and the former Nazi collaborator Maurice Papon, who was tried in France in the 1990s.[322]

A different phenomenon is that of Argentina's "truth trials," whose very purpose is to make known the truth and have it judicially validated. These trials are explicitly limited to investigation and documentation of crimes, without any possibility of prosecution or punishment.[323] Trials conducted in Chile under

319 Truth commissions and courts may both contribute to other objectives as well, such as deterrence, reconciliation, and the consolidation of peace and democracy. These are, however, less easily measured. A thorough analysis of them is outside the scope of this book.

320 *See, e.g.*, Robert Jackson, Opening Speech, *The Trial of German Major War Criminal by the IMT Sitting at Nuremberg* (HMSO, 1946), at 4: "Never before has an effort been made to bring within the scope of a single litigation, the developments, covering a whole continent, and involving a score of nations, countless individuals, and innumerable events." *See also* May and Wierda, *International Criminal Evidence*, above note 316, at 13, where it is noted that "the judgment of the [Tokyo Tribunal] comprised over 1,200 pages in total: 1,050 pages of this were devoted to a detailed analysis of Japanese history from 1928 to 1945, while only seven pages were spent on the judgment against the accused and 82 pages to individual verdicts."

321 *See generally* H. Arendt, *Eichmann in Jerusalem: A Report on the Banality of Evil* (New York: Penguin Books, 1963).

322 *See, e.g.*, D. Singer, "France on Trial," *The Nation*, 24 February 1999; R. Faurisson, "The Papon Trial" (May/June 1998) 17 *Journal for Historical Review* 3, at 14. "Show trials" of this sort are not necessarily lamentable. Mark Osiel suggests that trials in contexts of transition *should* spark public discussion. Provided they can guarantee due process, he argues that "trials should be unabashedly designed as monumental spectacles." He claims that this will also facilitate the building of a collective memory and possibly a national identity. M. Osiel, *Mass Atrocity, Collective Memory, and the Law* (New Brunswick, NJ: Transaction, 1997), at 3.

323 Orentlicher, "Promotion and Protection of Human Rights: Impunity," above note 316, at para. 16: "A decision by the Argentine Supreme Court rendered on 13 August 1998, which ruled that courts lacked jurisdiction to hold the proceedings as a result of the amnesty laws, led to submission of a case before the Inter-American Commission. In a friendly settlement resolving this case, the Government of Argentina accepted and undertook to guarantee 'the right to the truth, which involves the exhaustion of all means to obtain information on

the so-called Aylwin doctrine had a similarly strong truth-seeking dimension. That doctrine enabled Chilean courts to refuse to apply a sweeping national amnesty law until the facts of the case (including the identity of the presumed authors of the crime) were ascertained.[324] The ICTY's Rule 61 hearings in the 1990s in which victims – and only victims – publicly testified to their abuse constituted yet another model of truth telling in court. Rule 61 hearings had a deliberate focus on the truth and were in some respects analogous to truth commission public hearings.[325]

When one looks beyond the moment of trial to the other stages of a judicial proceeding, additional overlap in the area of truth seeking becomes apparent. For example, in the antecedent stages of a common law criminal trial, police and prosecutors – not to mention grand juries[326] or special prosecutors[327] – may perform important investigative functions analogous to those of truth

---

the whereabouts of the disappeared persons.' As a result, Argentine courts were allowed to carry on truth trials and an *ad hoc* Prosecutor's Commission on truth proceedings was established to investigate cases. In July 2001, approximately 3,570 human rights cases were being investigated." The trials are premised on the right of victims' families and society as a whole to know the truth, and the right of families to bury and mourn their dead (*derecho a duelo*).

324 Although former Chilean president Patricio Aylwin is credited with the articulation of this theory, it hardly required formal expression. Unless an amnesty explicitly ousts the jurisdiction of courts to investigate, a court has no choice but to do so, in order to determine whether the amnesty applies in a particular case. Variations of the Aylwin doctrine have been applied by courts in Guatemala, Peru, Argentina, and Ghana. *See, e.g.,* N. Roht-Arriaza and L. Gibson, "The Developing Jurisprudence on Amnesty" (1998) 20.4 *Human Rights Quarterly* 843.

325 Rule 61 of the ICTY's Rules of Procedure allows ICTY prosecutors to present an indictment, together with all its evidence, before a Trial Chamber in open court and in the absence of the accused. If the Trial Chamber is satisfied of the existence of reasonable grounds of the accused's guilt, it issues an international arrest warrant. If the accused's state of nationality fails or refuses to cooperate, the tribunal can report this to the Security Council for further action. If the accused is later arrested, the trial starts afresh before a new Trial Chamber, and the Rule 61 findings plays no part in deciding guilt or innocence. There were five Rule 61 hearings held in the early years of the tribunal, including those of wartime Bosnian Serb leader, Radovan Karadzic, and of his general, Ratko Mladic. No Rule 61 hearings have been held since 1996 due to the increase of the ICTY's caseload. *See* M. Freeman and M. Wierda, "The ICTY and the Pursuit of Justice in the Balkans," in G. Stamkoski, ed., *With No Peace to Keep*, 2d ed. (London: Volatile Media, 2002), at 259.

326 Grand juries are, in essence, juries of inquiry. Their responsibility is to receive accusations in criminal matters, hear the state's evidence, and then determine whether an indictment should be issued against the concerned individual. *See generally* S. S. Beale, ed., *Grand Jury Law and Practice*, 2d ed. (Minneapolis: West Group, 1997).

327 Special prosecutors have been appointed in many different countries to respond to allegations of human rights–related crimes, including in the United States, Colombia, Ethiopia, and Mexico, to name a few. *See, e.g.,* Hayner, *Unspeakable Truths*, above note 33, at 20, regarding the Special Prosecutor's Office in Ethiopia, which attempted (unsuccessfully) to

commissions. Plea bargaining arrangements, which involve the exchange of criminal confession and cooperation for leniency, also have a plain truth-seeking dimension.[328] The truth component is amplified when a plea bargain requires a public sentencing hearing.[329]

In common law civil proceedings, the case is not dissimilar: the common law's pretrial discovery process, for example, is devoted exclusively to truth seeking.[330] As for the civil law tradition, investigative magistrates (*juges d'instruction*) exercise truth-seeking functions akin to those of truth commissions.[331] This holds equally for pretrial judges in international criminal trials.[332] Judicial remedies such as habeas corpus (the right to a determination

---

merge truth telling and prosecution in a single process. *See also* P. Seils, *A Promise Unfulfilled? The Special Prosecutor's Office in Mexico* (International Center for Transitional Justice, 2004).

328   By circumventing the need for a trial, plea bargains also help save significant time and expense. In their absence, the costs associated with rendering justice – costs of courtrooms, staff, security, defense counsel for the indigent, jails, and so on – are generally much higher. In civil law systems, which usually lack a plea bargaining tradition, the closest equivalent is the "summary trial" and/or "summary penal order." Summary trials are different from plea bargains; they do not avoid trial, but merely curtail it. Also, summary trials may proceed exclusively in writing (*e.g.*, "trials by dossier" in Italy). Neither summary trials nor summary penal orders are available for serious violent crimes, but only for minor offenses. On summary trials, *see* R. Schlesinger and others, *Comparative Law* (New York: Foundation Press, 1998), at 529–30. On summary penal orders, *see ibid.*, at 528. *See also* S. C. Thaman, *Comparative Criminal Procedure* (Durham, NC: Carolina Academic Press, 2002), at 152–3 and 159–61.

329   For example, Biljana Plavsic, the former president of Republika Srpska (BiH), pleaded guilty to the charge of persecution before the ICTY. In exchange, the ICTY prosecutor dismissed other charges against her "with prejudice." The deal was made on the understanding that Plavsic would publicly acknowledge personal responsibility at her sentencing hearing, which she ultimately did. *See* Freeman, *Bosnia and Herzegovina*, above note 223, at 3. Note, however, that in the Plavsic case – as elsewhere – the plea bargain's truth is only partial. The truth of any facts not encompassed in the plea bargain (*e.g.*, the truth of any of the dismissed charges against Plavsic) receives no public airing.

330   Discovery is a procedure by which a civil litigant can obtain information from the opposing side to assist in trial preparation. Tools of discovery include depositions, written interrogatories, and the production of documents.

331   The civil law system's investigative magistrate is an official who conducts an impartial and independent study of incriminating and exculpatory evidence in criminal cases. (In some civil law jurisdictions, public prosecutors carry out this work rather than investigative magistrates.) The investigation, which may last years, typically encompasses sworn statements from, and rigorous *in camera* probing of, witnesses. The purpose of the investigation is to decide whether to commit the suspect for trial. If the magistrate ultimately decides a trial is warranted, a full report (*dossier*) is delivered to the trial chamber. *See, e.g.*, M. Glendon and others, *Comparative Legal Traditions*, 2d ed. (St. Paul, MN: West, 1999) at 99–100; May and Wierda, *International Criminal Evidence*, above note 316, at 250; Thaman, *Comparative Criminal Procedure*, above note 328, at 38.

332   *See* May and Wierda, *International Criminal Evidence*, above note 316, at 43–4.

of the validity of a person's detention) also have an underlying truth-seeking character.

Still, with few exceptions,[333] courts and other actors in the formal justice system rarely engage in the same breadth of investigation as a truth commission.[334] Broad investigation and public truth telling of the sort carried out by a truth commission can contribute to a "master narrative of oppression"[335] and help "reduce the number of lies that can be circulated unchallenged in public discourse."[336] Many truth commissions have also been instrumental in locating the whereabouts of hundreds or even thousands of missing persons who may have been forcibly disappeared – an outcome that lies wholly outside the customary scope of a court's remit.

One should not, however, overstate the truth-telling virtues of a truth commission. Because of time and resource limitations, truth commissions rarely examine more than a few hundred cases in any individual depth, and none in the same individual depth as a full-length criminal trial would.[337] Time and resource constraints also preclude most truth commissions from allowing more than a small percentage of victims willing to testify in public the opportunity to do so.[338] Finally, truth commissions are likely no better than courts at preventing a person from lying or misrepresenting facts.

Justice

If it is fair to say that courts fail to receive their full due in the area of truth, it is also fair to say that truth commissions infrequently receive their full due in the area of justice. For example, the work of truth commissions in assembling,

---

333 The ICTY's jurisprudence, for example, establishes a quite comprehensive historical account of the main conflicts in the former Yugoslavia.

334 One scholar writes, "Trials are generally ill-suited to deal with the task of providing a complete history of past violations. This is specifically a result of their adversary nature where the duty of the prosecutor is to focus on limited facts relevant to the guilt of the individual before the court, and the duty of the defense is to challenge the admissibility of the essential information." Bassiouni, "Accountability for Violations of International Humanitarian Law and Other Serious Violations of Human Rights," above note 246, at 32.

335 Phelps, *Shattered Voices*, above note 318, at 63.

336 M. Ignatieff, "Articles of Faith" (1996) 5 *Index on Censorship*, at 113. "In Argentina, [the truth commission's] work has made it impossible to claim, for example, that the military did not throw half-dead victims in the sea from helicopters. In Chile, it is no longer permissible to assert in public that the Pinochet regime did not dispatch thousands of entirely innocent people": *ibid*.

337 In point of fact, the final reports of all but a few truth commissions contain a recommendation for the establishment of a follow-up body to continue with investigations. An equivalent gesture by a court is hard to imagine. Courts must establish "final" truths in cases before them.

338 *See* Chapter 6.

organizing, and preserving evidence for use in ongoing or future prosecutions is often underappreciated.[339] Many times, the incriminating information contained in final reports or archives of truth commissions has found its way into courts.[340] Truth commissions also tend to make recommendations in their final reports about the need for criminal trials against presumed perpetrators.

At least one truth commission (*i.e.*, Argentina) was expressly conceived as a prelude to prosecution.[341] Other commissions (*e.g.*, Peru) went as far as to prepare and forward "ready" cases to the Attorney-General's office for prosecution.[342] And in perhaps the most innovative model to date, a truth commission in Timor-Leste operated in tandem with a hybrid criminal court. The court's Office of the General Prosecutor (OGP) had exclusive jurisdiction over "serious criminal offences," while the truth commission had jurisdiction over all other cases (*i.e.*, criminal and noncriminal "harmful acts"). The commission received confessions and then sent them to the OGP, which had fourteen days to make a decision on whether the application disclosed serious criminal offenses and whether the applicant would be prosecuted for those offenses.[343]

339   The ability of truth commissions to share nonconfidential exculpatory information is even more rarely acknowledged. By sharing such information with judicial and prosecutorial authorities, truth commissions can advance the cause of justice, precisely by helping to prevent its miscarriage.

340   For example, Nobel laureate Rigoberta Menchú Tum filed a case in Spain against former Guatemalan military leader José Efraín Ríos Montt for atrocities committed in Guatemala under his rule. She adduced the Guatemalan truth commission's final report as evidence in the case. P. Seils, "The Limits of Truth Commissions in the Search for Justice: An Analysis of the Truth Commissions of El Salvador and Guatemala and Their Effect in Achieving Post-Conflict Justice," in Bassiouni, *Post-Conflict Justice*, above note 1, at 791. Likewise, the final report of Chad's truth commission has been used in indictments brought against the former Chadian tyrant Hisseine Habré.

341   Teitel, *Transitional Justice*, above note 1, at 88–9. At times, Commonwealth commissions of inquiry have also functioned as calculated preludes to prosecution, almost serving as a kind of "state-sponsored 'pre-trial' discovery" process. R. A. Macdonald, "Interrogating Inquiries," in Manson and Mullan, *Commissions of Inquiry*, above note 78, at 478.

342   The Peruvian TRC was the first to establish a unit "charged with the task of organizing legal cases against specific individual perpetrators" so that cases could be presented for prosecution. The commission made the decision to establish the unit only after the first public hearings, in which many victims demanded criminal justice. E. G. Cueva, "The Contribution of the Peruvian Truth and Reconciliation Commission to Prosecutions," in Schabas and Darcy, *Truth Commissions and Courts*, above note 127, 55 at 62.

343   If the option of prosecution was declined by the OGP, the commission could then facilitate what was referred to as a "Community Reconciliation Process" (CRP) for the applicant, which involved a public hearing and then the arrangement of a "Community Reconciliation Agreement" (CRA) between the applicant and a "Community of Reception." The CRP process was designed to facilitate the reception of the perpetrator back into an affected community. The CRA, which could include an obligation to do community service or pay reparations, was registered with the relevant district court. Once the perpetrator had

Another way in which truth commissions are able to contribute to justice is by critically examining the role of the judiciary in failing to stem past abuse. This is a function that judges do not typically undertake. A majority of truth commissions, including those of Argentina, Chile, El Salvador, South Africa, and Sierra Leone, have examined the role of judges in tolerating or sanctioning past abuse.[344] Criticism of the courts was especially fierce in El Salvador, where the truth commission asserted the impossibility of a fair trial before domestic courts and called for the voluntary resignation of the members of the Supreme Court to permit the appointment of new judges who would uphold judicial independence and the rule of law. The president of the Supreme Court responded that "only God" could remove him prior to the end of his tenure. Under a revised constitutional formula, neither the president nor his colleagues was appointed to serve on a new Supreme Court created in the following year.[345]

Truth commissions are also able to make special contributions to justice because of their investigative character. For example, the more flexible evidentiary standards used by truth commissions (especially in comparison to common law criminal courts) can facilitate the objective of justice. While in court a guilty defendant might escape accountability by relying on the prohibition of retroactive criminalization (and on the corollary argument that the defendant's actions were legal at the time they were committed), that principle has no application before an investigative body such as a truth commission. Also, not being bound by exclusionary rules of evidence, truth commissions are able to accept any available evidence – an important freedom when one considers the widespread concealment of crime that is pervasive in times of war or repression (and, in the case of enforced disappearance, an intrinsic element of the crime itself).

At the same time, the value of a truth commission cannot replace the value of a trial.[346] There is also no guarantee that a commission's work will

---

fulfilled his obligations under the CRA, he became entitled to immunity from criminal and civil proceedings arising from the harmful acts to which he confessed. While the CRP system generally worked well (approximately 1,380 minor offenders completed the process), there were many difficulties with the prosecution of serious crimes. Also, "Many individuals who were denied participation in a CRP on the basis that the OGP intended to prosecute were never indicted." *See* M. Hirst and H. Varney, *Justice Abandoned? An Assessment of the Serious Crimes Process in East Timor* (International Center for Transitional Justice, 2005), http://www.ictj.org.

344 The commissions' analyses of the role of judges have helped to promote a "rich understanding of the requirements of the rule of law," one that denies the notion that law and politics are separable. *See* de Greiff, "Truth-Telling and the Rule of Law," above note 29.

345 Popkin, "El Salvador: A Negotiated End to Impunity," above note 143, at 210–11, 214–15.

346 *See, e.g.,* the Inter-American Commission on Human Rights' findings in *Ellacuría,* above note 12, at 229. The commission observed that "despite the important contribution that the [El Salvador] Truth Commission made in establishing the facts surrounding the most

stimulate prosecutions.[347] At the same time, it is important to acknowledge that in some extreme cases – for example, where an amnesty law effectively ousts the jurisdiction of local courts (*e.g.*, Ghana), or where the outgoing regime continues to wield significant military power (*e.g.*, Guatemala), or where domestic courts are highly corrupt or dysfunctional (*e.g.*, Chad) – a truth commission may represent the closest approximation to justice at a particular moment in time.[348] Indeed, in contexts of political or postconflict transition, often the choice – in the short term, at least – is "not between truth commissions and trials, but between truth commissions and nothing."[349]

Reparation

Both trials and truth commissions can make significant contributions to the cause of victim reparation.

In most civil law systems, a victim can become a formal party to a criminal trial (known in French as a *partie civile*) and obtain compensation upon the trial's conclusion.[350] In both common and civil law systems, compensation is also available quite directly through civil trials. In international criminal law,

---

serious violations, and in promoting national reconciliation, the role that it played, although highly relevant, cannot be considered as a suitable substitute for proper judicial procedures as a method for arriving at the truth."

347 *See, e.g.*, Seils, "The Limits of Truth Commissions in the Search for Justice," above note 340, where the author examines the limited impact of the Salvadoran and Guatemalan truth commissions on subsequent justice efforts.

348 The former South African TRC chair Bishop Desmond Tutu famously described truth commissions as a "third way" between national amnesia and criminal justice. *See generally* D. Tutu, *No Future Without Forgiveness* (New York: Doubleday, 1999).

349 J. D. Tepperman, "Truth and Consequences," at 145. Tepperman adds, "Critics of commissions too often make the best the enemy of the good and confuse the way they think the world ought be with the way it actually is. Of course the commissions reflect compromises among the various goals of new democracies, and of course the results are imperfect. But that is because the goals themselves . . . are often fundamentally irreconcilable. The commissions' imperfections stem from the imperfect situations out of which they arise." *Ibid. See also* P. Burgess, "Justice and Reconciliation in East Timor," in Schabas and Darcy, *Truth Commissions and Courts*, above note 127, at 134: "East Timor, like other fragile new democracies, does not have the luxury of working only with lofty theoretic ideals of justice and reconciliation . . . The available choices are to do nothing, holding smugly to a clean book of rules, or to face the real challenges and find new ways to make some progress, maintaining momentum, balance and morale whilst inevitably moving sideways and sometimes even backwards, with eyes firmly focused on the road ahead."

350 In France, Spain, and Argentina, the injured person may become a party acting alongside the prosecutor. If the prosecution is successful, the court may order the payment of civil damages to the injured party at the conclusion of the criminal trial; there is no need for a separate civil suit. Schlesinger and others, *Comparative Law*, above note 328, at 532–9; M. Glendon and others, *Comparative Legal Traditions*, above note 331, at 101.

the ICC has established a Victims Trust Fund, which can be used to deliver compensation payments to victims of crimes falling under the court's jurisdiction following a finding of guilt.[351]

Truth commissions almost invariably recommend comprehensive reparation packages for identified victims that, in some cases, have been adopted almost in their entirety. Yet even when not implemented, truth commission recommendations on reparation frequently become both a benchmark and a focal point for victim advocates. In Morocco, as previously noted, the truth commission itself had the power to award compensation.

Some truth commissions' work has also compelled national heads of state to issue broad public apologies (*e.g.*, Peru), or in some instances even individualized apologies to victims (*e.g.*, Chile). Some truth commission reports have helped prod acknowledgments of responsibility from foreign leaders too.[352] Depending on the perceived sincerity of such apologies, these may constitute a form of moral reparation for victims. Truth commissions invariably make important recommendations about victim monuments and memorials as well.

Reform

On the issue of reform, here again, both trials and truth commissions can make valuable contributions.

Plans to hold criminal or civil trials can prompt immediate reforms to the personnel within a justice system (*e.g.*, in prosecutorial services and in the judiciary), and to the laws they apply. The subsequent holding of trials can then serve to test the enacted reforms and, thereafter, generate the public will to make further needed adjustments to personnel or legislation.

As for truth commissions, time and again their final reports convincingly demonstrate that past abuse was institutionalized and systematic, as opposed to random and isolated. Their close study of patterns of past violence, and their relative independence from the institutions under review, also enables them to envisage rational and compelling recommendations for reform. Indeed, many truth commission reports have spurred important legal and institutional reforms (*e.g.*, Uganda).[353] A commission's recommendations on reform can

---

351 *See generally* http://www.icc-cpi.int/vtf.html.

352 Shortly after Guatemala's truth commission issued its final report, former US president Clinton acknowledged that previous American support for repressive local military forces and intelligence units was "wrong." "Clinton: Backing Dictators Was Wrong," BBC News (http://www.bbc.co.uk), 11 March 1999.

353 The Ugandan Human Rights Commission, for example, "exists as a direct result of the work of [Uganda's truth commission]." J. R. Quinn, "Dealing with a Legacy of Mass Atrocity: Truth Commissions in Uganda and Chile" (2001) 19.4 *Netherlands Quarterly of Human Rights* 383, at 401.

also serve as "pressure points" around which civil society or the international community can mobilize.[354]

Public debate

Courts and truth commissions can each add in significant ways to public discourse about a legacy of mass abuse.[355] To make such a contribution, however, it is generally important for the proceeding in question to have a high profile in the media. Trials or truth commissions that take place largely outside the public spotlight are unlikely to foment the kind of public debate that can lead either to greater social consensus or to empathy for victims, both of which may be preconditions for creating a lasting culture of human rights. In this regard, truth commission public hearings appear to be especially effective at engaging the public.[356] As for trials, the recent experiences of international and mixed criminal tribunals suggest that formal information and outreach programs can help increase the level of public interest and debate.[357] Even without such programs, however, major public trials tend to be widely reported in the media, albeit with varying levels of accuracy and sensitivity.

As to the different styles that public testimony can take, some find the quality of narration of a criminal trial uniquely compelling.[358] Others, by contrast, may find it quite dull and technical, especially in comparison to the emotional

---

354 Hayner, *Unspeakable Truths* above note 33, at 30. Commissions may recommend a variety of reforms, including "strengthened civilian oversight of intelligence agencies and the military; new appointment, tenure and disciplinary rules for the judiciary; the establishment of an independent and well-financed prosecutor's office; redesign of the electoral and political system; land reform; and new human rights training programmes for the police and armed forces." Freeman and Hayner, "Truth-Telling," above note 38, at 126.

355 The South African TRC saw public debate as an element of truth in itself, or more specifically, of what it called "social truth." It distinguished this from three other kinds of truth: factual (*i.e.*, forensic) truth, personal (*i.e.*, narrative) truth, and healing (*i.e.*, restorative) truth. Boraine, *A Country Unmasked*, above note 26, at 288–91.

356 *See* Chapter 6.

357 "Effective outreach programmes are essential to ensure that (a) citizens are aware of and understand important developments in respect of prosecutions for serious violations of human rights; (b) citizens understand why the prosecutor has brought charges for some offences but not others; (c) judicial officials are aware of how human rights prosecutions are perceived by citizens; and (d) public perceptions of prosecutions are not distorted either as a result of lack of information or because judicial officials have failed to counter revisionist interpretations of prosecutions. Initiatives undertaken by [the Sierra Leone Special Court] exemplify such efforts. The Registrar has established an Outreach Unit that seeks to ensure timely transmission of information to and from every district of the country despite a poor communications infrastructure." Orentlicher, "Promotion and Protection of Human Rights: Impunity," above note 24, at para. 40.

358 *See, e.g.*, Nino, *Radical Evil*, above note 272, at 146.

storytelling character of a modern truth commission's public hearing. According to one observer, the truth commission format may be more likely to foster a "process of national introspection that requires that everyone . . . examine [his or her] role in the conflicts of the past."[359] However, one must concede that truth commissions are generally less able, or less apt, to place the public spotlight on perpetrators.[360] In addition, the mere fact of seeing perpetrators held in the dock or hearing them testify – assuming they choose not to exercise the right to silence – can stimulate important public debates.

Validation of victim experiences

Both courts and truth commissions have valuable contributions to make in validating victim experiences.

In courtrooms, especially in the common law system, victims and witnesses can often face fierce probing or cross-examination. They may be regularly interrupted in the middle of answers by counsel seeking to identify inconsistencies in their testimony. Judges and juries, too, are generally obligated to treat testimony with skepticism. Yet there are other forms of victim participation in trial proceedings that can be more affirming, such as the ability in the civil law system to act as *partie civile*,[361] or the ability in common law systems to give "victim impact statements" at sentencing.[362] Also, for some victims, nothing may produce a greater sense of validation than to see their victimizers tried, sentenced, and imprisoned.

As purely investigative bodies, truth commissions can never achieve such a form of validation for victims. Yet they can contribute to victim dignity in other ways. In its statement-taking work, and at its public hearings, a truth commission usually accepts victim testimony with minimal probing. Indeed, at a commission's public hearings, victims can usually expect to speak without interruption.[363] Commissioners may even rise when the victim enters and

---

359 P. van Zyl, "Dilemmas of Transitional Justice: The Case of South Africa's Truth and Reconciliation Commission" (1999) 52 *Journal of International Affairs* 647, at 667. A common criticism of trials is that they allow a public that quietly tolerated or supported past human rights violations to evade introspection. Solely the persons on trial are seen to be responsible for the grave abuses of the past.

360 The obvious exceptions are the commissions of South Africa and Timor-Leste. The Sierra Leonean and Ghanaian truth commissions also managed to arrange an unusually high number of public testimonies by perpetrators.

361 The ICC has adopted a variation on the *partie civile* model. Victims are entitled to make submissions directly to the court or, alternatively, through counsel.

362 *See, e.g.*, S. Bandes, "Empathy, Narrative, and Victim Impact Statements" (1996) 63 *U. Chi. L. Rev.* 361.

363 For example, it was the policy of Morocco's truth commission to ask no questions of victims who testified at its public hearings. Its singular role was to listen.

leaves the hearing room – an exact reversal of what happens in a court of law.[364] Other commission acts of solidarity with victims may include attending reburials, praying alongside families, and similar gestures of support and empathy.

In conclusion, because courts and truth commissions have so many common functions, it is sometimes hard to understand the cause of many debates about their alleged incompatibility. Indeed, around the world the everyday establishment of commissions of inquiry – whether Commonwealth, presidential, parliamentary, or international – rarely generates controversy on the basis of alleged incompatibility with the cause of justice. By and large, courts and truth commissions ought to be seen as compatible and even mutually reinforcing. In the end, each is important, and neither is alone sufficient to achieve the varied objectives of transitional justice.

Interrelationship of courts and truth commissions

This final section of the chapter analyzes the interrelationship of courts and truth commissions, and offers some brief reflections about their increasing integration.

A number of observers have been critical of truth commissions, arguing that they tend to be created as surrogates for justice.[365] According to these critics, truth commissions are "deals with the devil . . . flawed compromises between those seeking justice and those trying to obstruct it."[366] In fact, this is rarely the case. As previously noted, truth commissions can be created as important precursors to prosecution, or as complements to ongoing prosecution. More to the point, in many instances prosecutions according to international fair trial standards are not even a realistic possibility. Thus, far from being a surrogate, a truth commission may constitute either a vital ingredient of justice or, in worst-case scenarios, its best available approximation. At the same time, a truth commission is not, and never can be, an adequate substitute for justice in the courts.

Another concern about truth commissions is that, rather than augmenting the likelihood of trials, they risk producing the opposite effect. For example, in Guatemala, the effect of the truth commission may have been to reduce international pressure on the government to conduct trials.[367] A truth commission

---

364 The victim focus may continue beyond the hearing as well. Several truth commissions offer follow-up emotional support to persons who testify at public hearings. *See* Chapter 6.

365 *See, e.g.,* R. Brody, "Justice: The First Casualty of Truth?" *The Nation,* 30 April 2001.

366 Tepperman, "Truth and Consequences," above note 137, at 131.

367 *See* P. Seils, "Reconciliation in Guatemala: The Role of Intelligent Justice" (2002) 44 *Race and Class* 33. *See also* Tepperman, "Truth and Consequences," above note 137, at 144.

may also risk prejudicing the possibility of a fair trial by, for example, attributing responsibility to a person who is subject to an ongoing or planned jury trial.[368] By employing lax practices in the preservation of evidence, or by making habitual grants of confidentiality or use immunity to victims, witnesses, and perpetrators, a truth commission can also potentially undermine the ability of investigative and judicial authorities to place subsequent reliance on the evidence and information gathered.[369] In addition, some victims and witnesses may be reluctant to give statements or testify as part of criminal proceedings that follow a truth commission process, because of either fatigue or fear of retraumatization (*e.g.*, if the commission's statement-taking procedure or public hearing format was highly inquisitorial or deficient in terms of emotional and psychological support). One must, therefore, concede that truth commissions could produce some negative effects on criminal justice efforts.

In most cases, however, there is a positive relation between truth commissions and criminal prosecutions. Fortunately, there is an increased recognition of the complementarity of both processes. There is, in fact, a noticeable trend toward increased harmonization of court and truth commission proceedings, and away from the simplistic notion that one must choose justice or truth but not both.[370] One could see this clearly in South Africa, where the truth-for-amnesty process depended on a palpable threat of prosecution. One could also observe it in Timor-Leste, with its integrated truth commission and hybrid criminal court.[371] In Peru, the truth commission entered into an "Institutional Cooperation Agreement" with the Prosecutor's Office; the agreement provided for cooperation in areas such as exhumations, witness protection, and access to information.[372]

But if greater harmonization is generally welcome, one must also concede that it adds complexity. For example, when the possibility of a truth commission

---

368 *See* Chapter 7. *See* also Matthews, *Jervis on Coroners*, above note 232, at 231, where the author explains that a coroner in the UK must generally adjourn an inquest when there is a contemporaneous criminal proceeding underway in which individual culpability for the death in question is being determined.

369 This has been the case to some extent in South Africa (on use immunity), Chad (in the preservation of evidence), and El Salvador (on confidentiality, though of course it had no choice).

370 *See, e.g.*, UN SC res. 1593 (2005). In referring the situation in Darfur, Sudan, to the ICC prosecutor – its first referral to that court – the Security Council emphasized "the need to promote healing and reconciliation and encourages in this respect the creation of institutions, involving all sectors of Sudanese society, such as truth and/or reconciliation commissions, in order to complement judicial processes and thereby reinforce the efforts to restore long-lasting peace, with African Union and international support as necessary . . . " *See also* SC res. 1470 (2003) concerning Sierra Leone.

371 *See generally* Hirst and Varney, *Justice Abandoned*, above note 343.

372 Agreement available in English at http://www.cverdad.org.pe.

in Bosnia and Herzegovina (BiH) was debated in the late 1990s, the ICTY voiced concern about its establishment, viewing it as both a threat to, and a partial duplication of, the tribunal's own efforts.[373] After significant modifications to the original proposal, the ICTY eventually articulated a vision of the complementary role a commission could play.[374] To date, however, no truth commission has been established in BiH.[375] In Sierra Leone, where a truth commission and hybrid criminal court operated alongside each other, the court restricted the commission's access to detainees it wished to call at public hearings.[376] In addition, many citizens remained confused about the distinct but complementary roles each body was playing.[377]

---

373 According to one proponent of the proposed BiH truth commission, the ICTY's concerns were: "(1) The TRC would get in the way of the work of the ICTY, including through the conduct of overlapping investigations. (2) Multiple statements by the same individual to the two bodies might contain inconsistencies that could be used by a defense attorney to impugn the ICTY testimony of the witness. (3) The TRC could be a source of competition for international resources and local attention. (4) The combination of the ICTY and the TRC would be confusing to those who are obliged to live with the legacy of the past on a day-to-day basis." N. Kritz, "Progress and Humility: The Ongoing Search for Post-Conflict Justice," in Bassiouni, *Post-Conflict Justice*, above note 1, at 62. Hayner points out additional ICTY concerns: "that the commission's findings of political responsibility might not be distinguished in the public's eye from those of criminal responsibility, thus leading to unreasonable demands for prosecutions; that there would be a danger that the commission and the Tribunal could arrive at contradictory findings of fact, given the commission's lower standards of evidence . . . and that the Tribunal already was providing the historical truth, so that a truth commission was not necessary": *Unspeakable Truths*, above note 33, at 208.
374 *See* full text of speech by ICTY president Claude Jorda, May 2001, available at http://www.icty.org. Jorda identified four areas of action that, in his view, could be better handled by a BiH truth commission than by the ICTY: dealing with "lower ranking executioners," victim reparations, historical analysis, and "the work of undiluted memory."
375 *See generally* Freeman, *Bosnia and Herzegovina*, above note 223. As of this writing, the prospect of a BiH truth commission is under active official consideration.
376 *Prosecutor v. Sam. Hinga Norman* (Case No. SCSL-2-3-08-PT), Sierra Leone Special Court, Appeal Chamber (28 November 2003). The background and content of the judgment are discussed in detail in Schabas, "A Synergistic Relationship," above note 127, at 40–50. According to Schabas, "the quarrel over testimony by indicted prisoners was the only significant dispute between the Truth Commission and the Special Court." *Ibid.*, at 5. As the Sierra Leonean TRC's final report puts it, "The Commission finds that the two institutions themselves [*i.e.*, the TRC and the Special Court] might have given more consideration to an arrangement or a memorandum of understanding to regulate their relationship." *Sierra Leone Truth and Reconciliation Commission Final Report (2004)*, vol. 2, ch. 2, para. 590.
377 *See* T. Cruvellier and M. Wierda, *The Special Court for Sierra Leone: The First Eighteen Months* (International Center for Transitional Justice, 2004), at 12. This occurred despite the fact that both bodies "repeatedly explained to the people of Sierra Leone that there was no cooperation between the two bodies, but that they respected the role of the other institution and appreciated its contribution to post-conflict justice." Schabas, "A Synergistic Relationship," above note 127, at 5.

Of comparable complexity is the emerging question of how the ICC prosecutor will view truth commissions. Under article 17 of the Rome Statute, a case is admissible before the ICC if a state party is unwilling or unable to genuinely investigate or prosecute.[378] In such instances, the prosecutor may initiate an investigation or prosecution.[379] However, in deciding whether to investigate, the prosecutor must first be satisfied that it would be in "the interests of justice" to do so.[380] It is not known to what degree the ICC prosecutor might choose not to prosecute a particular case on the basis that the interests of justice are being met by a truth commission (and/or other possible transitional justice mechanism).[381] Equally unknown, for now, is the relationship that an active truth commission would have with the ICC, and specifically whether, when, and how it would disclose information to the court.[382]

None of this added uncertainty or surely complexity should, however, provoke excessive concern. Over time, the issues will surely become better understood and thus less daunting. In the meantime, with each new political or postconflict transition, the general complementarity of truth commissions and trials is gradually being discovered and appreciated.

378 Article 17(1) provides: "Having regard to paragraph 10 of the Preamble and article 1, the Court shall determine that a case is inadmissible where: (a) The case is being investigated or prosecuted by a State which has jurisdiction over it, unless the State is unwilling or unable genuinely to carry out the investigation or prosecution; (b) The case has been investigated by a State which has jurisdiction over it and the State has decided not to prosecute the person concerned, unless the decision resulted from the unwillingness or inability of the State genuinely to prosecute; (c) The person concerned has already been tried for conduct which is the subject of the complaint, and a trial by the Court is not permitted under article 20, paragraph 3; (d) The case is not of sufficient gravity to justify further action by the Court."

379 As of this writing, the ICC prosecutor is conducting formal investigations into atrocities committed in the DRC, Uganda, and Sudan. The latter was a UN Security Council referral.

380 Article 53(1) provides in part: "The Prosecutor shall, having evaluated the information made available to him or her, initiate an investigation unless he or she determines that there is no reasonable basis to proceed under this Statute. In deciding whether to initiate an investigation, the Prosecutor shall consider whether: (a) The information available to the Prosecutor provides a reasonable basis to believe that a crime within the jurisdiction of the Court has been or is being committed; (b) The case is or would be admissible under article 17; and (c) Taking into account the gravity of the crime and the interests of victims, there are nonetheless substantial reasons to believe that an investigation would not serve the interests of justice."

381 *See* P. Seils and M. Wierda, *The International Criminal Court and Conflict Mediation* (International Center for Transitional Justice, 2005), at 13–14. *See also* H. Kaul, "Construction Site for More Justice: The International Criminal Court After Two Years" (2005) 99 *AJIL* 370, at 375.

382 *See* Hayner, *Unspeakable Truths*, above note 33, at 209. Note, in this regard, that a truth commission in the DRC is presently operating at the same time as an in-country team of ICC investigators.

CONCLUSIONS

This chapter has attempted to provide a cogent overview of the truth commission phenomenon. The account began with a description of the broader field into which truth commissions fit, namely, transitional justice. It then offered a detailed definition of what a truth commission is, drawing on, but also diverging from, Hayner's original formulation. Thereafter, the chapter provided a brief history of truth commissions, followed by an analysis of selected mandates and models and their perceived advantages and disadvantages. The chapter also offered an original taxonomy of human rights investigation in which truth commissions were compared and contrasted to other similar bodies, ranging from NGOs, to national human rights commissions, to multilateral human rights complaints procedures. The chapter concluded by distinguishing truth commissions from courts, and by assessing their relative strengths and weaknesses as tools of discovery and accountability.

In the next chapter, we turn to the second major theme of this book: procedural fairness. In it, there will be an attempt to articulate a conception of procedural fairness that corresponds to the specific political and legal character of truth commissions, and the difficult contexts in which these bodies must operate.

2

Procedural Fairness

INTRODUCTION

In any human rights investigation – judicial, quasi-judicial, or nonjudicial – there is a duty on the part of the investigating body to be fair. There is, however, no such thing as a universally applicable standard of fairness. Instead, what is fair in any investigation or proceeding will depend on many factors including, in particular, the nature and severity of the consequences that may result. Thus, the standard of fairness one will encounter in a criminal prosecution (where the worst consequence might be the death penalty or life imprisonment) will tend to be greater than that encountered in a civil suit in small claims court (where the worst consequence might be the loss of $25,000) or in a disciplinary process (where the worst consequence might be a loss of employment) or in a coroner's inquest (where the worst consequence might be reputational damage). The challenge is to define parameters and measures of fairness that are appropriate to the particular investigation or proceeding. The central purpose of this chapter is to make that assessment in the specific case of truth commissions.

The chapter begins with an overview of the international standards that are most relevant to a conception of procedural fairness for truth commissions, namely, human rights law, nontreaty standards concerning commissions of inquiry, and nontreaty standards concerning the treatment of victims of human rights violations. This is followed by an analysis of relevant standards of fairness in use in domestic jurisdictions. There is a special focus on three such standards: due process, natural justice, and the "cardinal principles" of procedural fairness articulated in the UK by Lord Justice Salmon (as he then was) in respect of Commonwealth commissions of inquiry. The chapter concludes with an original conception of procedural fairness for truth commissions.

SECTION 1: RELEVANT INTERNATIONAL STANDARDS

In examining standards of procedural fairness relevant to truth commissions, an obviously important source is international human rights law. After all, truth commissions are, in almost every sense, human rights investigators. As such, they should be expected to uphold core human rights standards and values. Moreover, as a matter of international law, the acts and omissions of truth commissions are attributable to the state, given that truth commissions are officially established bodies that tend to operate with the financial support, and under the general supervision, of the state.[1] Their misdeeds could, therefore, trigger international legal responsibility for the sponsoring state.

Article 38(1) of the Statute of the International Court of Justice 1945[2] is the most widely used basis for determining the sources of international law, and hence the sources of international human rights law. It identifies the following sources:

a. international conventions, whether general or particular, establishing rules expressly recognized by the contesting states;
b. international custom, as evidence of a general practice accepted as law;
c. the general principles of law recognized by civilized nations; and
d. . . . judicial decisions and the teachings of the most highly qualified publicists of the various nations, as subsidiary means for the determination of rules of law.

The article 38(1) list of sources is not comprehensive. For example, UN General Assembly and Security Council resolutions and a wide range of other relevant international statements and documents may also constitute sources of international law.[3]

---

1   On the rules of international law concerning attribution of responsibility to the state, *see* M. Freeman and G. van Ert, *International Human Rights Law* (Toronto: Irwin Law, 2004), at 343–4. *See also* Draft Articles on Responsibility of States for Internationally Wrongful Acts 2001 (Draft Articles), UN doc. A/CN.4/L.602/Rev. 1 (2001), art. 4.

2   The Statute is part of the United Nations Charter 1945, 59 Stat. 1031, TS 993, 3 Bevans 1153.

3   *See generally* Freeman and van Ert, *International Human Rights Law*, above note 1, at 54–5 and 68.

For the purposes of this section, the primary focus is on human rights treaties and other widely endorsed international instruments. It is acknowledged that a full interpretation of human rights law would require examination of all of the sources of international law, including the vast jurisprudence of international and regional courts, commissions, and treaty bodies – all of which have "read in" rights that are not made explicit in treaty law.[4] But that is beyond the scope or purpose of this book, as would be the examination of instruments covering the human rights–related fields of international labor, refugee, and humanitarian law.[5] As to relevant parts of international criminal law and procedure, and in particular those relating to the Rome Statute of the International Criminal Court 1998,[6] these are dealt with in Part II of the book. So too are the rules of procedure used by multilateral human rights mechanisms.[7]

Human rights standards

Human rights treaties cover a broad range of civil, political, economic, social, and cultural rights. This section, however, examines only rights that bear on the immediate subject of the book. Consequently, the focus is on rights in criminal proceedings, rights in civil and administrative proceedings, privacy and reputation rights, property rights, protection from discrimination, and the right to a remedy.

The primary source of international human rights law is the International Bill of Human Rights. It comprises the Universal Declaration of Human Rights 1948 (UDHR),[8] the International Covenant on Civil and Political Rights 1966

---

4   For example, the right against self-incrimination is not explicitly covered in the European Convention on Human Rights 1950. The European Court of Human Rights has, however, found that the right forms part of article 6's notion of fair procedure: *Murray v. United Kingdom* (1996) 22 EHRR 29, at para. 45; *Saunders v. United Kingdom* (1997) 23 EHRR 313, at para. 68.

5   Note, however, that each of these fields of human rights–related law encompasses most of the human rights described in this section, including rights in criminal proceedings (*e.g.*, art. 75(4)–(7) of Protocol I to the Geneva Conventions of 1949), property rights (*e.g.*, arts. 13 and 14 of the UN Convention Relating to the Status of Refugees 1951), protection from discrimination (*e.g.*, the Discrimination (Employment and Occupation) Convention (no. 111) 1958), and the right to a remedy (*e.g.*, art. 91 of Protocol I to the Geneva Conventions of 1949).

6   2187 UNTS 90, *entered into force* 1 July 2002.

7   Note, however, that the rules of procedure of multilateral human rights monitors and supervisory bodies generally offer little of relevance to this book.

8   GA res. 217A (III), UN doc. A/810 at 71 (1948). Although originally drafted as a nonbinding declaration, today most if not all of the UDHR has attained customary status.

(ICCPR),[9] the International Covenant on Economic, Social and Cultural Rights 1966 (ICESCR),[10] and the Optional Protocol to the ICCPR 1966.[11] There are many other important UN human rights instruments that complement the Bill of Human Rights. Of especial significance are: the International Convention on the Elimination of All Forms of Racial Discrimination 1966 (CERD);[12] the Convention on the Elimination of All Forms of Discrimination Against Women 1979 (CEDAW),[13] and its related protocol;[14] the Convention Against Torture and Other Cruel, Inhuman or Degrading Treatment or Punishment 1984 (CAT),[15] and its related protocol;[16] and the Convention on the Rights of the Child 1989 (CRC),[17] and its two related protocols.[18]

In addition to UN human rights instruments, there is an important corpus of regional human rights law in each of the Americas, Europe, and Africa. The key instruments of the human rights system of the Organization of American States are: the American Declaration on the Rights and Duties of Man 1948

9   999 UNTS 171, *entered into force* 23 March 1976. There are currently 155 states parties to the treaty.

10   993 UNTS 3, *entered into force* 3 January 1976. There are currently 152 states parties to the treaty.

11   999 UNTS 302, *entered into force* 23 March 1976. There are currently 105 states parties to the treaty. There is also a Second Optional Protocol to the ICCPR Aiming at the Abolition of the Death Penalty 1989, UN doc. A/44/49, *entered into force* 11 July 1991. It has 56 states parties.

12   660 UNTS 195, *entered into force* 4 January 1969. There are currently 170 states parties to the treaty.

13   GA res. 34/180, 34 UN GAOR Supp. (no. 46) at 193, UN doc. A/34/46, *entered into force* 3 September 1981. There are currently 180 states parties to the treaty.

14   Optional Protocol to the CEDAW 1999, GA res. 54/4, annex, 54 UN GAOR Supp. (no. 49) at 5, UN doc. A/54/49 (Vol. I) (2000), *entered into force* 22 December 2000. There are currently 76 states parties to the treaty.

15   GA res. 39/46, annex, 39 UN GAOR Supp. (no. 51) at 197, UN doc. A/39/51 (1984), *entered into force* 26 June 1987. There are currently 141 states parties to the treaty.

16   Optional Protocol to the CAT 2002, GA res. A/RES/57/199, *adopted* 18 December 2002 (*reprinted in* 42 I.L.M. 26 [2003]). There are currently 16 states parties to the treaty.

17   GA res. 44/25, Annex, 44 UN GAOR Supp. (no. 49) at 167, UN doc. A/44/49 (1989), *entered into force* 2 September 1990. There are currently 192 states parties to the treaty.

18   The Optional Protocol to the Convention on the Rights of the Child on the sale of children, child prostitution, and child pornography 2000, GA res. 54/263, Annex II, 54 UN GAOR Supp. (no. 49) at 6, UN doc. A/54/49, Vol. III (2000), *entered into force* 18 January 2002; Optional Protocol to the Convention on the Rights of the Child on the involvement of children in armed conflict 2000, GA res. 54/263, Annex I, 54 UN GAOR Supp. (no. 49) at 7, UN doc. A/54/49, Vol. III (2000), *entered into force* 12 February 2002. There are currently 103 and 104 states parties to the two treaties, respectively.

(AmDR);[19] the American Convention on Human Rights 1969 (ACHR),[20] and its two protocols;[21] the Inter-American Convention to Prevent and Punish Torture 1985;[22] the Inter-American Convention on the Prevention, Punishment and Eradication of Violence Against Women 1994;[23] the Inter-American Convention on Forced Disappearance of Persons 1994;[24] and the Inter-American Convention on the Elimination of All Forms of Discrimination Against Persons with Disabilities 1999.[25]

The principal instruments of the human rights system of the Council of Europe are: the revised European Convention for the Protection of Human Rights and Fundamental Freedoms 1950 (ECHR),[26] and its assorted protocols;[27] the revised European Social Charter 1996 (EurSC);[28] the European Convention for the Prevention of Torture and Inhuman or Degrading Treatment or Punishment 1987;[29] the European Charter for Regional or Minority Languages 1992;[30] and the Framework Convention for the Protection of National Minorities 1995.[31] The EU Charter of Fundamental Rights (EU Charter of Rights),

---

19 OAS Res. XXX, adopted by the Ninth International Conference of American States (1948), *reprinted in* Basic Documents Pertaining to Human Rights in the Inter-American System, OEA/Ser.L.V/II.82 doc.6 rev.1, at 17 (1992).

20 OAS TS no. 36.

21 Additional Protocol to the ACHR in the Area of Economic, Social and Cultural Rights 1988, OAS TS no. 69; and Protocol to the ACHR to Abolish the Death Penalty 1990, OAS TS no. 73.

22 OAS TS no. 67.

23 (1994) 33 ILM 1534.

24 (1994) 33 ILM 1429.

25 OAS GA res. 1608 (1999).

26 ETS no. 5. The text of the ECHR was amended by Protocols no. 3 (ETS no. 45), 5 (ETS no. 55), 8 (ETS no. 118), and 11 (ETS no. 155), which entered into force on 21 September 1970, 20 December 1971, 1 January 1990, and 1 November 1998, respectively.

27 There are fourteen protocols to the ECHR. The protocols cover, *inter alia*, rights to property and to free elections (Protocol 1), mobility rights and freedom from imprisonment for debt (Protocol 4), and rights to appeal in criminal cases and to receive compensation for wrongful conviction (Protocol 7).

28 ETS no. 163. The EurSC was preceded by the European Social Charter 1961 (ETS no. 35), the Additional Protocol to the Charter 1988 (ETS no. 128), the Protocol Amending the European Social Charter 1991 (ETS no. 142), and the Additional Protocol Providing for a System of Collective Complaints 1995 (ETS no. 158). The purpose of the EurSC was to bring all revisions up to date and introduce new rights such as the right to housing (art. 31) and the right to protection against sexual harassment in the workplace (art. 26).

29 ETS no. 126. There have been two protocols to the Convention: Protocol 1 (1993) ETS no. 151; and Protocol 2 (1993) ETS no. 152.

30 ETS no. 148.

31 ETS no. 157. On minority rights in Europe generally, *see* P. Cumper and S. Wheatley, eds., *Minority Rights in the "New" Europe* (The Hague: M. Nijhoff, 1999).

being Part II of the draft Treaty establishing a Constitution for Europe 2004,[32] may one day supplement these treaties.

The key instruments of the human rights system of the African Union are: the African Charter on Human and Peoples' Rights 1981 (AfrCHPR),[33] and its protocol on women's human rights;[34] and the African Charter on the Rights and Welfare of the Child 1990.[35]

Of the various UN and regional human rights instruments, two – the UDHR and the AmDR – include general limitations provisions applicable to all the rights and freedoms they proclaim.[36] Other instruments permit states to derogate from (*i.e.,* suspend) human rights during times of public or national emergency.[37] Neither general limitations provisions nor derogations are examined in this chapter; they are drawn to the reader's attention only because of their practical implications for the scope of the rights that are discussed here.

Rights in criminal proceedings

As indicated in Chapter 1, courts have a high level of formality and entail a broad and well-developed array of rights. Many of the rights belonging to

---

32 *Adopted* 29 October 2004, Notice no. 2004/C 310/01.

33 OAU doc. CAB/LEG/67/3 rev. 5.

34 Protocol to the AfrCHPR on the Rights of Women in Africa 2003 (AfrCHPR Women's Protocol), AU doc. CAB/LEG/23.18. The protocol is not yet in force. Fifteen ratifications are required for it to come into force.

35 OAU doc. CAB/LEG/24.9/49.

36 UDHR art. 29(2) provides: "In the exercise of his rights and freedoms, everyone shall be subject only to such limitations as are determined by law solely for the purpose of securing due recognition and respect for the rights and freedoms of others and of meeting the just requirements of morality, public order and the general welfare in a democratic society." AmDR art. 28 provides that all of its declared rights are "limited by the rights of others, by the security of all, and by the just demands of the general welfare and the advancement of democracy." The EU Charter of Rights art. 112(1) also provides a general limitations clause. These general limitations clauses are unusual in treaties. Most treaties only establish limitations of *specific* rights, as opposed to *all* rights. *See, e.g,* ICCPR art. 12(3), which allows states to limit freedom of movement and residence and the right to leave and return to a country of one's own when "necessary to protect national security, public order, public health or morals or the rights and freedoms of others . . ."

37 Derogation must be temporary, proportionate to the level of emergency, and nondiscriminatory in its application. Unlike a general limitations clause – which applies to all rights declared in an international instrument – a derogation is permitted only for a limited set of human rights. For example, states parties to the ICCPR are not allowed to derogate from the following: the prohibition on genocide (art. 6); limitations on capital punishment (art. 6); freedom from torture and cruel, inhuman, or degrading treatment or punishment (art. 7); freedom from slavery (art. 8); the right not to be imprisoned for debt (art. 11); the prohibition on *ex post facto* laws (art. 15); the right to personhood (art. 16); and the right to freedom of thought (art. 18). Compare with ECHR art. 15 and ACHR art. 27(2).

accused persons, in particular, are encompassed in international human rights instruments. These range from the right to know the offenses charged, to the right to trial within a reasonable time, to protection from retroactive application of criminal laws, to safeguards against double jeopardy (*i.e.*, against being tried twice for the same offense). This discussion covers only rights having direct relevance to the work of truth commissions. Although we have seen that truth commissions are not equivalent to criminal courts, the norms that will be discussed serve as standards to which truth commissions can sometimes aspire, especially in the context of public hearings.

The right to a fair and public trial by an impartial and independent tribunal. UDHR article 10 guarantees every individual "a fair and public hearing by an independent and impartial tribunal" in the determination of criminal charges. ICCPR article 14(1) affirms the same right, but also requires the tribunal to be competent and established by law. In addition, it permits the exclusion of the press and the public from all or part of a trial "for reasons of morals, public order (*ordre public*) or national security in a democratic society, or when the interest of the private lives of the parties so requires, or to the extent strictly necessary in the opinion of the court in special circumstances where publicity would prejudice the interests of justice . . ." The same basic right to a fair and public trial is guaranteed to children in CRC article 40(2)(b)(iii).[38] It is also guaranteed in AmDR articles 18 and 26, ACHR article 8(1) and 8(5), and ECHR article 6(1).[39] AfrCHPR articles 7(1) and 26 protect the right to have one's cause heard, but they leave out criteria of fairness, publicity, or judicial independence.

The presumption of innocence. The presumption of innocence is guaranteed in UDHR article 11(1) and ICCPR article 14(2), as well as in CRC article 40(2)(b)(i). It is equally protected in AmDR article 26, ACHR article 8(2), ECHR article 6(2),[40] and AfrCHPR article 7(1)(b).

The right to the assistance of legal counsel. The right to the assistance of legal counsel is guaranteed in ICCPR article 14(3)(a) and CRC article 37(d). ACHR article 8(2)(d) and (e), ECHR article 6(3)(c), and AfrCHPR article 7(1)(c) also affirm the right.

---

38 Concerning juveniles that face criminal proceedings, ICCPR art. 14(4) allows states parties to take account of their age and the desirability of promoting their rehabilitation. *See also* CRC art. 40(1) and (2).

39 *See also* EU Charter of Rights art. 107.

40 EU Charter of Rights art. 108(1) also affirms the presumption of innocence.

The right to examine witnesses and evidence. The right to examine witnesses and evidence is guaranteed in ICCPR article 14(3)(e) and CRC article 40(2)(b)(iv). It is also protected in ACHR article 8(2)(f) and ECHR article 6(3)(d).

The right against compelled self-incrimination. The right against compelled self-incrimination is guaranteed in ICCPR article 14(3)(g) and CRC article 40(2)(b)(iv). Two regional instruments protect the right too: ACHR article 8(2)(g) and AfrCHPR article 7(1)(d).

The right to an interpreter (if needed). This right to an interpreter is guaranteed in ICCPR article 14(3)(a) and (f) and CRC article 40(2)(b)(vi). ACHR article 8(2)(a) and ECHR article 6(3)(a) also protect the right.

Rights in civil and administrative proceedings

Under many of the leading international human rights instruments, the right to a fair and public hearing by an independent and impartial tribunal (and associated procedural guarantees) applies not only to criminal proceedings but also to civil proceedings. ICCPR article 14(1) explicitly applies to "suits at law." CRC article 12(2) requires states parties to afford children "the opportunity to be heard in any judicial and administrative proceedings" affecting them, either directly or through a representative.[41]

As to regional norms, ACHR article 8(1) provides, "Every person has the right to a hearing . . . in the substantiation of any accusation of a criminal nature made against him or for the determination of his rights and obligations of a civil, labor, fiscal, or any other nature." ECHR article 6(1) recognizes due process guarantees in proceedings in which the "determination of . . . civil rights and obligations" is at issue.

Privacy and reputation rights

Entitlements to privacy and respect for one's reputation are generally treated as a common right in international human rights instruments.[42] Such entitlements are relevant to all of the truth commission powers examined in Part II of the book.

---

41 Note also that CRC art. 3(1) requires all state actions concerning children – "whether undertaken by public or private social welfare institutions, courts of law, administrative authorities or legislative bodies" – to operate in the children's best interests.

42 Privacy protection in the context of criminal proceedings (*e.g.*, ICCPR art. 14(1)) was already noted above.

UDHR article 12 provides, "No one shall be subjected to arbitrary interference with his privacy, family, home or correspondence, nor to attacks upon his honour and reputation. Everyone has the right to the protection of the law against such interference or attacks." ICCPR article 17 is virtually identical; so too is CRC article 16. The ICCPR also treats reputation as a limit on freedom of expression in light of the "special duties and responsibilities" it entails; article 19(3)(a) and (b) permits restrictions provided by law and necessary for respect of, *inter alia*, the rights or reputations of others.

ECHR article 8(1) declares, "Everyone has the right to respect for his private and family life, his home and his correspondence."[43] However, article 8(2) permits governmental interference with this right where "necessary in a democratic society in the interests of national security, public safety or the economic well-being of the country, for the protection of health or morals, or for the protection of the rights and freedoms of others." The ECHR also treats reputation as a limit on freedom of expression: article 10(2) permits limitations "for the protection of the reputation or rights of others, for preventing the disclosure of information received in confidence, or for maintaining the authority and impartiality of the judiciary."

AmDR article 5 guarantees every person "protection of the law against abusive attacks upon his honour, his reputation, and his private and family life." In addition, AmDR articles 9 and 10 guarantee the inviolability of one's home and one's personal correspondence, respectively. As for the ACHR, article 11 ensures everyone's right "to have his honour respected and his dignity recognized" and to that end provides guarantees against arbitrary or abusive interference with private life, family, home, or correspondence. In addition, and of particular relevance for this book, ACHR article 14(1) guarantees to individuals injured by false or offensive public statements or ideas disseminated by publicly regulated media a "right to reply or to make a correction using the same communications outlet." Furthermore, for the "effective protection of honour and reputation," article 14(3) requires publishers and other media outlets to employ "a person responsible who is not protected by immunities or special privileges."

Property rights

International human rights instruments cover a broad array of property rights including intellectual property rights[44] and property rights related to the

---

43 Article 67 of the EU Charter is almost identical. It entitles everyone to "respect for his or her private and family life, home and communications."
44 *See, e.g.,* UDHR art. 27(2); ICESCR art. 15(c); AmDR art. 13.

exercise of the right to self-determination.[45] This discussion covers only those property rights directly relevant to truth commissions, and in particular to a commission's powers of search and seizure (discussed in Chapter 5).

UDHR article 17 guarantees the right to own property and to not be arbitrarily deprived of it. ICCPR article 26, ICESCR article 2(2), and CRC article 2(1) declare the right not to suffer discrimination on the ground of property. CERD article 5(d)(v) and (vi) and CEDAW articles 15(2) and 16(1)(h) preclude, respectively, discrimination against racial minorities and discrimination against women in the exercise of their property rights.

Article 1 of the ECHR First Protocol 1954[46] guarantees to natural and legal persons (*i.e.*, humans and corporations) the peaceful enjoyment of their possessions. It permits deprivations of those possessions only "in the public interest and subject to the conditions provided for by law and by the general principles of international law." These provisions are declared not to impair, among other things, the state's prerogative to enforce laws controlling the use of property in the general interest. Article 77(1) of the EU Charter of Rights would supplement the ECHR First Protocol by providing that deprivations of property would be subject to "fair compensation being paid in good time . . ."

ACHR article 21(1) guarantees individuals the right to the use and enjoyment of their property but subject to "the interest of society." Article 21(2), however, precludes deprivation of property "except in payment of just compensation, for reasons of public utility or social interest, and in the cases and according to the forms established by law."

Like the ECHR and the ACHR, the AfrCHPR protects property rights, subject to the public interest. In particular, AfrCHPR article 14 guarantees the right to property but permits limitations "in the interest of public need or in the general interest of the community and in accordance with the provisions of appropriate laws."

Protection from discrimination

The principle of nondiscrimination and its corollary, the guarantee of equality, lie at the heart of international human rights law. Beginning with the UN Charter itself, equality provisions appear in virtually all human rights instruments, and in the case of the CERD and the CEDAW, form the principal subject of the treaty. For present purposes, the discussion is limited to equality guarantees directly relevant to the work of truth commissions. Other equality

---

45   *See, e.g.*, ICCPR art. 47; ICESCR art. 25.
46   ETS no. 9.

provisions, including the obligation to undertake affirmative action measures,[47] are not reviewed here.

UDHR article 2 guarantees rights and freedoms to everyone "without distinction of any kind, such as race, colour, sex, language, religion, political or other opinion, national or social origin, property, birth or other status." UDHR article 7 also guarantees equality before the law and prohibits discrimination or incitement to discrimination. ICCPR article 26 does much the same: it declares the principles of equality before the law and prohibits discrimination "on any ground such as race, colour, sex, language, religion, political or other opinion, national or social origin, property, birth or other status."[48] ICCPR article 3 also requires states to ensure the equal rights of men and women. A similar provision appears in ICESCR article 3. CRC article 2 provides similar equality guarantees for children, including protection from discrimination by the child's parents, legal guardians, or family members.

Similarly broad equality and nondiscrimination provisions are found in the major regional human rights instruments, including AmDR article 1, ACHR articles 1 and 24, ECHR article 14 and ECHR Protocol no. 12 (2000), and AfrCHPR articles 2, 3(1), 3(2), and 18(3). Article 19 of the AfrCHPR guarantees equality to "peoples" too (as opposed to just individuals).[49] There are also several regional antidiscrimination treaties analogous to the CERD and the CEDAW, including the Inter-American Convention on the Elimination of All Forms of Discrimination Against Persons with Disabilities 1999,[50] the European Framework Convention for the Protection of National Minorities 1995,[51] and the Protocol to the AfrCHPR on the Rights of Women in Africa 2003.[52]

Right to a remedy

International human rights law treats the question of a remedy as an independent human right. States agree to respect and ensure the right in their domestic laws just like any other human right.

The relevance of the right for truth commissions is straightforward. Where a truth commission helps vindicate victims' rights to justice (*e.g.*, by preparing and forwarding case files to prosecutors for follow-up action), truth (*e.g.*, by discovering the fate of missing persons), reparation (*e.g.*, by recommending comprehensive reparation programs), or reform (*e.g.*, by making findings of

---

47   *See, e.g.,* CEDAW art 4(1).
48   *See also* ICCPR art. 2(1).
49   *See also* EU Charter of Rights arts. 80, 81, and 83.
50   Above note 25.
51   Above note 31.
52   Above note 34.

institutional responsibility in a final report and urging sectoral reforms), it plays a direct role in helping to fulfill a state's obligation to remedy serious human rights violations. But the right to a remedy is also relevant in an inverse sense. Where a truth commission itself violates an individual's human rights (*e.g.*, by arbitrarily violating the human right to privacy), the victim of the violation enjoys the right to a remedy.

The right to a remedy appears in most major human rights instruments. UDHR article 8 and ICCPR article 2(3) recognize the right to an "effective" remedy for the violation of human rights. Under the UDHR, domestic courts are responsible for ensuring effective remedies; by contrast, under the ICCPR, remedies may be ensured by "competent judicial, administrative or legislative authorities, or by any other competent authority provided for by the legal system of the State." Right-to-remedy provisions are also found in other UN instruments, including CERD article 6, CEDAW article 2(c), and CAT article 14 which guarantees torture victims redress and "an enforceable right to fair and adequate compensation, including the means for as full rehabilitation as possible."[53] Right-to-remedy provisions appear in several regional instruments too, including ACHR articles 10, 25 and 63(1), and ECHR articles 13 and 41.[54]

Standards concerning commissions of inquiry

Several human rights treaties explicitly require investigation of human rights violations. For example, CAT article 12 provides, "Each State Party shall ensure that its competent authorities proceed to a prompt and impartial investigation, wherever there is reasonable ground to believe that an act of torture has been committed in any territory under its jurisdiction." Similarly, article 8 of the Inter-American Convention to Prevent and Punish Torture 1985 declares that "if there is an accusation or well-grounded reason to believe that an act of torture has been committed within their jurisdiction, the States Parties shall guarantee that their respective authorities will proceed properly and immediately to conduct an investigation into the case and to initiate, whenever appropriate, the corresponding criminal process."[55] There are, however, no

---

53   The article also prescribes compensation for a torture victim's dependents in the event of the victim's death.

54   *See also* EU Charter of Rights art. 107.

55   *See also* draft International Convention for the Protection of All Persons from Enforced Disappearance, UN doc. E/CN.4/2005/WG.22/WP.1/REV.4 (23 September 2005), articles 3, 12, and 24(3). Article 12(1) provides: "Each State Party shall ensure that any individual who alleges that a person has been subjected to enforced disappearance has the right to report the facts to the competent authorities, which shall examine the allegation promptly and impartially..." Article 12(2) requires the investigation of a credible claim of forced disappearance even in the absence of a formal complaint.

human rights treaties that deal *per se* with truth commissions or commissions of inquiry, much less with the standards of procedural fairness that should apply in their proceedings. Instead, there are a few relevant non–human rights–related treaties on the subject, plus some noteworthy nontreaty human rights sources.

The 1899 and 1907 Hague Conventions for the Pacific Settlement of International Disputes

The first international codifications of fact-finding procedures appear to have been the Hague Convention for the Pacific Settlement of Disputes 1899[56] and the Hague Convention for the Pacific Settlement of Disputes 1907.[57] These treaties enable states parties to establish an International Commission of Inquiry to investigate the claims of each side in the event of a dispute.[58] Both conventions include a general set of rules of procedure for the inquiry. There are rules pertaining to the role of counsel,[59] the right to be heard,[60] the duty to cooperate with an inquiry,[61] the summoning and examination of witnesses,[62] the modalities of testifying,[63] and the form in which an inquiry must render its findings.[64]

Although the inquiry mechanism envisaged in these conventions is rarely used, least of all in the investigation of human rights claims,[65] their procedural standards continue to serve as benchmarks in the area of nonjudicial fact-finding.[66] Their influence is apparent in the design of the International Labour Organization (ILO) Commission of Inquiry mechanism,[67] as well as in the design of the International Humanitarian Fact-Finding Commission.[68] The content of the Declaration on Fact-Finding by the United Nations in the Field

---

56   1 Bevans 230.
57   36 Stat. 2199, TS no. 536.
58   Article 9 of both Conventions.
59   *E.g.,* articles 14, 21, 25, and 26 of the 1907 Convention.
60   *E.g.,* article 19 of the 1907 Convention.
61   *E.g.,* article 23 of the 1907 Convention.
62   *E.g.,* articles 25 and 26 of the 1907 Convention.
63   *E.g.,* articles 27 and 28 of the 1907 Convention.
64   *E.g.,* articles 33, 34, and 35 of the 1907 Convention.
65   Article 9 of both conventions specifies that the commission of inquiry mechanism covers only "disputes of an international nature involving neither honour nor vital interests." Allegations of human rights violations surely involve honor and possibly vital interests too.
66   This is true mostly at the international level, not the national level.
67   *See* Chapter 1, Section 3.
68   *See* Chapter 1, Section 3.

of Maintenance of International Peace and Security (1991) also reveals a similar influence.[69]

The Hague Conventions are now supplemented by the Permanent Court of Arbitration's Optional Rules for Fact-Finding Commissions.[70]

The UN Principles on the Effective Prevention and Investigation of Extra-Legal, Arbitrary and Summary Executions (1989)

The UN Principles on the Effective Prevention and Investigation of Extra-Legal, Arbitrary and Summary Executions,[71] though nonbinding, highlight some of the most important aspects of procedural fairness in the context of human rights investigations. The Principles are specifically directed at cases of extralegal, arbitrary, and summary executions. Many of the provisions can, however, be applied to other serious human rights violations as well.

Principle 9 declares that investigations are to be "thorough, prompt and impartial" and that governments must provide investigative offices and procedures to "determine the cause, manner and time of death, the person responsible, and any pattern or practice which may have brought about that death." The investigative body must have "the power to obtain all the information necessary to the inquiry," including the authority to issue summonses requiring alleged perpetrators to testify or produce evidence.[72] Investigative bodies are also entitled to "all the necessary budgetary and technical resources for effective investigation."[73]

The Principles recognize that standing investigative bodies of the state – whether police officers, investigating magistrates, or other officials – may sometimes lack the capacity or impartiality to conduct a fair investigation. In such instances, the Principles require governments to conduct an investigation by means of an "independent commission of inquiry or similar procedure"

---

69   GA res. A/RES/46/59 (1991). Section 2 of the Declaration defines fact-finding to mean "any activity designed to obtain detailed knowledge of the relevant facts of any dispute or situation which the competent United Nations organs need in order to exercise effectively their functions in relation to the maintenance of international peace and security." Section 3 provides that fact-finding must be "comprehensive, objective, impartial and timely." Fact-finding reports in this field are to be "limited to a presentation of findings of a factual nature" (section 17). As a guarantee of their independence, members of fact-finding missions are to be accorded "all immunities and facilities needed for discharging their mandate, in particular full confidentiality in their work and access to all relevant places and persons . . ." (section 23).

70   *See* http://pca-cpa.org/ENGLISH/BD/inquiryenglish.htm.

71   UN doc. E/1989/89 (1989).

72   Principle 10.

73   *Ibid.*

comprising members "chosen for their recognized impartiality, competence and independence as individuals."[74]

To ensure procedural fairness, the Principles require the protection of "[c]omplainants, witnesses, those conducting the investigation and their families" from threats and acts of violence or intimidation, and the removal of those potentially implicated by the investigation from positions of control or power over such persons.[75] Victims' families and their legal representatives have the right to be "informed of, and have access to, any hearing as well as to all information relevant to the investigation," and are likewise entitled to present other evidence.[76]

Upon conclusion of the investigation, a public report must be issued that includes "the scope of the inquiry, procedures and methods used to evaluate evidence as well as conclusions and recommendations based on findings of fact and on applicable law."[77] The report must also describe "specific events that were found to have occurred and the evidence upon which such findings were based, and list the names of witnesses who testified, with the exception of those whose identities have been withheld for their own protection."[78]

The UN Manual on the Effective Prevention and Investigation of Extra-Legal, Arbitrary and Summary Executions (1991)

The express purpose of the UN Manual on the Effective Prevention and Investigation of Extra-Legal, Arbitrary and Summary Executions[79] is to supplement the Principles just described. Of especial interest is the Manual's model protocol (called the "Minnesota Protocol"), much of which touches directly on questions of procedural fairness applicable to extrajudicial commissions of inquiry such as truth commissions.

---

74 Principle 11. Principle 11 also provides: "In particular, they shall be independent of any institution, agency or person that may be the subject of the inquiry. The commission shall have the authority to obtain all information necessary to the inquiry and shall conduct the inquiry as provided for under these Principles."

75 Principle 15. *Compare with* draft International Convention for the Protection of All Persons from Enforced Disappearance, UN doc. E/CN.4/2005/WG.22/WP.1/REV.4 (23 September 2005), article 12(4): "Each State Party shall take the necessary measures to prevent and sanction acts that hinder the conduct of the investigations. It shall ensure in particular that persons suspected of having committed an offence of enforced disappearance are not in a position to influence the progress of the investigations by means of pressure or acts of intimidation or reprisal aimed at the complainant, witnesses, relatives of the disappeared person or their defence counsel, or at persons participating in the investigation."

76 Principle 16.

77 Principle 17.

78 *Ibid.*

79 Available at http://www.mnadvocates.org/4Jun20046.html.

The Protocol stipulates that a commission's terms of reference should be "neutrally framed so that they do not suggest a predetermined outcome" and should "state precisely which events and issues are to be investigated and addressed in the commission's final report."[80] Article 11 provides that the public should be notified about the establishment of the commission through a broad publicity campaign and should be invited to submit relevant information or testimony. The same article goes on to suggest that commissions should have the discretion to amend the terms of reference ("to ensure that thorough investigation by the commission is not hampered by overly restrictive or overly broad terms of reference") provided that they inform the public of any amendments.[81]

The Protocol itemizes several additional powers that a commission should have beyond those listed in the UN Principles, including the power to issue a public report, conduct on-site visits to crime scenes, and receive evidence from abroad.[82] The Protocol also recommends the use of commission counsel, a practice associated with Commonwealth commissions of inquiry. Such counsel should be impartial experts and "insulated from political influence, as through civil service tenure, or status as a wholly independent member of the [legal] bar."[83]

The Protocol provides important guidelines for commission hearings and the treatment of evidence. In accordance with "general principles of criminal procedure," article 10 stipulates that closed, rather than public, proceedings may be conducted to protect the safety of witnesses, provided that the proceedings are recorded and that "the closed, unpublished record [is] kept in a known location."[84] Like the UN Principles, the Protocol recommends that a commission wield the power to compel persons to testify. But it also adds the power to impose fines or sentences for failure to comply with any summons or subpoena.[85]

The Protocol stipulates that commissions should permit all interested parties an opportunity to be heard, and compelled witnesses should have the right to appear through counsel if their testimony could expose them to criminal or civil liability.[86] For its part, the commission should question witnesses

---

80   Article 2.
81   In practice, truth commissions – and commissions of inquiry in general – rarely have the power to amend their terms of reference.
82   Article 3.
83   Article 6.
84   Article 10 also recognizes that in some instances complete secrecy may be necessary to encourage testimony. In such event "the commission will want to hear witnesses privately, informally and without recording testimony."
85   Article 12.
86   Article 13.

appearing before it.[87] In evaluating the evidence it acquires, the commission should assess its "relevance, veracity, reliability and probity."[88] It should seek to corroborate all evidence – especially hearsay evidence, *in camera* testimony, and testimony not subjected to cross-examination – failing which it may accord the evidence less weight.[89]

The "UN Set of Principles for the Protection and Promotion of Human Rights Through Action to Combat Impunity" (1996)

The "Set of Principles for the Protection and Promotion of Human Rights Through Action to Combat Impunity"[90] (hereafter Joinet Principles), elaborated by Louis Joinet in his former capacity as the UN's special rapporteur on the question of impunity, are in wide use among human rights practitioners. Their value was reaffirmed in 2004 in a study commissioned by the UN Secretary-General on "best practices, including recommendations, to assist States in strengthening their domestic capacity to combat all aspects of impunity, taking into account the [Joinet Principles] and how they have been applied, reflecting recent developments and considering the issue of their further implementation . . ."[91] In 2005, the Principles themselves were updated.[92] Unlike the original Principles, the updated Principles have yet to be formally adopted by the UN Commission on Human Rights.[93] Aspects of the updated Principles are taken up in Section 3 of this chapter.

The most relevant portion of the Joinet Principles concerns what their author describes (but never defines) as "extrajudicial commissions of inquiry." As guarantees of the independence and impartiality of such commissions, Principle 6 stipulates that they must be established by law or by negotiated accord, and be comprised of impartial members who serve "on conditions ensuring their independence, in particular by the irremovability of their members for the duration of their terms of office." Transparent funding and sufficient material and human resources are listed as additional factors that will guarantee

---

87   *Ibid.*
88   Article 14.
89   *Ibid.*
90   UN doc. E/CN.4/Sub.2/1996/18 (1996).
91   D. Orentlicher, "Promotion and Protection of Human Rights: Impunity," UN doc. E/CN.4/2004/88 (2004).
92   D. Orentlicher, "Updated Set of Principles for Promotion and Protection of Human Rights Through Action to Combat Impunity," UN doc. E/CN.4/2005/102/Add.1 (2005).
93   By Resolution 2005/66 ("Right to the Truth"), the Commission on Human Rights merely noted its "appreciation" of the updated set of Principles.

independence and impartiality.[94] The Joinet Principles also note the need to ensure the immunity of commission members from any defamation or other proceedings that might be launched against them for the findings published in their reports.[95]

In fulfilling their terms of reference, extrajudicial commissions of inquiry into human rights violations should exercise three main functions according to the Joinet Principles:

a) to analyse and describe the machinery of the State through which the violating system operated,

b) to identify the administrations, agencies and private entities involved and reconstruct their roles, and

c) to safeguard evidence for later use in the administration of justice.[96]

If the commission has the power to publicly ascribe individual responsibility for human rights violations, its information must be corroborated by "at least" two sources, and the implicated person must be given "the opportunity to make a statement setting out his or her version of the facts or, within the time prescribed by the instrument establishing the Commission, to submit a document equivalent to a right of reply for inclusion in the file."[97] The Joinet Principles also contain two important rules relating to "archives containing names" (*i.e.*, archives that permit the identification of the individuals to whom they relate):

> Everyone shall be entitled to know whether his or her name appears in the archives stored during the reference period, and, if it does, to use his or her right of access and subsequently to challenge the validity of the relevant information by exercising his or her right of reply. The document containing his or her version shall be attached to the document being challenged.

> Except where it relates to officials of the security services or persons working with them on an ongoing basis, the information in the security and information service archives containing names shall not by itself constitute incriminating evidence, unless it is corroborated by several different reliable sources.[98]

94   Principle 10.
95   Principle 12.
96   Principle 7(c).
97   Principle 8.
98   Principle 18.

The UN Principles on the Effective Investigation and Documentation of Torture and Other Cruel, Inhuman or Degrading Treatment or Punishment (2000)

In 2000, the UN General Assembly adopted the Principles on the Effective Investigation and Documentation of Torture and Other Cruel, Inhuman or Degrading Treatment or Punishment[99] – a set of principles very similar to the UN Principles on the Effective Prevention and Investigation of Extra-Legal, Arbitrary and Summary Executions 1989, discussed earlier. Principle 3 of the 2000 Principles is equivalent in content to Principle 10 of the 1989 Principles, Principle 4 to Principle 16, Principle 5(a) to Principle 11, and Principle 5(b) to Principle 17.

Standards concerning victims of human rights violations

In Chapter 1 it was explained that international human rights law recognizes a wide range of victim entitlements including the right to justice, the right to truth, the right to reparation, and the right to guarantees of nonrepetition. This subsection reviews some additional, if more general, victim entitlements under two important international instruments. Though not expressly prescribed in treaty law, these standards are relevant to this book's holistic conception of procedural fairness.

The UN Declaration of Basic Principles of Justice for Victims of Crime and Abuse of Power

The Declaration of Basic Principles of Justice for Victims of Crime and Abuse of Power[100] of the UN General Assembly, which at the time marked a watershed moment in the recognition of victims' rights, continues to serve as a reference point among scholars and practitioners alike. Several of its provisions bear mention. Principle 4 provides:

> Victims should be treated with compassion and respect for their dignity. They are entitled to access to the mechanisms of justice and to prompt redress, as provided for by national legislation, for the harm that they have suffered.

Principle 6 then provides examples of how judicial and administrative procedures can address the rights and needs of victims. These include, by:

---

99 GA res. 55/89 (2000).
100 GA res. 40/34 (1985).

(a) Informing victims of their role and the scope, timing and progress of the proceedings and of the disposition of their cases, especially where serious crimes are involved and where they have requested such information;

(b) Allowing the views and concerns of victims to be presented and considered at appropriate stages of the proceedings where their personal interests are affected, without prejudice to the accused and consistent with the relevant national criminal justice system; . . .

(d) Taking measures to minimize inconvenience to victims, protect their privacy, when necessary, and ensure their safety, as well as that of their families and witnesses on their behalf, from intimidation and retaliation . . .

Principles 14 and 15 then declare a general entitlement of victims that extends well beyond the context of judicial and administrative proceedings. Principle 14 provides:

Victims should receive the necessary material, medical, psychological and social assistance through governmental, voluntary, community-based and indigenous means.

Principle 15 provides:

Victims should be informed of the availability of health and social services and other relevant assistance and be readily afforded access to them.

A final provision of note is Principle 16, which provides for victim-sensitive training in key areas of service delivery for victims:

Police, justice, health, social service and other personnel concerned should receive training to sensitise them to the needs of victims, and guidelines to ensure proper and prompt aid.

"Basic Principles and Guidelines on the Right to a Remedy and Reparation for Victims of Violations of International Human Rights and Humanitarian Law"

As discussed in Chapter 1, the "Basic Principles and Guidelines on the Right to a Remedy and Reparation for Victims of Violations of International Human

Rights and Humanitarian Law"[101] (hereafter "Bassiouni Principles") constitute one of the most comprehensive international reference points on the rights and interests of victims of violations of human rights and humanitarian law.

Principle 8 broadly defines victims as

> persons who individually or collectively suffered harm, including physical or mental injury, emotional suffering, economic loss or substantial impairment of their fundamental rights, through acts or omissions that constitute gross violations of international human rights law, or serious violations of international humanitarian law. Where appropriate, and in accordance with domestic law, the term 'victim' also includes the immediate family or dependants of the direct victim and persons who have suffered harm in intervening to assist victims in distress or to prevent victimization.

Principle 9 further provides: "A person shall be considered a victim regardless of whether the perpetrator of the violation is identified, apprehended, prosecuted, or convicted and regardless of the familial relationship between the perpetrator and the victim."

Principle 10 declares that victims should be treated "with humanity and respect for their dignity and human rights." It also states that "appropriate measures should be taken to ensure their safety, physical and psychological well-being and privacy, as well as those of their families," and that "a victim who has suffered violence or trauma should benefit from special consideration and care to avoid his or her re-traumatization in the course of legal and administrative procedures designed to provide justice and reparation."

Principle 24 requires states to alert the public and especially victims of "all available legal, medical, psychological, social, administrative and all other services to which victims may have a right of access." The same Principle goes on to provide that "victims and their representatives should be entitled to seek and obtain information on the causes leading to their victimization and on the causes and conditions pertaining to the gross violations of international human rights law and serious violations of international humanitarian law and to learn the truth in regard to these violations." Principle 25 provides a general prohibition on discrimination.

SECTION 2: SELECTED DOMESTIC MODELS OF FAIRNESS

It is not possible to do justice to the diverse notions of fairness to be found in the world's nearly two hundred sovereign states with their distinctive political

---

101 Annexed to UN GA res. A/C.3/60/L.24.

and legal traditions. As a result, the notions of fairness discussed here are unavoidably selective. For purposes of this section, the focus is on relevant Anglo-American models. It is hoped that the reader will tolerate this emphasis in light of the previous (and complementary) treatment of international legal standards. Such standards, of course, represent the very closest approximation of a "universal" standard of fairness.

This section begins with a brief review of "due process" standards. The aim is to understand to what extent such standards could or should apply to truth commissions. This is followed by an examination of the "natural justice" standard applied to quasi-judicial and nonjudicial procedures in Commonwealth jurisdictions. Both of these concepts – due process and natural justice – fall within the broader concept of procedural fairness employed in this book. In the author's view, the term "procedural fairness" captures, better than any other, the commonplace but admirable idea that procedures that affect people's rights and interests should be fair in their design and operation. It is true that the term may have divergent meanings in particular jurisdictions.[102] But a full treatment of such distinctions is beyond the ambit of this book.[103] The section concludes with an analysis of the six so-called "cardinal principles" of fairness articulated by Lord Justice Salmon in his seminal 1966 report on Commonwealth commissions of inquiry.

Due process

The term "due process of law" (or simply "due process") will be familiar to any common law lawyer. Although due process may apply to a wide range of proceedings, it is a term that above all connotes the rights of accused persons at trial.

It would be unreasonable, as well as illogical, to hold truth commissions up to the standards of full due process. Truth commissions are not courts, and they make no determinations of guilt that would trigger binding civil or criminal penalties. The procedures they use do not, therefore, relate to due process in its traditional sense.

Yet truth commissions increasingly possess and exercise powers that raise a host of due process–like concerns. For example, a truth commission may have the power to subpoena witnesses for testimony and documents, and to conduct searches and seizures of private property. Alternatively, truth commissions may

---

102 In Canada, for example, the term "procedural fairness" is often used to describe a notion of fairness that goes beyond the traditional limits of natural justice. *See generally* D. Mullan, *Administrative Law* (Toronto: Irwin Law, 2001).

103 So too would be any in-depth treatment of related theories such as John Rawls's concept of "procedural justice." *See* J. Rawls, *A Theory of Justice* (Cambridge, MA: Harvard University Press, 1971).

adversely implicate perpetrators in a number of ways, including by disclosures at public hearings and by the publication of findings of individual responsibility for past crimes. Such powers and actions raise a host of issues: Should an implicated individual have the right to confront and cross-examine his or her accuser? Should victims have the right to accuse in anonymity? Should those implicated have the right to free legal counsel or the right not to be compelled to give self-incriminating testimony? These and other procedural issues are of importance to victims, witnesses, perpetrators, and the general public.

The assertion in this book is that where a right or legal entitlement implicated in a trial closely overlaps with one implicated in a truth commission procedure (*e.g.*, the right against compelled self-incrimination), due process standards provide a useful benchmark of fairness. In such instances, a truth commission should give serious consideration to the due process standard and, absent a compelling reason to do otherwise, apply it. Where such overlap is absent, however, the transfer of due process standards is generally inappropriate. Admittedly, the degree of overlap can sometimes be ambiguous. For example, both truth commissions and courts may hold public hearings, which at first glance might imply that truth commissions should adopt due process standards. But as previously explained, truth commission hearings are of a fundamentally different character; there are no disputing parties, there is no acting judge or jury, and there is no final judgment resulting in criminal or civil liability. The case for imposing all the due process standards on truth commission public hearings is, therefore, rather weak.

Due process standards derive from many sources: constitutions, statutes, jurisprudence, and international law. One of the earliest written expressions of the due process concept appeared in the Magna Carta 1215,[104] in which the king of England declared, "No Freeman shall be taken, or imprisoned, or be disseised of his Freehold, or liberties, or free Customs, or be outlawed, or exiled, or any otherwise destroyed; nor will we pass upon him, nor condemn him, but by lawful Judgment of his peers, or by the Law of the Land." Later English expressions of the concept can be found, for example, in the Petition of Right 1627[105] and the Bill of Rights 1689.[106] Comparable provisions may also

---

104 17 Joh.

105 3 Car. I c.1. The Petition was sent by Parliament to King Charles I complaining of a series of breaches of law. The Petition sought recognition of various principles, including the principle that there should be no imprisonment without cause. King Charles accepted the Petition.

106 1 Wm. & Mary, 2d Sess. (1689) c.2. The Bill's full title was "An Act Declaring the Rights and Liberties of the Subject and Settling the Succession of the Crown." It declared, *inter alia*, that "excessive bail ought not to be required, nor excessive fines imposed; nor cruel and unusual punishments inflicted."

be found, *inter alia*, in the French Declaration of the Rights of Man and of the Citizen 1789.[107]

Today, however, the term "due process of law" is predominantly used in, and associated with, the United States. The Fifth Amendment to the US Constitution, which applies to the federal government, its agencies, and its courts, provides:

> No person shall be held to answer for a capital, or otherwise infamous crime, unless on a presentment or indictment of a Grand Jury, except in cases arising in the land or naval forces, or in the Militia, when in actual service in time of War or public danger; nor shall any person be subject for the same offense to be twice put in jeopardy of life or limb; nor shall be compelled in any criminal case to be a witness against himself, nor be deprived of life, liberty, or property, without *due process of law*; nor shall private property be taken for public use, without just compensation. (Emphasis added.)

Section 1 of the Fourteenth Amendment to the US Constitution, which applies to state governments, their agencies, and their courts, uses almost identical language:

> No State shall make or enforce any law which shall abridge the privileges or immunities of citizens of the United States; nor shall any State deprive any person of life, liberty, or property, without *due process of law*; nor deny to any person within its jurisdiction the equal protection of the laws. (Emphasis added.)

The Sixth Amendment (which deals with rights in criminal trials),[108] the Seventh Amendment (which deals with rights in civil trials),[109] and the Eighth

---

107 The Declaration is appended to the French Constitution of 1791. Article 7 of the Declaration provides in part: "No person shall be accused, arrested, or imprisoned except in the cases and according to the forms prescribed by law."

108 "In all criminal prosecutions, the accused shall enjoy the right to a speedy and public trial, by an impartial jury of the State and district wherein the crime shall have been committed, which district shall have been previously ascertained by law, and to be informed of the nature and cause of the accusation; to be confronted with the witnesses against him; to have compulsory process for obtaining witnesses in his favor, and to have the Assistance of Counsel for his defense."

109 "In Suits at common law, where the value in controversy shall exceed twenty dollars, the right of trial by jury shall be preserved, and no fact tried by a jury, shall be otherwise re-examined in any Court of the United States, than according to the rules of the common law."

Amendment (which deals with proportionality of criminal punishments)[110] are also integral parts of the US notion of due process.

The US Supreme Court considers due process to have both a substantive and procedural dimension. Substantive due process minimally consists in the notion that laws must, in content as well as in application, be reasonable and fair (*i.e.*, there can be no *arbitrary* deprivation of life, liberty, or property). Procedural due process, by contrast, minimally consists in an individual's right to be heard concerning deprivations of life, liberty, or property, as well as the right to be notified of any charges or proceedings involving him or her.[111] The content of due process can, however, extend much further. It may encompass: (1) *pretrial rights* such as the prohibition on arbitrary arrest and detention, the right to know reasons for arrest, the right to legal counsel, *habeas corpus*, and the prohibition of torture and incommunicado detention; (2) *trial rights* such as equality of access to court, equality before the court, the right to a fair hearing, the right to a public hearing, the right to a presumption of innocence, the right to prompt notice of the nature and cause of adverse charges, the right to adequate time and facilities to prepare a defense, the right to trial without undue delay, the right to defend oneself with the assistance of counsel, the right to examine witnesses, the right to an interpreter, the right against self-incrimination, and the right against double jeopardy and retroactive punishment; and (3) *post-trial rights* such as the right to appeal and the right to compensation for any miscarriage of justice.[112]

Most, if not all, of these elements of due process apply in the context of criminal proceedings. However, in other instances – for example in civil, administrative, or inquisitorial proceedings – many of these same elements will not apply to the same extent. As noted earlier, the process that is "due" to an individual will depend on the nature of the proceeding, together with a wide range of other factors.

The US Supreme Court decision in *Hannah v. Larche*[113] provides an especially helpful articulation of the parameters of due process in noncriminal contexts. The case concerned the US Commission on Civil Rights, which was established in 1957 by the US Congress pursuant to the Civil Rights Act of 1957[114] for the purposes of investigating allegations of racial discrimination against

---

110 "Excessive bail shall not be required, nor excessive fines imposed, nor cruel and unusual punishments inflicted."

111 Without prior notification, the right to be heard would of course be a hollow principle.

112 *See generally* J. Orth, *Due Process of Law: A Brief History* (Lawrence, KS: University Press of Kansas, 2003); Human Rights First, *What Is a Fair Trial?: A Basic Guide to Legal Standards and Practice* (2000), available at http://www.humanrightsfirst.org/pubs/descriptions/fairtrialcontents.htm.

113 363 US 420, 442 (1960).

114 71 Stat. 634, 42 U.S.C. 1975–1975e.

black voters, examining and gathering relevant information, and reporting to the president and to Congress. The commission was empowered to subpoena witnesses and documents, as well as to conduct oral hearings. Controversially, the commission adopted rules of procedure that denied persons accused of discrimination the right to know the specific charges against them (or the identity of their accusers), and the right to cross-examine witnesses. The voting registrars in the state of Louisiana who were accused of racial discrimination challenged these procedures as violations of constitutional due process. However, the court rejected their petition, finding the commission's procedures consistent with the US Constitution.

In reaching this conclusion, Chief Justice Earl Warren, speaking for the majority, began by examining the particular nature of the commission's proceedings. He explained:

> It does not adjudicate. It does not hold trials or determine anyone's civil or criminal liability. It does not issue orders. Nor does it indict, punish, or impose any legal sanctions. It does not make determinations depriving anyone of his life, liberty, or property. In short, the Commission does not and cannot take any affirmative action which will affect an individual's legal rights. The only purpose of its existence is to find facts which may subsequently be used as the basis for legislative or executive action.[115]

He then went on to consider the scope of due process applicable to the commission. His analysis is worth quoting at length:

> "Due process" is an elusive concept. Its exact boundaries are indefinable, and its content varies according to specific factual contexts. Thus, when governmental agencies adjudicate or make binding determinations which directly affect the legal rights of individuals, it is imperative that those agencies use the procedures which have traditionally been associated with the judicial process. On the other hand, when governmental action does not partake of adjudication, as for example, when a general fact-finding investigation is being conducted, it is not necessary that the full panoply of judicial procedures be used. Therefore, as a generalization, it can be said that due process embodies the differing rules of fair play, which through the years, have become associated with differing types of proceedings. Whether the Constitution requires that a particular right obtain in a specific proceeding depends upon a complexity of factors. The nature of the alleged right involved, the nature of the proceeding, and the possible burden on that proceeding, are all

---

115 *Hannah v. Larche*, above note 113, at 441.

considerations that must be taken into account. An analysis of these factors demonstrates why it is that the particular rights claimed by the respondents need not be conferred upon those appearing before purely investigative agencies, of which the Commission on Civil Rights is one.

It is probably sufficient merely to indicate that the rights claimed by respondents are normally associated only with adjudicatory proceedings, and that since the Commission does not adjudicate, it need not be bound by adjudicatory procedures. Yet, the respondents contend, and the court below implied, that such procedures are required since the Commission's proceedings might irreparably harm those being investigated by subjecting them to public opprobrium and scorn, the distinct likelihood of losing their jobs, and the possibility of criminal prosecutions. That any of these consequences will result is purely conjectural. There is nothing in the record to indicate that such will be the case or that past Commission hearings have had any harmful effects upon witnesses appearing before the Commission. However, even if such collateral consequences were to flow from the Commission's investigations, they would not be the result of any affirmative determinations made by the Commission, and they would not affect the legitimacy of the Commission's investigative function.

On the other hand, the investigative process could be completely disrupted if investigative hearings were transformed into trial-like proceedings, and if persons who might be indirectly affected by an investigation were given an absolute right to cross-examine every witness called to testify. Fact-finding agencies without any power to adjudicate would be diverted from their legitimate duties and would be plagued by the injection of collateral issues that would make the investigation interminable. Even a person not called as a witness could demand the right to appear at the hearing, cross-examine any witness whose testimony or sworn affidavit allegedly defamed or incriminated him, and call an unlimited number of witnesses of his own selection. This type of proceeding would make a shambles of the investigation and stifle the agency in its gathering of facts.

In addition to these persuasive considerations, we think it is highly significant that the Commission's procedures are not historically foreign to other forms of investigation under our system. Far from being unique, the Rules of Procedure adopted by the Commission are similar to those which . . . have traditionally governed the proceedings of the vast majority of governmental investigating agencies.[116]

---

116 *Ibid.*, at 442–4.

As examples of analogous investigative proceedings, the Chief Justice cited the standard legislative committee (which has rarely "afforded the procedural rights normally associated with an adjudicative proceeding"), the Federal Trade Commission (which "could not conduct an efficient investigation if persons being investigated were permitted to convert the investigation into a trial"), the Securities and Exchange Commission (which limits due process in order to "prevent the sterilization of investigations by burdening them with trial-like procedures"), and the presidential commission.[117] But the court did not stop there. It proceeded to apply the same test to "the oldest and, perhaps, the best known of all investigative bodies, the grand jury."[118] The Chief Justice wrote:

> It has never been considered necessary to grant a witness summoned before the grand jury the right to refuse to testify merely because he did not have access to the identity and testimony of prior witnesses. Nor has it ever been considered essential that a person being investigated by the grand jury be permitted to come before that body and cross-examine witnesses who may have accused him of wrongdoing. Undoubtedly, the procedural rights claimed by the respondents have not been extended to grand jury hearings because of the disruptive influence their injection would have on the proceedings, and also because the grand jury merely investigates and reports. It does not try.[119]

Ultimately, the court concluded that the Civil Rights Commission's rules of procedure conformed to the requirements of due process because of "the purely investigative nature of the Commission's proceedings, the burden that the claimed rights would place upon those proceedings, and the traditional procedure of investigating agencies in general . . ."[120] In a concurring opinion, Justice Felix Frankfurter stated, "The precise nature of the interest alleged to be adversely affected or of the freedom of action claimed to be curtailed, the manner in which this is to be done and the reasons for doing it, the balance of individual hurt and the justifying public good – these and such like are the considerations, avowed or implicit, that determine the judicial judgment when appeal is made to 'due process.'"[121]

Justice John M. Harlan, in dissent, argued that the inquiry was tantamount to "government by Inquisition," involving the "farming out" of "pieces of

---

117 *Ibid.*, at 448.
118 *Ibid.*
119 *Ibid.*, at 448–9.
120 *Ibid.*, at 451.
121 *Ibid.*, at 487–8.

trials" to avoid the highest strictures of due process.[122] However, subsequent US Supreme Court jurisprudence in analogous cases has affirmed the reasoning of the majority in *Hannah v. Larche*.[123] Later, in Section 3 of this chapter, similar reasoning is employed in proposing a conception of procedural fairness for truth commissions.

Before leaving the subject of due process, a word must be said about the comparative criminal procedure of common law and civil law systems, for one would not wish to convey the impression that due process is exclusively an Anglo-American or common law preserve.

Common law criminal trials are usually described as "adversarial" or "accusatorial." The pretrial investigations, as well as the trial proceedings, are party-driven, often featuring vigorous cross-examination. Judges decide questions of law while juries, if any, decide questions of fact. There are many strict, exclusionary rules of evidence.[124] Great reliance is placed on testimonial evidence, and statements are invariably made under solemn oath or affirmation.

---

122 *Ibid.*, at 508.

123 *See, e.g., Cafeteria Workers v. McElroy*, 367 U.S. 886 (1961), at 894–5 ("The Fifth Amendment does not require a trial-type hearing in every conceivable case of government impairment of private interest . . . The very nature of due process negates any concept of inflexible procedures universally applicable to every imaginable situation. [C]onsideration of what procedures due process may require under any given set of circumstances must begin with a determination of the precise nature of the government function involved as well as of the private interest that has been affected by governmental action."); *Morrissey v. Brewer*, 408 U.S. 471 (1972), at 481 ("Whether any procedural protections are due depends on the extent to which an individual will be 'condemned to suffer grievous loss' . . . The question is not merely the 'weight' of the individual's interest, but whether the nature of the interest is one within the contemplation of the 'liberty or property' language of the Fourteenth Amendment . . . Once it is determined that due process applies, the question remains what process is due. It has been said so often by this Court and others as not to require citation of authority that due process is flexible and calls for such procedural protections as the particular situation demands . . . To say that the concept of due process is flexible does not mean that judges are at large to apply it to any and all relationships. Its flexibility is in its scope once it has been determined that some process is due; it is a recognition that not all situations calling for procedural safeguards call for the same kind of procedure."); *Board of Curators, Univ. of Mo. v. Horowitz*, 435 U.S. 78 (1978) ("We have emphasized many times that '[t]he very nature of due process negates any concept of inflexible procedures universally applicable to every imaginable situation' . . . what process is due will vary 'according to specific factual contexts.'").

124 One scholar explains the rationale for the common law's exclusionary rules as follows: "[T]he adversary system in its modern variant is inspired to a great extent by an attitude of distrust of public officials and its complementary demand for safeguards against abuse. Accordingly, the adversary system is quite tolerant of evidentiary barriers limiting the search for truth for fear of abuse of governmental power." M. Damaska, "Evidentiary Barriers to Conviction and Two Models of Criminal Procedure" (1973) 121 *U. Pa. L. Rev.* 506, at 583.

The determination of guilt is decided at a separate hearing from the determination of sentence. And the overall conduct of the trial is highly rigid and formal. Criminal trials in the civil law tradition are quite different. They tend to be described as "inquisitorial" rather than adversarial,[125] and rarely feature cross-examination. Pretrial investigations and trial proceedings are often judge-driven rather than party-driven.[126] Cases are decided by judges, or by judges and laypersons who together decide both questions of law and fact. There are fewer exclusionary rules of evidence because laypersons can make factual determinations only in concordance with judges. Great reliance is placed on documentary evidence (previously compiled by an investigative magistrate or prosecutor), and witnesses, when they appear, do not always testify under oath. Guilt and punishment are determined within a single proceeding, rather than at two separate proceedings. And the overall conduct of the trial is less rigid and formal than its common law counterpart.[127]

This is admittedly a superficial description of the common law and civil law approaches. In fact, within each tradition there is great diversity. In the common law world, for example, criminal trials in the United States operate differently from criminal trials in the United Kingdom, and both in turn operate differently from criminal trials in Uganda or Sri Lanka. In the civil law world, criminal trials in France run differently from criminal trials in Germany, and both in turn run differently from criminal trials in Chile or Senegal.[128] There

---

125 According to some scholars, a better term to describe the civil law's criminal trials is "non-adversarial." The term "inquisitorial" appears to derive from the comparatively active role played by the judge in such trials. *See* M. A. Glendon and others, *Comparative Legal Traditions*, 2d ed. (St. Paul, MN: West, 1999), at 99.

126 *See, e.g.,* s. 139 of Germany's Code of Civil Procedure, which has been called the "Magna Carta" of fair procedure. It obligates a judge to raise issues of law and fact not introduced by either party to trial, thus helping to ensure that cases are decided on their merits, and not on the quality of the lawyers who are appearing. *See also* IMT Charter art. 24(f), which entitled the Nuremberg Tribunal to "put any question to any witness and to any defendant, at any time." Under France's Code of Criminal Procedure (section 310), the presiding judge is able "to take all measures which he believes are useful to uncover the truth . . . During the course of the trial he may call, or if he wishes subpoena, and hear all persons or introduce any new piece of evidence which appears to him, according to the developments in court, to be useful for the determination of the truth . . ." Cited in S. C. Thaman, *Comparative Criminal Procedure* (Durham, NC: Carolina Academic Press, 2002), at 178 9. Note, however, that in some civil law jurisdictions (*e.g.,* Mexico), pretrial investigations and trial proceedings are prosecutor-driven, rather than judge-driven.

127 On the differences between criminal trials in the civil law and common law traditions generally, *see* Glendon and others, *Comparative Legal Traditions*, above note 125, at cc. 3 and 4; R. May and M. Wierda, *International Criminal Evidence* (Ardsley, NY: Transnational Publishers, 2003), at 17–18.

128 *See generally* R. Schlesinger and others, *Comparative Law* (New York: Foundation Press, 1998), at 509–39.

are also signs that the two traditions are beginning to influence each other, as some common law jurisdictions begin to adopt elements of the civil law model, and *vice versa.*[129] Still, the general descriptions of each tradition's criminal trial format hold.

In summary, then, the content of due process varies not only across but also within these two legal traditions, to say nothing of the Islamic legal tradition or the various hybrid traditions found throughout the developing world.[130] As one eminent scholar has explained, "Because the Anglo-American adversary-accusatory model is different from the inquisitorial-based model, and both are different from the Islamic model, the occurence, application, and effectiveness of [due process] rights will differ in the various systems."[131] Thus, for example the civil system's more informal, inquisitorial, and judge-driven format produces a rather different quality of due process than the common law. Yet it would be absurd to suggest that it produces less fair procedures or results. Instead, what the differences in common law and civil law approaches do suggest is that the objective of due process can be achieved by various means. There are, in short, different ways to conduct a fair trial.[132]

---

129   *Ibid.*, at 285, 526–9. The interface between the two traditions is also very much present in the field of international criminal law. International criminal tribunals have adopted a hybrid approach that borrows from both traditions. *See generally* May and Wierda, *International Criminal Evidence,* above note 127.

130   Because of colonialism, "almost every contemporary legal system has some characteristics associating it with either common law or civil law or both." Schlesinger and others, *Comparative Law,* above note 128, at 287. It is true that many legal systems (especially in Africa and Asia) retain significant components of non-European law. Also, in the Arab world, much law continues to be based in part on Islamic law. But the civil law and common law remain the touchstone legal traditions, with a few obvious exceptions, such as China and North Korea.

131   M. C. Bassiouni, "Human Rights in the Context of Criminal Justice: Identifying International Procedural Protections and Equivalent Protections in National Constitutions" (1993) 3 *Duke J. Comp. & Int'l L.* 235, at 274.

132   In point of fact, divergent state constitutions exhibit strongly overlapping commitment to due process or fair trial standards. A 1993 analysis of 139 constitutions revealed "an overwhelming affirmation" of such essential rights as the right to life, liberty, and security of the person (51 countries); the right to recognition before the law and equal protection of the laws (108 countries); the right to be free from arbitrary detentions (119 countries); the right to be free from torture and other cruel, inhuman, or degrading treatment or punishment (81 countries); the right to be presumed innocent (67 countries); the right to a fair trial (38 countries); the right to assistance of counsel (65 countries); the right to a speedy trial (43 countries); the right to an appeal (46 countries); the right to be protected from double jeopardy (51 countries); and the right to protection against *ex post facto* laws (96 countries). The same study further noted, "If the right to a fair trial (39 countries) is considered in conjunction with the right to a defense (45 countries), there exists a strong affirmation of the right to general fairness in criminal proceedings. The relatively high number of constitutions which guarantee the right to notice (51), to counsel of choice (47),

Natural justice

Any English or Commonwealth lawyer will instantly recognize the term "natural justice." Natural justice falls within, but short of, the broader concept of due process. It is intended to express the bare requirements of procedural fairness. Specifically, it concerns ideas derived from two Latin maxims: (1) *nemo debet esse judex in propia causa* (one should not be judge in one's own cause), and (2) *audi alteram partem* (both sides should be heard). The implication of the former is that one who is not impartial should not judge. The implication of the latter is that no one should be condemned, or have his or her rights adjudicated, without an opportunity to be heard.[133]

Although originally a concept that applied only to courts, today the term "natural justice" is most often associated with the field of administrative law, and in particular with the operation of administrative tribunals.[134] By design, administrative tribunal proceedings tend to be more informal, more inexpensive, and more expeditious than court proceedings, generally allowing greater flexibility in rules of evidence.[135] Like courts, however, administrative tribunals have an adjudicative function: they decide the merits of specific cases and make binding orders. In this respect, administrative tribunals are, in functional terms, more similar to courts than to truth commissions. There is, therefore, no suggestion that truth commissions be held *per se* to the procedural or evidentiary standards of administrative tribunals. Yet where a right or interest implicated in an administrative procedure overlaps with one implicated in a truth commission procedure – for example, where truth commissions hold public hearings or make factual determinations that could adversely affect individual reputations – natural justice, no less than due process, provides a relevant point of reference.

---

to a speedy trial (47), to appeal (59), and to protection against double jeopardy (59) also indicates that there is broad international acceptance of these more concrete aspects of the right to a fair trial." *Ibid.*, at 292. Without doubt, this overlap has much to do with the steady influence of human rights treaty law on domestic systems.

133 The principle may one day become constitutionally entrenched in European law. *See, e.g.,* EU Charter of Rights art. 101(2), wherein the "right to good administration" includes "the right of every person to be heard, before any individual measure which would affect him or her adversely is taken." Presumably such a right would not, however, preclude *ex parte* civil proceedings.

134 In English law, the decision of the House of Lords in *Ridge v. Baldwin* [1963] 2 All ER 66, marked the decisive turning point. In rejecting an approach focused on classifying a proceeding as either judicial (in which case natural justice applied) or nonjudicial (in which case it did not), the House of Lords held that the principles of natural justice encompassed any body making decisions that affected individual rights.

135 In common law jurisdictions, for example, administrative tribunals are generally not required to follow the best evidence rule, the rules of hearsay, or rules concerning opinion evidence.

The application of natural justice, though quite broad, is not infinitely elastic. Natural justice does not, in other words, apply in every situation. In particular, it tends not to apply "where the impugned conduct does not lead to a final determination of rights in issue but is merely of a preliminary or an advisory nature."[136] On its face, this basis for excluding the application of natural justice seems highly relevant to truth commissions, which, as we have seen, are investigatory bodies that generally lack the power to make final determinations.[137] Yet case law on natural justice does not provide a ready answer as to what is merely "preliminary," and hence outside its ambit. To be sure, in most if not all legal systems a prosecutor may decide to prosecute an alleged offender without providing him or her an opportunity to reply to the evidence at hand. Regulatory investigators may also not have to give implicated persons an opportunity to read or challenge a transcript containing adverse allegations before a final report is issued.[138] Yet, as the vast jurisprudence on natural justice makes clear, no two "preliminary" proceedings are alike; some may require natural justice, others may not. The answer in each case depends, *inter alia*, on the severity of the potential adverse consequences of the proceeding.[139]

Having said when natural justice might not apply, one must also specify when it surely does. As a general rule, natural justice applies "whenever the rights, property or legitimate expectations of an individual are affected."[140] *A fortiori* it applies to all judicial and quasi-judicial tribunals, because they each have an adjudicative function.[141] In addition, it generally applies to any proceeding where the following rights or interests are at stake: the right to liberty, property rights (especially realty), rights of employment and livelihood,[142]

---

136   G. A. Flick, *Natural Justice: Principles and Practical Application*, 2d ed. (Sydney: Butterworths, 1984), at 36. It may also not apply where there is a need to take urgent action (*ibid.*, at 37, 40–1) or where there is a right of appeal (*ibid.*, at 37, 41–3).

137   Here again, one must note the exceptions of South Africa (with its *sui generis* amnesty-granting power), Timor-Leste (with its *sui generis* power to formalize contracts of community service and reparation between perpetrators and communities), and Morocco (with its *sui generis* compensation-granting power). Each of these commissions made determinations of persons' civil rights and obligations.

138   Flick, *Natural Justice*, above note 136, at 43–4.

139   Mullan, *Administrative Law*, above note 102, at 395.

140   Flick, *Natural Justice*, above note 136, at 26–7.

141   D. Basu, *Comparative Administrative Law* (Calcutta: Sarkar and Sons, 1969), at 179; Mullan, *Administrative Law*, at 158. In some jurisdictions, such as Canada, the judicial/quasi-judicial distinction is no longer applied by courts. It has been replaced by a "functionalist" approach that eschews such categories and instead focuses on the character and context of the proceeding and the interests at stake. *Ibid.*, at 157–61.

142   Flick, *Natural Justice*, above note 136, at 29.

reputation rights,[143] economic privileges,[144] participation in clubs and other associations, and legitimate expectations.[145]

However, even if such rights or interests are present, one must still determine "how much" natural justice is required. Like due process, natural justice is a broad concept; depending on the case, all or only some of its components may apply.

The main components of natural justice are absence of bias, reasonable notice, cross-examination, legal representation, and the duty to give reasons. A brief discussion of each follows.

We have already observed that the absence of bias is the first leg of natural justice in English and Commonwealth law. The main forms of bias are the presence of a pecuniary interest in the matter at hand,[146] personal involvement arising from a prior or existing relationship, and prejudgment or predisposition.[147] The scope of the nonbias principle is, like other principles of law, a relative one. Depending on the jurisdiction and the case, one may be required to prove actual bias, a real likelihood or danger of bias, or merely a reasonable suspicion of bias.[148] Occasionally a person may directly express his or her prejudice before or during a proceeding, but in most cases actual bias will be difficult to establish. Courts, therefore, tend to focus on whether there is an appearance of bias.[149] The presence of bias triggers an automatic right to judicial review.

143 *Ibid.*, at 30–1. *See also* B. Jones and K. Thompson, "Administrative Law in the United Kingdom," in R. Seerden and F. Stroink, eds., *Administrative Law of the European Union, Its Member States and the United States* (Antwerp: Intersentia/Metro, 2002), at 247.

144 *See, e.g., Re Webb and Ontario Housing Corporation* (1978), 93 DLR (3d) 187 (Ontario Court of Appeal), in which persons benefiting from social assistance were entitled to a measure of natural justice when their continued eligibility for such assistance was in jeopardy.

145 Flick, *Natural Justice*, above note 136, at 33–6; Mullan, *Administrative Law*, above note 102, at 177–86 and 321–49.

146 The classic English case concerning this form of bias remains *Dimes v. Grand Junction Canal Properties* (1852) 3 House of Lords Cases 759 HL. The case was notably applied by the House of Lords in *Regina v. Bow Street Stipendiary Magistrate and Others Ex parte Pinochet Ugarte (no. 2)* [1999] 1 All ER 577 (H.L.), in which former Chilean president Augusto Pinochet was arrested in the UK pursuant to the request of a Spanish judge. Pinochet challenged the arrest on the basis that, as a former head of state, he enjoyed immunity from arrest and extradition. The House of Lords initially dismissed his claim, but the judgment had to be vacated because one of the judges on the panel was director of a charity division of Amnesty International, which was an intervening party in the proceeding.

147 Prejudgment can take at least two forms: preconceived opinions, or the commingling of investigative and adjudicative functions in one person or body. Flick, *Natural Justice*, at 177. *See also* Basu, *Comparative Administrative Law*, above note 141, at 179.

148 Flick, *Natural Justice*, above note 136, at 148.

149 The standard test in the UK remains what a "reasonable person" (*i.e.*, the judge) would think. Mullan, *Administrative Law*, above note 102, at 327–8.

The second main leg of natural justice is the *audi alteram partem* principle.[150] It consists of an obligation to provide reasonable notice to a person about a proceeding in which that person is adversely implicated, and to provide an opportunity for the person to present his or her case. To be "reasonable," the notice must generally specify the time, place, and format of the hearing or proceeding, and the legal and factual basis of the adverse allegations;[151] failing that, the notice will usually be deemed defective.[152] Concerning the format of any right of reply, there is no necessary obligation to afford an in-person, oral hearing. Provided a party is given a reasonable opportunity to present his or her case, and provided the possible adverse consequences to the individual's rights or interests are minor, it may be consistent with the *audi alteram* principle to permit only written representations. This helps preserve the parallel objective of procedural efficiency, without offending fairness.[153] Electronic hearings, another alternative, may also comply with the requirements of the *audi alteram* principle.[154]

Another component of the *audi alteram* principle, namely the right to cross-examine one's accusers, is subject to restrictions too. This is hardly surprising. The efficiency gains of quasi-judicial and nonjudicial mechanisms would quickly vanish if cross-examination was considered an essential component of natural justice in the way it is for courtroom trials in the common law world. Consequently, administrative tribunals and investigative bodies frequently prefer various alternatives to cross-examination, including written submissions, private interviews, oral submissions not involving cross-examination (*e.g.,*

---

150   The right to a hearing was considered as a general principle of European Community law in *Transocean Marine Paint Association v. Commission* [1974] E.C.R. 1063 ("a person whose interests are perceptibly affected by the decision taken by a public authority must be given the opportunity to make his point of view known").

151   It is not necessary to put tentative conclusions to the person in order to give him or her a chance to refute them. It may be sufficient to describe what has been said against him or her by other persons or in documents. *Maxwell v. Department of Trade and Industry* [1974] 1 Queen's Bench 523 (Court of Appeal).

152   Flick, *Natural Justice*, above note 136, at 67. Mullan states, "[T]he requirements of notice will be more rigorous the nearer the nature of the decision-making process in question comes to approximating the paradigmatic kind of case arising in ordinary criminal or civil litigation." *Administrative Law*, above note 102, at 233.

153   Flick, *Natural Justice*, above note 136, at 14–18; Mullan, *Administrative Law*, above note 102, at 245. In *Kindler v. Canada (Minister of Justice)* [1991] 2 SCR 779, the Supreme Court of Canada held that even an extradition could be carried out purely on the basis of written submissions. In a subsequent case, *Baker v. Canada (Minister of Citizenship and Immigration)* [1999] 2 SCR 817, the Court similarly held that a written submission would suffice in the case of a foreign national who stayed in Canada past the date of her visa and who, on humanitarian grounds, was seeking permission to apply for permanent residence without leaving Canada.

154   *See, e.g.,* the 1994 amendments to the Ontario *Statutory Powers Procedures Act*, RSO 1990, c.S.5.2 (as amended by SO 1994, c.27 and SO 1997, c.23).

prehearing conferences to define the areas of dispute), and the right to respond to adverse evidence and submit questions to witnesses through the adjudicator.[155] Alternatives to cross-examination are especially welcome when witness credibility is not a major concern, or when the security or well-being of a witness is not assured, as in cases involving sexual misconduct.[156]

As with the other components of natural justice, the right to counsel is also restricted in various ways in the context of quasi-judicial and nonjudicial proceedings. The reasons are no different. To allow an unrestricted role for counsel would amount to an invitation to re-create the court setting that the administrative or investigative procedure was meant to mitigate.[157] Where, however, a proceeding involves particularly complex legal and factual issues, there will tend to be a greater obligation to allow for legal representation.[158]

The final frontier of natural justice is the duty of an administrative or investigative body to give reasons for the decisions it makes. This is, it seems, the least settled aspect of natural justice. In common law jurisdictions, in contrast to most civil law jurisdictions,[159] there is still no duty to provide reasons in the absence of a statutory requirement to do so.[160] Such a requirement, it is argued, would create procedural delays in a setting that is intended to be more informal.[161] Yet the concept of a duty to give reasons is gaining favor, since it tends to advance an administrative or investigative body's transparency and accountability.[162] A duty to give reasons is most likely to be found where there

---

155 *See, e.g., Pergamon Press Ltd* [1971] 1 Chancery 388 (Court of Appeal), at 400, where inspectors appointed under the UK Companies Act were viewed as "masters of their own procedure" and hence not bound to provide a right of cross-examination to "a person who is at risk of being criticized" by them.

156 Mullan, *Administrative Law*, above note 102, at 287–90.

157 Flick, *Natural Justice*, above note 136, at 179.

158 Mullan, *Administrative Law*, above note 102, at 262.

159 *See* Thaman, *Comparative Criminal Procedure*, above note 126, at 189.

160 "The most common defence of this position was the argument by way of analogy to the situation in the regular courts. If the courts themselves did not have to give reasons in justification of their judgments, there was simply no basis for the imposition of such a requirement on other adjudicative fora let alone those charged with the exercise of broad statutory discretions." Mullan, *Administrative Law*, above note 102, at 306–7. *But see, e.g.,* section 33(2) of the South African Constitution, which provides: "Everyone whose rights have been adversely affected by administrative action has the right to be given written reasons." *See also* EU Charter of Rights art. 101(2), wherein the "right to good administration" includes "the obligation of the administration to give reasons for its decisions."

161 *See* Jones and Thompson, "Administrative Law in the United Kingdom," above note 143, at 248.

162 *Ibid.,* at 248–9; Flick, *Natural Justice*, above note 136, at 117. A duty to give reasons was affirmed in the case of *Baker v. Canada (Minister of Citizenship and Immigration),* above note 153. In continental Europe, the duty to give reasons is seen as a "guarantee against arbitrary justice." Thaman, *Comparative Criminal Procedure*, above note 126, at 207.

are fundamental interests or rights at stake.[163] At its most general level, the duty consists in setting out the key findings, and the factual and legal basis for making such findings.

Many of these principles arise again in Part II of the book. For present purposes, it is sufficient to reiterate that natural justice bears directly on many dimensions of truth commission work. At the same time, its demands – like the demands of due process – vary according to the particular body's composition and function, the severity of available sanctions, relevant statutory provisions, and the facts of the case.

Lord Justice Salmon's cardinal principles

In Chapter 1, there was a discussion of the Commonwealth commission of inquiry tradition. It is recalled that Commonwealth commissions of inquiry generally have all the powers of a court in relation to matters of attendance of witnesses and the production of documents and evidence. Witnesses appearing before such commissions also tend to enjoy the same privileges and immunities as in a court of law. Unlike a court or an administrative tribunal, however, a Commonwealth commission of inquiry does not resolve disputes between parties or make individual determinations of civil or criminal responsibility. It is a purely investigative procedure.

The Commonwealth commission of inquiry is the closest functional equivalent of a truth commission, and may sometimes be characterized as one even if it is not so titled.[164] As previously noted, however, there are many significant differences between a truth commission and a typical Commonwealth commission of inquiry. First, a truth commission usually conducts itself in a victim-centered manner. By contrast, Commonwealth commissions of inquiry tend to adopt a more lawyer-driven approach focused less on dignifying victims than on getting to the facts.[165] Second, truth commissions frequently cope with an acute caseload problem: their investigation will often cover thousands of individual cases committed over broad expanses of time and geography. In contrast, Commonwealth commissions of inquiry usually focus on a specific event, institution, or theme that is engulfed in public controversy.[166] Third,

---

163 *See* Mullan, *Administrative Law*, above note 102, at 309–10, where he reviews recent English case law on this point.

164 *See* Chapter 1, Section 2.

165 A major innovation of truth commissions, especially in the context of public hearings, is to make the role of lawyers much more peripheral while still preserving the solemnity and legality of the proceedings.

166 This fact also helps to explain why truth commissions tend to be much larger operations than standard Commonwealth commissions of inquiry. Truth commissions, especially contemporary ones, frequently establish multiple offices and employ much larger numbers of

because they tend to be established in times of political or postconflict transition, truth commissions often face much higher security risks in carrying out their mission than do Commonwealth commissions of inquiry. Fourth, truth commissions often comprise many commissioners coming from a wide range of disciplines and backgrounds, all of whom may be appointed through procedures that involve broad public input, including direct nominations. By contrast, a standard Commonwealth commission of inquiry is presided over by a single judge who is usually selected by the executive branch without any meaningful public consultation or involvement. Finally, it is predominantly in relation to truth commissions that additional (and unusual) functions are grafted on. For example, the truth commissions in South Africa, Timor-Leste, and Morocco wielded, respectively, the power to grant amnesty for human rights violations, the power to formalize contracts of community service with perpetrators, and the power to grant victim compensation. In Sierra Leone and the DRC, truth commissions were encouraged to involve themselves in the resolution of local conflicts.[167] As will be seen, these and other differences between truth commissions and Commonwealth commissions of inquiry have implications for this book's proposed conception of procedural fairness.

Most Commonwealth states have decades of experience in the use of Commonwealth commissions of inquiry. In some states, such as Canada, such commissions of inquiry are established with surprising frequency.[168] In the United Kingdom, by contrast, only a small number have been set up.[169] Many of those established up until the 1960s were apparently a source of public dissatisfaction.[170] This led the UK government to appoint a Royal Commission in 1966 to make recommendations on how to improve the functioning of inquiries.[171]

---

staff. Paradoxically, truth commissions tend to cost much less than Commonwealth commissions of inquiry – something that is explained less by differences in state finances than by the more limited role of legal counsel in truth commissions. The fees of legal counsel tend to comprise the largest category of expenditure of a typical Commonwealth commission of inquiry

167 *The Truth and Reconciliation Act 2000* (Sierra Leone), art. 7(2); *Law 04/018 (2004) Concerning the Organization, Powers and Functions of the Truth and Reconciliation Commission* (DRC), art. 5.

168 *See* Chapter 1, Section 3.

169 Since 1990, for example, only four have been established: the so-called Shipman Inquiry (Department of Health), the Bloody Sunday Inquiry (Northern Ireland Office), the Public Inquiry into the Shootings at Dunblane Primary School (Scottish Office), and the North Wales Child Abuse Inquiry (Welsh Office).

170 L. Blom-Cooper, "Public Inquiries" (1993) 46 *Current Legal Problems* 204, at 207.

171 Reform-oriented reviews of commissions of inquiry have been conducted in many Commonwealth states. In Canada alone, *see, e.g.,* Canada Law Reform Commission, Working Paper 17, *Administrative Law: Commissions of Inquiry* (Ottawa: The Commission, 1977); Ontario Law Reform Commission, *Report on Public Inquiries* (Toronto: The Commission,

Lord Justice Salmon (as he then was) headed the Royal Commission. In his final report, he laid down six "cardinal principles" of fair procedure that he urged all future commissions of inquiry to observe:

1. Before any person becomes involved in an inquiry the tribunal must be satisfied that there are circumstances which affect him and which the tribunal proposes to investigate.
2. Before any person who is involved in an inquiry is called as a witness he should be informed of any allegations which are made against him and the substance of the evidence in support of them.
3. (a) He should be given an adequate opportunity of preparing his case and of being assisted by legal advisors; (b) His legal expenses should normally be met out of public funds.
4. He should have the opportunity of being examined by his own solicitor or counsel and of stating his case in public at the inquiry.
5. Any material witnesses he wishes called at the inquiry should, if reasonably practicable, be heard.
6. He should have the opportunity of testing by cross-examination conducted by his own solicitor or counsel any evidence which may affect him.

Since the Royal Commission issued its report, these cardinal principles have profoundly influenced the procedures used by all manner of inquiries established in the United Kingdom.[172] For example, the "Salmon letter" – a letter giving prior notice of potential criticism that an individual could face in the course of the inquiry or in a final report – has become a standard feature of UK inquiry practice. The cardinal principles have also, it seems, influenced law and practice in other Commonwealth jurisdictions.[173]

On their face, Lord Justice Salmon's cardinal principles hardly seem objectionable. Indeed, they aim to set commendably high standards of procedural fairness. And yet, it is an open question to what extent the cardinal principles are well suited to the purely investigative character of a commission of inquiry.

The Royal Commission's report began, properly, with a clear distinction between common law court proceedings, which are adversarial, and

---

1992); and Alberta Law Reform Institute, Report no. 62, *Proposals for the Reform of the Public Inquiries Act* (Edmonton: The Institute, 1992).

172 R. Scott, "Procedures at Inquiries: The Duty to be Fair" (1995) 11 *LQR* 596, at 601. *See also* the Consultation Report to the *Inquiries Act*, 2005 (UK), at para. 83.

173 *See, e.g.*, Z. Segal, "The Power to Probe into Matters of Vital Public Importance" (1983–4) 58 *Tul. L. Rev.* 941, at 944–5; Canada Law Reform Commission, *Administrative Law; Du Preez and Another v. Truth and Reconciliation Commission* (South African Appellate Court), 1997 (3) SA 204, at 218.

Commonwealth commissions of inquiry, which are inquisitorial. The report states: "It is inherent in the inquisitorial procedure that there is no *lis*[suit] . . . There is no plaintiff or defendant, no prosecutor or accused; there are no pleadings defining issues to be tried, no charges, indictments or depositions."[174] It is all the more curious, therefore, that the Salmon principles are so adversarial in tone and content. They seem aimed at making inquiry procedures more, not less, courtlike.[175]

The second cardinal principle, for example, declares an individual's right to be informed of adverse "allegations" and the substance of the supporting evidence. The word "allegations" seems misplaced, there not being any parties in the litigation sense.[176] Also, a commission obligation to disclose the substance of its adverse evidence could seriously slow down its work. According to one seasoned observer, the strict application of this rule has turned inquiries in the United Kingdom into "a series of mini-trials" and "significantly lengthened the time taken to inquire and to report."[177]

The third principle – that an implicated individual should be given adequate opportunity to prepare his "case" and be assisted by legal advisors paid by the state – also seems like an importation from the court process. There is neither a true "case" (in the litigation sense) nor any legal consequence an inquiry could impose that would in each instance warrant a right to state-paid legal assistance. The individual is not on trial, but merely an interested party to an official investigation.

The same concern applies to the fourth principle. It prescribes the opportunity to be "examined" by one's own counsel and to publicly state one's "case" at the inquiry. This seems, once again, to transpose the adversarial features of a common law court onto a commission of inquiry. Sir Richard Scott, who

---

174 *Report of the Royal Commission on Tribunals of Inquiry*, 1966 (Cmnd 3121 London), at para. 30.

175 *See, e.g.*, A. Hegarty, "Truth, Law and Official Denial: The Case of Bloody Sunday," in W. A. Schabas and S. Darcy, eds., *Truth Commissions and Courts: The Tension between Criminal Justice and Truth* (Dordrecht: Kluwer, 2004), 199 at 237, where the author notes the following about the Bloody Sunday Inquiry's application of the Salmon cardinal principles: "Whilst the Inquiry regards itself as inquisitorial, the oral hearings are in fact highly adversarial, with the consequence that some witnesses have had the disadvantages of both approaches and the advantages of neither." She further notes, "For many of the civilian witnesses testifying before the Bloody Sunday Inquiry, the experience has been a traumatic, terrifying one. They are unable to come and simply 'tell their story': they are interrupted by questions and confronted by transcripts of interviews given years ago. Their incomplete memories, the differences however slight from statements made at the time or years later to journalists, are subtly proffered as reasons to disbelieve their evidence. Some have left the Inquiry feeling worse than before." *Ibid.*, at 242.

176 Scott, "Procedures at Inquiries," above note 172, at 603.

177 Blom-Cooper, "Public Inquiries," above note 170, at 215.

headed a UK inquiry into the export of defense equipment to Iraq, commented: "The distinction between examination-in-chief, cross-examination and re-examination is meaningless. All questions to the witness are part of the investigative process designed to uncover the truth about the matter under investigation. They are not designed to prove or disprove a 'case.'"[178]

The final Salmon principle, which would provide an implicated individual the unqualified right to cross-examine "any evidence which may affect him," goes the furthest of all. While cross-examination may occasionally be appropriate (*e.g.*, for inquiries focused on a specific event and affecting a small number of individuals), it would produce very ill effects for the vast majority of Commonwealth commissions of inquiry. It would cause significant, and ultimately self-destructive, delays.[179] It should be a privilege, not a right.[180]

In questioning Lord Justice Salmon's principles, there is no intention to diminish the importance of protecting an individual's right against arbitrary attacks on reputation. That right is, after all, a human right. But reputation rights do not exist in a vacuum; they must be balanced against legitimate public interests such as the right to know the truth about certain controversial or opprobrious events. It is also reasonable to question why a commission of inquiry should provide greater procedural protections for reputation rights than would a court. As Sir Richard Scott remarked:

> The reputation of a stranger to [a particular] litigation may be blackened by evidence given to the court by others. The witness . . . has no means of defending his or her reputation. He is not allowed to address the court nor to cross-examine the witnesses who have given the hurtful evidence nor to give evidence in rebuttal. In criminal cases, the victim of an assault may be outraged by allegations made by the accused about the circumstances that led to the assault . . . The victim has no right to intervene.[181]

---

178 Scott, "Procedures at Inquiries," above note 172, at 605.

179 *Ibid.*, at 609. At 610, Scott proposes a less extreme alternative: "Notice of any adverse evidence and an opportunity to those affected to give their own evidence in answer, coupled with an opportunity to make representations, including further evidence, on any proposed adverse conclusions, would, in my opinion, constitute in most cases adequate procedural safeguard against unfairness." At 612, Scott discusses the case of *Pergamon Press Ltd.* [1971] 1 Ch. 388 (Court of Appeal), in which Denning M. R. held that implicated persons in a corporate investigation could not see adverse transcripts, or cross-examine witnesses, or see proposed passages in a final report.

180 Blom-Cooper, "Public Inquiries," above note 170, at 216: "Cross-examination by parties of witnesses has never been a right, but only a privilege to be exercised under the control of the inquiring body."

181 Scott, "Procedures at Inquiries," above note 172, at 599.

For better or worse, Commonwealth commissions of inquiry have adopted a rather trial-like format consistent with the recommendations of the Salmon report. The typical commission of inquiry employs time-consuming public examination and cross-examination, treating public hearings primarily as engines for truth seeking, rather than for truth telling.[182] While this may produce a very public form of investigation and hence contribute to greater public trust, it can also produce delays and expenditures that undermine a commission's actual purpose.[183]

In a significant development, the UK parliament adopted the *Inquiries Act* in April 2005. The law aims to consolidate three kinds of inquiry under one statute: inquiries initiated by ministers under subject-specific legislation (*e.g.*, an inquiry launched pursuant to the *Police Act*), inquiries created by ministers on a nonstatutory basis (*e.g.*, the 2003 Hutton inquiry into the circumstances surrounding the death of Dr. David Kelly, the source of a BBC report that adversely implicated the government and its claims about Iraqi weapons), and inquiries established by ministers pursuant to the now repealed *Tribunals of Inquiry (Evidence) Act* of 1921. It is noteworthy that the law's express purpose is to provide a legal framework in which future inquiries, whether statutory or nonstatutory, can operate "in reasonable time and at a reasonable cost."[184] It is also noteworthy that article 18(3) of the *Act* requires the chair to "act with fairness and with regard also to the need to avoid any unnecessary cost (whether to public funds or to witnesses or to others)" in deciding on

---

182 Most Commonwealth commissions of inquiry seek to gather as much evidence at the public hearings as they do outside of them. "Public inquiries generally proceed through the 'trial' format: a process that proceeds through the oral questioning of a witness and then cross-examination, all in the presence of a presiding judge . . . The 'trial format' tends to be an extremely slow and tedious means of gathering and presenting information . . . It would be possible for inquiries to conduct at least the first part of their investigation by first assembling a comprehensive set of documents and written or videotaped testimony. Investigators for the inquiry could go out and separately and simultaneously interview a variety of witnesses." B. Schwartz, "Public Inquiries," in A. Manson and D. Mullan, eds., *Commissions of Inquiry: Praise or Reappraise?* (Toronto: Irwin Law, 2003), at 452. By contrast, truth commissions that conduct public hearings typically gather most of their evidence prior to, and outside of, the hearing process. The hearing itself is, in this respect, primarily a form for truth *telling* rather than truth *seeking*.

183 A perfect illustration is the so-called Saville Inquiry, named after its chair, the Rt. Hon. Lord Saville. The inquiry was established in 1998 by Prime Minister Tony Blair under the *Tribunals of Inquiry (Evidence) Act*, 1921 (UK), as amended. Its purpose was to investigate the 1972 event known as "Bloody Sunday," where 14 protesters were killed in Londonberry, Northern Ireland. Inquiry counsel's opening statement was 176 hours long. In total, over 900 witnesses gave oral evidence, and the inquiry cost approximately 155 million British pounds. Its final hearings concluded in 2004. "The Growth of Public Inquiries," *The Economist*, 12 February 2004, at 51.

184 HL Bill 7 (2004), preamble.

the procedure or conduct of an inquiry.[185] Oddly, however, the *Act* does not require an inquiry's terms of reference to specify a fixed end date; it is left optional.[186]

Concerning the Salmon principles in particular, the Consultation Paper that preceded the law's passage put the matter plainly: "The Government strongly believes that inquiries should be investigatory. The introduction of adversarial elements into the inquiry process, which are likely to increase costs and have potential to cause delays, should be avoided wherever possible. Adversarial elements should not be a significant feature of a process in which the main aim is to learn lessons, not apportion blame."[187]

The *Inquiries Act* will be sure to influence other Commonwealth jurisdictions, no less than the Salmon report did in its time. Although the law contains elements to enable greater procedural flexibility for those who run commissions of inquiry, it is too early to say whether the reforms are capable of returning inquiry practice to a nonadversarial inquisition model. Certainly the role of lawyers will have to be lessened.[188]

In Part II, we will see that truth commissions – which tend to be more inexpensive, more victim-centered, and more ambitious in scope – have much

---

185 The Explanatory Notes to the article further specify: "Each decision to admit evidence, to hold oral hearings, or to allow legal representation adds to the cost of the inquiry." *See also* art. 20(4)(d) of the *Act*, which allows a commission or its sponsoring minister to restrict public access to the inquiry if not doing so would be likely "to cause delay or to impair the efficiency or effectiveness of the inquiry, or . . . result in additional cost (whether to public funds or to witnesses or to others)."

186 Article 15(1). The lack of a fixed deadline is a regrettable hallmark of many Commonwealth commissions of inquiry in the UK and elsewhere. It is difficult to explain this continuing practice given the problems it creates, including the inability to regulate costs (which ultimately fall on the taxpayer), the need to seek repeated extensions from the political sponsor, and the risk of losing the public's attention over time. Truth commission practice seems superior in this regard. Though short extensions are common, rarely do truth commissions operate without a fixed deadline. In addition, extensions are usually contemplated within a truth commission's terms of reference (*e.g.*, a commission may be given 18 months to operate with a maximum possible extension of 6 months). Hayner noted the importance of deadlines in an early article on truth commissions: "A truth commission should be given a specific time limit to conclude its report. While this period should be extendable by agreement, it should never be open-ended." *See* P. Hayner, "Fifteen Truth Commissions – 1974 to 1994: A Comparative Study" (1994) 16 *Human Rights Quarterly* 597, at 652.

187 UK Department for Constitutional Affairs Consultation Paper, *Effective Inquiries*, May 2004, para. 82.

188 As noted earlier, legal costs tend to comprise the most significant part of the total cost of Commonwealth commissions of inquiry. The case is quite different with truth commissions.

to contribute to the reform of the Commonwealth commission of inquiry model.

SECTION 3: TOWARD A CONCEPTION OF PROCEDURAL FAIRNESS FOR TRUTH COMMISSIONS

Up to this point in the chapter, various international standards of procedural fairness have been examined. Three relevant domestic models of fairness have also been examined – namely, due process, natural justice, and Lord Justice Salmon's cardinal principles. Drawing from these and other models – as well as from the experiences and characteristics of truth commissions described in Chapter 1 – the elements of a conception of procedural fairness that corresponds to the specific objectives and constraints of truth commissions can now be developed.

Before doing this, however, two important points bear mention. First, as previously noted, there is no theory of fairness that is universal in its application. Fairness must be measured by a careful analysis of a wide range of factors including the nature of the proceeding, the rights at stake, the severity of the possible consequences, and so forth. There is, in consequence, no claim that this book's conception of procedural fairness applies to anything other than truth commissions. It may, but that is a matter for the reader to decide. Second, because the mandate and political context of each truth commission is unique, there is no pretense that the proposed conception will apply in identical fashion to every truth commission. To the contrary, depending on the truth commission, the conception may appear either excessively exigent or insufficiently so. For this reason, the conception is conceived not as a rigid benchmark, but as a constructive framework upon which truth commissions can draw and against which their practices can be evaluated.

The section begins with a description of the proposed guiding principles of fairness for a truth commission. This is followed by a description of competing objectives of truth commissions that are not necessarily components of fairness. The section concludes with a review of the main practical constraints that may impede the realization of fairness, or any other objectives that a truth commission may pursue.

An outline of the proposed conception is found in Table 2.1. Its application to specific truth commission powers and functions – namely, statement taking, subpoena powers, search and seizure powers, public hearings, and publication of findings of individual responsibility – is dealt with in Part II.

> ### Table 2.1: Conception of Procedural Fairness for Truth Commissions
>
> *Guiding Principles of Fairness*
> Independence
> Impartiality
> Accountability
> Competence
> Nondiscrimination
> Transparency
> Proportionality
> Dignity
> Accessibility
> Good faith
>
> *Competing Procedural Objectives*
> Efficiency
> Flexibility
> Victim-centeredness
> Accuracy
> Comprehensiveness
>
> *Practical Constraints*
> Time pressure
> Limited human and financial resources
> Excessive caseload
> Security concerns

Guiding principles of fairness

Independence

In Chapter 1, it was explained that "relative independence" from the state is a defining characteristic of a truth commission.[189] Independence, however, is not

189 *Recall also* Principle 11 of the Principles on the Effective Prevention and Investigation of Extra-Legal, Arbitrary and Summary Executions (1989), UN doc. E/1989/89, which requires governments to conduct an investigation by means of an "independent commission of inquiry or similar procedure" where the state cannot conduct a credible investigation through its standing organs. *See also* the Principles on the Effective Investigation and Documentation of Torture and Other Cruel, Inhuman or Degrading Treatment or Punishment, GA res. 55/89 (2000), Principle 5A.

merely a characteristic; it is also a core value. It takes on particular importance where a commission is operating in an environment of ongoing and systematic violence or abuse.[190]

There are many possible measures of a truth commission's level of independence. A first indicator of independence is political. A truth commission should not be subject to the direct control of any single political faction, nor should it be a mere branch or division of the government or sponsoring body.[191] A truth commission that is nothing more than an extension of government cannot be considered truly independent.[192] This does not mean it cannot have government actors within its membership; it simply means that the commission must not be comprised exclusively of them.[193]

A truth commission's charter should ensure a minimum level of security of tenure to commissioners. While commission sponsors must reserve the prerogative to remove commissioners,[194] that discretion must not be so broad

---

190   Several truth commissions have found themselves in this situation, including those of Uganda, Chad, and the DRC. In Sri Lanka, a truth commission (structured as three interconnected subcommissions) continued operating even upon the resumption of open armed conflict. "The ongoing war weakened the impact of the commissions, especially as the president was dependent on the support of the military as the war continued and thus apparently unwilling to criticize or confront the armed forces' human rights record." P. Hayner, *Unspeakable Truths: Facing the Challenge of Truth Commissions*, 2d. ed. (New York: Routledge, 2002), at 65.

191   *See, e.g., National Reconciliation Commission Act*, 2002, Act 611 (Ghana), section 8(1)(a): "The Commission shall, in the performance of its functions, be independent and not subject to the direction or control of any person or authority." *See also An Act to Establish the Truth and Reconciliation Commission of Liberia* (2005), s. 39(a): "The Commission, its commissioners and every member of staff shall function without political or other bias or interference and shall, unless this act expressly otherwise provides, be independent and separate from any party, government, administration, or any other functionary or body by directly or indirectly representing the interests of such entity." *Recall also* the Principles on the Effective Prevention and Investigation of Extra-Legal, Arbitrary and Summary Executions (1989), UN doc. E/1989/89, Principle 11, which provides that members of a commission of inquiry "shall be independent of any institution, agency or person that may be the subject of the inquiry."

192   For example, the committees of inquiry created in Algeria and Lebanon to establish the fate of disappeared persons (both of which were discussed in Chapter 1) were considered mere "interfaces" between the public and the government. They were perceived to be state-run bodies, rather than state-sponsored bodies operating at arm's length from their sponsor. This is one of the reasons why they were not viewed as truth commissions; the ingredient of independence was absent.

193   For instance, in Germany two-thirds of the truth commission members were parliamentarians, represented in proportion to their political parties' presence within parliament. The remaining third were experts from outside parliament. None of this appears to have negated the appearance of independence in the eyes of the public.

194   *See* "Accountability" below.

or unfettered as to undermine the appearance and reality of independence. Thus, commissioners should not be removable "at pleasure" (*i.e.*, without cause). Instead, they should be removable only for demonstrable "misbehavior, incapacity or incompetence."[195] Commission sponsors should be required to consult with the commission chair before effecting any removal and to follow transparent and fair procedures.[196] They should also be required to provide reasons for any removal.[197]

The selection of commissioners is also relevant to the issue of independence. To enhance the appearance and reality of independence, commissioners ought to be selected through a procedure that operates partly at arm's length from the sponsoring government.[198] A unilateral appointment process is more likely to reduce the appearance of independence – although it may be otherwise where, for example, a president is seen to be the highest moral authority in a state.[199]

Another indicator of independence concerns a commission's level of institutional autonomy. A truth commission that can, as a matter of law, be easily suspended, dissolved, or curtailed is one lacking in independence.[200] Commissions

---

195 *Promotion of National Unity and Reconciliation Act*, 1995 (South Africa), Chapter 2, s. 7(7). *See also* D. Orentlicher, "Updated Set of Principles," Principle 7(b): "They shall also be constituted in accordance with conditions ensuring their independence, in particular by the irremovability of their members during their terms of office except on grounds of incapacity or behaviour rendering them unfit to discharge their duties . . ."; and "Belgrade Minimum Rules of Procedure for International Human Rights Fact-Finding Missions" (1981) 75 *AJIL* 163, Rule 6: "Any person appointed a member of the fact finding mission should not be removed from membership except for reasons of incapacity or gross misbehaviour."

196 *See, e.g.*, Orentlicher, "Updated Set of Principles," above note 92, Principle 7.

197 *See, e.g.*, art. 13(7) of *Inquiries Act*, 2005 (UK).

198 For example, the mandate of Sierra Leone's TRC designated the special representative of the UN Secretary-General as "selection coordinator" and directed him to seek nominations from the general public. In addition, a selection panel was formed with representatives appointed by the president, the national human rights commission, the former rebel group, the nongovernmental interreligious council, and a coalition of human rights NGOs. This panel interviewed and ranked the finalists and then forwarded its recommendations to the selection coordinator, who chose the final four national candidates. (The commission also comprised three international commissioners. The UN High Commissioner for Human Rights selected the candidates.) Ultimately, the lists of both national and international candidates were submitted to the president for appointment. *See also An Act to Establish the Truth and Reconciliation Commission of Liberia* (2005), s. 9.

199 In South Africa, for example, the process of selecting commissioners was highly consultative, including public nominations and interviews of all candidates. However, to provide geographical and political balance, President Mandela added two members who did not pass through the full selection process. M. Freeman and P. Hayner, "Truth-Telling," in *Reconciliation After Violent Conflict: A Handbook* (Stockholm: Institute for Democracy and Electoral Assistance, 2003), at 129–30.

200 *But see Dixon v. Canada (Commission of Inquiry into the Deployment of Canadian Forces to Somalia)* (1997), 149 DLR (4th) 269, in which Canada's Federal Court of Appeal held that

should be suspended or curtailed only for legitimate and explicit reasons consistent with the public interest.[201]

In the context of an official body like a truth commission, the term "independence" also implies a level of financial security.[202] Primary or exclusive reliance on national government funding (as opposed to international funding) is generally desirable. It indicates a sense of local ownership and local political commitment to transitional justice efforts. Yet local ownership may conflict with the objective of independence. Some may view government funding as, above all, a means of control. Such a perception will be immediately reinforced if a government cuts a commission's funds at or around the same time a commission makes statements or findings that embarrass the government.[203] For this reason, and to the extent possible, it is useful to fix part of the commission's overall budget before, or shortly after, its inauguration.[204] All funding should be openly publicized in order to enhance the appearance of independence.[205]

In practice, however, most commissions rely on a mix of domestic and international funds, because domestic sources are alone insufficient. In rare

---

the length of a commission's mandate remains within the control of the sponsor, and that any decision to cut short its life produces political, but not legal, consequences.

201 See, e.g., article 14(1) of the *Inquiries Act*, 2005 (UK), which provides: "The Minister may at any time, by notice to the chairman, suspend an inquiry for such period as appears to him to be necessary to allow for (a) the completion of any other investigation relating to any of the matters to which the inquiry relates, or (b) the determination of any civil or criminal proceedings (including proceedings before a disciplinary tribunal) arising out of any of those matters."

202 *Recall* Principle 10 of the Principles on the Effective Prevention and Investigation of Extra-Legal, Arbitrary and Summary Executions (1989), UN doc. E/1989/89, which provides that investigative bodies require "all the necessary budgetary and technical resources for effective investigation." *See also* Principle 3 of the Principles on the Effective Investigation and Documentation of Torture and Other Cruel, Inhuman or Degrading Treatment or Punishment, GA res. 55/89 (2000).

203 T. Witelson, "Declaration of Independence: Examining the Independence of Federal Public Inquiries," in Manson and Mullan, *Commissions of Inquiry*, above note 182, at 314.

204 This practice, however, is rare in the case of truth commissions and is only partly explained by the reliance most commissions place on international funds. Typically, mandates omit any mention of budget, or make only general references to the sources of a commission's funds. *See, e.g.,* the "Final Provisions" of Supreme Decree no. 0065-2001-PCM (Peru), as amended: "The Truth Commission's resources are: (a) Those that may be transferred for such effect by the Ministry of the Economy and Finance. (b) Those that may be assigned in the General Budget of the Republic for the next fiscal period. (c) Those that may be obtained directly from international cooperation. (d) Others that may come from donations." (Unofficial translation by Lisa Magarrell.)

205 See, e.g., D. Orentlicher, "Updated Set of Principles," above note 92, Principle 11(b): "The commission shall be provided with [t]ransparent funding to ensure that its independence is never in doubt . . ." *See also* "Transparency" below.

cases, commissions have relied exclusively on international funds.[206] At first blush, one may assume that international financial participation will enhance the appearance or reality of independence. However, some foreign governments are implicated in past abuses in the country where a truth commission operates. Receipt of funds from such governments could undermine the domestic and international public's perception that an independent investigation is being conducted.[207]

Another aspect of financial independence concerns the size of a commission's budget. The total amount of funding should be sufficient to ensure the appearance and reality of independence.[208] The objective of independence is obviously undermined where truth commissions cannot operate due to a lack of funds.[209]

Concerning whether, and how much, commissioners should be paid for their services, divergent viewpoints may be argued with equal force. Commissioners who work on a volunteer basis are ostensibly less beholden

---

206 This was the case, for example, with the truth commissions in El Salvador and Timor-Leste. *See also* the 2003 Comprehensive Peace Agreement Between the Government of Liberia and the Liberians United for Reconciliation and Democracy (LURD) and the Movement for Democracy in Liberia (MODEL) and Political Parties, art. XIII(4): ". . . The Parties request that the International Community provide the necessary financial and technical support for the operations of the Commission." *But see An Act to Establish the Truth and Reconciliation Commission of Liberia* (2005), s. 36, which calls upon the government of Liberia to finance some of the commission's work.

207 For instance, the Guatemalan truth commission received financial support from various governments, including that of the United States. This might have limited the commission's perceived independence; however, its final report did end up addressing US responsibility. The commission found that for decades, the United States knowingly provided funds, training, and other vital support to Guatemalan military regimes that committed atrocities as a matter of official policy.

208 *See, e.g.,* D. Orentlicher, "Updated Set of Principles," above note 92, Principle 11(b): "The commission shall be provided with [s]ufficient material and human resources to ensure that its credibility is never in doubt." In Chapter 1, it was noted that contemporary truth commission budgets average between US$5 million and US$10 million.

209 Many truth commissions have experienced funding shortfalls. Consider the example of Uganda's truth commission: "[T]he Commission was desperately short of funds, and was forced at one point to suspend public hearings; a February 1988 Ford Foundation Grant enabled the CIVHR to resume those hearings. Commissioners reported being limited by serious shortages, including filing cabinets, stationery (at certain stages, those testifying before the Commission were asked to provide their own paper, files, and pens to the Commissioners in order that their testimony might be recorded), staff, and transportation. Consequently, the Commissioners worked only part-time on the CIVHR. Such constraints forced the Commission to delay the release of its report . . ." J. R. Quinn, "Dealing with a Legacy of Mass Atrocity: Truth Commissions in Uganda and Chile" (2001) 19.4 *Netherlands Quarterly of Human Rights* 383, at 393–4.

to their political master and hence more independent.[210] It could, however, be argued that commissioners who are paid a professional salary to work on a full-time basis are, like well-paid judges, more insulated from external influences and hence more likely be viewed as independent.[211]

A final issue concerns a commission's operational or administrative independence.[212] Independent truth commissions control various things including the use of their time, budget, and human resources; the interpretation of their terms of reference; and the selection of cases and locations for investigation or public hearings.[213] One may also say that investigative powers, such as the power to compel the giving of testimony and evidence, are indicative of greater operational independence. A commission investigation that is excessively reliant on state cooperation is less independent than one that is not.

Ultimately, however, a truth commission's level of independence cannot be measured on paper alone. The commission's actual conduct must also be assessed. Some truth commissions may enjoy considerable structural independence yet lack the ideological independence to conduct a truly independent investigation; by contrast, others lacking in structural independence may find ways to overcome such constraints and conduct a truly independent investigation.

Impartiality

The same factors that tend to increase the appearance and reality of independence will, in most instances, help increase the appearance and reality of

---

210 In some of the truth commission experiences in Latin America (*e.g.*, Chile), commissioners did not receive a salary. *See, e.g.*, article 9 of the *Decree Establishing the National Commission on Truth and Reconciliation*, Supreme Decree no. 355, 1990 (Chile), reprinted in N. Kritz, ed., *Transitional Justice: How Emerging Democracies Reckon with Former Regimes*, 3 vols. (Washington, DC: United States Institute for Peace Press, 1995), vol. 3, which stipulates that commissioners fulfill their duties *ad honorem*.

211 *See, e.g.*, s.12 of *An Act to Establish the Truth and Reconciliation Commission of Liberia* (2005): "Members of the TRC shall be employed by the Government of Liberia and shall render services on a full-time basis and receive remuneration in an amount determined not to be less than that received by Justices of the Supreme Court of Liberia." Note, however, that in 2004, proponents of a truth commission in BiH proposed that, in order to foster the appearance of independence, commission members should receive the same salaries as judges. This backfired. Many victim groups viewed the proposal as an attempt by the commission's proponents – some of whom would likely be appointed to the commission – to make themselves rich.

212 *See generally* Witelson, "Declaration of Independence," above note 203, at 322–34.

213 *See, e.g.*, Arusha Accord (2000), art. 8(3) concerning a proposed truth commission for Burundi: "The Commission must have the leeway to work independently, *inter alia* through autonomy in managing the material and financial resources to be allocated to it."

impartiality.[214] But independence and impartiality are not synonymous; an independent truth commission is not necessarily an unbiased one.

Some forms of bias, such as the presence of a pecuniary interest or prior personal involvement in cases under investigation, will taint almost any inquiry.[215] By contrast, the mere fact of public association with a particular cause should not automatically disqualify a person from the possibility of serving as a member of a truth commission. For example, having rebuked a government for its past human rights record does not make one biased; to defend human rights is to defend everyone's rights.[216] Similarly, having displayed concern or sympathy for victims does not necessarily betray a bias; it may reflect simple human compassion.[217]

Yet even if one displayed true bias of one form or another, this could potentially be overcome by ensuring equal representation, within the commission,

---

214 This fact is underscored by the proximate use of both terms in most human rights treaties. *See, e.g.,* UDHR art. 10 reference to "independent and impartial tribunal." *See also* CRC art. 40(2)(b)(iii), AmDR arts. 18 and 26, ACHR art. 8(1) and 8(5), ECHR art. 6(1), and AfrCHPR arts. 7(1) and 26.

215 *See, e.g.,* article 10(1) of the *Inquiries Act,* 2005 (UK), which provides: "The Minister must not appoint a person as a member of the inquiry panel if it appears to the Minister that the person has (a) a direct interest in the matters to which the inquiry relates, or (b) a close association with an interested party, *unless,* despite the person's interest or association, his appointment could not reasonably be regarded as affecting the impartiality of the inquiry panel." *See also* Rome Statute art. 41, which disqualifies a judge from hearing a case where he or she "has previously been involved in any capacity in that case before the Court or in a related criminal case at the national level involving the person being investigated or prosecuted." Additional possible grounds of disqualification are found in Rule 34(1) of the ICC Rules of Procedure and Evidence.

216 *See, e.g., Furundzija* (21 July 2000), Case no. IT-95-17/I-T, ICTY Appeals Chamber, where an ICTY judge's impartiality was challenged on the basis of her having acted as a representative of her country on the UN Commission on the Status of Women (UNCSW). The Appeals Chamber stated, at paras. 200–2: "[E]ven if it were established that Judge Mumba expressly shared the goals and objectives of the UNCSW . . . in promoting and protecting the human rights of women, that inclination . . . is distinguishable from an inclination to implement those goals and objectives as a Judge in a particular case. It follows that she could still sit on a case and impartially decide upon issues affecting women. [E]ven if Judge Mumba sought to implement the relevant objectives of the UNCSW, those goals merely reflected the objectives of the United Nations, and were contemplated by the Security Council resolutions leading to the establishment of the Tribunal . . . Concern for the achievement of equality for women, which is one of the principles reflected in the United Nations Charter, cannot be taken to suggest any form of pre-judgement in any future trial for rape. To endorse the view that rape as a crime is abhorrent and that those responsible for it should be prosecuted within the constraints of the law cannot in itself constitute grounds for disqualification." Impartiality claims based on past work in the field of human rights might, however, garner less success if the person in question regularly attacked a particular government but failed to criticize equally serious violations committed by other parties, such as rebel groups.

217 Experience working with victims would in fact be quite desirable in most cases, to the extent it increases the commission's overall competence. See "Competence" below.

of persons holding an opposite bias. This was the approach taken in Chile, where the truth commission comprised eight commissioners; half were known as public sympathizers of the military government, and half as its public opponents.[218] The more common approach, however, is to appoint commissioners who are representative of a broad cross-section of viewpoints and stakeholder groups in order to minimize public perceptions of a particular bias.[219] Another approach, especially prevalent in Commonwealth jurisdictions, is to appoint a judge as the head of the commission.[220] In still other cases – for example, in El Salvador, Guatemala, and Sierra Leone – states have opted for the appointment of foreign nationals.[221]

Once appointed, commissioners ought to serve in their personal capacities.[222] This does not always require resigning or temporarily abandoning an existing post. In fact, in many cases, truth commissioners have retained their prior posts and found a way to balance their competing commitments without undermining the appearance of impartiality. However, where there

218 H. Steiner, ed., *Truth Commissions: A Comparative Assessment* (Cambridge, MA: Harvard Law School Human Rights Program, 1997), at 21. Former Chilean TRC commissioner Jose Zalaquett often emphasizes that all of the commissioners were decent people. Presumably, no amount of parallel representation could salvage a commission comprised of unethical persons with totally closed minds.

219 *See, e.g.,* "On the Establishment of a Commission for Reception, Truth and Reconciliation in East Timor," UNTAET/REG/2001/01 as amended, section 4.1: "The Commission shall be composed of five to seven National Commissioners. National Commissioners shall be persons of high moral character, impartiality, and integrity who are competent to deal with the issues under the present Regulation and shall not have a high political profile, and have a demonstrated commitment to human rights principles. No National Commissioner may be the spouse or blood relative in the first degree of any other National Commissioner. At least thirty per cent (30%) of the National Commissioners shall be women."

220 Judges almost always head Commonwealth commissions of inquiry. The use of *sitting* judges on any commission of inquiry may, however, raise concerns about judicial independence and the principle of separation of powers. T. Witelson, "Interview with Mr. Justice Gilles Letourneau, Somalia Commission Chair," in Manson and Mullan, *Commissions of Inquiry*, above note 182, at 371.

221 Appointing foreign nationals can have potentially detrimental aspects. Describing El Salvador's truth commission, one author notes: "On the negative side, foreigners, especially staff, unfamiliar with El Salvador may not have been sufficiently attuned to perceive the relative importance of certain cases and issues as well as the consequences of some of their decisions and recommendations . . . Moreover, the international nature of the Commission became a target of attack from quarters dissatisfied with its findings and recommendations . . ." M. Popkin, "El Salvador: A Negotiated End to Impunity," in N. Roht-Arriaza, ed., *Impunity and Human Rights in International Law and Practice* (New York: Oxford University Press, 1995), at 207.

222 *See, e.g., Law 04/018 (2004) Concerning the Organization, Powers and Functions of the Truth and Reconciliation Commission* (DRC), art. 50. *See generally* T. Franck and H. S. Fairley, "Procedural Due Process in Human Rights Fact-Finding by International Agencies" (1980) 74 *AJIL* 308, at 314–15.

is a likelihood of frequent conflicts of interest, the commissioner in question ought to temporarily or permanently abandon the existing post or, alternatively, refuse the appointment to the truth commission.

As a more general practice to reinforce impartiality, it is advisable to have established rules about conflicts of interest applicable to all commissioners. These should require commissioners to disclose actual or apparent conflicts based on financial or personal interests, and to recuse themselves from decision making as and when appropriate.[223] Commissioners should also be required to pledge to act impartially in the exercise of their duties and in the assessment of evidence.[224]

While it is essential to ensure the impartiality of commissioners, it is also important to ensure the impartiality of commission staff. Hence the same considerations apply, *mutatis mutandis*, to the members of a truth commission's staff.

Another pernicious form of bias is what one might describe as institutional, as opposed to individual, bias. For example, any truth commission title or mandate that prejudges responsibility is at odds with the principle of impartiality.[225]

---

223 *See, e.g., National Reconciliation Commission Act,* 2002, Act 611 (Ghana), art. 6(5): "Where a member of the Commission discovers during any meeting or proceedings of the Commission that the member has or may have a financial or personal interest in the matter before the Commission which is likely to cause a conflict of interest for that member: (a) the member shall make a full disclosure of the nature of interest and shall not be present during the discussion of or participate in a decision on the matter; and (b) the disclosure shall be entered in the record of proceedings. (c) A member who does not comply with subsection (5), is liable to be removed form the Commission." *See also An Act to Establish the Truth and Reconciliation Commission of Liberia* (2005), s. 23; *Law 04/018 (2004) Concerning the Organization, Powers and Functions of the Truth and Reconciliation Commission* (DRC), art. 45.

224 *See, e.g,* On the Establishment of a Commission for Reception, Truth and Reconciliation in East Timor," UNTAET/REG/2001/01 as amended, s. 5.1: "Upon appointment, each National Commissioner shall make the following oath (or solemn declaration) before the Transitional Administrator: 'I swear (solemnly declare) that in carrying out the functions entrusted to me as a member of the Commission, I will perform my duties independently and impartially. I will, at all times, act in accordance with the dignity that the performance of my functions requires...'"

225 For example, the truth commission in Chad was entitled *Commission d'Enquête sur les Crimes et Détournements Commis par l'Ex-Président Habré, ses co-Auteurs et/ou Complices* (Commission of Inquiry on the Crimes and Misappropriations Committed by the Ex-President Habré, His Accomplices and/or Accessories). *See also* Franck and Fairley, "Procedural Due Process in Human Rights Fact-Finding," at 315–16, where the authors discuss the terms of reference for early UN investigations of alleged Israeli and South African violations of humanitarian law. The authors state: "In each of these instances, the terms of reference – the resolution establishing a mission – included conclusory language that palpably interfered with the integrity of the fact-finding process by violating the essential line between political assumptions and issues to be impartially determined." At page 344 of the article, the authors

Equally problematic would be a truth commission mandate that focused primarily or exclusively on the responsibility of only one side of a multisided conflict. Similarly, a truth commission charter that skipped over key periods of past abuse in a way that implied partisan or ethnic bias would tend to undermine the appearance of impartiality.[226] To be sure, truth commission mandates need not cover every period of history, nor examine violations committed up to the moment of the commission's creation. The mandate must simply avoid an overt and built-in bias.

As with the objective of independence, impartiality is a value that ultimately cannot be measured exclusively in the preceding terms. It must be evaluated by reference to a commission's actual conduct as well.[227]

Accountability

A truth commission is an official body. As such, it is accountable to members of the public and to elected and appointed representatives.

Commissioners should be answerable for the management of the commission and the execution of their mandated duties. They should also be accountable for the actions of staff and of persons who have been lawfully authorized or deputized to act in their stead.

Ideally, all commissioners and staff should be required to undertake an oath, or solemn declaration, of office. The oath should comprise a personal undertaking to carry out the commission's mandate in good faith; perform the

---

conclude: "A fact-finding mission should not begin its quest without clearly defined terms of reference that circumscribe the precise area in which it is to operate. These terms of reference should be neutrally stated in the form of questions of fact." *Recall also* article 2 of the UN Manual on the Effective Prevention and Investigation of Extra-Legal, Arbitrary and Summary Executions (1991), which provides that a commission of inquiry's terms of reference should be "neutrally framed so that they do not suggest a predetermined outcome," and should "state precisely which events and issues are to be investigated and addressed in the commission's final report."

226 The truth commission in Panama excited controversy for this reason. President Mireya Moscoso's decree establishing the commission authorized the examination of human rights violations committed during the period of military rule in Panama: from the *coup d'état* in October 1968 that brought Omar Torrijos to power through to the last days in 1989 when Manuel Noriega ruled the country. The mandate implicitly excluded examination of violations that may have been committed by the president's spouse (who was the last civilian president prior to the 1968 coup) or by the United States following its invasion of Panama in December 1989. *See* Executive Decree no. 2 creating the "Commission on the Truth," 2001 (Panama). The mandate of Ghana's truth commission excited similar controversy by requiring a special focus on periods of military rule. *See, e.g.,* "Reconciliation Process Is Partisan – Bishop," *Ghanaian Times,* 9 January 2003.

227 *See also* "Nondiscrimination" below.

assigned duties impartially, independently, and without discrimination; and fulfill any obligations to preserve confidentiality.[228] In addition, interpreters and translators retained by the commission should be required to declare that they will translate or explain documents and testimony to the best of their ability, and that they will not reveal the contents of such documents or testimony outside the commission.[229]

A commissioner should face appropriate legal penalties for any serious misbehavior.[230] At the same time, being a commissioner should not expose one to unreasonable legal risk. Commissioners as well as staff should have express immunity from adverse legal proceedings for all actions, decisions, and omissions made in good faith in the course of the inquiry.[231] This will help ensure that they report their findings to the government and the public without fear,[232] and that they are held accountable for misbehavior and not for uttering controversial statements or taking unpopular actions.

The commission's finances and accounts should be independently audited at the conclusion of its work.[233] This scrutiny will reinforce the credibility of the commission and the integrity of its procedures and results.

---

228   See, e.g., "On the Establishment of a Commission for Reception, Truth and Reconciliation in East Timor," UNTAET/REG/2001/01 as amended, sections 5.1 and 11.5. See also European Committee Against Torture, Rules of Procedure (1997), Rule 46(1): "Members of the Committee, experts and other persons assisting the Committee are required, during and after their terms of office, to maintain the confidentiality of the facts or information of which they have become aware during the discharge of their functions."

229   See, e.g., section 7 of the Tribunals of Inquiry Act, 1966, ch. 447, Laws of the Federation of Nigeria. See also ICC Rules of Procedure and Evidence, UN doc. PCNICC/2000/1/Add.1 (2000), Rule 6.

230   See, e.g., Law 04/018 (2004) Concerning the Organization, Powers and Functions of the Truth and Reconciliation Commission (DRC), art. 13.

231   See, e.g., Promotion of National Unity and Reconciliation Act, 1995 (South Africa), s.41(2): "No (a) commissioner, (b) member of the staff of the Commission; or (c) person who performs any task on behalf of the Commission, shall be liable in respect of anything reflected in any report, finding, point of view or recommendation made or expressed in good faith and submitted or made known in terms of this Act." See also Law 04/018 (2004) Concerning the Organization, Powers and Functions of the Truth and Reconciliation Commission (DRC), art. 47; Commissions of Inquiry Law, 1968, vol. 23 of the Laws of the State of Israel, s. 24, which provides that commissioners "have every immunity granted by law to a Judge."

232   See, e.g., Fayed v. The United Kingdom (17101/90) [1994] ECHR 27 (21 September 1994), at para. 81.

233   See, e.g., National Reconciliation Commission Act, 2002, Act 611 (Ghana), s. 25: "(1) The Commission shall maintain proper books of accounts and other records of account in a form determined by the Auditor-General. (2) The Commission shall not later than three months after it has submitted its report, submit to the Auditor-General, its books and records of account."

Competence

Competence is an implied requirement of fairness; without it, the likelihood of fair results is slim.

Commissioners, if not individually then certainly collectively, should be minimally competent and professionally qualified in the tasks that will be required of them.[234] Within the commission membership there should, for example, be expertise in human rights and related fields.[235] To the extent individual commissioners require training, it must be provided. Commission staff should be hired only if they attain a minimum level of competence in the particular position. They should receive appropriate training too, once hired. The same is true for any volunteers or contract workers who may be hired to work on behalf of the commission.

A due diligence standard should be used to evaluate whether a truth commission is carrying out its mission in a competent fashion. After all, those who operate truth commissions are not required to get everything right. Also, fact-finding work entails interpretation; reasonable people can sometimes disagree about how to interpret the same events based on the same evidence.

Commissioners and staff should, however, be expected to act in a rational and diligent manner and to make thoughtful choices about evidence or the use of limited time and resources. They should be expected to take account of relevant factors and discount irrelevant factors.[236] They should, in addition, fulfill their obligations in a reasonable and timely fashion.[237] They should also examine the experiences of previous truth commissions; it would be difficult to exonerate a commission whose lack of study results in the repetition of avoidable errors.

As applied to truth commissions, the principle of competence also implies a level of institutional authority. A truth commission that acquits itself with diligence may nevertheless lack competence in the sense of legal authority. Thus,

234 *See, e.g.,* section 9(1) of the *Inquiries Act,* 2005 (UK), which provides: "In appointing a member of the inquiry panel, the Minister must have regard (a) to the need to ensure that the inquiry panel (considered as a whole) has the necessary expertise to undertake the inquiry . . ."

235 *See, e.g.,* D. Orentlicher, "Updated Set of Principles," above note 92, Principle 7(a): "[Truth commissions and other commissions of inquiry] shall be constituted in accordance with criteria making clear to the public the competence and impartiality of their members, including expertise within their membership in the field of human rights and, if relevant, of humanitarian law."

236 To do otherwise would amount to an abuse of discretion. *See generally* Mullan, *Administrative Law,* above note 102, at 100–32.

237 *See, e.g.,* EU Charter of Rights art. 101(1) ("right to good administration"), which declares a right to have one's affairs handled "within a reasonable time" by EU institutions.

commissions with important investigative powers – for example, the power to compel the disclosure of evidence or to ensure the protection of witnesses and victims – can be described as more competent than those that lack the same powers.[238] This is not to say that commissions with weak investigative powers are incompetent; it is simply to recognize that full competence consists of more than talent, training, and good judgment.

Nondiscrimination

The principle of nondiscrimination is a core component of any proper notion of fairness. It is a principle recognized in every major human rights instrument.[239]

All parties who interact with, or are affected by, a truth commission should expect treatment free of discrimination on the basis of "race, colour, gender, sex, sexual orientation, age, language, religion, nationality, political or other opinion, cultural beliefs or practices, property, birth or family status, ethnic or social origin, or disability."[240] Generally speaking, a difference in treatment is considered discriminatory where it lacks an "objective and reasonable justification."[241]

Sometimes discriminatory intent is manifest and obvious, but more often than not it defies easy detection. The modern notion of equal treatment, however, does not rest on intent alone. Instead, it involves an evaluation of whether a particular action or policy produces discriminatory consequences or results.[242]

Whether a commission observes the principle of nondiscrimination must be assessed on the basis of actual conduct. It cannot be presupposed in the abstract.

---

238 *Recall* Principles 10 and 11 of the Principles on the Effective Prevention and Investigation of Extra-Legal, Arbitrary and Summary Executions, UN doc. E/1989/89 (1989), which provide that investigative bodies must have "the power to obtain all the information necessary to the inquiry," including the authority to issue summonses requiring alleged perpetrators to testify or produce evidence. *See also* Principle 3 of the Principles on the Effective Investigation and Documentation of Torture and Other Cruel, Inhuman or Degrading Treatment or Punishment, GA res. 55/89 (2000).

239 *See generally* Freeman and van Ert, *International Human Rights Law,* above note 1, at 283–6.

240 "On the Establishment of a Commission for Reception, Truth and Reconciliation in East Timor," UNTAET/REG/2001/01, s. 35.1(b).

241 *Belgian Linguistic Case (no. 2)* (1979) 1 EHRR 252, at para. 32.

242 *See, e.g., Andrews v. Law Society of British Columbia,* [1989] 1 SCR 143 (Supreme Court of Canada), at 174: "[D]iscrimination may be described as a distinction, whether intentional or not, but based on grounds relating to personal characteristics of the individual or group, *which has the effect of* imposing burdens, obligations, or disadvantages on such individual or group not imposed upon others, or which withholds or limits access to opportunities, benefits, and advantages available to other members of society." (Emphasis added.)

Transparency

As official bodies tasked with bringing past abuse to public light, truth commissions ought to conduct their work in the most transparent manner possible. Ideally, a truth commission's mandate should explicitly require it to act with maximal openness.[243]

Truth commissions should make the mandate and rules of procedure under which they are organized widely available to the public. These constitute the basis for the commission's authority, and announce its objectives and modalities of operation.[244] Salaries of commissioners and staff, as well as the expenses of operation, should be part of the public record too.[245] Truth commissions should also aim to establish websites, proactively engage international and national media, and provide reasons and explanations to the public for all significant actions and decisions.[246] Their final reports should also, of course, be made public.[247]

Proportionality

In law, proportionality signifies that the means elected to fulfill a valid objective ought to be proportionate to, or commensurate with, the objective itself.[248]

---

243 *See, e.g.,* "On the Establishment of a Commission for Reception, Truth and Reconciliation in East Timor," UNTAET/REG/2001/01 as amended, s. 13.3: "Once it is established, the Commission shall publicize the fact that it has been established and make the scope of its inquiries known by all possible means." Article 50 of Part I of the Treaty Establishing a Constitution for Europe, *adopted* 29 October 2004, Notice no. 2004/C 310/01, would make transparency a fundamental principle of EU actions.

244 Although truth commission mandates increasingly contain detailed information about rules of procedure, many mandates continue to leave the details to commissioners following their appointment, once they have assessed the magnitude of the tasks.

245 Many truth commissions are audited during and after their lifetime. An auditor's report on expenditures will normally become part of the public record. However, some commissions (*e.g.,* Peru and Timor-Leste) have published the salaries of all employees even without an audit.

246 *See generally* Chapter 3.

247 *See, e.g., An Act to Establish the Truth and Reconciliation Commission of Liberia* (2005), s. 43: "The TRC shall submit a final report containing recommendations at the end of its tenure to the National Legislature and have key findings of the report published simultaneous with its presentation in at least three local dailies in pursuit of transparency and public interest objectives."

248 While this section is focused on proportionality as a *component* of procedural fairness, the principle of proportionality also serves as a *limitation* on its scope (*i.e.,* the degree of fairness a truth commission can be expected to deliver should be proportionate to its objectives, powers, resources, etc.).

The principle of proportionality is particularly important when dealing with issues of human rights. As we have seen in this chapter, and as Part II of the book will demonstrate, the work of truth commissions is linked to many important human rights, ranging from reputation rights to property rights to remedial rights. A truth commission should infringe such rights as little as possible to attain its legitimate objectives. If it can attain any particular objective by less infringing means, it ought to do so. If a commission employs means that are patently out of proportion to a particular objective, it would be in violation of this book's notion of procedural fairness.

Truth commission charters ideally should make the proportionality of ends and means an explicit operational objective.[249]

Dignity

Notions of human dignity underpin the theory and practice of human rights. The preamble of the UDHR affirms that "recognition of the inherent dignity ... of all members of the human family" is the "foundation of freedom, justice and peace in the world ..." Likewise, the preambles to the ICCPR and the ICESCR declare that human rights stem from the "inherent dignity" of human beings. Article 61 of the EU Charter of Rights provides: "Human dignity is inviolable. It must be respected and protected."

A truth commission is a body whose core mission is, in almost every sense, the vindication of human rights. A truth commission must, therefore, respect the fundamental dignity of all of those persons it encounters or investigates.[250] A truth commission that, in practice, fails to affirm the dignity of the

---

249 This has rarely been done. *But see* "On the Establishment of a Commission for Reception, Truth and Reconciliation in East Timor," UNTAET/REG/2001/01 as amended, s. 28.2, which required that any terms of community service endorsed by the truth commission and formalized in a Community Reconciliation Agreement be "reasonably proportionate" to the criminal acts disclosed in the perpetrator's confession.

250 The mandates of the truth commissions in South Africa and Timor-Leste recognize this. *See Promotion of National Unity and Reconciliation Act*, 1995 (South Africa), s. 35.1(a), which provides that all persons "shall be treated with compassion and respect for their dignity ..." The Timor-Leste truth commission's mandate identically stipulates that "all persons shall be treated with compassion and respect for their dignity." "On the Establishment of a Commission for Reception, Truth and Reconciliation in East Timor," UNTAET/REG/2001/01 as amended, s. 35.1(a). *See also An Act to Establish the Truth and Reconciliation Commission of Liberia* (2005), s. 26(r). *Recall also* Principle 4 of the UN Declaration of Basic Principles of Justice for Victims of Crime and Abuse of Power, GA res. 40/34 (1985): "Victims should be treated with compassion and respect for their dignity"; and Principle 10 of the Bassiouni Principles, above note 101, which declares that victims should be treated "with humanity and respect for their dignity and human rights."

human person would be in contravention of the most rudimentary concept of fairness.

Accessibility

If truth commissions are to achieve the lofty objectives imposed on them by law and public expectation, they must be accessible. This means that, as much as possible, truth commissions need to afford reasonably available means for victims, witnesses, and the general public to interact with them.

At a minimum, all parties coming before a truth commission should have the right to communicate, and to be communicated to, in their own languages.[251] Though this may prove costly in some jurisdictions, it is a precondition to rendering a full and accurate account of past events, as well as a requirement of upholding the principle of nondiscrimination.

The objective of accessibility should preferably be made explicit in a truth commission's charter.[252]

Good faith

The requirement of good faith (*bona fides*) is undoubtedly a general principle of international law.[253] In law, the principle of good faith signifies that persons acting in an official capacity must do so without deceit, fraud, or malice. The principle connotes a state of mind marked by a spirit of "honesty, fairness and reasonableness."[254]

In the truth commission context, the good faith principle implies dutifully fulfilling one's mandated obligations, both in letter and in spirit.

251   *See, e.g., Promotion of National Unity and Reconciliation Act*, 1995 (South Africa), ch. 2, s. 11(f). *See also An Act to Establish the Truth and Reconciliation Commission of Liberia* (2005), s. 26(r)(iii): "The TRC shall take sufficient measures to allow victims to communicate in the language of their choice." *See also* art. 67(1)(f) of the Rome Statute for the International Criminal Court 1998, which entitles accused persons to have, "free of any cost, the assistance of a competent interpreter and such translations as are necessary to meet the requirements of fairness, if any of the proceedings of or documents presented to the Court are not in a language which the accused fully understands and speaks."

252   *See, e.g.,* Supreme Decree no. 065-2001-PCM (Peru) as amended, s. 6(f): "The Truth Commission shall establish channels of communication and mechanisms for the participation of the population, in particular those affected by the violence." (Unofficial translation by Lisa Magarrell.)

253   *See generally* J. F. O'Connor, *Good Faith in International Law* (Brookfield, VT: Dartmouth, 1991).

254   *Ibid.,* at 124.

Commissioners, staff, and others temporarily or voluntarily engaged by the truth commission ought to contractually pledge to perform their duties in good faith.[255]

The guiding principles just described are the key building blocks for any truth commission that aspires to be fair. For the most part, the principles are complementary to one another. This is not, however, always the case. For example, a truth commission must be independent, but not so independent as to be unaccountable. It must be transparent, but not to the point of violating the dignity or legitimate privacy interests of those who come before it.[256]

Competing procedural objectives

The guiding principles of fairness can be in tension with other core objectives of a truth commission that are related to, but not intrinsic components of, fairness. An examination of these competing procedural objectives follows.

Efficiency

Truth commissions tend to have broad mandates that must be fulfilled within relatively short timeframes and employing limited budgets. To be effective, truth commissions must be efficient; there is no other choice.

In the pursuit of efficiency, however, a truth commission must remain fair. At times this can present a serious dilemma. As any litigator or judge can attest, fairness and efficiency are inversely related: the more fair the procedure, the less efficient; the less fair the procedure, the more efficient. By way of illustration, trial procedures that are very permissive vis-à-vis requests for adjournment increase fairness at the expense of efficiency; by contrast, trial procedures that

---

255 *See, e.g., An Act to Establish the Truth and Reconciliation Commission of Liberia* (2005) s. 39(d)(i): "Notwithstanding any personal opinion, preference or former party affiliation, serve impartially and independently and perform his or her duties in good faith and without fear, favour, bias or prejudice."

256 *Recall*, in this regard, ICCPR art. 14(1): "All persons shall be equal before the courts and tribunals. In the determination of any criminal charge against him, or of his rights and obligations in a suit at law, everyone shall be entitled to a fair and public hearing by a competent, independent and impartial tribunal established by law. The press and the public may be excluded from all or part of a trial for reasons of morals, public order (*ordre public*) or national security in a democratic society, or when the interest of the private lives of the parties so requires, or to the extent strictly necessary in the opinion of the court in special circumstances where publicity would prejudice the interests of justice; but any judgement rendered in a criminal case or in a suit at law shall be made public except where the interest of juvenile persons otherwise requires or the proceedings concern matrimonial disputes or the guardianship of children."

are very restrictive vis-à-vis such requests increase efficiency at the expense of fairness.

The same dynamic applies to truth commission procedures. Burdening a truth commission with significant procedural fairness obligations has the potential to undermine the commission's ability to carry out the most essential duties. It could considerably slow the investigation process and restrain the commission's capacity to gather facts and evidence.[257]

Efficiency should not, however, function as an automatic trump over fairness, nor *vice versa*. Instead, a rational balance must always be found between the two objectives.

Flexibility

As *ad hoc* bodies established to pursue multiple worthy objectives, truth commissions require considerable flexiblity in the interpretation and fulfillment of their mandate. Often there is no road map to draw upon. Much is invented from scratch, with the commission's charter and selected foreign experiences as the primary points of reference.[258] Initially, a commission may not even have offices from which to work.[259] The result is that it can sometimes takes months

257 *See* earlier discussion of *Hannah v. Larche*.

258 The situation is, however, improving for truth commissions as a result of assistance from expert organizations such as the International Center for Transitional Justice. By contrast, multilateral commissions of inquiry (*e.g.*, those established by the UN Security Council) do not appear any better off today than they were in the past. M. C. Bassiouni, who headed a UN commission of experts investigating war crimes committed in the former Yugoslavia, lamented, "After fifty years, there is no standard operating procedure for fact-finding missions. Admittedly, any standard operating procedure needs to be tailored to the situation. But no manual exists to describe how an investigation should be conducted and there is no standard, though adaptable, computer program to input collected data. Worst of all, there is no continuity. In short, there is nothing to guide, instruct, or assist the heads and appointees to these missions of how to better carry out their mandates. It strains one's belief that in fifty years the most elementary aspects of standardized organization, planning, documentation, and reporting have not been developed. Thus, each mission has to reinvent the wheel and, in an organizational sense, has to reinvent itself as a mission." M. C. Bassiouni, "Appraising UN Justice-Related Fact-Finding Missions" (2001) 5 *Wash. U. J. L. & Pol'y* 35, at 40–1.

259 *See, e.g.*, Alex Boraine's description of the first weeks of work at the South African TRC: "Parliament had voted to establish a Commission, the President had announced the names of the commissioners, but that was where it stopped. As yet we had no budget, no offices, no staff, not even a paper clip. We had nothing. It was decided at the first meetings that I would be charged with the responsibility of getting the logistics in place, drawing up a staff complement, and initiating a search for key staff members. This was an extraordinarily difficult task... We stumbled from one vacant building to another, trying to find offices in the centre of Cape Town that would be modest and which would make a spectrum of visitors feel comfortable. We eventually found a building which looked like a vast barn,

for a commission to find its focus, by which point there is not a minute to lose. Even as the commissioners are meeting each other for the first time, public expectations are already high.[260]

In the early truth commission experiences, especially in Latin America, terms of reference were very brief, rarely exceeding a few pages and sometimes consisting of no more than a few short paragraphs.[261] This left commissioners with wide, almost untrammeled, discretion to establish the commission's workplan and procedures. Recent truth commission mandates have become more detailed, providing increased guidance to commissioners but also leaving them a narrower band of discretion. For example, the South African TRC's mandate contained forty-nine articles, many of them quite detailed and exacting.

Both of these approaches may go too far. This author recommends an intermediate approach similar to the terms of reference for the Sierra Leonean TRC.[262] It achieves a judicious balance between the objective of flexibility, on the one hand, and the principles of accountability and legality, on the other. It represents a model of what one might term "bounded discretion."

Ultimately, however, no mandate can prevent any clear abuse of discretion, such as improper fettering of discretion or acting under the instructions of someone without authority. This is why truth commissions must remain subject to judicial oversight, even if their exercise of discretionary powers will rarely incite broad censure.

---

with no internal walls and not too much flooring or ceiling. We called in a company to draw up plans and to renovate the building without delay. While this work was under way I visited a number of furniture factories and, working from a great deal of ignorance, placed orders so that the commissioners would at least have a desk, a chair, and the bare necessities to assist them with their work." *A Country Unmasked* (Oxford: Oxford University Press, 2000), at 83. *See also Nigeria: Judicial Commission of Inquiry for the Investigation of Human Rights Violations, Final Report (2002)*, vol. 1, ch. 2, para. 2.110: "The Commission has had to contend with enormous administrative and logistical problems in carrying out its assignment. These problems, which revolved around setting up a well-staffed, well-remunerated and functional secretariat . . . slowed down the take-off of the work of the Commission."

260   "[O]nce named, in many instances these commissioners may be unknown to each other, and will have to find for themselves a working dynamic and cohesive relationship. At the same time, the framers often find themselves 'working against the clock' in their bid to get the commission off the ground." J. R. Quinn and M. Freeman, "Lessons Learned: Practical Lessons Gleaned from Inside the Truth Commissions of Guatemala and South Africa" (2003) 25 *Human Rights Quarterly* 1117, at 1129.

261   For example, the El Salvador truth commission's mandate consisted of fourteen very short provisions. *See* Mexico Peace Agreements (1991), "Provisions Creating the El Salvador Commission on Truth." The mandate of the Argentine truth commission was equally short.

262   *See* Appendix 2.

Victim-centeredness

In Chapter 1, it was explained that truth commissions – especially more recent ones – tend to be victim-centered in attitude and in practice. They place a premium on victim experiences and feelings. This is in contrast to criminal court proceedings, wherein perpetrators, not victims, are the objects of primary focus.

For contexts marked by a legacy of mass violence or abuse, the objective of victim-centeredness is laudable. It may, however, be in tension with the objective of impartiality. Truth commissions might be attacked for being too sympathetic to victims, and for accepting their evidence at face value rather than approaching it with caution or skepticism. Elevated atttention to victim interests and perspectives may also make a commission less attentive to, or concerned about, important issues of procedural fairness for implicated persons, such as the need to afford a right of reply before attributing responsibility in a final report.[263] The key, ultimately, is for a truth commission to remain steadfast in its adherence to the guiding principles of procedural fairness while still allocating special attention to victims.

At times, the objective of transparency may also be in tension with a victim-centered orientation. This tension is explored in subsequent chapters, particularly Chapter 6.

Accuracy

Truth commissions are investigative bodies. They must search for evidence, sift through it, interpret it, corroborate it, and ultimately report findings. In this process, accuracy is – as one might expect – a central objective. Accuracy is not, however, a component of procedural fairness. Procedural fairness does not guarantee or require the accuracy of results. It only requires a fair process for arriving at those results.[264]

In considering the relationship between the objective of accuracy and the objective of fairness, there is no obvious tension between them. There is, however, a natural tension between the objectives of accuracy and efficiency, owing to the practical constraints described below.

Comprehensiveness

Respectable truth commissions aim to provide not only an accurate and impartial portrait of the abuses under investigation, but also a comprehensive

---

263 *See* Chapter 7.
264 Competence does not guarantee accurate results either; it only *increases* the probability of accuracy.

one.[265] Like the objective of accuracy, the objective of comprehensiveness is complementary to the guiding principles of fairness but in tension with the objective of efficiency, as explained in the next section.

Practical constraints

The guiding principles of fairness and other competing procedural objectives have now been laid out. A complete conception of procedural fairness for truth commissions must, however, take account of the practical constraints that limit a commission's capacity to comply with these divergent principles and objectives.

There are four main practical constraints: time pressure, limited human and financial resources, excessive caseload, and security concerns. Almost without exception, persons who manage truth commissions lament most or all of these constraints.[266] Other investigative bodies, such as international commissions of inquiry, frequently issue the same laments.[267]

These four constraints were previously noted in Chapter 1, but a few brief illustrations will serve to reinforce the point. The truth commission in Chad – a body tasked with investigating thousands of serious violations committed during eight years of authoritarian rule – lacked adequate human and financial resources and faced threats from former military personnel. It was unable to send investigators to the country's interior because it lacked a means of transport, and three-fourths of the original commissioners abandoned their posts and had to be replaced because of security threats.[268] The truth commission in Haiti – a commission that operated for nine months with a shoestring budget and 50 to 100 staff – was required to investigate thousands of human rights violations committed during three years of military rule, even as well-armed groups linked to the prior regime continued to threaten, and commit, serious acts of violence across the country.[269] The Guatemalan truth

---

265 *Recall* Principle 9 of the Principles on the Effective Prevention and Investigation of Extra-Legal, Arbitrary and Summary Executions (1989), UN doc. E/1989/89 (1989), which requires investigations to be "thorough, prompt and impartial."

266 *See, e.g.,* Quinn and Freeman, "Lessons Learned," above note 260, at 1117. Even the truth commission in Korea, which investigated a mere 83 cases, excused the incompleteness of its investigation due to "insufficient time." *A Hard Journey to Justice: First Term Report by the Presidential Truth Commission on Suspicious Deaths of the Republic of Korea* (2004), at 106 and 120.

267 *See, e.g., Report of the International Commission of Inquiry on Darfur to the United Nations Secretary-General* (2005), at paras. 18–19.

268 *See* Hayner, "Fifteen Truth Commissions," above note 186, at 624.

269 *See Si M Pa Rele (If I Don't Cry Out): Report of the National Commission of Truth and Justice,* Haiti (1996).

commission – which operated in a tense security environment – initially had a maximum of one year to investigate as many as two hundred thousand extrajudicial killings and enforced disappearances committed over thirty-four years. The TRC in Sierra Leone – which was created in law in February 2000 but not able to begin work until July 2002, primarily due to renewed armed conflict – was allocated less than two years to investigate tens of thousands of cases of brutal conflict-related violence committed between 1991 and 1999. Less than half of the funds pledged to the commission ended up reaching it, and serious security risks persisted throughout the period of its operation.[270] Compare any of these cases to that of a typical wrongful death inquiry in a developed Commonwealth state, in which an ordinary commission of inquiry may have a multimillion dollar budget and open-ended time frame to investigate a single incident of public controversy.[271]

Alone or in combination, these varied constraints – time pressure, limited human and financial resources, excessive caseload, and security concerns – directly affect the attainment of most of the cited truth commission objectives. For example, security concerns affect how accessible and transparent a truth commission can be. Time, budget, and caseload realities limit how accurate and comprehensive a truth commission can be.[272] Lack of resources limit how independent or efficient a truth commission can be.

As if these were not enough, there are still other factors that may affect the scope of procedural fairness that one can reasonably expect of a truth commission. There may be structural limitations in the truth commission's mandate, such as a lack of investigative powers (*e.g.*, Chile). There may be time-consuming, non-investigation-related obligations imposed on a commission, such as the need to take decisions on scores of applications for compensation (*i.e.*, Morocco) or to facilitate hundreds of contracts of community service for perpetrators (*i.e.*, Timor-Leste) or to fundraise the commission's operating budget (*e.g.*, Nigeria). A country may be too vast and undeveloped to cover in an exhaustive manner (*e.g.*, the DRC). There may be a dozen or more languages

---

270 *See generally Sierra Leone Truth and Reconciliation Commission Final Report* (2004), vol. I, Introduction.

271 *See* note 183 above, regarding the inquiry into the events of Bloody Sunday.

272 In practice, most commissions gather evidence on a fraction of the total number of actual cases. In addition, most commissions can examine in detail only a small subset of the cases on which they *do* have information. El Salvador's truth commission, for example, addressed in detail 32 of the many thousands of cases on which it had evidence. P. Seils, "The Limits of Truth Commissions in the Search for Justice: An Analysis of the Truth Commissions of El Salvador and Guatemala and Their Effect in Achieving Post-Conflict Justice," in M. C. Bassiouni, ed., *Post-Conflict Justice* (Ardsley, NY: Transnational, 2002), at 780.

and dialects spoken in the country (*e.g.*, South Africa). Levels of illiteracy may be quite high (*e.g.*, Sierra Leone). Lack of cooperation from state security agencies may also be a major impediment (*e.g.*, El Salvador).

Part II of this book examines five possible components of a truth commission's work: statement taking, the use of subpoena powers, the use of search and seizure powers, public hearings, and the publication of findings of individual responsibility. In doing so, all of the constraints just noted – together with previously discussed principles and objectives – are taken into account. To do otherwise would, in this author's view, result in a flawed standard of procedural fairness for truth commissions.

CONCLUSIONS

This chapter has explored a range of different standards of procedural fairness, including international human rights standards and a selection of domestic standards. We have seen that these diverse standards are instructive in different ways. Yet we have also noted that none is, as such, apposite for truth commissions.

In that respect, this chapter attempted to articulate a conception of procedural fairness corresponding to the particular nature of the truth commission. The concept is multilayered: it encompasses guiding principles, but it does not discount other legitimate and competing procedural objectives. Nor does the concept ignore the main practical constraints that truth commissions of all kinds tend to experience.

This inquiry has compelled the conclusion that there is tension *among* the various guiding principles of fairness, *between* those principles and other procedural objectives, and *between* both of these and the practical realities of truth commission work.

For truth commission sponsors and advocates concerned about fairness, the only sensible approach is to take into account all of these factors, providing clear directions and standards for the operation of the commission but also leaving a reserve of discretion to the commissioners who must balance and prioritize these factors on a day-to-day and case-by-case basis.[273]

At the same time, there is no getting around the fact that, as a human rights body, a truth commission must place a premium on fairness. It must deliver

---

273 *See, e.g.,* Franck and Fairley, "Procedural Due Process in Human Rights Fact-Finding," above note 222, at 310, describing early UN fact-finding bodies: "It is the position of the authors that fact-finding must be as impartial and as fair to the parties as procedural and evidentiary rules can render it without making the inquiry's task impossible, not merely for ethical reasons but in order to maximize the credibility and impact of the facts found."

the maximum amount of procedural fairness possible, both to perpetrators and victims.[274] The aim of subsequent chapters is to explain in practical terms how that may be done.

274 Victims, in fact, expect no less. As one author notes, "Psychologists and scholars of procedural justice who have studied victims of the Holocaust, state repression and torture note that victims derive more satisfaction from the way the procedure is conducted and its symbolic value than from its actual outcome." R. Mani, *Beyond Retribution: Seeking Justice in the Shadows of War* (Malden, MA: Polity, 2002), at 90. *See also* E. A Lind and T. R. Tyler, *The Social Psychology of Procedural Justice* (New York: Plenum Press, 1988), which examines the psychological impact of procedures that aspire to provide a sense of dignity, respect, and voice. *But see* M. Başoğlv and others, "Psychiatric and Cognitive Effects of War in Former Yugoslavia: Association of Lack of Redress for Trauma and Posttraumatic Stress Reactions" (2005) 294 *Journal of the American Medical Association* 523, which finds that post-traumatic stress disorder (PTSD) and depression in war survivors is mostly independent of a sense of injustice. Fear of threat to safety and loss of control over life appeared to be the most influential factors in PTSD and depression.

PART II

3

Statement Taking

INTRODUCTION

Truth commissions tend to collect most of their information through "statement taking." This term refers to private meetings and interviews conducted primarily by commission staff with persons wishing to make formal statements to the commission.[1]

Statement taking is important in at least two ways: it advances a commission's truth-seeking objectives, and it provides an opportunity for victims and others to describe their traumatic experiences within a caring and generally safe environment. In the absence of statement taking, it is very difficult for a truth commission to fulfill its mission. Truth commissions often find that there is a dearth of "hard" or direct evidence about the atrocities under inquiry. Records are often destroyed or falsified in the transfer of power, and those that remain are likely to be incomplete or unreliable.[2]

1　Some commissions have also hired NGOs to carry out significant statement-taking work on their behalf. For example, the South African TRC hired and trained "designated statement-takers." These were persons drawn from community-based and nongovernmental organizations. In total they collected almost 4,000 statements. A. Boraine, *A Country Unmasked* (Oxford: Oxford University Press, 2000), at 108. In Ghana, a local NGO (CDD-Ghana) assisted the truth commission to obtain statements in isolated regions. *Ghana National Reconciliation Commission Final Report* (2004), section 2.3.2.3.

2　*See, e.g.,* Boraine, *A Country Unmasked*, above note 1, at 109, regarding the South African TRC: "Over and over again, investigators would go to a police station in search

This is true not only in countries with truth commissions, but also in those without.[3]

Statement-taking work tends to begin shortly after a commission's installation and may continue through the life of the commission. For many commissions, statement taking is the primary activity in which it engages. As such, it also tends to be the activity wherein the commission interacts with the greatest number of people. Indeed, most truth commissions receive several thousand individual statements.[4] Other human rights-related investigations (*e.g.*, those by NGOs and UN war crimes commissions) also involve extensive statement taking.

Truth commission mandates generally allow for meetings with, and interviews of, any person.[5] Broadly speaking, however, there are four types of people from whom a commission will take statements: direct victims, persons making

---

of information, only to find that there were no proper records or that the records seemed to have been destroyed." *See also* R. Mani, *Beyond Retribution: Seeking Justice in the Shadows of War* (Malden, MA: Polity, 2002), at 106, where the author notes that the US military illegally impounded and later refused to release thousands of incriminating documents, videotapes, and photos from Haiti, which would have been invaluable sources of information for the truth commission there. The commission requested their release on many occasions, but without success. A similar situation occurred with the truth commission in Panama, which was unable to obtain thousands of documents seized and removed by US forces during their armed intervention of the country in 1989.

3 *See, e.g., Kayishema and Ruzindana*, Judgment, ICTR Trial Chamber, 21 May 1998, at para. 65: "[T]he organizers and perpetrators of the massacres that occurred in Rwanda in 1994 left little documentation behind." *See also* International Center for Transitional Justice, "Transitional Justice in the News" (http://www.ictj.org), 15 March 2004 ("Brazil: Government Burned All Documents Related to 1970s Counterinsurgency") and 15 November 2000 ("Iraq: Key Evidence of Human Rights Violations Lost").

4 For example, truth commissions in Argentina, Haiti, South Africa, Peru, Ghana, and Timor-Leste received approximately 7,000, 5,500, 23,000, 17,000, 4,000, and 7,900 individual statements, respectively. This obviously presents major challenges in organizing, reading, sharing, and meaningfully sifting through the information. In most countries, the actual number of violations is much higher than the number reported to the commission. *See* P. Hayner, "Fifteen Truth Commissions – 1974 to 1994: A Comparative Study" (1994) 16 *Human Rights Quarterly* 597, at 646.

5 *See, e.g.,* section 8(1)(c) of *The Truth and Reconciliation Act 2000* (Sierra Leone), giving the commission power "to interview any individual, group or members of organisations or institutions and, at the commission's discretion, to conduct such interviews in private." *Compare with* Inter-American Commission on Human Rights, Rules of Procedure (2002), Rule 55(a), which allows members of its on-site missions to "interview any persons, groups, entities or institutions freely and in private." Rule 55(d) similarly provides: "The members of the Special Commission shall have access to the jails and all other detention and interrogation sites and shall be able to interview in private those persons imprisoned or detained."

statements on behalf of direct victims,[6] third-party witnesses, and perpetrators (referred to, collectively, as "deponents").[7] Frequently commissions elicit statements from political or civic leaders to understand their perspective on past events too.[8]

Invariably, victims and their family members provide the lion's share of statements. Voluntary statements by perpetrators – though crucial[9] – are comparatively rare.[10] Commissions must, therefore, rely on a range of incentives and threats to get information from perpetrators, including offers to take their statements on a confidential basis, offers of use immunity, and threats to use powers of subpoena or search and seizure powers.[11]

---

6 As noted in Chapter 1, such persons may themselves be considered victims in some cases. *See, e.g.,* Principle 8 of the Bassiouni Principles: "Where appropriate, and in accordance with domestic law, the term 'victim' also includes the immediate family or dependants of the direct victim and persons who have suffered harm in intervening to assist victims in distress or to prevent victimization."

7 A person may, of course, belong to more than one category (*e.g.,* a torture survivor who witnessed abuses of fellow prisoners, or a child soldier who was forcibly recruited by rebel armies and later committed war crimes).

8 For example, the truth commission in Timor-Leste conducted "research interviews" with selected high-level figures from all sides of the prior conflict. Similarly, the truth commission in Peru interviewed leaders of political parties, terrorist groups, and important social movements.

9 For instance, a former member of Sri Lanka's truth commission commented: "The testimony of police and military officers is vital because it can tell us so much about the vertical structure of command. Civilians can tell us only about their local police sergeant or army private. The vertical structures become transparent only when people within the system come forward." Manouri Muttetuwegama, cited in H. Steiner, ed., *Truth Commissions: A Comparative Assessment* (Cambridge, MA: Harvard Law School Human Rights Program, 1997), at 54.

10 For example, the Chilean TRC received thousands of statements from victims and their families, but fewer than twenty military officers (all retired) came forward with confessions. This low level of perpetrator cooperation is all too common. P. Hayner, *Unspeakable Truths: Facing the Challenge of Truth Commissions,* 2d ed. (New York: Routledge, 2002), at 113. An exception to the rule is the TRC in Sierra Leone. It had unusually high participation levels by perpetrators, particularly child perpetrators who were as much victims as perpetrators. More than 13% of the approximately 8,000 statements taken by the TRC were from perpetrators. *See* P. Hayner, International Center for Transitional Justice, *The Sierra Leone Truth and Reconciliation Commission: Reviewing the First Year* (January 2004) at 3–4. Still, as the TRC's final report notes: "Perpetrators were reticent to talk to the Commission for various reasons. The main reasons articulated were the fear of being indicted by the Special Court or being called as a witness by the Court and the fear of reprisals in their communities." *Sierra Leone Truth and Reconciliation Commission Final Report* (2004), vol. 1, ch. 5, para. 123. The truth commissions in South Africa and Timor-Leste are also exceptions to the general rule of low perpetrator participation.

11 M. Freeman and P. Hayner, "Truth-Telling," in *Reconciliation After Violent Conflict: A Handbook* (Stockholm: Institute for Democracy and Electoral Assistance, 2003), at 137. "Another

The focus of this chapter will be on the following aspects of statement taking: publicity and outreach, accessibility, the need to provide information to deponents on possible consequences of providing a statement, procedures for taking and recording statements, procedures relating to the receipt and preservation of confidential and anonymous statements, and the provision of support mechanisms and referrals.

SECTION 1: PUBLICITY AND OUTREACH

It is generally desirable for a truth commission's mandate to impose publicity and outreach obligations on the commission. In Haiti, the truth commission was obligated to make its mandate as widely known as possible throughout the country.[12] In Timor-Leste, the truth commission's mandate required the commission to conduct two months of preparatory activities, which included the development of a "public education campaign."[13] Section 5(3) of the mandate of Sierra Leone's TRC obligated it to "undertake a public education campaign for the purposes and procedures of the Commission" during its preparatory phase.[14] Section 5(4) further provided, "Both during the preparatory period and after it commences operations, the Commission shall endeavour to inform the public of its existence and the purposes of its work, and, when appropriate, shall invite all interested parties who may wish to do so, to make statements or submit information to the Commission." Similarly, section 11(d) of the South African TRC's mandate provided that "victims

---

possibility is that truth commission sponsors could create a new punishable offence of failure by witnesses (other than victims) to come forward to the commission with information about past crimes." *Ibid.*

12   Presidential Executive Order Establishing the Truth and Justice Commission, 1995 (Haiti), art. 11.

13   Section 12. Section 13.3 of the mandate goes on to provide: "Once it is established, the Commission shall publicize the fact that it has been established and make the scope of its inquiries known by all possible means. Where appropriate, it shall invite interested parties to make statements or submit information to the Commission and provide assistance to persons wishing to provide statements to the Commission."

14   The commission's final report notes the following about its preparatory phase: "A Commissioner, accompanied by volunteer staff, spent an average of one week in each district, holding meetings and interacting with civil, community, chieftaincy and faith organizations." *Sierra Leone Truth and Reconciliation Commission Final Report* (2004), vol. 1, ch. 2, para. 49. It further notes at para. 53: "The visits brought home to the Commissioners the magnitude of the problems the Commission would be dealing with. For many people, this was the first time that an institution associated with the Government had visited them and their communities. It conveyed a message that the Commission cared and was willing to come to them as it implemented the processes."

shall be informed through the press and any other medium of their rights in seeking redress through the Commission, including information of: (i) the role of the Commission and the scope of its activities; (ii) the right of victims to have their views and submissions presented and considered at appropriate stages of the inquiry."[15]

Whether or not a mandate imposes publicity obligations, a truth commission should proactively reach out to potential deponents. An effective publicity campaign will serve at least two purposes. First, it will inform interested parties of the nature of the information the commission seeks and the modalities of participation. This will help to ensure that victims and others actualize their right to participation. Second, robust publicity will help stimulate public debate about the legacy of abuse that made the truth commission necessary in the first place.[16]

Truth commission mandates tend to be published in a government's gazette.[17] Official publication, however, is no substitute for an active outreach campaign. The official gazette may not be widely distributed, and many persons who have information or evidence relevant to a commission's investigation may not read it, or be able to read. Consequently, a commission should take other affirmative steps. If its resources are very limited, the commission should focus on forms of outreach that are more national in scale to maximize the impact of the effort. At the same time, a commission should undertake focused outreach in communities or regions where violations were known to be especially prevalent. This is based on both principle and pragmatism: most truth commissions are established on the ostensible basis of assisting victims, and it is victims who invariably provide the bulk of statements to the commission.[18]

---

15 *Recall also* article 11 of the UN Manual on the Effective Prevention and Investigation of Extra-Legal, Arbitrary and Summary Executions (1991), which provides that the public should be notified about the establishment of a commission of inquiry through a broad publicity campaign and invited to submit relevant information or testimony.

16 Kritz writes, "To achieve its goal, a truth commission must do more than merely research and document facts. If that is all it does, a truth commission can produce a completely accurate and objective report that will simply be relegated to an academic shelf. Instead, an effective truth commission process needs to engage and confront all of society in a painful national dialogue and search for a deep understanding of what they did to one another, and what to do about it." N. Kritz, "Progress and Humility: The Ongoing Search for Post-Conflict Justice," in M. C. Bassiouni, ed., *Post-Conflict Justice* (Ardsley, NY: Transnational, 2002), at 61.

17 *See, e.g., Tribunals of Inquiry Act* of 1966, Instrument Constituting a Judicial Commission of Inquiry for the Investigation of Human Rights Violations, published in the Federal Republic of Nigeria Official Gazette 86:56 (Statutory Instrument 8 of 1999).

18 For example, article 6(f) of the mandate of Supreme Decree no. 0065–2001-PCM (Peru), as amended, provides that the Peruvian TRC "shall establish channels of communication and

In furtherance of its publicity objectives, a truth commission might also solicit the assistance of civic and religious leaders in various communities to announce its mission and encourage participation.[19] This is especially important when victims reside predominantly in impoverished and isolated villages, since notices conveyed by customary forms of mass communication may be inaccessible to them. Commissions may also consider the possibility of partnering with or enlisting NGOs to help publicize the statement-taking process. In Peru, the truth commission entered into a written agreement with the National Human Rights Coordinator (a group of human rights NGOs) to "cooperate in disseminating the Commission's initiatives and organizing workshops and seminars to sensitize and train authorities, local leaders and the population at large on the functions, objectives and attributions of the Truth and Reconciliation Commission."[20] Similarly, the truth commission in Timor-Leste had a partnership with NGOs in West Timor (*i.e.,* outside of the country) for outreach and education purposes.[21] Such arrangements will not, however, be viable or appropriate in every context. Even if they support the truth commission's work, NGOs must retain their independence and freedom to monitor and criticize a commission.[22]

Concerning the format that outreach and publicity may take, there are a variety of possible approaches. A commission may post notices, posters, and pamphlets in public places, government offices, and community centers.[23] Advertisements in the popular media are also quite useful.[24] So too are media interviews undertaken by commissioners.[25] Establishing a media

---

mechanisms for the participation of the population, especially that which was affected by the violence." (Unofficial translation by Lisa Magarrell.)

19   This method was used by the Guatemalan truth commission, as well as by the REMHI project discussed in Chapter 1. *See* M. Ballengee, "The Critical Role of Non-Governmental Organizations in Transitional Justice: A Case Study of Guatemala" (2000) 4 *UCLA J. Int'l L. & Foreign Aff.* 477, at 492, 495.

20   Agreement available at http://www.cverdad.org/peru.

21   CAVR Update, August-September 2003 (http://www.easttimor-reconciliation.org).

22   Freeman and Hayner, "Truth-Telling," above note 11, at 133. More generally, *see* "Truth Commissions and NGOs: The Essential Relationship" (International Center for Transitional Justice, April 2004, available at http://www.ictj.org).

23   The truth commission in Sri Lanka posted over 5,000 notices. *Final Report of Commission of Inquiry into Involuntary Removal or Disappearance of Persons in the Western Southern and Sabaragamuwa Provinces*, September 1997, at Part 1, ch. 1, A(2).

24   During its preliminary phase, El Salvador's truth commission advertised in newspapers and on radio and television about its "open door" policy to the receipt of statements from the public. T. G. Phelps, *Shattered Voices: Language, Violence, and the Work of Truth Commissions* (Philadelphia: University of Pennsylvania Press, 2004), at 98. Panama's truth commission regularly published appeals in the country's main newspapers for information on cases. *Informe Final de la Comisión de la Verdad de Panamá* (2002), at 8.

25   Argentina's truth commission held more than thirty press conferences and gave over one hundred press, radio, and television interviews. *See Nunca Más: The Report of the Argentine*

liaison department within a commission will also facilitate the diffusion of information.[26]

Today especially, publicity is often carried out using the Internet. Most contemporary truth commissions have created their own websites as tools for publicity and outreach, and as a means to receive feedback or statements from interested parties. Examples include the truth commissions established in South Africa, Panama, Peru, the Republic of Korea, Timor-Leste, and Morocco.[27] The utility and feasibility of doing this will, however, vary according to context.[28]

A truth commission may also choose to publish periodic bulletins (or interim reports), as did the commissions in Sri Lanka, Timor-Leste, and Morocco. The truth commission in Timor-Leste also spread its message through the production and distribution of T-shirts and stickers, and by creating its own radio programs.

In general, the more diverse the forms of publicity, the more likely a truth commission is to reach a country's diverse communities and gain evidence from parties of every age, race, gender, socioeconomic class, and religious group.[29] In a country where multiple languages are spoken, outreach should ideally be conducted in each language, having regard to regional variation.

In some cases, victims and witnesses with useful information and evidence have relocated to other countries, often to escape persecution or violence. Such persons should also be notified about the commission statement-taking process so that they may participate.[30] Various truth commissions, including those of Argentina, Chile, Guatemala, Timor-Leste, and Morocco, have actively sought statements from exiles.[31]

National Commission on the Disappeared, trans. E. Canetti (New York: Farrar Straus Giroux, 1986), Part 4, at 432.

26   See J. R. Quinn and M. Freeman, "Lessons Learned: Practical Lessons Gleaned from Inside the Truth Commissions of Guatemala and South Africa" (2003) 25 *Human Rights Quarterly* 1117, at 1144 (describing the work of the South African TRC's media liaison department).

27   For a list of active truth commission websites, *see* http://www.ictj.org.

28   The truth commissions in Sierra Leone and Grenada did not establish websites. Also, as of this writing, the truth commissions in Paraguay, the DRC, and Liberia have not established websites.

29   Special outreach efforts may, however, be required to encourage more participation by women in contexts of widespread sexual violence. Underreporting by women in such contexts is a pervasive problem. Hayner, *Unspeakable Truths,* above note 10, at 77–9.

30   To that end, truth commissions might place announcements and advertisements in the community newspapers and other mass media in the countries where most expatriates reside.

31   National embassies, consulates, and high commissions usually assist in the receipt and delivery to the commission of statements from expatriates. *See, e.g., Law 04/018 (2004) Concerning the Organization, Powers and Functions of the Truth and Reconciliation Commission* (DRC), art. 34, which enables the DRC truth commission to obtain information from foreign sources through official diplomatic channels.

In all its public outreach and education work, a truth commission should articulate possible material consequences of *not* providing a statement. Specifically, if reparations are potentially contingent on participation in the truth commission's inquiry or on its conclusions about individual cases, such facts should be made known. This is especially the case when a truth commission's mandate explicitly, if imprecisely, establishes a link between truth commission participation and reparation eligibility.[32] A commission that fails to publicize such a link would deny victims the possibility of informed choice, leading to *ad hoc* results that would arbitrarily favor those in a position of greater knowledge about the advantages of choosing to come forward and make a statement.[33] The importance of publicizing the link is amplified if the truth commission follows a "closed list" policy whereby only those who give statements to the commission are eligible beneficiaries of the recommended reparation program.[34]

In this matter, however, a note of caution is in order. While publicizing a possible link between truth commission participation and reparation eligibility will generally lead to an increase in the quantity of statements, it may generate two possibly negative consequences. First, it could undermine the perceived quality of the statements in the public's eye.[35] Second, it could raise financial expectations that may not be fulfilled, either in whole or in part. This was to some extent the experience of the South African TRC.[36] It may

---

32   *See, e.g.,* the mandate of the South African TRC, which provides that the commission "shall make recommendations to the President with regard to – (i) the policy which should be followed or measures which should be taken with regard to the granting of reparation to victims or the taking of other measures aimed at rehabilitating and restoring the human and civil dignity of victims; (ii) measures which should be taken to grant urgent interim reparation to victims." In addition, section 15 provides: "(1) When the (Human Rights Violations) Committee finds that a gross violation of human rights has been committed and if the Committee is of the opinion that a person is a victim of such violation, it shall refer the matter to the Committee on Reparation and Rehabilitation for its consideration . . ." *Promotion of National Unity and Reconciliation Act*, 1995 (South Africa), s. 4(f). *See also An Act to Establish the Truth and Reconciliation Commission of Liberia* (2005), s. 38: "The TRC shall create a trust fund for the benefit of victims and survivors of the crises; appoint trustees and determine beneficiaries as part of the outcome of the proceedings, findings and recommendations of the TRC at the end of its tenure."

33   Note, however, that in two of the more prominent cases of victim reparation programs – those of Chile and Argentina – the programs were established after the commissions concluded their work and without any prior assurance of reparation. Hayner, *Unspeakable Truths*, above note 10, at 173 and 175.

34   In South Africa, the TRC publicly announced that only victims on its official list would be eligible for the reparation package it would eventually recommend. *Ibid.,* at 178.

35   *See, e.g.,* D. Orentlicher, "Promotion and Protection of Human Rights: Impunity," UN doc. E/CN.4/2004/88 (2004), at para. 19(c).

36   The recommendations on victim reparation that the TRC made in its 1998 final report were not implemented until 2004. The payments, totaling $97 million, fell well short of the $441

also become the fate of future truth commissions. Accordingly, as a matter of political prudence, a commission must be careful in how it publicizes any link between statement taking and future eligibility for reparations. It should not, in any case, promise substantial reparation in return for participation.[37] This concern even holds true for commissions such as the Sierra Leonean TRC and the Liberian TRC, whose ultimate recommendations are, at law, binding on the respective governments.[38]

A further linkage between outreach and statement taking pertains to families of forcibly disappeared persons. In some cases, during or after the operation of a truth commission, a state may deem missing persons "presumed dead" or "forcibly disappeared."[39] Such a designation is intended, *inter alia*, to enable families of the disappeared to access dormant bank accounts and to inherit and administer estates.[40] Truth commissions should consider publicizing this potential advantage of coming forward to provide a statement, particularly since its official findings will tend to increase the likelihood of obtaining such a designation.

RECOMMENDATIONS

- It is generally desirable for a truth commission's mandate to impose publicity and outreach obligations on the commission.
- Whether or not the mandate imposes such obligations, a commission should proactively advise the public as to when, how, where, and why it will be taking statements.

---

million that the TRC recommended. The 22,000 eligible victims received one-time payments of $4,400 each. *See* International Center for Transitional Justice, "Transitional Justice in the News," 30 November 2004. In other contexts, including Chad and Nigeria, the reparation recommendations made by their respective truth commissions remain unimplmented.

37 The only outlier in this discussion, as explained in previous chapters, is Morocco. That country's truth commission had the power to directly award compensation to eligible victims.

38 Past experience in El Salvador – where the truth commission's recommendations on reparation remain unimplemented – provides a cautionary tale in this respect

39 In Liberia, the truth commission itself can declare a missing person dead, though it cannot issue any attendant legal documentation. *See An Act to Establish the Truth and Reconciliation Commission of Liberia* (2005), s. 29: "Upon proper inquiry and investigation, the TRC may at any time prior to the end of its tenure *ad interim*, declare missing persons and others who were victims of mass murders and massacres, dead and recommend to the appropriate agency of government for issuance of certificates in testimony thereof as a form of immediate relief, consolation and reparation to survivors and relatives of victims."

40 In Argentina, the government created the status of "forcibly disappeared" rather than declaring persons dead. This was equivalent to a death certificate, and it applied to all victims documented by Argentina's truth commission. Hayner, *Unspeakable Truths*, above note 10, at 28–9, 177. The truth commission in Uruguay recommended the creation of an equivalent status: "absence on account of enforced disappearance." *Peace Commission Final Report* (10 April 2003), para. 76.

- Publicity may be carried out by use of private and public media, the Internet, posters, and pamphlets.
- Where resources are acutely limited, a commission should focus its outreach efforts on communities or regions where violations were known to be especially prevalent. On-site visits to such communities or regions should be considered.
- Truth commissions should consider enlisting the participation of respected NGOs and other civil society actors to publicize the statement-taking process.
- Nationals living abroad, particularly refugees, should be notified about the commission statement-taking process so that they may participate.
- In its public outreach work, a commission should articulate possible material consequences of failing to provide a statement. In particular, where a commission is mandated to develop a list of victims for a future reparation or compensation program, or to design and recommend such a program, or to do both, the commission should indicate whether failure to provide a statement could adversely affect eligibility.

SECTION 2: ACCESSIBILITY

A truth commission will best fulfill its mandate if the maximum number of potential deponents provides statements. The ease and convenience with which interested parties are able to access commission staff and make statements will significantly affect this number. The degree of accessibility will also affect the quality of the information gathered in statements.

Location is the primary factor that dictates parties' ability to access and participate in a commission. The places where statements are taken should establish a welcoming atmosphere. The statement-taking location should help deponents feel confident that their stories will be taken seriously. Location is also important to protect the confidentiality and privacy of deponents.

Statements may be taken at a single *centralized* location that deponents visit. This can help underscore the extent to which they are participating in a major official investigation. It is crucial, however, that any such location is considered neutral and safe. The truth commission in Chad was required to use unreconstructed former torture chambers as the central location for receiving statements. As a result, fewer victims came forward.[41] Also, it cannot be known if some deponents' memories of torture interfered with the completeness

---

41   A lack of office space forced the ill-funded Chadian truth commission "to set up its head-quarters in the former secret detention center of the security forces, where some of the worst

or accuracy of their statements. By contrast, when the truth commission in Timor-Leste chose a former prison as its new headquarters, it appeared to work well. The building was "exorcised" by a local soothsayer in a traditional cleansing ceremony before the staff arrived and began work.[42] In El Salvador, the commission put its main office in the center of the capital's most affluent neighborhood. Because many victims viewed it as a neighborhood where auto-crats and military officials resided, there was fear of approaching the office.[43]

Whatever its vices and virtues, in most cases a single location will be insuffi-cient. Truth commissions determined to hear from deponents throughout the country should generally seek to establish a *substantial presence in key regions* of the country. Several truth commission mandates have encouraged, or even required, the establishment of regional offices, with appropriate measures to ensure centralized oversight.[44] The truth commissions of South Africa and Guatemala appear to have found regional offices helpful in overcoming geo-graphical distances. The use of such offices enabled these commissions to focus greater attention on particular events in remote communities, whereas any attempt to limit their presence to a single national office would have severely limited accessibility and participation.[45] Subsequent commissions, such as those of Peru and Ghana, followed similar approaches.

A truth commission may gather statements in *local or private settings* too. For example, statement takers may visit remote communities or take statements directly in deponents' homes.[46] This approach may be needed to take statements from elderly persons and persons with disabilities, who might otherwise be unable to give statements to a commission. It may also help in obtaining testimony from more reticent or vulnerable persons who feel safer making statements in their communities or from their homes. The Guatemalan truth commission's staff managed to visit almost two thousand communities, registering more than seven thousand individual and collective

---

of the torture and killings had taken place, thus deterring many former victims from coming to give testimony." Hayner, *Unspeakable Truths*, above note 10, at 58.

42   CAVR Update, February–March 2003 (http://www.easttimor-reconciliation.org). The building is envisioned as a future human rights center and memorial.

43   Hayner, *Unspeakable Truths*, above note 10, at 149.

44   *See, e.g.*, the mandate of Timor-Leste's truth commission, which provides: "The Commission shall establish up to six Regional Offices of the Commission. The details of each Regional Office, including location and areas of responsibility, are to be published in the Official Gazette of East Timor." "On the Establishment of a Commission for Reception, Truth and Reconciliation in East Timor," UNTAET/REG/2001/01 as amended, 10.1.

45   Quinn and Freeman, "Lessons Learned," above note 26, at 1121–3.

46   *See, e.g.*, Boraine, *A Country Unmasked*, above note 1, at 108, describing the proactive approach to statement taking adopted by the South African TRC. The staff of the REMHI project in Guatemala (discussed in Chapter 1) took statements in parishes, houses, or wher-ever victims wished to talk. *See* Ballengee, "Critical Role of Non-Governmental Organiza-tions," above note 19, at 492.

testimonies.[47] Because access to victims was limited by geography and by ongoing fears of reprisals, this proactive effort was imperative. The earlier truth commission in Argentina also traveled to remote regions, where it took over fourteen hundred statements.[48]

Statements may be also taken in *confidential, undisclosed locations.* This is crucial in situations where deponents fear for their lives, as many did in El Salvador during the period of operation of that country's truth commission.[49] The use of undisclosed locations helps protect deponents' identities, and thus their safety. The statements of such deponents may provide vital information that would otherwise be missed because of fear of reprisals.

A truth commission may also choose to take *statements submitted in writing.* There may be a place to which completed statement forms can be mailed, typically the commission's main or regional offices. In addition, a commission's website may allow for statements to be electronically posted, whether openly or confidentially. Commissions often receive statements in the form of personal letters too.[50]

Overall, the best practice is to provide multiple means to access the commission in order to give a statement. This will help ensure that no one is unfairly excluded on the basis of geography, language, disability, personal finances,

47 Freeman and Hayner, "Truth-Telling," above note 11, at 142. A contrasting, and unfortunate, example is drawn from the truth commission in Chad, which recalled in its final report: "[L]ack of transport . . . paralyzed the Commission for a considerable time. At the start, the Commission was furnished two small urban vehicles, a 504 and a small Suzuki, whereas all-terrain vehicles were actually required for travel to the provinces . . . On 25 August 1991 a Toyota all-terrain vehicle was put at the disposal of the Commission. But during the events of 13 October 1991, unfortunately, the Toyota and the little Suzuki were taken off by combatants . . . This is why the Commission was unable to send investigators to the interior of the country during the entire initial period." Cited in Hayner, *Unspeakable Truths,* above note 10, at 58. *See generally Report of the Commission of Inquiry on the Crimes and Misappropriations Committed by the Ex-President Habre, His Accomplices and/or Accessories* (1992), as excerpted in N. Kritz, ed. *Transitional Justice: How Emerging Democracies Reckon with Former Regimes* (Washington, DC: US Institute for Peace Press, 1995), vol. 3, at 51–93. The Sierra Leonean TRC reported similar problems: "Each district team reported problems with the vehicles or the drivers assigned to them. Due to the frequency of breakdowns, the Commission terminated the vehicle hire contract and diversified the range of suppliers. Items such as audio recorders and tapes were difficult to come by. The Commission was unable to procure digital video cameras for the use of the statement takers until the last month of statement taking." *Sierra Leone Truth and Reconciliation Commission Final Report* (2004), vol. 1, ch. 4, para. 16.

48 Phelps, *Shattered Voices,* above note 24, at 84.

49 *See From Madness to Hope: The Twelve-Year War in El Salvador: Report of the Commission on the Truth for El Salvador,* UN doc. S/25500, Annex, 1993. Excerpts of the Salvadoran truth commission's final report are included in Appendix 2 to this book.

50 Within the few months of its establishment, the Moroccan truth commission received thousands of personal letters from victims and families across the country.

or similarly arbitrary grounds.[51] Multiple means of communicating with a commission will be particularly important where, for example, an ongoing conflict precludes the commission's direct access to parts of a country.[52] Yet even in more stable contexts, the existence of multiple access points will tend to enhance the process and product of a commission's work.

RECOMMENDATIONS

- Statements should be taken in locations, and using methods, that are physically and psychologically accessible. Accordingly, statements should be taken in neutral and convenient locations, during times that are considerate of deponents' schedules.
- A commission should make statement taking accessible to the public generally, and to victims in particular, by as many means as possible. This might include any one or more of the following: creating regional or local offices, using a website (to which statements can be directly posted), and carrying out site visits to take statements in remote communities and in deponents' homes. In exceptional circumstances, effective access may require that statements be taken in undisclosed locations. (*See* Section 5: Receipt and Preservation of Confidential and Anonymous Statements.)
- Deponents should be able to make statements in their native language.
- Commissions should consider special measures to facilitate statement taking for elderly persons and persons with disabilities.

SECTION 3: INFORMATION ON POSSIBLE CONSEQUENCES OF GIVING A STATEMENT

To guarantee that individuals are willingly and freely providing information or evidence, a truth commission should ensure that deponents are aware of

---

51 The South African TRC's mandate provides that "procedures for dealing with applications by victims shall be expeditious, fair, inexpensive and accessible." *Promotion of National Unity and Reconciliation Act,* 1995 (South Africa), s. 11(f).

52 Inaccessibility due to ongoing conflict has occurred in several instances, including in Uganda, Sri Lanka, and the DRC. *See, e.g.,* J. R. Quinn, "Dealing with a Legacy of Mass Atrocity: Truth Commissions in Uganda and Chile" (2001) 19.4 *Netherlands Quarterly of Human Rights* 383, at 394. *See also Final Report of Commission of Inquiry into Involuntary Removal or Disappearance of Persons in the Northern and Eastern Provinces,* September 1997, at ch. 1, s. 1.3: "Unlike other Commissions, this Commission had to investigate disappearances in areas of Military Operations. The Commission had to either cancel several sittings or postpone them due to the unsettled conditions caused by the ground situation. On one occasion in Batticaloa, the Commission found shells zooming over the Circuit Bungalow where it stayed and heard the rattle of gunfire for hours."

the possible subsequent uses of their statements. In other words, deponents should be put in a position whereby their decision to impart information to the commission is fully informed.

For a deponent, there are many possible consequences of providing a statement to a truth commission. Many of these are mostly or wholly within a truth commission's control. For example, whether a deponent's name ends up on the commission's official list of victims is a decision directly controlled by the commission.[53] In addition, subject to a deponent's consent, it is the commission that will decide whether to include excerpts from his or her statement in its final report.[54]

A different, but equally important, possible consequence of providing a statement is the prospect of its use in trial proceedings. Nonconfidential, self-incriminating information given voluntarily by a deponent during the statement-taking process will generally not be protected by the privilege against self-incrimination. To the contrary, a commission's mandate may require it to share such information with police, investigators, prosecutors, and courts during its investigation or upon the completion of its mandate.[55] Depending on the case, this could result in the deponent's being prosecuted, sued, disciplined, or compelled to serve as a witness at a future trial.

Many truth commissions have possessed and exercised the authority to share information in this way, including those of Argentina (which was required to submit evidence of criminal conduct to authorities for possible prosecution),[56] Uganda (which passed files to the police for further investigation),[57] Chile (which, despite an amnesty, had an explicit obligation to immediately send, under seal, evidence of criminal conduct to courts),[58] Haiti (which was

---

53   As previously noted, whether a government fulfills its promise to give just and meaningful reparation to those whose names appear on the list is another matter.

54   *See, e.g.,* Rules of Procedure of the International Humanitarian Fact-Finding Commission (1992), Rule 29: "No personal data shall be published without the express consent of the person concerned." *See also* European Committee Against Torture, Rules of Procedure (1997), Rule 45(2).

55   Although the issue is not examined here as such, it is worth noting that a truth commission might also have the discretion to forward such information to vetting bodies examining the past performance of personnel in public institutions such as the army, police, or judiciary.

56   Decree 187/83 (1983) Creating the National Commission on Disappeared Persons, art. 2(a). *See* R. Mattarollo, "Truth Commissions," in Bassiouni, *Post-Conflict Justice*, above note 16, at 317.

57   The Ugandan police were responsible for the investigation of criminal matters referred to it by the truth commission. If, following investigation, a case was deemed suitable for prosecution, it was to be passed to the director of public prosecutions. In the end, few cases made it to trial. *See* Hayner, *Unspeakable Truths*, above note 10, at 94.

58   Article 2 of Supreme Decree 355 (1990) Establishing the Commission on Truth and Reconciliation.

required to promptly forward information on any criminal acts that fell outside its remit),[59] the Republic of Korea (which had an obligation to forward cases involving criminal acts to the prosecutor general),[60] Peru (which sent cases to the public prosecutor during its investigation and upon the completion of its mandate),[61] and Timor-Leste (which forwarded statements and confessions indicating participation in international crimes to the Office of the General Prosecutor for possible prosecution).[62]

Other consequences for deponents who make statements to truth commissions are much less within a commission's control. For example, a truth commission is unable to determine whether the transfer of incriminating information will result in a trial; that is a matter for the receiving prosecutor to decide.[63] Also, a truth commission ordinarily will be unable to protect a deponent against any adverse action carried out by an employer as punishment for having provided a statement to the commission.[64]

Other consequences that are partly outside of a commission's control pertain to archives. Truth commission records – which contain information received, as well as generated, by it – will usually be preserved in some way long after the commission itself has dissolved. However, many truth commission mandates fail to specify anything concerning the disposition of a commission's files and records.[65] This is problematic. After a commission's dissolution,

---

59 Presidential Executive Order Establishing the Truth and Justice Commission, 1995 (Haiti), art. 12.

60 Article 25 of the *Special Act to Reveal the Truth Regarding Suspicious Deaths*, Act no. 6170, 15 January 2000, as amended. The commission also had a right to appeal any decision by the prosecutor general *not* to prosecute a referred case. Article 32.

61 The Peruvian TRC's mandate authorized it to establish "special cooperation agreements" with prosecutorial and judicial authorities. Supreme Decree no. 0065-2001-PCM (Peru) as amended, article 5.

62 *See* discussion in Chapter 1, Section 4.

63 For their part, truth commissions can at least ensure a proper chain of custody for evidence they acquire so as not to mitigate its possible use at any future trial.

64 *But see, e.g.,* the Ontario *Public Inquiries Act*, RSO 1990, as amended, s. 9.1(1) and (2): "(1) No adverse employment action shall be taken against any employee of any person because the employee, acting in good faith, has made representations as a party or has disclosed information either in evidence or otherwise to a commission under this Act or to the staff of a commission. (2) Any person who contrary to subsection (1) takes adverse employment action against an employee is guilty of an offence and on conviction is liable to a fine of not more than $5,000."

65 This may be because the matter is already regulated by other legislation, such as an archival law. *But see* article 7 of the Supreme Decree no. 0065-2001-PCM (Peru) as amended: "...At the end of its operation, the bank of documents gathered by the [Truth and Reconciliation] Commission throughout its term shall be turned over, under inventory, to the Ombudsman's Office, under strict reserve as to its contents..." (Unofficial translation by Lisa Magarrell.) *See also An Act to Establish the Truth and Reconciliation Commission of Liberia*

members of the public – including prosecutors, researchers, and perpetrators – may be able to access the commission's records under freedom of information or *habeas data* legislation.[66] Privacy laws or data-protection legislation (which governs, among other things, the management of personal data contained in computer systems) will not necessarily shield all of the commission's records from such public access.[67] Moreover, "even a trustworthy custodian may be subjected to irresistible pressures by an administratively superior body."[68] This is not a minor concern: in a worst-case scenario, access to a commission's records could lead to acts of private vengeance against perpetrators or, alternatively, against victims and witnesses who came forward to identify perpetrators. Accordingly, all deponents, but especially victims, should be consulted as to whether the commission's file on their cases can be reviewed by third parties after the commission's dissolution.[69]

The best general practice is for a truth commission to ask a deponent to indicate, *up front*, his or her consent to *various* possible subsequent uses of the information he or she provides to the commission. In Timor-Leste, for example, the truth commission informed every deponent of the range of possible subsequent uses of his or her statement. This was done through an information sheet that had a consent form at the bottom (all of which was attached to each statement). The consent form had a number of tickable boxes. Deponents had the right to decide, for example, whether the commission could use some or all of the statement in its final report, whether they wished to have their identity made known or kept confidential, whether they wished to

---

(2005), s. 47: "The archives of the TRC shall remain in the public domain except those records or documents classified by the TRC as 'confidential' which shall remain classified for 20 years following the retirement of the TRC. This restriction extends to commissioners, staff and persons privy to such confidential and closed information by virtue of employment, assignment or their involvement with the TRC or otherwise."

66   *See generally* T. H. Peterson, *Final Acts: A Guide to Preserving the Records of Truth Commissions* (Baltimore: Johns Hopkins University Press and the Woodrow Wilson International Center for Scholars, 2005), at 3, 17–18. *See also* International Council on Archives, *In Defense of Human Rights: Archives So We Do Not Forget* (2004), available at http://www.ica.org.

67   See Peterson, *Final Acts*, above note 66, at 3, 18–19.

68   *Ibid.*, at 31. The author cites an intriguing suggestion made by Transparency International on this issue, namely, to accord constitutional protection to a country's chief archivist. *Ibid.*, at 33.

69   Peterson recommends two guiding principles for handling the records of victims of human rights violations: "1. The victim has the right to know what information is in the file on his or her case. 2. The victim has the right to determine whether the file on his or her case can be consulted by third parties." The victim's rights of access are not, however, absolute. They must, for example, be balanced with the rights of third parties who are named as responsible for the violations and who may not have had an opportunity to view or contest the allegations. *Ibid.*, at 93–5.

have the identity of persons mentioned in the statement made known or kept confidential, and so forth.

RECOMMENDATIONS

- A commission should inform a deponent of all possible subsequent uses of his or her statement for purposes that are consistent with its mandate. Such uses may include listing the deponent's name in the final report, citing part of the deponent's statement in the final report, forwarding the statement to prosecutors or courts, and permitting public access to the statement after the commission's dissolution.
- Where appropriate, a commission should obtain a deponent's prior consent for any legally significant subsequent uses of his or her statement.

SECTION 4: PROCEDURES FOR TAKING AND RECORDING STATEMENTS

There are many possible approaches a truth commission may adopt when it comes to taking and recording statements from deponents. There are, however, at least two baseline rules a commission should follow no matter what approach it employs. First, a commission's statement-taking procedure should be implemented according to a predetermined format so that statements are recorded consistently and accurately for future use by the commission and other bodies. Second, the scope of a statement taker's questions should be confined to areas that fall within a commission's mandate, whether the person giving the statement is a victim, relative, third-party witness, or perpetrator.[70]

The use to which a commission intends to put deponents' statements has implications for the appropriate manner in which an interview should be conducted. Often commissions must balance the goals of respecting the dignity of deponents, on the one hand, and of acquiring information that is as complete and accurate as possible, on the other.

---

70 Limiting an inquiry to the scope of the mandate was referred to as "judicial pertinency" in *Watkins v. United States*, 77 US 1173 at 1189 (1957), a US Supreme Court case that dealt with the appropriate limits of the House Committee on Un-American Activities in the United States. *See also* Z. Segal, "The Power to Probe into Matters of Vital Public Importance" (1984) 58 *Tul. L. Rev.* 941, at 963, discussing the recommendation of the 1966 UK Royal Commission chaired by Lord Justice Salmon that before someone becomes a "target of an inquiry, the tribunal [of inquiry] must be satisfied that there is a link between that person and the specific matter under investigation."

In weighing these two objectives, one approach may be to emphasize dignity in the interview process. The act of statement taking can serve as a form of moral acknowledgment, both because a statement taker listens to a deponent's story, and because the story is recorded for posterity. Victims, in particular, may have a strong interest in this form of acknowledgment. For some victims, indeed, the mere fact of being listened to has moral and psychological value.[71] A victim-centered approach to statement taking tends to allow the deponent to recount his or her experiences with little interruption or guidance, and without undue repetition of the original trauma.[72] Such an approach is, however, often accompanied by a reluctance to probe deponents for factual clarifications, especially where the statement taker is on familiar terms with the deponent.[73]

A contrasting approach might emphasize detail and accuracy in the interview process. A truth commission that intends to publish findings of individual responsibility, for example, will need to employ a less passive statement-taking model – especially since deponent statements may constitute the only reliable source of evidence in some cases. A statement taker may have to require the deponent to return to subjects that he or she finds difficult to discuss, or to follow up with the deponent after an interview to elicit further information. The statement taker may also need to ask very pointed questions in order to acquire and accurately record the details of the events.

Whichever interview style is adopted, however, it is important to recognize that none can guarantee a statement's empirical veracity. Deponents of every

---

71   *See* Steiner, *Truth Commissions*, above note 9, at 25 (citing Elizabeth Kiss) and 26 (citing Tina Rosenberg).

72   This approach is endorsed, *inter alia*, in the UN Training Manual for Human Rights Monitoring (http://www1.umn.edu/humanrts/monitoring), c. VIII. *Recall also* Principle 10 of the Bassiouni Principles, which provides that "a victim who has suffered violence or trauma should benefit from special consideration and care to avoid his or her retraumatization in the course of legal and administrative procedures designed to provide justice and reparation."

73   *See, e.g.,* N. Roht-Arriaza, "Civil Society in Processes of Accountability," in Bassiouni, *Post-Conflict Justice*, above note 16, at 106, where she discusses the approach used by the REMHI project in Guatemala (discussed in Chapter 1): "REMHI trained local people, living in the communities that had suffered the brunt of the violence, to take testimonies from their neighbours according to an action research paradigm. Local interviewers were chosen to facilitate access and trust, minimize translation and cultural problems and give the project greater resonance with the collective nature of traditional Mayan society. On the other hand, the methodology involved dangers, including over-familiarity engendering leading questions and a tension between the need to both probe responses and be supportive."

kind may have reasons for telling more or less than the whole truth, and it will not always be easy to discover why.[74]

As to the recording of statements, there are several possible techniques a commission can adopt. One method is to have statement takers make intermittent notes during open-ended interviews with deponents and then write reports summarizing the substance of the statements later on, outside the deponent's presence. This method can help to cultivate a natural rapport between the deponent and the statement taker by allowing the interaction to be more like a conversation. At the same time, a statement taker's memory of details will be less exact than the actual interview notes. Accordingly, an alternative approach might be to take extensive notes throughout the interview. As one might expect, however, such an approach tends to reduce the free flow of ideas and information and diminish the "listening" quality of an interview.

Alternatively, or additionally, a commission may use prescribed forms or questionnaires that can be completed by deponents prior to an interview, or by statement takers during an interview. The use of forms allows for a higher level of standardization, making it more likely that deponents' statements will be treated in a similar manner, and that the commission obtains the precise information it seeks.[75] The use of forms may, however, result in the omission of important details that do not correspond to specific questions on the form. Deponents may have information about a number of different relevant incidents, but self-censor on written forms in an effort to tailor their responses to formulaic questions. This could limit the nature and quality of "truth" a commission would obtain.

---

74 *See, e.g.,* R. Shaw, "Rethinking Truth and Reconciliation Commissions: Lessons from Sierra Leone" (US Institute for Peace, February 2005), at 8–9: "Most people I asked during my research over four consecutive years, however, were very divided about the [Sierra Leonean] TRC and truth telling. Almost without exception, people wanted 'to forget,' even if such forgetting eluded them, often urging 'let's forgive and forget.' Some, intriguingly, were able to synthesize the TRC message of remembering with this prevailing understanding of healing and reconciliation as forgetting. But for others – including victims – the TRC was often an obstacle to healing and reconciliation. For some communities, such as a large village in which I worked in 2003 and 2004 that had held church ceremonies to reintegrate ex-combatants, the TRC disrupted their own practices of reconciliation. Sometimes whole communities agreed not to give statements or to give statements that withheld information that they thought might be damaging to the ex-combatant children of their neighbors. People thereby sought to protect their communities and their relationships from the potentially damaging consequences of publicly remembering violence."

75 The use of standardized forms also facilitates the work of a truth commission's data entry staff. This is not an insignificant concern for most commissions, given the volume of cases they handle. *See generally* P. Ball and others, eds., *Making the Case: Investigating Large Scale Human Rights Investigations* (Washington, DC: AAAS, 2000).

Another alternative, or additional, recording method is for interviews to be taped or video recorded.[76] This is often costly and will not usually be appropriate in commissions where security risks to deponents are particularly high.[77] Additionally, recording is never appropriate if the deponent has not given his or her express consent.

Whatever method is used, it is important for the deponent to make a solemn undertaking or affirmation about the truthfulness and completeness of the statement he or she gives.[78] The goal is to ensure that deponents are aware of the importance of recounting their experience in a forthright and honest manner, not least because of the subsequent reliance that the commission and others (*e.g.*, prosecutors) might place on it.[79] Ideally, written statements or summaries of oral statements should be signed by the deponent. Where they are not signed, the statement taker should note the reasons on the document.[80]

Another important procedural issue concerns the persons who may, or may not, be present at an interview. Generally speaking, a deponent should be able to have others present during the interview. This can help increase the level of participation in a truth commission's statement-taking process, and it may also improve the quality of the statements a commission receives. However, if the statement taker perceives that the presence of a third party is detrimentally affecting the quality of the statement, he or she might request the party to leave for a part of the interview and also note any concerns about the effect of the third party's presence in the case summary.

Statements do not always need to be made by individuals in private settings. They may also be taken in open group settings. Group settings will, however, be desirable only in a narrow set of circumstances. These circumstances may include, for example, when all members of the group were present for the same event, or when members of the group are reluctant to provide information except in the presence of the larger group.[81] The veracity of group statements is more questionable because group members will often influence each other's

---

76 Various commissions have audiotaped or videotaped their interviews. These include truth commissions in Bolivia, Haiti, South Africa, and the Republic of Korea. Peterson, *Final Acts*, above note 66, at 43.

77 UN Training Manual for Human Rights Monitoring, c. VIII, at paras. 20–22.

78 *See, e.g., An Act to Establish the Truth and Reconciliation Commission of Liberia* (2005), s. 27(c), which empowers the Liberian TRC to "administer oaths during investigation for the taking and making of statements the falsity of which is punishable for perjury."

79 To further support the likelihood of obtaining true statements, several commission mandates make it a punishable offense to knowingly provide false information. *See, e.g.*, section 22(e) of the *National Reconciliation Commission Act*, 2002, Act 611 (Ghana).

80 *See, e.g.*, Rule 111(1) of the ICC Rules of Procedure and Evidence.

81 *See, e.g.*, Ballengee, "Critical Role of Non-Governmental Organizations," above note 19, at 492.

recollections of events. Consequently, statement takers may need to conduct individual interviews as a follow-up to any group session.

A further issue concerns who is present to take the statement on behalf of the commission, whether in a private or group setting. If a particular statement taker is not perceived to be neutral, this will obviously interfere with the veracity and completeness of a deponent's statement.[82]

There are still other important considerations to bear in mind. These pertain to special categories of deponents. For example, if the deponent is a child, it is usually appropriate for a parent, close adult family member, or legal guardian to be present while the child makes a statement.[83] Also, there may be differences between the class and gender of the statement taker and the deponent that affect the dynamics of the interview. Such differences might, for example, cause the deponent to be deferential to the statement taker or to give an altered statement that he or she believes will win the statement taker's approval. Deponents in some countries may also be illiterate and, therefore, unable to affirm the accuracy of a written version of their statement without a trusted third party to read aloud the statement or case summary. Whether most deponents are literate also has implications for the use of forms and questionnaires. Illiterate persons should receive close assistance from commission staff in completing such forms. They may be able to indicate consent to the content of a completed form by means of a thumbprint.[84]

Special measures may also be needed for deponents who have been victims of sexual violence – whether women, men, or children.[85] The truth commission in Haiti was mandated to pay special attention to politically motivated crimes of a sexual nature committed against females.[86] The Sierra Leone TRC was required under its mandate to create a climate "which fosters constructive interchange between victims and perpetrators, giving special attention to the subject of sexual abuses and to the experiences of children within the armed

---

82   During the UN's "Henry Mission" to Israel and Palestine in the late 1970s, on-site interviews with Palestinians were conducted in the presence of official Israeli representatives. Their presence reportedly made many deponents reluctant to provide a statement. *See* T. Franck and H. S. Fairley, "Procedural Due Process in Human Rights Fact-Finding by International Agencies" (1980) 74 *AJIL* 308, at 331.

83   *See, e.g.,* ICC Rules of Procedure and Evidence, Rule 17(3): "The Victim and Witnesses Unit may also, with the agreement of the parents or the legal guardian, assign a child-support person to assist a child through all stages of the proceedings."

84   The truth commission in Ghana adopted this practice for illiterate deponents (or "petitioners," as they were called there). *See Ghana National Reconciliation Commission Final Report* (2004), vol. 2, at section 2.3.1.

85   More than half of those who reported sexual abuse to Ghana's truth commission were men.

86   Presidential Executive Order Establishing the Truth and Justice Commission, 1995 (Haiti), art. 3.

conflict."[87] It was also authorized to "implement special procedures to address the needs of such particular victims as children or those who have suffered sexual abuses as well as in working with child perpetrators of abuses or violations."[88] Ideally, female statement takers should be made available for female deponents who have experienced sexual violence.[89] The Peruvian TRC established a special gender unit that ensured the effective handling of such issues.[90]

Whether or not such practices are adopted, a truth commission's statement takers should receive uniform training. This will ensure that they carry out their work in a consistent and effective manner. All training should pay particular attention to how to handle issues of trauma,[91] and to how the experience of trauma may affect the accuracy of the information being gathered.[92] Training should also cover issues of security and confidentiality. The level of training that statement takers receive will, however, depend on the level of resources available in the commission's budget and the amount of time the commission has to fulfill its mandate.

RECOMMENDATIONS

- Statements should be taken following a predetermined format, and questions should be confined to areas that fall within the commission's mandate.
- A commission should take steps to ensure that statements are recorded consistently, accurately, and completely for future use, and in a manner that respects the dignity of the deponent.

---

87   *The Truth and Reconciliation Act 2000* (Sierra Leone), s. 6(2).

88   *Ibid.,* s. 7(4).

89   Hayner, *Unspeakable Truths,* above note 10, at 78. The mandate of Timor-Leste's truth commission provides that the commission has power "to make guidelines, including gender-aware policies, to be followed by all staff of the Commission concerning the performance of its functions." "On the Establishment of a Commission for Reception, Truth and Reconciliation in East Timor," UNTAET/REG/2001/01 as amended, s. 3.3.

90   *See also An Act to Establish the Truth and Reconciliation Commission of Liberia* (2005), s. 24: "The TRC shall [ensure] . . . that gender mainstreaming characterizes its work, operations and functions, ensuring therefore that women are fully represented and staffed at all levels of the work of the TRC and that special mechanisms are employed to handle women and children victims and perpetrators, not only to protect their dignity and safety but also to avoid re-traumatization."

91   *See, e.g.,* Roht-Arriaza, "Civil Society in Processes of Accountability," above note 73, at 106, where she describes the training used by the REMHI project: "Interviewers were trained in the history of the armed conflict, in mental health and in how to conduct interviews and how to report their results. Some 800 people were trained through 220 workshops." *See also* ICC Rules of Procedure and Evidence, Rule 16(1)(c).

92   *See* Hayner, *Unspeakable Truths,* above note 10, at 148–9.

- Deponents should be allowed to make statements in person or in writing.
- Security conditions and resources permitting, statements might be recorded on audiotape or videotape with the consent of the deponent.
- Deponents should generally be asked to give a solemn undertaking about the truthfulness and completeness of their statements.
- Whenever possible, statements should be signed by the deponent and by the statement taker, noting the date, time and place, and all persons present during the interview; where not signed, the reasons should be noted.
- To ensure effective participation, a commission should permit deponents to be accompanied by friends, family, or counsel.
- It is generally preferable to take statements in private, rather than in a group setting. However, taking statements in a group setting may be preferable in some instances, depending on the specific cultural setting and the nature of the commission's subsequent use of the statements.
- A commission should ensure specialized hiring and training measures to facilitate the effective interviewing of illiterate and underage deponents, and of victims of sexual violence.

SECTION 5: RECEIPT AND PRESERVATION OF CONFIDENTIAL AND ANONYMOUS STATEMENTS

Safety is a central issue for many truth commissions. Those who provide evidence – whether victims, next-of-kin, witnesses, or perpetrators – are sometimes targets of violence. The goal of effective participation may, therefore, require appropriate protective measures.[93]

Confidentiality is a way of protecting deponents where objective danger would arise from their participation in a truth commission's statement-taking process. Many truth commissions have allowed confidential statements, in most

---

93   A case in point is Sierra Leone. "[I]n a fragile security situation, and without any means of protecting for those who testified before the TRC, many civilians feared retaliation by ex-combatants. In particular, large numbers of ex-combatants have been inducted into the Sierra Leone army. The specter of rogue soldiers in the early years of the civil war (who became known as 'sobels' – soldier-rebels – due to their collaboration with the RUF rebels) and after the AFRC coup in 1997 made revenge attacks a frightening possibility for victims asked to give statements to the TRC. 'It's better to suffer once than to suffer twice,' I was often told." Shaw, "Rethinking Truth and Reconciliation Commissions," above note 74, at 5.

cases because of concerns for deponent and staff security. The, most recent truth commission mandates explicitly permit the taking of confidential testimony, including those of Guatemala,[94] Timor-Leste,[95] Peru,[96] and Sierra Leone.[97]

Assuming a truth commission is willing and able to receive confidential testimony, it should evaluate a number of factors in determining whether or not to do so in any individual instance. These include the degree of physical risk to the deponent, the commission's relative need for the information (having regard to what facts the commission has already learned on a nonconfidential basis, and what facts are already matters of public knowledge[98]), the anticipated reliability of the evidence, the extent to which confidentiality is necessary for the deponent to make full disclosure, the possibility that the statement concerns sensitive matters of national security, and the ability of the commission to prevent subsequent disclosure of the deponent's name or other identifying information.[99]

In any event, confidential treatment of a deponent's statement should be accorded on an exceptional basis only. It should not be granted automatically upon request without the reliable indication of a genuine threat or need by the deponent. Instead, a commission should generally encourage a deponent

94   Its mandate provides that "proceedings shall be confidential so as to guarantee the secrecy of the sources and the safety of deponents and informants." UN doc. A/48/954/S/1994/751, Annex II (1994).

95   Section 44.2: "At the discretion of the Commission, any person shall be permitted to provide information to the Commission on a confidential basis. The Commission shall not be compelled to release information, except on request of the Office of the General Prosecutor." UNTAET/REG/2001/01.

96   The mandate of the Peruvian TRC provides that the commission may "carry out investigative steps in a confidential manner with the capacity to maintain the confidentiality of identity of those who provide important information to it or participate in the investigations." Supreme Decree no. 0065-2001-PCM (Peru) as amended, art. 6(d). (Unofficial translation by Lisa Magarrell.)

97   Section 7(3): "At the discretion of the Commission, any person shall be permitted to provide information to the Commission on a confidential basis and the Commission shall not be compelled to disclose any information given to it in confidence." *The Truth and Reconciliation Act 2000* (Sierra Leone).

98   *See, e.g.,* Bloody Sunday Inquiry ruling on "Names in the Public Domain," 24 May 2001, available at http://www.bloody-sunday-inquiry.org/k/rulings/tribunal/Archive.

99   *Compare with Prosecutor v. Dusko Tadic,* Case no. IT-94-1, Decision (10 August 1995), in which the ICTY Trials Chamber, finding that there should be a balance between the defendant's interest in knowing and confronting his accuser and the witness's interest in security, held that the ICTY could allow confidential testimony where the witness's fear of retributive violence is credible. The Chamber relied heavily on a leading case of the English Court of Appeal, *R. v. Taylor,* [1994] TLR 484, which allowed confidential testimony where (a) the witness's fear is "real"; (b) the witness's testimony is important to the prosecution; (c) there is no *prima facie* evidence that the witness is untrustworthy; and (d) there is no effective witness protection program.

to consider giving some or all of his or her statement on a nonconfidential basis; information will be significantly more useful in subsequent truth, justice, reparation, and reform efforts if it does not remain confidential.[100]

For the sake of efficiency, a truth commission can delegate the decision on specific requests for confidentiality to the staff level. It can authorize decisions to be made "on the spot," in accordance with established criteria. Some cases may, however, be too sensitive to be left to staff (*e.g.*, a confession by a high-ranking military commander). In those cases, commissioners should generally intervene to make the final decision.

Before it can promise confidentiality, a truth commission must determine how to ensure it. At one extreme, a commission could choose not to record any identifying information during the interview.[101] A different approach would be to record, and then guard as confidential, a deponent's identifying information. Special identification codes, known only by members of the commission and accessible only on secure computer servers, could be employed to preserve confidentiality. Alternatively, a commission could simply redact names or other information that might indicate the identity of the deponent prior to publishing the testimony or releasing it to a third party.

Whichever approach is taken, the obligations of commissioners and staff to preserve confidentiality should be clearly articulated. For example, the mandate of the South African TRC provides:

1. Every commissioner and every member of the staff of the Commission shall, with regard to any matter dealt with by him or her, or information which comes to his or her knowledge in the exercise, performance or carrying out of his or her powers, functions or duties as such a commissioner or member, preserve and assist in the preservation of those matters which are confidential in terms of the provisions of this Act or which have been declared confidential by the Commission.

2. (*a*) Every commissioner and every member of the staff of the Commission shall, upon taking office, take an oath or make an affirmation in the form specified in subsection (6) . . .

---

100   In the case of the Sierra Leonean TRC, persons making confidential statements were asked if they would be willing to give part of their statement on a nonconfidential basis, in which case they would use two separate forms for the statement, one for the confidential portion and the other for the nonconfidential portion.

101   *Recall* article 10 of the UN Manual on the Effective Prevention and Investigation of Extra-Legal, Arbitrary and Summary Executions (1991), which recognizes that in some instances complete secrecy may be necessary to encourage testimony. In such instances "the commission will want to hear witnesses privately, informally and without recording testimony."

3. No commissioner shall, except for the purpose of the exercise of his or her powers, the performance of his or her functions or the carrying out of his or her duties or when required by a court of law to do so, or under any law, disclose to any person any information acquired by him or her as such a commissioner or while attending any meeting of the Commission.

4. Subject to the provisions of subsection (3) and sections 20(6) and 33, no person shall disclose or make known any information which is confidential by virtue of any provision of this Act . . .[102]

Similar, if less detailed, provisions are found in the mandates of the truth commissions of Timor-Leste,[103] Sierra Leone,[104] and Liberia.[105] Analogously, Rules 5 and 6 of the ICC Rules of Procedure and Evidence provide that judges, prosecutors, and staff should make solemn undertakings to respect the confidentiality of investigations. The Rules of Procedure of the International Humanitarian Fact-Finding Commission also create strict obligations to preserve the confidentiality of information once received.[106]

Another critical issue pertaining to the preservation of confidential information relates to the organization of a commission's archives and records. In general, a truth commission should maintain well-organized files in a secure location, with a system in place to ensure that, where confidentiality has been assured, deponent identities cannot be easily discovered. For example,

---

102 Section 38.

103 Section 44.1 of its mandate provides: "Every Commissioner and member of staff of the Commission or any person acting on behalf of the Commission shall, with regard to any matter or information which he or she becomes aware of in the exercise, performance or carrying out of his or her powers, functions or duties, preserve and assist in the preservation of the confidentiality of those matters which are confidential."

104 Article 14(3) of its mandate provides: "No member of the Commission or member of staff of the Commission shall make private use of or profit from any confidential information gained as a result of his work in the Commission or divulge such information to any other person except in the course of his functions as a member or staff of the Commission and any contravention of this provision may result in dismissal from the Commission."

105 Section 25 of its mandate provides: "Owing to their fiduciary relationship and duty to the TRC, no member of the TRC or its employees or agents, shall divulge confidential or other information obtained by virtue of their affiliation or work with the TRC, or use said information for profits or gains other than for reasons related to the duty and functions of the TRC. The TRC, all its employees, or agents shall be sworn to or execute sworn statements to hold all matters relating to the work of the TRC and coming to their knowledge confidential the breach of which shall constitute a second degree felony, punishable under Liberian laws."

106 Rule 29(2): "Members of the Commission, ad hoc members of the Chambers, experts and other persons assisting the Commission or a Chamber are under an obligation, during and after their terms of office, to keep secret the facts or information of which they have become aware during the discharge of their functions." *See* http://www.ihffc.org.

section 19(2) of the mandate of the Sierra Leone TRC provides that "before it is dissolved, the members of the Commission shall, among the final administrative activities of the Commission – a. organise its archives and records, as appropriate, for possible future reference, giving special consideration to (i) what materials or information might be made available to the public of Sierra Leone, either immediately or when conditions and resources allow; and (ii) what measures may be necessary to protect confidential information ..." Ideally, however, measures to preserve confidential information and files should be in place from the *beginning* of a commission's work, and not just upon its conclusion. At a minimum, the adopted measures must ensure a clear separation of confidential materials from other commission materials, and include safeguards against tampering and pilferage. In addition, where possible, computer systems, databases, and e-mail communications should be protected through technologies such as firewalls and encryption.[107]

A final matter concerns anonymous statements. Because the identity of an anonymous deponent is unknown even to the commission, his or her statement is inherently less reliable than a confidential statement. Nevertheless, anonymous statements might be permitted on an exceptional basis at the discretion of the commission.[108] Only very limited reliance should be placed on them for purposes of attributing responsibility.[109]

To offset reliability concerns about confidential and anonymous statements, statement takers should generally attempt to ask more probing questions than they would do in an ordinary interview.

RECOMMENDATIONS

- A truth commission should have established procedures and criteria to determine if it is appropriate for deponents to make confidential or anonymous statements. Criteria should include the degree of physical risk, the commission's relative need for the information (having regard to what information is already in the public realm and what information the commission has already secured from other deponents on a nonconfidential basis regarding a particular event or set of facts), the relevance and probative value of the information, and the

---

107 *See generally* http://www.benetech.org.
108 *See, e.g.,* D. Orentlicher, "Updated Set of Principles for the Protection and Promotion of Human Rights Through Action to Combat Impunity," UN doc. E/CN.4/2005/102/Add.1, Principle 10(d): "Requests to provide information to the commission anonymously should be given serious consideration, especially in cases of sexual assault, and the commission should establish procedures to guarantee anonymity in appropriate cases, while allowing corroboration of the information provided, as necessary."
109 *See generally* Chapter 5, Section 1.

capacity of the commission to prevent direct or indirect disclosure of the deponent's identity.

- Statements should be treated as confidential on an exceptional basis. Accordingly, deponents wishing to make confidential statements must formally request to do so. The ultimate decision on confidentiality is at the discretion of the commission.
- Prior to taking any confidential statement, a commission should explain the scope of its obligations and the degree of its capacity to preserve confidentiality.
- Where necessary to preserve confidentiality, a commission should consider using pseudonyms or expunging the deponent's name and all other identifying information from the public records of the commission.
- Anonymous statements are inherently less reliable than confidential statements, but they should be permitted at the discretion of the commission, provided that excessive reliance is not placed on them for purposes of attributing individual responsibility in a published final report. (*See* Chapter 7, "Publication of Findings of Individual Responsibility.")
- A truth commission should maintain well-organized files in a secure location, with a system in place to ensure the upholding of confidentiality obligations it has undertaken for specific deponents.

SECTION 6: SUPPORT AND REFERRALS

For many deponents, but especially for victims, making a statement to a commission can be a traumatic experience. Accordingly, if resources permit, a commission should make available persons to provide psychological, medical, or emotional support and assistance at the moment a statement is made.[110] For example, the truth commissions in Argentina and Chile both had psychologists and social workers present when family members of disappeared persons gave statements. Ghana's truth commission provided counseling free of charge to persons who experienced emotional difficulty in providing their statements. It also followed up with some needy victims at their homes and provided family counseling.[111] Timor-Leste's truth commission had a full-time

---

110 *Recall* Principle 14 of the UN Declaration of Basic Principles of Justice for Victims of Crime and Abuse of Power, GA res. 40/34 (1985), which provides: "Victims should receive the necessary material, medical, psychological and social assistance through governmental, voluntary, community-based and indigenous means."

111 *Ghana National Reconciliation Commission Final Report* (2004), vol. 1, ch. 2, at 2.3.3.5.2; and vol. 2, ch. 2, at 2.5.3.1.

"Reception and Victim Support Division" that provided support to victims not only during the statement-taking process, but in most other activities of the commission. Morocco's truth commission had a full-time, on-site medical unit at its central office.[112] But where resources to provide such support are lacking,[113] alternative and more culturally embedded forms of support might be considered, such as volunteer counseling by respected clergy, community elders, or spiritual leaders.

In addition to providing psychological, medical, or emotional support, a commission should train statement takers to provide specific information about, and make referrals to, available support services such as rehabilitation clinics, pension bureaus, and job-training facilities.[114] The moment of deposition is the logical occasion to make such referrals, because in the vast majority of cases it will be a deponent's only occasion of direct interaction with the commission.[115] The South African TRC, for example, established a referral system under which traumatized victims were referred to outside agencies for additional psychological support.[116] The truth commission in Timor-Leste also provided support and made referrals for victims with urgent needs.[117]

RECOMMENDATIONS

- To the extent resources permit, a commission should have, on staff or on site, persons to provide medical, psychological, or emotional support and assistance for deponents at the moment they give a statement.
- Commission staff should be competent to advise deponents regarding available public and private services for special medical, psychological, emotional, and economic support.

---

112 *See* http://www.ier.ma.
113 For example, as of 2002 there was only one psychologist in Sierra Leone. Hayner, *Unspeakable Truths*, above note 10, at 146. *See* Chapter 6, Section 10.
114 *Recall* Principle 15 of the UN Declaration of Basic Principles of Justice for Victims of Crime and Abuse of Power, GA res. 40/34 (1985), which provides: "Victims should be informed of the availability of health and social services and other relevant assistance and be readily afforded access to them." *Recall also* Principle 24 of the Bassiouni Principles, which requires states to alert the public and especially victims of "all available legal, medical, psychological, social, administrative and all other services to which victims may have a right of access."
115 Quinn and Freeman, "Lessons Learned," above note 26, at 1135.
116 It appears that this system, though well intended, did not function very well and was not widely used. Hayner, *Unspeakable Truths*, above note 10, at 140.
117 CAVR Update, December 2003–January 2004 (http://www.easttimor-reconciliation.org/). A total of 712 victims with urgent needs received US $200 each, together with assistance in accessing services and participation in healing workshops.

4

Subpoena Power

INTRODUCTION

Broadly speaking, there are two kinds of subpoenas that are common to courts and some truth commissions: *subpoenas ad testificandum* (subpoenas to testify) and *subpoenas duces tecum* (subpoenas compelling production of documents and other objects that are material and relevant and in the custody or control of a person). References to the term "subpoena" in this chapter refer to both kinds of subpoenas.[1]

If a truth commission is to have the ability to issue subpoenas, this must be specified in its terms of reference. In that respect, this chapter may be of particular relevance at the "design stage" of a commission, insofar as a commission cannot create its own subpoena power. Also, because a subpoena is a legal device found in all major legal systems, the design and exercise of a truth commission subpoena power will generally be guided and governed by the relevant standards and practices of the concerned state. Consequently, the chapter does not go into extensive detail regarding subpoena powers, but instead attempts to highlight some of the key fairness issues at stake.

---

1   Some truth commission mandates also refer to the power to "summon" individuals to testify. *See, e.g.,* s. 8(g) of *The Truth and Reconciliation Act 2000* (Sierra Leone). Used in this sense, the term "summon" is to be understood as synonymous with the term "subpoena."

Subpoenas can be useful in a number of situations. A person with relevant information or evidence may be unwilling to volunteer information or to comply with informal requests for it. Alternatively, a person may be willing to comply, but concerned about the possible consequences of disclosure in the absence of a binding subpoena.[2] A person may also be barred under statute from making any disclosures without an overriding obligation in the form of a subpoena.[3] At the same time, a subpoena power is not always a good thing to have, especially if it cannot be enforced.[4] Also, in some contexts, a subpoena power may even be unnecessary.[5]

To date, the following truth commissions have had subpoena powers: Uganda, Chad, Sri Lanka, Haiti, South Africa, Nigeria, Grenada, Timor-Leste, Ghana, Sierra Leone, Liberia, and the DRC.[6] One truth commission, namely that of the Republic of Korea, had a power functionally akin to a subpoena power. It could impose a fine of up to 10 million *won* on a person who refused a request to appear before the commission.[7] No truth commission, however, has possessed the power to issue letters rogatory.[8]

Other investigative bodies with a possible human rights focus, such as Commonwealth commissions of inquiry, may also wield subpoena powers. In Australia, commissioners have the power to summon evidence or testimony.[9] Commissions of inquiry in India are granted the powers of civil courts in

---

2   For example, a lawyer or doctor may be concerned about breaching professional confidence.

3   For example, a public official may possess national security information that can only be revealed pursuant to a subpoena.

4   Consider the case of Guatemala: "The post-war Guatemalan government was fragile, and even after the signing of the peace accords, right-wing elements remained extremely powerful in the country, especially within the military. The framers of the [truth commission] feared that an overly aggressive commission would be defied, thus complicating its work and undermining its legitimacy. Tomuschat put the dilemma simply: 'Even if we'd had subpoena power, people just wouldn't have shown up.'" J. D. Tepperman, "Truth and Consequences" (March/April 2002) *Foreign Affairs* 128, at 136–7.

5   For example, although it lacked a subpoena power, the Peruvian TRC – a truth commission that had unusually high moral authority in its particular context – appears to have obtained the institutional cooperation it required for purposes of its investigations.

6   See Appendix 1.

7   *A Hard Journey to Justice: First Term Report by the Presidential Truth Commission on Suspicious Deaths of the Republic of Korea* (2004), at 61. Seven persons, including public prosecutors and former presidents, were fined for failure to appear before the commission. *Ibid.*, at 90.

8   A letter rogatory is a formal request issued by a court in one jurisdiction to a court in another asking it to summon, examine, and later forward the evidence obtained from a witness resident in that state. Letters rogatory are common in civil and criminal cases. The execution of a letter rogatory is based on the comity of courts in different jurisdictions, or in some cases, on treaties providing for "mutual legal assistance."

9   *Parliamentary Commission of Inquiry Act*, no. 9 of 1986 (Australia).

respect of subpoena powers.[10] The New Zealand *Commissions of Inquiry Act* permits a commission or its designate(s) to require production of "documents, things, or information," and to summon witnesses to appear before it and to produce objects in their possession.[11] The commission of inquiry statutes of Canada and Israel also confer subpoena powers.[12] Most US congressional committees of investigation have full subpoena powers too.[13] Coroners also typically have powers of subpoena.[14]

Because they are among the most invasive powers exercised by truth commissions, subpoenas raise a host of fairness issues. In the context of a court proceeding, the purpose of a subpoena is, of course, to compel the disclosure of evidence "under penalty" (*sub poena*) for failure to comply.[15] Subpoenas serve the same purpose in truth commission investigations. Subpoenas issued by truth commissions may seek information comparable in content and volume to information sought in a criminal or civil case. A truth commission subpoena will, therefore, implicate similarly important individual interests such as privacy rights and the privilege against self-incrimination.[16] For these and other reasons, a subpoena should be used only as a last resort.[17]

10   *Commissions of Inquiry Act*, Act no. 60 of 1952 (India), as amended, arts. 4 and 5.
11   1908 § 4D (4 August 1908).
12   See *Inquiries Act*, RS 1985, c. I-11 (Canada), s. 8; *Commissions of Inquiry Law*, 1968, vol. 23 of the Laws of the State of Israel, s. 9. In addition, the public inquiry legislation of every Canadian province permits commissions of inquiry to subpoena witnesses and compel testimony. A. W. MacKay and M. G. McQueen, "Public Inquiries and the Legality of Blaming: Truth, Justice, and the Canadian Way," in A. Manson and D. Mullan, eds., *Commissions of Inquiry: Praise or Reappraise?* (Toronto: Irwin Law, 2003), at 261.
13   See *Hannah v. Larche*, 363 US 420, 442 (1960), in which the US Supreme Court attached a 32-page appendix to its judgment describing the powers of dozens of congressional investigative bodies.
14   P. Matthews, *Jervis on Coroners*, 12th ed. (London: Sweet & Maxwell, 2002), at 212–16. In the United Kingdom, however, a coroner lacks the prerogative to compel a witness to bring documents or other things in his or her possession or control. The coroner must obtain and serve a court summons. *Ibid.*, at 214–15 and 295.
15   In a standard common law trial, judges have the power to compel the attendance of witnesses, but it is usually the parties themselves who do so. This is consistent with the adversarial nature of a common law trial. *Ibid.*, at 212–13.
16   See Chapter 2, Section 1.
17   The South African TRC, for example, rarely made use of its subpoena power. "The power of subpoena was used more as a threat than anything else. We rarely had to make use of it, but in the case of P. W. Botha it was of vital importance that we had this power . . . Without the power of subpoena we would not have been able to bring so powerful a leader to answer to the law of the land . . . In the majority of cases the people who were invited, particularly from the police and the military, agreed to attend the hearings, and those who initially declined and were warned about the possibility of a subpoena very quickly changed their minds." A. Boraine, *A Country Unmasked* (Oxford: Oxford University Press, 2000), at 273. But Hayner

This chapter will focus on the following issues: procedures for issuing subpoenas, the possible scope of a subpoena, subpoena enforcement powers, and the rights of subpoena recipients.

SECTION 1: PROCEDURE FOR ISSUING
AND SERVING SUBPOENAS

A truth commission subpoena may issue from local judicial authorities or from the commission itself. The latter would be the most efficient option. It would allow a truth commission to control the speed at which subpoenas are issued, as well as their content. Decades of experience of Commonwealth commissions of inquiry support this practice. As well, in countries with a weak or corrupt judiciary, a reliance on the judiciary would disrupt a truth commission's ability to make use of its subpoena power. In general, therefore, it is preferable for a truth commission to have issuing authority. While it is true that judges do not head many truth commissions (in contrast to Commonwealth commissions of inquiry), it is possible to introduce sufficient safeguards into a commission's mandate to ensure that a subpoena power is properly used.[18]

The question of whom within a commission is granted authority to issue a subpoena raises important issues for consideration. Requiring the approval of a quorum of commissioners helps ensure that subpoenas are issued only as a last

notes, "The commission was also strongly criticized by human rights organizations for not issuing a subpoena against Minister of Home Affairs and Inkatha Freedom Party President Mangosuthu Buthelezi, a decision based largely on the commission's fear of a possible violent reaction." P. Hayner, *Unspeakable Truths: Facing the Challenge of Truth Commissions*, 2d ed. (New York: Routledge, 2002), at 42. *Compare with* the case of Sierra Leone's TRC: "The Commission had to issue subpoenas against five serving ministers and leaders of government institutions, including the Attorney General, and the chairman and secretary of the ruling political party. All this happened despite the president's public admonition to all public officials at the commencement of hearings to cooperate with the Commission . . . The former head of state, Capt. Valentine Strasser who had ignored the Commission's invitation on several occasions was also subpoenaed and compelled to testify." *Sierra Leone Truth and Reconciliation Commission Final Report* (2004), vol. 1, ch. 4, para. 38. The decision not to subpoena certain individuals appears to have been linked to a concern about undermining the related cause of national reconciliation. J. R. Quinn and M. Freeman, "Lessons Learned: Practical Lessons Gleaned from Inside the Truth Commissions of Guatemala and South Africa" (2003) 25 *Human Rights Quarterly* 1117, at 1126.

18   *See e.g., An Act to Establish the Truth and Reconciliation Commission of Liberia* (2005), s. 27(b)(i), which authorizes the Liberian TRC to recommend the appointment of an *ad hoc* "Special Magistrate" (ranking as a "Circuit Judge") who would "procure information and testimonies in furtherance of the work of the TRC . . ."

resort in the event that a person does not volunteer testimony or evidence that the commission considers relevant and necessary.[19] A quorum requirement also helps to ensure that subpoenas are not issued haphazardly and without reflection or debate. Ideally, there should be consensus among commissioners prior to issuing a subpoena. Where there is no consensus, however, decisions to issue subpoenas could be based on a simple majority vote.

There may be occasions in which a subpoena must be issued on an urgent basis (*e.g.*, where a person is about to flee the jurisdiction). It may, therefore, be useful for a commission chair to have the power to independently issue a subpoena on an exceptional and emergency basis. Such flexibility is particularly important in light of the fact that commissioners may be based in different parts of the country, meeting only infrequently.

Commission staff members, who are not formally appointed by the state and who are less accountable as a matter of law than are commissioners, should not have the power to issue subpoenas. This would present credibility problems for the commission and open the practice of issuing subpoenas to *ad hoc* decision making. On the other hand, commission staff – who often have detailed knowledge of particular cases – are in a good position to advise commissioners on the need for a subpoena in any specific case.

A subpoena may be served by mail to the most recent known address of the intended recipient, or to that person's designated legal representative. However, personal service is generally preferable. In such instance, the subpoena should be served directly at the person's residence or business place, either by a designated staff member of the commission or, alternatively, by a police or court official, provided the official is not implicated in the crime in question.[20] If the subject of the subpoena is evading service of the subpoena, a judge may also have the power to issue a warrant for the arrest of the person.

---

19   In Ghana, the truth commission initially invited former president Jerry Rawlings to testify in public. When he failed to confirm his appearance after successive invitations by the commission, a subpoena was issued compelling him to attend and testify. "Rawlings Appears at Rights Probe," BBC News, 12 February 2004.

20   *See, e.g.,* section 5(c) of the *Tribunals of Inquiry Act,* 1966, chapter 447, Laws of the Federation of Nigeria: "Summonses issued under this paragraph may be in Form A in the Schedule to this Act, and shall be served by the police or by such person as the members may direct." *See also* section 29(c) of the *Promotion of National Unity and Reconciliation Act,* 1995 (South Africa), which provides that subpoenas "shall be signed by a commissioner, shall be served by a member of the staff of the Commission or by a sheriff, by delivering a copy thereof to the person concerned or by leaving it at such person's last known place of residence or business, and shall specify the reason why the article is to be produced or the evidence is to be given."

RECOMMENDATIONS

- For efficiency reasons, it is best to have a subpoena power reside directly in the truth commission, rather than requiring the commission to apply to the judiciary.
- Subpoenas should be issued only as a last resort in the event that a person does not volunteer testimony or evidence that the commission considers relevant and necessary.
- A reasonable quorum among commissioners should be required prior to issuing a subpoena. Where consensus is not possible, decisions could be taken on the basis of a simple majority vote.
- The commission chair should have the power to independently issue a subpoena on an exceptional and urgent basis.
- Commission staff should not have authority to issue subpoenas.
- Ideally, a subpoena should be personally served on the individual in question. It should be served directly at the individual's residence or business place, either by a designated staff member of the commission or, alternatively, by any competent police officer or court official not personally implicated in the subject matter of the subpoena. A subpoena may alternatively be served by mail to the individual's most recent known address, or to his or her designated legal representative.

SECTION 2: SUBPOENA CONTENT AND SCOPE

A truth commission should have the power to issue subpoenas against natural persons. It should also be able to issue them against legal persons, such as corporations.[21]

Having regard to the standard scope of subpoenas used in judicial proceedings in most countries, a subpoena should cover both testimony and physical or documentary evidence. Such an approach conforms with the mandates of past and present truth commissions[22] and Commonwealth commissions of

---

21   This is consistent with the practice of international criminal tribunals. *See* R. May and M. Wierda, *International Criminal Evidence* (Ardsley, NY: Transnational Publishers, 2003), at 190.

22   *See, e.g.*, section 29(c) of the *Promotion of National Unity and Reconciliation Act*, 1995 (South Africa), which provides that the commission can "by notice in writing call upon any person to appear before [it] and to give evidence or to answer questions relevant to the subject matter of the hearing." *See also Law 04/018 (2004) Concerning the Organization, Powers and Functions of the Truth and Reconciliation Commission* (DRC), art. 38.

inquiry.[23] In the United States, most congressional and departmental committees of investigation are able to require attendance and testimony of witnesses, in addition to the production of documents relating to matters under investigation. Persons may also be required to furnish a written list of information in their possession.

In the American grand jury system, prosecutors may obtain "blank subpoenas" and issue them to any person with evidence relevant to an investigation.[24] The US Supreme Court has approved of grand jury subpoenas that are sweeping in scope, and it will uphold a relevancy challenge only where there is "no reasonable possibility that the category of material the Government seeks will produce information relevant to the general subject of the grand jury's investigation."[25] The rationale for permitting such latitude in the grand jury system applies with equal force to truth commissions: both bodies are investigative only, and neither can impose any formal legal punishment on those who come before it (though a grand jury, of course, has the power to indict).

Nevertheless, to curtail unwarranted intrusions on individual rights, truth commission subpoenas should be directly relevant to areas of investigation specified in the mandate.[26] Subpoenas that lack a rational relationship with the area of inquiry could undermine the truth commission's authority and unfairly harm the privacy rights of the recipient. In general, therefore, there should be an articulable relationship between the materials or testimony sought and the focus of the investigation. In addition, the subpoena should indicate the

---

23 *See, e.g., Inquiries Act,* RS 1985, c. I-11 (Canada), section 2: "The commissioners have the power of summoning before them any witnesses, and of requiring them to (a) give evidence, orally or in writing, and on oath or, if they are persons entitled to affirm in civil matters on solemn affirmation; and (b) produce such documents and things as the commissioners deem requisite to the full investigation of the matters into which they are appointed to examine." *See also* s. 22(1) and (2) of the *Inquiries Act,* 2005 (UK).

24 *See* S. Brenner, "Is the Grand Jury Worth Keeping?" (1998) 81 *Judicature* 190, at 192.

25 *Ibid.,* citing the US Supreme Court decision in *U.S. v. R. Enterprises, Inc.,* 498 US 292 (1992).

26 Relevance is the standard generally employed in Commonwealth commission of inquiry statutes. *See, e.g.,* section 7 of the Ontario *Public Inquiries Act,* RSO 1990, as amended: "A commission may require any person by summons, (a) to give evidence on oath or affirmation at an inquiry; or (b) to produce in evidence at an inquiry such documents and things as the commission may specify, *relevant* to the subject-matter of the inquiry[.]" *See also* section 4(d) of the *Commissions of Inquiry Act,* 1908 (New Zealand), as amended: "For the purposes of the inquiry the Commission may of its own motion, or on application, issue in writing a summons requiring any person to attend at the time and place specified in the summons and to give evidence, and to produce any papers, documents, records, or things in that person's possession or under that person's control that are relevant to the subject of the inquiry." Similarly, coroners may compel the attendance of witnesses only where relevant to the subject of inquiry. Matthews, *Jervis on Coroners,* above note 14, at 213.

nature of any adverse allegations made against the recipient and on which he or she may expect to be questioned.[27] The subpoena need not, however, list "particulars of time, place, person or circumstances as in a charge sheet before trial."[28]

Subpoenas for evidence and subpoenas for testimony involve slightly different considerations in terms of their proper scope. A subpoena for *evidence* should generally set out various particulars in order to be valid.[29] The subpoena should not be overly vague such that there is no limit to the evidence to which it pertains, or overly broad such that compliance with the subpoena is unduly burdensome. Evidence sought by means of such a subpoena may include, *inter alia*, written materials, maps, drawings, audio or video recordings, photographs, or physical evidence connected to a particular incident under investigation.

As a matter of efficiency and fairness, a subpoena for evidence should also indicate the time and place for delivery of the evidence to the commission. The ICTY's Rules of Procedure set out a useful framework for dealing with a party that seeks production of documents or information. Rule 54*bis* provides:

A party requesting an order under Rule 54 that a State produce documents or on shall apply in writing to the relevant Judge or Trial Chamber and shall: (i) identify as far as possible the documents or information to which the application relates; (ii) indicate how they are relevant to any matter in issue before the Judge or Trial Chamber and necessary for a fair determination of that matter; and (iii) explain the steps that have been taken by the applicant to secure the State's assistance.

27 *Recall* the second of Lord Justice Salmon's cardinal principles, discussed in Chapter 2: "Before any person who is involved in an inquiry is called as a witness he should be informed of any allegations which are made against him and the substance of the evidence in support of them."

28 J. S. Sarkar, *Commissions of Inquiry: Practice and Principle* (New Delhi: Ashish Publishing House, 1990), at 9. Speaking of Commonwealth commissions of inquiry, the author notes, "The commission is inquisitorial rather than accusatory and it is the business of the commission to find out whatever materials are available in connection with the subject-matter of the inquiry." *Ibid.*

29 *See, e.g.,* s. 29 of the *Promotion of National Unity and Reconciliation Act,* 1995 (South Africa), which provides: "(1) The Commission may for the purposes of or in connection with the conduct of an investigation or the holding of a hearing, as the case may be . . . (b) by notice in writing call upon any person who is in possession of or has the custody of or control over any article or other thing which in the opinion of the Commission is relevant to the subject matter of the investigation or hearing to produce such article or thing to the Commission . . ."

A subpoena for *testimony* may be more broad or general in nature than a subpoena for evidence. A subpoena for testimony should, however, contain at a minimum the time and place where testimony will be taken, as well as indicate the general subject matter. Further, the recipient should be given reasonable notice in order to make arrangements to attend. Resources permitting, his or her costs of attendance should be covered, since the person is being compelled to appear.[30]

Any subpoena issued by a truth commission, whether for evidence or testimony, should articulate the consequences of noncompliance and the procedure to be followed if a person is unable or unwilling to comply.[31] For example, if a legal fine or penalty could be imposed for noncompliance, the subpoena should clearly indicate that. Similarly, the subpoena should alert the recipient of any negative inference that might be drawn from his or her nonattendance.[32]

RECOMMENDATIONS

- A subpoena power should be capable of being exercised against natural persons or legal persons.
- A subpoena power should enable a commission to require the attendance of a person to give testimony, or to produce documents or other things in the person's custody or control that are relevant and necessary to the subject of the inquiry.
- A subpoena may be broad in scope, but it must establish an articulable relationship between the testimony or evidence sought, and the subject of the investigation. The subpoena should also inform the recipient of the nature of any adverse allegations about which he or she may expect to be questioned.
- A subpoena for *documentary evidence* should not be overly vague, such that there is no limit to the evidence to which it pertains. Neither should it be overly broad, such that compliance would be unduly burdensome. The subpoena should indicate a reasonable time and location for delivery of the evidence.

30   *See, e.g.,* section 8 (1)(d) of *The Truth and Reconciliation Act 2000* (Sierra Leone), which grants the commission the power "subject to adequate provision being made to meet his expenses for the purpose, to call upon any person to meet with the Commission or its staff, or to attend a session or hearing of the Commission . . ."

31   In this spirit, the mandate of Timor-Leste's truth commission provides: "[I]n any case in which the Commission has (exercised its subpoena power), persons shall be informed of the potential consequences of non-compliance with such order." "On the Establishment of a Commission for Reception, Truth and Reconciliation in East Timor," UNTAET/REG/ 2001/01 as amended, s. 35(f). *See also* s. 22(3) and (4) of the *Inquiries Act,* 2005 (UK).

32   In this author's view, no negative inference should be drawn from nonattendance; this would violate the presumption of innocence.

- The scope and content of a subpoena for *testimony* may be more general than a subpoena for documentary evidence. It should contain the time and place where testimony will be taken and indicate the relevant subject matter of the testimony. The recipient should receive reasonable notice to attend and testify.
- A subpoena should explain possible consequences of noncompliance, as well as the procedure to be followed if the person is unable or unwilling to comply.

SECTION 3: ENFORCEMENT POWERS

Truth commission legislation should make it an offense to fail to comply with a subpoena without a reasonable excuse, or to deliberately distort or conceal relevant information or evidence.[33] The mere creation of offenses will, however, rarely suffice. An effective mechanism of enforcement is also necessary.

Formal contempt of court is the method most widely used to enforce judicial subpoenas.[34] The same remedy may suit most truth commissions' needs.[35] But a commission should not have the final word in any case of alleged contempt. It is generally preferable for prosecutorial authorities to enforce subpoenas, upon the commission's showing of a *prima facie* case of noncompliance.

It is noteworthy that subpoena enforcement proceedings can allow a commission to do more than simply ensure compliance with the subpoena. Such proceedings can allow a commission to set out its full case against the noncompliant party. For example, in South Africa, persons who refused subpoenas issued by the TRC were subject to possible contempt proceedings. When former president P. W. Botha refused to comply with a TRC subpoena, the attorney general chose to prosecute. This provided an occasion for the TRC to publicly reveal its full evidence against the former president, because it had to justify the basis for having issued the subpoena in the first place.[36]

---

33 *See, e.g.*, s. 22 of the *National Reconciliation Commission Act*, 2002, Act 611 (Ghana). *See also* s. 36 of the *Inquiries Act*, 2005 (UK).

34 The same is true for coroners. Matthews, *Jervis on Coroners*, above note 14, at 29.

35 *See, e.g., An Act to Establish the Truth and Reconciliation Commission of Liberia* (2005), s. 27(b)(ii). Depending on the resources of the truth commission and the quality of the judiciary in its country of operation, informal methods of enforcement, such as publication of the names of recalcitrant subpoena recipients, may also be considered.

36 Botha defended himself by alleging bias on the part of the TRC, and the state paid 1.6 million Rand to cover his legal fees. Various witnesses appeared on behalf of the TRC, including TRC chair Desmond Tutu and a former police colonel, Eugene de Kock. *See* Boraine, *A Country Unmasked*, above note 17, at 198–220.

Although the TRC lost the legal battle,[37] the case demonstrated how a subpoena enforcement proceeding can contribute to accountability vis-à-vis the noncompliant party.[38] At the same time, one must appreciate that the quality of the justice system in many transitional contexts may preclude vigorous enforcement of this sort.

Truth commission mandates that include subpoena powers invariably make it a punishable offense for anyone to fail to comply without reasonable excuse. For example, section 20 of the mandate of Timor-Leste's truth commission provides:

> (1) It shall be an offence for any person to: (a) knowingly furnish the Commission with false or misleading information; (b) without reasonable excuse, fail to comply with an order issued by the Commission to appear and/or answer questions at a specified place, date and time; (c) without reasonable excuse, fail to comply with an order issued by the Commission to produce any object or item in his or her possession, custody or control. Any person who commits any of the acts listed in Subsection 20.1 shall be guilty of an offence and liable to a term of imprisonment not to exceed 1 year or a fine not to exceed US$3000, or both.

Similarly, section 39 of the South African TRC's mandate provides:

> Any person who . . . (e) (i) having been subpoenaed in terms of this Act, without sufficient cause fails to attend at the time and place specified in the subpoena, or fails to remain in attendance until the conclusion of the meeting in question or until excused from further attendance by the person presiding at that meeting, or fails to produce any article in his or her possession or custody or under his or her control; (ii) having been subpoenaed in terms of this Act, without sufficient cause refuses to be sworn or to make affirmation as a witness or fails or refuses to answer fully and satisfactorily to the best of his or her knowledge and belief any question lawfully put to him or her . . . [and] (h) destroys any article relating to or in anticipation of any investigation or proceedings in terms of this Act . . . shall be guilty of an offence and liable on conviction to a fine, or to imprisonment for a period not exceeding two years or to both such fine and such imprisonment.

---

37   Botha was initially convicted, but the judgment was overturned on appeal.
38   The mere prospect of enforcement proceedings can also serve as a deterrent to someone who is considering noncompliance with a subpoena, since the risk of refusal may be perceived to be greater than the risk of compliance.

Commissions of inquiry follow similar practices. For example, pursuant to the former UK *Tribunals of Inquiry (Evidence) Act*, a person who failed to appear, produce a document, or answer a question posed by the commission could be punished as if he or she were guilty of contempt of court.[39] The Australian *Parliamentary Commission of Inquiry Act* permits a commissioner to summon a person to appear and give evidence, and to produce documents and other things; a person who fails to appear may, at the court's demand, be arrested and detained for the purpose of compelling his or her appearance.[40] Such a person, in addition to being detained until after the appearance, may also be penalized with six months' imprisonment or a fine of one thousand dollars.[41]

Historically it is also standard for investigators for US congressional committees of inquiry to have the power to subpoena for testimony and evidence, and to enforce that power through contempt proceedings.[42] For example, the Louisiana Labor-Management Commission of Inquiry, an inquiry established in the late 1960s by the Louisiana legislature to investigate criminal allegations in the field of labor relations, had the power to compel the production of documents and testimony and to enforce that power by petition to state courts in contempt proceedings.[43]

But if truth commissions and similar bodies should have the ability to enforce subpoenas, recipients should have the ability to contest them. Valid defenses might include irrelevance (*i.e.*, the evidence sought is extraneous to the inquiry), incapacity, legal privilege,[44] unreasonable burden, or insufficient notice. For example, the mandate of Timor-Leste's truth commission provides at section 20.2:

> Without limiting the meaning of the term "reasonable excuse" in Subsection 20.1, it shall be regarded as a reasonable excuse that: (a) a person's testimony or production of an object or item in his or her possession was not relevant to the matters into which the Commission was inquiring;

---

39 Section 1(2). In India, certain officers of an Indian commission of inquiry are authorized to sign letters, notices, and summonses, as well as to compel attendance by threat of fine, arrest, or trial for perjury or contempt. *See Sarma Sakar Commission of Inquiry*, Regulation of Procedure, 1978 (India), cited in N. Kritz, ed., *Transitional Justice: How Emerging Democracies Reckon with Former Regimes* (Washington, DC: US Institute for Peace Press, 1995), *Sarma Sarkar Commission of Inquiry*, vol. 3, at 230–2.

40 Sections 11 and 17.

41 Section 24.

42 H. W. Ehrmann, "The Duty of Disclosure in Parliamentary Investigation: A Comparative Study" (1943–4) 2 *U. Chi. L. Rev.* 1, at 7.

43 *See Jenkins v. McKeithen*, 395 US 411 (1969).

44 *See generally* Chapter 6.

(b) a person was incapable of complying with an order of the Commission for reasons beyond his or her control; or (c) a person is given insufficient notice of the Commission's order to enable compliance with the order of the Commission.

As to whether a commission should have the power to enforce its own subpoenas, the Law Reform Commission of Canada recommended against such an approach in respect of commissions of inquiry, preferring that an order be obtained from the ordinary courts. Though a less efficient approach, the commission properly argued that it would violate the principle that one should not be judge in one's own case.[45] Thus, for example, section 8 of the Ontario *Public Inquiries Act* provides:

Where any person without lawful excuse, (a) on being duly summoned under section 7 as a witness at an inquiry, makes default in attending at the inquiry; or (b) being in attendance as a witness at an inquiry, refuses to take an oath or to make an affirmation legally required by the commission to be taken or made, or to produce any document or thing in his or her power or control legally required by the commission to be produced to it, or to answer any question to which the commission may legally require an answer; or (c) does any other thing that would, if the commission had been a court of law having power to commit for contempt, have been in contempt of that court, . . . the commission may state a case to the Divisional Court setting out the facts and that court may, on the application of the commission or of the Attorney General, inquire into the matter and, after hearing any witnesses who may be produced against or on behalf of that person and after hearing any statement that may be offered in defense, punish or take steps for the punishment of that person in like manner as if he or she had been guilty of contempt of the court.[46]

---

45   Canada Law Reform Commission, Working Paper 17, *Administrative Law: Commissions of Inquiry* (Ottawa: The Commission, 1977), at 48.

46   Section 16 of the same Act also provides for an arrest power in certain circumstances: "Upon proof to the satisfaction of a judge of the Ontario Court (General Division) of the service of a summons to appear at an inquiry upon a person and that, (a) such person has failed to attend or to remain in attendance at the inquiry in accordance with the requirements of the summons; (b) a sufficient sum for his or her fees and allowances has been duly paid or tendered to the person; and (c) his or her presence is material to achievement of the purposes of the inquiry, . . . the judge may, by warrant in Form 2 directed to any sheriff or police officer, cause such person to be apprehended anywhere within Ontario and forthwith to be brought before the commission conducting the inquiry and to be detained in custody as the judge may order until his or her presence as a witness before the inquiry is no longer

Other Commonwealth jurisdictions have not followed suit. For example, section 5(d) of the Nigerian *Tribunals of Inquiry Act* gives commissions:

[T]he power to issue a warrant to compel the attendance of any person who, after having been summoned to attend fails or refuses or neglects to do so and does not excuse such failure or refusal or neglect to the satisfaction of the tribunal, and to order him to pay all costs which may have been occasioned in compelling his attendance or by reason of his failure or refusal or neglect to obey the summons, and also to fine such person a sum not exceeding twenty naira, such fine to be recoverable in the same manner as a fine imposed by a magistrate's court.[47]

Israel's *Commissions of Inquiry Law* takes a similar approach.[48]

While this book recommends against a truth commission having the power to enforce its own subpoenas – especially when a judge is not acting as its chair – some mandates may confer upon a commission the same powers as a court with respect to subpoena enforcement. In such instances, the commission should attempt to adopt most, if not all, of the procedures employed by ordinary courts in the country.[49]

RECOMMENDATIONS

- A truth commission's mandate should make it an offense to fail to comply with a subpoena without a reasonable excuse, to deliberately distort or conceal relevant evidence, or to commit perjury.

required, or, in the discretion of the judge, to be released on a recognizance, with or without sureties, conditioned for appearance to give evidence."

47   Section 10 of the same Act, however, appears to contemplate a role for the court where the sanctions at issue are more serious: "Any person who, after service on him of a summons to attend as a witness or to produce a book, document or any other thing and, notwithstanding any duty of secrecy however imposed, fails or refuses or neglects to do so or to answer any question put to him by or with the concurrence of the tribunal shall be guilty of an offence, and liable on summary conviction to a fine of two hundred naira or to imprisonment for a term of six months."

48   Section 9 of the *Commissions of Inquiry Law*, 1968, vol. 23 of the Laws of the State of Israel.

49   The Nigerian truth commission had the power to issue arrest warrants against persons failing to comply with its subpoenas. However, "in the over-all interest of national reconciliation," the commission chose not to exercise this power, including against three former heads of state who failed to respond to the commission's summons to appear. *Nigeria: Judicial Commission of Inquiry for the Investigation of Human Rights Violations, Final Report (2002)*, Foreword by the Chairman, paras. 1.54 and 1.57. Later in the same report, the commission explained its decision thus: "The Commission is on a reconciliation process, and one does not reconcile under duress." *Ibid.* at vol. 4, ch. 8, para. 8.14.

- Truth commission subpoenas should be enforceable through pre-scribed procedures, including prosecution by public authorities at the behest, or upon the certification, of the commission.
- Contempt proceedings should be available for refusal to appear, refusal to produce documents, refusal to be sworn in as a witness, and improper refusal to answer questions.
- Subpoena recipients should be allowed to defend against contempt proceedings on the following grounds: irrelevance, incapacity, legal privilege, unreasonable burden, or insufficient notice.
- Penalties for noncompliance with a subpoena could include a fine, a short term in prison, and reimbursement of the commission's reasonable costs.

SECTION 4: RECIPIENT RIGHTS

A subpoena recipient should have more than the right to defend his or her refusal to comply with a subpoena. The recipient should also be able to seek to have the subpoena itself quashed, through a judicial process, and on the same grounds, namely, irrelevance, incapacity, legal privilege, unreasonable burden, or insufficient notice. But any such application should be required to be brought to court without undue delay.[50] This is to avoid unreasonable holdups in a commission's work.[51]

A subpoena recipient should also be entitled to a base level of confidentiality or privacy, heightened if the individual or his or her family can show the reasonable fear of a threat to physical safety or economic well-being. Thus, if a commission wishes to make public that it intends to subpoena a particular individual, it should have compelling reasons for doing so. Absent such reasons, the subpoena should be issued outside the public spotlight.

With respect to documents subpoenaed by truth commissions, if a document contains both relevant and irrelevant personal data, that which is personal and irrelevant should generally be sealed, redacted, or otherwise prevented from being publicized. This issue arises, for example, in the case of a person's private

---

50   *See, e.g.*, section 38 of the *Inquiries Act, 2005* (UK), which allows a maximum of 14 days to bring an application for judicial review of a decision by a member of any inquiry panel. *See also An Act to Establish the Truth and Reconciliation Commission of Liberia* (2005), s. 20: "[The TRC's] work and functions shall be regarded as a matter of national priority; all matters of the TRC appearing before the Supreme Court of Liberia shall be advanced for hearing and determination to the top of the Supreme Court's docket at all times without the slightest delay as a matter of first priority."

51   Applying the same logic, a subpoena recipient wishing to appeal the denial of a motion to quash should be required to bring the motion on an equally expeditious basis.

records or diaries. One method of protecting the privacy of the recipient might be for the commission to review all pages of a personal record or diary in the presence of the owner of the document, and to make a copy only of relevant pages. This would both prevent the commission from unfairly revealing the complete document and save the commission the burden of maintaining security to protect sealed documents.

Another right of subpoena recipients is financial in nature. A subpoena should not be financially onerous for the recipient. In Ontario, the recipient of a commission of inquiry's subpoena is entitled to be paid the same personal allowances for attendance at the hearing as those payable for the attendance of a witness summoned to attend court.[52] Section 13 of Nigeria's *Tribunals of Inquiry Act* similarly provides: "Witnesses and interpreters and any other person attending at the request of a tribunal or upon summons shall be paid such sums as allowances for expenses, as the case may be, as a tribunal may, with the approval of the proper authority, direct, and such sums shall be paid out of the public revenue."

While many truth commissions will not be in a position to use their limited funds for such purposes, a commission should make its best efforts to reimburse the reasonable costs of compliance with a subpoena. That is a reasonable *quid pro quo* for forcing persons to give testimony or evidence against their will.

Finally, objects and documents obtained through a subpoena for evidence should be returned to the subpoena recipient within a reasonable time, once the commission has had an opportunity to photocopy, photograph, or inspect them, as the case may be. They do not, under any circumstance, become commission property. Where, however, the objects and documents reveal evidence of criminal activity, prosecutors should have an opportunity to apply for the evidence.

RECOMMENDATIONS

- A subpoena recipient should be permitted the right to quash the subpoena on the same grounds as he or she would defend refusal, namely: irrelevance, incapacity, legal privilege, unreasonable burden, or insufficient notice. But any application for judicial review of a subpoena should be required to be brought expeditiously.
- A subpoena recipient should be entitled to a base level of confidentiality or privacy, heightened if the individual or the recipient's family can show a reasonable fear of a threat to physical safety or economic well being.

---

52   Section 7(2), Ontario *Public Inquiries Act*, RSO 1990, as amended.

- Resources permitting, a commission should reimburse the reasonable costs of compliance with a subpoena.
- Objects and documents obtained through a subpoena for evidence should be returned to the subpoena recipient within a reasonable time. Where, however, the objects and documents reveal evidence of criminal activity, prosecutors should have an opportunity to apply for the retention of the evidence.

5

Search and Seizure Power

INTRODUCTION

It is a fundamental principle of most, if not all, legal systems that state agents should not have unfettered authority to search persons or property. In the case of highly invasive searches, a standard safeguard is to require prior judicial authorization. In the common law, this is achieved by means of a "warrant," which generally consists of a written order issued by a court authorizing a limited power of search and seizure. The two most common types of warrants are *arrest warrants* and *search warrants*. This chapter deals only with the latter, since truth commissions and commissions of inquiry have, appropriately, lacked arrest warrant powers (*i.e.*, the power to seize *persons*).[1] References to "warrant" in this chapter should, therefore, be understood as references to search warrants only.

If a truth commission is to have the power to search property and seize relevant evidence, this must be specified in its mandate. A truth commission

---

1   *But see* section 13A of the *Commissions of Inquiry Act,* 1908 (New Zealand), as amended, which permits a commissioner, if he or she is a judge, to issue arrest warrants directly. *See also* s. 5(d) of the *Tribunals of Inquiry Act,* 1966, chapter 447, Laws of the Federation of Nigeria, which permits a commission to issue arrest warrants for failure to attend a hearing pursuant to a subpoena. Truth commissions have not, thus far, had the power to seek or enforce DNA warrants. Such warrants could, theoretically, be important to future truth commission investigations. They are not, however, examined in this book.

cannot unilaterally arrogate such a power unto itself.[2] Consequently, like the prior chapter, this chapter may be primarily relevant at the "design stage" of a commission. Also, because a power of search and seizure is found in all major legal systems, its exercise will generally be controlled by the relevant standards and practices of the particular state. For these reasons, this chapter focuses on only the key fairness issues at stake.

A standard search warrant authorizes a police officer or similar official to search and possibly seize any property that constitutes evidence of the commission of a crime (*actus reus*), or of the intention to be so used (*mens reus*). Search warrants are backed up by force and allow for inspections without prior notice. This is chiefly how they are to be distinguished from documentary subpoenas, which do not involve surprise inspections and generally leave the recipient time to voluntarily comply. Warrants, therefore, serve as an important fallback option for obtaining key evidence.

Powers of search and seizure are useful not only against individual perpetrators but also against unaccountable public authorities who refuse to cooperate with a commission's requests for information. Noncooperation of state security agencies has been a standard feature of the experience of the majority of truth commissions. In Argentina, Chile, and El Salvador, for example, requests for cooperation were generally turned down or ignored by the armed forces and police, despite statutory obligations to cooperate.[3] Even the South African TRC, which had a full warrant power, ultimately found that thousands of critical files were intentionally destroyed by state security forces and others.[4] Still, according to its deputy chairperson, the TRC's powers of search and seizure were "extremely useful and were used on a number of occasions, particularly with regard to the former South African Defence Force."[5]

To date, several truth commissions have wielded powers of search and seizure, including those of South Africa, Nigeria, Timor-Leste, Ghana, Sierra

---

2   *See* the famous English case proscribing against warrantless searches: *Entick v. Carrington* (1765), 19 St. Tr. 1030; 95 E.R. 807 (K.B.). This principle appears in different forms in most, if not all, contemporary legal traditions.

3   *See* P. Hayner, *Unspeakable Truths: Facing the Challenge of Truth Commissions*, 2d ed. (New York: Routledge, 2002), at 34 (Argentina), 36 (Chile), 39 (El Salvador). The Korean truth commission had the same experience. *See A Hard Journey to Justice: First Term Report by the Presidential Truth Commission on Suspicious Deaths of the Republic of Korea* (2004), at 15.

4   There is a chapter dedicated to this subject in the TRC's October 1998 final report. Hayner, *Unspeakable Truths*, above note 3, at 239.

5   A. Boraine, *A Country Unmasked* (Oxford: Oxford University Press, 2000), at 273.

Leone, Liberia, and the DRC.[6] This is part of a growing trend toward the inclusion of search and seizure powers in truth commission mandates.[7] A number of Commonwealth commission of inquiry statutes provide for search and seizure powers too, such as those of India, Israel, New Zealand, and Nigeria. Consistent with its inherently broad powers, a standard parliamentary or congressional committee of investigation would also normally enjoy such powers. Ombudsman offices sometimes possess powers of search and seizure too.[8] On an exceptional basis, even private plaintiffs in a common law civil suit may be able to exercise powers of search and seizure, such as when there is strong evidence that a defendant may destroy incriminating material.[9]

Even where truth commissions have lacked search and seizure powers, most have nevertheless enjoyed an explicit power to request documents from, and receive the full cooperation of, public authorities.[10] This, however, tends not to be a legally enforceable power. Accordingly, when cooperation is inadequate, a commission is left without remedy.

6   *See also* Decree no. 014/P.CE/CJ/90 (1990) Creating the Commission of Inquiry on the Crimes and Misappropriations Committed by the Ex-President Habré, His Accomplices and/or Accessories (Chad), reprinted in N. Kritz, ed. *Transitional Justice: How Emerging Democracies Reckon with Former Regimes* (Washington, DC: US Institute for Peace Press, 1995), vol. 3, at 48–50, art. 2: "The mission of the Commission is . . . to confiscate and secure under seal all objects and premises required for elucidating the truth."

7   *See* Appendix 1.

8   For example, the ombudsman offices in Victoria (Australia) and South Africa have search and seizure powers.

9   *See Anton Piller KG v. Manufacturing Processes Ltd.*, [1976] 1 All E.R. 779 (C.A.). The "Anton Piller" order, as it has come to be known in the UK and other common law jurisdictions, is only available where there is "clear evidence (1) of an extremely strong *prima facie* case (2) that damage, potential or actual, would have a very serious effect on it; and (3) that the defendants have in their possession incriminating documents or things and that there is a real possibility that they may destroy such material." G. Thompson, "Anton Piller Orders," CLE Society of British Columbia, available at http://www.cle.bc.ca. Anton Piller orders are distinguishable from search warrants used in criminal law cases. The orders do not permit the use of force to gain entry, but only the ability to return to court to obtain a contempt order. Also, defendants have the right to consult their legal representatives before permitting entry to their premises. *Ibid.*

10 *See, e.g.,* the Chilean TRC's mandate, which provides: "Within the scope of their competency, government authorities and agencies are to offer the Commission all the collaboration it may request, furnish the documents it may need, and provide access to such places as it may determine necessary to visit." Article 8 of the *Decree Establishing the National Commission on Truth and Reconciliation*, Supreme Decree no. 355, 1990 (Chile), reprinted in Kritz, *Transitional Justice*, vol. 3, at 104. A similar provision is found, *inter alia*, in the mandate of the Peruvian TRC. Supreme Decree no. 0065-2001-PCM (Peru) as amended, art. 6. (Unofficial translation by Lisa Magarell.) *See also* Presidential Executive Order Establishing the Truth and Justice Commission, 1995 (Haiti), art. 15.

Many truth commissions have also been given authority under their mandates to conduct on-the-spot searches.[11] This authority too, in practice, will be less effective than a full search and seizure power, for it permits only searches, not seizures.

In this chapter, the following issues will be examined: procedures for issuing search warrants, the possible scope of a warrant, procedures for executing a warrant, and the rights of the subject of the search.

SECTION 1: PROCEDURE FOR ISSUING WARRANTS

Several truth commissions have been authorized to exercise search and seizure powers without the need to apply for prior judicial authorization. For example, section 11(1) of the mandate of Ghana's truth commission provides: "The Commission shall have the powers of the police for the purposes of entry, search, seizure and removal of any document or article relevant to any investigation under this Act." Similarly, section 8(1)(b) of the Sierra Leonean TRC's mandate provides the commission with the power

> to visit any establishment or place without giving prior notice, and to enter upon any land or premises for any purpose which is material to the fulfillment of the Commission's mandate and in particular, for the purpose of obtaining information or inspecting any property or taking copies of any documents which may be of assistance to the Commission, and for safeguarding any such property or document.

Section 5(g) of the Nigerian *Tribunals of Inquiry Act* (the statutory basis for Nigeria's truth commission) provides inquiries with

> the power to enter upon any land or premises personally or by any agent or agents duly authorised in writing by the members, for any purpose which, in their opinion, is material to the inquiry, and in particular, for the purpose of obtaining evidence or information or of inspecting or taking copies of any documents required by, or which may be of assistance to, the tribunal, and for safeguarding any such document or property which in the opinion of the members ought to be safeguarded for any purpose of the inquiry.

---

11   For example, El Salvador's truth commission had the authority to "visit any establishment or place freely without giving prior notice." Mexico Peace Agreements (1991), Provisions Creating the El Salvador Commission on Truth, section 8.

By contrast, the mandate of Timor-Leste's truth commission provides at section 15.1: "The Commission may request an Investigating Judge of the District Court to issue a search warrant to enable police authorities to search premises considered to contain evidence relevant to a Commission inquiry."[12] Similarly, section 32(2) of the South African TRC's mandate provides:

> An entry or search warrant referred to in subsection (1) shall be issued by a judge of the Supreme Court or by a magistrate who has jurisdiction in the area where the premises in question are situated, and shall only be issued if it appears to the judge or magistrate from information on oath that there are reasonable grounds for believing that an article or thing mentioned in paragraph (a) or (b) of subsection (1) is upon or in such premises, and shall specify which of the acts mentioned in paragraph (b)(i) to (vi) of that subsection may be performed thereunder by the person to whom it is issued.[13]

While there are contexts in which it would not be useful or effective for a truth commission to rely on judicial authorities for the issuance of warrants, it is generally more consistent with conventional legal practice to have warrants so issued. This is the approach revealed in most Commonwealth commission of inquiry legislation. One must acknowledge, however, that in many transitional contexts, the judiciary may not be independent or effective. Where this is the case, a truth commission could itself be directly vested with a search and seizure power, in which case the recommendations in this chapter regarding judicially obtained warrants would apply, *mutatis mutandis*.[14]

A truth commission mandate may identify the essential elements to be contained in a warrant.[15] Alternatively, the content of a warrant may be determined

---

12   Section 15.2 goes on to provide: "An Investigating Judge of the District Court shall only issue a search warrant if he or she is satisfied that there are reasonable grounds to believe that such search would produce evidence necessary for the Commission's inquiry."

13   *See also An Act to Establish the Truth and Reconciliation Commission of Liberia* (2005), s. 27(b)(i), which authorizes the commission to recommend the appointment of an *ad hoc* "Special Magistrate" (ranking as a "Circuit Judge") who would "issue or cause to be issued a warrant of search and seizure ..."

14   The advisability of vesting such a significant power in a truth commission will vary from one context to another. It will generally be less desirable where no member of the commission possesses a judicial background.

15   *See, e.g.,* the mandate of Timor-Leste's truth commission: "The warrant shall contain the following: (a) identification of the Investigating Judge; (b) identification of the inquiry of the Commission relevant to the search; (c) identification of the locations and items to be searched; (d) the reason for the search; (e) the authority to search for and seize particular items; and (f) the hours of its execution and the duration of its validity." "On the

largely on the basis of local legal practice. In either case, the commission should be required to swear an oath or submit an affidavit setting out, at a minimum, the place to be searched, the reasons for the search, the things to be seized, and the proposed date and time for the search.

A warrant should generally be issued only where there are "reasonable grounds" for believing that there are, in any building or place, documents or things relevant to the subject matter of the inquiry.[16] (This is expressed slightly differently in the United States, where the constitutional standard of "probable cause" is applied.[17]) If reasonable grounds cannot be established, no warrant should issue and no search should be conducted. A search and seizure power is not to be used for the purpose of "fishing expeditions" (*i.e.,* open-ended investigations).

With respect to a commission's internal procedure, the recommendations in Chapter 4 ("Subpoena Power") are equally apt. Thus, a reasonable quorum of commissioners should be required prior to issuing or seeking a warrant. Also, for efficiency reasons, where consensus cannot be reached, warrants should be sought based on a simple majority vote. A commission chair should, however, have the power to independently issue or seek a warrant on an exceptional or emergency basis. Commission staff should not have independent authority to issue or seek warrants.

Establishment of a Commission for Reception, Truth and Reconciliation in East Timor," UNTAET/REG/2001/01 as amended, s. 15.3.

16   *See, e.g.,* section 17 of the Ontario *Public Inquiries Act,* RSO 1990, as amended: "Where a judge of the Ontario Court (General Division) is satisfied upon an application made without notice by a person appointed by a commission to make an investigation under this section, (a) that the commission conducting the inquiry has appointed the applicant to make an investigation under this section; and (b) that there are *reasonable grounds* for believing that there are in any building, receptacle or place, including a dwelling house, any documents or things relevant to the subject-matter of the inquiry, the judge may issue a warrant . . . to enter and search if necessary by force, such building, receptacle or place, for such documents or things." (Emphasis added.) The same standard is employed for judicially authorized searches of dwellings in Italy and England. S. C. Thaman, *Comparative Criminal Procedure* (Durham, NC: Carolina Academic Press, 2002), at 53.

17   The Fourth Amendment of the US Constitution provides that "no warrants shall issue, but upon probable cause, supported by oath or affirmation, and particularly describing the place to be searched, and the persons or things to be seized." Even the probable cause standard may be considered too low in some jurisdictions, particularly in relation to searches of private dwellings or private correspondence (as opposed to searches of privately owned vehicles). European jurisdictions, in particular, tend to provide higher procedural thresholds concerning searches of private dwellings and private writings. *See generally* Thaman, *Comparative Criminal Procedure,* above note 16, at 47–52 and 75–7. *Recall also* ECHR article 8(1): "Everyone has the right to respect for his private and family life, his home and his correspondence."

As a general rule, a warrant should be obtained in advance of any search.[18] This is especially important for truth commissions, which tend to work in contexts wherein the rule of law is only weakly upheld. On an exceptional basis, however, searches without a warrant should be permitted where the subject of the search freely consents, or where the prior obtaining of a warrant would defeat the purpose of the search.[19] In the latter case, however, a commission should be required to issue or seek a warrant within the twenty-four hours following the search.[20] The commission should be able to justify such a search only on the basis of exigent circumstances tantamount to a "now or never" situation.[21] However, if a commission ultimately fails to obtain such a *post hoc* warrant, neither it nor any future court should be able to rely on the seized evidence, and the evidence should be returned to the searched party.

RECOMMENDATIONS

- Where a judicial system is reasonably independent and effective, a truth commission should be required to apply to a judge for a warrant prior to conducting a search and seizure operation. Alternatively, where the judicial system is very weak or corrupt, a truth commission could be directly vested with a search and seizure power, in which case

---

18 In the absence of a state of emergency, a warrantless search is, in most if not all legal systems, presumptively unreasonable.

19 *See, e.g.,* Section 32(5) (a) of the *Promotion of National Unity and Reconciliation Act,* 1995 (South Africa), which created the TRC: "Any commissioner, or any member of the staff of the Commission or police officer at the request of a commissioner, may without a warrant enter upon any premises, other than a private dwelling, and search for, seize and remove any article or thing . . . (i) if the person who is competent to do so consents to such entry, search, seizure and removal, or (ii) if he or she upon reasonable grounds believes that (aa) the required warrant will be issued to him or her . . . if he or she were to apply for such warrant; and (bb) the delay caused by the obtaining of any such warrant would defeat the object of the entry, search, seizure and removal." *Recall also* ECHR article 8(2), which permits state interference with private property where "necessary in a democratic society in the interests of national security, public safety or the economic well-being of the country, for the protection of health or morals, or for the protection of the rights and freedoms of others."

20 *See, e.g.,* section 11(2) of the *National Reconciliation Commission Act,* 2002, Act 611 (Ghana): "[T]he Commission or a person authorized by the Commission may (a) with the consent of the occupier of the premises enter, search, seize and remove any document or article; or (b) where in the opinion of the Commission obtaining a warrant will defeat the purpose of the entry, seizure and removal of any article relevant to the investigations, enter, search, seize and remove the document or article without a warrant except that the warrant shall be obtained within twenty-four hours of the search, seizure and removal."

21 *See, e.g., Roaden v. Kentucky,* 413 US 496 (1973); *New York v. Belton,* 453 US 454 (1981).

the recommendations herein regarding judicially obtained warrants would apply, *mutatis mutandis.*

- A warrant should be issued only where there are reasonable grounds for believing that there are, in any building or place, documents or things relevant to the subject matter of the inquiry.
- Where a commission has authority to issue a search warrant, a reasonable quorum among commissioners should be required prior to issuing the warrant. Where consensus is not possible, decisions could be taken on the basis of a simple majority vote.
- The commission chair should have the power to independently issue a warrant on an exceptional and urgent basis.
- Commission staff should not have authority to issue a search warrant.
- Generally, a warrant should be obtained in advance of the search operation. On an exceptional basis, a search might be conducted without warrant where: (1) the subject of the search consents; or (2) obtaining a warrant in advance would defeat the purpose of the search, such as in cases of genuine exigency or probable destruction of evidence, and provided that the warrant is obtained within the twenty-four hours following the search.

SECTION 2: SCOPE OF A WARRANT

Where a warrant provides the basis for conducting a search, its duration should be limited to the time strictly necessary to achieve the intended purpose.[22] This is a necessary element of any reasonable search and seizure operation. If the lifetime of a warrant is too open-ended, a search may risk becoming arbitrary or unreasonable.[23]

A warrant should permit the removal and retention of objects for a reasonable period of time.[24] However, where possible, the commission should copy or photograph, rather than seize and withhold, evidence obtained pursuant to a warrant.

---

22   Section 32(8) of the *Promotion of National Unity and Reconciliation Act*, 1995 (South Africa): "A warrant issued in terms of this section may be issued on any day and shall be of force until – (a) It is executed; or (b) It is cancelled by the person who issued it or, if such person is not available, by any person with like authority; or (c) The expiry of one month from the day of its issue; or (d) The purpose for the issuing of the warrant has lapsed, whichever may occur first." Section 15.9 of the Timor-Leste truth commission's mandate is identical.

23   *See* Chapter 2, Section 1, regarding unreasonable searches.

24   Note that, depending on the case (and the relevant legal tradition), the warrant might be restricted to particular objects, rather than being open-ended.

A warrant should also permit – during and after the search – the inspection and examination of objects, the asking of pertinent questions to the person being searched, and the making of copies of all or part of any articles found or seized. These are standard elements of warrants in most, if not all, legal systems. They are also standard elements of the mandates of some truth commissions. For example, section 32(1) of the South African TRC's mandate provides:

> Any commissioner, member of the staff of the Commission or police officer authorized thereto by a commissioner may on the authority of an entry warrant . . . enter upon any premises in or upon which any article or thing – (a) which is concerned with or is upon reasonable grounds suspected to be concerned with any matter which is the subject of any investigation in terms of this Act; (b) which contains, or is upon reasonable grounds suspected to contain, information with regard to any such matter, is or is upon reasonable grounds suspected to be, and may on the authority of a search warrant . . . – (i) inspect and search such premises and there make such inquiries as he or she may deem necessary; (ii) examine any article or thing found in or upon such premises; (iii) request from the person who is in control of such premises or in whose possession or under whose control any article or thing is when it is found, or who is upon reasonable grounds believed to have information with regard to any article or thing, an explanation or information; (iv) make copies of or extracts from any such article found upon or in such premises; (v) seize any article or thing found upon or in such premises which he or she upon reasonable grounds suspects to be an article or thing mentioned in paragraph (a) or (b); (vi) after having issued a receipt in respect thereof remove any article or thing found on such premises and suspected upon reasonable grounds to be an article or thing mentioned in paragraph (a) or (b), and retain such article or thing for a reasonable period for the purpose of further examination or, in the case of such article, the making of copies thereof or extracts therefrom: Provided that any article or thing that has been so removed, shall be returned as soon as possible after the purpose of such removal has been accomplished.

Similarly, section 15.8 of the Timor-Leste truth commission's mandate provides:

> Police officers may, on the authority of a search warrant: (a) inspect and search the identified premises and there make such inquiries as he

or she may deem necessary; (b) examine any object or item (including documents) relevant to a Commission inquiry found in or upon such premises; (c) request from the person who is in control of such premises or in whose possession or under whose control any object or item . . . is when it is found, or who is upon reasonable grounds believed to have information with regard to any object or item, an explanation or information; (d) make copies of or extracts from any object or item found upon or in such premises; (e) seize any object or item found upon or in such premises which he or she upon reasonable grounds suspects to be an object or item within the meaning of Subsection 15.8 (b); (f) After having issued a receipt in respect thereof remove any object or item found on such premises and suspect upon reasonable grounds to be an object or item . . . and retain such object or item for a reasonable period for the purpose of further examination or, in the case of such article, the making of copies thereof or extracts thereof or extracts therefrom[.][25]

In terms of their scope of application, warrants should generally apply to both natural (*i.e.*, human) and legal (*i.e.*, corporate) persons.

RECOMMENDATIONS

- The duration of a warrant should not be open-ended. It should be limited to the time that is minimally necessary to achieve the stated purpose.
- A warrant should permit the removal and retention of objects for a reasonable period of time. It should also permit – during and after the search – the inspection and examination of objects, the making of copies of all or part of any articles found, and the asking of pertinent questions of the person being searched.
- Warrants should apply to all persons, natural or legal.

25 *Compare with* section 17(3) and (5) of the Ontario *Public Inquiries Act*, RSO 1990, as amended: "(3) A person making an investigation under this section may, upon giving a receipt therefor, remove any document or thing found in his or her investigation relevant to the subject-matter of the inquiry and deliver it to the commission which shall keep custody of it . . . (5) Where a document has been delivered to a commission by a person making an investigation under this section, the commission may cause the document to be photocopied and the photocopy may be filed in evidence in place of the document delivered to the commission and a copy of such document certified by the commission to be a true copy thereof, is admissible in evidence in proceedings in which the document so delivered is admissible, as evidence of the document so delivered."

SECTION 3: PROCEDURE FOR EXECUTING WARRANTS

While it is reasonable to give a truth commission the power to issue or obtain warrants, it is generally preferable to have the warrants executed by uniformed police officers, whether the officers are independent of the commission or temporarily employed by it.[26] A commissioner, or designated senior staff member of the commission, should accompany the police officer.[27] In a democracy, it is generally desirable that the exercise of such a highly invasive power falls within the purview of permanent public institutions, such as judicial bodies and the police, that are clearly identifiable and accountable to the public.

As we have already observed, however, in transitional contexts police officers may be corrupt or directly implicated in the crimes under investigation.[28] Commissioners or senior staff might, therefore, be able to conduct a search and seizure operation independent of the police, provided that they carry suitable identifying information such as a special commission badge.[29]

Search and seizure operations ideally should be carried out with the consent and cooperation of the investigated party. Where consent is not given, however, those executing the warrant should be permitted to apply reasonable force to enter the building or place, provided that (1) they first make audible demand

---

26 Taking this one step further, the Timor-Leste truth commission's mandate provides: "Any object or item seized by the police for retention under Subsection 15.8 shall remain in the custody and control of the police. Commission staff may be given access to such object or item on the premises of the police." "On the Establishment of a Commission for Reception, Truth and Reconciliation in East Timor," UNTAET/REG/2001/01 as amended, s. 15.10.

27 *See, e.g.,* section 17 of the Ontario *Public Inquiries Act,* RSO 1990, as amended, which authorizes a commission member, "together with such police officers as he or she calls upon to assist him or her," to carry out the warrant. The Timor-Leste truth commission's mandate provides: "The search should also be made in the presence of at least one Commission staff member." "On the Establishment of a Commission for Reception, Truth and Reconciliation in East Timor," UNTAET/REG/2001/01 as amended, s. 15.6.

28 *Recall also* Principle 15 of the Principles on the Effective Prevention and Investigation of Extra-Legal, Arbitrary and Summary Executions (1989), UN doc. E/1989/89, which requires the protection of "[c]omplainants, witnesses, those conducting the investigation and their families" from threats and acts of violence or intimidation, and the removal of those potentially implicated by the investigation from positions of control or power over such persons.

29 Section 22(7) of the mandate of the Republic of Korea's truth commission provides for the use of badges during on-site searches. *Special Act to Reveal the Truth Regarding Suspicious Deaths,* Act no. 6170, 15 January 2000, as amended.

of entry,[30] and (2) there is an independent witness to the use of force.[31] These criteria are essential. The sole purpose of a search should be to locate and, where necessary, seize relevant items. Searches that do not initially seek consensual accommodation from the investigated party will appear abusive and will serve to only discredit a truth commission.

The subject of the search should be entitled to accompany those conducting the search or, alternatively, to designate another person to serve as a witness during the search. Also, in some jurisdictions, the law may require the presence of a clerk, prosecutor, or other official during the search.[32] The officials conducting the search must exhibit the warrant for inspection if so asked.

Warrants should generally be executed by day and, exceptionally, at reasonable times of night. This is the practice in most legal systems, and it was also the approach required of at least two truth commissions, namely, South Africa[33] and Timor-Leste.[34] In addition, those executing the warrant should identify themselves properly, present or post a copy of the warrant, and address

---

30   See, e.g., Section 32(6)(a) of the *Promotion of National Unity and Reconciliation Act,* 1995 (South Africa): "Any person who may on the authority of a warrant issued in terms of subsection (2), or under the provisions of subsection (5), enter upon and search any premises, may use such force as may be reasonably necessary to overcome resistance to such entry or search. (b) No person may enter upon or search any premises unless he or she has audibly demanded admission to the premises and has notified the purpose of his or her entry, unless such person is upon reasonable grounds of the opinion that any article or thing may be destroyed if such admission is first demanded and such purpose is first notified."

31   See, e.g., the Timor-Leste truth commission's mandate, which provides: "If possible, the search will be made in the presence of the residents of the premises . . . Where there are no residents present at the time of the search, the police may provide for at least one independent witness. Such witness shall sign the record. In any case where the witness cannot read or write, the record shall be read out to the witness and the witness asked to make an identifying mark to verify the record." "On the Establishment of a Commission for Reception, Truth and Reconciliation in East Timor," UNTAET/REG/2001/01 as amended, s. 15.6. Other than in cases of urgency, a better approach may be to return on a separate occasion to conduct the search.

32   See Thaman, *Comparative Criminal Procedure,* above note 16, at 55 (discussing the approaches of Spain and Germany).

33   Section 32(3): "A warrant issued in terms of this section shall be executed by day unless the person who issues the warrant authorizes the execution thereof by night at times which shall be reasonable . . ."

34   Section 15.4: "Searches shall normally be made during daylight hours. The Commission may, however, request the Investigating Judge to authorize a night time search when there are reasonable grounds to believe that it is necessary for the effective execution of the warrant or for the safety of the persons involved in the search. Such grounds shall be recorded in the warrant."

any questions about their authority to execute the warrant.[35] Also, the subject of the warrant should be promptly informed of the potential consequences of noncompliance.[36]

Those conducting the search should make a detailed written record of the search, including all relevant dates and times, and a list of the seized objects. The written record should be signed by those who conducted the search, as well as by the subject of the search and a witness proposed by the subject. Truth commissions should also make a practice of videotaping all searches, both for their own benefit and for purposes of public accountability. For example, the mandate of Timor-Leste's truth commission provides at section 15.5:

> The police conducting the search shall make a written record of the search. Photographs, films or tape recordings may be part of the record. The written record shall contain the following: (a) identification of the recipient of the warrant; (b) a detailed description of the premises; (c) a list and description of the objects, and any other items at the premises that may be relevant for the investigation; (d) a detailed list of the physical evidence seized during the search; (e) identification and signature of persons claiming the ownership or possession of seized evidence, if any; and (f) identification of the persons present at the premises and their physical conditions, if relevant.

A truth commission should provide the subject of the search with a list of all seized evidence.[37] Also, to preserve the utility of the evidence at any future trial, a commission should meticulously record the chain of custody of the evidence until its return, if any, to the owner.

35   *See, e.g.,* section 32(4) of the *Promotion of National Unity and Reconciliation Act,* 1995 (South Africa): "Any person executing a warrant in terms of this section shall immediately before commencing with the execution – (a) identify himself or herself to the person in control of the premises, if such person is present, and hand to such person a copy of the warrant or, if such person is not present, affix such copy to a prominent place on the premises; (b) supply such person at his or her request with particulars regarding his or her authority to execute such a warrant." *See also* "On the Establishment of a Commission for Reception, Truth and Reconciliation in East Timor," UNTAET/REG/2001/01 as amended, s. 15.3.

36   *See, e.g.,* the Timor-Leste truth commission's mandate, which provides that "in any case in which the Commission has (exercised its search and seizure power), persons shall be informed of the potential consequences of non-compliance with such order." "On the Establishment of a Commission for Reception, Truth and Reconciliation in East Timor," UNTAET/REG/2001/01 as amended, s. 35.1(f).

37   This is an aspect of practice for Anton Piller orders. *See* G. Thompson, "Anton Piller Orders," above note 9.

Where, during the conduct of a search, the investigated party refuses inspection or removal of property on the basis that it contains privileged information, the matter should be referred to a local court or magistrate to have a prompt ruling issued on the matter.[38] In the interim, the property should be sealed and temporarily placed in the custody of a neutral third party, such as a court clerk or registrar.[39] Among other things, this rule will help to ensure that a commission does not seek to obtain indirectly (by warrant) what it is likely prohibited from obtaining directly (by subpoena).

Finally, while a commission should be permitted to keep custody of seized property for no longer than the warrant allows, a judge should have discretion to extend the period of retention upon application by a commission.[40] By corollary, judges should also have the discretion to shorten the period of retention.[41]

RECOMMENDATIONS

- Warrants should ideally be executed by uniformed police officers, whether they work independently of the commission or are temporarily employed by it. A commissioner or designated staff member should accompany the police officer.
- Where police officers are corrupt or implicated in the subject of the warrant, a member of the truth commission might have authority

---

38   *See* Chapter 6 (Section 7) concerning the different possible types of legal privilege. An inference that property is privileged cannot be drawn, however, simply from the fact that it was seized from the office of a lawyer or doctor. Specific evidence will ultimately need to be adduced, as the case may be, of a solicitor–client or doctor–patient relationship and privilege.

39   *See, e.g.,* Section 32(7) of the *Promotion of National Unity and Reconciliation Act,* 1995 (South Africa): "If during the execution of a warrant or the conducting of a search in terms of this section, a person claims that an article found on or in the premises concerned contains privileged information and refuses the inspection or removal of such article, the person executing the warrant or conducting the search shall, if he or she is of the opinion that the article contains information which is relevant to the investigation and that such information is necessary for the investigation or hearing, request the registrar of the Supreme Court which has jurisdiction or his or her delegate, to seize and remove that article for safe custody until a court of law has made a ruling on the question whether the information concerned is privileged or not."

40   There are various possible grounds for retaining the property. These might include the fact that it is physical evidence that cannot be readily copied in any way, or that it constitutes evidence of criminal conduct (and that its return would likely result in destruction by the owner).

41   See, e.g., Canada Law Reform Commission, Working Paper 17, *Administrative Law: Commissions of Inquiry* (Ottawa: The Commission, 1977), at 57.

to execute the warrant without police accompaniment, provided that suitable identifying information – such as a special commission badge – is employed.

- Those executing a warrant should identify themselves properly, present or post a copy of the warrant, and address any questions about their authority to execute the warrant. The subject of the search should be orally advised of the potential consequences of non-compliance.
- A search and seizure operation should ideally be carried out with the consent and cooperation of the subject of the search. Where consent is not given, those conducting the search should be permitted to apply reasonable force to enter the premises only if (1) they first make audible demand of entry, and (2) an independent witness to the entry is on the premises.
- The subject of the search should be entitled to accompany those conducting the search, or to designate another person to serve as a witness during the search.
- Warrants should generally be executed by day, unless there is a justified urgency for doing otherwise.
- Those conducting the search should make a detailed written record of the search and of any seized objects. The record should be signed by those who conducted the search, as well as by the subject of the search and a witness proposed by the subject. The search should also, ideally, be videotaped.
- Where, during a search, the subject refuses to permit removal of property on the basis that it contains privileged information, the matter should be referred to the courts, and the property sealed and temporarily placed in the custody of a neutral third party such as a court clerk or registrar.

SECTION 4: RIGHTS OF THE SUBJECT OF THE SEARCH

Where a warrant is defective, the investigated party should be able to seek to have it quashed through a judicial process. This right can be explicitly included in a truth commission's mandate.[42] The right should not, however, be too open-ended. The application should be required to be brought to court without undue delay.

---

42   If the right to quash the defective warrant is not included in the commission's mandate, the right to challenge it – and the grounds for doing so – should in any event be present in other domestic statutes or rules of procedure.

The subject of a search should have the right to a remedy when a search and seizure is conducted in an arbitrary or unreasonable fashion.[43] Reasonableness requires, *inter alia*, that the dignity and privacy of the subject be respected at all stages of the search and seizure operation. For example, section 32(3)(c) of the South African TRC's mandate emphasizes that search operations must be consistent with: "(a) a person's right to, respect for and the protection of his or her dignity; (b) the right of a person to freedom and security; and (c) the right of a person to his or her personal privacy."[44] The mandate of Ghana's truth commission stipulates: "A document, article or information obtained by the investigation unit shall not be made public unless authorized by the Commission."[45]

Where evidence has been improperly seized by police, national law may provide for an "exclusionary rule" by which illegally obtained evidence is barred from use in a trial against the person.[46] Variants of the rule are found in international human rights law[47] and international criminal law.[48] A similar rule should apply in respect of truth commission investigations and findings. Reliance upon evidence illegally obtained by a commission should be barred, subject to a possible "good faith exception."[49] As well, a subsequent referral, if any, of such evidence to a law enforcement or judicial body should be made with notification of the deficiency.

Finally, and as previously noted, once an object has been seized by or on behalf of a truth commission, the commission cannot hold it *ad infinitum*.

---

43   *See, e.g., Law 04/018 (2004) Concerning the Organization, Powers and Functions of the Truth and Reconciliation Commission* (DRC), art. 37. *See also* the discussion of privacy and reputation rights under international law in Chapter 2, Section 1.

44   Section 15.7 of the Timor-Leste truth commission's mandate is more or less identical.

45   *National Reconciliation Commission Act, 2002*, Act 611 (Ghana), s. 11(3). *See also Law 04/018 (2004) Concerning the Organization, Powers and Functions of the Truth and Reconciliation Commission* (DRC), art. 37.

46   Various jurisdictions provide for "nonusability" (or "nullification") of unlawfully seized evidence. *See* Thaman, *Comparative Criminal Procedure*, above note 16, at 103 and 111. In the United States, the same notion is described as the "fruit of the poisonous tree" doctrine.

47   *See* Chapter 2, Section 1.

48   *See, e.g.,* Rule 95 of the ICTY Rules of Procedure: "No evidence shall be admissible if obtained by methods which cast substantial doubt on its reliability or if its admission is antithetical to, and would seriously damage, the integrity of the proceedings." *See also* Rome Statute art. 69(7): "Evidence obtained by means of a violation of this Statute or internationally recognized human rights shall not be admissible if: (a) The violation casts substantial doubt on the reliability of the evidence; or (b) The admission of the evidence would be antithetical to and would seriously damage the integrity of the proceedings."

49   *United States v. Leon*, 468 US 897 (evidence can be used and relied upon where it was discovered by authorities acting in good faith and in the reasonable belief that their actions were authorized).

Instead, the object's owner has the right to have it returned within a reasonable time of its seizure.

RECOMMENDATIONS

- The subject of the search should have a right to challenge and quash a defective warrant, but any application for judicial review of a warrant must be brought expeditiously.
- The subject of the search should have a right to a remedy where the manner of search and seizure is arbitrary or unreasonable.
- Where a search is conducted in an arbitrary or unreasonable manner, a truth commission should be precluded from using or relying upon the seized evidence, and any subsequent referral of such evidence to a law enforcement or judicial body should either not be made, or be made with notification of the deficiency.

6

Public Hearings

INTRODUCTION

A significant number of truth commissions have conducted public hearings that were authorized, or alternatively required, by their terms of reference. The South African TRC, which catalyzed the global use of hearings by truth commissions, held several different types of public hearings: victim hearings, amnesty hearings, and special hearings focused on key institutions, themes, or events.[1] This chapter focuses only on victim hearings, and on related reply hearings by implicated persons. Much of this chapter will, nevertheless, be relevant to other types of commission hearings.[2]

Public hearings present an enormous administrative, logistical, and financial challenge for truth commissions.[3] Yet there is an increasing trend in favor

---

1   Similarly, the truth commissions in Peru and Timor-Leste held a mix of victim hearings, thematic hearings, regional hearings, and hearings on institutional responsibility. The Timorese commission also held reconciliation-focused public hearings, in which members of the relevant community were given the opportunity to put questions to perpetrators who confessed to low-level crimes.

2   For example, in a typical thematic hearing (*e.g.*, on the role of women in a past conflict), individual victims testify in much the same manner as they would at an "individual" hearing. The chief differences lie in the thematic focus of the hearing and in the common (but not invariable) practice of inviting experts and public figures to provide contextual testimony about the particular theme under consideration at the hearing.

3   *See* J. R. Quinn and M. Freeman, "Lessons Learned: Practical Lessons Gleaned from Inside

of their use because of several potential benefits. Public hearings can help provide a privileged public platform for victims, and thereby serve as an indirect form of acknowledgment and moral restoration for past suffering.[4] When they are broadcast on national television and radio, public hearings can also have an unrivaled impact on public awareness about past abuse. In the most successful cases, they can generate a society-wide debate, and foster greater public sympathy for victims.[5] This can in turn contribute to the process of reconciliation, and help secure public support for subsequent justice, reparation, and reform efforts. In societies with high rates of illiteracy, public hearings can bring the work of the truth commission to the ordinary citizen in a way that no final report can.[6] Public hearings in which victims recount their torment, often in moving fashion, also make it more difficult for culpable persons and institutions to deny the human impact of past abuse. It is much easier to attack statistics than to attack the testimony of a poor country widow whose life has been destroyed by the torture or disappearance of a loved one.

Public hearings can also considerably enhance the transparency of a truth commission's work. This is especially crucial after a long history of cover-ups

---

the Truth Commissions of Guatemala and South Africa" (2003) 25 *Human Rights Quarterly* 1117, at 1141.

4   Describing the South African TRC's first victim hearing, Alex Boraine writes: "Today they were no longer under siege, no longer harassed, but were protected by the police. They were guests of honour. They were in a liberated zone." A. Boraine, *A Country Unmasked* (Oxford: Oxford University Press, 2000), at 99. Several of those who testified before Peru's TRC viewed their public testimony as an opportunity to clean (*limpiar*) their honor and that of their families, and to affirm their innocence. See "El Impacto de las Audiencias Públicas en los Participantes" (http://www.cverdad.org.pe).

5   The Peruvian TRC viewed public hearings as a "stimulator of solidarity" (*un estímulo a la solidaridad*). See "El Impacto de las Audiencias Públicas en los Participantes" (http://www.cverdad.org.pe). Another objective of the public hearings was to convert the testimonies into a pedagogical instrument that would stimulate a permanent public dialogue that could contribute to national reconciliation. TRC Regulation on Public Hearings, art. 5. See also M. Freeman, "Whose Truth?" (2005) 385 *New Internationalist* 7, at 8: "In Peru, the truth commission's hearings put the pain of the past on full display for city dwellers who knew little about the bloodshed in the countryside."

6   See e.g., *Nigeria: Judicial Commission of Inquiry for the Investigation of Human Rights Violations, Final Report (2002)*, Synoptic Overview, ch. 2, para. 63: "For a population that is largely illiterate, the public hearings provided them the best opportunity to see things with their own eyes." The Nigerian commission's report also notes that "except for some celebrated individuals who were prominent in society, the majority of victims who were not so well known languished in jails and detention centers without any mention by the media. They lived under very harsh and inhuman conditions. The public hearings gave them and the society a chance to hear the stories." *Ibid.*, Synoptic Overview, ch. 3, at 60.

and official secrecy.[7] Just as importantly, public hearings can put the victim, rather than any individual commissioner, at the center of public attention.[8] When recorded on tape or video, public hearings can also serve as a powerful and enduring resource for teaching future generations about the country's legacy of abuse.

Yet public hearings – and public truth telling more generally – will not be possible or desirable in every context. In some cases, victims, witnesses, and their families may still fear reprisal by known and unknown perpetrators and thus balk at the opportunity to give public testimony.[9] Similarly, public hearings may present security risks for commissioners and commission staff. Time constraints and resource limitations may militate against public truth telling too.[10] There may even be cultural factors at play that make public hearings seem inappropriate, such as a local disdain or disinclination for public displays of emotion or grief.

Sponsors and advocates of truth commissions will need to carefully weigh all of the foregoing considerations. They should, in addition, be aware of certain practical realities concerning public hearings. First, in most instances, only a small percentage of the total number of persons wishing to publicly testify will have the opportunity to do so. This is true even for commissions with comparatively large resources and lengthy periods of operation. Second, for some victims the opportunity to give public testimony may be psychologically empowering, whereas for others it may be psychologically debilitating.[11] There should,

---

7   *See generally* J. Allen, "Media Relations and the South African TRC – Riding a Tiger," available from the International Center for Transitional Justice (http://www.ictj.org).

8   The focus on the victim is, however, diminished where commissioners begin to cry while listening to testimony. *See, e.g.,* Boraine, *A Country Unmasked,* above note 4, at 104. It is natural to have a strong emotional reaction to stories of torture and similar suffering. But, as Boraine notes, "We had a job to do and that job was to keep the focus on the victims and as far as possible to keep the attention away from ourselves."

9   For this reason public hearings would have been unimaginable in the case of the truth commission in El Salvador, for example.

10   Discussing the case of the South African TRC, Hayner notes, "Instead of investigating, investigators were asked to cull victim statements to select witnesses for the next hearings, organize logistics, and prepare summary material for the commissions on each panel." P. Hayner, *Unspeakable Truths: Facing the Challenge of Truth Commissions,* 2d ed. (New York: Routledge, 2002), at 227.

11   For example, in 1997, the *New York Times* reported on a study which found that nearly 60% of those who testified at public hearings of the South African TRC felt worse after testifying. Cited in R. Shaw, "Rethinking Truth and Reconciliation Commissions: Lessons from Sierra Leone" (US Institute for Peace, February 2005), at 7. At one public hearing of Ghana's truth commission, a victim actually had a heart attack while giving testimony, and later died. *Ghana National Reconciliation Commission Final Report* (2004), vol. 2, ch. 2, at 14. Subsequently, the commission adopted the practice of measuring the blood pressure of anyone scheduled to testify in public. It also arranged for ambulances to be on hand at the site of any hearing. Similarly, in the case of the Sierra Leonean TRC, "Red Cross volunteers

therefore, be no automatic presumption that public hearings will be therapeutic for those able to testify.[12] Third, as noted earlier in the book, the contemporary truth commission public hearing does not have a strong truth-*seeking* dimension.[13] Although new and important information can emerge at the hearing, it is not primarily a tool for searching out the truth; rather it is primarily a tool for publicizing the truth. With rare exceptions, those selected to testify have already recounted their story to a truth commission during the statement-taking process (*i.e.*, the facts of the cases were already known to the commission). The public hearing, then, is an opportunity to make a similar statement on a public stage. It is above all a moment for truth *telling*. As such, it is not customarily a moment in which the veracity of a statement will be challenged.[14]

To date, the following truth commissions have held public hearings: Uganda, Germany, Sri Lanka, South Africa, Nigeria, Grenada, Timor-Leste, Ghana, Sierra Leone, Peru, Morocco, and Paraguay. The truth commission in Liberia will also hold public hearings.

Many other investigative bodies conduct public hearings too. For example, all Commonwealth commission of inquiry statutes permit, and often encourage, the holding of public hearings. Some nongovernmental bodies have also organized public hearings.[15] Coroners often hold public hearings as part of their inquest procedures too.

The particular focus of this chapter is on the following aspects of a truth commission's public hearings: the selection of those who will appear, rules of notification to implicated persons, the nature and scope of the right of reply, the taking of oaths or solemn undertakings, the right to legal representation, evidentiary rules at hearings, legal privileges based on contexts and relationships

---

and medical personnel from the district hospitals were also present at every hearing." *Sierra Leone Truth and Reconciliation Commission Final Report* (2004), vol. 1, ch. 5, para. 207.

12   *See generally* Hayner, *Unspeakable Truths*, above note 10, at 141–4. This has not, however, stopped truth commissions from promoting the supposed healing effect of public and private truth telling. In Sierra Leone, posters proclaimed "Truth today! Peaceful Sierra Leone Tomorrow" and "Blo Maind to TRC en ge Pis" (Blow mind to the TRC and get peace).

13   Exceptions to the contemporary trend are the truth commissions of Nigeria and Ghana, both of which followed a more classic Commonwealth inquiry model. In each case, the commission treated public hearings as occasions to ferret out the facts, including through questioning and cross-examination of those who testified. *See* discussion below.

14   For this reason, a victim hearing should not be undertaken unless or until a commission is sure that the victim's statements can be generally presumed to be true. The case is, however, different for public hearings of those persons suspected of wrongdoing who choose, or are compelled, to testify. In such cases, the hearing is used as more of an investigative tool, with significant probing and questioning by the commission or counsel or both.

15   For example, NGOs in Morocco organized public hearings before the advent of a national truth commission, and later in parallel to it. M. Freeman and V. Opgenhaffen, *Transitional Justice in Morocco: A Progress Report*, International Center for Transitional Justice (November 2005), at 12 and 18.

of confidentiality, use immunity and the privilege against self-incrimination, protective measures for victims and witnesses, and victim emotional and psychological support.

SECTION 1: SELECTION AND PREPARATION
OF THOSE WHO WILL APPEAR

As revealed in the introduction to this chapter, public hearings entail many complex moral, legal, and political considerations. One such consideration is the selection of those who will have the opportunity to give public testimony. Decisions on witness selection may involve a degree of external consultation, but a commission must ultimately retain sole discretion to choose who will testify in public.

While no person has an absolute right to testify at a truth commission public hearing, a general presumption of competency should be applied to parties willing to testify. This will help ensure that the commission gives due consideration to the broadest range of possible candidates. Like all presumptions, however, this one is rebuttable. For example, persons who are severely mentally or physically incompetent may be excluded from consideration if it appears they would be unable to understand the nature or possible consequences of the proceeding. Indeed, to put evidently incompetent people on the stand would run foreseeable, and ultimately unnecessary, risks both for the person and for the commission.[16]

In the matter of witness selection, children should be treated as a special case in accordance with international standards. In conformity with article 1 of the Convention on the Rights of the Child 1989 (CRC),[17] a truth commission should consider persons under eighteen years of age as children. Although in many cases it will not be possible, practical, or appropriate for a commission to obtain testimony from witnesses who were children at the time the human rights violations occurred, nevertheless a truth commission should seek to address the unique interests of children and youth.[18] The Sierra Leonean TRC's mandate, for example, explicitly required the commission to

16   While many victims suffer from degrees of Post-Traumatic Stress Disorder (PTSD), this is not necessarily a ground for incompetence to testify at a public hearing. To make it so would be inconsistent with the reason for organizing victim hearings in the first place. *See Prosecutor v. Furundzija*, ICTY Judgment, Case T-95-17/1-T (10 December 1998), at para. 109: "There is no reason why a person with PTSD cannot be a perfectly reliable witness."

17   GA res. 44/25, annex, 44 UN GAOR Supp. (no. 49) at 167, UN doc. A/44/49 (1989), *entered into force* 2 September 1990.

18   *Recall also* that CRC art. 12(2) obligates states parties to provide children, either directly or through a representative, "the opportunity to be heard in any judicial and administrative proceedings" affecting them. Though a truth commission is simply an investigative

pay special attention to children and youth.[19] In conformity with this mandate, the commission allowed many children to testify at its public hearings, many of whom were also perpetrators of atrocities. In the case of the South African TRC, by contrast, it was decided that children under the age of eighteen would not testify.[20] However, during its special hearing on children and youth, the TRC accepted testimony from individuals who were "eighteen years or younger when the gross human rights violations occurred."[21] A commission might also consider allowing parents or legal guardians to stand in for children and testify on their behalf.

Within the pool of competent candidates, a truth commission will usually be able to accommodate only a small percentage of the total number of victims who may wish to testify.[22] Even the South African TRC, which held more public hearings than any other truth commission, only enabled some nine percent of the total pool of victims to testify.[23] In Sierra Leone and Nigeria, it was less than five percent.[24] In Morocco, it was less than one percent.[25] As a matter of procedural fairness, therefore, a truth commission ought to acquire a reasonably

---

proceeding, it may nevertheless be in the "best interests" (CRC art. 3) of particular children to allow them a chance to testify in public.

19 See Section 6(2): "It shall be the function of the Commission to ... work to help restore the human dignity of victims and promote reconciliation by providing an opportunity for victims to give an account of the violations and abuses suffered and for perpetrators to relate their experiences, and by creating a climate which fosters constructive interchange between victims and perpetrators, giving special attention to the subject of sexual abuses and to the experiences of children within the armed conflict." See also Section 7(4): "The Commission shall take into account the interests of victims and witnesses when inviting them to give statements, including the security and other concerns of those who may wish to recount their stories in public and the Commission may also implement special procedures to address the needs of such particular victims as children or those who have suffered sexual abuses as well as in working with child perpetrators of abuses or violations."

20 Instead, NGOs and other child care professionals were requested to testify on their behalf. See Truth and Reconciliation Commission of South Africa Report (1998), vol. 4, ch. 9, Special Hearing: Children and Youth, at para. 7, http://www.polity.org.za/govdocs/commissions/1998/trc/4chap9.htm.

21 Ibid., at para. 1.

22 One prominent exception is the truth commission in Ghana, which convened hearings for close to 50% of the total number of cases presented to it. Ghana National Reconciliation Commission Final Report (2004), vol. 1, ch. 5, at 5.01.

23 The TRC received statements from approximately 23,000 victims. Of these, approximately 2,000 were granted the opportunity to appear at a public hearing. M. Freeman and P. Hayner, "Truth-Telling," in Reconciliation After Violent Conflict: A Handbook (Stockholm: Institute for Democracy and Electoral Assistance, 2003), at 140.

24 Approximately 350 of the 7,700 persons who made statements to the TRC in Sierra Leone were allowed to testify in public. P. Hayner, International Center for Transitional Justice, The Sierra Leone Truth and Reconciliation Commission: Reviewing the First Year (2004), at 4. The truth commission in Nigeria heard 340 of the approximately 10,000 petitions it received.

25 Freeman and Opgenhaffen, Transitional Justice in Morocco, above note 15, at 18.

large set of victim statements and perform minimal investigation or due diligence regarding the content of those statements prior to making any final selections. Such an approach is also prudential. A person who testifies in error or in bad faith will damage not only the commission's reputation, but also, potentially, the reputations of those who may be unfairly or inaccurately implicated by the testimony.

The criteria a commission may adopt for the selection of those who testify will ordinarily correspond to the objectives set out in its mandate. In general, commissions tend to adopt rather broad criteria. For example, there is usually a strong interest in selecting a mix of persons who will reflect the country's regional, ethnic, racial, and religious diversity. Gender parity may also be deemed important. Less well-known cases (or their larger surrounding contexts) may be given precedence over those that are already familiar to the public. Diversity in the periods of history represented or in the types of violations may be other objectives.[26] In deciding on the overall balance of cases, it may also be important to take into account the proportional victimization of different groups.[27] Other, more practical, criteria may include the "readiness of a case for hearing due to timely conclusion of investigations."[28]

Victims tend to comprise the primary category of persons a truth commission will invite to testify. Rarely, however, are they the only parties a commission will invite. A commission may also see fit to invite family members, witnesses, and presumed perpetrators to testify, as well as other special categories of persons such as experts, academics, and current and former heads of state. Truth commissions in South Africa, Nigeria, Peru, Ghana, Sierra Leone, and Timor-Leste took this approach.

Whatever the final criteria for witness selection, it is essential for a truth commission to provide similar consideration to similar cases, and to avoid any

---

26 These and other objectives were all included in the criteria employed by the truth commission in Morocco for selecting victims to testify. The specific criteria employed were gender balance, regional representation (based on historical events, type of violations, and location of detention centers), clarity and significance of the specific story, psychological strength of the particular victim, and diversity of stories (to avoid repetition). See http://www.ier.ma. The Sierra Leonean TRC applied similarly broad criteria, including to ensure a good balance in terms of "region, ethnic group, age group, political affiliation and gender," the "range of violations," and the "range of perpetrator factions." *Sierra Leone Truth and Reconciliation Commission Final Report* (2004), vol. 1, ch. 5, para. 203.

27 For example, in Peru most victims were indigenous persons living in rural zones of the country. The TRC ensured that the proportion of those testifying at public hearings reflected that fact.

28 Ghana's truth commission employed this criterion. Its other three criteria were "the principle of first-come, first-served; severity of the violation; [and] lack of need for investigations." *Ghana National Reconciliation Commission Final Report* (2004), vol. 2, ch. 2, at 2.5.5.1.

bias or discrimination in making selections. In addition, the selection criteria should be made public, consistent with the principle of transparency.

It goes without saying that victims who testify at public hearings should do so on a voluntary basis only.[29] The principle of consent is, indeed, an essential criterion for victim hearings. As to presumed perpetrators, they should first be requested to appear, if at all, on a voluntary basis.[30] However, where they decline, and where their public testimony is considered highly relevant and necessary,[31] they may (mandate permitting) be subpoenaed.[32] The same is true for material third-party witnesses.

All victims who will appear at public hearings should be provided with a briefing at which the hearing procedure and any corresponding rights or duties are explained.[33] Most commissions that have held public hearings, including those in South Africa, Peru, Timor-Leste, Sierra Leone, and Morocco, have provided such briefings. A briefing should also encompass a realistic appraisal of the personal and legal implications of giving testimony.[34] In addition, it should include an honest account of the capacity of the commission to provide protection against repercussions that might arise from giving public evidence. This is especially important in circumstances in which a commission allows a victim to identify the name of his or her alleged victimizer. In such an instance, providing an accurate briefing about the commission's inability to protect against private vengeance or defamation suits is essential. The victim must be

---

29   D. Orentlicher, "Updated Set of Principles for the Protection and Promotion of Human Rights Through Action to Combat Impunity," UN doc. E/CN.4/2005/102/Add.1, Principle 10(a): "Victims and witnesses testifying on their behalf may be called upon to testify before the commission only on a strictly voluntary basis."

30   Such an approach demonstrates good faith on the part of the commission. It gives an opportunity for compliance, rather than presuming noncompliance.

31   For their public testimony to be necessary, the commission must be satisfied that merely private testimony would not serve the public interest.

32   See Chapter 4.

33   Such rights encompass not only those discussed throughout this chapter, but also the right to have the reasonable costs of providing testimony (e.g., the costs of transport) paid for by the state. See, e.g., Orentlicher, "Updated Set of Principles," above note 29, Principle 10(c): "All expenses incurred by those giving testimony shall be borne by the State."

34   In Sierra Leone, the TRC communicated some of the possible implications as early as the statement-taking process. Deponents were asked if they were willing to testify at a public hearing, and if so, whether they would mention names of perpetrators. If they indicated they might, the statement taker would alert the deponent that the TRC could inform any person so named, and offer to him or to her the chance of stating a defense at the hearing (though not any opportunity to question or cross-examine his or her accuser). The Peruvian TRC had victims and witnesses sign a "declaration of informed consent" before testifying in public. The declaration form explained, inter alia, that prosecutors could make use of the testimony and that anyone who felt "affected" by it could exercise a right of reply before the commission.

able to make an informed choice, and should harbor no illusions that there will be effective and ongoing post-hearing protection against legal or personal threats from named persons.[35]

RECOMMENDATIONS

- Truth commissions should have full discretion to select those who will appear at public hearings.
- There should be a general presumption of competency for any adult who might testify at a public hearing. Children may be deemed competent on an exceptional basis.
- A truth commission should acquire, and ensure the reliability of, a substantial number of statements prior to making any decisions about which victims will have the opportunity to testify at a public hearing.
- The criteria for selection of all those who will testify should be publicized, and they should reflect the objectives set out in the commission's mandate.
- Regarding the selection of any perpetrators or third-party witnesses whose public testimony is of interest to a truth commission, such persons should first be requested to appear on a voluntary basis. Where they decline and where their testimony is deemed significant, relevant, and necessary, they could (mandate permitting) be subpoenaed by the commission.
- Victims who testify at public hearings should be provided with a prior briefing at which the hearing procedure and any corresponding rights or duties are explained.

SECTION 2: NOTIFICATION TO IMPLICATED PERSONS: TIMING, METHOD, AND CONTENT

This section examines the timing, method, and content of public hearing notifications delivered by truth commissions to adversely implicated parties.

Timing of notification

If possible, prior to a victim hearing a truth commission should give notice of the hearing to any adversely implicated individual to enable him or her to attend. Such notice is a precondition to a meaningful right of reply (*see* Section 3),

---

35   It is worth noting that the Peruvian TRC identified "informed consent" as one of its guiding principles for public hearings. *See* TRC Regulation on Public Hearings, art. 3. Copy on file with the author. Concerning protective measures, *see* Section 9 below.

and it is arguably a requirement of both natural justice[36] and international human rights law.[37] Prior notice will also help mitigate the possibility of false accusation. It will allow the person to hear the adverse evidence and observe the behavior of the relevant witness.[38] Admittedly, the provision of such notice creates an enormous administrative burden on a commission, and may even create the appearance of siding with perpetrators.[39] Nevertheless, it should be considered and attempted.

Prior notice will be most practicable where an individual is implicated in a previously gathered statement given to a commission. However, even if a person is adversely implicated for the first time at the public hearing itself (*i.e.*, where the person was not implicated in a deponent's prior statement to the commission), the commission has the option to suspend proceedings until proper notice can be provided to the implicated person. Although suspension may be disruptive and inefficient, in some cases it may be necessary as a matter of fairness to the implicated person. (By corollary, an implicated individual should have a right to seek to suspend a public hearing before it takes place where he or she can demonstrate that notice was demonstrably inadequate and that the harm to his or her interests would be substantial and hard to reverse.)

In determining the amount of prior notice to be given, the key condition is that the notice must be "reasonable." Following a formal legal challenge to the notification procedures of the South African TRC, the commission was required to provide notice twenty-one days prior to a public hearing – an amount of time the South African Appellate Court considered reasonable.[40] This may be more notice than is required or reasonable in some contexts; it may be too little in others.

In exceptional circumstances, a commission may be justified in omitting any prior notice, and instead informing the implicated person after the fact. But such situations should be limited to cases of genuine exigency or emergency in which, for example, prior notice would likely lead to death threats against the testifying victim, or against the commission itself.[41]

---

36 *See* Chapter 2, Section 3.
37 *See* Chapter 2, Section 1. *See also, e.g.,* the decisions of the European Court of Human Rights in *Jordan v. United Kingdom* 24746/94 [2001] ECHR 327 (4 May 2001), at paras. 133, 134, and 142; and *McShane v. United Kingdom* 43290/98 [2002] ECHR 469 (28 May 2002), at paras. 122–3.
38 *Recall* the sinternational law guarantees against arbitrary attacks on reputation. *See* Chapter 2, Section 1.
39 *See, e.g.,* Boraine, *A Country Unmasked,* above note 4, at 113.
40 *See Du Preez and Another v. Truth and Reconciliation Commission* (South African Appellate Court) 1997 (3) SA 204, at 230–5. *See also Truth and Reconciliation Commission of South Africa Report* (1998), vol. 1, ch. 7, Legal Challenges, at para. 50, http://www.polity.org.za/govdocs/commissions/1998/trc/1chap7.htm.
41 *See* D. Mullan, *Administrative Law* (Toronto: Irwin Law, 2001), at 250–1.

A commission may also be justified in omitting any prior notice where the testifying victim agrees in advance of the public hearing that he or she will not use the opportunity to make individual accusations. Such an agreement would, of course, have to be voluntary. This approach was employed by the truth commission in Morocco.[42]

Method of delivery of notification

Truth commissions may send notification to the individual concerned or, alternatively, to his or her designated legal representative. Where an effective postal system exists, it is generally sufficient for notice to be delivered by means of ordinary or registered mail. In other cases, however, commissions may need to do more. For example, if there is a significant risk that the letter would not be delivered (meaning that the individual would receive no notice) or that the letter would be read prior to delivery (thus breaching the individual's privacy), a commission may prefer not to rely on the postal service. Courier services would be a second option. Personal delivery would be yet another option. The latter would, however, constitute an unreasonably onerous burden for most commissions.

Where the implicated individual cannot be located,[43] or where resource constraints are especially acute, a truth commission could consider making general public announcements in appropriate places, including in newspapers and on radio or TV. The announcement could simply state the names of the persons who will testify (provided they so consent), and invite anyone who has reason to believe he or she might be implicated in a human rights violation related to those persons to contact the commission.[44] Alternatively, a blanket,

---

42   Victims selected to give public testimony were asked to respect the rules set out in the commission's "pact of honor," namely, (1) to attend preparatory meetings in order to understand the purpose and form of the hearing, (2) to refrain from using the hearing as an opportunity to defend or attack a political group, and (3) to abstain from naming any individual who they considered responsible for the violations they experienced. The pact of honor is posted on the commission's website: http://www.ier.ma. Timor-Leste's truth commission allowed victims to name perpetrators at its public hearings. In at least one case, after naming someone as responsible for her abuse, the victim and her family suffered threats and violence.

43   See, e.g., Truth and Reconciliation Commission of South Africa Report (1998), vol. 1, ch. 7, Legal Challenges, http://www.polity.org.za/govdocs/commissions/1998/trc/1chap7.htm, at para. 53: "In many instances, the alleged perpetrators were no longer in the same employment as previously and their addresses were not easily available."

44   In this regard, see the mandate of Timor-Leste's truth commission: "The Commission shall endeavour to publicise, by all available means, the location and timing of hearings convened by the Commission to allow interested parties to participate in the hearing." "On

rather than individualized, form of notice may be used, though this will usually be insufficient.

Content of notification

Truth commissions are not required to disclose all relevant material in their possession.[45] Full discovery would undermine the efficient conduct of a commission's work and increase the length of proceedings. It could also turn the process into an "unstructured pseudo-litigation."[46] But the notice a truth commission provides to an implicated individual should, at a minimum, give the person enough information to formulate a reply to the allegations.[47] It should also, of course, be written in a language the person understands.

The notice should ideally describe the nature of the alleged acts, the date and approximate time when the acts are alleged to have occurred, and the identities of any others who are accused of participation in the same acts. The notice should also specify the types of evidence that support the allegation (*e.g.*, whether eyewitness testimony, documentation in police records, or a third-party report). In addition, the notice should set out the date and time of the planned hearing, and the modalities and restrictions for exercising a right of reply. Where notice is not provided until *after* the hearing, a commission should consider providing a complete transcript or recording of the testimony.

Until the date of the hearing, commissions must be especially careful about guarding the identities of victims or witnesses who made adverse allegations during the statement-taking process. If the names of accusers are made available to alleged perpetrators in advance of the hearing, this may raise serious harassment or security concerns and possibly life-threatening consequences. Also, if victims or witnesses are aware that their names are to be disclosed prior to the hearing, they may be reluctant to come forward at all. In the *Du Preez* case in South Africa, the Appellate Division Court held that "procedural fairness demands not only that a person implicated be given reasonable and

---

the Establishment of a Commission for Reception, Truth and Reconciliation in East Timor," UNTAET/REG/2001/01 as amended, s. 16.5.

45 *See, e.g., Labbe v. Canada (Commission of Inquiry into the Deployment of Canadian Troops to Somalia)* (1997), 146 DLR (4th) 180 (Federal Court Trial Division, Canada).

46 P. Matthews, *Jervis on Coroners*, 12th ed. (London: Sweet & Maxwell, 2002), at 227 (describing the reluctance of coroners to give full prehearing disclosure).

47 In *Re Pergamon Press Ltd* [1971] 1 Chancery 388 (Court of Appeal), at 400, Lord Denning suggested that the "gist" of adverse allegations should be revealed. *See also Doody v. Secretary of State for the Home Department and Other Appeals* [1993] 3 All ER 92 (HL) at 106: "Since the person affected usually cannot make worthwhile representations without knowing what factors may weigh against his interests, fairness will very often require that he is informed of the gist of the case which he has to answer."

timely notice of the hearing, but also that he or she is at the same time informed of the substance of the allegations against him or her, with sufficient detail to know what the case is all about."[48] Yet the judgment was careful to note that the commission could, where necessary, withhold the identity of the source of the allegation.[49] Similarly, in *Hannah v. Larche*,[50] the US Supreme Court concluded that nothing in the Civil Rights Act 1957 required the US Civil Rights Commission "to afford persons accused of discrimination the right to be apprised as to the specific charges against them or as to the identity of their accusers[.]"[51] In that case, the Civil Rights Commission determined that the need to protect the identity of accusers outweighed the due process rights of alleged perpetrators; notice was provided of the charges, but no names were disclosed.[52]

RECOMMENDATIONS

- *Timing:* (1) A commission should make reasonable efforts to notify a person that he or she has been adversely implicated in a deponent's statement whenever that deponent has been granted the opportunity to testify at a public hearing. Reasonable prior notice should be provided. (2) In exceptional circumstances, a commission may be justified in foregoing prior notice and instead informing the implicated person after the fact. A commission may also be justified in foregoing prior notice where the person scheduled to testify agrees in advance not to make individual accusations in his or her public testimony. (3) Where a person is adversely implicated for the first time at the public hearing itself (*e.g.*, where the person was not implicated in a deponent's prior statement to the commission), the commission may suspend proceedings until reasonable notice can be provided and a new hearing date set.
- *Method:* The form of notice should be written. It should be delivered by mail to the most recent known address of the implicated individual, preferably by registered mail. Notification could be sent to the individual concerned or to the individual's designated legal representative. If the postal service is particularly unreliable, courier service or

---

48 See *Du Preez*, above note 40, at 234. The court added that "What is sufficient information would depend upon the facts of each individual case." *Ibid. See also Truth and Reconciliation Commission of South Africa Report* (1998), vol. 1, ch. 7, Legal Challenges, at para. 44, http://www.polity.org.za/govdocs/commissions/1998/trc/1chap7.htm.

49 *Du Preez*, above note 40, at 234–5.

50 363 U.S. 420 (1960).

51 *Ibid.* at 420.

52 *Ibid.* at 424.

personal service should be considered. Where the implicated individual cannot be located or where resource constraints are especially acute, a commission could consider making general public announcements in appropriate places.

- *Content:* Notice to an implicated individual should include sufficient detail to allow the person to understand the nature and scope of the adverse allegations. At minimum, a summary of the allegations, together with a list of the types of evidence, should be provided. Information about the source of the allegations may be withheld where the commission considers it necessary or prudent to do so. The notice should set out the location, date, and time of the planned hearing, and the modalities and restrictions for exercising a right of reply.

SECTION 3: NATURE AND SCOPE OF THE RIGHT OF REPLY

A person adversely implicated prior to, or during, a public hearing is entitled to a formal right of reply; after all, he or she should be presumed innocent.[53] However, that right can be exercised in a variety of possible ways, consistent with a commission's mandate and its investigative character.

Ordinarily, the impulse to provide a right of reply emanates from the *audi alteram* principle, discussed in Chapter 2, Section 2. However, at least one truth commission – that of Sierra Leone – made a point of contacting adversely implicated persons for an altogether different reason, namely, "to allow a facilitated exchange between victim and perpetrator, if the victim wished."[54]

Irrespective of the form it takes, the reply of the implicated individual should be voluntary and waived by silence. A reasonable number of days should, however, be required to elapse before the commission can treat any right of reply as having been waived.

In determining the various possible modalities of reply (assuming it is not waived), a truth commission will need to balance various considerations, including the need to preserve the victim-centered character of hearings without sacrificing fairness or accuracy. A truth commission public hearing that is structured too much like a trial will tend to undermine the objective of victim-centeredness. However, a hearing that adversely implicates an individual in public without permitting a reciprocal form of reply will undermine the competing objective of fairness. The final report of the South African TRC,

---

53   *See* Chapter 2, Section 1, concerning the presumption of innocence in international law.
54   International Center for Transitional Justice, *The Sierra Leone Truth and Reconciliation Commission*, above note 24, at 4.

for example, concluded that "[i]n general, the Commission sought to be both therapeutic in its processes and rigorous in its findings, but sometimes the effort to satisfy one objective made it more difficult to attain the other."[55] All truth commissions that organize public hearings will, in fact, have to face the same tension when determining the modalities of a right of reply.

As a first consideration, a truth commission may need to determine whether an implicated party should be entitled to cross-examine his or her accuser.[56] As a general rule, the right of reply should not extend that far. Cross-examination should be a last resort, allowed only where the credibility of the accuser is in serious doubt and where nothing less would suffice to permit the implicated party to refute the allegations.[57]

Allowing cross-examination will generally detract from the ability of victims to simply relate their stories, uninterrupted, and without intimidation. It will tend to produce lengthier proceedings too.[58] It will also result in more traumatic proceedings that could produce a chilling effect on the number and type of victims willing to participate in the public hearings. In addition, allowing cross-examination tends to create the erroneous, and potentially counterproductive, impression of a trial. While cross-examination is acknowledged to be an important device to elicit the truth, a truth commission has many other means of doing so, including independent investigation of the alleged facts and the provision of a separate opportunity for the implicated individual to refute the alleged facts (as discussed below).

During the victim hearings conducted by South Africa's TRC, victims were rarely questioned by the commission: "[U]nless there were glaring

---

55 See *Truth and Reconciliation Commission of South Africa Report* (1998), vol. 1, ch. 6, Methodology and Process, Regional Prefindings, at para. 28, http://www.polity.org.za/govdocs/commissions/1998/trc/1chap6.htm.

56 Though they pertain to criminal proceedings, it is worth recalling the provisions of international law concerning the right to examine adverse witnesses and evidence. *See* ICCPR art. 14(3)(e), CRC art. 40(2)(b)(iv), ACHR art. 8(2)(f), and ECHR art. 6(3)(d).

57 *Recall* that the Consultation Paper that preceded the promulgation of the *Inquiries Act*, 1985 (UK) provided: "The introduction of adversarial elements into the inquiry process, which are likely to increase costs and have potential to cause delays, should be avoided wherever possible. Adversarial elements should not be a significant feature of a process in which the main aim is to learn lessons, not apportion blame." Para. 82.

58 *Recall Hannah v. Larche*, at 443–4: "[T]he investigative process could be completely disrupted if investigative hearings were transformed into trial-like proceedings, and if persons who might be indirectly affected by an investigation were given an absolute right to cross-examine every witness called to testify. Fact-finding agencies without any power to adjudicate would be diverted from their legitimate duties and would be plagued by the injection of collateral issues that would make the investigation interminable. Even a person not called as a witness could demand the right to appear at the hearing, cross-examine any witness whose testimony or sworn affidavit allegedly defamed or incriminated him, and call an unlimited number of witnesses of his own selection. This type of proceeding would make a shambles of the investigation and stifle the agency in its gathering of facts."

inconsistencies and falsehoods, their oral testimony was generally accepted."[59] As a result, the interaction of the vast majority of victims with the TRC was, in its words, "a positive and affirming experience."[60] The truth commissions of Peru and Morocco adopted the same nonconfrontational approach. By contrast, the experiences of victims at the public hearings of the Ugandan and Nigerian truth commissions – both of which permitted cross-examination – were quite different. Some victims were aggressively cross-examined, thus diminishing the potential for any therapeutic effect.[61] To some extent, this was also the case with the truth commission in Ghana, which also permitted cross-examination.[62]

Other proceedings analogous to truth commissions have often excluded a right of cross-examination. For example, cross-examination was considered unnecessary in the case of the US Civil Rights Commission. In *Hannah v. Larche*,[63] the US Supreme Court concluded that the commission's investigative process "could be completely disrupted if investigative hearings were transformed into trial-like proceedings" and that the absence of cross-examination was consistent with most other similar US investigative bodies.[64] Similarly, in *United States v. Fort*,[65] the Court of Appeals for the District of Columbia Circuit held that the refusal of Congress to permit a subpoenaed street gang member the opportunity to cross-examine those who had allegedly defamed him did not violate constitutional due process because the particular proceeding was merely investigative and not judicial in nature.

By contrast, Commonwealth commissions of inquiry generally allow for cross-examination. Cross-examination was permitted during the Krever Commission in Canada,[66] the Bloody Sunday Inquiry in Northern Ireland,[67] and

---

59   See *Truth and Reconciliation Commission of South Africa Report* (1998), vol. 1, ch. 6, Methodology and Process, Regional Prefindings, at para. 28, http://www.polity.org.za/govdocs/commissions/1998/trc/1chap6.htm. It was not so, however, in all instances. Winnie Madikizela-Mandela's hearing, which lasted nine days and looked and functioned like a trial, saw victims and other witnesses aggressively cross-examined by Mandela's counsel. Oddly, it also saw TRC chair Desmond Tutu embrace and declare his admiration for Madikizela-Mandela. Such actions opened the TRC to charges of bias. *See* Boraine, *A Country Unmasked*, at 252–3.

60   *Ibid.*

61   Hayner, *Unspeakable Truths*, above note 10, at 69–70. The ANC's 1993 commission of inquiry also allowed implicated individuals to confront their accusers. *Ibid.*, at 63–4.

62   *See, e.g.,* "Assassie-Gyimah Tortured Me," *Accra Mail* (http://www.ghanaweb.com), 4 March 2003.

63   363 U.S. 420 (1960).

64   *Ibid.*, at 443–4.

65   443 F.2d 670 (1970), *cert. denied* 91 S.Ct. 2255 (1971).

66   M. J. Trebilcock and L Austin, "The Limits of the Full Court Press: Of Blood and Mergers" (1998) 48 *Univ. of Toronto L.J.* 1, at 21.

67   *See* http://www.bloody sunday-inquiry.org.uk.

the Sarma Sakar Commission of Inquiry in India,[68] to give only a few examples. Some of the reasons for this preference for cross-examination reflect the different purposes of such inquiries in comparison to contemporary truth commissions. As previously noted, the public hearings of Commonwealth commissions of inquiry generally reflect an emphasis on investigation and accuracy over catharsis and acknowledgment, while those of truth commissions tend to reflect the reverse emphasis. In addition, because Commonwealth commissions of inquiry tend to deal with far fewer cases, the impact of cross-examination on the efficiency of the process is less debilitating.

In light of the foregoing, alternatives to cross-examination are, in all but the most extreme cases, preferable for truth commissions and perfectly consistent with procedural fairness. Of the many possible alternatives, two stand out. First, the implicated individual might be entitled to present his or her version of the facts in writing before or after the hearing takes place.[69] Second, the person might be allowed to present his or her arguments at a separate public or private hearing or interview, subject to a commission's mandate and resources and the dictates of fairness in the particular instance.[70] In the case of a separate hearing, the person whose testimony triggered the need for such a hearing should receive an equivalent form of notification – in terms of timing, method, and content – to that received by the implicated person.[71] In such instance, the modalities of notification described earlier in Section 2 would apply, *mutatis mutandis*.[72]

If, instead, an implicated party is granted a right of "instant rebuttal"[73] or cross-examination, a commission must exert strict control over the proceedings. To do so, a commission requires the authority to impose restrictions on the extent, nature, and line of questioning so that victims are not harassed and

---

68 *See Sarma Sakar Commission of Inquiry*, Regulation of Procedure, 1978 (India), cited in Kritz, *Transitional Justice*, vol. 3, at 231.

69 *Recall* that, under the principles of natural justice, there is no necessary obligation on the part of an administrative or investigative body to afford an in-person, oral reply to an adverse allegation. It may in some cases be sufficient to permit only written representations. *See* Chapter 2, Section 1.

70 The truth commission in Ghana permitted written replies and ensured the assistance of counsel of choice in preparing such replies. It also permitted responses at separate public hearings. See *Ghana National Reconciliation Commission Final Report* (2004), at 2.3.3.4.1.

71 An entitlement of this sort is prescribed in the mandates of the truth commissions in South Africa, Timor-Leste, and Ghana.

72 *Recall also* Principle 16 of the Principles on the Effective Prevention and Investigation of Extra-Legal, Arbitrary and Summary Executions (1989), UN doc. E/1989/89, which requires the protection of "[c]omplainants, witnesses, those conducting the investigation and their families" from threats and acts of violence or intimidation.

73 *Du Preez*, above note 40, at 219.

so that proceedings progress efficiently.[74] This is particularly important in the cases of children and victims of sexual crimes who testify.[75]

Restrictions on cross-examination might take many forms. For example, a commission could require that cross-examination be limited to certain witnesses or to certain questions. At the Bloody Sunday Inquiry, parties had to apply for leave to cross-examine, setting out the reasons "why cross-examination is required, the nature of the cross-examination proposed, and the material (including its source) upon which it is proposed to base the cross-examination."[76] Another approach is to permit the implicated party an opportunity to submit a list of questions that the commission may itself put to the victim at the hearing. For example, the US Civil Rights Commission's mandate precluded ordinary cross-examination, but it provided that

> counsel may submit in writing any question or questions he/she wishes propounded to his/her client or to any other witness. With the consent of the majority of the Members of the Subcommittee present and voting, such question or questions shall be put to the witness by the Chairman, or by a Member of the Subcommittee either in the original form or in modified language. The decisions of the Subcommittee as to the admissibility of questions submitted by counsel for a witness, as well as to their form, shall be final.

A related practice derives from the Commonwealth commission of inquiry tradition, in which commission counsel, on behalf of the commission, habitually put most of the questions to any witness. This allows the commission, and not outside lawyers, to control the overall proceedings.

RECOMMENDATIONS

- A person adversely implicated prior to, or during, a public hearing is entitled to a formal right of reply.
- The reply of the implicated individual should be voluntary and waived by silence, provided that a minimum and reasonable period of time

---

74   *See, e.g.*, Section 34(2) of the *Promotion of National Unity and Reconciliation Act*, 1995 (South Africa), which provides: "The Commission may, in order to expedite proceedings, place reasonable limitations with regard to the time allowed in respect of the cross-examination of witnesses or any address to the Commission." *See also* section 17(2) of the *National Reconciliation Commission Act*, 2002, Act 611 (Ghana): "The Commission may limit the time allowed for cross-examination."

75   *See, e.g.*, Rule 88 of the ICC's Rules of Procedure and Evidence, which empowers the ICC to protect such victims from harassment and intimidation while testifying.

76   *See* Bloody Sunday Inquiry, Rulings and Judgments, October 1999, Rulings and Observations, http://www.bloody-sunday-inquiry.org.uk/index2.asp?p=3.

be required to elapse before the commission may treat any right of reply as having been waived.

- The reply might be exercised in a variety of ways, all of which can be outlined in the truth commission's mandate or left to the commission's reasonable discretion.
- The right of reply should rarely include a right of cross-examination. Instead, an implicated individual should be entitled to present his or her version of the facts (1) in writing to the commission before or after the hearing takes place, or (2) at a separate public or private hearing or interview, subject to a commission's mandate and resources, and the dictates of fairness in the particular case. If an implicated person is given the opportunity to reply to allegations at a separate public hearing, the person whose testimony caused the need for such a hearing should receive an equivalent form of notification (in terms of timing, method, and content) to that received by the implicated person.
- If cross-examination is permitted, a truth commission should have authority to impose restrictions on the extent, nature, and line of questioning so as to avoid any harassment or intimidation of victims or witnesses, paying particular attention to attacks on children and victims of sexual crimes who testify.
- As a further alternative to cross-examination, the implicated individual could be permitted to submit a list of questions that the commission might, at its reasonable discretion, put to the victim before, during, or after the hearing.

SECTION 4: OATHS AND AFFIRMATIONS

It is common for investigative proceedings – whether truth commissions,[77] Commonwealth inquiries,[78] or similar bodies – to require persons to testify at

---

[77] For example, the truth commission in Ghana required all those who appeared at public hearings to "swear an oath or affirm in accordance with their religious beliefs." *Ghana National Reconciliation Commission Final Report* (2004), vol. 1, ch. 2, at 2.6.2.1. Similarly, Timor-Leste's truth commission had the authority to require "that a person attending a hearing of the Commission give their statement or answer under oath or affirmation and to administer such oath or affirmation . . . " "On the Establishment of a Commission for Reception, Truth and Reconciliation in East Timor," UNTAET/REG/2001/01 as amended, section 14.1(d). The Sierra Leonean TRC also required all testimony to be given under oath.

[78] For example, section 7(1) of the Ontario *Public Inquiries Act*, RSO 1990, as amended, provides that a commission of inquiry may require any person to give evidence by oath or affirmation at a public hearing.

public hearings under oath or affirmation. An oath or affirmation commonly consists of an undertaking to "speak the truth, the whole truth, and nothing but the truth."[79] For interpreters and translators, the oath or affirmation may consist of a pledge to interpret or translate truthfully.

An oath sometimes carries religious connotations. That is why affirmations are allowed as an alternative form of undertaking. There is, however, no practical difference between an oath and an affirmation. In both cases, the rationale is to underscore the duty of truthfulness,[80] and to enhance the reliability of the testimony in the event it is needed as evidence at a future proceeding, whether against the person who testified (*e.g.,* for perjury) or against a third party. Ordinarily, in a court of law, this requires issuing a warning about the consequences of giving false testimony.[81] But in the case of a truth commission's victim hearings, it is probably inappropriate and unnecessary to issue such a warning given the noninvestigative character of such hearings.

An exception to the requirement of an oath or affirmation is generally made for children and other persons who may not understand the nature of such an undertaking. A truth commission should have the discretion to waive the requirement of an oath or affirmation for such persons.[82]

RECOMMENDATIONS

- An oath or affirmation should be administered to any person testifying at a public hearing of a truth commission. At a commission's reasonable discretion, exceptions may be made for children or other similar categories of persons, or where an oath or affirmation would be counterproductive to a legitimate commission objective.
- The oath or affirmation should consist of simply promising to tell the whole truth.
- Interpreters and translators should also be required to give an oath or affirmation.

79   *See* ICTY Rule 90(B).
80   *See, e.g.,* Rule 603 of the US Federal Rules of Evidence.
81   *See, e.g.,* Rule 66 of the ICC Rules of Procedure and Evidence, which requires such a warning to be given to every witness.
82   *See, e.g.,* ICC Rules of Procedure and Evidence, Rule 66(2), which provides that "a person under the age of 18 or a person whose judgment has been impaired and who . . . does not understand the nature of a solemn undertaking may be allowed to testify without this solemn undertaking if the Chamber considers that the person is able to describe matters of which he or she has knowledge and that the person understands the meaning of the duty to speak the truth."

SECTION 5: RIGHT TO LEGAL REPRESENTATION

Unless its mandate so stipulates, a truth commission will need to decide whether to allow, or possibly provide, counsel to the persons appearing before it. In determining the scope of any right to counsel, the commission must consider various interests and factors, including the rights of victims and implicated parties, and the possible impact – negative or positive – that counsel will have on achieving the hearings' broad truth-telling objectives.[83]

Counsel permitted

The right to legal representation in judicial proceedings is considered fundamental in almost any legal system. Truth commissions, however, are investigative bodies and therefore lawyers may not be required for many aspects of a truth commission's work, including its public hearings.[84]

Legal representation has been permitted at the public hearings of numerous truth commissions. Usually, however, it is limited to cases of persons appearing at the commission's request or under subpoena.[85] Counsel is also generally permitted before Commonwealth commissions of inquiry, including in New Zealand,[86] Australia,[87] and Israel.[88] In the United States, counsel is permitted at congressional investigations.[89] Legal representatives are also permitted during

---

83   International law contains provisions on the right to assistance of legal counsel, but those provisions pertain to the context of a courtroom trial. Nevertheless, they offer a standard to which truth commissions may choose to aspire. *See* Chapter 2, Section 1.

84   *Recall* the discussion of natural justice in Chapter 2, Section 2, in which it was noted that the right to counsel is restricted in various ways in the context of quasi-judicial and nonjudicial proceedings.

85   *See, e.g,* section 34(1) of the *Promotion of National Unity and Reconciliation Act,* 1995 (South Africa): "Any person questioned by an investigation unit and any person who has been subpoenaed or called upon to appear before the Commission is entitled to appoint a legal representative." *See also* section 181 of "On the Establishment of a Commission for Reception, Truth and Reconciliation in East Timor," UNTAET/REG/2001/01 as amended; section 17(1) of the *National Reconciliation Commission Act,* 2002, Act 611 (Ghana); and section 31 of *An Act to Establish the Truth and Reconciliation Commission of Liberia* (2005).

86   "Every person entitled, or given an opportunity, to be heard under this section may appear in person or by his counsel or agent." *Commission of Inquiry Act* 1908 (New Zealand), as amended, section 4A.

87   *Royal Commissions Act* 1902 (Australia), section 6FA; *Special Commissions of Inquiry Act* 1983 (New South Wales), section 12(2).

88   *Commissions of Inquiry Law,* 1968, vol. 23 of the Laws of the State of Israel, section 15(b).

89   S. Levinson, "Trials, Commissions, and Investigating Committees: The Elusive Search for Norms of Due Process," in R. Rotberg and D. Thompson, eds., *Truth v. Justice* (Princeton, NJ: Princeton University Press, 2000), at 226.

grand jury proceedings, although their participation is normally restricted to consulting with their clients outside of the deliberating room.

Generally speaking, a truth commission should allow a person testifying at a public hearing to consult with counsel and have counsel present at the hearing. At the discretion of the commission, counsel may also speak on behalf of the person. At the same time, the participation of counsel will, in all likelihood, extend the length of the proceedings and make them resemble court proceedings. The participation of counsel may also limit the ability of a truth commission to control the budget of its proceedings.[90] At the same time, the rights of implicated parties, as well as of victims, will sometimes require the protection that only an attorney can provide.

Counsel provided

Providing counsel to persons testifying at public hearings can give rise to potential inequities and can be extremely resource-intensive. Significant funds would be required to cover legal fees, and significant time would be required to determine who ought to receive legal assistance. In general, therefore, a truth commission should not be required to cover the costs of counsel acting for persons appearing at public hearings.

A commission could, however, provide counsel where the person is indigent and appearing under subpoena, and where there is a risk of substantial harm that would be difficult to reverse.[91] For example, section 34(3) of the South African TRC mandate provides:

> The Commission may appoint a legal representative to appear on behalf of [a person appearing under subpoena] if it is satisfied that the person is not financially capable of appointing a legal representative himself or herself, and if it is of the opinion that it is in the interests of justice that the person be represented by a legal representative.

In implementing this power, the TRC operated a very expensive legal assistance scheme based on the national model of legal aid. The commission could prescribe and pay the costs of legal services for both victims and implicated parties. Like the South African mandate, the law establishing Ghana's truth commission provides: "The Commission may appoint a lawyer if the individual appearing before the Commission cannot afford one, and representation

---

90   Trebilcock and Austin, "The Limits of the Full Court Press," above note 66, at 50.

91   *Recall, e.g.,* article 13 of the UN Manual on the Effective Prevention and Investigation of Extra-Legal, Arbitrary and Summary Executions (1991), which stipulates that all compelled witnesses of a commission of inquiry should have the right to appear through counsel if their testimony could expose them to criminal or civil liability.

by a lawyer is necessary in the interests of justice."[92] Similarly, the mandate of Timor-Leste's truth commission authorizes payment of legal representation where a person required to attend is not financially capable of appointing legal counsel and the commission considers that it is in the interests of justice that the person be represented by counsel.[93]

Most Commonwealth commissions of inquiry have provided counsel to indigent persons, but this is not always the case. For example, the Bloody Sunday Inquiry did not accept that the cost of legal representation of indigent civilian witnesses should always be met from public funds. It recommended that the reasonable costs of legal representation should be met "in any cases where [the tribunal] is persuaded that the interests of justice require legal representation," adding that "[an] obvious case for representation is where a witness is facing serious allegations."[94]

In the United States, at grand juries, witnesses are not provided with lawyers. Even in civil litigation, free counsel is not a constitutional right.[95] Similarly, no one subpoenaed to appear before a congressional committee of investigation is ever provided with counsel, and "that has not been viewed as a denial of due process."[96]

In any event, whether counsel is permitted or provided by a truth commission, persons appearing at public hearings should be promptly informed of their right, if any, to legal representation.[97]

On a final and more general note, truth commissions should adopt appropriate guidelines concerning acceptable conduct for counsel. This will assist a truth commission in controlling the proceedings, preventing unnecessary delay, reducing trauma to victims, and ensuring that the proceedings remain faithful to the commission's investigative mandate. To that end, a commission may use any of the methods recommended in Section 3 of this chapter.

92   Section 17(3).
93   Section 18.2. Section 18.3 goes on to provide: "If in the opinion of the Commission there is a significant possibility that a person will incriminate him or herself in evidence given to the Commission it shall ensure that such person is represented by a legal representative, unless such person declines to be so represented." As will be argued in Section 8 below, this appears to go further than necessary to reasonably protect the privilege against self-incrimination.
94   See http://www.bloody-sunday-inquiry.org.uk/index2.asp?p=3.
95   A legislative compromise occurred in the 1970s, when Congress created the Legal Services Corporation to provide free legal assistance to the indigent in certain types of civil proceedings. However, in the words of one observer, the US Supreme Court has "been strikingly unwilling to find [free counsel] guarantees in regard to civil litigation." Levinson, "Trials, Commissions, and Investigating Committees," above note 89, at 224–5.
96   Ibid., at 226.
97   See, e.g., Section 34(4) of the Promotion of National Unity and Reconciliation Act, 1995 (South Africa): "A person . . . shall be informed timeously of his or her right to be represented by a legal representative."

RECOMMENDATIONS

- A truth commission should allow a person testifying at a public hearing to retain counsel and have counsel present at the hearing. At the discretion of the commission, counsel may be allowed to speak on behalf of the person.
- A truth commission should generally not, itself, be required to provide counsel to persons appearing at public hearings. However, counsel could be provided where the person is indigent and appearing under subpoena, and where there is a risk of substantial harm that would be difficult to reverse.
- Persons appearing at public hearings should be promptly informed of the scope and content of their right to counsel.
- Truth commissions should adopt guidelines concerning acceptable conduct for counsel in order to effectively control the proceedings, prevent unnecessary delay, and avoid any trauma to victims and witnesses who testify.

SECTION 6: ADMISSIBLE EVIDENCE

Truth commissions are generally free to admit any evidence that passes a base level of relevance and reliability.[98] This approach is in keeping with their inquisitorial character. It is also consistent with practice of analogous proceedings, such as those of Commonwealth commissions of inquiry[99] and of coroner inquests.[100] It conforms to practice in the field of international criminal law

---

98 An exception, however, is the mandate of the Ugandan truth commission, which provides that it "shall in the course of its inquiry, so far as is practicable, apply the law of evidence, and shall in particular conform with the following instructions, that is to say, (a) that any person desiring to give evidence to the Commission shall do so in person; (b) that hearsay evidence which adversely affects the reputation of any person or tends to reflect in any way upon the character or conduct of any person shall not be received; (c) that no expression of opinion on the character, conduct or motives of any person shall be received in evidence; (d) that any who in the opinion of the Commissioners is adversely affected by the evidence given before the Commission shall be given an opportunity to be heard and to cross-examine the person giving such evidence . . ." Legal Notice no. 5 (1986) Creating the Commission of Inquiry into Violations of Human Rights, pursuant to the *Commission of Inquiry Act* (Uganda).

99 For example, in New Zealand, commissions of inquiry may accept any relevant evidence "whether or not it would be admissible in a Court of law." *Commissions of Inquiry Act*, 1908 (New Zealand), as amended.

100 Matthews, *Jervis on Coroners*, above note 46, at 282.

too, in which relevance is the primary criterion of admissibility.[101] A broad approach to the admission of evidence is also consistent with the practice of civil law systems, which tend to operate according to the principle of "free evaluation of evidence."[102] A similar approach to the admission of evidence has also been adopted in some common law trial proceedings.[103] Thus, the current truth commission trend of allowing victims to testify with little or no interruption may be perfectly sound.[104]

It follows from the foregoing considerations that hearsay evidence (*i.e.*, evidence about an absent third party's statement that is offered up as proof of the substantive content of the statement) should generally be admissible at a public hearing. Hearsay evidence is excluded from most common law courts, unless the evidence in question fits into one of the many exceptions to the general rule against its admission.[105] The rationale for the prohibition on hearsay in common law courts is that the third party who made the statement did not do so under oath and is not available to be interrogated, thus limiting the statement's reliability and possibly causing prejudice to a criminal defendant. However, truth commissions are commissions of inquiry, not courts. There is, in consequence, no obvious reason why such evidence should be impermissible. Strict adherence to the hearsay rule would in fact thwart a commission's truth-seeking purposes while producing little gain in procedural

---

101   *See* R. May and M. Wierda, *International Criminal Evidence* (Ardsley, NY: Transnational Publishers, 2003), at 93–4. *See also* ICTY Rule 89, which affords wide discretion to the judge trying a particular case. It provides, in part: "(C) A Chamber may admit any relevant evidence which it deems to have probative value. *See also* ICTR Rule 89 and Rome Statute art. 69(4).

102   S. C. Thaman, *Comparative Criminal Procedure* (Durham, NC: Carolina Academic Press, 2002), at 123, 139, 152, 189.

103   *See, e.g.,* the decision of the Supreme Court of Canada in *R. v. Finta* [1994] 1 SCR 701. The case concerned a person accused of war crimes dating back to the Second World War. The Court held (at 707): "It is essential in a case where the events took place 45 years ago that all material evidence be put before the jury. With the passage of time it becomes increasingly difficult to get at the truth of events: witnesses die or cannot be located, memories fade, and evidence can be so easily forever lost. It is then essential that in such a case all available accounts are placed before the court. The argument that all cases pose difficulties in presenting a defence fails to recognize that this case, because of the time elapsed, presents very real difficulties for the defence in getting at the truth which is not comparable to other cases."

104   Morocco's truth commission, for example, asked no questions of any victim who testified at a public hearing. *See* http://www.ier.ma. In South Africa, by contrast, commissioners sometimes asked questions to verify and corroborate facts (*e.g.,* asking a victim to describe his or her torture). Boraine, *A Country Unmasked*, above note 4, at 103.

105   Classic exceptions include "dying declarations" (*i.e.,* declarations made by the third party on his or her deathbed), declarations or statements against interest, and official statements and records. Some common law courts have, however, relaxed the prohibition on hearsay in the context of war crimes trials. *See* May and Wierda, *International Criminal Evidence*, above note 101, at 115.

fairness. Indeed, even international criminal tribunals accept most hearsay evidence.[106]

Along with hearsay evidence, physical and documentary evidence should also generally be admissible at a truth commission's public hearings. However, most physical and documentary evidence will be properly submitted outside of the formal proceedings to avoid unnecessary delays.

Concerning documents, there should be no requirement to submit originals.[107] However, parties might be encouraged to submit notarized copies of original documents to enable the commission to accord greater weight to the evidence.

As to the rights of parties to call witnesses to appear on their behalf at public hearings, it may be noted that Commonwealth commissions of inquiry often permit parties to do so.[108] Under the Ontario *Public Inquiries Act*, for example, those with a direct interest in the inquiry are entitled "to call and examine or cross-examine witnesses personally or by counsel on evidence relevant to the person's interest."[109] Such permissiveness is, however, inappropriate to a prototypical truth commission hearing, whose character is more expressive than investigative. A truth commission should, nevertheless, retain discretion to allow persons to call their own witnesses at public hearings on an exceptional basis. In addition, a truth commission should generally permit the introduction of witness affidavits, since they may provide useful information to the commission without causing delays.

RECOMMENDATIONS

- Truth commissions should adopt a broadly permissive approach to the admission of evidence at public hearings. Relevance should be the primary criterion of admissibility.
- In addition to oral testimony, the introduction of physical and documentary evidence should be permitted at a public hearing.

---

106 *See ibid.* at 116–19. The ICTR, for instance, decided that hearsay was not *per se* inadmissible, "even when it cannot be examined at its source or when it is not corroborated by direct evidence." *Prosecutor v. Musema*, Case no. ICTR-96-13-T, Judgment and Sentence (27 January 2000), at para. 51. *See also* ICTY Rule 92*bis* concerning the admission of written hearsay evidence.

107 The common law's "best evidence rule" provides that, where an original piece of writing is available, it (and not a copy of it) must be adduced. The rule is still applied in trials in many common law jurisdictions.

108 *Recall* the fifth of Lord Justice Salmon's cardinal principles, discussed in Chapter 2: "Any material witnesses [that a subpoenaed person] wishes called at the inquiry should, if reasonably practicable, be heard."

109 Section 5 (1).

- There should be no requirement to submit original documents as proof of any fact.
- Hearsay evidence should generally be admissible.
- Except at a commission's reasonable discretion, there should be no right to call witnesses to appear on one's behalf at a public hearing. Witness affidavits should, however, be permitted.

SECTION 7: PRIVILEGES BASED ON CONTEXTS AND RELATIONSHIPS OF CONFIDENTIALITY

Victims appearing at public hearings will almost always appear on a voluntary basis. Implicated parties and other witnesses may, however, be appearing under subpoena. Issues pertaining to the existence of legal privileges will, therefore, be especially pertinent to them.

John H. Wigmore's classic test for determining the existence of a legal privilege involves four criteria: (1) the communication must originate with an expectation that it will not be disclosed; (2) the element of confidentiality must be essential to the effective maintenance of the relationship between the parties; (3) the relationship must be one that, in the opinion of the community, ought to be fostered; and (4) the injury that would inure to the relationship by the disclosure of the communication must be greater than the advantage that would be gained for the correct disposal of litigation by virtue of its disclosure.[110]

A truth commission is an investigative body, and its public hearings are nonjudicial in character. Yet it is still desirable for a privileged communication to be respected in the context of such hearings absent a compelling and overriding public interest. The interests of justice are arguably better served in the long run by creating the conditions under which such confidential communications are reliably protected. Recognizing established privileges demonstrates respect and understanding for the confidential nature of certain relationships, and may also engender greater confidence and comfort with a truth commission's proceedings.[111]

Probably the oldest and best recognized privilege is the lawyer-client privilege.[112] Communications between spouses, doctor and patient, and

---

110 J. H. Wigmore, *Evidence in Trials at Common Law*, vol. 8 (McNaughton rev. ed.) (Boston: Little, Brown & Co., 1961), section 2285, at 527.

111 *But see Law 04/018 (2004) Concerning the Organization, Powers and Functions of the Truth and Reconciliation Commission* (DRC), arts. 35 and 36. These articles require persons summoned by the commission to provide full disclosure notwithstanding any applicable privileges or immunities.

112 *See, e.g.,* ICTY Rules of Procedure and Evidence, Rule 97. In the United States, in addition to communications with counsel, federal courts have extended the privilege to client

clergy and penitent are also widely regarded as privileged.[113] Depending on the context, journalistic, parent-child, parliamentary, or executive privileges may also be recognized.[114] There are also *sui generis* privileges and immunities, such as those pertaining to staff or officials of the International Committee of the Red Cross,[115] or staff of international tribunals such as the ICC,[116] or staff of multilateral institutions such as the United Nations.[117]

Commonwealth commission of inquiry statutes typically recognize, on a global basis, the privileges that exist in domestic law. The Ontario *Public Inquiries Act*, for example, recognizes the same privileges as those used in judicial proceedings.[118] Similarly, under the New Zealand *Commissions of Inquiry Act*, every person giving evidence, and every counsel or agent or other person appearing before an inquiry, is entitled to the same privileges and immunities

---

communications with agents for counsel where those communications are "in confidence for the purpose of obtaining legal advice from the lawyer." *See U.S. v. Schwimmer*, 892 F. 2d 237 (2d Cir. 1989). However, the attorney-client privilege does not apply when counsel acts in a nonadvisory capacity. *See, e.g., U.S. v. Evans*, 113 F. 3d 1457 (7th Cir. 1997).

113 *See, e.g.*, Rule 73(3) of the ICC Rules of Procedure and Evidence. *See also* May and Wierda, *International Criminal Evidence*, above note 101, at 90.

114 In many US jurisdictions, grand juries recognize a reporter's privilege and executive privilege, and a few recognize a parent-child privilege. *See* S. Brenner, "Is the Grand Jury Worth Keeping?" (1998) 81 *Judicature* 190, at 193. *See also* ICC Rules of Procedure and Evidence, Rule 75, regarding privileges for family members. On journalists' privileges, see the ICTY case involving Jonathan Randal, a *Washington Post* reporter who successfully opposed a Trial Chamber subpoena on the basis of a "war correspondent" privilege. The Appeals Chamber asked and answered three questions: "Is there a public interest in the work of war correspondents? If yes, would compelling war correspondents to testify before a tribunal adversely affect their ability to carry out their work? If yes, what test is appropriate to balance the public interest in accommodating the work of war correspondents with the public interest in having all relevant evidence available to the court and, where it is implicated, the right of the defendant to challenge the evidence against him?" (para. 34). It answered the first two questions in the affirmative. On the third question, the chamber established a two part test before ultimately setting aside the subpoena: "First, the petitioning party must demonstrate that the evidence sought is of direct and important value in determining a core issue in the case. Second, it must demonstrate that the evidence sought cannot reasonably be obtained elsewhere" (para. 50). *See Prosecutor v. Brdjanin and Zupljanin*, IT-99-36-AR73.9, Decision on Interlocutory Appeal (Appeals Chamber), 11 December 2002.

115 *See, e.g.*, Rule 73(4)–(6) of the ICC Rules of Procedure and Evidence.

116 *See* May and Wierda, *International Criminal Evidence*, above note 101, at 90.

117 *See, e.g.*, the Convention on the Privileges and Immunities of the United Nations 1946, UNTS, vol. 1, at 15.

118 Section 11: "Nothing is admissible in evidence at an inquiry that would be inadmissible in a court by reason of any privilege under the law of evidence."

as witnesses and counsel in courts of law.[119] In the majority of US states, federal grand juries observe common law privileges between lawyers and clients, clergy and penitents, doctors and patients, and spouses.[120]

Truth commissions that hold public hearings have also, in general, afforded broad recognition and protection for legal privileges. For example, the South African TRC's mandate provides: "[T]he law regarding privilege as applicable to a witness summoned to give evidence in a criminal case in a court of law shall apply in relation to the questioning of a person[.]"[121] Similarly, the Ghanaian truth commission's mandate provides: "Witnesses are entitled to the same privileges as witnesses appearing before the High Court."[122] The mandate of the truth commission in Timor-Leste, by contrast, lists the specific communications that must be protected, namely, those between family members,[123] lawyer and client,[124] medical professional and patient,[125] and clergy and penitent.[126] Some truth commission mandates, however, are silent on the question of privileges. This is the case for the mandates of the truth commissions in Sierra Leone and Peru, for example, both of which held public hearings.

Whatever privileges apply in any particular instance, it must be made clear that none is absolute. For example, a privilege can ordinarily be waived by consent of the party holding the privilege (*e.g.*, the client, patient, penitent). Also, a privilege may be deemed waived where the party holding the privilege voluntarily reveals the content of the privileged communication to a third party who then gives evidence of that disclosure.[127]

---

119   Section 6.
120   Brenner, "Is the Grand Jury Worth Keeping?," above note 114, at 192.
121   Section 34(1).
122   Section 17(1).
123   Section 17.2: "No witness may be compelled to incriminate the witness' spouse or partner, parents, children, or relatives within the second degree." This is broader than usual. While spousal communications are protected in most if not all national jurisdictions, the additional family categories are less commonly protected.
124   Section 17.4: "Unless a client consents to the disclosure, a lawyer should refuse to answer questions concerning information provided by a client."
125   Section 17.5: "Unless the patient consents to the disclosure, a medical professional shall refuse to answer questions in relation to information provided by a patient in the course of delivery of medical services to such a person. For purposes of the present Section, the term 'medical professional' includes, without limitation, medical doctors, psychiatrists, psychologists, counselors and their professional assistants.'"
126   Section 17.3: "Unless the person who has provided information consents to the disclosure, a duly ordained priest or monk shall refuse to answer questions concerning information revealed during the course of religious duties rendered by that priest or monk."
127   *See, e.g.*, Rule 73 of the ICC Rules of Procedure and Evidence. *See also* the prior discussion about hearsay evidence.

RECOMMENDATIONS

- Communications between spouses, between lawyer and client, between medical professional and patient, and between religious clergy and penitent should be regarded as privileged and immune from compulsory disclosure.
- Journalistic, parent-child, parliamentary, or executive privileges may also apply. In addition, privileges may attach to officials of multilateral institutions such as the International Committee of the Red Cross or the various international criminal tribunals.
- No privilege is absolute. Privileged communications should be admissible at a public hearing (1) by consent, or (2) where the person in question voluntarily revealed the content of the communication to a third party who then gives evidence of that disclosure.

SECTION 8: USE IMMUNITY AND THE PRIVILEGE AGAINST SELF-INCRIMINATION

There are at least two broad forms of immunity that are potentially relevant to truth commission public hearings: "use immunity" and "transactional immunity." *Black's Law Dictionary* defines each as follows:

> "Use immunity" prohibits witness' compelled testimony and its fruits from being used in any manner in connection with criminal prosecution of the witness; on the other hand, "transactional immunity" affords immunity to the witness from prosecution for the offense to which his compelled testimony relates.

The closest equivalent to transactional immunity in the context of truth commissions is the form of amnesty offered to eligible applicants under the South African TRC's amnesty process. However, transactional immunity exceeds what is necessary to preserve the privilege against self-incrimination. Use immunity is sufficient, and more consistent with international law.[128]

---

128 *See, e.g., Report of the International Commission of Inquiry on Darfur to the United Nations Secretary-General* (2005), at para. 618: "'Use immunity' may be held to be acceptable in international law, at least in the circumstances of a [truth commission]: it contributes to the revelation of truth. Perpetrators are constrained to reveal all, albeit on the limited assurance that their testimonies at the [truth commission] will not be used against them in criminal proceedings. Nevertheless, society can hold them accountable for the crimes they admit to have committed, and they may still be prosecuted, the only evidence not usable against them being the one they gave at the [truth commission] hearings."

Protection against self-incrimination is sometimes characterized as a right,[129] and other times as a privilege.[130] In many respects this is a distinction without a difference, since it may be waived in either case.

In international criminal trials, the right against self-incrimination is not absolute. Witnesses can be compelled to answer questions that may be self-incriminating, provided their answers are covered by use immunity (*i.e.*, provided the witness cannot be prosecuted on the basis of his or her own compelled, self-incriminating testimony or evidence).[131]

Consistent with the approach of international criminal law, it is generally acceptable for truth commissions to have the power to compel persons to make self-incriminating statements or deliver self-incriminating evidence, provided that use immunity attaches by law or mandate to any to such testimony or evidence. Yet a commission should only exercise such a power where it is reasonable, just, and necessary to do so, and where there is no manifest security risk to the compelled person. Exercise of such a power might also be conditioned on the prior consent of an appropriate government minister. Such limitations can help ensure that such an extraordinary power is used only on an exceptional and non-prejudicial basis.[132]

What of the scope of use immunity itself? In this author's view, the protection of use immunity should extend beyond the context of future criminal trials. Specifically, the use of compelled testimony and evidence should be prohibited in relation to subsequent *or contemporaneous* proceedings against the compelled person, and whether of a criminal, *civil, or disciplinary* character. Public authorities should, nonetheless, be able to use compelled, self-incriminating statements and evidence against that person in prosecutions for perjury, as well

---

129 See, e.g., ICCPR art. 14(3)(g). It provides that in the determination of any criminal charge everyone has the "right" not to be compelled to testify against himself or herself or to confess guilt. See also CRC art. 40(2)(b)(iv), ACHR art. 8(2)(g), and AfrCHPR art. 7(1)(d).

130 For example, US law generally protects the "privilege" against self-incrimination, even though it is a constitutional right under the Fifth Amendment to the US Constitution.

131 See, e.g., ICTY and ICTR common Rule 90(E).

132 "As a practical matter, [compelled self-incriminating] information may strengthen the resolve of police to lay or persist with charges and will also assist them in finding and marshalling admissible evidence that they can use to convict that person. It may be impossible to select a truly impartial jury if an effusion of allegations and innuendo has already poisoned the minds of most members of the public. Even if judges are all so intellectually honest that they would never consciously take into account inadmissible testimony, they may be unconsciously influenced by the forbidden 'knowledge' they have acquired from public inquiries. Jurors, untrained in the art of 'disabusing' themselves, may be more vulnerable." B. Schwartz, "Public Inquiries," in A. Manson and D. Mullan, eds., *Commissions of Inquiry: Praise or Reappraise?* (Toronto: Irwin Law, 2003), at 445.

as for the giving of contradictory evidence (*i.e.,* for the purpose of impeaching credibility).[133] In addition, authorities should be permitted to make reasonable "derivative" uses of such statements or evidence. Specifically, investigative authorities should be permitted to use the statements or evidence to further investigations regarding the underlying offenses to which each relates, provided that they can ultimately prove that the evidence offered at a future trial could reasonably have been discovered in the absence of the compelled testimony or evidence.[134] Finally, there should be no bar on the use of compelled testimony and evidence in legal proceedings brought against third parties, such as co-conspirators.

The South African TRC's mandate contained a detailed provision on self-incrimination. It provided that the TRC could compel persons to give self-incriminating statements or evidence, subject to applicable privileges for protected communications.[135] It further stipulated that a person could be

---

133 *See, e.g.,* section 13 of the *Canadian Charter of Rights and Freedoms*: "A witness who testifies in any proceedings has the right not to have any incriminating evidence so given used to incriminate that witness in any other proceedings, except in a prosecution for perjury or for the giving of contradictory evidence." At times, however, the line between using a prior statement to incriminate and using a prior statement to cross-examine can be tenuous. *See, e.g., R. v. Noël,* [2002] 3 S.C.R. 433, in which the Supreme Court of Canada held that under section 13 of the Canadian Charter, an accused cannot be cross-examined on the basis of prior compelled testimony unless there is no realistic danger that the individual's prior testimony could be used to incriminate him or her.

134 *See generally* the decision of the Supreme Court of Canada in *R. v. S.(R.J.)* (1995), 36 C.R. (4th) 1. *Compare with* A. R. Amar, "Taking the Fifth Too Often," *New York Times,* 18 February 2002, in which the author decries the inability to make derivative use of compelled testimony in the United States: "[S]ometimes a truth-seeking society needs to be able to compel a person to speak outside his trial – in grand jury rooms, civil cases and legislative hearings, for example. One solution is to require the person to testify in these specific places, but then exclude this compelled testimony from any later prosecution brought against him. This way, he would never become a witness against himself 'in a criminal case.' This rule would offer Congressional witnesses a narrow type of testimonial immunity. While the testimony itself would be excluded from the criminal trial, evidence that might be drawn indirectly from the testimony would be admissible at a later trial. This would allow prosecutors to use any reliable leads that the testimony might generate. Courts today allow government lawyers to force people to give voice samples and take breath tests for alcohol because these are not considered forms of self-incrimination prohibited by the Fifth Amendment. If prosecutors can compel defendants to provide these kinds of evidence, they should also be allowed to introduce reliable evidence that is found as a result of earlier immunized testimony . . . Current case law ignores the Constitution's words, distorts constitutional structure and overprotects the guilty."

135 Section 31(1): "Any person who is questioned by the Commission in the exercise of its powers in terms of this Act, or who has been subpoenaed to give evidence or to produce any article at a hearing of the Commission shall, subject to the provisions of subsections (2), (3) and (5), be compelled to produce any article or to answer any question put to him or her

compelled to answer a question or to produce an article that may incriminate him or her, but only after the commission:

(a) consulted with the attorney-general who has jurisdiction;

(b) satisfied itself that to require such information from such a person is reasonable, necessary and justifiable in an open and democratic society based on freedom and equality; and

(c) satisfied itself that such a person has refused or is likely to refuse to answer a question or produce an article on the grounds that such an answer or article might incriminate him or her.[136]

In relation to any such compelled testimony or evidence, the mandate afforded broad use immunity, but it excluded any derivative uses of the information.[137]

The mandate of the truth commission in Timor-Leste had a more restricted notion of the right against self-incrimination. Section 17.1 provided:

> No witness may be compelled to incriminate himself or herself. Every person who is invited or required to come before the Commission shall be informed of such right. If at any time it appears to the Commission that a question asked of a witness is likely to elicit a response that might incriminate the witness, the Commission shall readvise the witness of his or her right not to answer the question.

In this author's view, the provision takes the principle too far. Permitting someone to refuse absolutely to provide self-incriminating testimony amounts to a complete right to silence. Such an approach is excessive and counterproductive for an investigative body such as a truth commission.

Issues of self-incrimination have a long pedigree in the United States that is worthy of special mention. The Fifth Amendment to the US Constitution articulates the privilege against self-incrimination as follows: "No person . . . shall be compelled in any criminal case to be a witness against himself." Although

---

with regard to the subject-matter of the hearing notwithstanding the fact that the article or his or her answer may incriminate him or her."

136 Section 31(2).

137 Section 31(3): "[Any] incriminating answer or information obtained or incriminating evidence directly or indirectly derived from a questioning in terms of subsection (1) shall not be admissible as evidence against the person concerned in criminal proceedings in a court of law or before any body or institution established by or under any law: Provided that incriminating evidence arising from such questioning shall be admissible in criminal proceedings where the person is arraigned on a charge of perjury or a charge contemplated in section 39 (d)(ii) of this Act or in section 319(3) of the Criminal Procedure Act, 1955 (Act No. 56 of 1955)."

the text would seem to limit the privilege only to criminal proceedings, "The Supreme Court broadly interprets 'criminal case' to include any proceeding, including a grand jury proceeding, in which a witness' testimony might render that witness liable in a subsequent criminal prosecution."[138] Further, the Fifth Amendment "applies only when the accused is compelled to make a *testimonial* communication that is incriminating."[139] Thus, it does not protect physical evidence such as handwriting and fingerprints. In the federal grand jury system, a prosecutor can prevent a target of investigation from asserting a privilege against self-incrimination by giving use immunity to the individual. The Supreme Court has held that this kind of immunity is constitutional because it puts the compelled person in the same position he or she would have been in had he or she not been required to testify.[140]

Despite its wide recognition, the Fifth Amendment, like all privileges, may be waived. In the United States, a leading case on waiving the Fifth Amendment privilege is *Rogers v. U.S.*[141] In that case, the Supreme Court held that the treasurer of the Communist Party waived the Fifth Amendment in her testimony before a grand jury by admitting that she was in possession of certain party records, including membership lists. She asserted the Fifth Amendment as to the identity of the person to whom she transferred the records.[142] Relying on two prior cases, the Court held that "[i]f petitioner desired the protection of the privilege against self-incrimination, she was required to claim it" and "[t]he privilege 'is deemed waived unless invoked.'"[143] As well, the Court famously observed that "[d]isclosure of a fact waives the privilege as to the details."[144] Thus, Rogers was found to have waived her Fifth Amendment privilege by answering incriminating questions.[145]

In the case of truth commissions, the issue of waiver may be avoided by having use immunity attach *automatically,* by mandate, to any compelled statement or evidence that is self-incriminating. In this way, a compelled person would not need to affirmatively invoke the privilege, and the commission would not need to provide the person with a caution. While a requirement of invocation may make sense in a courtroom, it is ill-suited to an investigative body such as

---

138 "Compelled Production of Evidence," 24 *Am. Crim. L. Rev.,* at 802.

139 *Baltimore City Dep't of Soc. Svcs. v. Bouknight,* 493 U.S. 549, at 554 (1990) (emphasis in original text) (citing *Fisher v. U.S.,* 425 U.S. 391, at 408 (1976)).

140 Brenner, "Is the Grand Jury Worth Keeping?," above note 114, at 194.

141 340 U.S. 367 (1951).

142 *Ibid.,* at 368.

143 *Ibid.,* at 370–1.

144 *Ibid.,* at 373–4 (citing *McCarthy v. Arndstein,* 262 U.S. 355 (1923)).

145 *Ibid.,* at 374–5. The Fifth Amendment may also be waived by inference. There is, however, disagreement among federal courts as to the scope and application of inferred waiver, particularly when waiver is inferred based on testimony in a prior proceeding.

a truth commission, which is often run by nonjudges, and which is intended to operate differently from a formal criminal trial.

Some Commonwealth inquiry legislation takes the automatic immunity approach one step further by having use immunity attach automatically to *any* testimony or evidence, whether voluntary or compelled, and whether or not self-incriminating. For example, section 8 of the Nigerian *Tribunals of Inquiry Act* provides: "Evidence taken under this Act shall be inadmissible against any person in any civil or criminal proceedings whatever, except in the case of a person charged with giving false evidence before the members." Similarly, section 14 of Israel's *Commissions of Inquiry Law* provides that "testimony given before a commission of inquiry or before a person entrusted with the collection of material . . . shall not be evidence in any legal proceeding, other than a criminal action in respect of the giving of that testimony." The mandate of the Liberian truth commission provides more or less the same.[146]

While such an approach maximizes the incentive for broad disclosure, arguably it goes further than necessary or desirable. First, immunity should attach only to *compelled* testimony or evidence. No use immunity should attach to voluntary testimony that is self-incriminating; instead, voluntary testimony should act as a waiver of the privilege.[147] In this manner, future options in the realm of criminal justice are preserved without any abridgment of the person's rights. Second, use immunity should not attach to all compelled testimony and evidence. Instead, it should attach only to the part that was self-incriminating, as determined by a court of law.

---

146 *See An Act to Establish the Truth and Reconciliation Commission of Liberia* (2005), s. 30: "The TRC shall grant immunity to all persons or groups of persons, organizations or institutions from prosecution or tort actions on account of statements made or evidence given before the TRC in advancement of the public interest objective inherent in the functions and objects of the TRC and pursuant to the successful execution of its mandate, and which, therefore, shall not be used in any court of law against the person making the statement." *See also Terms of Reference for the Truth and Reconciliation Commission* (Grenada), 7 April 2000, s. 2.

147 Alternatively, as is done in some jurisdictions, use immunity may be accorded to voluntary testimony on a case-by-case basis. For example, in the United Kingdom, the attorney general has occasionally given inquiry-specific undertakings such as the following: "To undertake in respect of any person who provides evidence to the inquiry that no evidence he or she may give before the inquiry, whether orally or by written statement, nor any written statement made preparatory to giving evidence nor any document produced by that person to the inquiry will be used in evidence against him or her in any criminal proceedings, except in proceedings where he or she is charged with having given false evidence in the course of this inquiry or having conspired with or procured others to do so." *See* para. 48 of Explanatory Notes to the draft UK *Inquiries Bill* (now the *Inquiries Act*). *See* http://www.dca.gov.uk/legist/inquiries.htm#background.

RECOMMENDATIONS

- A commission could have the power to compel persons to make self-incriminating statements or deliver self-incriminating evidence, subject to any applicable privileges, and provided that "use immunity" attaches by law or by mandate to any compelled testimony or evidence (as already explained). Absent this safeguard, a commission should not have the power to compel the giving of self-incriminating testimony or evidence.
- A power to compel persons to give self-incriminating testimony or evidence should be exercised only where it is reasonable, just, and necessary to do so, and where there is no manifest security risk to the compelled person. Exercise of the power may also be conditioned on the prior consent of an appropriate government minister.
- The scope of use immunity for compelled self-incriminating statements or evidence should be broad. Specifically, the use of such statements and evidence should be prohibited in relation to contemporaneous or subsequent criminal, civil, or administrative proceedings against that person, *except* in prosecutions for perjury or for the giving of contradictory evidence (*i.e.*, for the purpose of impeaching credibility).
- Compelled self-incriminating testimony and evidence should be admissible in legal proceedings brought against third parties, such as co-conspirators.
- Public authorities should be barred from making "derivative" use of such statements and evidence to further investigations regarding the underlying offenses to which each relates, unless it can be proved that any evidence ultimately introduced in court could reasonably have been discovered in the absence of the compelled testimony or evidence.
- Use immunity should attach only to *compelled* testimony. No use immunity should attach to voluntary testimony that is self-incriminating; instead, voluntary testimony should act as a waiver of the privilege against self-incrimination.
- Use immunity should attach *automatically* to compelled testimony or evidence that is self-incriminating; consequently, there should be no obligation for the compelled person to affirmatively invoke the privilege against self-incrimination, nor should there be any obligation for the commission to provide a caution.
- Use immunity should not attach to all compelled testimony and evidence, but only to the part that is self-incriminating, as determined by a court.

SECTION 9: PROTECTIVE MEASURES

The success of public hearings will depend to a large extent on the physical and psychological safety of persons who testify. Those who have suffered human rights abuses will generally be reluctant to come forward and testify if the risks associated with participation in the proceedings are high. They will also be more likely to recant testimony after having provided it.[148]

Formal protective measures should be prescribed only in response to a formal request or application. Truth commissions should accept such requests on a *prima facie* basis and review them in a confidential manner. Formal protective measures should be granted only on an exceptional basis, and they should always be weighed against the public interest in hearing open and public testimony. Informal protective measures, such as the enforcement of rules for audience members at a hearing, do not, however, require special requests or exemptions.[149]

A useful set of criteria for determining eligibility for formal protective measures is found in the mandate of Timor-Leste's truth commission. Section 36.1 requires the commission to

> take appropriate measures to protect the safety, physical and psychological well being, dignity and privacy of victims and witnesses who are to appear before the Commission [having regard to] all relevant factors, including age, gender, health and the nature of the crime, in particular, but not limited to, where the crime involves sexual or gender violence or violence against children or where there exists a credible threat against the safety of a victim or witness.

The specific measures that are possible or appropriate in any particular case are left to the discretion of the commission.[150]

---

148 In Uganda, "witnesses would sometimes return after a hearing to withdraw their testimony, sometimes flatly denying what they had said even when it was recorded on video- or audiotape. It was clear that they had been pressured to recant their story, particularly if they named perpetrators." Hayner, *Unspeakable Truths*, above note 10, at 95.

149 As a means of psychological comfort and protection for victims who testified, the truth commission in Morocco distributed to each audience member a set of instructions. The instructions prohibited applause, taking photos, using cell phones, speaking or addressing questions to victims during their testimony, or leaving the room prior to the end of the hearing. The rules are posted on the commission's website: http://www.ier.ma.

150 *See also* Charter of the Women's International War Crimes Tribunal on Japan's Military Sexual Slavery (2000), art. 13: "The Tribunal shall take appropriate measures to protect the safety, physical and psychological well-being, dignity and privacy of those victimized and witnesses of sexual violence and any other person at risk on account of their testimony, having regard to the nature of crimes being dealt with and taking trauma into account . . ."

Threats against family members should be considered as possible grounds of eligibility for protective measures.[151] Equally valid grounds include national security concerns,[152] or the need to preserve privileged communications given in the course of a legally protected relationship.[153] Children who testify should also tend to be treated as presumptively eligible for protective measures, consistent with legal practice in most domestic jurisdictions. In Sierra Leone, for example, children testified in closed sessions only.[154] Cases involving acts of sexual violence will almost always be deserving of protective measures too, given the social trauma and stigmatization that so often accompanies public disclosure of such acts.[155] Victims of sexual violence, however, may not always prefer protective measures.[156]

151 *See, e.g.,* Rome Statute art. 68(5): "Where the disclosure of evidence or information pursuant to this Statute may lead to the grave endangerment of the security of a witness or his or her family, the Prosecutor may, for the purposes of any proceedings conducted prior to the commencement of the trial, withhold such evidence or information and instead submit a summary thereof. Such measures shall be exercised in a manner which is not prejudicial to or inconsistent with the rights of the accused and a fair and impartial trial." *See also* Matthews, *Jervis on Coroners,* above note 46, at 245 (regarding coroner inquests).

152 *See, e.g.,* ICTY Rule 54*bis*, which enables a state to object to a "binding order" (*i.e.,* a subpoena for evidence) on the basis of national security concerns. The Trial Chamber may, however, require the state to disclose its evidence, depending on the case. May and Wierda, *International Criminal Evidence,* at 60–1. The Rome Statute inverts decision-making. Before the ICC, the state has the final decision about whether to withhold subpoenaed evidence on the basis of national security interests. *See* Rome Statute arts. 72(4) and 93(4).

153 *See, e.g.,* ICC Rules of Procedure and Evidence, Rule 72.

154 International Center for Transitional Justice, *The Sierra Leone Truth and Reconciliation Commission,* above note 24, at 4.

155 *See, e.g., An Act to Establish the Truth and Reconciliation Commission of Liberia* (2005), s. 26(o): "The TRC shall employ specialists in children and women's rights and shall ensure that special measures or mechanisms are employed that will enable women and children to provide testimony to the TRC, while at the same time protecting their safety and not endangering or delaying their social reintegration or psychological recovery." *See also* May and Wierda, *International Criminal Evidence,* at 185.

156 *See, e.g.,* International Center for Transitional Justice, *Truth Commissions and Gender: Principles, Policies and Procedures* (forthcoming): "[M]oving forward with the default assumption that sexual violence requires *in camera* testimony alone is also problematic. These were the rules in operation in the Sierra Leone TRC – yet to the surprise of the commission many women who came to give testimony about sexual violence proactively asked for an opportunity to narrate their experience in public for all to hear about the abuses they suffered. In response to their requests, the commission then channeled their testimony for public hearings. For many, the public denunciation of this crime is important to fighting the stigma associated with it; privatizing it calls on the victim to bear the full burden of the crime – once again coding it in shame and secrecy. While many knew the statistical accounts of widespread sexual abuse in Sierra Leone, it was public testimony that most powerfully and evocatively evidenced these widespread and systemic patterns and the enormity of their impact on the lives of Sierra Leonean women."

Protective measures may take diverse forms. A particularly robust form is a witness protection program. Such programs generally offer the most secure protection to a vulnerable witness. However, they are often infeasible for a truth commission because of the immense human and financial resources they absorb. The South African TRC used a formal witness protection program modeled on one used in Italy for mafia trials. The program employed a number of tactics. Depending on the individual case, these included the use of "safe houses" and bodyguards, a visible increase in community and state policing, and other similar measures.[157] Any required witness resettlement after the hearing was arranged by the state; as a temporary body, the commission could not guarantee or pay for long-term protection.[158] Pursuant to an "Institutional Cooperation Agreement" with the Prosecutor's Office, the Peruvian TRC also arranged for witness protection. The agreement obligated the Prosecutor's Office to "immediately take the necessary measures to protect the identity, domicile, profession and any other witness information" for any "appropriately grounded and documented" request of the commission.[159] The Liberian TRC authorizes the design and use of witness protection programs "on a case by case basis."[160] Timor-Leste's truth commission arranged for a police presence at all of its public hearings, and arranged special protective measures for witnesses in appropriate cases.

There are other important, and often less costly, ways to protect the identity or location or both of a person who may testify at a public hearing. For example,

---

157   Hayner, *Unspeakable Truths*, above note 10, at 245–7. "Although we had a witness protection programme, there was never any serious threat to those who received such protection." Boraine, *A Country Unmasked*, above note 4, at 293.

158   A commission can, however, alert the witness to certain possible eventualities. "When a commission with a witness protection program closes, it needs to notify all protected witnesses that it intends to transfer its witness protection program records to the government agency operating the witness protection program. The protected witness should be given an opportunity to raise any objections to the transfer of his or her file. If a witness objects, the file should be transferred to the archives and closed, except to the witness. The files should be opened only upon the death of the witness or, if the date of death is unknown, fifty years from the initiation of witness protection. Files in the custody of the operating office should be transferred to the archives at the time of the death of the witness or in fifty years, whichever comes first." T. H. Peterson, *Final Acts: A Guide to Preserving the Records of Truth Commissions* (Baltimore: Johns Hopkins University Press and the Woodrow Wilson International Center for Scholars, 2005), at 99.

159   Agreement available in English at http://www.cverdad.org.pe. According to the Peruvian commission's final report, there were few cases of serious danger to victims who testified, whether before, during, or after their testimony. Nevertheless, many victims expressed fear of reprisals. When a victim mentioned the name of an alleged perpetrator at a hearing, the commission took no chances: it solicited protective measures from the Prosecutor's Office.

160   *An Act to Establish the Truth and Reconciliation Commission of Liberia* (2005), s. 26(n).

in the case of Nigeria's truth commission, women were sometimes permitted to provide public testimony with their faces covered. In Northern Ireland, the Bloody Sunday Inquiry used witness "screening," meaning that witnesses were visible only to the tribunal, counsel, and other legal representatives; members of the public and media could only *hear* the evidence being delivered. The tribunal also withheld from the public domain the addresses and telephone numbers of soldiers and the addresses of other witnesses.[161] Coroners, similarly, have the power to prohibit the publication of the name, address, or school of any child or youth who is a witness at a public inquest.[162]

In the field of international criminal law, the ICC Rules of Procedure and Evidence allow for live testimony by means of audio or video-link technology, the expunging of names from public records, and the use of pseudonyms.[163] They also provide for the possibility of sealing some of the records of proceedings.[164] Other basic security measures, such as the use of metal detectors and security guards, are also commonly used in the context of international and domestic criminal trials.

Another category of protective measure that could be considered by a truth commission is the use of *in camera* (private) hearings. Such hearings should be used as a last resort, only where it is not possible to conduct all or part of the hearing in public by using one of the methods just discussed.[165] Indeed, members of the public may, with good reason, view private hearings with distrust.[166]

---

161 *See* Bloody Sunday Inquiry, Rulings and Judgments, Ruling on Home Addresses, February 1999, http://www.bloody-sunday-inquiry.org.uk/index2.asp?p=3. "Nobody is being prosecuted before this Tribunal, nor is it our function to do justice between the parties competing in an adversarial contest. Our task is to do justice by ascertaining, through an inquisitorial process, the truth about what happened on Bloody Sunday. The proper fulfillment of that task does not necessarily require that the identity of everyone who gives evidence to the Inquiry should be disclosed in public . . ." Bloody Sunday Inquiry, Rulings and Judgments, July 1998, Matters Raised at the Preliminary Hearing, http://www.bloody-sunday-inquiry.org.uk/index2.asp?p=3.

162 Matthews, *Jervis on Coroners*, above note 46, at 242. Exceptionally, coroners may also permit witnesses to remain anonymous. *Ibid.*, at 243.

163 Rules 67 and 87.

164 *See* Rule 74(7) of the ICC Rules of Procedure and Evidence.

165 *See, e.g.*, Recommendation 11 of the *Report of the Task Force on the Establishment of a Truth, Justice and Reconciliation Commission*, Republic of Kenya (2003). In the case of Ghana's truth commission, *in camera* hearings were allowed only (1) "where the security of the state may be jeopardized," (2) "where the personal safety of a witness or other person may be compromised," or (3) "where public decency or morality may be gravely offended by the nature of the testimony." *Ghana National Reconciliation Commission Final Report* (2004), vol. 1, ch. 2, at 2.6.4.2.

166 "In much of Africa, for example, much more so than Latin America, the public tends to be skeptical of hearings that take place behind closed doors." Hayner, *Unspeakable Truths*, above note 10, at 225.

Still, sometimes the use of private hearings may be the only feasible way to obtain information that a truth commission deems essential to its inquiry.[167] Alternatively, a private hearing may be the only way to empower certain categories of persons – for example, female victims of sexual violence – to testify.[168] There may, in addition, be a compelling public interest justification for holding a hearing out of the public eye.[169]

However, *ex ante*, a commission should consider whether something less than a formal private hearing would be reasonable in the case at hand. For example, it may suffice to arrange a private interview with a commission staff member. This will take less time and use fewer resources than a private hearing, which implies the use of a special room, the presence of legal counsel, and an appearance before a formally constituted panel of commissioners.

Assuming, however, that an *in camera* hearing is required, it appears that most recent truth commission mandates provide for such a possibility. For example, section 33(1) of the South African TRC's mandate provides:

> If the Commission, in any proceedings before it, is satisfied that – (i) it would be in the interest of justice; or (ii) there is a likelihood that harm may ensue to any person as a result of the proceedings being open, it may direct that such proceedings be held behind closed doors and that the public or any category thereof shall not be present at such proceedings or any part thereof: Provided that the Commission shall permit any victim who has an interest in the proceedings concerned, to be present.

The mandate further provides in section 33(2) that:

> Where the Commission under subsection (1)(b) on any grounds referred to in that subsection directs that the public or any category thereof shall not be present at any proceedings or part thereof, the Commission may . . . (a) direct that no information relating to the proceedings, or any part thereof held behind closed doors, shall be made

---

167 For example, death threats against victims who appeared at public hearings forced one division of the Sri Lankan truth commission to hold its hearings in private. *Ibid.*, at 227.

168 For example, some truth commissions – including those of Sierra Leone, South Africa, Peru, and Timor-Leste – arranged "women's hearings" at which female victims testified before private audiences exclusively comprised of other women (including female commissioners, staff, and audience members). D. Orentlicher, "Promotion and Protection of Human Rights: Impunity," UN doc. E/CN.4/2004/88 (2004), at para. 18(f).

169 *Recall* ICCPR art. 14(1), which allows the exclusion of the press and the public from all or part of a trial "for reasons of morals, public order (*ordre public*) or national security in a democratic society, or when the interest of the private lives of the parties so requires, or to the extent strictly necessary in the opinion of the court in special circumstances where publicity would prejudice the interests of justice . . ."

public in any manner; (b) direct that no person may, in any manner, make public any information which may reveal the identity of any witness in the proceedings; (c) give such directions in respect of the record of proceedings as may be necessary to protect the identity of any witness: Provided that the Commission may authorize the publication of so much information as it considers would be just and equitable.

The mandates of the truth commissions in Ghana,[170] Timor-Leste,[171] and Liberia[172] contain similar provisions.

Commonwealth commissions of inquiry also generally allow *in camera* hearings, again on an exceptional basis. The Ontario *Public Inquiries Act*, for example, provides:

All hearings on an inquiry are open to the public except where the commission conducting the inquiry is of the opinion that, (a) matters involving public security may be disclosed at the hearing; or (b) intimate financial or personal matters or other matters may be disclosed at the hearing that are of such a nature, having regard to the circumstances, that the desirability of avoiding disclosure thereof in the interest of any person affected or in the public interest outweighs the desirability of adhering to the principle that hearings be open to the public, in which

170 Section 12.1: "(1) The proceedings of the Commission shall be held in public except that the Commission may for good cause have private hearings . . . (3) The Commission shall in its proceedings both private and public permit the presence of the victim in the matter and such other persons whose presence the Commission considers necessary. (4) Where proceedings are held in private, the Commission may direct that (a) no information from the proceedings shall be made public; (b) a person shall not disclose the identity of a witness in the proceedings; (c) records of proceedings be kept in such manner as to protect the identity of a witness, except that the Commission may for good reason direct otherwise."

1/1 Section 16.2. "If the Commission, in relation to any hearing it has convened, is satisfied that: (a) it would be in the interests of justice; or (b) there is a likelihood that harm may ensue to any person as a result of the proceedings being open, it may direct that such proceedings be held behind closed doors and that the public or any category thereof shall not be present at such proceedings or any part thereof; provided that the Commission shall permit any victim who has an interest in the proceedings concerned, to be present." *See also* section 16.3: "Where the Commission directs that the public or any category thereof shall not be present at any proceedings or part thereof, the Commission may: (a) direct that no information relating to the proceedings, or any part thereof held behind closed doors, shall be made public in any manner; (b) direct that no person may, in any manner, make public any information which may reveal the identity of any witness in the proceedings; (c) give such directions in respect of the record of proceedings as may be necessary to protect the identity of any witness."

172 *An Act to Establish the Truth and Reconciliation Commission of Liberia* (2005), s.26(p).

case the commission may hold the hearing concerning any such matters in the absence of the public.[173]

In a slight departure, Israel's *Commissions of Inquiry Law* allows *in camera* hearings, but only if they are necessary to protect the security of the state, to safeguard morality, or to safeguard the welfare of a minor.[174] The same law also usefully specifies that individuals who publish any part of an *in camera* proceeding may be sentenced to six months' imprisonment.[175] Coroner inquests must be conducted in public, except where matters of national security are implicated.[176]

Modern international criminal procedure also allows for *in camera* proceedings in certain circumstances. The ICTY allows for the protection of victims and witnesses by means of *in camera* proceedings.[177] The ICC Rules of Procedure and Evidence contemplate a wide variety of possible occasions and reasons for *in camera* hearings too, including to consider the relevance or admissibility of evidence (Rule 72), to handle self-incriminating evidence (Rule 74), to protect victims and witnesses (Rule 87), and to "facilitate the testimony of a traumatized victim or witness, a child, an elderly person or a victim of sexual violence" (Rule 88).

RECOMMENDATIONS

- Having regard to its available resources, a commission should undertake or arrange protective measures to ensure the physical safety and privacy of anyone who testifies publicly and who would (or whose family would) face significant security risks on account of testimony.
- Truth commissions should accept all applications for protective measures on a *prima facie* basis. Applications for protective measures should be considered in private by the commission.
- Truth commissions should have the discretion to provide or to deny protective measures in accordance with established criteria that

---

173 Section 4.
174 Section 18(a).
175 Section 26. *See also Law 04/018 (2004) Concerning the Organization, Powers and Functions of the Truth and Reconciliation Commission* (DRC), art. 40, which creates an obligation on the part of the DRC's truth commission to preserve the confidentiality of any evidence given at an *in camera* hearing. *Recall also* article 10 of the UN Manual on the Effective Prevention and Investigation of Extra-Legal, Arbitrary and Summary Executions (1991), which provides that, in accordance with "general principles of criminal procedure," *in camera* proceedings of a commission of inquiry be recorded, and "the closed, unpublished record kept in a known location."
176 Matthews, *Jervis on Coroners*, above note 46, at 241. A decision to hold a coroner inquest *in camera* must be decided in private, and is subject to judicial review.
177 ICTY Statute (2000), article 22.

recognize the need to assure public and individual security, and witness dignity and privacy.

- There are several ways to protect the identity or location or both of a person who may testify at a public hearing. These include using a witness protection program, expunging the person's name and other identifying information from public records of the commission, using pseudonyms, employing witness voice and picture alteration devices, using videoconferencing technology, using closed-circuit television, limiting those who may attend, and restricting how a hearing may be publicly reported.

- A commission should have the power to conduct *in camera* hearings at its discretion in accordance with established criteria, provided that (1) every effort is made to hold hearings in public using one or more of the aforementioned measures to protect the identity or location or both of a witness, and (2) something short of a formal *in camera* hearing (*e.g.*, a private interview) would not be sufficient to ensure fairness.

- No information from any *in camera* proceeding should be made public without the consent of the person who testified. There should be penalties for anyone who breaches the confidentiality of an *in camera* hearing.

SECTION 10: VICTIM EMOTIONAL AND PSYCHOLOGICAL SUPPORT

Participation in a public hearing is fraught with emotion. Victims, in particular, are often forced to relive the horror of their experiences in all its grisly detail. Many of them may also be unaccustomed to the public spotlight. Without effective emotional support, some victims will be unable to complete their testimony or recount their experience accurately.[178]

Because the possibility of trauma is foreseeable, truth commissions have a duty to be prepared and to create a positive ambience for victims.[179] They

---

178 *See, e.g.*, D. Orentlicher, "Updated Set of Principles," above note 29, Principle 10(b): "Social workers and/or mental health-care practitioners should be authorized to assist victims, preferably in their own language, both during and after their testimony, especially in cases of sexual assault."

179 Creating such an ambience involves many considerations beyond those discussed in this section. For example, a commission must be careful in its selection of the venues for hearings and in its organization of seating arrangements. Morocco's truth commission, for example, placed many victims – specifically those who would not have the opportunity to testify in public – on stage behind those who testified. This served as a form of moral support and solidarity for those testifying, and as a form of recognition for those who would not have an

should also make an effort to keep the person's emotional and other expectations in check. Indeed, testifying at a public hearing does not guarantee later justice, reparation, or reform.[180]

The South African TRC provided emotional and psychological support mechanisms to victims who testified. The work was largely assigned to a handful of staff members, called "briefers." Chosen because they had a general background in counseling, briefers were assigned to carry out the difficult task of preparing and following up with victims who would testify at public hearings. Their work was based on the system of critical incident stress management used in treating trauma victims all over the world. While there were some serious limitations to the work of the TRC's briefers,[181] there was no doubt as to the program's utility.

The Peruvian TRC followed South Africa's lead and provided important emotional and psychological support to victims in the context of its public hearings. In fact, the commission identified emotional and social sustainability for victims as one of its guiding principles for public hearings.[182] Each person who testified was accompanied by a mental health professional before, during, and after giving testimony, except where the person voluntarily declined such support. The commission also carried out a midterm survey of some of the victims who testified to find out what impacts – positive and negative – the act of public testimony had had on them. Other truth commissions, including those of Timor-Leste,[183] Sierra Leone, Ghana, and Morocco, have also provided

---

equivalent opportunity. Another example comes from the truth commission in Timor-Leste, which began many public hearings with choirs and prayers. See CAVR Update, December 2003–January 2004 (http://www.easttimor-reconciliation.org). The truth commission in Ghana created a special prayer, which it read aloud before each public hearing. The prayer included the following passage: "We also pray to You, God, Ever-Faithful, and True, to grant all those who come before this Commission, Your spirit of truth, honesty and a deep sense of love and desire for peace, healing and reconciliation in our dear country, Ghana."

180 In Peru, one person who testified apparently believed that the small sum of money she received to enable her to attend the hearing represented the state's compensation for her lost husband. See "El Impacto de las Audiencias Públicas en los Participantes" (http://www.cverdad.org.pe).

181 There were only fourteen briefers across the entire country, they received no specialized training appropriate to the type of trauma they encountered, and they were largely unable to meet the needs of many of those who appeared before the public hearings. Eventually they called for and received some support on a volunteer basis from outside professionals and community workers, who were able to see to the needs of some of those in greatest need of emotional support. However, even this fell short of what was needed. N. Roht-Arriaza, "Civil Society in Processes of Accountability," in M. C. Bassiouni, ed., *Post-Conflict Justice* (Ardsley, NY: Transnational, 2002), at 105.

182 TRC Regulation on Public Hearings, art. 3.

183 The Timor-Leste truth commission's mandate provides: "The Commission shall allow for special measures be taken in hearings which involve testimonies from special groups of

valuable emotional and psychological supports before and after public hearings.[184] Modern international criminal tribunals have begun to make greater use of emotional and psychological support mechanisms too.[185]

Support need not consist mostly, or only, of health care professionals. Truth commissions might also consider facilitating alternative forms of assistance, such as interventions by religious clerics and elders, self-help support groups, and special community or family support arrangements.[186] Such forms of assistance may be sufficient to the task in some contexts. They are also less demanding on a commission's typically limited resources.

RECOMMENDATIONS

- Consistent with the resources and mandate of a truth commission, victims should receive appropriate medical, psychological, or emotional support services to help them testify effectively at public hearings. The commission should also follow up with victims after their public testimony to ensure that their well-being was not compromised as a result of testifying.
- Alternative forms of assistance, such as religious or spiritual support by clerics and elders, self-help support groups, and special community or family support arrangements, could also be considered.
- In all other respects, Chapter 3, Section 6 ("Support and Referrals") applies, *mutatis mutandis.*

---

victims, such as women and children. Such hearings may allow for accompaniment of victims by relevant victim support workers." "On the Establishment of a Commission for Reception, Truth and Reconciliation in East Timor," UNTAET/REG/2001/01, as amended, s. 16.4.

184 In Sierra Leone, children testified only at *in camera* hearings of the TRC. But the commission still ensured appropriate emotional support: "A social worker was always present at a child hearing, sitting next to the child and offering any emotional or other support required. After the hearing, the social worker conducted further visits to the child, to ensure no adverse consequences from his or her participation." *Sierra Leone Truth and Reconciliation Commission Final Report* (2004), vol. 1, ch. 5, para. 210.

185 *See, e.g.,* ICC Rules of Procedure and Evidence, Rule 17(2)(a)(3), which provides that the ICC Victim and Witnesses Unit must assist all witnesses who appear before the Court in obtaining "medical, psychological and other appropriate assistance."

186 *See, e.g.,* section 7(2) of *The Truth and Reconciliation Act 2000* (Sierra Leone): "The Commission may seek assistance from traditional and religious leaders to facilitate its public sessions and in resolving local conflicts arising from past violations or abuses or in support of healing and reconciliation." The identical provision appears in *An Act to Establish the Truth and Reconciliation Commission of Liberia* (2005), s. 26(q).

7

Publication of Findings of Individual Responsibility

INTRODUCTION

The decision by a truth commission to publish findings of individual responsibility in a final report will always be controversial. Although most have lacked the explicit power to do so, the urge to "name names" often remains strong, especially when to refrain from doing so might reinforce a broader environment of impunity.[1]

While a truth commission's public attribution of individual responsibility is distinct from a legal judgment, it raises significant procedural fairness issues. At the heart of these issues is a tension between individual privacy and reputation rights on the one hand,[2] and the victims' and public's right to know the truth

---

1 Describing the Salvadoran truth commission's decision to name names, one author writes, "Having formed the view that criminal justice was almost certainly not going to occur in El Salvador, at least in the reasonably foreseeable future, the Commission took the view that not to name names would effectively pass up the only opportunity to establish the guilt of those responsible, at least in the court of public opinion." P. Seils, "The Limits of Truth Commissions in the Search for Justice: An Analysis of the Truth Commissions of El Salvador and Guatemala and Their Effect in Achieving Post-Conflict Justice," in M. C. Bassiouni, ed., *Post-Conflict Justice* (Ardsley, NY: Transnational, 2002), at 781.

2 *See* the discussion of privacy and reputation rights in Chapter 2. *See also Jenkins v. McKeithen*, 395 U.S. 411 (1969), where the US Supreme Court noted the capacity of nonjudicial bodies to impose sanctions by publicizing its findings in individual cases. The case looked at the Louisiana Labor-Management Commission, whose function was "to find persons guilty

on the other.[3] The stakes are high for all concerned. A wrongly accused person could see his or her reputation forever tarnished. Being named could also make it more likely that the person will be prosecuted or sued, especially where a commission is consciously established, and publicly viewed, as a precursor to justice in the courts. For the commission, a false accusation might greatly undermine its credibility, as well as the reception of its overall findings of fact. For victims, the public attribution of individual responsibility may be viewed as an essential, if incomplete, form of justice.

The question of naming names is a familiar one for publishers, who must take into consideration relevant laws on defamation (and corollary defenses such as fair comment) prior to attributing responsibility to any individual in a publication.[4] One could, therefore, argue that truth commissions should approach the issue in the same manner as publishers. For a variety of reasons, however, a higher standard of fairness should be observed by truth commissions. First, while it is true that publishers frequently name names in publications, the public will often attach greater credibility to the findings of a truth commission – whether because of public respect for individual commissioners, the perceived depth of investigation, or the official character of a commission's proceedings. Even the media itself may wrongly treat a truth commission's findings as dispositive.[5] Second, unlike publishers, members of truth commissions often enjoy personal immunity for acts and omissions made in good faith in carrying out their mandate. Consequently, those falsely named will tend to have fewer options of legal redress.[6] Third, in some cases, the recommendations of a

---

of violating criminal laws without trial or procedural safeguards, and to publicize those findings." *Jenkins*, at 424. As the Court reasoned, "It is no answer that the Commission has not itself tried to impose any direct sanctions on appellant; it is enough that the Commission's alleged actions will have a substantial impact on him." *Jenkins*, at 424.

3   *See* discussion of the right to truth in Chapter 1.

4   There are two traditional forms of defamation: slander (*i.e.,* oral defamation) and libel (*i.e.,* written defamation). In most jurisdictions, a publisher will be protected from actions for defamation if the publication in question constituted fair comment on a subject of legitimate public concern. Even if the attribution in question is mistaken, it is generally permitted – provided that it is an honest, as opposed to a willful, error.

5   *See, e.g., Report of the International Commission of Inquiry on Darfur to the United Nations Secretary-General* (2005), at para. 527: "Were the Commission to [publicly] name those persons, the world media might indeed be inclined to jump to conclusions and hold that such persons were outright guilty, and not simply suspected of bearing responsibility."

6   This is very significant insofar as it gives a commission a largely unfettered freedom of expression, which is in tension with the reasonable limitations placed on that freedom by international law. *See, e.g.,* ECHR art. 10(2), which permits limitations on freedom of expression "for the protection of the reputation or rights of others, for preventing the disclosure of information received in confidence, or for maintaining the authority and impartiality of the judiciary." *See generally* discussion in Chapter 2, Section 1.

truth commission may create implementation or reporting obligations on the part of government.[7] In the publishing world, there is no equivalent to this; publishers cannot bind governments.

A salient case on the publication of findings of individual responsibility by an investigative body is the decision of the European Court of Human Rights in *Fayed v. The United Kingdom*.[8] It concerned the publication in the United Kingdom of a report by government-appointed inspectors investigating the acquisition of a company. The applicants complained that the publication of the report, in which they were criticized, amounted to a violation of various rights including the right to a fair trial under article 6(1) of the European Convention on Human Rights 1950. Specifically, they alleged that the inspectors' actions substantially harmed their reputations, and thus "determined" their civil right to honor and reputation. The Court rejected this argument, finding that the inspectors' role was not determinative of the complainants' rights, making article 6(1) inapplicable. In citing the US Supreme Court judgment in *Hannah v. Larche*,[9] the Court found that the inspectors' functions were, "in practice as well as in theory, essentially investigative"; that they "did not adjudicate, either in form or in substance"; that they said in their own report "that their findings would not be dispositive of anything"; and that "they did not make a legal determination as to criminal or civil liability" concerning the complainants' civil rights to honor and reputation.[10] In the Court's opinion, the limited purpose of the inspectors' inquiry was "to ascertain and record facts which might subsequently be used as the basis for action by other competent authorities – prosecuting, regulatory, disciplinary or even legislative."[11] This case underscores what was said in Chapter 2, namely, that investigative bodies – whether company inspectors or truth commissions – should not be held to the standard

---

7   For example, the recommendations of El Salvador's truth commission were legally binding on the government, as were those of the Sierra Leonean TRC. The Sierra Leonean mandate also requires the establishment of an official follow-up body to the truth commission. Its responsibility is "to monitor the implementation of the recommendations of the Commission and to facilitate their implementation." *The Truth and Reconciliation Act 2000* (Sierra Leone), s. 18. In addition, the government is required to provide the follow-up body with quarterly reports summarizing the steps that the government has taken to implement the recommendations. For its part, the follow-up body is required to publish the reports of the government and to submit to the public quarterly reports evaluating state efforts in regard to implementation. *Ibid.* As of this writing, the government has not established the follow-up body.

8   17101/90 [1994] ECHR 27 (21 September 1994).

9   *See* discussion of this case in Chapter 2, Section 2.

10   Para. 61.

11   *Ibid.*

of a fair trial, including for purposes of naming names. Still, they must act fairly.[12]

There are three principal justifications in favor of naming. First, the assignment of individual responsibility is arguably part and parcel of the commission's obligation to tell the truth; evidence of individual culpability is just as much a part of the truth as evidence of victims' suffering. Second, naming perpetrators can serve a parallel function to criminal prosecution. By assigning responsibility, a truth commission can express society's repudiation of individual criminal behavior.[13] Indeed, a truth commission's attribution of individual responsibility is sometimes the best approximation to criminal justice where prosecution is legally, politically, or economically infeasible. Third, by assigning individual responsibility, a commission may enhance victims' sense of justice. Naming perpetrators can help to bring victims' experiences out of the shadow of official denial or social silence, and confirm that what victims know to have happened to them *did* in fact happen. The acknowledgment of a generic description of abuses by "security forces" or "the government" is less concrete than a specific designation of those responsible for the abuse.

Yet even where a commission is empowered to name names, there may be a range of legitimate reasons for it to refrain from doing so. First, attributing individual responsibility may be impracticable. It is widely agreed, for example, that before a commission attributes responsibility to an individual, it should provide him or her with some form of prior notice and an opportunity to rebut the substance of the allegations.[14] This procedural requirement can deplete precious time and resources, as it involves locating alleged perpetrators, serving notice on them, providing them with an account of the incriminating evidence, granting them an opportunity to refute the evidence, and assessing their responses.[15] Second, where a truth commission is established

---

12 *See, e.g., Re Pergamon Press Ltd* [1970] 3 All ER 535 at 539 (describing an investigator's power to attribute individual responsibility under the UK's *Companies Act*): "Seeing that their work and their report may lead to [serious] consequences, I am clearly of the opinion that the inspectors must act fairly."

13 Naming of individuals may have another virtue akin to criminal prosecution: it ascribes responsibility to individuals, rather than to collectives. *See, e.g.,* Human Rights Watch and Federation of International Human Rights, *Leave None to Tell the Story: Genocide in Rwanda* (March 1999), at 736.

14 *See, e.g.,* Principle 8 of the Joinet Principles.

15 *See, e.g., Sierra Leone Truth and Reconciliation Commission Final Report* (2004), vol. 1, ch. 5, para. 64, discussing arguments against naming names: "The strongest argument was the lack of time and human resources to engage in the investigations necessary for naming perpetrators. The process of naming perpetrators would include notifying them of the allegations against them, providing all necessary proof and giving them sufficient time to respond." The Sierra Leonean TRC did ultimately name names in its final report.

in an attempt to create or consolidate a new consensus after political conflict, naming perpetrators may excessively strain the truce between parties or factions. Perpetrators who have agreed to a negotiated solution may attempt to disrupt the process if faced with personal assignments of responsibility.[16] Accused perpetrators may also seek to prevent publication of the final report.[17] Third, in countries with widespread participation in abuses, from East Germany's domestic spying to Sierra Leone's internecine conflict, the naming of individual perpetrators can amount to an arbitrary exercise. A truth commission will lack the time and the resources, and may in any event lack the evidence, to accurately identify *all* of those bearing responsibility for serious abuse. Naming only those individuals to whom the commission can definitively attribute responsibility may, therefore, excite legitimate resentment and perceptions of unfairness.[18] This concern can, however, be partly overcome by

---

16   In El Salvador, prior to the issuance of the truth commission's final report, the country's president led an aggressive national and international campaign to prevent the commission from naming names, occasionally hinting about a possible military coup. When the commission ultimately named several ranking officials as perpetrators, military leaders denounced the commission on national television. P. Hayner, *Unspeakable Truths: Facing the Challenge of Truth Commissions*, 2d ed. (New York: Routledge, 2002), at 115.

17   In South Africa, the ruling African National Congress (ANC) tried to block the release of the TRC's report in 1998. The report criticized the ANC for human rights abuses committed in its guerilla "training camps." *See also* "Transitional Justice in the News" (http://www.ictj.org), 15 January 2005, where it is reported that the three-year delay in the release of the Nigerian truth commission's fianl report was "primarily due to pressure from those named in the document."

18   *See, e.g.,* the *Report of the Arbour Commission of Inquiry into Certain Events at the Prison for Women in Kingston, Ontario, Canada* (1996), at xii: "During the entire process of this inquiry, and in particular in the writing of this report, I have concluded that it would not be fair for me to embark upon a personal attribution of responsibility, for many reasons. Many persons were not called to testify and had therefore no opportunity to address allegations that might have been made against them . . . Attribution of personal blame would suggest personal, rather than system, shortcomings and justifiably demoralize the staff, while offering neither redress nor hope for a better system in the future." *See also* Seils, "The Limits of Truth Commissions in the Search for Justice," at 789, where the author notes of Guatemala's truth commission, "In the circumstances of an investigation that dealt directly with over 40,000 deaths, it might be argued that the naming of certain individuals responsible for particular deaths would have verged on the arbitrary." Of El Salvador's truth commission, one commentator has argued, "I believe that the other Salvadoran commission, the truth commission, was wrong to name individual culprits. It investigated only a small subset of the ten thousand cases, and named only two of the five guerrilla commanders." José Zalaquett, cited in H. Steiner, ed., *Truth Commissions: A Comparative Assessment* (Harvard Law School Human Rights Program, 1997), at 62. The Salvadoran commission did not name any of the civilian leaders widely presumed to have a connection with the death squads that had terrorized the country.

emphasizing in the final report that the list of suspected perpetrators is not exhaustive.[19] There are still further possible reasons to desist from publishing findings of individual responsibility. For example, doing so may trigger genuine security risks for commissioners, victims, witnesses, perpetrators, and their respective family members. This was a major concern, *inter alia*, for Haiti's truth commission.[20] Alternatively, the attribution of individual responsibility may complicate the possibility of future national prosecution against a named person, especially where jury trials are a right of the defendant. A named person can easily argue that the reputation damage resulting from being named has made a fair trial impossible.[21] At least one truth commission has also rejected the idea of naming names on the basis of the commission's nonjudicial character and lack of robust investigative powers.[22]

Naming can also sometimes be tantamount to a "high-tech lynching" in the eyes of the average citizen.[23] This can cause family members, neighbors, and

---

19   This is probably essential for any truth commission that names individuals, not least because of the inevitable dearth of direct evidence against the "highest level planners and organizers of the atrocities." S. Kemp, "The Inter-Relationship between the Guatemalan Commission for Historical Clarification and the Search for Justice in National Courts," in W. A. Schabas and S. Darcy, eds., *Truth Commissions and Courts: The Tension between Criminal Justice and Truth* (Dordrecht: Kluwer, 2004), at 86. Indeed, even if a victim knows the full names of his or her direct victimizers (something that is far from certain), it is uncommon for a victim to know the names of those who, from afar, may have given the original orders.

20   Describing the decision by the truth commission in Haiti not to publish names of presumed perpetrators, Hayner writes: "The commission feared that there could be retaliation against named perpetrators, especially if the public assumed the possibility of courtroom justice was extremely remote, a reasonable conclusion given the dismal record of trials in Haiti for these kinds of crimes." *Unspeakable Truths*, above note 16, at 123. By contrast, a former commissioner of Sri Lanka's truth commission suggested that naming names can deter, rather than encourage, private vengeance. "One police sergeant who worked in an area rife with political rivalry denied his participation in abuses. He was stabbed fifty-two times on a train. If people are not permitted to name names, they may take measures in their own hands." Manouri Muttetuwegama, cited in Steiner, *Truth Commissions*, above note 18, at 62.

21   *See, e.g., Phillips v. Nova Scotia*, [1995] 2 SCR 97, in which the Supreme Court of Canada notes that adverse and excessive publicity generated by a commission of inquiry can make a fair trial by jury impossible.

22   *See* J. Zalaquett, "Balancing Ethical Imperatives and Political Constraints: The Dilemma of New Democracies Confronting Past Human Rights Violations" (1992) 43 *Hastings L.J.* 1426, at 1435, describing the approach of the Chilean TRC: "Naming culprits through an official commission appointed by the executive, which did not have subpoena powers and could not conduct trials, would have been analogous to publicly indicting individuals without due process."

23   US Supreme Court justice Clarence Thomas coined the expression "high-tech lynching." He used it to describe the judicial confirmation hearing in which a former colleague, Anita Hill, accused him of sexual improprieties.

work colleagues to spurn the named individual.[24] It might also lead to a loss of one's position in the public service, a temporary prohibition on reemployment within it, or denial of future promotions.[25] As a result of such consequences, the political will to prosecute, rather than being increased, can instead be sapped, as the public perceives that something close to justice has been meted out. In a worst-case scenario, the act of naming could also indirectly prompt a government to pass a broad amnesty that ousts the jurisdiction of courts to conduct criminal trials against named (and even unnamed) individuals.[26]

In light of the preceding considerations, the best practice is to permit, but not require, truth commissions to make findings of individual responsibility. Truth commissions that have had authority to name names pursuant to their mandates include those of El Salvador, Chad, Sri Lanka, South Africa, Grenada, Peru, Timor-Leste, Ghana, Sierra Leone, the DRC, and Liberia. Many Commonwealth commissions of inquiry frequently possess and exercise an explicit naming power too.[27] Article 2 of the new UK *Inquiries Act* is more nuanced. It provides: "(1) An inquiry panel is not to rule on, and has no power to determine, any person's civil or criminal liability. (2) But an inquiry panel is not to be inhibited in the discharge of its functions by any likelihood of liability being inferred from facts that it determines or recommendations that it makes." Several international commissions of inquiry have also had the authority or

---

24   For a discussion of the social sanctions engendered by adverse public disclosures of past abuse in the context of a truth commission, *see, e.g.,* K. Greenawalt, "Amnesty's Justice," in R. Rotberg and D. Thompson, eds., *Truth v. Justice* (Princeton, NJ: Princeton University Press, 2000), at 189–98.

25   *See* the discussion of truth commissions' contributions to justice and reform in Chapter 1, Section 4.

26   This occurred in El Salvador. "[I]t is clear that the quick passage of the amnesty legislation was in direct response to the commission's naming perpetrators in its report...": Hayner, *Unspeakable Truths*, at 93. In Guatemala, the inability of the truth commission to name names was accepted as part of the mandate "because of fears that specific accusations would lead the military to insist on an amnesty for all crimes – as had happened a few years before in neighboring El Salvador." J. D. Tepperman, "Truth and Consequences" (March/April 2002) *Foreign Affairs* 128, at 137.

27   A well-known example of a Commonwealth commission of inquiry that named names is the so-called Kahan Commission of Inquiry in Israel. Its mandate was "to investigate all the facts and factors connected with the atrocity which was carried out by a unit of the Lebanese Forces [known as Phalangists] against the civilian population of the Shatilla and Sabra camps." Regarding Ariel Sharon (Israel's defense minister at the time), the commission held: "It is our view that responsibility is to be imputed to the Minister of Defense for having disregarded the danger of acts of vengeance and bloodshed by the Phalangists against the population of the refugee camps, and having failed to take this danger into account when he decided to have the Phalangists enter the camps. In addition, responsibility is to be imputed to the Minister of Defense for not ordering appropriate measures for preventing or reducing the danger of massacre as a condition for the Phalangists' entry into the camps."

obligation to identify perpetrators.[28] Nongovernmental bodies have occasionally named names as part of their activities too.[29]

From this brief discussion, it should be clear that the practice of naming names raises a plethora of complex issues. This chapter, however, focuses only on the following: the types of evidence to be considered, the standard of proof to be applied, the modalities of prior notification, the scope of reply owed to an implicated party, the scope of a commission's obligation to investigate any reply, modes of naming in a final report, and judicial review.

While the chapter focuses on findings of individual responsibility, some of it will also be relevant to so-called institutional findings made by truth commissions (*i.e.*, findings highlighting the responsibility of institutions, rather than of individuals). The final reports of truth commissions almost always include such findings. In some contexts, attributing responsibility to institutions may represent the best available approximation to naming names, especially where a commission lacks the mandate to make findings of individual responsibility.[30] Such findings are less sensational, yet they have the virtue of focusing public attention on the institutionalized form that mass abuse invariably takes.[31]

---

28   See, e.g., *Report of the International Commission of Inquiry on Darfur to the United Nations Secretary-General* (2005). That commission ultimately decided to withhold names from the public realm. It gave three reasons for this decision in its final report: "1) the importance of the principles of due process and respect for the rights of the suspects; 2) the fact that the Commission has not been vested with investigative or prosecutorial powers; and 3) the vital need to ensure the protection of witnesses from possible harassment and intimidation" (para. 645). Instead, the commission delivered a list of names to the UN Secretary-General in a sealed file, and recommended that he forward it to competent prosecutors for use in their investigations. When the UN Security Council later referred the situation in Darfur to the ICC, the Secretary-General sent the list to the ICC. BBC News, "Court Probes Sudan 'War Crimes,'" http://www.news.bbc.co.uk, 6 June 2005.

29   For example, *see* the Brazilian *Nunca Mais* report, discussed in Chapter 1. *See also* art. 14(2) of the Charter of the Women's International War Crimes Tribunal on Japan's Military Sexual Slavery (2000): "The judgment shall state clearly whether the accused has been found guilty or not guilty of the alleged crime or whether there is insufficient evidence available ... and shall give reasons for the particular judgment."

30   The Moroccan truth commission, for example, was barred from making determinations of individual responsibility but was obligated to make findings of institutional responsibility. *See Dahir no. 1.04.42 (2004) Approving the Texts of the Fairness and Reconciliation Commission* (Morocco), arts. 6 and 9(3).

31   Writing about the Guatemalan truth commission, which made significant findings of institutional responsibility but lacked the power to attribute individual responsibility, one author writes: "[T]here is something to be said for an approach that highlighted the responsibility of the social, military and political institutions of the State rather than individuals. This is not to suggest that institutions rather than individuals are responsible. Even if the Commission had been able to go down the same road as the Salvadoran Truth Commission in naming names, it is doubtful that it would have had a significant added value for the report. By not naming names, the report was able to transmit a sense of the massive institutional nature of

Institutional findings can also be critical to providing the "big picture" in terms of overall responsibility for past abuse. For example, Guatemala's truth commission attributed ninety-three percent of the documented violations to the military or state-backed paramilitary forces, and three percent to the guerilla forces.[32]

Sometimes, however, a commission may make an institutional finding that is tantamount to an attribution of individual responsibility (*e.g.*, where the size of an institution or unit is so small that a blanket attribution of responsibility would be tantamount to an attribution of individual responsibility).[33] In such a case, the fairness considerations examined in this chapter may be directly relevant.[34] They might also be relevant where a commission attributes responsibility to a former combatant group that has become a legally registered political party.[35]

SECTION 1: TYPES OF EVIDENCE

Truth commissions invariably have broad investigative mandates empowering them to consider almost any evidence that will shed light on the events under inquiry. Commissions should use this to their advantage. At the same time, they should have a protocol for measuring the quality of the various types

---

genocide and other crimes." P. Seils, "The Limits of Truth Commissions in the Search for Justice," above note 1, at 788.

32 *See* Hayner, *Unspeakable Truths*, above note 16, at 48. Several other truth commissions have made equivalent findings.

33 Courts in most countries will, however, rarely recognize defamation suits filed by groups. The typical rule is that defamation applies only to individuals, not to collectives. *But see* "Transitional Justice in the News" (http://www.ictj.org), 31 October 2003, which reports on slander claims brought against several commissioners of the Peruvian TRC.

34 Describing the mandate of the Guatemalan truth commission, Hayner writes: "In fact, most of the restrictions built into the commission's mandate were open to interpretation; even those who signed the accord recognized that the names of the military unit, and the position of the commanding officer who was responsible, could be listed in the report, if the commissioners so chose, and that the persons' names could then be matched up by the press or nongovernmental organizations..." *Unspeakable Truths*, above note 16, at 275.

35 For example, in South Africa, the African National Congress (ANC) insisted on an oral right of reply before having responsibility attributed to it for gross violations of human rights. When this right was denied, the ANC unsuccessfully sought an injunction preventing the publication of the TRC's findings against it. A. Boraine, *A Country Unmasked* (Oxford: Oxford University Press, 2000), at 306–7, 314. As Hayner notes, "Outlining wide-scale abuses by guerilla forces, which perhaps converted into a political party at the end of the conflict, might dampen the group's credibility with the international community or its popular support at home." *Unspeakable Truths*, above note 16, at 230.

of evidence they obtain and will consider for the purpose of naming names. Decisions about the use of evidence for such purpose should be guided by three principal criteria: relevance, probative value, and reliability.[36] There are many possible definitions of each of these terms. For present purposes, each may be understood as follows:

1. *Relevance* refers to the tendency of the evidence to make more or less likely any fact that is of consequence in deciding whether to assign responsibility to an individual.[37] Evidence that does not bear on the question of responsibility – no matter how unflattering to the implicated party – should not be considered.

2. *Probative value* refers to the power the evidence has to show the truth or falsehood of a question, weighed against its prejudicial effect. For instance, a lengthy record of a divorce proceeding that refers in passing to a predilection for violence might introduce so much extraneous information about an individual that the whole record should be excluded. Evidence about the character of the alleged perpetrator, even when it is somewhat relevant to the question of responsibility, creates temptations to punish the individual for being a bad person, rather than for the act at issue in the particular inquiry.[38]

3. *Reliability* refers to the source of the evidence: Does it come from persons who are likely to know the circumstances they describe? Are the descriptions of events the person's own, or do they relate the experiences of others? If the evidence comes from documents, were the writers unbiased or partisan? Who was their intended audience? And were they aware that their writings might become the object of investigation? Questions such as these are especially relevant where an investigation follows a history of conflict in which official stories and popular counternarratives circumscribe certain events, and loyalty to one narrative or another becomes a mark of membership in a particular political or ethnic community.[39]

---

36 *Compare with* article 14 of the UN Manual on the Effective Prevention and Investigation of Extra-Legal, Arbitrary and Summary Executions (1991), which stipulates that in evaluating the evidence it acquires, a commission of inquiry should assess its "relevance, veracity, reliability and probity."

37 *See, e.g.,* R. May, *Criminal Evidence* (London: Sweet & Maxwell, 1999), at para. 1–13.

38 *See, e.g, Mahon v. Air New Zealand* [1985] Appeal Cases 808 (Privy Council), at 820–1 (finding that a person managing an investigation must base his or her findings on material having probative value).

39 Note that even where the source of the evidence has no evident bias, truth commissions should also bear in mind the ordinary errors involved in transcribing, copying, or otherwise handling information. These too can affect a document's reliability.

The primary source of evidence for most truth commissions is the information acquired through the statement-taking process.[40] But truth commissions also tend to place great reliance on external sources of evidence, not all of which will be dependable.[41] Particular reliance is often placed on the published reports of international and national human rights NGOs. These reports tend to include an abundance of relevant information, documentation, and testimony. Truth commissions in Argentina, Chile, Haiti, El Salvador, South Africa, Guatemala, Peru, and Timor-Leste, among others, placed significant reliance on files submitted to them by NGOs.

In judging how to use NGO materials – which, technically, constitute hearsay – truth commissions need to consider several factors. These include: the credibility and independence of the particular NGO, whether the report consists of first-hand testimony or analysis synthesized by the NGO's staff members, and whether the NGO's interview techniques are consistent with the commission's statement-taking standards. Where an NGO's research techniques meet or exceed the standards of a truth commission, they may be relied upon and will help reduce the cost of the commission's investigation, allowing the commission to shift resources to other areas of its work. But in no case should a truth commission name an individual solely on the basis of previous NGO work. Fairness and prudence dictate that truth commissions should at least corroborate such evidence if it is to be relied upon for the purpose of naming.[42]

---

40   *See* Chapter 3.

41   Describing the challenge of reliance on external sources of information and evidence, the member of a former UN war crimes commission noted, "[T]here were data-entry and analysis problems because sources varied significantly in terms of quality and content, in part reflecting their different data-gathering methodologies and goals. More specifically, spellings of names and locations were inconsistent due to transliteration or translation into the reporting language. Locations were, at first, difficult to pinpoint due to a lack of specific geographical information. Reports of the same incident sometimes varied in the numbers of persons involved and in the outcome described. Property damage reports rarely indicated more than the type of property affected; the location and value of property were rarely included. Numbers of victims, properties, and other variables were often reported in numerical ranges (for instance, 100–1,000). Names of victims, perpetrators, and witnesses were often altered or omitted from the reports." M. C. Bassiouni, "The Commission of Experts Established Pursuant to Security Council Resolution 780: Investigating Violations of International Humanitarian Law in the Former Yugoslavia" (1994) 5 *Crim. L. Forum* 279, at 301–2.

42   *See* N. Roht-Arriaza, "Civil Society in Processes of Accountability," in Bassiouni, *Post-Conflict Justice,* above note 1, at 104. *See also* R. McGrath, "Problems of Investigations into War Crimes and Crimes Against Humanity During and After Ethnic Conflicts," in *ibid.,* at 902, where the author describes challenges faced by the ICTY in placing reliance on NGO materials: "On the ground in the Balkans, statements given to human rights workers by witnesses were sometimes found to be inconsistent with those given by the same witnesses to investigators

Several truth commissions – including those in Haiti, El Salvador, South Africa, Guatemala, Panama, and Peru – have organized or conducted exhumations of mass graves as part of their overall investigation. The work of forensic experts can provide an additional and unique source of reliable physical evidence for a commission. At the same time, the benefits may often be outweighed by the slow process and high costs entailed by such work. Also, becoming engaged in exhumations and other forensic activity risks eclipsing other, and potentially more important, forms of data collection. Accordingly, each commission should evaluate the relative importance of this type of evidence in light of its constraints in terms of human and material resources.

Additional and important sources of evidence used by many truth commissions include:

- Police records
- Court records and trial transcripts from relevant domestic and international civil and criminal proceedings
- The testimonies, case files, and reports generated by:
  - National human rights commissions and ombudsman offices
  - National vetting and lustration bodies
  - National compensation and reparation bodies
  - Multilateral human rights monitors
  - Multilateral human rights complaint procedures
  - Other commissions of inquiry, whether national or multilateral[43]
- Local and foreign press reports
- Individual birth and death certificates
- X-rays, dental photographs, and morgue records
- Crime scene artifacts, such as bits of cloth or plastic[44]

---

of the [ICTY]. This is significant because inconsistent prior statements can be used to 'impeach', or call into question the relationship between the criminal investigators and the NGOs."

43   Surprisingly, the ICTY and the ICTR have both taken judicial notice of (*i.e.,* accepted as "fact") the content of various UN documents, including reports of international commissions of inquiry. *See* R. May and M. Wierda, *International Criminal Evidence* (Ardsley, NY: Transnational Publishers, 2003), at 136. In this author's view, such an approach is not recommended for truth commissions, let alone courts, given the significant limitations on the investigative powers of most UN bodies. A more balanced approach might be simply to accord significant weight to such documents. Taking judicial notice of "adjudicated facts," by contrast, seems perfectly reasonable, presuming that an impartial and independent tribunal adjudicated and presuming the exhaustion of appeals.

44   *Compare* this list with the Charter of the Women's International War Crimes Tribunal on Japan's Military Sexual Slavery (2000), art. 9: ". . . The following shall be admitted as evidence: (a) *documentation*: Written evidences such as official documents, affidavits/depositions,

RECOMMENDATIONS

- Truth commissions should examine and make use of as many different sources of evidence as possible before publishing findings of individual responsibility in a final report.
- Every piece of evidence – whether generated internally or externally – should attain a minimum threshold in terms of its relevance, probative value, and reliability in order to justify reliance on it for the purpose of attributing individual responsibility.
- In all other respects, Chapter 6, Section 6 ("Admissible Evidence") applies, *mutatis mutandis.*

SECTION 2: STANDARD OF PROOF

One of greatest dangers in naming names is the possibility of attributing responsibility to an innocent person, whether by nonmalicious error or by negligence. In addition to damaging the reputation of the named individual and potentially putting him or her at greater risk of prosecution or of physical violence, a few highly visible cases of erroneous naming could also do grave damage to a truth commission's public standing. Consequently, a truth commission needs to meet a rather high standard of proof before ascribing responsibility to any individual.

The difficulty is that, in some cases, a truth commission may not have much evidence on hand to prove individual responsibility. Indeed, many crimes leave no witnesses. Alternatively, the only proof of a crime may be the testimony of a single victim, as in a case of sexual assault or prison torture.

While a single source may in some cases be sufficient as a basis for a truth commission to name names – for example, where the source is a compelling "statement against interest"[45] – such cases will be rare. Instead, it is always preferable for a truth commission to rely on *more than one* direct and reliable source for purposes of attributing individual responsibility.[46] Corroborating the report of a criminal act by another source enhances fairness and helps ensure

---

signed statements, diaries, letters/notes or other documents, experts' views, photos and other visual documents; (b) *personal evidence*: Written or oral testimonies of survivors and witnesses, statements of expert witnesses; and (c) *material evidence*: Other relevant physical and material evidence."

45   A statement against interest may come directly from the perpetrator. It may, alternatively, come from a rape victim who publicly confesses to having been raped even though it is sure to lead to significant social shame for the victim, his or her family, and his or her community.

46   This is especially important in light of recent research on the prevalence of errors and distortions in memory input and output. *See, e.g.*, E. Loftus, *Eyewitness Testimony* (Cambridge,

greater accuracy, thus minimizing the risk of naming innocent individuals as perpetrators.[47] It is true that there is no formal requirement of corroboration in modern international criminal law.[48] Indeed, international criminal tribunals have convicted defendants on the basis of a single piece of evidence.[49] But corroboration is more important for truth commissions, because they do not offer the same wide array of procedural safeguards as a criminal trial does.

El Salvador's truth commission required that each factual finding in support of a decision to name a perpetrator should be based on two credible and independent sources.[50] The commission created three categories to measure the strength of its evidence: "overwhelming evidence," "substantial evidence," and "sufficient evidence." The commission did not assign individual responsibility where the evidence was merely "sufficient." In cases with substantial or overwhelming evidence, the commission named the parties on the premise that the purpose of the commission was to ensure that the truth was not only discovered but also made known.[51] The requirement of two sources reflected the commission's concern that implicated persons had not had the opportunity to confront their accusers; indeed, pursuant to its terms of reference, all testimony

---

MA: Harvard University Press, 1996); D. Schacter, *Memory Distortion* (Cambridge, MA: Harvard University Press, 1997).

47 *See* D. Orentlicher, "Updated Set of Principles for the Protection and Promotion of Human Rights through Action to Combat Impunity," UN doc. E/CN.4/2005/102/Add.1, Principle 9(a): "The commission must try to corroborate information implicating individuals before they are named publicly." *Recall also* article 14 of the UN Manual on the Effective Prevention and Investigation of Extra-Legal, Arbitrary and Summary Executions (1991), which provides that a commission of inquiry should seek to corroborate all evidence – especially hearsay evidence, *in camera* testimony, and testimony not tested by cross-examination – failing which it may accord the evidence less weight.

48 *See* May and Wierda, *International Criminal Evidence*, above note 43, at 120–1.

49 The ICTR, for example, held that it could make a ruling on the basis of a single testimony if it found that testimony to be relevant and credible. *See, e.g., Prosecutor v. Musema*, Case no. ICTR-96-13-T, at para. 43.

50 The requirement of two credible and independent sources is a standard commonly applied in civil law systems. *See, e.g., Prosecutor v. Jean-Paul Akayesu*, Case no. ICTR-96-4-T (2 September 1998), at 132. *See also* Joinet Principles, UN doc. E/CN.4/Sub.2/1996/18 (1996). Principle 8 provides that if a commission of inquiry intends to publicly attribute individual responsibility for human rights violations, its information should be corroborated by "at least" two sources.

51 *See From Madness to Hope: The Twelve-Year War in El Salvador: Report of the Commission on the Truth for El Salvador*, UN doc. S/25500, annex, 1993. Taking its cue from the Salvadoran model, the Sierra Leonean TRC made findings of individual responsibility only where it was "satisfied that the information or evidence at its disposal pointed overwhelmingly to a certain conclusion." *Sierra Leone Truth and Reconciliation Commission Final Report* (2004), vol. 2, ch. 2, at para. 5.

received by the commission was private and the identities of all witnesses were kept confidential. The use of two sources was, therefore, a compromise measure to ensure greater accuracy.[52]

The South African TRC approached the issue somewhat differently. When the identities of the individuals and the institutions involved were unclear, or when the commission could not locate the individual to give him or her prior notice, it attributed neither individual nor institutional responsibility. Where the institution's responsibility could be verified, but not that of the individual, the commission attributed institutional responsibility only. Finally, where there was sufficient evidence to make a finding of individual and institutional responsibility on the balance of probabilities,[53] and where the individuals in question received reasonable prior notification of the basis for the commission's intended finding, the commission attributed both individual and institutional responsibility.[54] Unlike El Salvador's truth commission, however, the TRC required only one reliable source, both for corroborating victims' accounts and for determining individual responsibility.[55]

Haiti's truth commission named perpetrators in a confidential report delivered to the president, with a recommendation to make the list public only after the initiation of prosecutions against named individuals.[56] The commission

---

52   In the cover letter to its final report to the UN Secretary-General, the commission noted that it expected there to be accusations of bias and error regarding its findings. It anticipated that its sources of evidence would be considered less trustworthy than "those which are subjected to the normal judicial tests for determining the truth and to other related requirements of due process of law," including cross-examination. In this respect, the commission stated that it felt a special responsibility "to take all possible steps to ensure the reliability of the evidence used to arrive at a finding . . . and insisted on verifying, substantiating and reviewing all statements of facts, checking them against a large number of sources whose veracity had already been established." Copy of letter on file with the author.

53   The balance of probabilities standard is also sometimes referred to as the "preponderance of evidence" standard. It means that the existence (or truth) concerning a particular fact is more probable than its nonexistence. In most common law jurisdictions, coroners use the balance of probabilities standard to make findings of "unlawful killing." P. Matthews, *Jervis on Coroners*, 12th ed. (London: Sweet & Maxwell, 2002), at 314.

54   *See Truth and Reconciliation Commission of South Africa Report* (1998), vol. 1, ch. 4, para. 157, available at http://www.polity.org/za/govdocs/commisssions/ 1998/trc/1chap4.htm. The Sierra Leonean TRC also applied a standard "akin to the preponderance or balance of probabilities." *Sierra Leone Truth and Reconciliation Commission Final Report* (2004), vol. 2, ch. 2, at para. 7.

55   Hayner, *Unspeakable Truths*, above note 16, at 130.

56   *Ibid.*, at 67. The Peruvian TRC, for certain files, took the exact opposite approach: "The commission [turned] over a number of cases to the attorney general's office for prosecution. It did not name the suspected perpetrators, but recommended that their names be made public if Peru's attorney general *fails* to carry out prompt and exhaustive investigations of the cases." (Emphasis added.) Human Rights Watch, "Peru – Prosecutions Should Follow Truth

initially considered assigning responsibility only to individuals whose names appeared in more than twenty victim statements, but it ended up using the same standard employed by El Salvador's truth commission.[57]

The recent International Commission of Inquiry on Darfur, which was authorized to name names, took a different approach. The relevant part of its final report explains:

In view of the limitations inherent in its powers, the Commission decided that it could not comply with the standards normally adopted by criminal courts (proof of facts beyond a reasonable doubt), or with that used by international prosecutors and judges for the purpose of confirming indictments (that there must be a *prima facie* case). It concluded that the most appropriate standard was that requiring a reliable body of material consistent with other verified circumstances, which tends to show that a person may reasonably be suspected of being involved in the commission of a crime.[58]

These are only a few examples. In the future, truth commissions may adopt other standards. For example, the civil law magistrate's intimate conviction (*intime conviction*) standard, the common law prosecutor's requirement of establishing a *prima facie* case, or the ICC prosecutor's preindictment requirement of establishing "substantial grounds" of the defendant's criminal responsibility[59] may be suitable alternative standards to apply. The substantive distinction between the balance of probabilities standard and any of these other standards is, in any case, difficult to discern. For simplicity's sake, the present recommendation is to employ the balance of probabilities standard, or close functional equivalents thereof. Certainly there is no cause to employ the common law's criminal trial standard of proof beyond a reasonable doubt. The consequences of criminal conviction, in general, far exceed the consequences of being named in a commission's final report.

Commission Report," 28 August 2003, http://www.hrw.org. In total, the TRC forwarded 47 case files to domestic prosecutors, which involved a total of approximately 400 perpetrators and 3,500 victims. Prosecutions are underway in several of these cases.

57 *See* art. 16 of the Haitian truth commission's internal regulations. The so-called all-islands commission in Sri Lanka, which succeeded the three regional commissions that comprised Sri Lanka's truth commission, also submitted a confidential list of "names of individuals in respect of whom there is credible material indicative of their responsibility for disappearances of certain persons." *Final Report of the Commission of Inquiry into Involuntary Removal and Disappearance of Certain Persons (All Island)*, ch. 3, section 1.

58 *Report of the International Commission of Inquiry on Darfur to the United Nations Secretary-General* (2005), at para. 15.

59 Rome Statute art. 61(5), (7).

RECOMMENDATIONS

- To maximize fairness and accuracy, it is preferable to rely on more than one direct and credible source of evidence before attributing individual responsibility in a final report. In some cases it may, however, be acceptable to rely on a single direct and reliable source.
- The common law's balance of probabilities standard, or something akin to it, is an appropriate minimum standard for a truth commission to employ in making any attribution of individual responsibility. A higher standard should, however, be applied where all or most of the investigation is conducted confidentially, or where reasonable notice and an opportunity to reply are not provided, or where the potential consequences for the named person are especially dire.

SECTION 3: NOTIFICATION OF INTENT TO NAME: TIMING, METHOD, AND CONTENT

Before publishing its final report, a truth commission should provide notice to all those against whom it intends to attribute individual responsibility for past violations. As previously observed, such an attribution can have profound consequences.[60] If a truth commission has followed transparent procedures and is regarded as an impartial body, the public may view the attribution as equivalent to a court conviction. Also, if the commission enjoys legal immunity for the contents of its final report, a named person will be unable to seek a remedy in defamation. The protection against false condemnation that prior notice provides is, therefore, essential. One anecdote may be sufficient to make the point. Describing the notification process used by the South African TRC prior to naming suspected perpetrators, commissioner Richard Lyster explained, "If the written response from the (alleged) perpetrator did contain material or information which tended to change the contemplated finding, this was done, and in a number of instances, the person's name was dropped from the list of perpetrators."[61]

Notice to implicated individuals is often a time-intensive activity for a truth commission. Prior notice comprises several stages: first, locating the

---

60 It may be recalled from Chapter 2, Section 1, that the applicability of natural justice (which includes the right of reply) depends on the severity of the possible consequences attendant to the proceeding at issue.

61 Cited in Hayner, *Unspeakable Truths*, above note 16, at 126. The Peruvian TRC, likewise, abandoned some of its planned findings of individual responsibility on account of exculpatory evidence given by persons in the course of exercising their right of reply.

individual; second, preparing the documents and delivering the notice; and third, processing the responses of the individual.[62]

A truth commission may sometimes conclude that it should name perpetrators without prior notice. The commission's decision may be prompted by a severe lack of resources, or by the impossibility of locating perpetrators who have gone into hiding or left the country. It may also be motivated by a concern that such notice could generate security risks for victims or commission members,[63] or alternatively end up stalling or impeding the release of the final report.[64] Yet an absence of notice will increase the risk of condemning innocent individuals and endanger the commission's legitimacy. Thus, it is preferable that truth commissions not name an individual unless there has been a reasonable effort to provide notice. Indeed, a commission should not attribute individual responsibility where such an effort is not genuinely and manifestly made.

Surprisingly, no truth commission mandate has articulated an obligation to provide, or attempt to provide, prior notice to the suspected perpetrators a commission intends to name in a public final report. There is, however, jurisprudence on the subject. The South African Appellate Division Court held that where the TRC "contemplated making a finding against a person to their detriment in the report, the person would need to be notified of the decision contemplated as well as afforded the opportunity to make written representations to the Commission."[65] Unable to comply with this requirement in some cases, the TRC was compelled to abandon a significant number of positive findings of individual responsibility.[66] Future truth commission sponsors would do well to study the South African case. They may also examine Commonwealth commission of inquiry statutes for appropriate standards,[67] as well as the vast jurisprudence on the *audi alteram* principle discussed in Chapter 2.

---

62   *See* Section 5 below, "Investigation of Replies."

63   This was a concern of the truth commission in Haiti. Hayner, *Unspeakable Truths*, above note 16, at 122 3.

64   *See, e.g.,* "Transitional Justice in the News", http://www.ictj.org, 31 January 2003: "The [South African] Truth and Reconciliation Commission has agreed to amend some sections of its final report that blamed the Inkatha Freedom Party (IFP) for human rights abuses during the final years of apartheid. A court challenge by the IFP has delayed the publication of the report, and an out-of-court settlement now clears the way for the report's publication."

65   *See Truth and Reconciliation Commission of South Africa Report* (1998), vol. 1, ch. 7, Legal Challenges, at para. 55.

66   P. van Zyl, "Unfinished Business: The Truth and Reconciliation Commission's Contribution to Justice in Post-Apartheid South Africa," in Bassiouni, *Post-Conflict Justice*, above note 1, at 751. Former TRC Deputy Chairperson Alex Boraine notes that more than 400 notices were sent out in total. *A Country Unmasked*, above note 35, at 301–2.

67   *See, e.g.,* Ontario *Public Inquiries Act*, RSO 1990, as amended, s. 5 (2): "No finding of misconduct on the part of any person shall be made against the person in any report of a

Timing of notification

A truth commission's notice to an implicated individual should provide ample opportunity for him or her to respond, even if this slows down the work of the commission. Five criteria should influence the timing of the notice that a truth commission should give to those it intends to name:

1. *The amount of time the commission will require to prepare the notice.* In some cases, it could take weeks to prepare a single notice. This reality must be borne in mind if prior notice is to be delivered in a timely manner.

2. *The amount of time the commission will require to find the implicated party.* It is not at all uncommon to experience difficulty in tracking down presumed perpetrators, some of whom may have relocated within or outside of the country for perfectly ordinary reasons, others of whom may have done so precisely in order not to be found.

3. *The amount of time the individual will need to respond to the allegations.* Some implicated persons may have participated at earlier stages in an investigation, whether in the context of a public hearing or in the course of making a private statement to the commission. If so, less time may be needed for the individual to respond to the truth commission's evidence. If not, the commission should provide reasonable additional time to respond, as determined by the amount and complexity of the evidence in the case.

4. *The amount of time the truth commission requires for reviewing the individual's response to the allegations.* The commission will have to set aside sufficient time to review the individual's reply. It should not assume that a *pro forma* review will suffice. The implicated individual may provide previously unknown evidence that the truth commission will need to consider, and his or her reply could potentially be quite lengthy and complex. The choice to abandon or reformulate a finding could take significant time for a commission to decide.

5. *The likelihood that the individual will publicly release the truth commission's preliminary findings.* In some cases, suspected perpetrators have denounced the commission's work on learning that they were to be named. This eventuality raises serious concerns for a commission intent on meeting its reporting deadline. Also, if the individual is a powerful public figure, the denunciation may undermine the reception of the commission's final report. The individual could even bring a legal

---

commission after an inquiry unless that person had reasonable notice of the substance of the alleged misconduct . . ."

action to enjoin the commission from releasing its report or naming him or her in it.[68] Where such scenarios are foreseeable, a commission may decide to forego written notice altogether and instead simply invite the alleged perpetrator to meet and discuss the allegations in the days before the commission finalizes its report.

In the end, the best practice may be to give notice early (and often). Still, as the Supreme Court of Canada observed in the case of a federal inquiry into a public health scandal, "Although the notices should be given as soon as it is feasible, it is unreasonable to insist that the notice of misconduct must always be given early. There will be some inquiries, such as this one, where the Commissioner cannot know what the findings may be until the end or very late in the process... The timing of notices will always depend upon the circumstances. Where the evidence is extensive and complex, it may be impossible to give the notices before the end of the hearings. In other situations, where the issue is more straightforward, it may be possible to give notice of potential findings of misconduct early in the process."[69]

Method of delivery of notification

The recommendations and analysis of Chapter 6, Section 2 (on the method of notifying an implicated individual of a planned public hearing) apply, *mutatis mutandis.*

Content of notification

The recommendations and analysis of Chapter 6, Section 2 (on the content of a truth commission's notice of a planned public hearing to an implicated individual) apply, *mutatis mutandis.*

RECOMMENDATIONS

* Before publishing findings of individual responsibility in a final report, a truth commission should make a reasonable effort to provide

---

68   For example, F. W. de Klerk successfully enjoined the South African TRC from naming him in its October 1998 report. *See* Hayner, *Unspeakable Truths*, above note 16, at 44. "The outcome of the court action taken by De Klerk was that the Commission had to remove in one way or another the page containing its findings on the former State President... All copies of Volume 5 were removed and the so-called 'finding page' excised and reprinted." Boraine, *A Country Unmasked*, above note 35, at 304.

69   *Canada (Attorney General) v. Canada (Commission of Inquiry on the Blood System)*, [1997] 3 S.C.R. 440, 1997 CanLII 323 (S.C.C.), at para. 69–70.

notice to all those it intends to name. A commission should not attribute individual responsibility in the absence of such effort.

- Five criteria should influence the timing of any such notice: (1) the amount of time the commission will require to prepare the notice, (2) the amount of time the commission will require to find the implicated party, (3) the amount of time the individual will need to respond to the allegations, (4) the amount of time the commission will require to consider the individual's reply, and (5) the risk that the individual will publicly release the truth commission's provisional finding.
- In all other respects, the recommendations of Chapter 6, Section 2 ("Notification to Implicated Persons: Timing, Method, and Content") apply, *mutatis mutandis.*

SECTION 4: NATURE AND SCOPE OF THE RIGHT OF REPLY

An individual who may be named by a truth commission as responsible for specific offenses should have the opportunity to reply to the allegations before publication of the commission's findings.[70] Indeed, prior notice of intent to name would be pointless if the alleged perpetrator did not have the opportunity to respond to the substance of the charges.

The form of reply may be flexible, so long as it permits the implicated person an opportunity to present the substance of his or her defense. In general, it is preferable for individuals to be required to provide their replies in writing.[71] A commission should also be entitled to place reasonable limits on the length of the reply.[72] The implicated individual should not be entitled to a private meeting with the commission except at its reasonable discretion.[73]

---

70 *See, e.g., Fayed v. UK,* above note 8, at para. 78: "In arriving at their findings of fact or conclusions, the inspectors were under a duty to act fairly and to give anyone whom they proposed to criticise in their report a fair opportunity to answer the allegations against them. Although the investigation was administrative and not judicial in nature, the Inspectors were bound by what are known under English law as 'the rules of natural justice.'"

71 The truth commission in Ghana permitted written replies and ensured the assistance of counsel of choice in preparing such replies. *See Ghana National Reconciliation Commission Final Report* (2004), vol. 2, at 2.3.3.4.1. *See also* Principle 8 of the Joinet Principles, discussed in Part I. It provides: "[T]he person implicated shall have the opportunity to make a statement setting out his or her version of the facts or . . . to submit a document equivalent to a right of reply for inclusion in the file."

72 F. W. de Klerk filed a 2,000-page reply to the commission as part of a lawsuit brought against the South African TRC the day before it issued its 1998 report. Hayner, *Unspeakable Truths,* above note 16, at 127.

73 *See, e.g.,* article 30(2) of the *Promotion of National Unity and Reconciliation Act,* 1995 (South Africa), which provides: "If during any investigation by or any hearing before the

An implicated party should not be allowed to impede a truth commission process by refusing to reply to charges. Consequently, the reply should be voluntary and deemed to be waived by non-response.[74] This, however, presumes that the individual has received reasonable notice. It would clearly be improper for a commission to provide inadequate notice to an individual, and then to deem his or her right of reply as waived by non-response.

Finally, an implicated individual should have the right, at law, to prevent a commission from adversely naming him or her in a final report, where the individual can demonstrate that notice was inadequate or that his or her rights were otherwise violated by the commission's process.[75]

RECOMMENDATIONS

- An individual to whom a truth commission intends to attribute responsibility in a final report should have a prior opportunity to reply to the adverse evidence and allegations.
- The implicated person should be entitled to provide the commission with a written statement, together with any contradictory or exculpatory evidence that he or she can adduce. The implicated party should not be entitled to a private meeting with the commission except at its reasonable discretion and in accordance with established criteria.
- The implicated individual's reply should be voluntary and waived by silence, provided that a commission may not draw any adverse inference from a failure to reply.

Commission – (b) the Commission contemplates making a decision which may be to the detriment of a person who has been implicated . . . shall if such person is available . . . afford him or her an opportunity to submit representations to the Commission within a specified time with regard to the matter under consideration *or* to give evidence at a hearing of the Commission." It is noteworthy that various administrative proceedings with potentially worse consequences than being named (*e.g.*, parole revocation by a parole board, deportation by an immigration board, denial of a license to work by a regulatory agency) do not require oral hearings. *See* D. Mullan, *Administrative Law* (Toronto. Irwin Law, 2001), at 268–75.

74 *See, e.g.*, art. 39 of the Inter-American Commission on Human Rights Rules of Procedure (2002): "The facts alleged in the petition, the pertinent parts of which have been transmitted to the State in question, shall be presumed to be true if the State has not provided responsive information during the maximum period set by the Commission under the provisions of Article 38 of these Rules of Procedure, as long as other evidence does not lead to a different conclusion."

75 In some instances, there may also be reasonable grounds to believe that the commission is likely to exceed its jurisdiction. *See, e.g.*, M. J. Trebilcock and L. Austin, "The Limits of the Full Court Press: Of Blood and Mergers" (1998) 48 *Univ. of Toronto L.J.* 1. *See also* section 7 below.

- The implicated person should have the right to contest and possibly enjoin a commission from publicly attributing responsibility to him or her in a final report, where it can be demonstrated that notice was inadequate or that his or her rights were otherwise violated by the commission's process.

SECTION 5: INVESTIGATION OF REPLIES

A truth commission should enjoy considerable discretion in its treatment of replies. It should not, for example, have to pursue every new lead or source of information.[76] It should, however, consider all credible contradictory or exculpatory evidence presented to it. Indeed, exculpatory evidence must receive the same attention as incriminating evidence.

Commissions should follow a consistent procedure toward replies. A commission should weigh at least three factors in setting its policy: the foreseeable consequences of being named in the final report, the weight of the evidence it has on hand in assigning responsibility, and the extent of its resources (bearing in mind the costs associated with investigation). Where the potential consequences of being named are grave, the commission should conduct much more than a cursory review.[77] Where the potential consequences are less dire, the scope of an investigation may be narrower. Similarly, where the commission's existing evidence is substantial and consistently points in one direction, it can more easily justify a cursory investigation. Where its evidence is less substantial or consistent, additional investigation should be undertaken.

It is likely that no commission would opt to investigate all replies, since some are certain to be frivolous. Where feasible, however, a commission should try to assess, by investigation, the veracity of the information contained in credible replies. It must be evenhanded, however, in its investigation of replies. All case files with roughly the same balance of evidence for and against them should receive roughly the same consideration from the commission.

---

76   Describing a coroner's duty of investigation, a leading authority on the subject writes: "[I]t is for him to decide how best to allocate his limited resources . . . he is not to be criticized in a particular case if he does not pursue every possible source of information or personally peruse every document available, provided that he has made reasonable and appropriate efforts to obtain the information and evidence which he reasonably considers that he needs for the inquest in question." Matthews, *Jervis on Coroners*, above note 53, at 226.

77   As previously noted, implicated parties may have objective reason to fear private vengeance in the event of being named in a commission's final report. This is a matter that could be raised in an individual reply, and it should not be dismissed without some assessment of the actual level of risk to the individual.

RECOMMENDATIONS

- A truth commission has an obligation to investigate any new and credible contradictory or exculpatory evidence received from an implicated individual prior to publicly attributing responsibility to him or her in a final report.
- A commission should weigh at least three factors in setting its policy for consideration of replies: (1) the foreseeable consequences of being named in the final report, (2) the weight of the evidence it has on hand in assigning responsibility, and (3) the extent of its resources.
- All case files with roughly the same balance of evidence for and against them should receive roughly the same consideration from a commission.

SECTION 6: MODE OF NAMING IN A FINAL REPORT

The mode of naming an individual perpetrator can be either *express* or *implied*, or a combination thereof. The first mode describes an approach whereby a truth commission, speaking in its own voice, makes a direct finding of individual responsibility, whether for acts or for omissions.[78] The finding can be made public in a final report, as was the case with truth commissions such as those of El Salvador, Chad (which went so far as to include photos of the named individuals), South Africa, Sierra Leone, and Peru. Alternatively, the findings can be communicated in a more confidential manner by, for example, submitting them in confidence to the commission's sponsor, as was done by the truth commissions in Argentina, Haiti, and Morocco.

The second mode of naming (*i.e.*, implied naming) is where a truth commission provides a basis for the public to infer the responsibility of a given perpetrator. This is especially prevalent among truth commissions that lack the explicit power to publish findings of individual responsibility.[79] For example,

---

78   See, e.g., *Sierra Leone Truth and Reconciliation Commission Final Report* (2004), vol. 2, ch. ?, at para. 279: "Nonetheless, the Commission finds that the War Council and the President were fully and timeously apprised of events that were taking place on the ground in Sierra Leone during their period in exile. They did not act to stop the violations being carried out by CDF elements nor did they speak out against them. As such, they are held responsible for the acts of their agents on the ground."

79   Many truth commissions – especially in Latin America – have been expressly forbidden to name names. See, e.g., the mandate of the Chile TRC, which provides that the commission "will not have the power to take a position on whether particular individuals are legally responsible for the events that it is considering." Article 2 of the *Decree Establishing the National Commission on Truth and Reconciliation*, Supreme Decree no. 355, 1990 (Chile), reprinted in N. Kritz, ed., *Transitional Justice: How Emerging Democracies Reckon with Former*

in its final report, Argentina's truth commission published unedited witness transcripts in which alleged perpetrators were identified by name. Generally this practice is inadvisable, because it blurs the distinction between the commission's findings of responsibility and the mere accusation. Where a commission takes this step, it should be explicit that the quoted testimony is *not a finding* of the commission.[80] It should also indicate whether the testimony has been corroborated to any degree; mere quoting of witnesses should not supplant the truth commission's independent assessment of the witnesses' accounts. Finally, a commission should only ever publish quotations from testimony that it considers highly reliable.

Another way to imply individual responsibility is to assign collective responsibility in a manner that taints specific individuals. For example, the truth commission in Chile did not name individuals as responsible for crimes, but instead provided detailed information about certain groups, such as specific military units or institutions. It left it to readers to make any inference about the responsibility of individuals whom they might know to be members of a given group or unit. The commission stated that despite its conclusions about collective bodies, it "had not presumed that government agents were involved in the deaths of individuals."[81] Other commissions have set out specific crimes and then, alongside such crimes, listed the individuals or units who, at the relevant time, were in charge of the area where the crimes occurred.[82] This approach serves as an indirect way of naming both low-level perpetrators and those who have "command" or "superior" responsibility for crimes.[83] In some

---

Regimes (Washington, DC: US Institute for Peace Press, 1995), vol. 3, at 104. *See also* the Agreement on the Establishment of the Commission to Clarify Past Human Rights Violations and Acts of Violence That Have Caused the Guatemalan Population to Suffer, UN doc. A/48/954/S/1994/751, annex II (1994): "The Commission shall not attribute responsibility to any individual in its work, recommendations and report nor shall these have any judicial aim or effect."

80   To its credit, the truth commission in Argentina made this point in its final report. Hayner, *Unspeakable Truths*, above note 16, at 111.

81   *Report of the Chilean National Commission on Truth and Reconciliation*, trans. P. E. Berryman, 2 vols. (Notre Dame, IN: University of Notre Dame Press, 1993). Original report published in 1991.

82   For example, the truth commissions in Peru and Sierra Leone did this in their respective final reports. *See, e.g., Sierra Leone Truth and Reconciliation Commission Final Report* (2004), vol. 1, Introduction, para. 34: "At the end of each section addressing the role played by a particular government, faction or group, the names and positions of persons found to have been its key office-holders are listed. In circumstances where a finding pertained to the actions of the government, faction or group in question, those office-holders were by implication held responsible."

83   The Rome Statute defines such responsibility as follows: "*(a)*_ A military commander or person effectively acting as a military commander shall be criminally responsible for crimes within the jurisdiction of the Court committed by forces under his or her effective command

contexts, this approach may represent the best available approximation of naming. It may also be defended on the basis that the information is, in any case, part of the public domain (*i.e.*, the commission is not, *per se*, saying anything unknowable). Yet it risks assigning guilt by association, sometimes to individuals who were connected with criminal institutions but did not themselves behave criminally, or at least cannot be proved to have done so.

Ultimately, the decision as to which mode of naming is most appropriate and fair – whether express or implied – will be determined by a commission's mandate, as well as by the many other considerations discussed in this book. Generally, however, express naming should be preferred over implied naming when a mandate so permits. If there is not sufficient evidence for a truth commission to ground an express finding of culpability, then it should preferably avoid impeaching individual reputations by subtle implications or insinuations.[84]

The mode of publication of a finding of individual responsibilty involves still other considerations. First, the precise nature of the evidence against each named individual in respect of each attributed crime should be made explicit in the final report.[85] In addition, a truth commission should distinguish

---

and control, or effective authority and control as the case may be, as a result of his or her failure to exercise control properly over such forces, where: (i) That military commander or person either knew or, owing to the circumstances at the time, should have known that the forces were committing or about to commit such crimes; and (ii) That military commander or person failed to take all necessary and reasonable measures within his or her power to prevent or repress their commission or to submit the matter to the competent authorities for investigation and prosecution. *(b)* With respect to superior and subordinate relationships not described in paragraph (a), a superior shall be criminally responsible for crimes within the jurisdiction of the Court committed by subordinates under his or her effective authority and control, as a result of his or her failure to exercise control properly over such subordinates, where: (i) The superior either knew, or consciously disregarded information which clearly indicated, that the subordinates were committing or about to commit such crimes; (ii) The crimes concerned activities that were within the effective responsibility and control of the superior; and (iii) The superior failed to take all necessary and reasonable measures within his or her power to prevent or repress their commission or to submit the matter to the competent authorities for investigation and prosecution."

84 It would, however, be reasonable for a truth commission to issue a general attribution of responsibility to the (unnamed) "leadership" of a large public institution such as the army. The truth commission in Guatemala, among others, made such a finding in its final report. *See Memoria del Silencio: Informe de la Comisión para el Esclarecimiento Histórico de Guatemala* (1999) and *Peru Truth and Reconciliation Commission Final Report* (2003), http://www.cverdad.org.pe/ingles/ifinal.

85 *Recall* Principle 17 of the Principles on the Effective Prevention and Investigation of Extra-Legal, Arbitrary and Summary Executions (1989), UN doc. E/1989/89, which provides that a commission of inquiry's final report must describe "specific events that were found to have occurred and the evidence upon which such findings were based . . ." *See also* the Principles

carefully among levels and types of responsibility. For example, it should clarify whether the named individual ordered, carried out, or incited specific abuses.[86] Conflating different types of responsibility fails the standard of specificity to which a truth commission should aspire in naming names.[87] An imprecise assignment of responsibility also reduces a commission's integrity as a finder of fact, which may compromise its perceived legitimacy. It could risk injuring the legitimate reputation rights of alleged perpetrators too, including by complicating their ability to seek judicial review.[88] Admittedly, the nature of the crimes in question may sometimes make it difficult to be precise. However, as a general rule, a commission's assignment of individual responsibility – if there is to be one – should be at least as specific as a criminal indictment.[89]

---

on the Effective Investigation and Documentation of Torture and Other Cruel, Inhuman or Degrading Treatment or Punishment, GA res. 55/89 (2000), Principle 5(b). More generally, *see* discussion in Chapter 2, Section 2, concerning the duty to give reasons (as a component of natural justice).

86   For various forms of criminal responsibility or participation, *see, e.g.,* art. 25(3) of the Rome Statute: "In accordance with this Statute, a person shall be criminally responsible and liable for punishment for a crime within the jurisdiction of the Court if that person: (a) *Commits* such a crime, whether as an individual, jointly with another or through another person, regardless of whether that other person is criminally responsible; (b) *Orders, solicits or induces* the commission of such a crime which in fact occurs or is attempted; (c) For the purpose of facilitating the commission of such a crime, *aids, abets or otherwise assists* in its commission or its attempted commission, including providing the means for its commission; (d) *In any other way contributes* to the commission or attempted commission of such a crime by a group of persons acting *with a common purpose.* Such contribution shall be intentional and shall either: (i) Be made with the aim of furthering the criminal activity or criminal purpose of the group, where such activity or purpose involves the commission of a crime within the jurisdiction of the Court; or (ii) Be made in the knowledge of the intention of the group to commit the crime; (e) In respect of the crime of genocide, directly and publicly *incites others to commit* genocide; (f) *Attempts to commit* such a crime by taking action that commences its execution by means of a substantial step, but the crime does not occur because of circumstances independent of the person's intentions. However, a person who abandons the effort to commit the crime or otherwise prevents the completion of the crime shall not be liable for punishment under this Statute for the attempt to commit that crime if that person completely and voluntarily gave up the criminal purpose." (Emphasis added.)

87   A regrettable example comes from Sierra Leone. In the TRC's final report, it made the following imprecise finding about leaders mentioned by name elsewhere in the report: "The Commission finds the leadership of the RUF, the AFRC, the SLA and the CDF to be responsible for *either* authorizing or instigating human rights violations against civilians; *alternatively* by failing to stop such practices or to speak out against them; *and* for failing to acknowledge the atrocities committed by their followers or members." (Emphasis added.) *Sierra Leone Truth and Reconciliation Commission Final Report* (2004), vol. 2, ch. 2, para. 27.

88   *See* Section 7 below.

89   This does not, of course, mean that the finding should be *phrased* or *framed* as an indictment – only that it should use the same level of precision. Indeed, it would be highly problematic for an investigative body such as a truth commission to present anything that too closely

Regarding the treatment of an implicated party's replies, there is no obligation for a commission to publish his or her version of the facts. Part of the purpose of a truth commission is to establish a clear factual record around which a national consensus can emerge. A report representing multiple, conflicting claims about its core topic undermines one of the commission's essential functions. There is really no need for such a tacked-on gesture at fairness. If the commission is not sure of its facts, then it should not publish a finding of individual responsibility in the first place.

No matter what approach it takes, a truth commission that names individuals should expect to confront accusations of arbitrariness and unfairness. Like the exercise of prosecutorial discretion in a context of mass abuse, the exercise of naming individual culprits is necessarily imperfect: no prosecutor or truth commission can punish or shame *all* wrongdoers, and accordingly the final list of offenders will tend to reflect not so much the worst offenders, but rather the worst of those caught. Consequently, commissions might consider providing a disclaimer in their reports to the effect that (1) there is no claim to have named every perpetrator, and (2) not being named does not prove innocence.

In characterizing the responsibility of specific individuals, a commission should clearly and prominently declare that its attributions of individual responsibility constitute findings of fact, not of law, and that only a court – with its superior evidentiary and procedural safeguards – can make a definitive determination of criminal or civil culpability.[90] This is especially important for truth commissions required to investigate violations that are defined crimes in international or domestic law, such as "torture" or "genocide." In such circumstances, the line between a finding of fact and a finding of law quickly becomes blurred and a truth commission can, in the public mind, be equated to a formally constituted court or jury. For this reason, a truth commission should generally avoid the *legal* characterization of offenses.[91]

---

resembled a criminal indictment. On indictments by international criminal tribunals, *see* May and Wierda, *International Criminal Evidence*, above note 43, at 42–3.

90　*See, e.g., Sierra Leone Truth and Reconciliation Commission Final Report* (2004), vol. 2, ch. 2, at para. 7: "The Commission did not make findings on questions of innocence or guilt. It made factual findings in relation to responsibility and accountability." *See also* Human Rights Watch and Federation of International Human Rights, *Leave None to Tell the Story,* above note 13, at 28: "We understand the limitations of even the most careful investigative techniques and recognize that despite our best efforts this work may contain errors. We stress that this work does not and is not meant to establish 'judicial truth' as to the guilt or innocence of any person, which is the responsibility of legally established national and international tribunals." The value of such a principle is, however, less apparent in contexts where the available national courts are very weak or corrupt, and where there is no available recourse to an international or mixed criminal tribunal.

91　*See, e.g., Re Nelles and Grange* (1984), 46 OR (2d) 210 (Ontario Court of Appeal), where Grange J. held that a commission's finding of a "non-accidental" lethal dosage to a patient

Instead, it might simply and neutrally summarize the evidence against the particular individual.[92]

Where its mandate covers defined international crimes – thus clouding the distinction between findings of fact and of law – a truth commission might consider setting out the legal elements of the crimes alongside the evidence against the named individual, while leaving to the public, and to prosecutors who may later seek an indictment in the case on the basis of the commission's and their own investigations, the judgment about their correspondence. A commission may also consider making findings of "moral" or "political" – as opposed to legal – responsibility for such violations.[93] Indeed, it would be difficult to rebuke a commission that limits itself to findings of political and moral responsibility and that leaves findings of legal or criminal responsibility to the courts. A commission could also underscore in its final report that its rules of evidence and procedure "are very different from those of the courts . . . [and] may not necessarily be the same as those which would be reached in a court."[94]

In several truth commission experiences, attribution of individual responsibility has been effected through deliberate or unintentional press leaks.[95] This is especially likely to occur where sections of a final report (*e.g.,* a confidential

---

was tantamount to a finding of civil or criminal responsibility. The commission's terms of reference prohibited "any conclusion of law regarding civil or criminal liability." *See also Canada (Attorney General) v. Canada (Commission of Inquiry on the Blood System)*, [1997] 3 S.C.R. 440, 1997 CanLII 323 (S.C.C.), at para. 52, in which the Supreme Court of Canada held that "commissioners should endeavour to avoid making evaluations of their findings of fact in terms that are the same as those used by courts to express findings of civil liability. As well, efforts should be made to avoid language that is so equivocal that it appears to be a finding of civil or criminal liability."

92   Hayner, *Unspeakable Truths*, above note 16, at 131–2.

93   For example, the South African TRC found Winnie Madikizela-Mandela "accountable, politically and morally, for the gross violations of human rights committed by the Mandela United Football Club." But the TRC did not stop there. It also found that Madikizela-Mandela herself "was responsible for committing such gross violations of human rights." TRC Final Report, vol. 5, at 244. The commission also made similar findings of "political responsibility" in respect of various individuals. Such distinctions are reminiscent of Karl Jaspers' oft-cited categories of guilt: criminal, political, moral, and metaphysical. *See generally* K. Jaspers, *The Question of German Guilt* (New York: The Dial Press, 1947).

94   *Canada (Attorney General) v. Canada (Commission of Inquiry on the Blood System)*, [1997] 3 S.C.R. 440, 1997 CanLII 323 (S.C.C.), at para. 54.

95   For example, this occurred in the case of the truth commissions of Argentina, Haiti, and Ghana. It also occurred in the case of a recent UN commission of inquiry into civil war–related violations in the Ivory Coast. "Radio France International first reported Friday that a highly confidential annex to the report contained the names of 95 individuals allegedly responsible for committing rights abuses, inciting violence or blocking the country's peace process. It includes Simone Gbagbo, a top rebel leader and the head of a pro-government militia." *See* C. Lynch, "Ivory Coast First Lady Leads Death Squad, Report Alleges," *Washington Post*, 29 January 2005.

annex in which individual perpetrators are identified) have not been made public. If such a leak occurs, it is essential that the commission (or in the event it has been dissolved, its former commissioners) promptly and publicly criticize the act of publication. In some cases – for example, where the identification of a presumed perpetrator is likely to result in acts of physical violence by or against the individual – it may also be appropriate to publicly renounce the relevant portion of the published report.[96] Commissions that intend to name individuals in confidential reports should, of course, take precautionary measures to minimize the chance of press leaks in the first place. Still, given the impossibility of achieving complete control over leaks, a truth commission should satisfy a high evidentiary threshold even when its intention is to compile only a private list of names.

RECOMMENDATIONS

- The mode of identifying any individual perpetrator can be express or implied. *Express identification* is where a truth commission, speaking in its own voice, makes a direct finding of individual responsibility. *Implied identification* is where a truth commission provides the basis for an inference of individual responsibility, for example, by publishing unedited witness transcripts that name alleged perpetrators or by assigning collective responsibility in a way that indirectly taints specific individuals.
- Except where a mandate precludes a commission from making explicit findings of individual culpability, express identification should be preferred over implied identification. If there is not sufficient evidence for a truth commission to ground an express finding of culpability, then it should generally avoid impeaching an individual's reputation by implication.
- The precise nature of the evidence against any named individual for any particular offense should be made explicit in the final report. The precise nature of a person's alleged participation in the offenses should also be noted.
- A commission is under no obligation to publish the version of facts alleged by the named individual.

---

96   *Recall also* ACHR article 14(1), which guarantees to individuals injured by false or offensive public statements or ideas disseminated by publicly regulated media a "right to reply or to make a correction using the same communications outlet." In addition, for the "effective protection of honour and reputation," ACHR article 14(3) requires publishers and other media outlets to employ "a person responsible who is not protected by immunities or special privileges."

- Because a truth commission will generally be unable to establish a comprehensive list of all offenders, its final report should explain that (1) not every perpetrator has been named, and (2) not being named does not prove innocence.
- A commission's final report should emphasize that attributions of individual responsibility constitute findings of fact, not of law, and that they remain to be proven definitively in court.
- Where a truth commission attributes individual responsibility in a confidential report that is leaked to the press and ultimately to the public, the commission (or its former members) should promptly and publicly criticize the act of publication and, if appropriate, renounce the relevant portion of the published report.

SECTION 7: JUDICIAL REVIEW

There is no inherent unfairness in vesting truth commissions with the power to publish findings of individual responsibility. Although the risk of injury to individual reputations is undeniable, that risk must be weighed against the competing public interest in the truth. As the European Court of Human Rights stated in *Fayed v. UK*:

> The risk of some uncompensated damage to reputation is inevitable if independent investigators in circumstances such as those of the present case are to have the necessary freedom to report without fear, not only to the authorities but also in the final resort to the public. It is in the first place for the national authorities to determine the extent to which the individual's interest in full protection of his or her reputation should yield to the requirements of the community's interest in independent investigation of the affairs of large public companies. The applicants' argument would amount to reading into Article 6 para. 1 (art. 6-1) an entitlement to have a report such as the one in the present case not published until after a full judicial hearing repeating, doubtless over a longer time-scale, the same fact-finding exercise as that already carried out by the Inspectors. Such an entitlement could effectively destroy the utility of informing the public of the results of the administrative investigations provided for under section 432(2) of the Companies Act 1985. Having found the aim of not only making but also publishing Inspectors' reports to be legitimate, the Court cannot apply the test of proportionality in such a way as to render publication impracticable.[97]

---

97   *Fayed v. UK*, above note 8, para. 81.

Named individuals should, nevertheless, be entitled to judicial review of a truth commission's published finding against them. Whether this is possible is purely a matter of national law. There is, in any case, no truth commission mandate that, *ex ante,* precludes judicial review.

Judicial review helps ensure that a truth commission has complied with the imperatives of procedural fairness. Judicial review will be especially necessary where a commission's mandate provides personal immunity for commissioners and staff from adverse civil claims related to their actions, statements, and decisions. The absence of a right to judicial review in such circumstances would leave the named person without legal recourse.[98]

The right to judicial review should be required to be exercised within a short and fixed time frame following the official public release of a truth commission's final report.

Grounds for review should be limited. Recourse to courts should be available only where the act of naming involved a clear error in law (*e.g.,* the commission exceeded its mandate), a perverse error of fact (*e.g.,* a case of mistaken identity), or a fundamental breach of procedural fairness (*e.g.,* a failure to have an opportunity to adduce exculpatory evidence).

Concerning the relief available in the event of a successful review, at a minimum a court should be able to declare the attribution of responsibility unlawful or invalid and to order the commission or its sponsor to publicly retract the finding. Judicial review should not, however, encompass a right to disclosure of private communications that took place between commissioners and staff. That would violate "the principle of deliberative secrecy that protects decision-makers from revealing the deliberations that led to the decision."[99]

The quality of judicial review will, of course, depend on the quality of the judiciary in any particular state. But that should not preclude the remedy's availability in law.

RECOMMENDATIONS

- Persons who have been adversely named in the published final report of a truth commission should have recourse to judicial review.
- Any right to judicial review should be required to be promptly exercised.

---

98 *Recall,* in this regard, the international legal right to a remedy. Where a truth commission violates an individual's human rights, the subject of the violation enjoys the right to a remedy. *See* Chapter 2, Section 1.

99 A. W. MacKay and M. G. McQueen, "Public Inquiries and the Legality of Blaming: Truth, Justice, and the Canadian Way," in A. Manson and D. Mullan, eds., *Commissions of Inquiry: Praise or Reappraise?* (Toronto: Irwin Law, 2003), at 270.

- Grounds for review should be limited to cases in which there was a clear error in law, a perverse error of fact, or a significant violation of procedural fairness.
- A court should be able to declare a particular attribution of responsibility unlawful or invalid, and order the commission or its sponsor to review or reconsider the finding and, where appropriate, formally retract it.

Summary of Recommendations

STATEMENT TAKING

Publicity and outreach

- It is generally desirable for a truth commission's mandate to impose publicity and outreach obligations on the commission.
- Whether or not the mandate imposes obligations, a commission should proactively advise the public as to when, how, where, and why it will be taking statements.
- Publicity may be carried out by use of private and public media, the Internet, posters, and pamphlets.
- Where resources are acutely limited, a commission should focus its outreach efforts on communities or regions where violations were known to be especially prevalent. On site visits to such communities or regions should be considered.
- Truth commissions should consider enlisting the participation of respected NGOs and other civil society actors to publicize the statement-taking process.
- Nationals living abroad, particularly refugees, should be notified about the commission statement-taking process so that they may participate.
- In all its public outreach work, a commission should articulate possible material consequences of not providing a statement. In particular, where a commission is mandated to develop a list of victims for a future reparation or compensation program, or to design and recommend such a program,

or to do both, the commission should indicate whether failure to provide a statement could adversely affect eligibility.

Accessibility

- Statements should be taken in locations, and using methods, that are physically and psychologically accessible. Accordingly, statements should be taken in neutral and convenient locations, during times that are considerate of deponents' schedules.
- A commission should make statement taking accessible to the public generally, and to victims in particular, by as many means as possible. This might include any one or more of the following: creating regional or local offices, using a website (to which statements can be directly posted), and carrying out site visits to take statements in remote communities and in deponents' homes. In exceptional circumstances, effective access may require that statements be taken in undisclosed locations. (*See* "Receipt and Preservation of Confidential and Anonymous Statements.")
- Deponents should be able to make statements in their native language.
- Commissions should consider special measures to facilitate statement taking for elderly persons and persons with disabilities.

Information on possible consequences of giving a statement

- A commission should inform a deponent of all possible subsequent uses of his or her statement for purposes that are consistent with its mandate. Such uses may include listing the deponent's name in the final report, citing part of the deponent's statement in the final report, forwarding the statement to prosecutors or courts, and permitting public access to review the statement after the commission's dissolution.
- Where appropriate, a commission should obtain a deponent's prior consent for any legally significant subsequent uses of his or her statement.

Procedures for taking and recording statements

- Statements should be taken following a predetermined format, and questions should be confined to areas that fall within the commission's mandate.
- A commission should take steps to ensure that statements are recorded consistently, accurately, and completely for future use, and in a manner that respects the dignity of the deponent.
- Deponents should be allowed to make statements in person or in writing.

- Security conditions and resources permitting, statements might be recorded on audiotape or videotape with the consent of the deponent.
- Deponents should generally be asked to give a solemn undertaking about the truthfulness and completeness of their statements.
- Whenever possible, statements should be signed by the deponent and by the statement taker, noting the date, time and place, and all persons present during the interview; where not signed, the reasons should be noted.
- To ensure effective participation, a commission should permit deponents to be accompanied by friends, family, or counsel.
- It is generally preferable to take statements in private rather than in a group setting. However, taking statements in a group setting may be preferable in some instances, depending on the specific cultural setting and the nature of the commission's subsequent use of the statements.
- A commission should ensure specialized hiring and training measures to facilitate the effective interviewing of illiterate and underage deponents, and of victims of sexual violence.

Receipt and preservation of confidential and anonymous statements

- A truth commission should have established procedures and criteria to determine if it is appropriate for deponents to make confidential or anonymous statements. Criteria should include the degree of physical risk, the commission's relative need for the information (having regard to what information is already in the public realm and what information the commission has already secured from other deponents on a non-confidential basis regarding a particular event or set of facts), the relevance and probative value of the information, and the capacity of the commission to prevent direct or indirect disclosure of the deponent's identity.
- Statements should be treated as confidential on an exceptional basis. Accordingly, deponents wishing to make confidential statements must formally request to do so. The ultimate decision on confidentiality is at the discretion of the commission.
- Prior to taking any confidential statement, a commission should explain the scope of its obligations and the degree of its capacity to preserve confidentiality.
- Where necessary to preserve confidentiality, a commission should consider using pseudonyms or expunging the deponent's name and all other identifying information from the public records of the commission.

- Anonymous statements are inherently less reliable than confidential statements, but they should be permitted at the discretion of the commission, provided that excessive reliance is not placed on them for purposes of attributing individual responsibility in a published final report. (*See* "Publication of Findings of Individual Responsibility.")
- A truth commission should maintain well-organized files in a secure location, with a system in place to ensure the upholding of confidentiality obligations it has undertaken for specific deponents.

Support and referrals

- To the extent resources permit, a commission should have, on staff or on site, persons to provide medical, psychological, or emotional support and assistance for deponents at the moment they give a statement.
- Commission staff should be competent to advise deponents regarding available public and private services for special medical, psychological, emotional, and economic support.

SUBPOENA POWER

Procedure for issuing and serving subpoenas

- For efficiency reasons, it is best to have a subpoena power reside directly in the truth commission, rather than requiring the commission to apply to the judiciary.
- Subpoenas should be issued only as a last resort in the event that a person does not volunteer testimony or evidence that the commission considers relevant and necessary.
- A reasonable quorum among commissioners should be required prior to issuing a subpoena. Where consensus is not possible, decisions could be taken on the basis of a simple majority vote.
- The commission chair should have the power to independently issue a subpoena on an exceptional and urgent basis.
- Commission staff should not have authority to issue subpoenas.
- Ideally, a subpoena should be personally served on the individual in question. It should be served directly at the individual's residence or business place, either by a designated staff member of the commission or, alternatively, by any competent police officer or court official not personally implicated in the subject matter of the subpoena. A subpoena may alternatively be served by mail to the individual's most recent known address, or to his or her designated legal representative.

Subpoena content and scope

- A subpoena power should be capable of being exercised against natural persons or legal persons.
- A subpoena power should enable a commission to require the attendance of a person to give testimony or to produce documents or other things in the person's custody or control that are relevant and necessary to the subject of the inquiry.
- A subpoena may be broad in scope, but it must establish an articulable relationship between the testimony or evidence sought, and the subject of the investigation. The subpoena should also inform the recipient of the nature of any adverse allegations about which he or she may expect to be questioned.
- A subpoena for *documentary evidence* should not be overly vague, such that there is no limit to the evidence to which it pertains. Neither should it be overly broad, such that compliance would be unduly burdensome. The subpoena should indicate a reasonable time and location for delivery of the evidence.
- The scope and content of a subpoena for *testimony* may be more general than a subpoena for documentary evidence. It should contain the time and place where testimony will be taken and indicate the relevant subject matter of the testimony. The recipient should receive reasonable notice to attend and testify.
- A subpoena should explain possible consequences of noncompliance, as well as the procedure to be followed if the person is unable or unwilling to comply.

Enforcement powers

- A truth commission's mandate should make it an offense to fail to comply with a subpoena without a reasonable excuse, to deliberately distort or conceal relevant evidence, or to commit perjury.
- Truth commission subpoenas should be enforceable through prescribed procedures, including prosecution by public authorities at the behest, or upon the certification, of the commission.
- Contempt proceedings should be available for refusal to appear, refusal to produce documents, refusal to be sworn in as a witness, and improper refusal to answer questions.
- Subpoena recipients should be allowed to defend against contempt proceedings on the following grounds: irrelevance, incapacity, legal privilege, unreasonable burden, or insufficient notice.

- Penalties for noncompliance with a subpoena could include a fine, a short term in prison, and reimbursement of the commission's reasonable costs.

Recipient rights

- A subpoena recipient should be permitted the right to quash the subpoena on the same grounds as he or she would defend refusal, namely: irrelevance, incapacity, legal privilege, unreasonable burden, or insufficient notice. But any application for judicial review of a subpoena should be required to be brought expeditiously.
- A subpoena recipient should be entitled to a base level of confidentiality or privacy, heightened if the individual or the recipient's family can show a reasonable fear of a threat to physical safety or economic well being.
- Resources permitting, a commission should reimburse the reasonable costs of compliance with a subpoena.
- Objects and documents obtained through a subpoena for evidence should be returned to the subpoena recipient within a reasonable time. Where, however, the objects and documents reveal evidence of criminal activity, prosecutors should have an opportunity to apply for the retention of the evidence.

SEARCH AND SEIZURE POWER

Procedure for issuing warrants

- Where a judicial system is reasonably independent and effective, a truth commission should be required to apply to a judge for a warrant prior to conducting a search and seizure operation. Alternatively, where the judicial system is very weak or corrupt, a truth commission could be directly vested with a search and seizure power, in which case the recommendations herein regarding judicially obtained warrants would apply, *mutatis mutandis.*
- A warrant should be issued only where there are reasonable grounds for believing that there are, in any building or place, documents or things relevant to the subject matter of the inquiry.
- Where a commission has authority to issue a search warrant, a reasonable quorum among commissioners should be required prior to issuing the warrant. Where consensus is not possible, decisions could be taken on the basis of a simple majority vote.
- The commission chair should have the power to independently issue a warrant on an exceptional and urgent basis.
- Commission staff should not have authority to issue a search warrant.

- Generally, a warrant should be obtained in advance of the search operation. On an exceptional basis, a search might be conducted without warrant where: (1) the subject of the search consents; or (2) obtaining a warrant in advance would defeat the purpose of the search, such as in cases of genuine exigency or probable destruction of evidence, and provided that the warrant is obtained within the twenty-four hours following the search.

Scope of a warrant

- The duration of a warrant should not be open-ended. It should be limited to the time that is minimally necessary to achieve the stated purpose.
- A warrant should permit the removal and retention of objects for a reasonable period of time. It should also permit – during and after the search – the inspection and examination of objects, the making of copies of all or part of any articles found, and the asking of pertinent questions of the person being searched.
- Warrants should apply to all persons, natural or legal.

Procedure for executing warrants

- Warrants should ideally be executed by uniformed police officers, whether they work independently of the commission or are temporarily employed by it. A commissioner or designated staff member should accompany the police officer.
- Where police officers are corrupt or implicated in the subject of the warrant, a member of the truth commission might have authority to execute the warrant without police accompaniment, provided that suitable identifying information – such as a special commission badge – is employed.
- Those executing a warrant should identify themselves properly, present or post a copy of the warrant, and address any questions about their authority to execute the warrant. The subject of the search should be orally advised of the potential consequences of noncompliance.
- A search and seizure operation should ideally be carried out with the consent and cooperation of the subject of the search. Where consent is not given, those conducting the search should be permitted to apply reasonable force to enter the premises only if (1) they first make audible demand of entry, and (2) an independent witness to the entry is on the premises.
- The subject of the search should be entitled to accompany those conducting the search, or to designate another person to serve as a witness during the search.
- Warrants should generally be executed by day, unless there is a justified urgency for doing otherwise.

- Those conducting the search should make a detailed written record of the search and of any seized objects. The record should be signed by those who conducted the search, as well as by the subject of the search and a witness proposed by the subject. The search should also, ideally, be videotaped.
- Where, during a search, the subject refuses to permit removal of property on the basis that it contains privileged information, the matter should be referred to the courts, and the property sealed and temporarily placed in the custody of a neutral third party such as a court clerk or registrar.

Rights of the subject of the search

- The subject of the search should have a right to challenge and quash a defective warrant, but any application for judicial review of a warrant must be brought expeditiously.
- The subject of the search should have a right to a remedy where the manner of search and seizure is arbitrary or unreasonable.
- Where a search is conducted in an arbitrary or unreasonable manner, a truth commission should be precluded from using or relying upon the seized evidence, and any subsequent referral of such evidence to a law enforcement or judicial body should either not be made, or be made with notification of the deficiency.

PUBLIC HEARINGS

Selection and preparation of those who will appear

- Truth commissions should have full discretion to select those who will appear at public hearings.
- There should be a general presumption of competency for any adult who might testify at a public hearing. Children may be deemed competent on an exceptional basis.
- A truth commission should acquire, and ensure the reliability of, a substantial number of statements prior to making any decisions about which victims will have the opportunity to testify at a public hearing.
- The criteria for selection of all those who will testify should be publicized, and they should reflect the objectives set out in the commission's mandate.
- Regarding the selection of any perpetrators or third-party witnesses whose public testimony is of interest to a truth commission, such persons should first be requested to appear on a voluntary basis. Where they decline and where their testimony is deemed significant, relevant, and necessary, they could (mandate permitting) be subpoenaed by the commission.

- Victims who testify at public hearings should be provided with a prior briefing at which the hearing procedure and any corresponding rights or duties are explained.

Notification to implicated persons: timing, method, and content

- *Timing:* (1) A commission should make reasonable efforts to notify a person that he or she has been adversely implicated in a deponent's statement whenever that deponent has been granted the opportunity to testify at a public hearing. Reasonable prior notice should be provided. (2) In exceptional circumstances, a commission may be justified in foregoing prior notice and instead informing the implicated person after the fact. A commission may also be justified in foregoing prior notice where the person scheduled to testify agrees in advance not to make individual accusations in his or her public testimony. (3) Where a person is adversely implicated for the first time at the public hearing itself (*e.g.*, where the person was not implicated in a deponent's prior statement to the commission), the commission may suspend proceedings until reasonable notice can be provided and a new hearing date set.
- *Method:* The form of notice should be written. It should be delivered by mail to the most recent known address of the implicated individual, preferably by registered mail. Notification could be sent to the individual concerned or to the individual's designated legal representative. If the postal service is particularly unreliable, courier service or personal service should be considered. Where the implicated individual cannot be located or where resource constraints are especially acute, a commission could consider making general public announcements in appropriate places.
- *Content:* Notice to an implicated individual should include sufficient detail to allow the person to understand the nature and scope of the adverse allegations. At minimum, a summary of the allegations, together with a list of the types of evidence, should be provided. Information about the source of the allegations may be withheld where the commission considers it necessary or prudent to do so. The notice should set out the location, date, and time of the planned hearing, and the modalities and restrictions for exercising a right of reply.

Nature and scope of the right of reply

- A person adversely implicated prior to, or during, a public hearing is entitled to a formal right of reply.
- The reply of the implicated individual should be voluntary and waived by silence, provided that a minimum and reasonable period of time be required

to elapse before the commission may treat any right of reply as having been waived.

- The reply might be exercised in a variety of ways, all of which can be outlined in the truth commission's mandate or left to the commission's reasonable discretion.
- The right of reply should rarely include a right of cross-examination. Instead, an implicated individual should be entitled to present his or her version of the facts (1) in writing to the commission before or after the hearing takes place, or (2) at a separate public or private hearing or interview, subject to a commission's mandate and resources, and to the dictates of fairness in the particular case. If an implicated person is given the opportunity to reply to allegations at a separate public hearing, the person whose testimony caused the need for such a hearing should receive an equivalent form of notification (in terms of timing, method, and content) to that received by the implicated person.
- If cross-examination is permitted, a truth commission should have authority to impose restrictions on the extent, nature, and line of questioning so as to avoid any harassment or intimidation of victims or witnesses, paying particular attention to attacks on children and victims of sexual crimes who testify.
- As a further alternative to cross-examination, the implicated individual could be permitted to submit a list of questions that the commission might, at its reasonable discretion, put to the victim before, during, or after the hearing.

Oaths and affirmations

- An oath or affirmation should be administered to any person testifying at a public hearing of a truth commission. At a commission's reasonable discretion, exceptions may be made for children or other similar categories of persons, or where an oath or affirmation would be counterproductive to a legitimate commission objective.
- The oath or affirmation should consist of simply promising to tell the whole truth.
- Interpreters and translators should also be required to give an oath or affirmation.

Right to legal representation

- A truth commission should allow a person testifying at a public hearing to retain counsel and have counsel present at the hearing. At the discretion of the commission, counsel may be allowed to speak on behalf of the person.

- A truth commission should generally not, itself, be required to provide counsel to persons appearing at public hearings. However, counsel could be provided where the person is indigent and appearing under subpoena, and where there is a risk of substantial harm that would be difficult to reverse.
- Persons appearing at public hearings should be promptly informed of the scope and content of their right to counsel.
- Truth commissions should adopt guidelines concerning acceptable conduct for counsel in order to effectively control the proceedings, prevent unnecessary delay, and avoid any trauma to victims and witnesses who testify.

Admissible evidence

- Truth commissions should adopt a broadly permissive approach to the admission of evidence at public hearings. Relevance should be the primary criterion of admissibility.
- In addition to oral testimony, the introduction of physical and documentary evidence should be permitted at a public hearing.
- There should be no requirement to submit original documents as proof of any fact.
- Hearsay evidence should generally be admissible.
- Except at a commission's reasonable discretion, there should be no right to call witnesses to appear on one's behalf at a public hearing. Witness affidavits should, however, be permitted.

Privileges based on contexts and relationships of confidentiality

- Communications between spouses, between lawyer and client, between medical professional and patient, and between religious clergy and penitent should be regarded as privileged and immune from compulsory disclosure.
- Journalistic, parent-child, parliamentary, or executive privileges may also apply. In addition, privileges may attach to officials of multilateral institutions such as the International Committee of the Red Cross or the various international criminal tribunals.
- No privilege is absolute. Privileged communications should be admissible at a public hearing (1) by consent, or (2) where the person in question voluntarily revealed the content of the communication to a third party who then gives evidence of that disclosure.

Use immunity and the privilege against self-incrimination

- A commission could have the power to compel persons to make self-incriminating statements or deliver self-incriminating evidence, subject to any applicable privileges, and provided that "use immunity" attaches by law or by mandate to any compelled testimony or evidence. Absent this safeguard, a commission should not have the power to compel the giving of self-incriminating testimony or evidence.

- A power to compel persons to give self-incriminating testimony or evidence should be exercised only where it is reasonable, just, and necessary to do so, and where there is no manifest security risk to the compelled person. Exercise of the power may also be conditioned on the prior consent of an appropriate government minister.
- The scope of use immunity for compelled self-incriminating statements or evidence should be broad. Specifically, the use of such statements and evidence should be prohibited in relation to contemporaneous or subsequent criminal, civil, or administrative proceedings against that person, *except* in prosecutions for perjury or for the giving of contradictory evidence (*i.e.*, for the purpose of impeaching credibility).
- Compelled self-incriminating testimony and evidence should be admissible in legal proceedings brought against third parties, such as co-conspirators.
- Public authorities should be barred from making "derivative" use of such statements and evidence to further investigations regarding the underlying offenses to which each relates, unless it can be proved that any evidence ultimately introduced in court could reasonably have been discovered in the absence of the compelled testimony or evidence.
- Use immunity should attach only to *compelled* testimony. No use immunity should attach to voluntary testimony that is self-incriminating; instead, voluntary testimony should act as a waiver of the privilege against self-incrimination.
- Use immunity should attach *automatically* to compelled testimony or evidence that is self-incriminating; consequently, there should be no obligation for the compelled person to affirmatively invoke the privilege against self-incrimination, nor should there be any obligation for the commission to provide a caution.
- Use immunity should not attach to all compelled testimony and evidence, but only to the part that is self-incriminating, as determined by a court.

Protective measures

- Having regard to its available resources, a commission should undertake or arrange protective measures to ensure the physical safety and privacy of anyone who testifies publicly and who would (or whose family would) face significant security risks on account of testimony.
- Truth commissions should accept all applications for protective measures on a *prima facie* basis. Applications for protective measures should be considered in private by the commission.

- Truth commissions should have the discretion to provide or to deny protective measures in accordance with established criteria that recognize the need to assure public and individual security, and witness dignity and privacy.
- There are several ways to protect the identity or location or both of a person who may testify at a public hearing. These include using a witness protection program, expunging the person's name and other identifying information from public records of the commission, using pseudonyms, employing witness voice and picture alteration devices, using videoconferencing technology, using closed-circuit television, limiting those who may attend, and restricting how a hearing may be publicly reported.
- A commission should have the power to conduct *in camera* hearings at its discretion in accordance with established criteria, provided that (1) every effort is made to hold hearings in public using one or more of the aforementioned measures to protect the identity or location or both of a witness, and (2) something short of a formal *in camera* hearing (*e.g.*, a private interview) would not be sufficient to ensure fairness.
- No information from any *in camera* proceeding should be made public without the consent of the person who testified. There should be penalties for anyone who breaches the confidentiality of an *in camera* hearing.

Victim emotional and psychological support

- Consistent with the resources and mandate of a truth commission, victims should receive appropriate medical, psychological, or emotional support services to help them testify effectively at a public hearing. The commission should also follow up with victims after their public testimony to ensure that their well-being was not compromised as a result of testifying.
- Alternative forms of assistance, such as religious or spiritual support by clerics and elders, self-help support groups, and special community or family support arrangements, could also be considered.
- In all other respects, the "Statement Taking" summary ("Support and Referrals" section) applies, *mutatis mutandis*.

PUBLICATION OF FINDINGS OF INDIVIDUAL RESPONSIBILITY

Types of evidence

- Truth commissions should examine and make use of as many different sources of evidence as possible before publishing findings of individual responsibility in a final report.

- Every piece of evidence – whether generated internally or externally – should attain a minimum threshold in terms of its relevance, probative value, and reliability in order to justify reliance on it for the purpose of attributing individual responsibility.
- In all other respects, the "Public Hearings" summary ("Admissible Evidence" section) applies, *mutatis mutandis.*

Standard of proof

- To maximize fairness and accuracy, it is preferable to rely on more than one direct and credible source of evidence before attributing individual responsibility in a final report. In some cases it may, however, be acceptable to rely on a single direct and reliable source.
- The common law's balance of probabilities standard, or something akin to it, is an appropriate minimum standard for a truth commission to employ in making any attribution of individual responsibility. A higher standard should, however, be applied where all or most of the investigation is conducted confidentially, or where reasonable notice and an opportunity to reply are not provided, or where the potential consequences for the named person are especially dire.

Notification of intent to name: timing, method, and content

- Before publishing findings of individual responsibility final report, a truth commission should make a reasonable effort to provide notice to all those it intends to name. A commission should not attribute individual responsibility in the absence of such effort.
- Five criteria should influence the timing of any such notice: (1) the amount of time the commission will require to prepare the notice, (2) the amount of time the commission will require to find the implicated party, (3) the amount of time the individual will need to respond to the allegations, (4) the amount of time the commission will require to consider the individual's reply, and (5) the risk that the individual will publicly release the truth commission's provisional finding.
- In all other respects, the "Public Hearings" summary ("Notification to Implicated Persons: Timing, Method, and Content" section) applies, *mutatis mutandis.*

Nature and scope of the right of reply

- An individual to whom a truth commission intends to attribute responsibility in a final report should have a prior opportunity to reply to the adverse evidence and allegations.

- The implicated person should be entitled to provide the commission with a written statement, together with any contradictory or exculpatory evidence that he or she can adduce. The implicated party should not be entitled to a private meeting with the commission except at its reasonable discretion and in accordance with established criteria.
- The implicated individual's reply should be voluntary and waived by silence, provided that a commission may not draw any adverse inference from a failure to reply.
- The implicated person should have the right to contest and possibly enjoin a commission from publicly attributing responsibility to him or her in a final report, where it can be demonstrated that notice was inadequate or that his or her rights were otherwise violated by the commission's process.

Investigation of replies

- A truth commission has an obligation to investigate any new and credible contradictory or exculpatory evidence received from an implicated individual prior to publicly attributing responsibility to him or her in a final report.
- A commission should weigh at least three factors in setting its policy for consideration of replies: (1) the foreseeable consequences of being named in the final report, (2) the weight of the evidence it has on hand in assigning responsibility, and (3) the extent of its resources.
- All case files with roughly the same balance of evidence for and against them should receive roughly the same consideration from a commission.

Mode of naming in a final report

- The mode of identifying any individual perpetrator can be express or implied. *Express identification* is where a truth commission, speaking in its own voice, makes a direct finding of individual responsibility. *Implied identification* is where a truth commission provides the basis for an inference of individual responsibility, for example, by publishing unedited witness transcripts that name alleged perpetrators or by assigning collective responsibility in a way that indirectly taints specific individuals.
- Except where a mandate precludes a commission from making explicit findings of individual culpability, express identification should be preferred over implied identification. If there is not sufficient evidence for a truth commission to ground an express finding of culpability, then it should generally avoid impeaching an individual's reputation by implication.
- The precise nature of the evidence against any named individual for any particular offense should be made explicit in the final report. The precise

nature of a person's alleged participation in the offenses should also be noted.

- A commission is under no obligation to publish the version of facts alleged by the named individual.
- Because a truth commission will generally be unable to establish a comprehensive list of all offenders, its final report should explain that (1) not every perpetrator has been named, and (2) not being named does not prove innocence.
- A commission's final report should emphasize that attributions of individual responsibility constitute findings of fact, not of law, and that they remain to be proven definitively in court.
- Where a truth commission attributes individual responsibility in a confidential report that is leaked to the press and ultimately to the public, the commission (or its former members) should promptly and publicly criticize the act of publication and, if appropriate, renounce the relevant portion of the published report.

Judicial review

- Persons who have been adversely named in the published final report of a truth commission should have recourse to judicial review.
- Any right to judicial review should be required to be promptly exercised.
- Grounds for review should be limited to cases in which there was a clear error in law, a perverse error of fact, or a significant violation of procedural fairness.
- A court should be able to declare a particular attribution of responsibility unlawful or invalid, and order the commission or its sponsor to review or reconsider the finding and, where appropriate, formally retract it.

APPENDIX 1

Table of Truth Commissions

Truth commissions are listed in chronological order according to their dates of inauguration. Excluded from this table are several commissions of inquiry that P. Hayner, in *Unspeakable Truths: Facing the Challenge of Truth Commissions*, 2d ed. (New York: Routledge, 2002) describes as truth commissions, but that I do not: Uganda (1974), Zimbabwe (1984), Uruguay (1985), African National Congress (1992 and 1993), and Burundi (1995).

The table begins on the next page.

Table A.1: Truth Commissions and Their Key Powers

Country	Title of truth commission	Source of mandate	Year in which work began[a]	Total period of operation[b]	Commissioners[c]	Subject of investigation[d]	Subpoena power	Search and seizure power	Public hearings	Publication of findings of individual responsibility
Bolivia	Comisión Nacional de Investigación de Desaparecidos	Presidential decree	1982	Disbanded in 1984	8	Forced disappearances committed during prior period of military rule from 1967 to 1982	No	No	No	Report never completed
Argentina	Comisión Nacional para la Desaparición de Personas	Presidential decree	1983	9 months	13	Forced disappearances committed during prior period of military rule from 1976 to 1983	No	No	No	No
Uganda	Commission of Inquiry into Violations of Human Rights	Created by minister of justice pursuant to Commission of Inquiry statute	1986	Nearly 9 years (with intervening stoppages)	6	Serious human rights violations committed from 1962 to 1986	Yes	No	Yes	No

Nepal	Commission of Inquiry to Find the Disappeared Persons during the Panchayat Period[e]	Created by president pursuant to Commission of Inquiry statute	1990	1 year	4	Forced disappearances committed between 1961 and 1990	No	No	No	No	No
Chile	Comisión Nacional para la Verdad y Reconciliación	Presidential decree	1990	9 months	8	Disappearances and various extrajudicial killings committed during prior period of military rule from 1973 to 1990	No	No	No	No	No
Chad	Commission d'Enquête sur les Crimes et Détournements Commis par l'Ex-Président Habré, ses co-Auteurs et/ou Complices	Presidential decree	1991	1 year, 5 months	12–16	Violations of various human rights and related economic crimes committed from 1982 to 1990 by outgoing regime	Yes	No[f]	No	No	Yes

Country	Title of truth commission	Source of mandate	Year in which work began	Total period of operation	Commissioners	Subject of investigation	Subpoena power	Search and seizure power	Public hearings	Publication of findings of individual responsibility
Germany	Enquete Kommission Aufar Beitung von Geschichte und Folgen der SED-Diktatur in Deutschland	Act of Parliament	1992	3 years	27	Repression in former East Germany from 1949 to 1989 under socialist rule	No	No	Yes	No
El Salvador	Comisión de la Verdad	Peace accord	1992	8 months	3 (all of whom were foreign nationals)	Serious acts of violence committed between 1980 and 1991 during the country's civil war	No	No	No	Yes
Sri Lanka	Commissions of Inquiry into the Involuntary Removal or Disappearance of Persons^g	Created by president pursuant to Commission of Inquiry statute	1994	2 years, 10 months	3	Involuntary removals and forced disappearances between 1988 and 1994	Yes	No	Yes	No
Haiti	Commission Nationale de Vérité et Justice	Presidential decree	1995	9 months	7 (three of whom were foreign nationals)	Serious human rights violations and crimes against humanity committed between 1991 and 1994 under military rule	Yes	No	No	No

Country	Commission	How established	Year	Duration	Members	Mandate				
South Africa	Truth and Reconciliation Commission	Act of Parliament	1995	2 years, 6 months (plus additional 3 years, 6 months focused on amnesty process)	17	Gross violations of human rights committed under apartheid rule between 1960 and 1994	Yes	Yes	Yes	Yes
Ecuador	Comisión de Verdad y Justicia	Established by Ministry of Government and Police	1996	Disbanded in 1997	7 (three of whom were foreign nationals)	Human rights violations concerning life, liberty, and personal security committed between 1979 and 1996	No	No	No	Report never completed
Guatemala	Comisión para el Esclarecimiento Histórico	Peace accord	1997	1 year, 6 months	3 (one of whom was a foreign national)	Human rights violations and acts of violence connected to the country's civil war between 1962 and 1996	No	No	No	No
Nigeria	Judicial Commission of Inquiry for the Investigation of Human Rights Violations	Created by president pursuant to Commission of Inquiry statute	1999	3 years	8	Gross human rights violations committed between 1966 and 1999	Yes	Yes	Yes	Yes

Country	Title of truth commission	Source of mandate	Year in which work began	Total period of operation	Commissioners	Subject of investigation	Subpoena power	Search and seizure power	Public hearings	Publication of findings of individual responsibility
Republic of Korea	Presidential Truth Commission on Suspicious Deaths	Act of Parliament	2000	2 years (plus a further 2-year extension to complete remaining cases)	9	"Suspicious deaths" connected with the democratization movement during prior period of authoritarian rule	Power to impose fine on anyone refusing an invitation to testify	No	No	No
Uruguay	Comisión de la Paz	Presidential resolution	2000	2 years, 7 months (but mandate extended after final report issued)	6	Disappearances committed during prior period of military rule from 1973 to 1985	No	No	No	No
Panama	Comisión de la Verdad	Presidential decree	2001	1 year, 3 months	7	Serious human rights violations committed during military rule between 1968 and 1989	No	No	No	No
Federal Republic of Yugoslavia (later Serbia and Montenegro)	Komisije Za Istinu I Pomirenje	Presidential decision	2001	Disbanded in 2003	15–24	Human rights violations and war crimes committed during the armed conflicts in the former Yugoslavia in the 1990s	No	No	Had power to hold public hearings but never did so	Report never completed

	Commission	Created by	Year	Duration	Commissioners	Mandate				
Grenada	Truth and Reconciliation Commission	Created by Governor-General pursuant to Commission of Inquiry statute	2001	Ongoing (focused on preparation of final report since 2004)	3 (two of whom were foreign nationals)	Violent political events that occurred between 1976 and 1991	Yes	No	Yes	Power to do so
Peru	Comisión de la Verdad y Reconciliación	Presidential decree	2001	2 years, 3 months	12	Violations of human rights and other serious acts of violence committed between 1980 and 2000	No	No	Yes	Yes
Timor-Leste	Commission for Reception, Truth, and Reconciliation	UN Transitional Administration for East Timor	2002	3 years, 6 months	7 (plus 29 regional commissioners)	Violations of human rights and humanitarian law committed during period of Indonesian occupation between 1974 and 1999	Yes	Yes	Yes	Yes (full report due to be published in 2006)
Ghana	National Reconciliation Commission	Act of Parliament	2002	2 years	9	Human rights violations committed between 1957 and 1993, especially during periods of military rule	Yes	Yes	Yes	Yes

Country	Title of truth commission	Source of mandate	Year in which work began	Total period of operation	Commissioners	Subject of investigation	Subpoena power	Search and seizure power	Public hearings	Publication of findings of individual responsibility
Sierra Leone	Truth and Reconciliation Commission	Peace accord followed by implementing statute	2002	2 years, 3 months	7 (three of whom were foreign nationals)	Violations of human rights and humanitarian law related to the armed conflict between 1991 and 1999	Yes	No	Yes	Yes
Morocco	Instance Equité et Réconciliation	Royal dahir	2004	23 months	17	Forced disappearances and arbitrary detentions committed between 1956 and 1999	No	No	Yes	No (full report due to be published in 2006)
Paraguay	Comisión de Verdad y Justicia	Act of Parliament	2004	Ongoing	9	Serious human rights violations committed between 1954 and 2003	No	No	Yes	Not authorized to do so
Democratic Republic of Congo (DRC)	Commission Vérité et Réconciliation	Peace accord followed by implementing statute	2004	Ongoing	21	Political crimes and massive violations of human rights and humanitarian law committed since 1960	Yes	Yes	Power to do so	Power to do so

| Liberia | Truth and Reconciliation Commission | Peace accord followed by implementing statute | 2005 | Ongoing | 9 | Gross violations of human rights and humanitarian law committed between 1979 and 2003 | Yes | No | Power to do so | Power to do so |
| Indonesia | Truth and Reconciliation Commission | Act of Parliament (signed into law by president) | 2005 | Not yet underway | 21 (members not yet appointed) | Acts of genocide and crimes against humanity committed between 1965 and 1998 | No | No | Not mentioned in mandate | Not mentioned in mandate |

a The year in which a commission's work begins does not always correspond to the year in which the terms of reference are established. Sometimes the terms of reference are established several months prior to the commission's actual start date.

b It is sometimes difficult to describe a commission's precise duration of operation. For example, some have "preparatory phases" that may not form an official part of the "period of operation." Also, the operation of commissions is sometimes interrupted, whether because of funding shortages or increased security risks. Accordingly, the total periods of operation of the commissions listed in this table are approximate figures.

c Except where otherwise indicated, commissioners are all nationals.

d In the case of commissions established following civil war, violations committed by state and nonstate actors are investigated.

e The Panchayat system of governance operated for nearly three decades in Nepal. It banned all political parties, with the exception of the Royalist Rastriya Panchayat.

f The commission did, however, have the power to "confiscate and secure under seal all objects and premises required for elucidating the truth": article 2 of its mandate.

g The Sri Lankan "truth commission" actually comprised three subcommissions. These were succeeded in 1998 by a follow-up body entitled the "all-islands commission." It had the same mandate as the original subcommissions, and was tasked with finalizing work they had left incomplete. The all-islands commission completed its work in 2000, and its findings were made public in 2002. Of the three original subcommissions, only one held public hearings.

Primary Materials on Truth Commissions

THE TRUTH AND RECONCILIATION COMMISSION ACT 2000 (SIERRA LEONE)

Being an Act to establish the Truth and Reconciliation Commission in line with Article XXVI of the Lome Peace Agreement and to provide for related matters.

Enacted by the President and Members of Parliament in this present Parliament assembled.

PART 1 – PRELIMINARY

1. In this Act, unless the context otherwise requires –
   "Chairman" means the Chairman of the Commission appointed under subsection (3) of section 3;

   "Commission" means the Truth and Reconciliation Commission established by section 2;

"Lome Peace Agreement" means the Peace Agreement between the Government of Sierra Leone and the Revolutionary United Front of Sierra Leone signed in Lome on 7th July, 1999;

"Moral Guarantors" means the Moral Guarantors referred to in Article XXXIV of the Lome Peace Agreement;

"Selection Coordinator" means the UN Special Representative of the Secretary-General in Sierra Leone;

"Selection Panel" means the selection panel of six persons referred to in subparagraph (iii) of paragraph (a) of the schedule composed of one member appointed by each of the following: – The President, the Revolutionary United Front of Sierra Leone, the erstwhile Armed Forces Revolutionary Council, the Inter-Religious Council, the National Forum for Human Rights and the National Commission for Democracy and Human Rights (or the Human Rights Commission, as set out in the Lome Peace Agreement, if such a Commission has been inaugurated).

PART II – ESTABLISHMENT OF COMMISSION

2. (1) There is hereby established a body known as the Truth and Reconciliation Commission.

    (2) The Commission shall be body corporate having perpetual succession and capable of acquiring, holding and disposing of any property, whether moveable or immovable and of suing and being sued in its corporate name and, subject to this Act, of performing all such acts as bodies corporate may by law perform.

    (3) The Commission shall have a common seal the use of which shall be authenticated by the signatures of the Chairman and the Deputy Chairman or by any other members designated in that behalf by the Commission.

3. (1) The Commission shall consist of seven members, four of whom shall be citizens of Sierra Leone and the rest shall be non-citizens, all of whom shall be appointed by the President after being selected and recommended in accordance with the procedure prescribed in the schedule.

(2) The members of the Commission shall be –

    a. persons of integrity and credibility who would be impartial in the performance of their functions under this Act and who would enjoy the confidence generally of the people of Sierra Leone; and

    b. persons with high standing or competence as lawyers, social scientists, religious leaders, psychologists and in other professions or disciplines relevant to the functions of the Commission.

(3) The Commission shall have a Chairman and a Deputy Chairman both of whom shall be appointed by the President from among persons recommended by the Selection Coordinator and the United Nations High Commissioner for Human Rights.

(4) Where a vacancy occurs in the membership of the Commission because of the death, disability, resignation or dismissal of a member, the President shall appoint a replacement –

    a. where the vacancy is in respect of a citizen of Sierra Leone, from among the short-listed persons considered by the Selection Panel in accordance with the Schedule, giving due consideration to the rankings and comments of the Selection Panel, if any; and

    b. where the vacancy is in respect of a non-citizen, a person recommended by the United Nations High Commissioner for Human Rights.

(5) A member of the Commission may resign his office by written notice to the President and may be removed from office but only for inability to perform the functions of his office, whether arising from infirmity of body or mind or for a misconduct under this Act.

4. Members of the Commission shall work full-time or nearly as full-time as possible and shall, accordingly, be paid such remuneration as the President may determine, on the recommendation of the Selection Coordinator, acting on the advice of the United Nations High Commissioner for Human Rights.

5. (1) The Commission shall be inaugurated within two weeks of the appointment of its members and shall operate for one year. Provided that for good cause shown, the President may, by statutory instrument, extend the term of the Commission for a further six months.

(2) Before the commencement of the period of one year specified in subsection (1), the Commission shall have a preparatory period of three months during which it may undertake all tasks necessary to ensure that it is able to work effectively from the commencement of its operations.

(3) The tasks to be undertaken during the preparatory period shall include procurement of office space, preparing a budget, securing funds for the Commission, hiring staff, discussing questions of methodology, designing and undertaking a public education campaign for the purposes and procedures of the Commission, designing and putting in place a database, undertaking a preliminary background research, collecting supporting materials for its investigations and prioritising its work.

(4) Both during the preparatory period and after it commences operations, the Commission shall endeavour to inform the public of its existence and the purposes of its work, and, when appropriate, shall invite all interested parties who may wish to do so, to make statements or submit information to the Commission.

PART III – FUNCTIONS OF COMMISSION

6. (1) The object for which the Commission is established is to create an impartial historical record of violations and abuses of human rights and international humanitarian law related to the armed conflict in Sierra Leone, from the beginning of the Conflict in 1991 to the signing of the Lome Peace Agreement; to address impunity, to respond to the needs of the victims, to promote healing and reconciliation and to prevent a repetition of the violations and abuses suffered.

(2) Without prejudice to the generality of subsection (1), it shall be the function of the Commission –

   a. to investigate and report on the causes, nature and extent of the violations and abuses referred to in subsection (1) to the fullest degree possible, including their antecedents, the context in which the violations and abuses occurred, the question of, whether those violations and abuses were the result of deliberate planning, policy or authorisation by any government, group or individual, and the role of both internal and external factors in the conflict;
   b. to work to help restore the human dignity of victims and promote reconciliation by providing an opportunity for victims to give an

account of the violations and abuses suffered and for perpetrators to relate their experiences, and by creating a climate which fosters constructive interchange between victims and perpetrators, giving special attention to the subject of sexual abuses and to the experiences of children within the armed conflict; and

c. to do all such things as may contribute to the fulfilment of the object of the Commission.

7. (1) The Commission shall, subject to this Act, solely determine its operating procedures and mode of work with regard to its functions which shall include the following three components: –

a. undertaking investigation and research into key events, causes, patterns of abuse or violation and the parties responsible;
b. holding sessions, some of which may be public, to hear from the victims and perpetrators of any abuses or violations of from other interested parties; and
c. taking individual statements and gathering additional information with regard to the matters referred to in paragraphs (a) or (b).

(2) The Commission may seek assistance from traditional and religious leaders to facilitate its public sessions and in resolving local conflicts arising from past violations or abuses or in support of healing and reconciliation.

(3) At the discretion of the Commission, any person shall be permitted to provide information to the Commission on a confidential basis and the Commission shall not be compelled to disclose any information given to it in confidence.

(4) The Commission shall take into account the interests of victims and witnesses when inviting them to give statements, including the security and other concerns of those who may wish to recount their stories in public and the Commission may also implement special procedures to address the needs of such particular victims as children or those who have suffered sexual abuses as well as in working with child perpetrators of abuses or violations.

(5) Decisions of the Commission shall, as far as possible, be taken by consensus and in the absence of consensus, by the majority vote of members

of the Commission and the Chairman shall cast the deciding vote where there is a tie.

(6) During the course of its operations, the Commission may provide information or recommendations to or regarding the Special Fund for War Victims provided for in Article XXIV of the Lome Peace Agreement, or otherwise assist the Fund in any manner the Commission considers appropriate but the Commission shall not exercise any control over the operations or disbursements of that Fund.

8. (1) The Commission shall have power generally to organise its work and shall, in its operations, have power –

    a. to gather, by means it deems appropriate, any information it considers relevant, including the ability to request reports, records, documents or any information from any source, including governmental authorities, and to compel the production of such information as and when necessary;

    b. to visit any establishment or place without giving prior notice, and to enter upon any land or premises for any purpose which is material to the fulfilment of the Commission's mandate and in particular, for the purpose of obtaining information or inspecting any property or taking copies of any documents which may be of assistance to the Commission, and for safeguarding any such property or document;

    c. to interview any individual, group or members of organisations or institutions and, at the Commission's discretion, to conduct such interviews, in private;

    d. subject to adequate provision being made to meet his expenses for the purpose, to call upon any person to meet with the Commission or its staff, or to attend a session or hearing of the Commission, and to compel the attendance of any person who fails to respond to a request of the Commission to appear and to answer questions relevant to the subject matter of the session or hearing;

    e. to require that statements be given under oath or affirmation and to administer such oath or affirmation;

    f. to request information from the relevant authorities of a foreign country and to gather information from victims, witnesses, government officials and others in foreign countries;

    g. to issue summonses and subpoenas as it deems necessary in fulfilment of its mandate; and

h. to request and receive police assistance as needed in the enforcement of its powers.

(2) Failure to respond to a summons or subpoena issued by the Commission, failure to truly or faithfully answer questions of the Commission after responding to a summons or subpoena, or intentionally providing misleading or false information to the Commission shall be deemed equivalent to contempt of court and may, at the discretion of the Commission, be referred to the High Court for trial and punishment.

9. (1) All persons, including members and officers of the Government and political parties, shall cooperate with and provide unrestricted access for the Commission and its staff for any purposes necessary in the fulfilment of the Commission's mandate under this Act, as determined by the Commission.

(2) Any person who wilfully obstructs or otherwise interferes with the Commission or any of its members or officers in the discharge of the Commission's functions under this Act, commits an offence and shall be liable on conviction to a fine not exceeding one million leones or to a term of imprisonment not exceeding one year or both such fine and imprisonment.

PART IV – ADMINISTRATIVE PROVISIONS

10. (1) To assist it in the performance of its functions, the Commission may appoint such committees as it may consider necessary.

(2) A committee under this section shall include persons who are not members of the Commission but who are appointed, taking into account gender representation and regional participation in the work of the Commission.

(3) A member of a committee who is not a member of the Commission shall be paid such allowances as the Commission may determine.

11. (1) The Commission shall have such offices and may employ such staff, including citizens of Sierra Leone, as it may consider necessary for the efficient performance of its functions.

(2) Public officers may be seconded or otherwise render assistance to the Commission.

(3) The staff of the Commission shall be employed on such terms as the Commission shall, after consultation with the Selection Coordinator, determine.

12. (1) The operations of the Commission shall be financed by a fund consisting of moneys and other resources –

   a. paid or made available to the Commission by the Government; and
   b. obtained by the Commission as gift or donation from foreign governments, intergovernmental organisations, foundations and non-governmental organisations.

(2) In accordance with the Lome Peace Agreement, the Commission shall seek technical assistance from the international community, as it deems appropriate.

13. (1) The funds of the Commission shall be utilized only on the basis of the budget prepared under subsection (3) of section 5.

(2) The Commission shall keep proper books of account and other records in relation to the operation of the Commission and shall prepare quarterly statements of accounts in a form designed to –

   a. indicate monthly expenditures;
   b. provide data for up-to-date budget control based on the management information system of the Commission; and
   c. ensure correct use of the funds of the Commission.

(3) The accounts of the Commission kept under subsection (2) shall be audited by an auditor, being a professional accountant of high standing, appointed by the Commission and the statement of accounts together with the auditor's report thereon shall be submitted to the Government and other contributors to the funds of the Commission.

14. (1) Subject to this Act, the Commission shall, in the performance of its functions under this Act, not be subject to the direction or control of any person or authority.

(2) Each member of the Commission and member of staff of the Commission shall serve in his individual capacity, independent of any political party, government or other organisational interests, and shall avoid

taking any action which could create an appearance of partiality or otherwise harm the credibility or integrity of the Commission.

(3) No member of the Commission or member of staff of the Commission shall make private use of or profit from any confidential information gained as a result of his work in the Commission or divulge such information to any other person except in the course of his functions as a member or staff of the Commission and any contravention of this provision may result in dismissal from the Commission.

(4) No member of the Commission or staff of the Commission shall be held liable for any acts carried out within the scope of his duties.

(5) Any member or member of staff of the Commission who contravenes subsection (2) shall be guilty of misconduct and liable to be dismissed from the Commission.

PART V – REPORT AND RECOMMENDATIONS

15. (1) The Commission shall submit report of its work to the President at the end of its operations.

(2) The report shall summarise the findings of the Commission and shall make recommendations concerning the reforms and other measures, whether legal, political, administrative or otherwise, needed to achieve the object of the Commission, namely the object of providing impartial historical record, preventing the repetition of the violations or abuses suffered, addressing impunity, responding to the needs of victims and promoting healing and reconciliation.

16. (1) Immediately upon submitting the report to the President, the Commission shall publish the report in *The Gazette* by the insertion of the appropriate Government Notice and in such other publications as it may consider appropriate and shall, in collaboration with the Government of Sierra Leone, make copies of the report or summaries thereof, widely available to the public.

(2) The President shall –

    a. immediately upon receiving the report of the Commission, submit a copy to the United Nations Secretary-General with a request that it be tabled before the Security Council of the United Nations within thirty days; and

b. within thirty days of receiving the report of the Commission, submit a copy to Parliament with a request that it be lodged in the archive of Parliament.

17. The Government shall faithfully and timeously implement the recommendations of the report that are directed to state bodies and encourage or facilitate the implementation of any recommendations that may be directed to others.

18. (1) The Government shall, upon the publication of the report of the Commission, establish a committee or other body, including representatives of the Moral Guarantors of the Lome Peace Agreement, hereinafter referred to as "the follow-up Committee" to monitor the implementation of the recommendations of the Commission and to facilitate their implementation.

(2) The Government shall, during the period of eighteen months or such longer or shorter period after the establishment of the follow-up Committee as that Committee shall determine, provide quarterly reports to the follow-up committee summarising the steps it has taken towards implementation of the recommendations of the Commission.

(3) The follow-up Committee shall publish the reports of the Government under subsection (2) in the appropriate form and submit quarterly reports to the public evaluating the efforts of the Government and the efforts of any other person or body concerned to implement the recommendations of the Commission.

19. (1) The President shall, not later than three months after the submission of the report of the Commission to him, dissolve the Commission by notice in a statutory instrument.

(2) Before it is dissolved, the members of the Commission shall, among the final administrative activities of the Commission –

a. organise its archives and records, as appropriate, for possible future reference, giving special consideration to –
   (i) what materials or information might be made available to the public of Sierra Leone, either immediately or when conditions and resources allow; and

(ii) what measures may be necessary to protect confidential information; and

b. organise the disposal of the remaining property of the Commission.

SCHEDULE – (SUBSECTION (1) OF SECTION 3)

Procedure for the Selection of Nominees for Appointment to the Commission

To best ensure the Commission's independence and credibility, the members of the Commission shall be selected through a consultative process relying on both national and international expertise as follows:

(a) The four national members of the Commission shall be selected as follows:–

    i. Nominations, which may be put forward by anyone within or outside Sierra Leone, should be submitted to the United Nations Special Representative of the Secretary-General in Sierra Leone, who will serve as Selection Coordinator.

    ii. With the assistance of an advisory committee, and after broad consultation with a cross-section of Sierra Leonean society and with the United Nations High Commissioner for Human Rights, the Selection Coordinator shall draw up a list of 10 to 20 finalists. The advisory committee shall include a representative of the National Council of Paramount Chiefs, a representative of the Inter-Religious Council, and a member of the international community based in Sierra Leone, and perhaps others, at the discretion of the Selection Coordinator.

    iii. Each of the finalists will be interviewed by a Selection Panel of six persons, composed of one member appointed by each of the following: – the President, the Revolutionary United Front, the erstwhile Armed Forces Revolutionary Council, the Inter-religious Council, the National Forum for Human Rights and the National Commission for Democracy and Human Rights (or the Human Rights Commission, as set out in the Lome Peace Agreement, if such a Commission has been inaugurated).

    iv. The Selection Panel shall then rank and provide comments regarding each of the finalists to the Selection Coordinator on a confidential basis. Where possible, the Selection Panel should submit consensus views on finalists, though rankings and comments may be submitted individually by each panelist if views differ. In addition, the Selection Panel should suggest a possible Chair for the

Commission, especially if consensus can be reached on such recommendation. The Selection Coordinator shall assist the Selection Panel as needed and may establish a deadline for its submission.

v. Based on the recommendations from the Selection Panel and the criteria established in subsection (2) of section 3, the Selection Coordinator shall recommend four citizen's members for appointment to the Commission, and will suggest a possible Chair. Both the Selection Panel and the Selection Coordinator should take into account gender representation and regional considerations in making their selections. While the four members might not necessarily be from each of the four regions of the country, the Commission as a whole should represent the interests and perspectives of the country at large. If further regional representation is later desired, the Commission itself might co-opt representatives from each of the country's four regions.

(b) Suggestions for non-citizen members may be submitted directly to the United Nations High Commissioner for Human Rights, or to the Selection Coordinator who will forward them to the High Commissioner. Giving due consideration to those suggestions, but not limited to those, the High Commissioner for Human Rights will recommend three persons who are not citizens of Sierra Leone for appointment to the Commission, including one person proposed as possible Chair. The High Commissioner for Human Rights shall first submit these recommendations to the Selection Panel, with an invitation to make comments, before submitting them to the President.

SOLOMON E. BEREWA
Attorney-General and Minister of Justice

FEBRUARY 2000
MEMORANDUM OF OBJECTS AND REASONS (ATTACHED TO THE BILL)

The object of this Bill is to establish the Truth and Reconciliation Commission proposed by Article XXVI of the Lome Peace Agreement as part of the process of healing the wounds of the armed conflict which began in 1991. By clause 2 of the Bill, the Commission is being established as a body corporate.

Section 1 of Article XXVI of the Peace Agreement envisaged the proceedings of the Commission as a catharsis for constructive interchange between the victims and perpetrators of human rights violations and abuses and from this catharsis the Commission is to compile 'a clear picture of the past'. Accordingly, by clause 6, the principal function of the Commission is to create an impartial historical record of events in question as the basis for the task of preventing their recurrence.

To best ensure the Commission's independence and impartiality, the members of the Commission are to be appointed after a selection process involving both national and international expertise as stipulated in the Schedule to the Bill and involving a Selection Panel on which all the protagonists to the conflict and other interested parties are represented; (clause 3). By clause 5, the Commission shall operate for one year preceded by a period of three months during which the Commission is to carry out all the ground work necessary for its effectiveness when operations begin. For good cause shown, the term of the Commission may be extended by the President by statutory instrument for a period of six months.

Under clause 12, the Commission is required to raise the funds to finance its operations from both governmental and international non-governmental sources to which it is required to submit quarterly reports to account for the moneys donated (clause 13). Under clause 15, the Commission reports to the President who will then arrange to send copies of the report to the U.N. and Parliament. By clause 18, the Government is required to set up a follow-up Committee to monitor and stimulate the progress of the implementation of the Commission's findings. Under clause 19, the President is required to dissolve the Commission by notice in a statutory instrument not later than three months after the submission of the Commission's report.

FROM MADNESS TO HOPE: THE 12-YEAR WAR IN EL SALVADOR – REPORT OF THE COMMISSION ON THE TRUTH FOR EL SALVADOR (1993)

Excerpts:
Part I – Introduction (Parts A to I)
Part II – Mandate (Part C)

I. INTRODUCTION

Between 1980 and 1991, the Republic of El Salvador in Central America was engulfed in a war which plunged Salvadorian society into violence, left it with thousands and thousands of people dead and exposed it to appalling crimes, until the day – 16 January 1992 – when the parties, reconciled, signed the Peace Agreement in the Castle of Chapultepec, Mexico, and brought back the light and the chance to re-emerge from madness to hope.

A. Institutions and Names

Violence was a fire which swept over the fields of El Salvador; it burst into villages, cut off roads and destroyed highways and bridges, energy sources and transmission lines; it reached the cities and entered families, sacred areas and educational centres; it struck at justice and filled the public administration with victims; and it singled out as an enemy anyone who was not on the list of friends. Violence turned everything to death and destruction, for such is the senselessness of that breach of the calm plenitude which accompanies the rule of law, the essential nature of violence being suddenly or gradually to alter the certainty which the law nurtures in human beings when this change does not take place through the normal mechanisms of the rule of law. The victims were Salvadorians and foreigners of all backgrounds and all social and economic classes, for in its blind cruelty violence leaves everyone equally defenceless.

When there came pause for thought, Salvadorians put their hands to their hearts and felt them pound with joy. No one was winning the war, everyone was losing it. Governments of friendly countries and organizations the world over that had looked on in anguish at the tragic events in that Central American country which, although small, was made great by the creativity of its people – all contributed their ideas to the process of reflection. A visionary,

Javier Pérez de Cuéllar, then Secretary-General of the United Nations, heeded the unanimous outcry and answered it. The Presidents of Colombia, Mexico, Spain and Venezuela supported him. The Chapultepec Agreement expressed the support of the new Secretary-General, Mr. Boutros Boutros-Ghali, for the search for reconciliation.

B. The Creative Consequences

On the long road of the peace negotiations, the need to reach agreement on a Commission on the Truth arose from the Parties' recognition that the communism which had encouraged one side had collapsed, and perhaps also from the disillusionment of the Power which had encouraged the other. It emerged as a link in the chain of reflection and agreement and was motivated, ultimately, by the impact of events on Salvadorian society, which now faced the urgent task of confronting the issue of the widespread, institutionalized impunity which had struck at its very heart: under the protection of State bodies but outside the law, repeated human rights violations had been committed by members of the armed forces; these same rights had also been violated by members of the guerrilla forces.

In response to this situation, the negotiators agreed that such repugnant acts should be referred to a Commission on the Truth, which was the name they agreed to give it from the outset. Unlike the Ad Hoc Commission, so named because there was no agreement on what to call the body created to purify the armed forces, the Commission on the Truth was so named because its very purpose and function were to seek, find and publicize the truth about the acts of violence committed by both sides during the war.

The truth, the whole truth and nothing but the truth, as the oath goes. The overall truth and the specific truth, the radiant but quiet truth. The whole and its parts, in other words, the bright light shone onto a surface to illuminate it and the parts of this same surface lit up case by case, regardless of the identity of the perpetrators, always in the search for lessons that would contribute to reconciliation and to abolishing such patterns of behaviour in the new society.

Learning the truth and strengthening and tempering the determination to find it out; putting an end to impunity and cover-up; settling political and social differences by means of agreement instead of violent action: these are the creative consequences of an analytical search for the truth.

C. The Mandate

Furthermore, by virtue of the scope which the negotiators gave to the agreements, it was understood that the Commission on the Truth would have to examine systematic atrocities both individually and collectively, since the flagrant human rights violations which had shocked Salvadorian society and the international community had been carried out not only by members of the armed forces but also by members of the insurgent forces.

The peace agreements were unambiguous when, in article 2, they defined the mandate and scope of the Commission as follows: "The Commission shall have the task of investigating serious acts of violence that have occurred since 1980 and whose impact on society urgently demands that the public should know the truth". Article 5 of the Chapultepec Peace Agreement gives the Commission the task of clarifying and putting an end to any indication of impunity on the part of officers of the armed forces and gives this explanation: "acts of this nature, regardless of the sector to which their perpetrators belong, must be the object of exemplary action by the law courts so that the punishment prescribed by law is meted out to those found responsible".

It is clear that the peace negotiators wanted this new peace to be founded, raised and built on the transparency of a knowledge which speaks its name. It is also clear that this truth must be made public as a matter of urgency if it is to be not the servant of impunity but an instrument of the justice that is essential for the synchronized implementation of the agreements which the Commission is meant to facilitate.

D. "Open-Door" Policy

From the outset of their work, which began on 13 July 1992 when they were entrusted with their task by the Secretary-General of the United Nations, the Commissioners could perceive the skill of those who had negotiated the agreements in the breadth of the mandate and authority given to the Commission. They realized that the Secretary-General, upon learning from competent Salvadorian judges of the numerous acts of violence and atrocities of 12 years of war, had not been wrong in seeking to preserve the Commission's credibility by looking beyond considerations of sovereignty and entrusting this task to three scholars from other countries, in contrast to what had been done in Argentina and Chile after the military dictatorships there had ended. The Commissioners also saw a glimmer of hope dawn in the hearts of the Salvadorian people when it became clear that the truth would soon be revealed, not through bias or pressure but in its entirety and with complete impartiality, a fact which helped to restore the faith of people at all levels that justice would be effective and fitting. Accordingly, in their first meeting with the media upon arriving in El Salvador, the Commissioners stated that they would not let themselves be pressured or impressed: they were after the objective truth and the hard facts.

The Commissioners and the group of professionals who collaborated with them in the investigations succeeded in overcoming obstacles and limitations that made it difficult to establish what had really happened, starting with the brief period of time – six months – afforded them under the Chapultepec Agreement. Given the magnitude of their task, this time-frame, which seemed to stretch into Kafkaesque infinity when they embarked upon their task, ultimately seemed meagre and barely sufficient to allow them to complete their work satisfactorily.

Throughout its mandate and while drafting its report, the Commission consistently sought to distance itself from events that had not been verified before it reached any conclusions. The whole of Salvadorian society, institutions and individuals familiar with acts of violence were invited to make them known to the Commission, under the guarantee of confidentiality and discretion provided for in the agreements. Paid announcements were placed in the press and on the radio and television to this end, and written and oral invitations were extended to the Parties to testify without restriction. Offices of the Commission were opened in various departmental capitals, including Chalatenango, Santa Ana and San Miguel. Written statements were taken, witnesses were heard, information from the sites of various incidents (e.g. El Calabozo, El Mozote, Sumpul river and Guancorita) was obtained. The Commission itself went to various departments with members of the professional team, occasionally travelling overland but more often in helicopters provided promptly and efficiently by ONUSAL. As the investigation moved forward, it continued to yield new pieces of evidence: anyone who might have been involved was summonsed to testify without restriction as to time or place, usually in the Commission's offices or in secret locations, often outside El Salvador in order to afford witnesses greater protection.

The Commission maintained an "open-door" policy for hearing testimony and a "closed-door" policy for preserving confidentiality. Its findings illustrate the horrors of a war in which madness prevailed, and confirm beyond the shadow of a doubt that the incidents denounced, recorded and substantiated in this report actually took place. Whenever the Commission decided that its investigation of a specific case had yielded sufficient evidence, the matter was recorded in detail, with mention of the guilty parties. When it was determined that no further progress could be made for the time being, the corresponding documentation that was not subject to secrecy was delivered to the courts or else kept confidential until new information enabled it to be reactivated.

One fact must be squarely denounced: owing to the destruction or conceal-ment of documents, or the failure to divulge the locations where numerous persons were imprisoned or bodies were buried, the burden of proof occa-sionally reverted to the Commission, the judiciary and citizens, who found themselves forced to reconstruct events. It will be up to those who administer the new system of justice to pursue these investigations and take whatever final decisions they consider appropriate at this moment in history.

Inevitably, the list of victims is incomplete: it was compiled on the basis of the complaints and testimony received and confirmed by the Commission.

E. A Convulsion of Violence

The warped psychology engendered by the conflict led to a convulsion of violence. The civilian population in disputed or guerrilla-controlled areas was automatically assumed to be the enemy, as at El Mozote and the Sumpul river. The opposing side behaved likewise, as when mayors were executed, the killings justified as acts of war because the victims had obstructed the delivery of supplies to combatants, or when defenceless pleasure-seekers became military targets, as in the case of the United States marines in the Zona Rosa of San Salvador. Meanwhile, the doctrine of national salvation and the principle of "he who is not for me is against me" were cited to ignore the neutrality, passivity and defencelessness of journalists and church workers, who served the community in various ways.

Such behaviour also led to the clandestine refinement of the death squads:

the bullet which struck Monsignor Romero in the chest while he was celebrating mass on 24 March 1980 in a San Salvador church is a brutal symbol of the nightmare the country experienced during the war. And the murder of the six Jesuit priests 10 years later was the final outburst of the delirium that had infected the armed forces and the innermost recesses of certain government circles. The bullet in the portrait of Monsignor Romero, mute witness to this latest crime, repeats the nightmare image of those days.

F. Phenomenology of Violence

It is a universally accepted premise that the individual is the subject of any criminal situation, since humans alone possess will and can therefore take decisions based on will: it is individuals that commit crimes, not the institutions they have created. As a result, it is to individuals and not their institutions that the corresponding penalties established by law must be applied.

However, there could be some situations in which the repetition of acts in time and space would seem to contradict the above premise. A situation of repeated criminal acts may arise in which different individuals act within the same institution in unmistakably similar ways, independently of the political ideology of Governments and decision makers. This gives reason to believe that institutions may indeed commit crimes, if the same behaviour becomes a constant of the institution and, especially, if clear-cut accusations are met with a cover-up by the institution to which the accused belong and the institution is slow to act when investigations reveal who is responsible. In such circumstances, it is easy to succumb to the argument that repeated crimes mean that the institution is to blame.

The Commission on the Truth did not fall into that temptation: at the beginning of its mandate, it received hints from the highest level to the effect that institutions do not commit crimes and therefore that responsibilities must be established by naming names. At the end of its mandate, it again received hints from the highest level, this time to the opposite effect, namely, that it should not name names, perhaps in order to protect certain individuals in recognition of their genuine and commendable eagerness to help create situations which facilitated the peace agreements and national reconciliation.

However, the Commission believes that responsibility for anything that happened during the period of the conflict could not and should not be laid at the door of the institution, but rather of those who ordered the procedures for operating in the way that members of the institution did and also of those who, having been in a position to prevent such procedures, were compromised by the degree of tolerance and permissiveness with which they acted from their positions of authority or leadership or by the fact that they covered up incidents which came to their knowledge or themselves gave the order which led to the action in question. This approach protects institutions and punishes criminals.

G. The Recovery of Faith

As this Commission submits its report, El Salvador is embarked on a positive and irreversible process of consolidation of internal peace and modification of conduct for the maintenance of a genuine, lasting climate of national coexistence. The process of reconciliation is restoring the nation's faith in itself and in its leaders and institutions. This does not mean that all the obstacles and difficulties in implementing the commitments made in the negotiations have been overcome: the particular sensitivity of some of these commitments, such as the commitment to purify the armed forces, is creating resistance to the administrative action which must be taken by President Alfredo Cristiani, who on many counts deserves widespread recognition as the driving force behind the peace agreements.

One fundamental element of the agreements, and one which is critical for El Salvador's democratic future, is the unreserved, unconditional subordination of the military authorities to civilian authority, not only on paper but in reality: in a democratic system based on respect for the constitutional order and governed by the rule of law, there is room neither for conditions, personal compromises or the possibility of subverting order for personal reasons, nor for acts of intimidation against the President of the Republic who, by virtue of his office, is the Commander-in-Chief of the armed forces.

H. The Risk of Delays

The purification which is to follow the reports of the Ad Hoc Commission and the Commission on the Truth may seem inadvisable in cases where a person guilty of a serious crime in the past rectified his behaviour and contributed to the negotiated peace. This, however, is the small price that those who engage in punishable acts must pay, regardless of their position: they must accept it for the good of the country and the democratic future of the new Salvadorian society. Moreover, it is not up to the Commission to act on complaints, requests for pardon or pleas of attenuating circumstances from persons dismissed from the armed forces, because it has no binding judicial powers. It is not by resignation but by its creative attitude towards its new commitments and the new order of democratic coexistence that Salvadorian society as a whole will ultimately strike a balance in dealing with those who must take the blame for what they did during the conflict but deserve praise for what they did in the peace process.

El Salvador needs new souls. By its response to the murder of the Jesuits, 10 years after the assassination of Monsignor Romero by that nightmarish creation the "death squads", the military leadership showed just how far its position had hardened in daring to eliminate those it viewed as opponents, either because they were opponents or because they voiced concern, including church workers and journalists. In the uproar that followed, the most perverse sentiments came to the fore and the most absurd obfuscation was used in an attempt to cover up the truth as to who had given the orders.

What is more, it would tarnish the image of the armed forces if they were to retain sufficient power to block the process of purification or impose conditions on it: if the guilty were not singled out and punished, the institution itself would be incriminated; no other interpretation is possible. Those who would have the armed forces choose this course must weigh the price of such an attitude in the eyes of history.

I. Foundation for the Truth

The mass of reports, testimony, newspaper and magazine articles and books published in Spanish and other languages that was accumulated prompted the establishment within the Commission on the Truth itself of a centre for documentation on the different forms of violence in El Salvador. The public information relating to the war (books, pamphlets, research carried out by Salvadorian and international bodies); testimony from 2,000 primary sources referring to more than 7,000 victims; information from secondary sources relating to more than 20,000 victims; information from official bodies in the United States and other countries; information provided by government bodies and FMLN; an abundant photographic and videotape record of the conflict and even of the Commission's own activities; all of this material constitutes an invaluable resource – a part of El Salvador's heritage because (despite the painful reality it records) a part of the country's contemporary history – for historians and analysts of this most distressing period and for those who wish to study this painful reality in order to reinforce the effort to spread the message "never again".

What is to be done with this wealth of material in order to make it available to those around the world who are seeking peace, to bring these personal experiences to the attention of those who defend human rights? What is to be done when one is bound by the requirement of confidentiality for documents and testimony? What use is to be made of this example of the creativity of the United Nations at a time in contemporary history which is fraught with conflict and turmoil and for which the parallels and the answers found in the Salvadorian conflict may be of some relevance?

To guarantee the confidentiality of testimony and of the many documents supplied by institutions and even by Governments and, at the same time, to provide for the possibility of consultation by academic researchers while preserving such confidentiality, the Commission obtained the agreement of the Parties and the consent and support of the International Rule of Law Center of George Washington University in Washington, D.C., which, since 1992, has been administering and maintaining the collection of documents relating to the transition to peace in countries under the rule of oppression and countries emerging from armed conflicts. In addition, the Commission has already sought the cooperation of Governments, academic institutions and international foundations, always on the clear understanding that it holds itself personally responsible for guaranteeing confidentiality before finally handing the archives over to their lawful owners.

The Foundation for the Truth would be a not-for-profit academic body governed by statutes conforming to United States law. It would be managed by an international Board of Directors, with Salvadorian participation; a representative of the Secretary-General of the United Nations and the members of the Commission would also be members of the Board. The Foundation would be operated under the direction of Professor Thomas Buergenthal and would maintain close contacts with leaders and researchers in El Salvador, with the group of European, United States and Latin American professionals who worked with the Commission, and with scientists from around the world. For those documents which were not subject to secrecy, duplicate copies and computer terminals for accessing the collection would be available in Salvadorian institutions requesting them.

The Foundation would be inaugurated in June 1993, in Washington, with a multidisciplinary encounter to discuss the report of the Commission on the Truth.

. . .

II. THE MANDATE

. . .

C. Methodology

In determining the methodology that would govern the conduct of the investigations essential to the preparation of this report, the Commission took a number of factors into account.

The text of its mandate was a binding condition and a starting-point for the Commission, in that it stated the Parties' intentions in this connection. The preamble to the mandate indicates that the Commission was established because the Parties recognized "the need to clear up without delay those exceptionally important acts of violence whose characteristics and impact . . . urgently require that the complete truth be made known . . .".

In establishing the procedure that the Commission was to follow in performing its functions, paragraph 7 of the mandate provided that the Commission would conduct its activities "on a confidential basis". Paragraph 5 established that "The Commission shall not function in the manner of a judicial body". Paragraph 8 (a) stipulated that "The Commission shall be completely free to use whatever sources of information it deems useful and reliable", while paragraph 8 (b) gave the Commission the power to "Interview, freely and in private, any individuals, groups or members of organizations or institutions". Lastly, in the fourth preambular paragraph of the mandate, the Parties agreed that the task entrusted to the Commission should be fulfilled "through a procedure which is both reliable and expeditious and may yield results in the short term, without prejudice to the obligations incumbent on the Salvadorian courts to solve such cases and impose the appropriate penalties on the culprits".

In analysing these provisions of the mandate, the Commission thought it important that the Parties had emphasized that "the Commission shall not function in the manner of a judicial body". In other words, not only did the Parties not establish a court or tribunal, but they made it very clear that the Commission should not function as if it were a judicial body. They wanted to make sure that the Commission was able to act on a confidential basis and receive information from any sources, public or private, that it deemed useful and reliable. It was given these powers so that it could conduct an investigation procedure that was both expeditious and, in its view, reliable in order to "clear up without delay those exceptionally important acts of violence whose characteristics and impact . . . urgently require that the complete truth be made known."

So it is clear that the Parties opted for an investigation procedure that, within the short period of time allotted, would be best fitted to establishing the truth about acts of violence falling within the Commission's sphere of competence, without requiring the Commission to observe the procedures and rules that normally govern the activities of any judicial or quasi-judicial body. Any judicial function that had to be performed would be reserved expressly for the courts of El Salvador. For the Parties, the paramount concern was to find out the truth without delay.

Another important overall consideration which influenced the Commission's methodology was the reality of the situation in El Salvador today. Not only was this reflected in the Commission's mandate, but it also had a profound impact on the Commission's investigation process and modus operandi. It forced the Commission to gather its most valuable information in exchange for assurances of confidentiality.

It was not just that the Parties authorized the Commission, in the peace agreements, to act on a confidential basis and to receive information in private; the reality of the situation in El Salvador forced it to do so for two reasons: first, to protect the lives of witnesses and, secondly, to obtain information from witnesses who, because of the climate of terror in which they continue to live, would not have provided such information if the Commission had not guaranteed them absolute confidentiality.

The situation in El Salvador is such that the population at large continues to believe that many military and police officers in active service or in retirement, Government officials, judges, members of FMLN and people who at one time or another were connected with the death squads are in a position to cause serious physical and material injury to any person or institution that shows a readiness to testify about acts of violence committed between 1980 and 1991. The Commission believes that this suspicion is not unreasonable, given El Salvador's recent history and the power still wielded or, in many cases, wielded until recently by people whose direct involvement in serious acts of violence or in covering up such acts is well known but who have not been required to account for their actions or omissions.

Even though the fears expressed by some potential witnesses may have been exaggerated, the fact is that in their minds the danger is real. As a result, they were not prepared to testify unless they were guaranteed absolute secrecy. It should be pointed out that many witnesses refused to give information to other investigatory bodies in the past precisely because they were afraid that their identity would be divulged.

The Commission can itself testify to the extreme fear of reprisals frequently expressed, both verbally and through their behaviour, by many of the witnesses it interviewed. It is also important to emphasize that the Commission was not in a position to offer any significant protection to witnesses apart from this guarantee of confidentiality. Unlike the national courts, for instance, the Commission did not have the authority to order precautionary measures; neither, of course, did it have police powers. Besides, it is the perception of the public at large that the Salvadorian judicial system is unable to offer the necessary guarantees.

The Commission also received reports from some Governments and international bodies, on condition that the source was not revealed. This information was subjected to the same test of reliability as the other information received and was used principally to confirm or verify personal testimony and to guide the Commission in its search for other areas of investigation.

From the outset, the Commission was aware that accusations made and evidence received in secret run a far greater risk of being considered less trustworthy than those which are subjected to the normal judicial tests for determining the truth and to other related requirements of due process of law, including the right of the accused to confront and examine witnesses brought against him. Accordingly, the Commission felt that it had a special obligation to take all possible steps to ensure the reliability of the evidence used to arrive at a finding. In cases where it had to identify specific individuals as having committed, ordered or tolerated specific acts of violence, it applied a stricter test of reliability.

The Commission decided that, in each of the cases described in this report, it would specify the degree of certainty on which its ultimate finding was based. The different degrees of certainty were as follows:

1. Overwhelming evidence – conclusive or highly convincing evidence to support the Commission's finding;
2. Substantial evidence – very solid evidence to support the Commission's finding;
3. Sufficient evidence – more evidence to support the Commission's finding than to contradict it.

The Commission decided not to arrive at any specific finding on cases or situations, or any aspect thereof, in which there was less than "sufficient" evidence to support such a finding.

In order to guarantee the reliability of the evidence it gathered, the Commission insisted on verifying, substantiating and reviewing all statements as to facts, checking them against a large number of sources whose veracity had already been established. It was decided that no single source or witness would be considered sufficiently reliable to establish the truth on any issue of fact needed for the Commission to arrive at a finding. It was also decided that secondary sources, for instance, reports from national or international governmental or private bodies and assertions by people without first-hand knowledge of the facts they reported, did not on their own constitute a sufficient basis for arriving at findings. However, these secondary sources were used, along with circumstantial evidence, to verify findings based on primary sources.

It could be argued that, since the Commission's investigation methodology does not meet the normal requirements of due process, the report should not name the people whom the Commission considers to be implicated in specific acts of violence. The Commission believes that it had no alternative but to do so.

In the peace agreements, the Parties made it quite clear that it was necessary that the "complete truth be made known", and that was why the Commission was established. Now, the whole truth cannot be told without naming names. After all, the Commission was not asked to write an academic report on El Salvador, it was asked to investigate and describe exceptionally important acts of violence and to recommend measures to prevent the repetition of such acts. This task cannot be performed in the abstract, suppressing information (for instance, the names of persons responsible for such acts) where there is reliable testimony available, especially when the persons identified occupy senior positions and perform official functions directly related to violations or the cover-up of violations. Not to name names would be to reinforce the very impunity to which the Parties instructed the Commission to put an end.

In weighing aspects related to the need to protect the lives of witnesses against the interests of people who might be adversely affected in some way by the publication of their names in the report, the Commission also took into consideration the fact that the report is not a judicial or quasijudicial determination as to the rights or obligations of certain individuals under the law. As a result, the Commission is not, in theory, subject to the requirements of due process which normally apply, in proceedings which produce these consequences.

Furthermore, the Commission's application of strict criteria to determine the degree of reliability of the evidence in situations where people have been identified by name, and the fact that it named names only when it was absolutely convinced by the evidence, were additional factors which influenced the Commission when it came to take a decision on this analysis. As a result, the Commission is satisfied that the criteria of impartiality and reliability which it applied throughout the process were fully compatible with the functions entrusted to it and with the interests it had to balance.

The considerations which prompted the Commission to receive confidential information without revealing the source also forced it to omit references from both the body and the footnotes of the reports on individual cases, with the exception of references to certain public, official sources. As a result, reference is made to official trial proceedings and other similar sources, but not to testimony or other information gathered by the Commission. The Commission took this approach in order to reduce the likelihood that those responsible for the acts of violence described herein, or their defenders, would be able to identify the confidential sources of information used by the Commission. In some of the reports on individual cases, the Commission also omitted details that might reveal the identity of certain witnesses.

. . .

APPENDIX 3

Primary Materials on Other Commissions of Inquiry

UK INQUIRIES ACT (2005)

[Excerpts: Sections 1–26, 35–40]

An Act to make provision about the holding of inquiries.

[7th April 2005]

BE IT ENACTED by the Queen's most Excellent Majesty, by and with the advice and consent of the Lords Spiritual and Temporal, and Commons, in this present Parliament assembled, and by the authority of the same, as follows: –

CONSTITUTION OF INQUIRY

1 Power to establish inquiry

(1) A Minister may cause an inquiry to be held under this Act in relation to a case where it appears to him that –

    (a) particular events have caused, or are capable of causing, public concern, or

    (b) there is public concern that particular events may have occurred.

(2) In this Act "Minister" means –

(a) a United Kingdom Minister;
(b) the Scottish Ministers;
(c) a Northern Ireland Minister;

and references to a Minister also include references to the National Assembly for Wales.

(3) References in this Act to an inquiry, except where the context requires otherwise, are to an inquiry under this Act.

2 No determination of liability

(1) An inquiry panel is not to rule on, and has no power to determine, any person's civil or criminal liability.

(2) But an inquiry panel is not to be inhibited in the discharge of its functions by any likelihood of liability being inferred from facts that it determines or recommendations that it makes.

3 The inquiry panel

(1) An inquiry is to be undertaken either –

(a) by a chairman alone, or
(b) by a chairman with one or more other members.

(2) References in this Act to an inquiry panel are to the chairman and any other member or members.

4 Appointment of inquiry panel

(1) Each member of an inquiry panel is to be appointed by the Minister by an instrument in writing.

(2) The instrument appointing the chairman must state that the inquiry is to be held under this Act.

(3) Before appointing a member to the inquiry panel (otherwise than as chairman) the Minister must consult the person he has appointed, or proposes to appoint, as chairman.

5   Setting-up date and terms of reference

(1) In the instrument under section 4 appointing the chairman, or by a notice given to him within a reasonable time afterwards, the Minister must –

   (a) specify the date that is to be the setting-up date for the purposes of this Act; and
   (b) before that date –
      (i) set out the terms of reference of the inquiry;
      (ii) state whether or not the Minister proposes to appoint other members to the inquiry panel, and if so how many.

(2) An inquiry must not begin considering evidence before the setting-up date.

(3) The Minister may at any time after setting out the terms of reference under this section amend them if he considers that the public interest so requires.

(4) Before setting out or amending the terms of reference the Minister must consult the person he proposes to appoint, or has appointed, as chairman.

(5) Functions conferred by this Act on an inquiry panel, or a member of an inquiry panel, are exercisable only within the inquiry's terms of reference.

(6) In this Act "terms of reference", in relation to an inquiry under this Act, means –

   (a) the matters to which the inquiry relates;
   (b) any particular matters as to which the inquiry panel is to determine the facts;
   (c) whether the inquiry panel is to make recommendations;
   (d) any other matters relating to the scope of the inquiry that the Minister may specify.

6 Minister's duty to inform Parliament or Assembly

(1) A Minister who proposes to cause an inquiry to be held, or who has already done so without making a statement under this section, must as soon as is reasonably practicable make a statement to that effect to the relevant Parliament or Assembly.

(2) A statement under subsection (1) must state –

(a) who is to be, or has been, appointed as chairman of the inquiry;
(b) whether the Minister has appointed, or proposes to appoint, any other members to the inquiry panel, and if so how many;
(c) what are to be, or are, the inquiry's terms of reference.

(3) Where the terms of reference of an inquiry are amended under section 5(3), the Minister must, as soon as is reasonably practicable, make a statement to the relevant Parliament or Assembly setting out the amended terms of reference.

(4) A statement under this section may be oral or written.

7 Further appointments to inquiry panel

(1) The Minister may at any time (whether before the setting-up date or during the course of the inquiry) appoint a member to the inquiry panel –

(a) to fill a vacancy that has arisen in the panel (including a vacancy in the position of chairman), or
(b) to increase the number of members of the panel.

(2) The power to appoint a member under subsection (1)(b) is exercisable only –

(a) in accordance with a proposal under section 5(1)(b)(ii), or
(b) with the consent of the chairman.

(3) The power to appoint a replacement chairman may be exercised by appointing a person who is already a member of the inquiry panel.

8   Suitability of inquiry panel

(1) In appointing a member of the inquiry panel, the Minister must have regard –

(a) to the need to ensure that the inquiry panel (considered as a whole) has the necessary expertise to undertake the inquiry;

(b) in the case of an inquiry panel consisting of a chairman and one or more other members, to the need for balance (considered against the background of the terms of reference) in the composition of the panel.

(2) For the purposes of subsection (1)(a) the Minister may have regard to the assistance that may be provided to the inquiry panel by any assessor whom the Minister proposes to appoint, or has appointed, under section 11.

9   Requirement of impartiality

(1) The Minister must not appoint a person as a member of the inquiry panel if it appears to the Minister that the person has –

(a) a direct interest in the matters to which the inquiry relates, or

(b) a close association with an interested party,

unless, despite the person's interest or association, his appointment could not reasonably be regarded as affecting the impartiality of the inquiry panel.

(2) Before a person is appointed as a member of an inquiry panel he must notify the Minister of any matters that, having regard to subsection (1), could affect his eligibility for appointment.

(3) If at any time (whether before the setting-up date or during the course of the inquiry) a member of the inquiry panel becomes aware that he has an interest or association falling within paragraph (a) or (b) of subsection (1), he must notify the Minister.

(4) A member of the inquiry panel must not, during the course of the inquiry, undertake any activity that could reasonably be regarded as affecting his suitability to serve as such.

10   Appointment of judge as panel member

(1) If the Minister proposes to appoint as a member of an inquiry panel a particular person who is a judge of a description specified in the first column of the following table, he must first consult the person specified in the second column.

Description of judge	Person to be consulted
Lord of Appeal in Ordinary	The senior Lord of Appeal in Ordinary
Judge of the Supreme Court of England and Wales, or Circuit judge	The Lord Chief Justice of England and Wales
Judge of the Court of Session, sheriff principal or sheriff	The Lord President of the Court of Session
Judge of the Supreme Court of Northern Ireland, or county court judge in Northern Ireland	The Lord Chief Justice of Northern Ireland

(2) In this section "sheriff principal" and "sheriff" have the same meaning as in the Sheriff Courts (Scotland) Act 1971 (c. 58).

11   Assessors

(1) One or more persons may be appointed to act as assessors to assist the inquiry panel.

(2) The power to appoint assessors is exercisable –

    (a) before the setting-up date, by the Minister;
    (b) during the course of the inquiry, by the chairman (whether or not the Minister has appointed assessors).

(3) Before exercising his powers under subsection (2)(a) the Minister must consult the person he proposes to appoint, or has appointed, as chairman.

(4) A person may be appointed as an assessor only if it appears to the Minister or the chairman (as the case requires) that he has expertise that makes him a suitable person to provide assistance to the inquiry panel.

(5) The chairman may at any time terminate the appointment of an assessor, but only with the consent of the Minister in the case of an assessor appointed by the Minister.

12   Duration of appointment of members of inquiry panel

(1) Subject to the following provisions of this section, a member of an inquiry panel remains a member until the inquiry comes to an end (or until his death if he dies before then).

(2) A member of an inquiry panel may at any time resign his appointment by notice to the Minister.

(3) The Minister may at any time by notice terminate the appointment of a member of an inquiry panel –

   (a) on the ground that, by reason of physical or mental illness or for any other reason, the member is unable to carry out the duties of a member of the inquiry panel;

   (b) on the ground that the member has failed to comply with any duty imposed on him by this Act;

   (c) on the ground that the member has –
      (i) a direct interest in the matters to which the inquiry relates, or
      (ii) a close association with an interested party, such that his membership of the inquiry panel could reasonably be regarded as affecting its impartiality;

   (d) on the ground that the member has, since his appointment, been guilty of any misconduct that makes him unsuited to membership of the inquiry panel.

(4) In determining whether subsection (3)(a) applies in a case where the inability to carry out the duties is likely to be temporary, the Minister may have regard to the likely duration of the inquiry.

(5) The Minister may not terminate a member's appointment under subsection (3)(c) if the Minister was aware of the interest or association in question when appointing him.

(6) Before exercising his powers under subsection (3) in relation to a member other than the chairman, the Minister must consult the chairman.

(7) Before exercising his powers under subsection (3) in relation to any member of the inquiry panel, the Minister must –

- (a) inform the member of the proposed decision and of the reasons for it, and take into account any representations made by the member in response, and
- (b) if the member so requests, consult the other members of the inquiry panel (to the extent that no obligation to consult them arises under subsection (6)).

13 Power to suspend inquiry

(1) The Minister may at any time, by notice to the chairman, suspend an inquiry for such period as appears to him to be necessary to allow for –

- (a) the completion of any other investigation relating to any of the matters to which the inquiry relates, or
- (b) the determination of any civil or criminal proceedings (including proceedings before a disciplinary tribunal) arising out of any of those matters.

(2) The power conferred by subsection (1) may be exercised whether or not the investigation or proceedings have begun.

(3) Before exercising that power the Minister must consult the chairman.

(4) A notice under subsection (1) may suspend the inquiry until a specified day, until the happening of a specified event or until the giving by the Minister of a further notice to the chairman.

(5) Where the Minister gives a notice under subsection (1) he must –

- (a) set out in the notice his reasons for suspending the inquiry;
- (b) lay a copy of the notice, as soon as is reasonably practicable, before the relevant Parliament or Assembly.

(6) A member of an inquiry panel may not exercise the powers conferred by this Act during any period of suspension; but the duties imposed on a member of an inquiry panel by section 9(3) and (4) continue during any such period.

(7) In this section "period of suspension" means the period beginning with the receipt by the chairman of the notice under subsection (1) and ending with whichever of the following is applicable –

(a) the day referred to in subsection (4);
(b) the happening of the event referred to in that subsection;
(c) the receipt by the chairman of the further notice under that subsection.

14   End of inquiry

(1) For the purposes of this Act an inquiry comes to an end –

(a) on the date, after the delivery of the report of the inquiry, on which the chairman notifies the Minister that the inquiry has fulfilled its terms of reference, or
(b) on any earlier date specified in a notice given to the chairman by the Minister.

(2) The date specified in a notice under subsection (1)(b) may not be earlier than the date on which the notice is sent.

(3) Before exercising his power under subsection (l)(b) the Minister must consult the chairman.

(4) Where the Minister gives a notice under subsection (1)(b) he must –

(a) set out in the notice his reasons for bringing the inquiry to an end;
(b) lay a copy of the notice, as soon as is reasonably practicable, before the relevant Parliament or Assembly.

CONVERSION OF INQUIRIES

15   Power to convert other inquiry into inquiry under this Act

(1) Where –

(a) an inquiry ("the original inquiry") is being held, or is due to be held, by one or more persons appointed otherwise than under this Act,

(b) a Minister gives a notice under this section to those persons, and

(c) the person who caused the original inquiry to be held consents,

the original inquiry becomes an inquiry under this Act as from the date of the notice or such later date as may be specified in the notice (the "date of conversion").

(2) The power conferred by this section is exercisable only if the original inquiry relates to a case where it appears to the Minister that –

(a) particular events have caused, or are capable of causing, public concern, or

(b) there is public concern that particular events may have occurred.

(3) Before exercising that power the Minister must consult the chairman.

(4) A notice under this section must –

(a) state that, as from the date of conversion, the inquiry is to be held under this Act;

(b) in the case of an inquiry panel consisting of more than one member, identify who is to be chairman of the panel;

(c) set out what are to be the terms of reference of the inquiry.

(5) The terms of reference set out under subsection (4) may be different from those of the original inquiry.

(6) The Minister may at any time after setting out the terms of reference under this section amend them if he considers that the public interest so requires.

(7) The Minister must consult the chairman before –

(a) setting out terms of reference that are different from those of the original inquiry, or

(b) amending the terms of reference under subsection (6).

(8) Section 6 applies, with any necessary modifications, in relation to –

(a) converting an inquiry under this section, or

(b) amending an inquiry's terms of reference under subsection (6), as it applies in relation to causing an inquiry to be held, or amending an inquiry's terms of reference under section 5(3).

16   Inquiries converted under section 15

(1) This section applies where an inquiry (the "original inquiry") is converted under section 15 into an inquiry under this Act.

(2) The appointment of a person who at the date of conversion is –

  (a) one of the persons holding, or due to hold, the original inquiry (an "original member"),
  (b) an assessor, counsel or solicitor to the inquiry, or
  (c) a person engaged to provide assistance to the inquiry,

continues as if made under this Act, and for the purposes of section 12(5) is treated as made by the Minister on the date of conversion.

(3) Any obligation arising under an order of the original inquiry, or otherwise in connection with that inquiry, is enforceable only as it would be if the original inquiry had not been converted.

(4) No rights or obligations arise under or by virtue of this Act before the date of conversion.

INQUIRY PROCEEDINGS

17   Evidence and procedure

(1) Subject to any provision of this Act or of rules under section 41, the procedure and conduct of an inquiry are to be such as the chairman of the inquiry may direct.

(2) In particular, the chairman may take evidence on oath, and for that purpose may administer oaths.

(3) In making any decision as to the procedure or conduct of an inquiry, the chairman must act with fairness and with regard also to the need to avoid any unnecessary cost (whether to public funds or to witnesses or others).

18 *Public access to inquiry proceedings and information*

(1) Subject to any restrictions imposed by a notice or order under section 19, the chairman must take such steps as he considers reasonable to secure that members of the public (including reporters) are able –

    (a) to attend the inquiry or to see and hear a simultaneous transmission of proceedings at the inquiry;

    (b) to obtain or to view a record of evidence and documents given, produced or provided to the inquiry or inquiry panel.

(2) No recording or broadcast of proceedings at an inquiry may be made except –

    (a) at the request of the chairman, or

    (b) with the permission of the chairman and in accordance with any terms on which permission is given.

Any such request or permission must be framed so as not to enable a person to see or hear by means of a recording or broadcast anything that he is prohibited by a notice under section 19 from seeing or hearing.

(3) Section 32(2) of the Freedom of Information Act 2000 (c. 36) (certain inquiry records etc exempt from obligations under that Act) does not apply in relation to information contained in documents that, in pursuance of rules under section 41(1)(b) below, have been passed to and are held by a public authority.

(4) Section 37(1)(b) of the Freedom of Information (Scotland) Act 2002 (asp 13) (certain inquiry records etc exempt from obligations under that Act) does not apply in relation to information contained in documents that, in pursuance of rules under section 41(1)(b) below, have been passed to and are held by a Scottish public authority.

19 *Restrictions on public access etc*

(1) Restrictions may, in accordance with this section, be imposed on –

    (a) attendance at an inquiry, or at any particular part of an inquiry;

    (b) disclosure or publication of any evidence or documents given, produced or provided to an inquiry.

(2) Restrictions may be imposed in either or both of the following ways –

(a) by being specified in a notice (a "restriction notice") given by the Minister to the chairman at any time before the end of the inquiry;

(b) by being specified in an order (a "restriction order") made by the chairman during the course of the inquiry.

(3) A restriction notice or restriction order must specify only such restrictions –

(a) as are required by any statutory provision, enforceable Community obligation or rule of law, or

(b) as the Minister or chairman considers to be conducive to the inquiry fulfilling its terms of reference or to be necessary in the public interest, having regard in particular to the matters mentioned in subsection (4).

(4) Those matters are –

(a) the extent to which any restriction on attendance, disclosure or publication might inhibit the allaying of public concern;

(b) any risk of harm or damage that could be avoided or reduced by any such restriction;

(c) any conditions as to confidentiality subject to which a person acquired information that he is to give, or has given, to the inquiry;

(d) the extent to which not imposing any particular restriction would be likely –

(i) to cause delay or to impair the efficiency or effectiveness of the inquiry, or

(ii) otherwise to result in additional cost (whether to public funds or to witnesses or others).

(5) In subsection (4)(b) "harm or damage" includes in particular –

(a) death or injury;

(b) damage to national security or international relations;

(c) damage to the economic interests of the United Kingdom or of any part of the United Kingdom;

(d) damage caused by disclosure of commercially sensitive information.

20   *Further provisions about restriction notices and orders*

(1) Restrictions specified in a restriction notice have effect in addition to any already specified, whether in an earlier restriction notice or in a restriction order.

(2) Restrictions specified in a restriction order have effect in addition to any already specified, whether in an earlier restriction order or in a restriction notice.

(3) The Minister may vary or revoke a restriction notice by giving a further notice to the chairman at any time before the end of the inquiry.

(4) The chairman may vary or revoke a restriction order by making a further order during the course of the inquiry.

(5) Restrictions imposed under section 19 on disclosure or publication of evidence or documents ("disclosure restrictions") continue in force indefinitely, unless –

> (a) under the terms of the relevant notice or order the restrictions expire at the end of the inquiry, or at some other time, or
> (b) the relevant notice or order is varied or revoked under subsection (3), (4) or (7).

This is subject to subsection (6).

(6) After the end of the inquiry, disclosure restrictions do not apply to a public authority, or a Scottish public authority, in relation to information held by the authority otherwise than as a result of the breach of any such restrictions.

(7) After the end of an inquiry the Minister may, by a notice published in a way that he considers suitable –

> (a) revoke a restriction order or restriction notice containing disclosure restrictions that are still in force, or
> (b) vary it so as to remove or relax any of the restrictions.

(8) In this section "restriction notice" and "restriction order" have the meaning given by section 19(2).

21   *Powers of chairman to require production of evidence etc*

(1) The chairman of an inquiry may by notice require a person to attend at a time and place stated in the notice –

(a) to give evidence;
(b) to produce any documents in his custody or under his control that relate to a matter in question at the inquiry;
(c) to produce any other thing in his custody or under his control for inspection, examination or testing by or on behalf of the inquiry panel.

(2) The chairman may by notice require a person, within such period as appears to the inquiry panel to be reasonable –

(a) to provide evidence to the inquiry panel in the form of a written statement;
(b) to provide any documents in his custody or under his control that relate to a matter in question at the inquiry;
(c) to produce any other thing in his custody or under his control for inspection, examination or testing by or on behalf of the inquiry panel.

(3) A notice under subsection (1) or (2) must –

(a) explain the possible consequences of not complying with the notice;
(b) indicate what the recipient of the notice should do if he wishes to make a claim within subsection (4).

(4) A claim by a person that –

(a) he is unable to comply with a notice under this section, or
(b) it is not reasonable in all the circumstances to require him to comply with such a notice,

is to be determined by the chairman of the inquiry, who may revoke or vary the notice on that ground.

(5) In deciding whether to revoke or vary a notice on the ground mentioned in subsection (4)(b), the chairman must consider the public interest in the information in question being obtained by the inquiry, having regard to the likely importance of the information.

(6) For the purposes of this section a thing is under a person's control if it is in his possession or if he has a right to possession of it.

22   Privileged information etc

(1) A person may not under section 21 be required to give, produce or provide any evidence or document if–

(a) he could not be required to do so if the proceedings of the inquiry were civil proceedings in a court in the relevant part of the United Kingdom, or
(b) the requirement would be incompatible with a Community obligation.

(2) The rules of law under which evidence or documents are permitted or required to be withheld on grounds of public interest immunity apply in relation to an inquiry as they apply in relation to civil proceedings in a court in the relevant part of the United Kingdom.

23   Risk of damage to the economy

(1) This section applies where it is submitted to an inquiry panel, on behalf of the Crown, the Financial Services Authority or the Bank of England, that there is information held by any person which, in order to avoid a risk of damage to the economy, ought not to be revealed.

(2) The panel must not permit or require the information to be revealed, or cause it to be revealed, unless satisfied that the public interest in the information being revealed outweighs the public interest in avoiding a risk of damage to the economy.

(3) In making a decision under this section the panel must take account of any restriction notice given under section 19 or any restriction order that the chairman has made or proposes to make under that section.

(4) In this section –

"damage to the economy" means damage to the economic interests of the United Kingdom or of any part of the United Kingdom;
"revealed" means revealed to anyone who is not a member of the inquiry panel.

(5) This section does not prevent the inquiry panel from communicating any information in confidence to the Minister.

(6) This section does not affect the rules of law referred to in section 22(2).

INQUIRY REPORTS

24 Submission of reports

(1) The chairman of an inquiry must deliver a report to the Minister setting out –

(a) the facts determined by the inquiry panel;
(b) the recommendations of the panel (where the terms of reference required it to make recommendations).

The report may also contain anything else that the panel considers to be relevant to the terms of reference (including any recommendations the panel sees fit to make despite not being required to do so by the terms of reference).

(2) In relation to an inquiry that is brought to an end under section 14(1)(b), the duty imposed by subsection (1) to deliver a report is to be read as a power to do so.

(3) Before making a report under subsection (1) the chairman may deliver to the Minister a report under this subsection (an "interim report") containing anything that a report under subsection (1) may contain.

(4) A report of an inquiry must be signed by each member of the inquiry panel.

(5) If the inquiry panel is unable to produce a unanimous report, the report must reasonably reflect the points of disagreement.

(6) In subsections (4) and (5) "report" includes an interim report.

25 Publication of reports

(1) It is the duty of the Minister, or the chairman if subsection (2) applies, to arrange for reports of an inquiry to be published.

(2) This subsection applies if –

    (a) the Minister notifies the chairman before the setting-up date that the chairman is to have responsibility for arranging publication, or

    (b) at any time after that date the chairman, on being invited to do so by the Minister, accepts responsibility for arranging publication.

(3) Subject to subsection (4), a report of an inquiry must be published in full.

(4) The person whose duty it is to arrange for a report to be published may withhold material in the report from publication to such extent –

    (a) as is required by any statutory provision, enforceable Community obligation or rule of law, or

    (b) as the person considers to be necessary in the public interest, having regard in particular to the matters mentioned in subsection (5).

(5) Those matters are –

    (a) the extent to which withholding material might inhibit the allaying of public concern;

    (b) any risk of harm or damage that could be avoided or reduced by withholding any material;

    (c) any conditions as to confidentiality subject to which a person acquired information that he has given to the inquiry.

(6) In subsection (5)(b) "harm or damage" includes in particular–

    (a) death or injury;

    (b) damage to national security or international relations;

    (c) damage to the economic interests of the United Kingdom or of any part of the United Kingdom;

    (d) damage caused by disclosure of commercially sensitive information.

(7) Subsection (4)(b) does not affect any obligation of the Minister, or any other public authority or Scottish public authority, that may arise under the Freedom of Information Act 2000 (c. 36) or the Freedom of Information (Scotland) Act 2002 (asp 13).

(8) In this section "report" includes an interim report.

26   *Laying of reports before Parliament or Assembly*

Whatever is required to be published under section 25 must be laid by the Minister, either at the time of publication or as soon afterwards as is reasonably practicable, before the relevant Parliament or Assembly.

. . .

SUPPLEMENTARY

35   *Offences*

(1) A person is guilty of an offence if he fails without reasonable excuse to do anything that he is required to do by a notice under section 21.

(2) A person is guilty of an offence if during the course of an inquiry he does anything that is intended to have the effect of –

(a) distorting or otherwise altering any evidence, document or other thing that is given, produced or provided to the inquiry panel, or
(b) preventing any evidence, document or other thing from being given, produced or provided to the inquiry panel,

or anything that he knows or believes is likely to have that effect.

(3) A person is guilty of an offence if during the course of an inquiry –

(a) he intentionally suppresses or conceals a document that is, and that he knows or believes to be, a relevant document, or
(b) he intentionally alters or destroys any such document.

For the purposes of this subsection a document is a "relevant document" if it is likely that the inquiry panel would (if aware of its existence) wish to be provided with it.

(4) A person does not commit an offence under subsection (2) or (3) by doing anything that he is authorised or required to do –

(a) by the inquiry panel, or
(b) by virtue of section 22 or any privilege that applies.

(5) Proceedings in England and Wales or in Northern Ireland for an offence under subsection (1) may be instituted only by the chairman.

(6) Proceedings for an offence under subsection (2) or (3) may be instituted –

> (a) in England and Wales, only by or with the consent of the Director of Public Prosecutions;
> (b) in Northern Ireland, only by or with the consent of the Director of Public Prosecutions for Northern Ireland.

(7) A person who is guilty of an offence under this section is liable on summary conviction to a fine not exceeding level three on the standard scale or to imprisonment for a term not exceeding the relevant maximum, or to both.

(8) "The relevant maximum" is –

> (a) in England and Wales, 51 weeks;
> (b) in Scotland and Northern Ireland, six months.

36   Enforcement by High Court or Court of Session

(1) Where a person –

> (a) fails to comply with, or acts in breach of, a notice under section 19 or 21 or an order made by an inquiry, or
> (b) threatens to do so,

the chairman of the inquiry, or after the end of the inquiry the Minister, may certify the matter to the appropriate court.

(2) The court, after hearing any evidence or representations on a matter certified to it under subsection (1), may make such order by way of enforcement or otherwise as it could make if the matter had arisen in proceedings before the court.

(3) In this section "the appropriate court" means the High Court or, in the case of an inquiry in relation to which the relevant part of the United Kingdom is Scotland, the Court of Session.

37   *Immunity from suit*

(1) No action lies against –

  (a) a member of an inquiry panel,
  (b) an assessor, counsel or solicitor to an inquiry, or
  (c) a person engaged to provide assistance to an inquiry,

in respect of any act done or omission made in the execution of his duty as such, or any act done or omission made in good faith in the purported execution of his duty as such.

(2) Subsection (1) applies only to acts done or omissions made during the course of the inquiry, otherwise than during any period of suspension (within the meaning of section 13).

(3) For the purposes of the law of defamation, the same privilege attaches to –

  (a) any statement made in or for the purposes of proceedings before an inquiry (including the report and any interim report of the inquiry), and
  (b) reports of proceedings before an inquiry,

as would be the case if those proceedings were proceedings before a court in the relevant part of the United Kingdom.

38   *Time limit for applying for judicial review*

(1) An application for judicial review of a decision made –

  (a) by the Minister in relation to an inquiry, or
  (b) by a member of an inquiry panel,

must be brought within 14 days after the day on which the applicant became aware of the decision, unless that time limit is extended by the court.

(2) Subsection (1) does not apply where an earlier time limit applies by virtue of Civil Procedure Rules or rules made under section 55 of the Judicature (Northern Ireland) Act 1978 (c. 23).

(3) Subsection (1) does not apply to –

(a) a decision as to the contents of the report of the inquiry;
(b) a decision of which the applicant could not have become aware until the publication of the report.

In this subsection "report" includes any interim report.

(4) This section does not extend to Scotland.

39 Payment of inquiry expenses by Minister

(1) The Minister may agree to pay to –

(a) the members of the inquiry panel,
(b) any assessor, counsel or solicitor to the inquiry, and
(c) any person engaged to provide assistance to the inquiry,

such remuneration and expenses as the Minister may determine.

(2) The Minister must pay any amounts awarded under section 40.

(3) The Minister must meet any other expenses incurred in holding the inquiry, including the cost of publication of the report and any interim report of the inquiry (whether or not the chairman has responsibility for arranging publication).

(4) Subsection (5) applies where the Minister –

(a) believes that there are matters in respect of which an inquiry panel is acting outside the inquiry's terms of reference, or is likely to do, and
(b) gives a notice to the chairman specifying those matters and the reasons for his belief.

(5) Subject to provision made by rules under section 41, the Minister is not obliged under this section or otherwise to pay any amounts or to meet any expenses in so far as they are referable –

(a) to any matters certified by the Minister, in accordance with such provision, to be outside the inquiry's terms of reference, and

(b) to any period falling after the date on which the notice under sub-section (4) was given.

(6) Within a reasonable time after the end of the inquiry the Minister must publish the total amount of what he has paid (or remains liable to pay) under this section.

40   Expenses of witnesses etc

(1) The chairman may award reasonable amounts to a person –

(a) by way of compensation for loss of time, or
(b) in respect of expenses properly incurred, or to be incurred,

in attending, or otherwise in relation to, the inquiry.

(2) The power to make an award under this section includes power, where the chairman considers it appropriate, to award amounts in respect of legal representation.

(3) A person is eligible for an award under this section only if he is –

(a) a person attending the inquiry to give evidence or to produce any document or other thing, or
(b) a person who, in the opinion of the chairman, has such a particular interest in the proceedings or outcome of the inquiry as to justify such an award.

(4) The power to make an award under this section is subject to such conditions or qualifications as may be determined by the Minister and notified by him to the chairman.

. . .

REPORT OF THE INTERNATIONAL COMMISSION OF INQUIRY ON DARFUR TO THE UNITED NATIONS SECRETARY-GENERAL (2005)

[Excerpts: Executive Summary; Introduction (paras. 1–39)]

Pursuant to Security Council Resolution 1564 of 18 September 2004

Geneva, 25 January 2005

EXECUTIVE SUMMARY

Acting under Chapter VII of the United Nations Charter, on 18 September 2004 the Security Council adopted resolution 1564 requesting, inter alia, that the Secretary-General 'rapidly establish an international commission of inquiry in order immediately to investigate reports of violations of international human-itarian law and human rights law in Darfur by all parties, to determine also whether or not acts of genocide have occurred, and to identify the perpetra-tors of such violations with a view to ensuring that those responsible are held accountable'.

In October 2004, the Secretary General appointed Antonio Cassese (Chair-person), Mohamed Fayek, Hina Jilani, Dumisa Ntsebeza and Therese Striggner-Scott as members of the Commission and requested that they report back on their findings within three months. The Commission was supported in its work by a Secretariat headed by an Executive Director, Ms. Mona Rishmawi, as well as a legal research team and an investigative team composed of investigators, forensic experts, military analysts, and investigators specializing in gender vio-lence, all appointed by the Office of the United Nations High Commissioner for Human Rights. The Commission assembled in Geneva and began its work on 25 October 2004.

In order to discharge its mandate, the Commission endeavoured to fulfil four key tasks: (1) to investigate reports of violations of international humanitarian law and human rights law in Darfur by all parties; (2) to determine whether or not acts of genocide have occurred; (3) to identify the perpetrators of violations of international humanitarian law and human rights law in Darfur; and (4) to suggest means of ensuring that those responsible for such violations are held accountable. While the Commission considered all events relevant to the current conflict in Darfur, it focused in particular on incidents that occurred between February 2003 and mid-January 2005.

The Commission engaged in a regular dialogue with the Government of the Sudan throughout its mandate, in particular through meetings in Geneva and in the Sudan, as well as through the work of its investigative team. The Commission visited the Sudan from 7–21 November 2004 and 9–16 January 2005, including travel to the three Darfur States. The investigative team remained in Darfur from November 2004 through January 2005. During its presence in the Sudan, the Commission held extensive meetings with representatives of the Government, the Governors of the Darfur States and other senior officials in the capital and at provincial and local levels, members of the armed forces and police, leaders of rebel forces, tribal leaders, internally displaced persons, victims and witnesses of violations, NGOs and United Nations representatives.

The Commission submitted a full report on its findings to the Secretary-General on 25 January 2005. The report describes the terms of reference, methodology, approach and activities of the Commission and its investigative team. It also provides an overview of the historical and social background to the conflict in Darfur. The report then addresses in detail the four key tasks referred to above, namely the Commission's findings in relation to: i) violations of international human rights and humanitarian law by all parties; ii) whether or not acts of genocide have taken place; iii) the identification of perpetrators; and iv) accountability mechanisms. These four sections are briefly summarized below.

I. Violations of international human rights law and international humanitarian law

In accordance with its mandate to 'investigate reports of violations of human rights law and international humanitarian law', the Commission carefully examined reports from different sources including Governments, intergovernmental organizations, United Nations bodies and mechanisms, as well as nongovernmental organizations.

The Commission took as the starting point for its work two irrefutable facts regarding the situation in Darfur. Firstly, according to United Nations estimates there are 1.65 million internally displaced persons in Darfur, and more than 200,000 refugees from Darfur in neighbouring Chad. Secondly, there has been large-scale destruction of villages throughout the three states of Darfur. The Commission conducted independent investigations to establish additional facts and gathered extensive information on multiple incidents of violations affecting villages, towns and other locations across North, South and West Darfur. The conclusions of the Commission are based on the evaluation of the facts gathered or verified through its investigations.

Based on a thorough analysis of the information gathered in the course of its investigations, the Commission established that the Government of the Sudan and the Janjaweed are responsible for serious violations of international human rights and humanitarian law amounting to crimes under international law. In particular, the Commission found that Government forces and militias conducted indiscriminate attacks, including killing of civilians, torture, enforced disappearances, destruction of villages, rape and other forms of sexual violence, pillaging and forced displacement, throughout Darfur. These acts were conducted on a widespread and systematic basis, and therefore may amount to crimes against humanity. The extensive destruction and displacement have resulted in a loss of livelihood and means of survival for countless women, men and children. In addition to the large scale attacks, many people have been arrested and detained, and many have been held incommunicado for prolonged periods and tortured. The vast majority of the victims of all of these violations have been from the Fur, Zaghawa, Massalit, Jebel, Aranga and other so-called 'African' tribes.

In their discussions with the Commission, Government of the Sudan officials stated that any attacks carried out by Government armed forces in Darfur were for counter-insurgency purposes and were conducted on the basis of military imperatives. However, it is clear from the Commission's findings that most attacks were deliberately and indiscriminately directed against civilians. Moreover even if rebels, or persons supporting rebels, were present in some of the villages – which the Commission considers likely in only a very small number of instances – the attackers did not take precautions to enable civilians to leave the villages or otherwise be shielded from attack. Even where rebels may have been present in villages, the impact of the attacks on civilians shows that the use of military force was manifestly disproportionate to any threat posed by the rebels.

The Commission is particularly alarmed that attacks on villages, killing of civilians, rape, pillaging and forced displacement have continued during the course of the Commission's mandate. The Commission considers that action must be taken urgently to end these violations.

While the Commission did not find a systematic or a widespread pattern to these violations, it found credible evidence that rebel forces, namely members of the SLA and JEM, also are responsible for serious violations of international human rights and humanitarian law which may amount to war crimes. In particular, these violations include cases of murder of civilians and pillage.

II. Have acts of genocide occurred?

The Commission concluded that the Government of the Sudan has not pursued a policy of genocide. Arguably, two elements of genocide might be deduced from the gross violations of human rights perpetrated by Government forces and the militias under their control. These two elements are, first, the actus reus consisting of killing, or causing serious bodily or mental harm, or deliberately inflicting conditions of life likely to bring about physical destruction; and, second, on the basis of a subjective standard, the existence of a protected group being targeted by the authors of criminal conduct. However, the crucial element of genocidal intent appears to be missing, at least as far as the central Government authorities are concerned. Generally speaking the policy of attacking, killing and forcibly displacing members of some tribes does not evince a specific intent to annihilate, in whole or in part, a group distinguished on racial, ethnic, national or religious grounds. Rather, it would seem that those who planned and organized attacks on villages pursued the intent to drive the victims from their homes, primarily for purposes of counter-insurgency warfare.

The Commission does recognise that in some instances individuals, including Government officials, may commit acts with genocidal intent. Whether this was the case in Darfur, however, is a determination that only a competent court can make on a case by case basis.

The conclusion that no genocidal policy has been pursued and implemented in Darfur by the Government authorities, directly or through the militias under their control, should not be taken in any way as detracting from the gravity of the crimes perpetrated in that region. International offences such as the crimes against humanity and war crimes that have been committed in Darfur may be no less serious and heinous than genocide.

III. Identification of perpetrators

The Commission has collected reliable and consistent elements which indicate the responsibility of some individuals for serious violations of international human rights law and international humanitarian law, including crimes against humanity or war crimes, in Darfur. In order to identify perpetrators, the Commission decided that there must be 'a reliable body of material consistent with other verified circumstances, which tends to show that a person may reasonably be suspected of being involved in the commission of a crime.' The Commission therefore makes an assessment of likely suspects, rather than a final judgment as to criminal guilt.

Those identified as possibly responsible for the above-mentioned violations consist of individual perpetrators, including officials of the Government of Sudan, members of militia forces, members of rebel groups, and certain foreign army officers acting in their personal capacity. Some Government officials, as well as members of militia forces, have also been named as possibly responsible for joint criminal enterprise to commit international crimes. Others are identified for their possible involvement in planning and/or ordering the commission of international crimes, or of aiding and abetting the perpetration of such crimes. The Commission also has identified a number of senior Government officials and military commanders who may be responsible, under the notion of superior (or command) responsibility, for knowingly failing to prevent or repress the perpetration of crimes. Members of rebel groups are named as suspected of participating in a joint criminal enterprise to commit international crimes, and as possibly responsible for knowingly failing to prevent or repress the perpetration of crimes committed by rebels.

The Commission has decided to withhold the names of these persons from the public domain. This decision is based on three main grounds: 1) the importance of the principles of due process and respect for the rights of the suspects; 2) the fact that the Commission has not been vested with investigative or prosecutorial powers; and 3) the vital need to ensure the protection of witnesses from possible harassment or intimidation. The Commission instead will list the names in a sealed file that will be placed in the custody of the UN Secretary-General. The Commission recommends that this file be handed over to a competent Prosecutor (the Prosecutor of the International Criminal Court, according to the Commission's recommendations), who will use that material as he or she deems fit for his or her investigations. A distinct and very voluminous sealed file, containing all the evidentiary material collected by the Commission, will be handed over to the High Commissioner for Human Rights. This file should be delivered to a competent Prosecutor.

IV. Accountability mechanisms

The Commission strongly recommends that the Security Council immediately refer the situation of Darfur to the International Criminal Court, pursuant to article 13(b) of the ICC Statute. As repeatedly stated by the Security Council, the situation constitutes a threat to international peace and security. Moreover, as the Commission has confirmed, serious violations of international human rights law and humanitarian law by all parties are continuing. The prosecution by the ICC of persons allegedly responsible for the most serious crimes in Darfur would contribute to the restoration of peace in the region.

The alleged crimes that have been documented in Darfur meet the thresholds of the Rome Statute as defined in articles 7 (1), 8 (1) and 8 (f). There is an internal armed conflict in Darfur between the governmental authorities and organized armed groups. A body of reliable information indicates that war crimes may have been committed on a large-scale, at times even as part of a plan or a policy. There is also a wealth of credible material which suggests that criminal acts were committed as part of widespread or systematic attacks directed against the civilian population, with knowledge of the attacks. In the opinion of the Commission therefore, these may amount to crimes against humanity.

The Sudanese justice system is unable and unwilling to address the situation in Darfur. This system has been significantly weakened during the last decade. Restrictive laws that grant broad powers to the executive have undermined the effectiveness of the judiciary, and many of the laws in force in Sudan today contravene basic human rights standards. Sudanese criminal laws do not adequately proscribe war crimes and crimes against humanity, such as those carried out in Darfur, and the Criminal Procedure Code contains provisions that prevent the effective prosecution of these acts. In addition, many victims informed the Commission that they had little confidence in the impartiality of the Sudanese justice system and its ability to bring to justice the perpetrators of the serious crimes committed in Darfur. In any event, many have feared reprisals in the event that they resort to the national justice system.

The measures taken so far by the Government to address the crisis have been both grossly inadequate and ineffective, which has contributed to the climate of almost total impunity for human rights violations in Darfur. Very few victims have lodged official complaints regarding crimes committed against them or their families, due to a lack of confidence in the justice system. Of the few cases where complaints have been made, most have not been properly pursued. Furthermore, procedural hurdles limit the victims' access to justice. Despite the magnitude of the crisis and its immense impact on civilians in Darfur, the Government informed the Commission of very few cases of individuals who have been prosecuted, or even disciplined, in the context of the current crisis.

The Commission considers that the Security Council must act not only against the perpetrators but also on behalf of the victims. It therefore recommends the establishment of a Compensation Commission designed to grant reparation to the victims of the crimes, whether or not the perpetrators of such crimes have been identified.

It further recommends a number of serious measures to be taken by the Government of the Sudan, in particular (i) ending the impunity for the war crimes and crimes against humanity committed in Darfur; (ii) strengthening the independence and impartiality of the judiciary, and empowering courts to address human rights violations; (iii) granting full and unimpeded access by the International Committee of the Red Cross and United Nations human rights monitors to all those detained in relation to the situation in Darfur; (iv) ensuring the protection of all the victims and witnesses of human rights violations; (v) enhancing the capacity of the Sudanese judiciary through the training of judges, prosecutors and lawyers; (vi) respecting the rights of IDPs and fully implementing the Guiding Principles on Internal Displacement, particularly with regard to facilitating the voluntary return of IDPs in safety and dignity; (vii) fully cooperating with the relevant human rights bodies and mechanisms of the United Nations and the African Union; and (viii) creating, through a broad consultative process, a truth and reconciliation commission once peace is established in Darfur.

The Commission also recommends a number of measures to be taken by other bodies to help break the cycle of impunity. These include the exercise of universal jurisdiction by other States, re-establishment by the Commission on Human Rights of the mandate of the Special Rapporteur on human rights in Sudan, and public and periodic reports on the human rights situation in Darfur by the High Commissioner for Human Rights.

INTRODUCTION

I. The Role of the Commission of Inquiry

1. Establishment of the Commission

1. The International Commission of Inquiry on Darfur (henceforth the Commission) was established pursuant to United Nations Security Council resolution 1564 (2004), adopted on 18 September 2004. The resolution, passed under Chapter VII of the United Nations Charter, requested the Secretary-General rapidly to set up the Commission. In October 2004 the Secretary-General appointed a five member body (Mr. Antonio Cassese, from Italy; Mr. Mohammed Fayek, from Egypt; Ms Hina Jilani, from Pakistan; Mr. Dumisa Ntsebeza, from South Africa, and Ms Theresa Striggner-Scott, from Ghana), and designated Mr. Cassese as its Chairman. The Secretary-General decided that the Commission's staff should be provided by the Office of the High Commissioner for Human Rights. Ms Mona Rishmawi was appointed Executive Director of the Commission and head of its staff. The Commission assembled in Geneva and began its work on 25 October 2004. The Secretary-General requested the Commission to report to him within three months, i.e. by 25 January 2005.

2. Terms of reference

2. In § 12, resolution 1564 (2004) sets out the following tasks for the Commission: "to investigate reports of violations of international humanitarian law and human rights law in Darfur by all parties"; "to determine also whether or not acts of genocide have occurred"; and "to identify the perpetrators of such violations"; "with a view to ensuring that those responsible are held accountable". Under the resolution, these tasks must be discharged "immediately".

3. The first of the above tasks implies that the Commission, rather than investigating alleged violations, must investigate "reports" of such violations committed by "all parties". This means that it is mandated to establish facts relating to possible violations of international human rights and humanitarian law committed in Darfur. In this respect the Commission must act as a fact-finding body, beginning with an assessment of information contained in the various reports made by other bodies including Governments, United Nations bodies, organs of other intergovernmental organizations, as well as NGOs.

4. It also falls to the Commission to characterize, from the viewpoint of international criminal law, the violations of international human rights law and humanitarian law it may establish. This legal characterization is implicitly required by the further tasks of the Commission set out by the Security Council, namely (i) to establish whether those violations amount to genocide, and (ii) to identify the perpetrators. Clearly, the Commission may not be in a position to fulfil these tasks if it has not previously established (a) whether the violations amount to international crimes, and, if so, (b) under what categories of crimes they fall (war crimes, crimes against humanity, genocide, or other crimes). This classification is required not only for the purpose of determining whether those crimes amount to genocide, but also for the process of identifying the perpetrators. In order to name particular persons as suspected perpetrators, it is necessary to define the international crimes for which they might be held responsible.

5. The second task with which the Security Council entrusted the Commission is that of legally characterizing the reported violations with a view to ascertaining whether they amount to genocide.

6. The third task is that of "identifying the perpetrators of violations" "with a view to ensuring that those responsible are held accountable". This requires the Commission not only to identify the perpetrators, but also to suggest possible mechanisms for holding those perpetrators accountable. The Commission

therefore must collect a reliable body of material that indicate which individuals may be responsible for violations committed in Darfur and who should therefore be brought to trial with a view to determining their liability. The Commission has not been endowed with the powers proper to a prosecutor (in particular, it may not subpoena witnesses, or order searches or seizures, nor may it request a judge to issue arrest warrants against suspects). It may rely only upon the obligation of the Government of the Sudan and the rebels to cooperate. Its powers are therefore limited by the manner in which the Government and the rebels fulfil this obligation.

7. In order to discharge its mandate in conformity with the international law that it is bound to apply, the Commission has to interpret the word "perpetrators" as covering the executioners or material authors of international crimes, as well as those who may have participated in the commission of such crimes under the notion of joint criminal enterprise, or ordered their perpetration, or aided or abetted the crimes, or in any other manner taken part in their perpetration. The Commission has included in this inquiry those who may be held responsible for international crimes, under the notion of superior responsibility, because they failed to prevent or repress the commission of such crimes although they a) had (or should have had) knowledge of their commission, and b) wielded control over the persons who perpetrated them. This interpretation is justified by basic principles of international criminal law, which provide that individual criminal responsibility arises when a person materially commits a crime, as well as when he or she engages in other forms or modalities of criminal conduct.

8. Furthermore, the language of the Security Council resolution makes it clear that the request to "identify perpetrators" is "with a view to ensuring that those responsible are held accountable". In § 7 the resolution reiterates its request to the Government of the Sudan "to end the climate of impunity in Darfur" and to bring to justice "all those responsible, including members of popular defence forces and Janjaweed militias" for violations of human rights law and international humanitarian law (emphasis added). Furthermore, the tasks of the Commission include that of "ensuring that those responsible are held accountable". Thus, the Security Council has made it clear that it intends for the Commission to identify all those responsible for alleged international crimes in Darfur. This is corroborated by an analysis of the objective of the Security Council: if this body aimed at putting an end to atrocities, why should the Commission confine itself to the material perpetrators, given that those who bear the greatest responsibility normally are the persons who are in command, and who either plan or order crimes, or knowingly condone or acquiesce in their perpetration?

9. This interpretation is also in keeping with the wording of the same paragraph in other official languages (for instance, the French text speaks of "auteurs de ces violations" and the Spanish text of "los autores de tales transgresiones"). It is true that in many cases a superior may not be held to have taken part in the crimes of his or her subordinates, in which case he or she would not be regarded as a perpetrator or author of those crimes. In those instances where criminal actions by subordinates are isolated episodes, the superior may be responsible only for failing to "submit the matter to the competent authorities for investigation and prosecution". In such instances, unquestionably the superior may not be considered as the author of the crime perpetrated by his or her subordinates. However, when crimes are committed regularly and on a large scale, as part of a pattern of criminal conduct, the responsibility of the superior is more serious. By failing to stop the crimes and to punish the perpetrators, he or she in a way takes part in their commission.

10. The fourth task assigned to the Commission therefore is linked to the third and is aimed at ensuring that "those responsible are held accountable". To this effect, the Commission intends to propose measures for ensuring that those responsible for international crimes in Darfur are brought to justice.

11. As is clear from the relevant Security Council resolution, the Commission is mandated to consider only the situation in the Darfur region of the Sudan. With regard to the time-frame, the Commission's mandate is inferred by the resolution. While the Commission considered all events relevant to the current conflict in Darfur, it focused in particular on incidents that occurred between February 2003, when the magnitude, intensity and consistency of incidents noticeably increased, until mid-January 2005 just before the Commission was required to submit its report.

3. Working methods

12. As stated above, the Commission started its work in Geneva on 25 October 2004. It immediately discussed and agreed upon its terms of reference and methods of work. On 28 October 2004 it sent a Note Verbale to Member States and intergovernmental organizations, and on 2 November 2004 it sent a letter to non-governmental organizations, providing information about its mandate and seeking relevant information. It also posted information on its mandate, composition and contact details on the web-site of the Office of the High Commissioner for Human Rights (www.ohchr.org).

13. The Commission agreed at the outset that it would discharge its mission in strict confidentiality. In particular, it would limit its contacts with the media to

providing factual information about its visits to the Sudan. The Commission also agreed that its working methods should be devised to suit each of its different tasks.

14. Thus, with regard to its first and second tasks, the Commission decided to examine existing reports on violations of international human rights and humanitarian law in Darfur, and to verify the veracity of these reports through its own findings, as well as to establish further facts. Although clearly it is not a judicial body, in classifying the facts according to international criminal law, the Commission adopted an approach proper to a judicial body. It therefore collected all material necessary for such a legal analysis.

15. The third task, that of "identifying perpetrators", posed the greatest challenge. The Commission discussed the question of the standard of proof that it would apply in its investigations. In view of the limitations inherent in its powers, the Commission decided that it could not comply with the standards normally adopted by criminal courts (proof of facts beyond a reasonable doubt), or with that used by international prosecutors and judges for the purpose of confirming indictments (that there must be a prima facie case). It concluded that the most appropriate standard was that requiring a reliable body of material consistent with other verified circumstances, which tends to show that a person may reasonably be suspected of being involved in the commission of a crime. The Commission would obviously not make final judgments as to criminal guilt; rather, it would make an assessment of possible suspects that would pave the way for future investigations, and possible indictments, by a prosecutor.

16. The Commission also agreed that, for the purpose of "identifying the perpetrators", it would interview witnesses, officials and other persons occupying positions of authority, as well as persons in police custody or detained in prison; examine documents; and visit places (in particular, villages or camps for IDPs, as well as mass grave sites) where reportedly crimes were perpetrated.

17. For the fulfilment of the fourth task the Commission deemed it necessary to make a preliminary assessment of the degree to which the Sudanese criminal justice system has been able and willing to prosecute and bring to trial alleged authors of international crimes perpetrated in Darfur, and then consider the various existing international mechanisms available. It is in the light of these evaluations that it has made recommendations on the most suitable measures.

4. Principal constraints under which the Commission has operated

18. There is no denying that while the various tasks assigned to the Commission are complex and unique, the Commission was called upon to discharge them under difficult conditions. First of all, it operated under serious time constraints. As pointed out above, given that the Security Council had decided that the Commission must act urgently, the Secretary-General requested that the Commission report to him within three months of its establishment. The fulfilment of its complex tasks, in particular those concerning the finding of serious violations and the identification of perpetrators, required the Commission to work intensely and under heavy time pressure.

19. Furthermore, both its fact-finding mission and its task of identifying perpetrators would have benefited from the assistance of a great number of investigators, lawyers, military analysts and forensic experts. Given the scale and magnitude of incidents related to the conflict in Darfur, the establishment of facts and the collection of credible probative elements for the identification of suspected perpetrators are difficult tasks, which are not to be taken lightly. The Commission's budget did not allow for more than thirteen such experts. Having said this, the Commission nevertheless was able to gather a reliable and consistent body of material with respect to both the violations that occurred and the persons who might be suspected of bearing criminal responsibility for their perpetration. The Commission thus considers that it has been able to take a first step towards accountability.

5. Brief account of the Commission's visits to the Sudan

20. The Commission first visited the Sudan from 8 to 20 November 2004. It met with a number of high level officials including the First Vice-President, the Minister of Justice, the Minister for Foreign Affairs, the Minister of Interior, the Minister of Defence, the Minister of Federal Affairs, the Deputy Chief Justice, the Speaker of Parliament, the Deputy Head of the National Security and Intelligence Service, and members of the Rape Committees. It met with representatives of non-governmental organizations, political parties, and interested foreign government repesentatives in the Sudan. In addition, it held meetings with the United Nations Advance Mission in the Sudan (UN-AMIS) and other United Nations representatives in the country. The Commission also visited Kober prison (See Annex 2 for a full list of meetings).

21. From 11 to 17 November 2004, the Commission visited Darfur. It divided itself into three teams, each focusing on one of the three states of Darfur. Each

team met with the State Governor (Wali) and senior officials, visited camps of internally displaced persons, and spoke with witnesses and to the tribal leaders. In addition, the West Darfur team visited refugee camps in Chad and the South Darfur team visited the National Security Detention Center in Nyala.

22. The Commission's investigation team was led by a Chief Investigator and included four investigators, two female investigators specializing in gender violence, four forensic experts and two military analysts. Investigation team members interviewed witnesses and officials in Khartoum and accompanied the Commissioners on their field mission to the three Darfur States. The investigation team was then divided into three sub-teams which were deployed to North, South and West Darfur.

23. One Commission member and Commission staff, acting on behalf of the Commission, visited Eritrea from 25–26 November 2004. They met with representatives of two rebel groups: The Sudan Liberation Movement/Army (SLM/A) and the Justice and Equality Movement (JEM). They also met with former Sudanese officials who are now residing in Eritrea. Two members of the Commission, accompanied by two staff members, travelled to Addis Ababa from 30 November to 3 December 2004. The objectives were: to obtain a thorough assessment from the African Union (AU) on the situation in Darfur, the African Mission in the Sudan (AMIS) and the Inter-Sudanese talks in Abuja; and to discuss with the AU leadership ways and modalities for the Commission to strengthen its working cooperation. The delegation met with high level officials of the AU, including the newly appointed Special Representative for the Sudan. The delegation also had the opportunity to meet extensively with the Chair and some key members of the AU Integrated Task Force on Darfur.

24. A second visit to the Sudan took place between 9 and 16 January 2004. During this visit, the Commission focused on interviewing witnesses particularly in detention centres, and also met with some officials, members of civil society, and UN staff in Khartoum.

25. With the assistance of a team of five legal researchers and one political affairs officer, who were led by the Executive Director, the Commission analysed the information provided. It reviewed and analysed published, public reports on Darfur, other reports that were brought to the attention of the Commission in response to its requests for information, as well as other types of information. In order to manage the more than 20,000 pages of material it received, the Commission developed a database in which it recorded bibliographic and evidentiary details. The incidents' analysis carried out by the research team

also was recorded in the database as a way to facilitate swift access by the Commissioners and staff to resource material and source information.

6. Cooperation of the Sudanese authorities and the rebels

26. Security Council resolution 1564 (2004) was adopted under Chapter VII of the United Nations Charter. The Security Council (SC) had previously determined (already in resolution 1556 (2004), at preambular § 21) that the situation in the Sudan constitutes a "threat to international peace and security and to stability in the region" under Article 39 of the United Nations Charter.

27. § 12 of the resolution, which requests the Secretary-General to establish an international commission of inquiry, also "calls on all parties to cooperate fully with such a commission". The Commission considers that, by the very nature of the Commission and its mandate, both the Government of the Sudan and the rebels are under a bona fide obligation to cooperate with it in the discharge of its various functions. In any event, both the Government of the Sudan and the rebel groups have willingly accepted to cooperate with the Commission.

(i.) Criteria for appraising cooperation

28. The Commission set forth the following criteria for evaluating the degree of cooperation of both the Government and the rebels: (i) freedom of movement throughout the territory of the Sudan; (ii) unhindered access to all places and establishments, and freedom to meet and interview representatives of governmental and local authorities, military authorities, community leaders, non-governmental organizations and other institutions, and any such person whose testimony is considered necessary for the fulfilment of its mandate; (iii) free access to all sources of information, including documentary material and physical evidence; (iv) appropriate security arrangements for the personnel and documents of the Commission; (v) protection of victims and witnesses and all those who appear before the Commission in connection with the inquiry and, in particular, guarantee that no such person would, as a result of such appearance, suffer harassment, threats, acts of intimidation, illtreatment and reprisals; and (vi) privileges, immunities and facilities necessary for the independent conduct of the inquiry. A letter was sent to the Government outlining these criteria.

(ii.) Cooperation of the Government

29. As mentioned above, since its inception the Commission has engaged in a constant dialogue with the Government of the Sudan through meetings in Geneva and the Sudan, and through the work of its investigative team.

30. Generally speaking the attitude of the Government authorities towards the Commission has been cooperative. The authorities appointed an efficient liaison official in Khartoum, Dr Abdelmonem Osman Taha, who organized all the meetings with senior Government officials requested by the Commission. In addition, the Minister of Interior as the President's representative on Darfur appointed a Committee presided over by Major-General Magzoub and consisted of six senior officials from the Ministries of Defence and Interior, as well as the National Security and Intelligence Service. The Commission met the Committee and received relevant documents about the Government's views on the conflict in Darfur.

31. Moreover, in his report dated 3 December 2004 (S/2004/947), the Secretary-General referred to a meeting of the Joint Implementation Mechanism (JIM) held on 12 November 2004, during which the Minister of Justice provided the following assurances regarding the work of the Commission: a) the Government would accept the report of the Commission, whatever its findings; b) witnesses of incidents would not be subjected to maltreatment; and c) following strict instruction from the President, Omer Hassan Al-Bashir, no Sudanese officials would obstruct the Commission's investigations.

32. Furthermore, the Government did not impede the conduct of the Commission's work in the Sudan. In November 2004, a middle-level officer of the National Security Services refused to allow the Commission to have access to a number of persons being held in detention in Nyala (South Darfur). The Commission's Chairman requested the assistance of the liaison officer in Khartoum, and, subsequently, the Commission was able to interview the detainees without any hindrance. The Commission underwent a similar experience in Khartoum in January 2005, during its second visit to the Sudan. When some middle-level authorities refused to allow the Commission access to the National Security's Detention Centre in Khartoum, the Chairman requested the immediate intervention of higher authorities and the Commission was eventually allowed access to the Centre.

33. However, one issue must be raised regarding the minutes of the meetings of the Security Committees at the locality and State levels. In a meeting with the First Vice-President Ali Osman Mohammed Taha held in Khartoum on 10 November 2004, the Commission asked to review the records of the various Government agencies in Darfur concerning decisions relating to the use of armed forces against rebels and measures concerning the civilian population. The Commission promised to keep its scrutiny of such records strictly confidential. During the same meeting, First Vice-President Taha assured the Commission that it would be able to have access to and examine the minutes

of the meetings of the Security Committees in the three States of Darfur and their various localities. However, when requested to produce those minutes, each of the Governors of the three States asserted that no such minutes existed and instead produced a selected list of final decisions on general issues. According to reliable sources, minutes and reports of such meetings are in fact produced by the Security Committees, and some of them relate to the operations conducted in Darfur to oppose the rebels or to deal with displaced persons. In spite of its requests, the Commission did not see copies of these documents.

34. An episode bearing on cooperation relates to another request by the Commission. In a meeting held on 9 November 2004 with Bakri Hassan Salih, Minister of Defence, and other senior Ministry of Defence officials, the Commission requested access to records of the deployment of military aircraft and helicopter gunships in Darfur since February 2003. Again, the Commission undertook to treat such records confidentially. The Minister of Defence agreed to comply with the request and promised that the Commission would obtain the records in Darfur from the relevant authorities. When the Commission did not obtain copies of these records in Darfur, it reiterated its request in a meeting with the Committee on Darfur on 20 November 2004. The Chairman of the Committee promised to provide those records and subsequently provided the Commission with an incomplete file, promising that it would be supplemented with further information. After further requests by the Commission, a number of records related to the use of aircraft in Darfur between February 2003 and January 2005 were produced. However, a complete set of the records requests was never provided to the Commission.

35. The Commission also wishes to stress that there have been episodes indicative of pressure put by some regional or local authorities on prospective witnesses, or on witnesses already interviewed by the Commission. For instance, in the first week of November 2004, in El Fashir (North Darfur) a government official, reportedly the chief of the local office of the National Security and Intelligence Service, gave money to some IDPs and urged them not to talk to the Commission. It was also reported to the Commission that the Sudanese authorities had deployed infiltrators posing as internally displaced persons (IDPs) into some camps such as Abushouk. In the same camp various eyewitnesses reported an episode that could be taken to amount to witness harassment. On 19 December 2004, around 12.30 in the afternoon, approximately twenty vehicles and three trucks drove through the camp. They stopped in the centre of the camp and started shouting: "We killed the Torabora (a common word used for indicating the rebels). We killed your fathers, your brothers. You have to sleep forever." Women and children in the vicinity ran away, returning

only after the soldiers had left the area. People in the camp were very worried about the safety of the entire camp.

36. In other instances, local authorities refused to allow the Commission's investigative team entry into a camp to interview witnesses. However these cases were settled in due course, after negotiations with the authorities.

(iii.) Cooperation of the Rebels

37. The Commission was in contact only with the two main rebel movements, the JEM and the SLM/A, and generally considers that both groups co-operated with the Commission. The Commission met with representatives and members of the two groups on a number of occasions in the Sudan, as well as outside the country. It met with the leadership of SLM/A and JEM in Asmara (Eritrea), including the Secretary-General and military commanders of the SLM/A, Minnie Arkawi Minawi, the chief negotiator of the SLM/A at the AU-sponsored talks, Dr. Sherif Harir, and the Chairman of the JEM, Dr. Khalil Ibrahim, as well as other senior officials of both groups. Discussions were open and frank, and both organisations provided responses to queries presented by the Commission. In Darfur, the Commission met, on several occasions, with various representatives of the two rebel groups.

38. The Commission received a number of documents from both groups, which included information of a more general nature about Darfur and the Sudan, as well as detailed documentation on specific incidents including names of victims allegedly killed in attacks. However, the Commission was led to believe that the documentary information provided by the rebels would be more extensive and detailed than what in fact was obtained.

39. The Commission was never refused access to areas under the control of the rebels and was able to move freely in these areas. The rebel groups did not interfere with the Commission's investigations of reported incidents involving the rebels.

. . .

Index

abbreviated trial, *See* summary trial
administrative tribunals, 14, 41, 69, 90, 95,
    106–108, 112, 119, 122–124, 238, 257,
    289
adversarial proceedings, 24, 116–117, 126,
    127, 130, 190, 236, 248, 261
affirmative action, 98, 113
Afghanistan, 5, 51, 66
African Charter on Human and Peoples'
    Rights, 93–95, 97–98, 138, 252
    Protocol on the Rights of Women in
    Africa, 93, 98
African Charter on the Rights and Welfare of
    the Child, 93
African Commission on Human and
    Peoples' Rights, 53, 68
African Committee of Experts on the Rights
    and Welfare of the Child, 53, 68
African Court on Human and Peoples'
    Rights, xiii, 68, 71
African National Congress, 18, 45, 272,
    317
African Union, 53, 61, 68, 84, 93
    See also Organization of African Unity
Albania, 48, 66
Algeria, 19–20, 25, 133
alternative dispute resolution, 71
American Convention on Human Rights, 8,
    67, 92–99, 138, 236, 252, 297

Additional Protocol in the Area of
    Economic, Social and Cultural Rights,
    52, 92
    Protocol to Abolish the Death Penalty, 92
American Declaration on the Rights and
    Duties of Man, 67, 92–94, 96, 98, 138
Amin, Idi, 21, 22
amnesty, xv, 6, 10, 15, 17, 26, 34–35, 38–40,
    43, 73–74, 79, 84, 120, 125, 172, 222,
    251, 274, 321
Amnesty International, 43, 61, 121
anonymity, 110, 162, 181, 185–186, 204, 261,
    303
Anton Piller orders, 207, 217
apartheid, 16, 285, 321
apologies, 30, 39, 55, 57, 75, 80
arbitration, 71
Argentina, 16, 21, 24–25, 31, 33, 39, 43,
    44–45, 48, 57, 62–63, 73–74, 76–79,
    150, 160, 164–167, 170, 172, 186, 206,
    278, 291–292, 296, 318, 342
Argentine Forensic Anthropology Team, 44
Armenia, 56
Australia, 48, 189, 199, 207, 242
Austria, 48, 69
Aylwin, Patricio, 74

balance of probabilities standard, 282–284,
    314

Bassiouni Principles, 6, 9, 17, 108, 146, 161, 176, 187
Belgium, 55, 65
Belgrade Minimum Rules of Procedure for International Human Rights Fact-Finding Missions, 134
beyond a reasonable doubt standard, 72, 283
bias, 19, 38, 55, 121, 133, 138–141, 148, 197, 229, 237, 277, 282, 342, 386
Bloody Sunday Inquiry, 55, 125, 127, 129, 153, 182, 237, 239, 244, 261
Bolivia, 24, 178, 318
Bosnia and Herzegovina, 7, 10, 25, 56, 66, 70, 74–75, 84–85, 137
    Republika Srpska, 55, 75
    Srebrenica, 7–8, 55
Botha, P. W., 190, 197–198
Brazil, 18, 40, 42–43, 49, 63, 160, 275
Burundi, 13–14, 18, 25, 60, 70, 137, 317

Cambodia, 5, 10, 44, 70
Canada, 23, 25, 31, 47–48, 54, 56, 64, 71, 109, 120, 122–123, 125–126, 134, 144, 190, 194, 200, 218, 233, 237, 246, 253, 272–273, 287, 296
Carnegie Endowment for International Peace, 60
Chad, 16, 24, 77, 79, 84, 133, 140, 152, 167–168, 170, 189, 207, 274, 291, 319, 377–378
child/children, rights and interests of, 36, 49, 57, 91, 94–95, 98, 148, 161, 177, 179–180, 226–227, 239–241, 249–251, 258–259, 261, 264, 267, 310–311
Chile, 5, 16, 20–21, 24–27, 30, 33, 39, 44–45, 63, 73–74, 76, 78, 80, 117, 121, 137, 139, 153, 161, 165–166, 172, 186, 206–207, 273, 278, 291, 292, 319, 342
China, 46, 118
civil law tradition, 58, 75, 79, 82, 116–118, 246, 281
Cold War, xiii, 59, 65
Colombia, 41, 45, 48, 74, 341
colonialism, 118
command responsibility, 292, 380
Commission of the Black Book of Fascism (Portugal), 56
Commission on the Responsibility of the Authors of the War and on Enforcement of Penalties, 59
Commission on the Status of Women, 51, 138
common law tradition, xv, xvi, 58, 74–75, 78, 82, 109, 111, 116–119, 122–123,

126–127, 190, 205, 207, 246–247, 250, 282–284, 314
Commonwealth, 30, 34, 53, 109, 119, 121, 125, 130, 139, 195, 201
Commonwealth commissions of inquiry, 22–25, 32, 53–54, 59, 77, 83, 89, 103, 109, 124–125, 127–131, 139, 153, 189, 191, 193–195, 201, 207, 209, 225, 237–240, 242, 244–245, 247, 249, 256, 263, 274, 285
compensation for human rights violations, xvi, 6, 8–9, 15, 19, 35–37, 41, 62–65, 79–80, 92, 97, 99, 111–112, 125, 153, 167–168, 266, 279, 301, 375, 381
confidentiality, 24, 42, 84, 96, 101, 142, 161–162, 168, 170, 174–175, 180–186, 189, 202–203, 226, 248–249, 258, 264–265, 269, 282–284, 291, 296–298, 303–304, 306, 311, 313–314, 343–344, 347–350, 352, 385, 390–391
Convention Against Torture and Other Cruel, Inhuman or Degrading Treatment or Punishment, 42, 50, 91, 99
Convention on the Elimination of All Forms of Discrimination Against Women, 50–51, 91, 97–99
Convention on the Rights of the Child, 50, 91, 94–98, 138, 226–227, 236, 252
    Optional Protocol on the involvement of children in armed conflicts, 91
    Optional Protocol on the sale of children, child prostitution, and child pornography, 91
coroners, xvi, 41, 58–59, 84, 88, 190, 194, 197, 225, 233, 245, 259, 261, 264, 282, 290
corroboration of evidence, 40, 62, 68, 104–105, 151, 185, 246–247, 278–279, 281–282, 292
Council of Europe, 52, 68, 92
cross-examination, 72, 82, 104, 110, 113–117, 121–123, 126, 128–129, 225, 229, 236–240, 245, 247, 253, 281–282, 310
Czech Republic, 66
Czechoslovakia, 54, 57

defamation, 105, 114, 229, 236–237, 269, 276, 284
Democratic Republic of Congo, 12, 14–15, 18, 25–27, 29, 33–34, 86, 125, 133, 139–140, 142, 153, 165, 171, 189, 193, 207, 220, 248, 264, 274, 324
democratization, 4–6, 65, 79
derogations in human rights treaties, 93

due diligence, 143, 228
due process, 73, 88, 95, 109–119, 121, 124,
   131, 234, 237, 244, 273, 275, 282,
   350–352, 380
   procedural due process, 112
   substantive due process, 112
duty to give reasons, 121, 123, 294

Ecuador, 24, 321
Eichmann, Adolf, 73
El Salvador, 4–5, 16, 18, 24–29, 31, 39, 42, 48,
   51, 62, 66, 68, 71, 77–79, 84, 136, 139,
   150, 153–154, 164, 167, 169–170, 206,
   208, 224, 268, 270, 272, 274–276,
   278–279, 281, 282–283, 291, 320,
   340–352, Appendix 2
enforced disappearances, 7–8, 14, 17, 19–20,
   33, 44, 48–49, 51, 63, 71, 76, 78, 92,
   99, 102, 133, 153, 167, 186, 223
Ethiopia, 74
EU Charter of Rights, 92–94, 97–99, 119,
   123, 143, 146
European Charter for Regional or Minority
   Languages, 52, 92
European Commission against Racism and
   Intolerance, 52
European Committee for the Prevention of
   Torture and Inhuman or Degrading
   Treatment or Punishment, 52
European Committee of Social Rights, 52, 68
European Convention for the Prevention of
   Torture and Inhuman or Degrading
   Treatment or Punishment, 92
European Convention for the Protection of
   Human Rights and Fundamental
   Freedoms, 92–99, 138, 142, 210–211,
   236, 269
European Court of Human Rights, 68, 70,
   90, 270
European Framework Convention for the
   Protection of National Minorities, 52,
   92, 98
European Social Charter, 52, 92

Fiji, 25–26, 35
First World War, 59
Ford Foundation, 31, 136
Former Yugoslav Republic of Macedonia, 62
France, 65, 73, 79, 117, 296
French Declaration of the Rights of Man and
   of the Citizen, 111

gender considerations, 14, 29–31, 37, 46, 51,
   53, 93, 97–98, 138–139, 144, 165,

179–180, 222, 228, 258–259, 261–262,
   267, 388
genocide, 10, 51, 60–61, 69, 70, 93, 276,
   294–295, 376–380, 383
Germany, 11, 15, 24, 28–29, 32, 45, 63, 65,
   69, 73, 117, 133, 216, 225, 272, 320
Ghana, 5, 15, 22–24, 29, 48, 74, 79, 82, 133,
   140–142, 159–160, 169, 178–179, 186,
   189, 192, 197, 206, 208, 211, 220,
   224–225, 227–228, 237–240, 242–243,
   250, 261, 263, 266, 274, 288, 296, 323
grand juries, 74, 111, 115, 194, 243–244,
   249–250, 253, 255
Greece, 5, 56, 65
Greensboro Truth and Reconciliation
   Commission, 42
Grenada, 26, 165, 189, 225, 256, 274, 323
Guatemala, 5, 16, 18, 25, 29, 32, 34, 44–45,
   48, 51, 74, 77, 79–80, 83, 136, 139,
   152–153, 164–165, 169, 176, 182,
   189, 272, 274–276, 278–279, 292–293,
   321

habeas corpus, 62, 75, 112
Habré, Hisseine, 77, 140, 207, 319
Hague Conventions for the Pacific
   Settlement of Disputes, 100–101
Haiti, 15, 24, 51, 62, 71, 152, 160, 162, 172,
   173, 178–179, 189, 207, 273, 278–279,
   282–283, 285, 291, 296, 320
Hayner, Priscilla, xiv, 12–15, 17–18, 20–25,
   85, 87, 130, 190, 224, 276, 317
hearsay evidence, 104, 119, 245–248, 250,
   278, 281, 311
Holocaust, 45, 63, 155
Honduras, 8, 25, 48
human rights archives, 39, 43, 56, 77, 105,
   173–174, 184–185, 260
Human Rights Watch, 43, 45
Hungary, 65

India, 55, 189–190, 199, 207, 238
Indonesia, 16, 25–27, 35, 60, 164, 323, 325
institutional responsibility, 63, 65, 92, 94, 99,
   222, 245, 275, 282
Inter-American Commission on Human
   Rights, 50, 52, 62, 67, 73, 78, 160,
   289
Inter-American Convention on the
   Elimination of All Forms of
   Discrimination Against Persons with
   Disabilities, 92, 98
Inter-American Convention on the Forced
   Disappearance of Persons, 7, 92

Inter-American Convention on the
    Prevention, Punishment and
    Eradication of Violence against
    Women, 92
Inter-American Convention to Prevent and
    Punish Torture, 92, 99
Inter-American Court of Human Rights, xiii,
    8, 62, 67, 70
International Bar Association, 44
International Center for Transitional Justice,
    24, 42, 149
International Commission on Missing
    Persons, 49
International Committee of the Red Cross,
    44, 224, 249, 251, 311
International Convention on the Elimination
    of All Forms of Racial
    Discrimination, 50, 91, 97–99
International Convention on the Protection
    of the Rights of All Migrant Workers
    and Members of Their Families, 51
International Court of Justice, 61, 70, 89
International Covenant on Civil and Political
    Rights, 50, 90–91, 93–99, 146, 148,
    236, 252, 262
    First Optional Protocol, 91
    Second Optional Protocol, 50, 91
International Covenant on Economic, Social
    and Cultural Rights, 50, 91, 96–98,
    146
International Criminal Court, xxii, 10, 70,
    72, 80, 82, 84, 86, 90, 138, 142, 147,
    178–180, 184, 239, 241, 249, 250, 259,
    261, 264, 267, 275, 283, 380
International Criminal Tribunal for Rwanda,
    xiii, 10, 69, 160, 246–247, 252, 279,
    281
International Criminal Tribunal for the
    former Yugoslavia, xiii, 10, 62, 69–70,
    74–76, 85, 138, 182, 195, 220, 226,
    241, 246–249, 252, 259, 264, 278–279
International Humanitarian Fact-Finding
    Commission, 61, 100, 172, 184
international humanitarian law, 9, 14, 19, 34,
    60–61, 90, 108, 140, 143, 376–380,
    383–384, 386
International Labour Organization, 53, 61,
    67, 100
investigative magistrates, 58, 75, 101, 117,
    283
Iran, 45, 64
Iran–United States Claims Tribunal, 64
Iraq, 25, 44, 51, 54, 66, 128–129,
    160

Islamic legal tradition, 118
Israel, 51, 55, 73, 140, 142, 179, 190, 201, 207,
    242, 256, 264, 274
Italy, 48, 65, 75, 210, 260
Ivory Coast, 61, 296

Jamaica, 54–55
Japan, 46, 64, 73, 258, 275, 279
Joinet Principles, 6, 9, 104–105, 271, 281, 288
judges, xv, 9–10, 17, 30, 51, 58, 65–66, 70, 75,
    78, 82, 110, 116–119, 121, 125, 129,
    137–138, 139, 184, 190–192, 195,
    200–201, 205, 209–211, 218, 252, 283,
    306, 342, 350, 382, 384, 386
judicial review, 121, 202–203, 221, 264, 275,
    294, 298–300, 306, 308, 316

Kenya, 15, 28, 33, 261
Korea, Republic of, 17, 152, 165, 173, 178,
    189, 206, 215, 322
Kosovo, 10, 46, 70

Lebanon, 20, 55, 133, 274
legal privileges, 96, 111, 121, 124, 199,
    202–203, 218, 225–226, 248–251, 259,
    297, 305–306, 308, 311–312, 389
    see also privilege against
    self-incrimination
letters rogatory, 189
Liberia, 16, 18, 25–26, 29–31, 66, 133–134,
    136–137, 140, 145–148, 166–167, 173,
    178, 180, 184–185, 189, 191, 197, 202,
    207, 209, 225, 242, 256, 259–260, 263,
    267, 274, 325
Libya, 16
lustration, 6, 41, 64–66, 279

Malawi, 63
media, 42, 45–46, 65, 68, 81, 96, 127, 145,
    164–165, 168, 223, 249, 251, 261–262,
    269–270, 297, 301, 311, 343–344,
    385
mediation, 14, 47, 71
medical examiners, 41, 58
Mexico, 25, 49, 71, 74, 117, 150, 208, 340–341
Morocco, xv, 16, 24, 27–29, 30, 32, 35–36, 43,
    47, 63, 82, 120, 125, 153, 165, 167,
    170, 187, 225, 227–229, 232, 237, 246,
    258, 265–266, 275, 291, 324
Mozambique, 5, 16, 39

Namibia, 16, 25
national human rights commissions, xvi, 19,
    41, 46–50, 87, 134, 279

natural justice, 88, 109, 119–124, 131, 231, 238, 242, 284, 288, 294
audi alteram partem, 119, 122, 235, 285
nemo debet esse judex in propia causa, 119, 121
Nazis, 42, 49, 57, 63, 65, 73
Nepal, 23, 49, 319, 325
New Zealand, 190, 194, 205, 207, 242, 245, 249, 277
NGOs, xvi, 19, 24, 31–32, 36, 43–46, 50, 55, 67–68, 87, 134, 159–160, 164, 168, 225, 227, 278–279, 301, 377, 383
Nigeria, 15, 23, 27, 29, 31, 142, 150, 153, 163, 167, 189, 192, 201, 203, 205–208, 223, 225, 227–228, 237, 256, 261, 272, 321
nondiscrimination under international law, 97, 98, 144
North American Agreement on Labor Cooperation, 53
North Korea, 118

oaths, 62, 116–117, 140–141, 183, 194, 200, 209–210, 225, 240–241, 246, 310
ombudsman offices, 41, 46–50, 207, 279
Open Society Institute, 31
Orentlicher, Diane (anti-impunity principles), 6, 8–9, 14, 19, 29, 49, 73, 81, 104, 134–136, 143, 166, 185, 229, 262, 265, 281
Organization for Security and Cooperation in Europe, 52
    High Commissioner for National Minorities, 52–53
    Representative on Freedom of the Media, 53
Organization of African Unity, 61
    See also African Union
Organization of American States, 61–62, 91

Palestinians, 179
Panama, 5, 24, 28, 45, 141, 160, 164–165, 279, 322
Papon, Maurice, 73
Paraguay, 24–25, 165, 225, 324
Paris Principles, 47
partie civile, 79, 82
peacebuilding, 6
perjury, 178, 199, 201, 241, 252–254, 257, 305, 312
Permanent Peoples' Tribunal, 46
Peru, 5, 16, 24, 31, 33–34, 36, 38, 49, 71, 74, 77, 80, 84, 135, 145, 147, 160–161, 163–165, 169, 173, 180, 182, 189, 207, 222–223, 225, 228–230, 237, 250, 260,

262, 266, 274, 276, 278–279, 282, 284, 291–292, 323
Philippines, 12, 47
Pinochet, Augusto, 45, 76, 121
plea bargaining, 75
Poland, 45–46, 48–49, 66
Polish Institute of National Remembrance, 49
Portugal, 56, 65
presumption of innocence, 94, 112, 118, 196, 235, 280–281, 285
pretrial discovery, 75
privacy rights and interests, xiv, 8, 44, 63, 90, 94–96, 99, 103, 105, 107–109, 111, 116, 122, 146, 148, 159–161, 168–169, 178–179, 181, 183, 190, 194, 202–203, 207, 210–211, 220, 225, 229, 232, 238, 240, 248, 258, 261–265, 268, 282, 286, 288–289, 297, 299, 301, 303–304, 306, 310, 312–313, 315
privilege against self-incrimination, 90, 95, 110, 112, 172, 190, 226, 244, 251–257, 264, 311, 312
probative value of evidence, 185, 246, 277, 280, 303, 314
procedural fairness, xiv–xvi, 34, 40–41, 87–89, 100–102, 106, 109, 116, 119, 125–126, 131, 145–146, 149, 151–155, 227, 233, 238, 268, 299, 300, 316
property rights, 90, 96–97, 120, 146
Protocol Additional to the Geneva Conventions of 12 August 1949, and relating to the Protection of Victims of International Armed Conflicts (Protocol I), 7, 61, 90

reasonable notice, 121–122, 196–197, 231, 234, 284, 286, 289, 305, 309, 314
reconciliation, xiv, 6, 10, 12, 14, 27, 33–36, 38–40, 56, 72–73, 79, 84, 191, 201, 222–223, 227, 267, 341, 345, 382
Recovery of Historical Memory Project (REMHI), 44, 164, 169, 176, 180
reparation for human rights violations, xiv, xv, 4, 6, 8–9, 11, 20, 31, 34–35, 38–41, 57, 62–64, 73, 77, 79–80, 85, 98, 106–108, 120, 125, 153, 166–168, 172, 176, 183, 223, 266, 279, 301, 381
restorative justice, 71
right of reply, 96, 105, 120, 122, 151, 222, 225, 229–230, 233, 235, 236–240, 275–276, 284, 286, 288–291, 297, 309, 310, 314–315
Romania, 48

Rome Statute of the International Criminal
Court, 72, 86, 90, 138, 147, 220, 246,
259, 283, 292, 294, 380
Royal Commission on Aboriginal Peoples
(Canada), 23, 56
Rwanda, xiii, 10, 18, 59–61, 69–70, 160,
271
gacaca, 70

Salmon principles of procedural fairness, 89,
109, 124, 126–131, 175, 195, 247
Second World War, 4, 45–46, 49, 57, 64–65,
246
Senegal, 117
sentencing circles, 71
Serbia and Montenegro, 5, 19, 28, 322
sexual violence, 31, 46, 56, 58, 92, 123, 144,
165, 179, 180–181, 185, 227, 239–240,
258–259, 262, 264, 265, 275, 279–280,
303, 310, 378
show trials, 73
Sierra Leone, 4–5, 10, 15–16, 18, 23–24,
27–30, 35–36, 39, 51, 70, 78, 81–82,
84–85, 125, 134, 139, 150, 153–154,
160–162, 165, 167, 170, 177, 179,
181–185, 187–189, 191, 196, 207–208,
224–229, 235, 240, 250, 259, 262,
266–267, 270–272, 274, 281–282,
291–295, 324, Appendix 2
Slovenia, 48
Somalia, 23, 51, 139
sources of international human rights law, 89
South Africa, xiv–xv, 3, 5, 11–12, 16–18,
22–30, 32, 34–37, 39, 45, 48, 63, 72,
78–79, 81–82, 84, 120, 123, 125–126,
134, 140, 142, 146–147, 149–150, 154,
159–162, 165–166, 169, 171, 178, 183,
187, 189, 190–193, 195, 197–198,
206–207, 209, 211–213, 216–218, 220,
222–225, 227–229, 231–239, 242–244,
246, 250–251, 253, 260, 262, 266, 272,
274, 276, 278–279, 282, 284–285,
287–288, 291, 296, 321
Spain, 5, 25, 48, 57, 77, 79, 121, 216
Special Committee to Investigate Israeli
Practices Affecting the Human Rights
of the Palestinian People and Other
Arabs of the Occupied Territories, 51
special prosecutors, 74–75
Sri Lanka, 23–24, 48, 55, 80, 117, 133, 161,
164–165, 171, 189, 225, 262, 273–274,
283, 320, 325
Sudan, 59–60, 69, 84, 86, 275, Appendix 3
summary penal order, 75

summary trial, xv, 75
Sweden, 46–47, 62, 69

Timor-Leste, xv, 5, 10, 12, 16–17, 24–25, 28,
30, 32–37, 60, 70, 77–79, 82, 84, 120,
125, 136, 139–140, 142, 145–146, 153,
160–162, 164–165, 169, 173–174, 180,
182, 184, 186–187, 189, 196, 198–199,
206, 209–210, 212–213, 215–217, 220,
222, 225, 228–229, 232–233, 238, 240,
242, 244, 250, 254, 258, 260, 262–263,
266–267, 274, 278, 323
Togo, 50, 60–61
torture, 8, 14–15, 20, 23, 30, 33, 39, 42, 60,
63, 71–72, 93, 99, 112, 118, 155, 161,
168–169, 223–224, 246, 280, 295
transactional immunity, 251
transitional justice, xiv, 3–6, 9–10, 62, 64, 83,
86–87, 135
Transparency International, 174
trauma of victims, 84, 108, 127, 155, 159,
176, 180, 186–187, 226, 236, 244–245,
258–259, 264–266, 311
trials by dossier, 75
truth commissions
accessibility of, 132, 147, 153, 162,
168–171, 183, 302
accountability of, 123, 132, 141–142, 148,
150, 192, 215, 217
accuracy of, 43, 132, 147, 151–153, 169,
175–176, 179–180, 228–229, 235, 238,
272, 281–282, 284, 302, 314
archives, 39, 77, 105, 173–174, 184–185,
260, 348
competence of, 102, 132, 134, 138–139,
143–144, 151, 187, 193, 304
comprehensiveness of, 151–153
dignity, respect for, xi, 82, 96, 108, 132,
146, 148, 155, 166, 175–176, 180, 220,
227, 258, 265, 302, 313
efficiency of, 115, 122, 132, 148–149,
151–153, 183, 191, 193, 195, 200, 210,
231, 233, 238–239, 304
emotional support by, 83–84, 186–187,
226, 265–267, 304, 313
establishment of, 27–28
final reports of, xiv–xvi, 20, 24, 36, 39, 68,
76–77, 80, 85, 99, 136, 145, 151,
161–162, 166, 170, 172, 174–175, 186,
206, 223, 235, 260, 302, 304, 313–316,
322
flexibility of, 38, 78, 149–150
funding (costs), 30–31, 38, 104, 135–136,
325

good faith of, 29, 42, 132, 141–142,
147–148, 173, 220, 229, 269
impartiality of, 29–30, 39, 101–102,
104–105, 132, 138–143, 148, 151–152,
284, 343, 352
in camera hearings, 104, 259, 261–265,
267, 281, 313
independence of, 17, 28, 30, 38, 132–142,
148, 153, 164
legal representation, 26, 110, 125, 181,
192–193, 225, 231–232, 234, 237–238,
242–245, 262, 303–304, 309–311
memory (of victims and witnesses), 39,
80, 127, 168, 280–281
nondiscrimination, 132, 144, 147
outreach efforts by, 36, 162–168, 301
practical constraints, 131–132, 151–152,
154, 224
proportionality, 112, 132, 145–146
protective measures, 181, 226, 230,
258–265, 312–313
public hearings, xiv–xv, 11, 24–26, 32,
34–36, 38, 43, 71–72, 74, 77, 81–85,
94, 110, 112, 119, 124, 131, 136–137,
154, 222–267, 286, 308–313
publication of findings of individual
responsibility, i, xiv–xv, 34, 42, 54, 65,
105, 110, 131, 154, 176, 186, 268–300,
304, 313–316, 345, 352, 380
search and seizure power, xiv–xv, 27, 34,
97, 127, 131, 154, 161, 205–221,
306–308
statement taking, xv, 16, 36, 40, 82, 84,
131, 154, 159–187, 225, 229, 233, 278,
301–304
subpoena power, xiv–xv, 24, 28, 34, 109,
131, 154, 161, 188–206, 218, 229–230,
242–243, 245, 247–249, 273, 304–306,
308, 311, 384
transparency of, 132, 134–135, 145, 148,
151, 153, 223, 229, 284
victim-centeredness of, xiii, 17–18,
24–26, 32, 47, 54, 67, 72, 124, 130,
132, 151, 176, 235
Turkey, 56, 57
Tutu, Desmond, 79, 197, 237

Uganda, 21–24, 29, 32, 80, 86, 117, 133, 136,
171–172, 189, 225, 237, 245, 258,
317–318
United Nations (UN), xiii–xiv, 5–9, 13, 16,
18, 27–28, 30, 32, 42, 50–53, 59–61,
64, 66–67, 69–70, 86, 89–91, 93, 97,
99–100, 104, 106, 108, 134, 138, 140,

142–144, 146, 149, 152, 154, 160, 163,
166, 170, 176, 178–179, 183, 185–187,
215, 226, 229, 238, 243, 249, 262,
264–265, 275, 277–279, 281–282,
292–293, 296, 323, 347, 377, 382–383,
387
UN Children's Fund (UNICEF), 36
UN Commission on Human Rights, xiv, 7,
50–51, 59–60, 67, 104
1503 procedure, 50–51
Working Group on Enforced or
Involuntary Disappearances, 51
UN Committee against Torture, 50, 142
UN Committee on Economic, Social and
Cultural Rights, 50
UN Committee on the Elimination of
Discrimination against Women,
50
UN Committee on the Elimination of Racial
Discrimination, 50
UN Committee on the Protection of the
Rights of All Migrant Workers and
Members of Their Families, 51
UN Committee on the Rights of the Child,
50
UN Declaration of Basic Principles of Justice
for Victims of Crime and Abuse of
Power, 106–107, 146, 186, 187
UN Declaration on Fact-finding by the
United Nations in the Field of
Maintenance of International Peace
and Security, 100–101
UN Educational, Scientific and Cultural
Organization, 67
UN General Assembly, 51, 89, 106
UN Human Rights Committee, 50
UN Manual on the Effective Prevention and
Investigation of Extra-Legal, Arbitrary
and Summary Executions, 102–104,
141, 163, 183, 243, 264, 277, 281
UN Peacebuilding Commission, 6
UN Principles on the Effective Investigation
and Documentation of Torture and
Other Cruel, Inhuman or Degrading
Treatment or Punishment, 106, 132,
135, 144, 294
UN Principles on the Effective Prevention
and Investigation of Extra-Legal,
Arbitrary and Summary Executions,
101, 106, 132–133, 135, 144, 152, 215,
238, 293
UN Security Council, 59–61, 69, 74, 84, 86,
89, 138, 149, 275, 278, 376, 380–385,
387, 389

UN Special Adviser on the Prevention of
Genocide, 51
United Kingdom, 16, 22, 54–55, 64, 69, 84,
89, 121, 123, 125–130, 134–135,
138, 143, 175, 190, 194, 196–197,
199, 202, 207, 236, 256, 270–271,
274, Appendix 3
United States, 16, 42–43, 45, 54–55, 57,
63–64, 68, 71, 74, 80, 111–118, 136,
141, 160, 175, 190, 194, 199, 210, 220,
234, 237, 239, 241–242, 244, 248–250,
252–255, 268, 270, 273
Commission on Civil Rights, 112, 114
congressional committees of
investigation, 53, 190, 194, 199, 207,
242, 244, 253

Universal Declaration of Human Rights, 90,
93–94, 96–99, 138, 146
universal jurisdiction, 70, 71, 382
Uruguay, 21, 24, 43, 167, 317, 322
use immunity, 84, 161, 226, 251–257,
311–312

vetting, xvi, 6, 41, 64–66, 172, 279
Vietnam, 45, 55

Women's International War Crimes
Tribunal, 43, 46, 258, 275, 279

youth, rights and interests of, 226–227, 261

Zimbabwe, 21, 23, 317